Paul, Covenant Killer

Paul, Covenant Killer

His Legal Letters Explained
Arranged in a Compendium and Translated from the Greek with
Commentary and Notes

Timothy L. Parrott

RESOURCE *Publications* · Eugene, Oregon

PAUL, COVENANT KILLER
His Legal Letters Explained

Copyright © 2021 Timothy L. Parrott. All rights reserved. Except for brief quotations in critical publications or reviews, no part of this book may be reproduced in any manner without prior written permission from the publisher. Write: Permissions, Wipf and Stock Publishers, 199 W. 8th Ave., Suite 3, Eugene, OR 97401.

Resource Publications
An Imprint of Wipf and Stock Publishers
199 W. 8th Ave., Suite 3
Eugene, OR 97401

www.wipfandstock.com

PAPERBACK ISBN: 978-1-5326-4242-5
HARDCOVER ISBN: 978-1-5326-4243-2
EBOOK ISBN: 978-1-5326-4244-9

11/02/21

Contents

What's in a Title?	*ix*
Persecutor, Persecuted, Prosecutor	*xi*
Comments, Structure, and Study Notes	*xvii*
A Review of the Legal Themes and Purpose within the Letters	*xxv*

SECTION I: ANNULING THE OLD, INSTITUTING A NEW

Romans
Commentary	3
Romans as a Letter	6
Romans Study Notes	25
Romans in Verse	35

I Corinthians
Commentary	67
I Corinthians as a Letter	71
I Corinthians Study Notes	88
I Corinthians in Verse	95

II Corinthians
Commentary	126
II Corinthians as a Letter	128
II Corinthians Study Notes	139
II Corinthians in Verse	145

Galatians
Commentary	165
Galatians as a Letter	168
Galatians Study Notes	175
Galatians in Verse	185

SECTION II: A MERGER, AN AFFIRMATION OF ENTITLEMENT

Ephesians
- Commentary — 199
- Ephesians as a Letter — 203
- Ephesians Study Notes — 210
- Ephesians — 216

Philippians
- Commentary — 227
- Philippians as a Letter — 230
- Philippians Study Notes — 235
- Philippians — 239

Colossians
- Commentary — 248
- Colossians as a Letter — 252
- Colossians Study Notes — 257
- Colossians in Verse — 262

SECTION III: AN EXTRACT AND A REBUTTAL

I Thessalonians
- Commentary — 273
- I Thessalonians as a Letter — 276
- I Thessalonians Study Notes — 280
- I Thessalonians in Verse — 284

II Thessalonians
- Commentary — 291
- II Thessalonians as a Letter — 294
- II Thessalonians Study Notes — 297
- II Thessalonians in Verse — 301

SECTION IV: PROOF OF CHRIST'S ENTITLEMENT AND AUTHORITY

Hebrews
- Commentary — 309
- Hebrews as a Letter — 318
- Hebrews Study Notes — 332
- Hebrews in Verse — 352

CONTENTS

SECTION V: A WILL AND TESTAMENT, THE TRANSFER OF AUTHORITY

I Timothy
    Commentary   379
    I Timothy as a Letter   381
    I Timothy Study Notes   386
    I Timothy in Verse   391

II Timothy
    Commentary   400
    II Timothy as a Letter   402
    II Timothy Study Notes   406
    II Timothy in Verse   411

SECTION VII: POWER OF ATTORNEY ASSIGNMENT

Titus
    Commentary   421
    Titus as a Letter   423
    Titus Study Notes   426
    Titus in Verse   429

SECTION IIX: A TORT

Philemon
    Commentary   435
    Philemon as a Letter   437
    Philemon Study Notes   439
    Philemon in Verse   442

SUMMARY AND CLOSING

Summary and Closing Comments   445
Honorarium and Acknowledgments   449

What's in a Title?

LIKE MANY INTERESTING JOURNEYS, this book is not unlike a trip to a foreign land where one must adapt to unexpected challenges, change, put away comforts or standards, and possibly accept the foreign. As most travelers that journey abroad know upon a visit to a new country, one never comes back from such trips without one's perspective being profoundly challenged and altered. This transpired with me as I started on a path of simply studying words, idioms, language, and culture foreign in time and place to an English speaker. Little was I ready for the journey and challenges of trying to understand the original business language of the period or the lingua franca of the time being Aramaic. It did not take long to perceive and realize, however, that what I was studying was a legal system and organization distinct and quite separate from what the standard world of religion, theology, and perspectives many have and continue to perpetuate, claim, preach, and teach.

What about the title chosen for this manuscript? I chose this for its layers of meaning for the reader to discover within this offering. One is a parallelism, as in the title of king; the law of the land replaced by another, whether by force of nature, natural or unnatural, or by the divine, if willing to consider the possibility. No two kings, rulers, legislative bodies, or outgoing or incoming legal systems perform, behave, or enact as their predecessor. So as a king passes away and is replaced with a new one, so has the "Law of the Land"—or rather the Law of Moses—plus the added and endless trivial regulations and practices of the ruling class by each era of any of the active kingdoms. The Law of Moses was the king of the kingdoms. It served as the foundation for both the kingdoms of Judah and Israel from their inception. A series of parallels occur in dramatic fashion from King Saul, to King David (and even with those within David's lineage), to the ending of the original covenant with Israel, and now a new institution by the Risen Christ, the one called Jesus. This new covenant is as distinctive as day and night, especially since it is universal in scope and purpose. This statement is more shocking than one may imagine upon a close examination of what Paul writes. Paul was guided, was actually created, to make this clear and to instruct and teach what it means to be within this new compact.

The conversion, actions, legal discourses, and discussions of Paul soar dramatically above what the original Twelve Apostles and leadership operating from Jerusalem knew, had in mind, or understood. It took a very long time for the original

Jewish leadership and Jewish Ecclesia to overcome the singular nationalistic thinking and realize that the immediate anticipated coming kingdom was completely different and broader in scope, purpose, and activities. The Jerusalem Counsel meeting about what to do with the Gentiles was not the casual conversation and decision-making edict and agreement it appears to be by the shortened report by Luke in the Book of Acts. It was hotly and passionately discussed, and all were in panic because all understood that this was literally a world-changing shift in the thinking and current paradigm by God's Spirit through obvious and undeniable revelation and circumstances. All of them were quite uncertain what the result of Gentile inclusion was going to mean, but they clearly realized that it was not within their limited, parochial Jewish understanding.

Bringing this shifting thought and understanding required someone with one foot in the Israelite world with a deep knowledge of its systems and information and one foot in the Gentile world to bring clarity to what was occurring both in the present and for the future. Paul was that individual, a known assassin legally working within the old covenant, but the strongest defender, instructor, and revelator once inside the new. Paul was and is the man for all ages extinguishing the old law and bringing in the new law—the one based on the spirit, not on written laws.

Persecutor, Persecuted, Prosecutor

PAUL AND THE LAW OF THE COMING KINGDOM

What could one possibly mean the by the Persecutor, Persecuted, and Prosecutor? How could such a one exist? Could one man have claimed all three titles or performed in all three capacities that this heading quandaries? Did such an individual exist somewhere in time? Who could have experienced such a diversity of descriptors?

There was such an individual created for such a purpose, and it was not Jesus. Jesus never persecuted anyone, although he did prosecute those in power, who in the end were the ones that persecuted him in a state-sponsored and empire-approved crucifixion and murder. Amazingly, though, Christ did know this man, and this man knew Christ. They were contemporaries. Both were aware of each rubbing shoulders from time to time. This man knew Christ as the blasphemer, one professing and calling himself equal to The-God, and then later he came to call him The-Savior Anointed. Only one man in history has fulfilled all three roles and can claim all three titles. That man is Saul, who became Paul.

So how does one make such a claim that Paul is the man this book is being written about? In defense of this statement, I offer the following short review of Paul's life.

THE PERSECUTOR

Paul comes with a unique background. Unlike the other apostles, first and foremost he could claim dual citizenship as a Roman and a Jew. But Roman citizenship was not the hammer he elected to use first. Second, he came from the finest stock out of the lineage of Benjamin, a preeminent tribe elected by God Himself, the One to have the first King of Israel. Paul's mother was of royal ancestry, and no doubt his father was a high-ranking citizen within the empire. His mother is the one who carries the power and influence in Jewish society, which is why Paul uses his Israelite privileges first. We know practically nothing on the patriarchal side, other than by researching what secular sources explain about what it meant to be a Roman citizen. But we do know Paul will claim his rights and freedom as a Roman citizen, thinking it will free him and allow him to continue spreading the name and message of Christ, The-Messiah, and his coming kingdom.

Other facts exist about Paul's uniqueness and trained background. Nobody would have had the ability to sit at the feet and be taught by the great teacher Gamaliel, the "Pharisee Doctor of Jewish Law"[1] unless one had credentials, cash, and intellectual capability. Paul's stock met all of these requirements. Later in his life as he addresses the false preachers claiming "lineage and using it to force demands on people within the Ecclesia," he will publicly challenge all and any to step forward and see if they can match his. I find nothing where any individuals do that. The pages of the Bible and history are deathly and eerily silent for the challenge, and correctly so. James, Jesus' half-brother, would have come the closest via heritage. Nobody in that audience steps forward and proves they had more preeminence in their name or their family or the Jewish culture. Paul just didn't come from a well-to-do family; he came from an exceptionally well-to-do family and one that was known in the Roman and Jewish culture.

Additionally, Paul had direct access to the Pharisees and Sadducees anytime he so desired. In Acts 23:6, he splits both governing bodies over the matter of death. For either side to take a position, these two governing bodies would have had to expose themselves in ignorance and self-condemnation. Both parties in this lawsuit were livid when Paul, in a stunning reversal of accusation, turned their lawsuit against themselves him into their own public condemnation and humiliation. They absolutely wanted him dead for the shameful public embarrassment and brow-beating both governances took and for spreading the sedition of another kingdom, that of Christ's, which was not the one the ruling class understood and desired to submit to. The acceptance of Christ would be a condemnation of the entire society as the priestly class, the ruling classes, and the nation would have been accountable for the slaying of the anticipated Promised One.

Paul came and went into the temple anytime he wanted because he had the right to do so. I ask that the reader please remember this concept of having the right to do so. Many readers may not be aware that Christ also had the same access through his mother, Mary, along with Jesus' half-brothers James and Judas and the others. Christ and his physical half-brothers were also well-educated, which explains one reason Christ was found in the temple talking to the elders at the age of twelve. Because of Paul's access to and his zeal (in reality, super-jingoism—Paul did everything in life in the superlative) for the Law of Moses, he was the "Golden Boy" within the rank-and-file membership. Paul was a clear social climber and likely had only one goal in mind early in his life: to sit at the top of all governing bodies within the Jewish culture. Paul talks about this zeal in his letters. So, what we have here is an individual who has been taught by the finest legal minds in one of the world's best education centers, the Temple of Jerusalem in Judea. Paul was a ranking lawyer (not so much as our perception in this era) as well as a politician.

---

1 Wikipedia article: "Gamaliel."

THE PROSECUTOR

Within this framework, because of his background in the law and having been trained with a legal mind, Paul confesses that he had every right within the Law of Moses to be the persecutor and prosecute those abandoning the faith of the Jews and the traditions of Israel. He would be accurately correct in this. To step outside the faith and culture was certain death if it could be proved to those passing judgment. Paul was as close as could be to being the primary legal trial and prosecuting attorney for the Jewish culture. He apparently had executioner authority also. But this is not where Paul spends or ends his career as that lawyer; Paul is flipped to the "opposing counsel," and that "law firm" displays his soaring talents, abilities, and knowledge for Christ's purposes.

Be very clear about something: Paul was a real individual, a real contemporary of Jesus, just like the other apostles. He probably voted for, or at least encouraged the scourging and crucifixion of Christ being a prominent Jewish religious leader and zealot. Speculation could even put him as one of the ones who spit or slapped Jesus, and he almost certainly visited the death scene. He probably was one of the Sanhedrin that voted to tell Peter to stop preaching Jesus (see Acts 4:5–22), clearly stands convicted in helping to stone Stephen the first martyr (see Acts 7; 8:1), and initially retained the chief position in a religious "Gestapo," a brutal killing machine and organization (Acts 8:1–4). He was on his way to Damascus to capture and kill another prominent leader of Christ when confronted.

He clearly knew Christ personally before his conversion, and Paul stands up before all people, and confesses openly with shame that he was the Chief Persecutor and Prosecutor of The Body of Christ (The "Body" being a legal entity).

THE PERSECUTOR

Then something happens to the spinning coin, if I may borrow such a phrase. Out of that whirling, spinning malaise, the coin lands on heads, and the road to Damascus takes on a whole new life and purpose for Paul. It is not my intention within this book to review all the physical acts of Paul. I leave that to the reader to go through the Book of Acts, Paul's letters, John's letters, and Peter's letters to piece together the historical chronology of his trips and the towns that he will frequent over the years. But I will say this: after spending three-and-a-half years in one-on-one discussion, debates, instructions, and counseling with "The Head" of the once "opposing counsel," Paul is not the same man at all anymore. Paul will emerge on the scene like a testosterone-driven young lion whelp with just as much zeal and fervor for Christ as he had when he opposed him. I am deliberate in using the word *opposed* here, and I do not mean that in the sense of fighting The Christ physically. While he had been doing that at one time, the reader needs to understand that Paul was opposing Christ legally through the Law of Moses; in effect, he was a prosecuting attorney using every legal lawsuit and claim he could to bring death to those that had left the culture and the faith. Paul was doing nothing more than seeking the death sentence for anyone outside of his "perfect world." Not walking away quite yet from the theme of the young lion whelp, like all young lions feeling their way through the pride, making lots of noise and wreaking havoc, Paul now is wreaking havoc within the Jewish culture; he uses the Law of Moses to demonstrate that this law is ineffective, dead. Within his letters he began prosecuting the Jews—not to destroy them but to bring life to them. Paul was still first a Jew, and he reached out to the Jews first until it became clear that it was Christ's intention that he be sent to and for the Nations. This has severe consequences.

THE PERSECUTED

During this flip-flop from the Jewish culture to the culture of Christ, Paul now became the persecuted, and you, the reader, have the opportunity to read about this. He was left for dead, stoned, whipped and scourged, stripped naked, left to freeze, left to bake in the sun to die, left for robbers and thieves, had an entire Roman garrison surround a city capture him to bring him to death, and he also was thrown into a lion's den (some would suggest it is a euphemism for Nero Caesar). I have not been able to find in my research anybody who has gone through more beatings and abuses only to live through them to tell the tale—and in the process, defend and spread the word of The Belief in Christ. Paul now has become the persecuted; in fact, the one-time hunter has become the hunted with a bounty on his head. The lion is now being stalked.

THE PROSECUTOR

Within the swirling dervish of all his adventures, Paul takes on his most important role—one that has been ignored and overlooked as far as I have been able to research. Paul, in the process of all of this, does not function as a "corporate attorney" for the Pharisees and Sadducees climbing up the ladder in the Jewish culture; however, he is to become the Attorney General for the Ecclesia of God.

The purpose of this book is to demonstrate that Paul's letters are not just letters to a group of people to be read as if in everyday conversation. Paul's letters are in fact legal briefs, summations, claims, accusations, proofs, reasons, and logic for the way things are to be done within the Ecclesia. Paul's letters are all legal documents serving as the foundational basis and tenets for all the "Called-Out" by God through Christ. These are the principles and foundations that every son and daughter of God is expected to know and understand how to apply and live by. If you will accept such a concept, Paul's letters are in fact articles associated with the Declaration of Independence in Christ—just as the Declaration of Independence of the United States declares your personal rights and freedoms, your expected behavior, and your future reward for being true and loyal.

Persecutor, Persecuted, Prosecutor

With this in mind, my hope is that you'll see the letters of Paul with a much different perspective. Are you in or out? Do you believe in observing and living by this new constitution or not? Will you accept the citizenship or not? This includes The-Secret that was delivered not just to Paul, but also was given to several other elders, apostles, and members of the Ecclesiae. Such divine instructions were never given to a single individual alone. The practical reasons for this should be clearly evident. No one should believe in any one man claiming to have the only direct revelation from God. Many at that time claimed that they alone were receiving direct revelations, and in the process were removing whole Ecclesiae. Imposters, imitators, and copycats were everywhere. Divine revelations in the early Ecclesia were common and not hidden under a basket. They were distributed among several people in several different ways, all within a time frame that made it obvious that something new had occurred or needed to be addressed. There were prophets in the early Ecclesiae, and Timothy is an example of someone those prophets recognized as needing to be separated to carry on the work of Paul. It is stated with certainty that this was the way it occurred with something as big as The-Secret. This was not revealed to just two or three people, and it was not just Paul in the end. Other Commissioners (apostles) received The-Secret as well, though several struggled with the information before accepting the revelation.

Today you are presented with all of Paul's legal briefs and subject matter, assembled in one compendium for evaluation, research, proof or rebuttal. But somewhere in here choices will be made: either freedom that leads to life, or enslavement that leads to death.

People doubt the validity of Paul's report, life, and teachings, a man who willingly gave up his life in service to become a willing slave to serve The-Master[2] (as he often refers to Jesus with devotion and affection, in humble gratefulness and adoration). Paul uses the literal word *slave* everywhere, but today this has been watered down or transposed as "servant"). Paul knew Christ. He knew Christ so well that he willingly accepted the "Crown of Martyrdom" and considered himself nothing in the sight of all men. I reflect on the potential mountain of guilt this man probably carried with him for his entire life even though he was/is forgiven by The-Savior and handpicked for Jesus' purposes. Look at how he devoted the rest of his existence to Jesus. So, the pregnant and enormous question arises: Is Paul a liar? If you believe so, then all his words become vain and empty. But if you recognize that Paul had a relationship with Christ like no one else and served the Ecclesiae, the Body of Christ, like none other, I suggest that you consider his actions.

In conclusion, The-Persecutor became The Persecuted and then returned to become The-Prosecutor. He is serving you and me today as the Chief Attorney General, Prosecutor, and first Legal Counsel under Christ. He is still in our presence now through his words, which live into the ages and are guaranteed to still be in existence

---

2. Note: Throughout, the hyphen is added intentionally for emphasis and with purpose; here it is meant to distinguish Jesus as the only such person in God's plan.

at the return of Christ. The young lion whelp, the voracious hunter, in his later years became the hunted aging lion, and in the process, he has left a lasting legacy for us all.

My hope is that this book will stimulate discussion, debate, rebuttal, or acceptance using scriptural proof combined with cultural, historical, and logical analysis over what I know is a controversial subject, a controversial person, and a controversial theology and doctrines. I tell all men, "I am a liar until you prove me correct." I do this so that in the Day of Judgment if I have led you astray, I will confess to having misled you, but I will have done it in sincerity and Godly-love and a concerned heart for you. I am doing no more than the apostle Paul, or as I prefer to call him, The-Commissioner, the one sent to you and me, to the Nations. But if you prove me to be truthful and honest in what I am presenting and claiming, I hope you pause to reflect on what is going on within you and around you.

Comments, Structure, and Study Notes

COMMENTS

This private translation of the letters of Paul from the Greek is intended for your personal use. The process used for this translation involved a series of downloaded programs from the internet: Interlinear Scripture Analyzer 2 [basic], *Strong's Concordance with Hebrew and Greek Lexicon*, Blue Letter Bible Lexicon, Treasury of Scriptural Knowledge—Bible Concordance, the King James Version of the Bible, and the Concordant Version Bible. All but the King James Version of the Bible were located through a simple search via the internet and downloaded.

Because this is a private translation, I encourage you to study the Scriptures, words, phrases, and topics to assure yourself that what I have done is accurate and true to the intent as it may be in The-God's will. Prove all things. Reject the incorrect and unacceptable; hold fast to that which is accurate and true.

This project started while I was doing research to develop a chronological line prior to, during, and after the life of Christ. That work has been submitted to the ASKELM organization[1] for peer and scholarly review. In the process, the letters and writings of Paul began to intrigue me since he has much historical data and knowledge sprinkled throughout his works. It was clear to me that Paul had become the central figure in delivering the theology and message (i.e., well-message [gospel]) of "The-God," and "Jesus-The-Anointed-Son" to all the nations outside of Israel. This historical fact can be found in the book of Acts in addition to hundreds of secular materials in existence.

My intention was not just to read the myriad of other translations in existence today and rewrite in my own words the letters of Paul. My interest was translating directly from the Greek into a language we use today. It was my intention to follow as closely as possible not only each word or phrase, but also not add or delete a word as intended and written by Paul. I believe the Scripture that warns about doing that, and I pray that has not been done intentionally. Yet once started, I realized that the sentence structure was so awkward that rearrangement was necessary to make the text read somewhat properly and be understood by English readers.

1. http://www.askelm.com.

Comments, Structure, and Study Notes

While reviewing the words and sentence structures, it became apparent that the popular King James Version (KJV), purposefully or unwittingly as it may have been, has obscured and conveniently dropped modifiers, did not express fully the active and progressive tenses of words and phrases, and often used a single word to serve as a catch-all, not distinguishing singular or plural entities, beings, or concepts. A perfect example of this is the way the KJV uses the word *God*, which can be both singular and plural and requires a thorough investigation to determine exactly what or who is meant by "god/God/The-God."

After completing this effort and beginning to read the Scriptures straight through, several of the common doctrinal teachings received over the years have now disappeared as taught by many institutions. Paul's letters are direct and simple; if you pause on each word or two, then each sentence, then each theme, you have to stop and ask yourself, "Can that be what is really meant?" Hopefully a question like that will get you reading on the topic or idea that strikes you to resolutely settle in your mind what is correct or needs correcting.

Because of this, I've added under "Study Notes" some ideas that struck me while investigating various words or concepts. An example of this is how many of the words Paul uses are directly related to military terms and concepts. He makes it clear we are in a fight, a real fight. As he says: "For we wrestle not against flesh and blood, but against principalities, against powers, against the rulers of the darkness of this world, against spiritual wickedness in high places" (Eph 6:12, KJV). One of Paul's themes is that we are in a real spiritual warfare, not just a physical one.

STRUCTURE

I used the following conventions for clarity:

[ ] equivalent or expanded concordant, lexicon, thesauri or clarifying word/phrase

( ) word added by most translations or translators to add clarity to topic or idea but not found in original

{ } my personal comments added for clarity relevant to topic but not found in the original

ITALICIZED and or CAPITALIZED WORDS used to distinguish titles and personages for clarity

Italicized scriptural quotes given by Paul but not provided with a scriptural reference

Bold scriptural quotes with scriptural references

Words-connected-by-hyphens: In Greek this is a singular word delivering a commonly understood concept or idea in the period, but in English it requires hyphenating to capture the fuller and complete dynamics and sweeping breadth of the meaning.

The reader should realize that the Bible in verse form is quite arbitrary, not only in creating each verse but also each chapter. There is nothing inside the Scriptures that demonstrates by God's authority that the Bible as a whole is intended to be in this format. Logically one should know that everything was composed in running prose or poetry format. However, being in verse and chapter only positively demonstrates God's ability to send out his message in whatever format is being used; this includes what you have in your hand now. While I referenced the King James as the skeletal for creating the letters in verse, as a reader you will see that I deviated in several places from that "standard." The original documents distributed locally from Jerusalem and into the rest of the Judean area would have been in Aramaic but then provided in the business language of the day: Greek Koine. The Greek spoke especially to Paul's audience, but as the gospel spread, eventually all letters from Mark to Revelation were translated and transcribed. Most interesting, though, is that Paul in the first letter to Timothy asks Timothy to come back to him quickly along with the carrying case containing the "scrollets"—little rolled up papers of Paul's and probably letters of the other Apostles too, a mini-library of sorts. In haste Paul was looking to combine for sure his letters in final form (fourteen in all for Paul, but twenty-seven for the Second Testament in total) into one scroll. Now think about copying dozens of separate originals into a single document and then copying that into dozens and dozens of documents. These may have inspired books in the format we know today: single pages with writing on the front and back, small, manageable, and much easier to reproduce. Such a form of distribution may have had its roots in Paul assembling everything (including Peter and eventually John and the Elders John supervised who will finalize the entire Covenant we know today) before his career closes and he disappears into history. This is interesting speculation.

Also of speculation is Paul's death in Rome. Paul states in Romans that he had Christ's blessing to go to Spain after the delivery of goods for the Ecclesia in Jerusalem and he would pass into Rome on his way to Spain. While it is true Paul was under house arrest in Caesar's household, if Paul in fact did have Christ's blessing to go to Spain, Paul would have gone, and the tradition of Paul's beheading in Rome may be a legend—for there is also speculation that he was martyred not in Spain but in Britain. History, in my opinion, has yet to resolve this.

The reader should also be aware the current letter's order and arrangement in the Second Testament as offered in the King James and nearly all other translations is not the original sacred order of the letters. Paul's writings would have come after the Jewish writers of Jude, Peter, and John (called the Universal or Catholic Epistles). The Jews had the preeminence in all activities related to God, the first in blessings or punishments, the first "to believe," the first to receive the spirit-of-God (the Holy-spirit), and they would have come first in the sacred writings too. Their order today in most Bibles is a perversion that God still overcomes. With this in mind, the reader should be aware there are two orders associated with the letters of the Second Covenant: the historical order and the Sacred Order. Paul's letters in this document are arranged in the original Sacred Order. For a scholarly presentation and historical defense of the order of the letters and for that matter the order and arrangement of the First Covenant (as they, too, are out of Sacred Order in the King James and many other translations), see *Restoring the Original Bible* by Dr. Earnest L. Martin, PhD, which can be ordered at any book retailer or found on the ASKELM website www.askelm.com.

PAUL'S WRITINGS

During the translation exercise, it became apparent quickly that Paul writes in the superlative in all of his letters. Words such as *super-abounding, much-greater, far-more,* and *above-and-beyond* are salted all throughout his letters. My engineering background could not help but see such mathematical phrases associated with his writing as *to the power of, exponentially,* and *infinity*. I could have just as easily substituted these concepts in place of several of the adjectives describing the topic Paul is discussing, but instead will leave it to the reader to reflect on where this may occur. For those with a proclivity to study numbers or biblical numerology, Paul's letters would be an interesting study.

Paul's letters, however, are foremost legal arguments, rhetorical dissertations, and historical panoramas of what has occurred in the Heavens and in this eon of Man. I am quite purposeful in stating this in this manner. Paul's direct use of legal words such as *title, name, spirit, body* (meaning a corporation or business entity as well as private enterprise), *indictment, justice, award, accounting,* and *credit* predominates his writings. Every one of his letters should be read first as a defense, or as a prosecuting attorney making an opening statement—a series of defense or attack arguments and debates supporting or proving his statements followed then with closing arguments, leaving you as a jurist to be convinced thoroughly in your mind about Paul's testament. Romans, which opens Paul's writing, could not be more classical in this structure and approach. I will say more about this in the Roman's Commentary. It is also highly suggested that the reader take the time to slow down and grasp such concepts of The-Originals, The-Elements, gods, and lords. It will reshape your thinking about eons and time periods, of which there have been several, and many overlapping and still in parallel within this era. A study of eons will also demonstrate and prove, as Paul does, concerning the power, plan, existence, purpose, and supremacy of The-One-God.

I claim that the Book of Hebrews is written by Paul because of the sophistication of the writing and because Hebrews is again a dissertation to an audience by a prosecuting attorney predicting the death and closure of the First Covenant as delivered by the Angels who had the power of attorney to bring it into effect and manage it. (You can understand this as the "State's Attorney" telling the jury that a criminal is guilty of something and demanding a death sentence, only here Paul is predicting the death of the First Covenant.) I know of no other apostle with the training and background who could have delivered such a letter to an audience. There are other reasons for this statement that I will address in the commentary section of Hebrews.

What about the theology contained in Paul's writings? I do not claim to be a scholar, but over the ages from the time John assembled the Bible we have today, theology has certainly crept in either by design of man or the influence of Satan. I used the word *crept* intentionally. Words with "similar" meaning are found everywhere in all translations, and unfortunately the King James Version—which is the "standard," if you wish to call it this—is replete with "almost" near the bull's-eye words but not directly to the point. Therefore, you will see plenty of hyphenated phrases and words throughout this compendium, and I will state directly here that while reading this, you will be closer to that bull's-eye than most but still not as close as the original Aramaic or Greek. The audience of that day would have had no doubts or uncertainty about clearly understanding the approach and message. That is why one should, in this era and in their lifetime, continue studying other translations and interpretations. The good news is that God will reach whomever He will by all who contribute to his purpose, so study. Now, what about the theology Paul intended all to know?

Paul's theology is called everywhere by him "The-Belief." The Greek is tou pisto, *ton pistos*, which is "the-belief." Realize that because of the need to conserve paper or vellum (animal skins), the writing structure of that day carried no capitalization, commas, or quotes. Those are our inventions for our clarity, which is another reason to understand that a misplaced comma or a capitalized word can change the entire context of what was meant in the original. It is for this reason that all works of this modern age of are truly in the hands of God and his purpose. So, what is "The-Belief" of Paul? Prove me wrong, but I state it thus: Christ is the purpose and cause of God's creation. God created all things for him, bringing him into existence at the precise time and place to fulfill God's plan of salvation. Born as a man, a man as you and I, made of flesh and blood, Christ was tempted in all manner of men and poured out his blood as a sacrifice in the method of a crucifixion (state and world-sponsored). He was dead as any other man is dead or who has died, was in the grave for a full three days, and was resurrected by the power of God after day three. He was presented to God for judgment in the flesh and found to be innocent, blameless, and flawless, not guilty of breaking any of The-Laws of Moses. He is now exalted with the highest pre-eminent position, title, and authority; he is filled with the full divinity and authority of God and is now a man filled with the full shining glory and spirit of GOD. He holds all and everything together in its place and is in dominance of any and all powers, sovereignties, and authorities that have or will exist into the eons. It is because of Christ's blood and acceptance by GOD that "all" (literally meaning every living or dead being, entity, creature, or creation with a conscience that understands there is a God) will be resurrected and willingly and with full acknowledgment gladly and openly confess that GOD is The-God of any gods. You and I are to be given the full divinity, form, nature, authority, and power that Christ has, and we as GOD's sons and daughters are destined to help restore, rule, and manage all of GOD's creations into the eons.

This is what I understand Paul's theology to be. Do not get lost by "near" words like *faith, righteousness, hope* or other such "religious" terms. Paul never used those, being instead direct and blunt.

Lastly it is important to discuss a topic I've hinted at, which is the Sacred Order of the Scriptures especially associated with this topic. Paul's letters start with the concept of freedom and end in Philemon with freedom. What occurs in between is a progressive set of proposals, reasons for those proposals, statements supporting or dismissing arguments for and against, rebuttals, corporate orders and directives, information concerning the development of those proposals (historical, theological, correcting misunderstandings), and a call to action to perform what is expected within "The-Body," The-Family-Corporation. Paul's letters are progressive in matters, and therefore it is important to understand the flow and mechanics of the letters in context to the whole. For without understanding the whole, the part becomes its own beast without rhyme, real reason, and rationale. What I have supplied is a table strictly associated with the Second Compact, not the First Testament that many will recognize by name. My contention is that Paul is arguing in favor of the new and improved compact, the one in which The-Secret has been revealed and enhancing the compact Christ made at "The Last Supper," which was sealed and witnessed with the deliverance of God's Holy-spirit and not blood. That is, the spirit being a far superior mechanism in all respects.

The flow associated with the twenty-seven New Testament letters is first The Gospel of Christ and his direct words and teachings. Next are the epistles written to the Jewish converts, which when read following Christ's material make logical sense since they were the first converts still transitioning between the Law of Moses and its associated appurtenances while slowly moving entirely into the Body of Christ. Next comes Paul's letters to the nations, completing the transition for all "Called-Out" and really "The-All" (The-Secret, universal salvation being offered to all who are dead and those yet to be born) into the Body of Christ and entirely away from the Law of Moses. Finally follows the information of the end time of the current eon and with the first Resurrection millennia period information in last position. For this reason, I offer for discussion and in support of the material and proposal a table to study and review as proof that Paul's writing are the legal writings and directives for the Ecclesiae, The-Called-Outs, The-Body-of-Christ.

It all makes perfectly good sense when viewed in proper order, and I agree with Dr. Earnest L. Martin's research and historical proofs for the proper and original arrangement of the New Testament. The table I have provided comes from his material, and I credit him within what is an abbreviated version given here. The table provides the credited data, book, and organization responsible for managing Dr. Martin's material with the exception of where I may not be in 100 percent agreement with his proposals. That primarily is in slight instances with some dates, since accurate dates are impossible to directly determine but historical and secular data leave very reasonable and believable time frames. Again, I support his material, and in the table I embellish where noted and support his claims.

Enter the Heavenly and Worldly System's Courts. Meet The-Satan, The-Death, The-Originals, The-Master-Savior-Anointed, THE-GOD, but mostly meet Paul, The Persecutor, The Persecuted, and the Prosecutor for you and me.

Current Order by Jerome	Chronology Order*	Approx. Date C.E.	Sacred Order		
Matthew	Mathew	35	Matthew	1	Of Christ
Mark	James	41	Mark		
Luke	Mark	42	Luke		
John	I Thessalonians	50	John		
Acts	II Thessalonians	51	Acts		
Romans	Galatians	53	James	2	"To the Jews First"
I Corinthians	I Corinthians	56	I Peter		
II Corinthians	Romans[1][2][3]	57	II Peter		
Galatians	Luke	57	I John		
Ephesians	II Corinthians	58	II John		
Philippians	Hebrews[4]	61	III John		
Colossians	Ephesians	63	Jude		
I Thessalonians	Philippians	63	Romans	3A	"Then to the Nations" Corporate Letters to the Ecclesiae
II Thessalonians	Colossians	63	I Corinthians		
I Timothy	Philemon	63	II Corinthians		
II Timothy	Titus	63	Galatians		
Titus	I Timothy	63	Ephesians	3B	
Philemon	Acts	63	Philippians		
Hebrews	I Peter	64	Colossians		
James	I John	64	I Thessalonians	4	
I Peter	II John	65	II Thessalonians		
II Peter	II Peter	66	Hebrews	5	
I John	III John	67	I Timothy	6	
II John	Jude	68	II Timothy		
III John	II Timothy	68	Titus		
Jude	John	94	Philemon		
Revelation	Revelation[5]	96	Revelation	7	

see—http://www.askelm.com/restoring/res000a.pdf

* All material, suggested data, dates and arrangements credited to Dr. E.L. Martin, PhD, unless noted, *Restoring the Original Bible*, ASK Organization.

1 Original Letter, date as offered by Dr. E.L. Martin.
2 Addition of The-Secret ~ 63 C.E. Date offered mine.
3 Post Script ~ 68 C.E. Date offered mine.
4 I offer 63 CE as the date.
5 Revelation has two written periods, pre-63 C.E and approximately 96 C.E.

Notes:
The numbers 1 -7 represent completeness or Of God. Each number represents a concept or value within Biblical numerology.

3A Foundational Principles and Instructions.

3B Advanced, specifically The-Secret addition.

A Review of the Legal Themes and Purpose within the Letters

PAUL'S LETTERS CAN BE broken into seven distinct categories, each letter building upon the next within each set or standing on its own. My contention with this book is that Paul is the old Covenant and Law destroyer and yet will bring and help establish a new and better covenant relationship with those called by God and given to Christ. Paul is given the task of developing and fully explaining the offering of salvation and responsibilities within a sure-to-come new government—not based on any written laws, whether religious or civil, of the past or present age of man, or the class of beings called the Originals.

Part 1: ANNULING THE OLD COVENANT, INSTITUTING A NEW AGREEMENT

ROMANS—GALATIANS

I characterize these letters as the beginning of the legal arguments for the dissolving and elimination of the Covenant and Law, which is no longer valid due to the death of an individual having executed it correctly and properly, all necessary requirements. All of it has been fulfilled and executed, meaning the Law including the Commandments, sacrifices, and circumcision. The Covenant having its effect on civilizations and peoples would never had ended until one of two parties came to death, having served and completed all necessary legal requirements, all of them in perfect obedience and practice. Paul here uses the example of the death of the husband releasing his authority, grip, and ownership over the wife. She is free to do as she desires; there are no legal requirements or demands on her or her actions or any future relationships she may end up having. It is the creation of a widow or widower. Either God or a man was required to release the grip of the consequences of the covenant's demands, the primary one being death. It was The-Sin who controlled the covenant and controlled The-Death through that compact. I use Paul's words here for the entities that are identified as such by him while providing a synopsis of his statements and declarations. With the death of one of the parties, the compact was now void, meaningless, with no power, no authority. Not to mention the defects within the covenant being imperfect in intention and application creating nearly impossible restrictions for any man to accomplish—that is, but one.

Christ's death brought to a close the covenant designed to prevent a man from becoming a Savior setting free mankind from a bondage contract designed to bring death. Christ—not a god turned man then restored as a god—but a man. The covenant's death required a man to fulfill the Law and its appurtenances and stand before The-God without blame or blemish. So begins Paul's arguments on the imperfection of the Law, that circumcision and sacrifices bring not salvation but rather certain death, with its effects still continuing to this day.

Also, within these letters Paul develops the new relationship all Creation will have with God—one based on spirit, with spiritual laws resulting in actions based on Godly-love and the forgiveness of errors based on the gracious gift of forgiveness by God. It has nothing to do with man's actions, or laws that must be physically written for the benefit of yourself or those around you.

Part 2: A MERGER WITH ROLES AND RELATIONSHIP

EPHESIANS—COLOSSIANS

These letters serve to explain two activities within the government of God and Christ. The first is the complete acceptance and integration of the Gentiles into the government of God with a direct relationship individually with God previously not available until the acceptance of Christ. God, revealing his acceptance of those outside of Israel with whom He had nothing to do with, no interest in, or any apparent reason to have a relationship with—i.e., anyone not of Israelite heritage, those without any knowledge of, legal matter with, methodology, or access to God Himself. None, apparently, in the conscience of God other than those fulfilling God's will and purpose.

Second to this acceptance and direct relationship are the role and responsibilities within the government—the revealing of the restoration of the heavens with authority and power in addition to the restoration of the physical earth. It's divinity and royalty within the framework of the Body of Christ. I see the Body of Christ as a corporation, a family-operated business, and as a son or daughter of that business, your presence and influence matters, affecting those you will be managing and ruling.

Part 3: AN EXTRACT AND A REBUTTAL

I AND II THESSALONIANS

These two letters essentially serve as a legal summary, an extract, of the previous letters, and they add more information around the expanded role within the government of God as well as details associated with the return of the Savior. Thessalonians will finalize the roles, responsibilities, and charge to the Out-Called, the Ecclesiae, with instruction on what to avoid, what to defend, and how to behave. Small and compact, it's essentially an extract to those it's intended for—those already having the full knowledge and understanding of God's purpose and will and Christ within this master plan.

Both letters of Thessalonians also have another purpose. In addition to focusing the reader's attention on standards and behavior, it focuses them on the future and pulls them directly into the spirit realm. These letters are the first to draw more attention to another world in operation. This other world has been marching in parallel with the physical world, with its own activities and occasional interferences, impact, and influence on our world that challenged Christ's authority and ownership.

Where Paul has been establishing the credentials of Christ in his previous letters, I Thessalonians will declare the authority of Christ over all Creation. It's a legal declaration or claim to the ownership of this right and privilege. What stands behind this letter, however, is II Thessalonians, which has the appearance of a rebuttal by challengers of Christ who assert that they qualify as the rightful heir and owner. II Thessalonians reviews a future takeover attempt, an assumption, a coup by The-Lawless One to stand in a future Temple and declare himself to be the one and only legal authority. Paul then writes that Christ is the one to stand supreme, the only being with the proper credentials who has ultimate authority.

Just because Paul declares it is Christ, is it so? Where is the factual evidence to prove that Christ is the only one to lay claim and be accepted as such legally? That lies in the next division of Paul's letters.

Part 4: LEGAL PROOF THAT CHRIST IS THE-HEIR AND POSSESSES ALL AUTHORITY

Hebrews

The book of Hebrews sits in the middle of Paul's letters. It is the apex of his work and shows his brilliance as a scholar, debater, and prosecuting attorney. In my opinion, this is what Paul was created to do in addition to laying the legal framework for the coming government of God. Hebrews is a lawsuit brought against the Originals in Heaven and any and all of their minions. It accuses them of fraud, deceit, blackmail, and murder. Paul demands that they prove they are the rightful owners and heirs of Creation. Paul says in effect, "Prove you are what Christ is, was created as, was intended to be, what he sacrificed; what he accomplished by fulfilling the legal demands of God on a man. Fulfilling all rites, ceremonies, prophecies, demands, and arriving at the expected time. Fully and passionately believing in God and all He is and does. Whether of angels or any other entity in Heaven, who are you? Where are you? Come forth or remain silent and obedient." Hebrews is the proof of Christ being the heir, the cause, the purpose of Creation, and all is to be (and is) assigned to him legally with full ownership, titles, and entitlements, divinity, and authority. This is the reason the letter appears out of time and beyond the general comprehension of readers. It continues to piggyback on the legal letters of Paul, and unless one realizes that Paul has been laying the foundation of a government and the authority associated with it, the reader glosses over the true theme. Volumes need to be written about this letter. It is not intended for a general audience, although it is sent as such and clears up the general misunderstandings about angels. The letter is much greater in scope and purpose. This is a man accusing and prosecuting the entities in Heaven. Unheard of! Profound.

Part 5: PROXY TRANSFER OF AUTHORITY

I and II Timothy

These letters serve to transfer the authority of Paul to Timothy. Essentially these letters are Paul's last will and testament to and for Timothy. Paul's transfers his authority and leadership to Timothy by proxy. This is a series of tenderly written letters, yet they are quite direct in reminding Timothy how he received this enhanced recognition, his expanded role, and the fact that he is now the primary authority over the entire Gentile Ecclesia. The letters contain what to do, how to do it, and reminders and warnings. Timothy now stands in Paul's place. Timothy is Paul's heir in government and civil matters within the Ecclesiae, particularly within the Gentile world.

Part 6: POWER OF ATTORNEY LETTER

Titus

Titus is a power of attorney letter. Paul is authorizing Titus to reestablish the Ecclesiae on Crete. This letter would have been carried to all those existing households and any new ones being created to establish Titus' authority and to let those groups affected know what Titus was charged to perform and what they could expect. Apparently there were individuals in authority within the Ecclesiae on the island that didn't just oppose the original teachings and doctrines delivered and established, but abused the authority they carried. Titus was sent to do a house cleaning, reestablish the foundational teachings and doctrines, and oppose an individual called a "prophet" for a group not associated with the Ecclesiae but certainly imposing his actions and doctrine on the households.

In another respect, as a reader you can well sense that the first thirty years of establishing the new lifestyle and culture of Christ was already beset with frauds, fakes, fornication, and crumbling Ecclesiae. Once-true believers and others emerged who saw an opportunity to take advantage of the weak-minded, perverting the true knowledge and teachings for their own gain. If Paul and the other Apostles were losing the battle so soon within this time period, can you imagine how far from the original individuals and institutions certainly must be today?

Part 7: A TORT

PHILEMON

Philemon is a tort. What is a tort? Per the *Legal Dictionary*, a tort is:

> A body of rights, obligations, and remedies that is applied by courts in civil proceedings to provide relief for persons who have suffered harm from the wrongful acts of others. The person who sustains injury or suffers pecuniary damage as the result of tortious conduct is known as the plaintiff, and the person who is responsible for inflicting the injury and incurs liability for the damage is known as the defendant or tortfeasor.[1]

Paul admits to being the tortfeasor in this letter, willing to make reparations to Philemon for the use of his slave without having Philemon's permission to do so. And Onesimus the slave is willing to admit his wrongful actions and accept Philemon's judgment concerning him because of his alliance with Paul. The fault (sin?) is entirely on Paul, and he is willing to make full restitution at personal cost to himself for both. Philemon simply needs to issue his judgment and demand.

But this letter is crafty in its admission, offering, and request. Paul uses a play on words with the name of the slave he has been using for his purpose. Paul places in the open letter an underlying theme, another legal concern that is still in debate and in practice to this day: slavery and its counterpoint freedom. This has been a fundamental core topic in all of Paul's letters starting with Romans, and he will finish his epistles with this same theme in Philemon. How does a slave in Christ own a slave who is a slave of Christ? For that matter, can one man really own another? The letter may be short in length, but its implications are enormous, and it continues to carry into time, even to our current period. This letter, like Hebrews, displays Paul's brilliance as a legal defender—or as I see it, subtlety incriminates Philemon in his ownership of slaves. Paul, the ever-present prosecutor and brilliant legal tactician, prosecutes and condemns himself first only to turn the tables in identifying and prosecuting just one of the several failing institutions in The-System. How does Philemon respond? That, too, is a timeless question.

---

1. http://legal-dictionary.thefreedictionary.com/Tort+Law.

Section I

ANNULING THE OLD, INSTITUTING A NEW

The Letters of Romans, Corinthians, and Galatians

Defense of Believing versus the Law of Moses
Legal Arguments and Proofs

Principles of Behavior and Living within The-Body-of-Christ
Corporate Directives and the "Employees Handbook"

Nature and Quality of GOD
Who the Owner Is, How He Operates, and through Whom

Your Legal Contract with GOD
What You Are to Do and What GOD Will Do

ROMANS COMMENTARY

ROMANS, THE THUNDERING OPENING letter to all Nations outside of Israel and the Jews (Paul never uses the word *Gentiles* directly, but "Nations" giving honor and dignity to these audiences—something a Jew would never do in the era of Paul and many in our times don't either) opens with a bang and immediately begins a debate of how man's salvation is not accomplished by The-Law of Moses, by its demanded ordinances and regulations, or by any action or deed you perform with the exception of believing in the sacrifice and blood of The Savior and Messiah, Jesus Christ.

You are the jurist. You must decide. You are in a seat of judgment. Will your tithes, taking in the homeless, time spent working in soup kitchens and performing other "selfless actions" gain your salvation or is salvation only won by believing that which Paul claims? You must decide, thumbs-up or thumbs-down, as Nero would have. Make your choice wisely.

Thus, after a brief establishment of his authority and offering praises to God and Christ, Paul, as the prosecuting attorney, brings forward his indictments and opening arguments against The Law of Moses and its appurtenances (circumcision taking the position of the dominant interference) in opposition to believing in God and Christ in order to be saved (see Romans 1:8–25). The original letter to the Romans is a rhetorical legal argument being held in the court of public opinion . . . *your* opinion.

Then follows a series of debates—the pros and cons and proofs of not by The-Law and its decrees and ordinances. Paul shows that only by believing is an individual saved and that belief is a gift directly given by God Himself so that no man or other being may boast in themselves as having achieved salvation by their might, will, power, or purpose (see Romans 2:1—7:25).

Romans 8:1—9:6 (notice that I ignore the King James chapter break) contains Paul's closing argument, bringing the charge that The-Law and all of its practices make it impossible to lead anyone to salvation. Therefore the law must die; it must disappear. It must be written out of the record books. With logic and the Scriptures, Paul demonstrates beyond any doubt and proves conclusively that only by believing will anyone be saved.

So ends the original distributed letter from Paul to the Romans. As a jurist, you are obligated to take a stand today on the position you will yield. What is your decision? Thumbs-up, thumbs-down—which is your master?

Section I

But wait... there is more. There was Timothy and something else.

Time has passed (estimates range from four to ten years), and something revolutionary happened in the Ecclesia, to the Apostles and all The-Chosen-Ones. What Paul calls specifically *The-Secret* has been divinely revealed to many, and the entire Ecclesiae is aware of this teaching. Paul needs to add something more to his original letter, specifically for the Romans but really for the Nations as a whole. Apparently, this revealed knowledge had gone to the Nations' heads, and they were thinking they were now in a superior position over the Jews in dominance of leadership, blessings, and sonship in Christ. I would also postulate that this battle over circumcision and The-Law still had not resolved itself and died, so in a "republishing" of the letter, not only is the original letter rehearsed, but Paul also corrects the Nations for taking a posture that they were greater now than the Jews. He refutes their likely self-imposed claim of "God-Ordained Authority" by exercising lordship over the Jews, which is not scriptural or correct. Paul reinstructs the Jews first and then the Nations; they are both equal, but the Nations are in the second position (for there is neither Jew nor Gentile in the Kingdom and both are to bear the same fruit).

Romans 9:7—11:36 is a discourse of what God intended for the Jews to bring salvation to the Nations. He explains that, in the process, the Jews also needed salvation for themselves, and so the two groups of peoples, in harmony and unison, were meant to help one another achieve the purpose and will of God. Neither is in domination to the other, and Christ is clearly the Head of All; He is the only Dominant-One.

I have distinguished this separation of themes by a time stamp in the letter and verse formats so the reader can properly transition in thinking and understanding about what Paul is correcting when it comes to both entities. Both parties were debating about which was greater, and so this addition to the letter should also help us understand what our position as members of the Nations was with God, is currently, and will be in the future.

But wait, there is even more...

Timothy has now returned with the scrollets that include both Paul's original and modified letters to the Ecclesiae. Why? Here is the interesting part. Paul, under house arrest, had already escaped Caesar once from the death sentence, but it was pretty clear that Paul would not be so fortunate this time unless (as he states) it was in Christ's will to allow him to go to Spain. We really do not know what occurred (to Spain, to Britain, or to beheading in Rome), but we know this. Starting in chapter 12 is a third edition added to Romans. It is a last plea and a series of instructions to all his readers. Paul is clearly reiterating living in Christ and in the spirit of God. Any reader can research all the rest of Paul's letters—specifically Galatians where Paul lays down the expectations of the principles of living and one's personal conduct. (Romans 13:9 quotes the "Golden Rule" as attributed to Christ.) Paul is repeating past instructions and adding future ones in this last will and testament of his. "Do this, act like that; take care of my relatives if I die." Paul to his last day remained the lawyer's lawyer in the

Ecclesiae. All of Paul's writings are legal documents in some form and fashion. He has written all sorts of legal briefs for you and me to research and take a stand on in his fourteen letters. Enjoy your internship as you grow in grace and knowledge.

As much as Paul thunders onto the scene in Romans, I would argue that this first letter is also his last and final writings to all; Romans not only opens but seals his works. All of Paul's other writings fall neatly into Romans and support the three major pivotal themes inside this letter (believing, The-Secret, and daily living). Chapters 12 through 16 can just as easily had been added to the end of Philemon as a separate letter as a passionate plea to you and me to stay loyal and true, live the lifestyle, and believe that Christ came in the flesh, is sitting on a throne to the right of our FATHER GOD now, and has guaranteed our resurrection.

So, in one complete letter, Paul delivers three major tenets: 1) salvation is through believing, not works or any actions you display or think you cause; 2) the revelation of The-Secret and our relationship within this Secret; and 3) how to live and demonstrate the spirit of God and behavior for His Kingdom while still in the form of man. No other letter offers all three themes with such detail. If one was to carry but one letter of Paul, Romans would be the first, last, and obvious choice.

ROMANS AS A LETTER

PAUL A SLAVE OF *Savior-Anointed*, a Commissioner, called and specifically-separated for the Well-Message of *GOD* that *HE* promised in-the-past, through the holy-writings by the-prophets of *HIM* about *The-Son-of-HIM*. *The-One* coming out of the seed of David in flesh designated-and-designed-to-be *The-Son-of-God* with unlimited-inherent-power with the spirit-of-holiness by the Resurrection from the dead-ones. *Savior-Anointed*, *The-Master* of us through whom we obtain grace and commissioned in faithful obedience to all The-Nations for the sake of *The-Name* of *Him* among whom you are also the Called-Ones of *Savior Anointed*.

To all those in Rome loved-by-God and called Holy-Ones of *GOD*, grace, and peace to you from *GOD* our *FATHER* and *Master-Savior-Anointed*.

First in order I-give-thanks *THE-GOD* of mine through *Savior-Anointed* over all of you that The-Belief of yours is announced in the-whole-System. For *THE-GOD* is my witness whom I divinely serve in the-spirit of mine in the-well-message of *The-Son*-of-*HIM*, how I unceasingly make mention of you always in my prayers. Asking-and-pleading at length somehow to find a way in the-will of *THE-GOD* to come to you. I greatly desire to see you that I may share spiritual gifts with you so you will be standing-firm, that is together you and I will be encouraged and strengthened together by our belief.

For I am not willing for you to be ignorant, Brothers. Many times I have purposed to come to you and was forbidden until now so that I should have some fruit among you as among the-rest of the Nations. To both Greeks and barbarians, both wise and foolish I am obligated-under-gratitude-for-a-favor-received. Thus, I have eagerness in me to bring to you, The-Ones in Rome, to bring the well-message. Because I am not ashamed of the-well-message of *The-Anointed* for in it is *GOD'S* unlimited-inherent-power bringing salvation to everyone who believes. To Jews first before to Greeks for the justice of *GOD* is revealed in it from-not believing into believing. As it has been written stating, "The-Just shall-be-living by believing."

For the anger of *GOD* is revealed from heaven on all ungodliness and injustice of men, The-Ones who suppress *The-Truth* in injustice. Because that which is known about *THE-GOD* is clearly-made-visibly-apparent among them for *GOD* has openly-shown it to them. For the-unseen-things of *HIM* from the Creation-of-the-System are still being understood and described by things that are made along-with his imperceptible inherent-unlimited-power and divinity. So, they are defenseless because they knew *THE-GOD*. They did not glorify him or thank him as *GOD* but they became vain in their own reasoning, unintelligent and darkened in their hearts. Alleging themselves to be wise, they are made stupid, and they changed the-glory of *THE-INCORRUPTIBLE-GOD* into the likeness and image of decaying-dying-sinful men, of flying creatures, four footed beasts, and of reptiles. Therefore *THE-GOD* has given up on them because-of the-unclean-lusting of the-hearts of them and for the-dishonoring of their bodies among themselves. Whom altering *The-Truth* of *THE-GOD* into a lie and venerating-and-worshipping and offering-divine-service to The-Creation rather than *THE-ONE CREATING* who is to be blessed into the-eons. Amen.

Because of this *THE-GOD* has given them over to their vile passions, for even their females have changed their natural use against nature. Likewise, also the-males are leaving the-natural use of a woman burning in their craving for another man, males in males acting indecently receiving the-reward of their deceptions in them as is only natural-and-fitting. Accordingly, they test *THE-GOD*, behaving like they have no knowledge of him. And *THE-GOD* gives over to them an unsound mind to be doing those things that are not fitting, having been filled with every unjustness, prostitution, wickedness, greed, extreme evil envy, murder, strife, fraud, depravity, whisperers, backbiters, God detesters, outrageous, proud, ostentatious, inventors of evil, disobedient to parents, unintelligent, promise breakers, unloving, truce breakers, unmerciful, The-Ones who recognize the-justice of *THE-GOD*. The-Ones which commit such things deserve death, not only doing the same, but also endorsing the-ones-committing them.

Therefore, you are without any excuses, oh man! For everyone that judges, for that-which you are judging the-different-one, you condemn yourselves as the-one-committing-and-practicing-the-same things. For we are aware that The-Judgment of *THE-GOD* is executed-with truth opposing the-ones who are practicing such things. And you can count on this, oh man; the-one-judging those practicing such while you are doing the same will not escape The-Judgment of *THE-GOD*. Do you despise the-riches of the-kindness of *HIM* and of the-tolerance and the-patience? Do you not comprehend the-kindness of *THE-GOD* is leading you to repentance? But in accordance with your hardened and unrepentant heart you are hoarding up righteous-fury for yourself when *THE-GOD* reveals *HIS* judgment in that Day-of-Indignation who will repay each one in accordance with his acts. Indeed, to the-ones who by patient endurance are doing acts of honor and glory and incorruption, eonian life. But to the-ones that are stubborn and full of strife, ignoring the-truth, committed to do the-injustice: fury and wrath, affliction, and distress on every soul of man that does evil. First to Jews and then the Nations. But glory and honor and peace to everyone that works well. To Jew first and then to Greek.

For there is no partiality with *THE-GOD*, for whoever has sinned without The-Law will-also perish without The-Law and for whoever has sinned in The-Law

Section I

through The-Law shall be judged. For listeners of The-Law are not just {innocent, without guilt or flaw} before THE-GOD, but the-doers of The-Law are being justified. For whenever Nations not having The-Law by nature are doing The-Law, they are a law to themselves who are openly-demonstrating the-acts of The-Law written in their hearts. Their conscious testifying as a witness in reasoning accusing or excusing themselves. In that-Day THE-GOD will be judging the-hidden things of men according-to my well-message through *Savior Anointed*.

Understand you called a Jew and are contently-relying in The-Law and boasting about THE-GOD. And note as well those who are testing the-things that are "most excellent" being instructed out of The-Law. You have confidence that you are to be a leader of blind-ones, a light to the-ones in darkness, a disciplining teacher of unbelieving-foolish ones, of minors, having a form of the-knowledge and of the-truth in The-Law. The-one teaching another are you not teaching yourself? The-one proclaiming to not be stealing you are stealing. The-one saying to not be committing adultery you are committing adultery. The-one hating idols you defile The-Sanctuary! Who is boasting in The-Law yet side stepping The-Law you are dishonoring THE-GOD. For as it was written, "THE-NAME of THE-GOD because of you is being blasphemed among the Nations." Indeed, circumcision is beneficial if you may be practicing The-Law but if you are a transgressor of The-Law circumcision has become un-circumcision. If ever then the-un-circumcised keeps the-just requirements of The-Law shall not his un-circumcision be counted for circumcision? And the-un-circumcision who is not-set-apart-as-holy meets-the-demands-of The-Law, he shall be judging you, you of The-Letter and circumcision that transgresses The-Law. For he is not The-Jew who is one outwardly nor circumcised which is done outwardly on the-flesh but he is The-Jew inwardly and circumcised of the heart, in spirit, not in the Letter whose praise is not from men but from THE-GOD.

What then is the-Jew's advantage, what benefit if any is in circumcision? Great and in every way! For without argument first they believed and were entrusted with The-Oracles of THE-GOD.

So-what if some disbelieved? Does their disbelief void the-belief in THE-GOD? Never, no way, no how! THE-GOD is true and every man a liar for as it is written, "So that YOU may be justified always in YOUR words," and, "You should be an over-comer when you are to be judged."

For if the-injustice of us upholds the-justice of GOD what are we to argue? THE-GOD is unjust who brings punishment? What logic is there in that? No, how else shall THE-GOD be judging The-System? For if The-Truth-of-THE GOD is super-glorified through my lying why am I also a sinner still being judged? And why not do evil so that good may come of it as we have been slanderously accused of and some claim that we have said? Their condemnation is assured. What then are we better-and-different-than-them? No, without a doubt, for we have charged both Jews and Greeks, all are under sin.

As it is written, "There is no just one, not even one." "There is no one who understands, there is no one who seeking out THE-GOD." "All avoid him simultaneously, they are useless." "There is not even one doing kindness." "Their larynx has been opened like a sepulcher, their tongues they defraud with, the venom of asps under their lips." "Their mouth is being crammed with vile cursing and bitterness." "Their feet fast to pour out blood, crushing and extreme callousness is their way," and, "The way of peace they know not." "There is no fear of God before their eyes."

For we are aware that whatever The-Law says it is speaking to those under The-Law, that every mouth may be being stopped and The-entire-System is becoming guilty and subject to the just-verdict of THE-GOD. Therefore, by none of The-Law's acts shall no flesh be justified at all in the sight of HIM for through The-Law is knowledge-and-recognition of sin.

But now apart from The-Law the justice of GOD has been made apparent being attested to by The-Law and The-Prophets. For GOD'S justice is through believing in *Savior Anointed* to all and on all, The-Ones-believing for there is no distinction. For all have sinned and come short of The-Esteem-of-*THE-GOD*. Being unreservedly-and-wholeheartedly justified by *HIS* grace through the-deliverance of and in *Anointed Savior* whom *THE-GOD* purposed as a conciliatory-atonement-offering through The-Belief in *His* blood and showing the-justice of *Him*. Because *THE-GOD* in mercy is passing over of the-penalties-of-sins that have previously occurred, *THE-GOD* in his mercy at this time is displaying the-justice of *HIM* and a *JUSTIFYING-ONE* of the-one who has belief in *Savior*.

Where is the-boasting then? There is no place for it! Because of which law? Or works? No! But through The-Law-of-Believing. We logically conclude then a man is justified by believing apart from the-acts of The-Law. Is *THE-GOD* only to Jews and not to the other Nations too? Yes, also to the other Nations since it is *THE-ONE-GOD* who shall be justifying circumcision by believing and un-circumcision through believing. Are we claiming-The-Law-has-no-authority-or-power because of believing? No way! No, we continue to-stand-by-the-authority-of The-Law.

What shall we be declaring then of our Father Abraham having been seen in the flesh? For if Abraham was justified out of works, he would be boasting but not about *THE-GOD*. For what does The-Writings say? "Abraham believed *THE-GOD* and it is accounted to him for justice." Yet for the-one-working there is the-wage which is but a payment-due which is not being accounted for grace. For the-one who is not working yet believing on *THE-ONE-JUSTIFYING* the-ungodly, his belief is accounted as just. Even as David has also said, "Happy is the-man whom from *THE-GOD* is accounted as just apart from works." "Happy are they who are pardoned from lawless acts and sins are covered over." "Happy is the-man whom the Lord will not be recognizing his sin."

Does this blessing come on circumcision or only the-uncircumcision? We are stating that Abraham's righteousness is accounted to him by believing. How then is this reasoned? While being in circumcision or in un-circumcision? Not in circumcision but in un-circumcision. And the sign he obtained was circumcision, the seal of the-righteousness of belief while-being in un-circumcision. That he is to be Father of all the-ones-believing while uncircumcised that righteousness may be credited to them also and the father of those circumcised. And it not only to the-ones-of-circumcision, but the-ones-observing and walking in the-footprints of The-Belief-of-The-Father of us Abraham while he was in the-un-circumcision-condition.

For The-Law did not offer The-Promise for Abraham or his seed to be the-Enjoyer-of-the-Allotment of the-Coming-System but through righteousness by-believing. For if they are Enjoyers-of-The-Allotment because of The-Law, believing is voided and the-Promise has been voided. The-Law is-producing anger-because-of-its-punishments. Also, where there is no law there are neither transgressions.

For out of this believing by grace the-Promise is to be confirmed to the-entire-seed, not only for the-ones by The-Law but also to the-ones because of the-Belief-of-Abraham who is Father of all of us. As it is written, while in the presence of God, he believed *THE-ONE-MAKING-LIVE* the-dead-ones and *THE-ONE-CALLING* into existence those things which do not exist as though they are, "I have appointed you the Father-of-Many-Nations." Who beyond reason-and-understanding believed with anticipated-assurance that he was to become the father of many nations according-to having been declared, "So will your seed be."

With no weakness in believing, he did not consider his body as having already been dead when he was about one hundred years old or even Sara's womb dead. He never doubted the-Promise-of-*THE-GOD* but was invigorated by believing giving esteem and honor to *THE-GOD* and being fully convinced for that which had been promised *HE* was able to do. Therefore, "It is accounted to him for righteousness." Not only is it written because of him for his own credit, but also because of us to whom it is being credited as the-ones believing in *THE-ONE* who raised *Savior-The-Master* of us from the dead who was sacrificed because of the-offenses of us and was raised for The-Justification.

Being justified, then, by believing, we are having peace with *THE-GOD* through *The-Master* of us *Savior-Anointed*. Through whom also we have access by-believing into The-Grace in which we remain and in which we are boasting about The-Expectation-of-The-Glory-of-*THE-GOD*. Not only that but we are boasting about the-Afflictions having perceived that the-Afflictions is producing patience. By tested endurance and testing, The-Expectation.

Now The-Expectation is not mortifying, knowing that the-Godly-love of *THE-GOD* has been poured out in the-hearts of us through the-Holy-spirit being given to us. Still for us the strength-less, *Anointed,* according-to the appointed season died for-the-sake-of the ungodly. For hardly for-the-sake of a just man shall anyone die, perhaps for-a-good-man would one even be daring to die. Yet *GOD* is demonstrating *HIS* Godly-love for us that while we were still sinners *The Anointed* died for-the-sake-of us.

Much more than being justified now by the-blood of *Him*, we shall be saved through *Him* from The-Judgment. For when being enemies we were reconciled to *THE-GOD* through the-death of *HIS Son*, we shall be saved in The-Life-of-*Him*. Not only that, but also glorying in *THE-GOD* through *The-Master* of us *Savior-Anointed* through whom now we have obtained The-Atonement. Because of this, even as Sin entered into The-System through one man and through Sin entered The-Death and in-this-manner death is passed through into all men for all have sinned. Before The-Law Sin was in the System, but Sin was not being {had no authority} without existence of The-Law. Still The-Death reigned from Adam to Moses and over the-ones that had not sinned as in the-likeness of Adam's transgression who is a type of *The-One* that was coming. But the-free gift is not like the-offense. For if the-offense of one caused many to die, much more the-gift of *THE-GOD* and by the-grace *The-One-Man, Savior-Anointed* super-abounds in the-many. And not as the-one sinning comes the-gift. Indeed, out of that one is The-Judgment-of-Condemnation for that gift out of the many offenses results in its just award. For if by The-One-Man's offense The-Death dominates, how much more for The-Ones through *The-One* super-abounds grace and the-gift of obtaining The-Justice-of-Life and shall be reigning through *The-One-Savior-Anointed*? By logic, then, since through one offense all men are condemned, therefore also through *The Just-One* is justification of life for all men.

Just as through the-disobedience of one man many sinners were created-and-caused, also through the-obedience of *The One* shall the-many be made just. For the Law crept in increasing the-offenses and increasing the-sins and-yet The-Grace super-exceeds-in-domination. For even as The-Death reigns through the-sin, even greater The-Grace is to be reigning through justice into life eonian through *Savior Anointed, The-Master* of us.

What shall we declare then? Shall we be remaining in sin that grace should be more abundant? NO! What message does that send? We who have died in sin shall still be living in her? Or do you not realize that as many of us that are immersed into *Anointed Savior* are baptized in the-death of *Him*? We were together then entombed by baptism into-the-death with *Him*. Further even as *Christ* was revived up-out-of the dead-ones through The-Glory-of-*THE-FATHER*, so then we should be walking in newness of life. For not-only-have we have become a-planted-seed together in the-likeness of the-death-of-*Him*, but also in The-Resurrection shall we also be like *Him*. Knowing this that the-old-man in us was impaled so-that The-Body-of-The-Sin may be destroyed, by no means then should we still be-slaving to The-Sin. For the-one-dying from sin has been pardoned-and-released. Yet if we died together with *Christ*, we are believing that we shall be living together also with *Him*. With-the-knowledge that *Anointed* is arisen out of the dead-ones and is no-longer dying, Death is no longer being-a-lord.

For who *He* died, *He* died once for sin, but for whom *He* is living; *He* is living for *THE-GOD*. Thus, also you be indeed recognizing yourself dead to The-Sin yet alive for *THE-GOD* and *Anointed Savior, The-Maste*r of us. Do not let The-Sin be reigning

Section I

in your mortal body and obeying her, in the-lusts of it. Nor yet be presenting your members as implements of unjustness for sin but present yourselves to *THE-GOD* as living out of the dead and your members as implements of justice for *THE-GOD*. For Sin shall not be mastering over you for you are not under the Law but under grace.

What-then? Shall we continue sinning then seeing that we are not under the Law but under grace? NO WAY! Are you not aware that to whom you are presenting yourselves you are slaves to obey? You are slaves to whom you are obeying, whether of sin for death or to obedience for justice. But thanks be to *THE-GOD* that while you were slaves to sin, you out of the heart obeyed the teaching that was given to you. Being freed from The-Sin you are enslaved to justice. As a man I am saying this because of the-weakness of your flesh for you present your members as slaves for uncleanliness and for lawlessness into greater-lawlessness. Now present yourself and your members as slaves for justice, for holiness. For when you were slaves to sin, you were not-associated-with justice.

What fruit then did you have-on-which you are now feeling guilty about? For the-complete-finish of those things is death. And now being freed from The-Sin, being enslaved to *THE-GOD* you are having your fruit in holiness and also ending in life eonian. For the-purchased-wages of sin—death, but the-gracious-gift of *THE-GOD* is life eonian in *Anointed Savior, The-Master* of us.

Or are you being ignorant, Brothers? For I am speaking to the ones with-knowledge about the Law that The-Law is dominating the-man for as much time as he-is-living, just-as a woman by The-Law is in-servitude-and-shackled-to the-living-man. She is exempt from the-law of her husband if he is dead. This is why she shall be called an adulterous if the-man is yet living and she establishes-a-marital-relationship-with a different man. But if her man may be dead, she is free from The-Law; she is not an adulteress if she establishes a marital-relationship with a different man. So now, my Brothers, you also were caused to die in The-Law through The-Body-of-*The Anointed* that you should be married to a different one who is raised from the dead-ones. That we should be bearing fruit to *THE-GOD* for when we were in the-flesh, the-passions of the-sins through The-Law operated inside our members to bear fruit for The-Death. But we were exempted from The-Law in which we were held captive for death so that in the newness of spirit we are to be serving and not to the passing-away of The-Writings.

What shall we declare then? Is The-Law sin? No way! I would not know The-Sin but for the Law. I would not have been aware of coveting if The-Law had not said, "You shall not be coveting." But The-Sin gaining-a-strategic-position through The-Commandment produces in me all manner of coveting for without the Law, Sin is dead. Now I was-once-alive not-having-the Law but when The-Commandment came, Sin revived-and-gained-strength-and-dominating-control and I died. And I realized-and-was-given understanding The-Commandment made for life really delivers death. For Sin rushed in through The-Commandment seducing me and through it slays-and-murders me. So The-Law indeed is holy and The-Commandment holy and just and good. Then "being-good" has become death for me? No way! But The-Sin that it may be made-to-be-recognized-as sin by "being-good" is sentencing me to death. That The-Sin through The-Commandment makes-one-an-infinitely-greater sinner.

For we are aware that The-Law is spiritual, but I am of-the-flesh, having been sold-and-discarded-for-trash under Sin. For that which I am doing I don't understand because that which I want-and-desire to do this I am not practicing, but that which I hate, this I am doing. But if I am doing this which I-do-not-desire, I am positively-confirming that The-Law is ideal.

For it is still no longer I doing it but Sin making its home in me. I am aware that nothing good is making its home in me, this flesh of mine. For to be doing-good is inside me, but how to do the-ideal I am not finding. For I desire to do good, but I do not. I do not desire to do that which is evil, and this I am practicing. But if I am doing that which I do not want to do, it is no longer I doing it but Sin that is making its home in me. Consequently, I am finding The-Law in me willing to be doing the-ideal but finding the-evil is present with me. Now I am gratified about The-Law-of-*THE GOD* concerning the-inward-man, but I am observing a different law in my members warring against The-Law-of-my-mind and leading me into captivity to The-Law-of-Sin which is in my members.

I am a wretched man! Who is the-deliverer of me from The-Death in the-body? I am thankful to *THE-GOD* through *Savior Anointed, The-Master* of us. Consequently, then I am indeed in my mind slaving to the Law-of-*GOD* but in the-flesh the Law-of-Sin.

In conclusion, nothing condemns the-ones in *Anointed Savior*. They are not walking according-to the flesh but according-to the spirit. For The-Law-of-The-Spirit of the-life in *Anointed Savior* frees me from The-Law-of-Sin and of The-Death. For it is impossible for The-Law because it was hindered through the-flesh. *THE-GOD* sending *HIS* own *Son* in the likeness of sinful flesh and for Sin condemns Sin in the-flesh. That the-requirement of The-Law may be fulfilled and the-ones are not passing-their-life in companionship with the flesh but with the spirit. For the-ones being in the-flesh think about the fleshly things, but the-ones in union with the spirit the things of-the-spirit. For the nature of the-flesh: death, yet the nature of the-spirit — life and peace. Because the-nature of the-flesh is hatred toward God for it is not subject to The-Law-of-*THE-GOD* for it is unable to. So the-ones being in the-flesh are not able to please *GOD*. But you are not of flesh but of spirit, that is if the spirit of *GOD* is making its home in you. Because if anyone is not having the spirit of *Anointed*, this one is not of *Him*. For indeed if *Anointed* is in you, the body is dead because of sin but the spirit is alive because of justification. For if the-spirit that raised up *Savior* out of dead-ones is making its home in you, *THE-ONE-ROUSING The-Anointed* out of the-dead-ones shall be making alive your mortal bodies because of *HIS* spirit making its home in you.

Therefore, Brothers, we are debtors not to the-flesh or to live according-to flesh, for if you are living according-to the flesh, you shall die. Yet if the-spirit is causing

Section I

the-practices of the-body to die, you shall be living. For whoever is being led by the-spirit of *GOD*, these are Sons-of-*GOD*. For you have not gotten a spirit-of-Slavery again to fear, but you got the spirit-of-Sonship in which we are calling aloud exclaiming-and-imploring ABBA, *THE-FATHER*. The-spirit itself is together witnessing with our spirit that we are offspring of *GOD*, and since offspring, also Enjoyers-of-the-Allotment. Without-a-doubt Enjoyers-of-the-Allotment-of-*GOD* and joint Enjoyers of The-Allotment-of-*Anointed*, if it be that we are suffering together that also we should be being glorified together.

For I am accounting that the-emotional-sufferings of the-current-season are not worthy of the glory to be revealed in us. For the-desire-and-expectation of The-Creation is waiting for the-unveiling of The-Sons-of-*THE-GOD*. For Creation was not voluntarily subjugated to decay but through The-One-Subjecting her in expectations. And that same Creation shall be freed from the-slavery-of-corruption into the-glorious-freedom by The-Offspring-of-*THE-GOD*. We are aware that The-entire-Creation is groaning together and with-birthing-pains together even now. But not only this, but we ourselves also The-First-Fruits-of-the-spirit. We ourselves also are groaning, waiting for our sonship and from the-unchaining-and-deliverance from our body. We were saved for The-Expectation by expectation. For expecting what is being observed is not expectation. Why? For what one sees why does he need to expect it?

But through endurance we are waiting, expecting what we do not see. Similarly, also the-spirit is together supporting the-weakness of us, and what for? Because we are not aware of what we should be praying according-to that which must be. But this-same-spirit is exceedingly-pleading for-the-sake-of us with inarticulate groaning. Yet *THE-ONE-SEARCHING* the-hearts is aware of the-way-and-manner of the-spirit that in union with *GOD* is pleading for-the-sake-of the Holy-Ones. We are aware that all are working together for good for The-Ones-Godly-Loving *THE GOD*, for the-ones being called according for-this purpose. That whom *HE* already had knowledge of and also predetermined to be conformed into the-image of *The-Son*-of-*HIM*, *First-born* among many brethren. For whom *HE* predetermined these *HE* also calls, these also *HE* justifies, whom *HE* justifies these *HE* also glorifies.

What if anything-more shall we declare toward these things? If *THE-GOD* protects-and-rules us, who is against us? Who truly did not spare *HIS* own *Son* but sacrificed *Him* for all our sakes, how not also together with *Him* for us shall *HE* be graciously granting all things? Who shall be prosecuting-and-accusing against The Chosen-Ones of *GOD*? *GOD* is *THE ONE-JUSTIFYING*. Who is the-one condemning *Anointed* who died? Even better, who has risen and is at the right hand of *THE-GOD* who also is pleading-and-interceding for-the-sake-of us? What shall be separating us from the-Godly-love of *The-Anointed*? Affliction or distress or persecution or famine or nakedness or danger or sword? As it is written, "That on account-of you, we are being slaughtered the-whole-day, we are counted as sheep for the slaughter."

No, in all these things we are more than conquering through *THE-ONE godly-loving* us, for I have been persuaded that neither death, nor life, nor angels, nor sovereignties, nor powers, nor anything present, nor anything about to come, nor height, nor depth, nor any different creation shall be able to separate us from the-Godly-love of *THE GOD* in *Anointed Savior, The-Master* of us.

I am telling the truth in Christ; I am not lying. My conscience together with Holy-spirit is a witness for me that in me is great sorrow and unceasing pain in my heart. Wishing this about myself that I was specifically-set-aside-away from *The-Anointed* for my brothers, my relatives by birth. Any who are Israelites to whom was given The-Sonship and The-Glory and The-Covenants and The-Legislations and The-Divine-Service and The-Promises. By whom out of The-Fathers came *The Anointed*, in the flesh, *The One-Being-Over-All*.

GOD be blessed into The-Eons.

Amen.

FIRST ADD TO THE ORIGINAL LETTER CIRCULATED ~ 65 C.E.

The Relationship of Jew and Gentile within THE REVELATION OF THE-SECRET

At no time has the-word of *THE-GOD* fallen short. For not all of The-Ones out of Israel are Israelites, neither are they all that are of Abraham's seed offspring but, "in Isaac shall your seed be called." Meaning not the-offspring of the-flesh. Those are not the children of *THE-GOD* but The-Offspring of The-Promise is accounted as the seed. For this is *The-Word-of-Promise*, according-to this, "I shall be coming in the-season and there shall be a son for Sarah." And not only this, but also out of Rebecca, the-one having bedded with Isaac The-Father for those of us not being born yet, nor yet practicing anything good or evil that accordingly the-purposeful-choice of *THE-GOD* may be permanent-and-accomplished. Not by acts but by *THE-ONE-CALLING*. It was declared to her, "That the-elder shall be slaving to the-younger." Further as it has been written, "The-Jacob I love and The-Esau I hate."

What shall we be declaring then, there is only injustice with *THE-GOD*? NO WAY! For to Moses *HE* is saying, "I shall be having mercy to whomever I may be merciful," and, "I shall have compassion on whomever I may have compassion." Consequently then, it is not the-one-choosing or the-one-trying-to-perform but out of *GOD* being merciful. For the scripture says about The-Pharaoh, "That for this purpose-and-cause, I created-and-prepared you up so that I should be displaying in you my ability-and-power," and, "So that my name should be being known-published-declared everywhere in the-land."

So then to whom *HE* chooses *HE* is being merciful to; whom *HE* chooses *HE* hardens. Why then are you protesting to me that *HE* is not treating me as expected?

Section I

For who can comprehend-and-understand the-intention-and-reasoning of *HIM*? For which indeed are any of you oh man, the-one to challenge-and-open-a-legal-claim against *THE-GOD*? Shall the-one-which-is-molded say to *THE-ONE-MOLDING*, "Why have you made me this way?" Does not the-potter have all-authority over the-mud? Out of the same clay lump to make one vessel which indeed has value but to another no value? For if *THE-GOD* is willing to show *HIS* anger and to make known the-unlimited-inherent-power of *HIM* and carries in great patience vessels-of-indignation having been adapted for destruction, then also *HE* should be making known the-riches of *HIS* glory on vessels-of-mercy which *HE* had prepared before for glory. Us, whom *HE* calls. Not only out of Jews but also out of Nations.

Further as *HE* is also saying in Hosea, "I will call them my people who were not people of mine," and, "Her beloved who was not beloved." And, "It will come to pass in the-place where it was declared to them; "You are not my people," there they will-be-being called Sons-of-*LIVING-GOD*." For Isaiah is crying over Israel, "If, ever it may be that, the-number of The-Sons-of-Israel are as the-sand of-the-sea, The-Remnant will be saved." "For in justice *HE* will precisely-and-concisely finish accounting," "*MASTER* of the-land will cut short that accounting." And according as Isaiah has declared before, "Unless the *MASTER OF HOST-OF-THE-ARMIES* had left-remaining for us a *Seed*, we have forever become like Sodom and forever likened as Gomorrah."

What are we claiming, then? That The-Nations not chasing justice have overtaken-and-secured justice, even righteousness without-believing? But Israel, pursuing the Law-of-Justice has not attained the Law-of-Righteousness? How is this to be understood? Because of not seeking or by any believing but only-going-through-the-motions-of-doing the Law for they stumbled at *The-Stumbling-Stone*. Recall as it has been written, "Perceive! I am placing in Jerusalem a stone of stumbling and a rock of entrapment," and, "Everyone believing on *Him* shall not be disgraced."

Brothers, it is the-delight of my heart and the-petition toward *THE-GOD* for The-Israel to be saved and to testify for them. They have a boiling-zeal for God but not according-to understanding. For they are ignorant of the-goodness of *THE-GOD* and are seeking to establish their own goodness. They were not submitting themselves to the-justice of *THE-GOD*. Out of justice *Anointed* ended the Law for everyone believing. For Moses had written of the-justice out of The-Law, "That the-man doing them, mandated to live by them."

For from believing comes righteousness that is said in this manner, "In the-heart of yours do not be asking who shall be ascending into The-Heaven." Meaning who is to be leading *Anointed* down-from-above. Or, "Who shall be descending into The-Abyss?" That is who is to be leading *Anointed* up from the dead-ones. For what does it say? "*The-Word* is near you, in your mouth and in the-heart of you."

This is The-Declaration-of-Belief we are proclaiming: that you always should vow-confess-and-claim with your mouth the *Master* is the *Savior* and should be believing in your heart that *THE-GOD* that raised *Him* out of dead-ones shall be saving you. For it is a believing heart making-available righteousness and a confessing mouth that saves. For The-Writings say this, "Everyone believing on *Him* shall not be disgraced."

For there is no distinction between Jew and Greek for *The-same-MASTER-OF-ALL* is generous to all of The-Ones-calling on *HIM*. For every one whoever should be calling on *THE-NAME* of *THE MASTER* shall be saved.

Then how shall they be called to whom they do not believe? Further, how shall they believe about whom they have not heard? And apart from preaching, how shall they be hearing? Now, how shall they be preached to if no one is being sent? As it is written, "How beautiful are the-feet of the-ones-bringing-the-message of-peace, of the-ones-bringing-the-good-message of good!"

For not all have accepted The-Good-Message. Isaiah is saying, "Lord! Who believes our report?"

Consequently, believing comes from hearing and hearing through the-declaration of *GOD*.

But I am asking do they not understand what was said? Indeed, most assuredly, "From every land comes an utterance from them," and, "to The-Ends of the-inhabited earth by the-declarations of them."

But I am asking how could Israel not know? First Moses said, "I shall be provoking you to jealousy using an insignificant Nation. I shall be vexing you by a foolish Nation." And Isaiah said very boldly without fear, "*I* was found by the-ones that were not seeking *ME*; *I* became available to-the-ones that were not asking for *ME*." Further about Israel *HE* has said, "*I* have stretched out *MY* hands toward a stubborn and belligerent people."

Am I not suggesting then *THE-GOD* has cast away His people? No way! For I am an Israelite coming out of the seed of Abraham of the Tribe-of-Benjamin. *THE-GOD* has not thrust away *HIS* people whom *HE* had foreknowledge of, or have you not understood what Elijah is saying by this scripture to *THE-GOD* as he is pleading against Israel saying, "*MASTER*! They have killed *YOUR* prophets and the-sacrifice-places of *YOURS* they are undermining," and, "*I* was reserved alone and they are seeking the-soul of *me*." But what is the divine-reply to him? "*I* have reserved for *MYSELF* seven thousand men who have not now bent the knee to The-Baal." Even so today there has come to be a Remnant according-to The-Lottery by grace in this season now.

Now if by grace, it is no longer out of works or-else grace no longer becomes grace. And if out of works, it is still not grace or-else the work is no longer work.

Why then is Israel still seeking this which she has not encountered but The-Lottery has encountered it? Because the remaining were blinded. Just as it has been written, "*THE-GOD* gives to them a spirit-of-stupor, eyes to not be observing and ears to not be hearing to this very day," and David is saying, "Let their table be-turned into a trap and into a mesh and into a snare and into a repayment to them." "Let the-eyes of them become darkened that they may not be observing and continually bowing together the-backs of them."

Section I

I ask, then, have they stumbled that they should be unable to return? No way! For by those that offended, salvation has come to The-Nations to provoke a jealousy in them. For if the-offense of them benefits the System and their being abandoned benefits the Nations, how much-greater The-Restoration of them? And I am saying to you, to The-Nations, that I am indeed commissioned for the Nations and through my service I am honored if somehow through my flesh I should provoke them to jealousy and should be saving any of them.

For if the-casting-away of them legally-resolves-the-situation for the System, how do they return if there is no life from the dead-ones?

For if *The-First-Fruit* is *Holy* so-also the dough-lump, and if *The-Root* is *Holy* so also the-Boughs. For if some of The-Boughs are pruned out and you being wild olives grafted in among them and Joint-Participants-of-*The-Root*, you become the olive tree and bear ripened fruit.

You do not taunt-and-consider-yourself-better-than The-Boughs! For if you are boasting, you are not reflecting-and-imitating *The-Root*; you are your own root. Shall you be declaring that *The-Boughs* are pruned out that I may be grafted in? For a purpose they are pruned by disbelief, and you have remained by faith? Do not be extremely haughty! For you should be in great fear. For if *THE-GOD* did not spare the natural branches, be aware *HE* should not be sparing you. Be aware then of the kindness and cutting-harshness of God! Indeed, on those falling—harshness. Yet on you, kindness if you may be always remaining in *HIS* kindness, or else you shall be hewn out. Also, for those that continue remaining in disbelief shall be able to be grafted in, for *THE-GOD* is able to again graft them. For if you are of the wild olive according by nature and hewn out and grafted in to a cultivated olive, how much easier these, the-natural-ones, shall be grafted back into their own olive tree?

For I am not willing for you to be ignorant, Brothers, about The-Secret so that in your wisdom you may not be arrogantly haughty! That in part the blindness to Israel has come to them until the-full-complement of The-Nations is completed.

And therefore, all Israel shall be saved, just it has been written, "Out of Sion *The-One-Rescuing* shall be arriving," and, "*He* shall be turning away the ungodliness from Jacob" and, "This to them is *MY* covenant, at-a-time *I* should be eliminating them from their sins."

Indeed, according-to the-good-message enemies because of you but according-to The-Lottery beloved because of The-Fathers.

For the-gracious-effects and the-calling of *THE GOD* are not to be repented of. For even as you also were once unpersuaded-and-did-not-believe in *THE-GOD*, but now you have been shown mercy through their disbelief. Therefore, these now unbelieving through mercy given to you, that they also may be obtaining mercy. For *THE-GOD* has The-All locked up together into disbelief that *HE* should be being merciful to The-All.

OH, the depth of riches and wisdom and knowledge of *GOD*! How unsearchable the-judgments of *HIM* and how untraceable are *HIS* ways! "For who knew the mind of

THE MASTER?" "Who has become *HIS* adviser?" Or, "Who has given to *HIM* first and it shall be repaid by *HIM*?" Seeing that out of *HIM* and through *HIM* and in *HIM* all!

To *HIM* The-Glory into The-Eons.

Amen.

SECOND ADD: THE CLOSING OF PAUL'S CAREER ~ 66–68 C.E.

A Call to Remain Loyal and True as One Entity, Be Self-Governing in Behavior and Selfless toward Others

I am entreating you now, Brothers! By the-mercies of *THE-GOD* that you present your bodies a living sacrifice, holy, well pleasing to *THE-GOD* which is the-logical divine-service of you. And you do not be configured to this eon but be renewing the-mind of yours. Testing what is the-good and well-pleasing and the perfect will of *THE-GOD*.

For I am saying through the-grace being given to me for every person among you to not think-highly-about-yourself beyond your-limit of-who-you-suppose-you-are but thinking-soberly about the measure of belief as *THE GOD* imparts to each. For even as we have many members in one body, yet not every member has the-same function. Though many, we are one body in Christ, and yet we with-each-member-operating-independently but having gracious-diverse-gifts according-to the-grace being given to us. Whether excelling in prophecies according-to the-proportion of belief, or through service in ministering, or the teacher in teaching, or the-one-calling in encouragement, or the-one-giving in generosity, the-one-managing-and-leading in diligence or the one being merciful in cheerfulness.

Let Godly-love be unhypocritical, detesting-utterly the-wicked, clinging to the-good. Let brotherly affection be a natural fond affection for each other, honor another one first. In diligence, do not be slothful being fervent in the-spirit slaving for *The-Master*, rejoicing in The-Expectation, enduring the-affliction, persevering in prayer, contributing to the needs of The-Holy-Ones, pursuing hospitableness.

Be blessing the-ones-persecuting you; be blessing and not cursing. Be rejoicing with the-ones-rejoicing and weep with the-ones-lamenting. Think of the-same about one another, not the-high-minded but the-humble, not being led away with thinking-and-conceited in yourselves. Render to no one evil for evil; be honest in-the-sight-of all men. If able, as much as is in you, with all men be at peace. Beloved do not avenge yourself but set aside anger. As it is written says the Lord, "Vengeance is mine, I shall be repaying." "If ever your enemy may be hungering be-giving-him-the-morsel, if he maybe thirsting, be-getting-him-the-drink. For doing this you will be heaping embers of fire on his head." Do not be conquered by the-evil but you be conquering the-evil with the-good.

Let every soul be subject to superior authorities. For there is no authority that is not from *GOD*. The-ones in authority have been set there by *THE-GOD*. So then, an

Section I

individual-resisting the-authority has withstood the mandate of *THE-GOD* for the-ones having resisted shall be receiving judgment on themselves. For The-Magistrates are not in fear of the-good acts but of the-evil ones. But do not be fearful of The-Authority. Do good. Then by you doing the-good, you shall be having praise out of it. For *GOD*'s servant is for you for the-good. Yet if you may be doing evil, you be fearful. For the servant of *GOD* is not wearing the-sword for show; it is for punishing in anger to the-ones-committing the-evil.

Therefore, be subject out-of necessity, not only because of The-Indignation, but also because of the-conscience. Because of this you also supply the taxes, for they are officials of *GOD* preserving this same-thing. Be then giving to-the-one all which is obligated, the-taxes to-the-one taxing, the-custom to-the-one's custom, the-respect to-the-ones of respect, honor to-the-one of honor.

To no one owe anything! Be loving to one another for the-one Godly-loving a different one has fulfilled the Law. For you shall not be committing adultery, you shall not be murdering, you shall not be stealing, and you shall not be testifying falsely, you shall not be coveting, and if any other different direction it is summed up in this saying as: "You shall Godly-love the-near-one as yourself." The-Godly-love is not acting evil to-the-one near, it is-the-fullness-and-completion-then-of The-Law-of-Godly-Love.

Also be aware of this, the-season, that hour is already now for us to-be aroused out of sleep for our salvation is nearer for us than we believe. The-night progresses, but The-Day has drawn near and we should be putting off the-acts of the-darkness and we should be outfitting The-Battle-Armor-of-Light. We should be walking respectfully as in The-Day, not in revelries and drunkenness, not in fornication and lewdness-and-vices, not in strife and jealousy. But you put on *The-Master Savior Anointed* and be avoiding at all costs the opportunity for lusts of the-flesh.

Yet for the-weak in The-Belief, gather them to you not by prejudicial reasoning. Indeed, one believes all things can be eaten and the-weak-one eats herbs. The-one that eats is not-to-be scorning the-one not eating and the-one that is not eating do-not-be judging the-one that eats, for *THE-GOD* has become a close companion to them for *HIMSELF*.

Who are you to be judging another's servant? He is standing or he is falling to his own master, but he is able to stand for it is *THE-GOD* to stand him.

Who, indeed, is deciding this day over that day? Who yet is deciding every day? Let each one be fully assured in his own mind. The-one-convinced The-Day is for *Master* is disposed to that, the one convinced The-Day is not *Master's* is disposed to that. And the-one eating to *Master*, he-is-thanking THE GOD and the-one not eating to *Master* is thanking THE-GOD. Understand not one of us lives to himself, and no one dies to himself. If ever we may be living for *The-Anointed* we are living, if ever we may be dying for *The-Master* we are dying, for whether we are living or dying we are *The-Master's*. For this purpose, *Anointed* died and rose and revives and that for the living-ones and the dead-ones *He* should be *Master*.

So why are you judging your brother? Or why are you also scorning your brother? We shall all be presented at The-Judgment-Platform-of-*The-Anointed*. For it has been written, "As *I* am living says the LORD, every knee shall be bowing to me," and, "every tongue shall be avowing to THE-GOD." Consequently, then, each of us will be giving an account concerning himself to THE-GOD. Then by no means still should we be judging one another, but rather you decide this, to not put in place a stumbling block or snare toward the-brother.

I have been taught and I know personally from the *Master Savior* that nothing of itself is contaminated-and-unclean. But if the-one-reckons-and-reasons anything as unclean, to that one it is unclean. Yet if over food you have offended-and-not-considered your brother, you are no longer walking according-to Godly-love. Do not be destroying him for whose sake *Anointed* died because of your food. Do not let your good be spoken as if evil, for The-Kingdom-of-*THE-GOD* is not food and drink but of justice and peace and joy in the Holy-spirit. For the-one slaving in these things to *The-Anointed* well pleases *THE-GOD* and is approved by men.

Consequently, we should then be pursuing peace and the-edification of one another. There should be no demolishing the-work of *THE-GOD* because of food. Indeed, all is clean, but evil to the-man through eating causing the-one to fall. Ideally do not be eating meats or be drinking wine in which your brother stumbles, is snared, or is being weakened. Do you have belief? You should be living-in-it to yourself as seen by *THE-GOD*. Happy is the-one who does not judge himself in which he is allowing. But for the-one doubting whatever he eats is condemned seeing that it is not out of believing, for whatsoever is not out of believing is sin.

For we ought to be able to bear the-infirmities of the-weak and not to be pleasing ourselves. For each of us, let him be pleasing the-near one toward good edification. For also *The-Anointed* pleased not himself but according as it has been written, "The-reproaches of The-Ones reproaching *YOU* fell on *Me*."

For whatever was written before was written ahead of our time for our teaching that through the-endurance and through the-support of The-Scriptures we may be given The-Expectation. Yet may *THE-GOD* of endurance and comfort-support-and-relief be granting you the-same-mind-and-approach to one another just as *Anointed Savior*. That with one accord with one mouth glorifying *THE-GOD* and *FATHER* of *The-Master* of us *Savior Anointed*. Therefore, be talking to one another accordingly and also as *The-Anointed* firmly lock-grasped us to himself for the glory of *GOD*.

Now I am saying *Savior Anointed* had to become a servant of The-Circumcision for-the-sake-of The-Promise made by *GOD* to confirm The-Promises to The-Fathers and for The-Nations to glorify *THE-GOD* for-the-sake-of *HIS* mercy. Accordingly it has been written, "Because of this *I* shall be acclaiming *YOUR* name among the Nations," and, "To *YOUR* name *I* shall play music," and elsewhere, "You be-making merry-and-rejoice Nations along with *HIS* people." And again be-praising, "the Nations be praising *HIM, THE-MASTER*! All you peoples be lauding *HIM*!" And also,

Section I

Isaiah says, "There shall be *The-Root-of-Jesse*, *The-One* rising up being-*Chief-of-the-Nations*, on *Him* the Nations shall be trusting-and-have-hope."

Now may THE-GOD-of-*The-Expectation* be filling you with all joy and peace in believing, that you be super-abounding in *The-Expectation* by the unlimited-ability-and-power of the Holy-spirit.

Now I have been persuaded, my Brothers, about you also myself, that you are bloated full of goodness having the-full-truth-and-understanding also being able to be caring-and-preserving one another. But more openly-and-boldly have I written to you Brothers as a part of reminding you because of the-gracious-gift-of-divine-service and-authority being given to me by THE-GOD. To me as The-Official of *Savior Anointed* to The-Nations acting as a priest of The-Well-Message of THE-GOD that it may be carried toward The-Nations. Properly received having-been-made-holy by the Holy-spirit.

Through *The-Anointed Savior* I then have boasting about *GOD*. For I dare not be speaking of any other acts which *The Anointed* has not spoken or performed through me for the training-and-teaching of the Nations. In mighty-overwhelming-undisputable-power of signs and of miracles and the unlimited-ability-and-power of the spirit-of-*GOD* from Jerusalem and all around to The-Illyricum by me has The-Well-Message of *The-Anointed* been completely-preached. Thus I-am being ambitious to-not-be-bringing-the-well-message to where *Anointed* is already-known so that I am not building on another's foundation. But as it is written, "To whom it was not informed concerning *Him* they shall not be seeing," and "of *Whom* they have not heard, they shall understand."

For this reason I was greatly hindered from coming to you. While still not having a place in the-area but having had a longing to-be-coming to you for many years and if I ever may be going to Spain, I will come to you first. For I am expecting to gaze upon you as I am going through and by you being first filled by your hospitality, then parting from there being provided for but now I am going into Jerusalem serving The-Holy-Ones.

For Macedonia and Achaia delighted to make some contribution to the-poor-ones of The-Holy-Ones in Jerusalem. They are delighted and debtors to them. For if The-Nations are able to participate in their spiritual things, they also have a duty to them to minister in the-needs-of-the-flesh. After finishing this blessing to them, I will be coming through you into Spain. I have perceived that when coming to you, I shall be coming with the-full-blessing of *The-Anointed* for The-Well-Message. I am entreating you, Brothers, through *The-Master* of us *Savior Anointed* through the-Godly-love of the-spirit, struggle-together with me in the-prayers over-the-sake-of me toward THE-GOD that I should be rescued from The-Stubborn-and-Unpersuaded in Judea. That through my service for them in Jerusalem it may be well received by The-Holy-Ones that I may be coming to you in joy through the will of *GOD* and with you, should be together refreshed.

Now THE GOD-OF-PEACE with all of you. Amen.

ROMANS AS A LETTER

Post Script: Closing Goodbyes, Acknowledgments, and Last Warnings and Blessings

Also, I am commending to you Phoebe, The-Sister of us, being a server of the Ecclesia in Cenchrea. You should be receiving her in *The Master*, worthy of The-Holy-Ones and they would be standing by her in whatever matter she may be needing from you. For she has become a patroness to many and to me myself. You welcome Priscilla and Aquila, fellow workers of mine in *Anointed Savior*, who for the-sake-of my life jeopardized their necks, whom not only I am thanking but also all of The-Called-Out-of-The-Nations and also The-Out-Called from their home. You welcome Epanetus, my beloved, who is The-First-Fruit of Achaia in *Anointed*.

You greet Mary, who toiled greatly over us. You welcome Andronicus and Junia, the-relatives of mine. Also my fellow captives who are the Notable-Ones among The-Apostles who were also in *Anointed* before me.

Greet you Amplias, my beloved in *Master*. Salute Urbanas, our fellow worker in *Anointed* and Stachys, my beloved. Salute Apelles, tested in *Anointed*. Salute the-ones of the-ones from Aristobulus. Greet Herodian, my relative. Greet you the-ones of the-ones of Narcissus, the-ones being in *Master*. Salute Tryphena and Tryphosa, the-ones toiling in *Master*. Salute Persis, the-beloved who toils much in *Master*.

Salute Rufus, the-one-called by *Master*, and his mother and mine. Welcome Asyncritus, Phlegon, Hermas, Patrobas, Hermes, and The-Brothers with them. Salute Philologus, and Julia, Nereus, and his sister, and Olympas, and together with all Holy-Ones with them. Greet one another with a holy brotherly-kiss. The-Called-Outs of *The-Anointed* are greeting you.

Now am I entreating you Brothers to take note of The-Ones-of-Dissensions and the-snares against the-teaching which you learned and avoid them! For they are not slaving such to *The-Master* of us *Savior Anointed* but for their own belly, by compliments and praising they are seducing the-hearts of-the-simple.

I am rejoicing over all of you for your obedience has reached far to all yet, I am desiring that you would indeed be wise to that which is good yet guileless to evil and *THE-GOD-of-Peace* shall-be-crushing under your feet The-Adversary in swiftness.

The-Grace of *The-Master* of us *Savior Anointed* be with you.

Amen.

Greeting you are Timotheus, my fellow worker with Lucius and Jason and Sosipater, my relatives. I, Tertius, the-one-writing the-letter in *Master*, am greeting you. Gaius, The-Lodger of mine and of all The-Called-Out, greet you. Erastus, The-Administrator-of-The-City, and Quartus his brother are greeting you.

The-Grace of *The-Master* of us *Savior Anointed* be with all of you.

Amen.

Now to *THE-ONE* being able to establish you in accordance with The-Well-Message of mine and The-Proclamation of *Savior Anointed* in accordance with The-Revelation-of-The-Secret having been kept-silent-and-unknown from time eonian

Section I

but is now-being-made-to-be understood-and-known through prophetic scriptures according-to the court-ordered-royal-decree of *THE-EONIAN-GOD* being made known to all The-Nations for obedience by-believing.

To the *ONLY-WISE-GOD* through *Savior-Anointed* the-glory into The-Eons. Amen.

ROMANS STUDY NOTES

Note: Through my many translations I have come to believe that the phrase or associated phrasing of "inheritance" [ex: Col 1:12] accurately translated as "The-Allotment" in Scripture is not a good or proper translation (i.e., inheritance). Paul makes it clear we are to be family members (I state: royal and godly) destined to be with HIM and HE with us and we in Christ and He in us. Inheritance has an implied connotation, an accepted concept that someone has died. THE-GOD is certainly not dead or about to die, and Christ has risen to life eonian (there are times of times of times) as well. I see this as a watering down of the intent and meaning of the Scriptures and have dropped using the word *inheritance* when speaking of THE-GOD's plan and purpose for us. We are to take rulership in an active kingdom/government with Christ at the head of the realm and we under Him with THE-GOD over all of us.

Note   The Greek word *agapen* translated as "love" in most translations is missing that this is Godly in nature and not of men or any other such creature or creation. I have therefore carried the adjective to add clarity to the meaning of this word throughout this translation.

Note: In my research, nearly all translations have dropped "the" as a modifier, but the Greek word for "the" (*tov*) is in every text and not meant to be ignored or deleted. It is often specifically singular, and when attached to the noun, it is describing that noun as unique, one of a kind, a specific thing, the original, the one and only. It is for this reason I carry "the" everywhere it appears in all translations. Whether of God, Jesus, Satan, or any other entity, concept, or idea, this modifier "the" clears up a lot of generalized words, ideas, concepts, and entities.

Note: The word or root of the word *pnuemia*, a word translated as "spirit, wind, or breath," has no gender identity since this is a word that is neuter in gender. *Pnuemia* is an "it." The Greeks, as we of the English language, often fix a gender to objects and things—for example: cars, boats, the moon, the sun. For the Greeks, *pnuemia* at times has a male gender affixed to it. *Pnuemia* in the Scriptures is never capitalized or designated as a stand-alone being, entity, principality, or sovereignty when used as the word "spirit." It is simply the

Section I

power inherent in the being, whether of man, or God, or Christ, or any other entity. If anything is living, "it" possesses a spirit. The "Holy-spirit" is simply the power from and of The-God, giving and renewing life and performing The-God's will.

Note: Paul constantly claims and mentions "principles, powers, authorities, sovereignties not of our world." He quite clearly claims that these beings are the ones that certainly influence at a minimum and control or direct (predominately in a negative way) the systems of this world, people of the nations, and individuals directly. You can find this concept also contained in The Old Testament through the implications of the First Commandment. This claim and concept of the warring factions in heaven makes a fascinating study.

Note: *Time periods, eons, ages, millennia, eons* and *eons*. I stayed true to the Greek words associated with time and what we still use today in our common language. A study of time periods is fascinating and also an area to cause confusion. The-God always works on some kind of a timetable, but understanding which is which and when is when is a bit of a mystery and can cause confusion. Some timetables are only known to The-God and made clear to man at God's will.

Note What is the difference between *expectation* and *hope*? Nearly all translations adopt the word *hope* for *expectation*, but Paul uses almost exclusively the word *expectation*. The reason I constantly use *expectation* is that having an expectation means you have no doubt at all. It is sure and certain with no ambiguity. Having a *hope* means you are not 100 percent convinced and convicted. I can tell you that Paul is undeniably convinced and convicted in what he delivers and talks about. Using *hope* sends a message there is some possibility for "wiggle room," doubt, error, or an excuse.

Even worse, much of the use of the word *expectation* in Paul's writings has the modifier "the" attached to it, forming the proper translation and singular concept of "The-Expectation." This makes "The-Expectation" an event, not a philosophy or theological premise. Not recognizing "The-Expectation" as an event will lead the reader immediately down an incorrect understanding of what is being offered or discussed.

1:1 The Greek word *christou* often translated as "Christ" is properly translated as "Anointed" and hence used throughout this translation. *Strong's Concordance* defines anointed as "distinguished from or set apart." When one begins to use of the word "anointed" with the above understanding of the dynamics of relationships, the intent and purpose concerning The-Savior take on a whole new dimension of understanding, and clarity occurs.

1:4 The Greek word *kuriou*, often translated as "Lord," is properly translated as "Master" and hence used throughout this translation.

Use of the word *master* during apostolic times carried two implications. In a social sense, it was a title of highest respect and honor; the Roman emperor was also known as Master, as in "Master of the World." To attribute such a title to Jesus Christ, or rather "Master Anointed," not only was an insult to Rome but secondly was seen as a military threat since this title also applied to military leaders, especially the current reigning Caesar. With the "Jews" openly talking about a coming kingdom, in a constant state of ready revolt, and the return of "The Master," all of the Roman Empire was alert to this "internal threat."

In a broader theological or spiritual sense, Satan's rule is now over as "Ruler/Master of this world" with all its implications.

Immediately within the first four versus of Romans, we get a hint of the struggle of two separate kingdoms/governments: one of those on earth (physical) and one of those in heaven (spiritual).

1:8 The words *The System* are translated in nearly all other translations as "world." The direct translation is, in fact, "the-system," and in all but a few instances I have left it as such. One cannot but think that Paul is making direct references to all the world's systems—banking, education, religion, social customs, entertainment, people, et al. They all are corrupted and belong to the Ruler of this world. The use of the word *world* masks what Paul wrote and what his audience understood.

1:9 In Greek, the use of the word "*tov*" is a definite article translated every time as "the." As a definite article, it always denotes a singular, particular one-of-a-kind item, thing, being, or pronoun. It is never used as a collective article. Paul is quite clear in his writings to distinguish people, places, and things using the word *tov*. He writes "The God," "The Master," and even such entities as "The Death." Paul is clearly telling his audience there is not a pantheon of gods that today we would call a "trinity," but rather a series of beings, distinguished from each other and other gods, powers, and principalities. When Paul spoke to the Greeks at Mars Hill, they were familiar and had a relationship with a wide pantheon of gods, but not the "Unknown God." Rome also had its counterparts. Paul distinguishing the Unknown God as "The God" sent a very clear message to his audience that this is the principle GOD—my capitalizing is for honor and respect and to distinguish separately—"The GOD of the gods" and "The (One and Only) Anointed" (parenthesis mine). Each separate, each definable, each identifiable. Consequently, I have used the hyphenation approach where *tov* occurs to add emphasis to this concept of singularity and uniqueness wherever *tov* occurs.

Note: Paul's writings are nearly always in an active tense—i.e., not only in the past but for now and for the future. This structuring of the verb tenses is often lost in many translations but not so in the original Greek. Here I remain true to

Section I

the Greek without prejudice or intentionally changing tenses or unknowingly missing the translation, even though it may sound a little awkward when reading the texts.

2:1 The Geek word *anthropos* (and all related derivations) has the meaning or root of man or men not "human." "Human" is a corrupted translation. The "Hu" portion is a shortened form, aberration, possibly a nickname of Cush, the grandson of Noah. Cush, known as a corrupter after the flood (he organized the city of Babylon) and the father of the Egyptian nation among others, was deified within that race and became a cult figure, a "god." Hence to be a follower of "Hu" meant you are a "hu-man" and not a follower of God. The influence of Cush during the early regeneration of the family of man was far-reaching, and the term and influence remain to this day in forms not fully investigated, understood, or explained. I prefer to think of myself as a man and not a follower of an ancient religious substitute for The-God.

2:21 Paul here is accusing the priesthood who were discussing stealing by pointing out the fact that the priesthood was stealing and robbing their own kinsmen or brothers—not just because of the forced commanded acts of the sacrificial and offering system within the Law, but also willfully in the exchanging that was taking place in the temple. Recall Christ's cleansing of the money changers, which included the swapping of a perfectly good sacrificial animal for a "better and purer" animal for sacrifice. Both the priest and sellers were profiting twice.

2:22 Paul's instructions concerning worshipping idols and corrupting the sanctuary are interesting. Despite God's instructions to have no idols, he placed two cherubim images in the Holy of Holies that became objects of adoration and worship within the Jewish society. It is as if The-God placed them there as a temptation, but we know that The-God had a greater purpose for the images to be there.

2:24 The use of both "Nations" and "Greeks" are interchangeable with the word *gentile*—that is, any person or nation not believing in The-God of Israel.

2:24 The Law was delivered by a representative of The-God. This entity was recognized by the Jews as a high-ranking angel under the authority and approval of The-God. This fact can also be proved through scholarly research. As Paul recognized, and his audience did as well, there is a difference between "God" versus "The-God," where "God" can be angels, sons of God, men, other principalities, and powers associated with nations outside of Israel and Judah.

3:3 *"So-what if some disbelieved?"* Paul begins his defending belief in The-God by setting up the first of several arguments. Notice in this sentence the way the question is presented. His audience already had knowledge of those who challenged God in the wilderness wanderings who refused to accept God's authority or move into the land upon the encouraging return of the Israelite spies.

3:5–9 These passages talk about justice. Its simplest definition is to render a decision or act in a matter of dispute without prejudice or without a preconceived purpose that serves and satisfies the intent of all involved; to render a decision or act in a manner or method that is fair, balanced, with full knowledge of all the facts. Justice is recognized and accepted by all involved to completely and correctly satisfy the needs and the desires of all. The interesting discussion about "being-just" or "justice" is whether divinity is intended and involved as a secondary subject matter in these passages. Is substituting the word *righteousness* or its cognitive in place of "just, justice, justification" an acceptable, correct, and proper translation to use? Nearly all translations reference and review the use of "righteousness" or some form of this within these passages; however, the root of the Greek is "just." It sounds at first like a great "alternative" or "equivalent definition" to substitute "righteous" for "just," but I am not convinced that in these passages by Paul he is justifying whether God is righteous or not. The verses all must logically conclude that God is nothing but righteous by virtue of His divinity and His character alone, yet this does not mean that judging is equivalent to righteousness. I have held to using the word *just* with its cognitives with the understanding that in judging and delivering a verdict, it is done without prejudice since God knows the thoughts, intents, and purposes of any individual and is not a "respecter of persons."

Here Paul is providing this opening proposal or topic of debate: increasing bad behavior causes and creates not only proper and appropriate behavior but even greater proper and appropriate behavior. That proposal for debate should freeze the brain and lead one to logically conclude that there is no way to "justify" these diverse ideas that the "bad" one creates the "good"—or even a "better" one. That is what Paul will eventually declare also. Therefore, in these passages I have stayed with the Greek so we can observe and understand that Paul is performing as a prosecuting attorney making his arguments before you as a jurist.

One of the bigger discussions in Romans is the newfound freedom of not being under "The-Law." This includes both Mosaic and man-made government laws. Converts were going about doing their own thing without regard or understanding of the damage they were doing to the name and gospel of Christ, God, or those they met. And while Paul does say that those in Christ are not legally subject to the laws of the land or Moses because they are citizens of the Kingdom of God, they needed to still participate in the laws of the land, thus setting a proper example as an ambassador for God's Kingdom. Paul in general does not tell those in Christ to exercise a form "diplomatic immunity." He was keenly aware that the current governments were

Section I

not going to permit such freewheeling actions. The Kingdom, after all, is a threat to them, and Christ's Kingdom was not yet to arrive. Paul encourages the Ecclesiae to live within the rule of law of the land without compromising their citizenship in Heaven.

3:9   The Greek word here is *proetiasametha*, fully translated as "we-previously-charged" where the word "charge" implicates being charged with murder, not just erring in one's way.

4:14   The discussion here is about timing; the Law had nothing to do with Abraham.

5:11   The word *obtained* has a connotation of a forceful taking, as in a war or battle.

5:12   "The-Death" is not only a concept of dying, but also implies an entity or a being. Paul's use of the definite article *tov (ton)*—Greek for "the"—brings attention to the reader that Death is a life form (see also verses 14, 17; 8:2).

5:13   This implies that sin was not counted as a negative condemnation against an individual.

6:4   If one is not careful, one can overlook the double witness being presented by Paul—the death in the watery grave as well as the physical one we participate in through Christ.

6:5   The proper translation is "injected semen." The word *planted* is a euphemism. Also suggested is life is carried by the man in his seed.

6:12   The proper translation is the word *her*, often replaced by "it" by translators since the Greek language attaches gender appointments to nearly every noun or concept. We have "Mother Earth," ships are christened as a "her," and the moon is given a feminine appellation among the myriad of male assigned gender ideas and nouns.

7:1–6   This passage talks about the covenant of marriage as legally being nullified for a woman (notice there is no restriction on the man during a marriage) upon the death of her husband. Christ's death would also symbolize the dissolving of the original covenant (Law and all) with God and Israel, making way for marriage to his new "bride," the Ecclesiae. This is but one of a several doctrinal issues associated with the crucifixion of Christ.

7:8   The phrase "gained a strategic advantage" is recognized by scholars as being a direct military concept and reference.

7:11   Is it not interesting that the Law says "You shall not murder," yet itself does exactly that? This is a true paradox.

7:16   Paul's discussion about his conscience being self-convicting is another proof of God's spirit already being in us and the failure of the written Law. God has truly written his laws "in the heart" of all men as stated.

7:21   The words *is lying beside me* is meant as a husband and wife have marital sex. Hence the concept Paul reiterates is that the "two shall become one flesh" has more meaning than one first understands; a special bonding occurs.

7:24   *"Who shall-deliver [rescue, is the Deliverer of] me"* (underline mine). The Greek word *rhyomai* according to *Strong's* G4506 has two definitions depending on where one places the accent and pronunciation of the word. Both definitions are related to the concept of "to rescue, deliver." Strong's second definition is simply stated as "the deliverer." The reader can surely see how this definition drops into place just as properly and as an appropriate usage in this sentence since it sets up verse 25 as a declaration by Paul as Christ as The-Deliverer. Paul's use of the Greek language is often done in the superlative and intended with the greater, fuller, and often the more mature understood concept, but not directly stated in intent and meaning. Traditional translations take a certainly correct but "low path" in leading the reader to the first definition of save, rescue, deliver. I have opted to supply the second and let the reader make the choice what Paul intended.

8:1   The other information being supplied here is that a conversion of the mind takes place, with the spirit beginning to dominate and control the flesh.

8:11   A direct statement that the spirit is God's spirit.

8:13   This verse is as much a promise as it is an explanation of what occurs between the two opposing forces.

9:1   The Greek word *pnuemati* translated as "spirit" is never capitalized when associated with the word holy as in "Holy spirit." The word is assigned a male gender but is neutral in meaning like the word *army* or the word *corporation*. The Holy spirit is the power that emanates from The-God and is not a being or entity as popularly preached and taught. Paul makes this clear once the word *spirit* is properly rendered.

9:23   "*HE should be making known <u>the-riches</u> of HIS esteem [glory] on instruments*" (underline mine). I understand the phrase "the-riches" to not only be spiritual in nature, meaning God's character, wisdom, approach, and demeanor, but also related to the promises made of being a son and daughter with divinity within His family, whether a vessel for "good" or for "bad."

10:1–6   Paul opens this next discussion intending to demonstrate that Israel—more specifically those attached to and demanding that the new Gentile converts observe the Mosaic Law (and the especially hot topic of circumcision)—could not find *justice* (lasting goodness and true justice). I want to also include *righteousness*, by simply performing the actions demanded by The-Law (italics mine). I make the distinction of both words intentionally because nearly all translations have interchanged these words as if they have the same meaning and interpretation. This is a bit like foisting one's own doctrine into the passages. Think about this: while justice and righteousness may be conjoined because of the Godhead's attributes, they are distinctive within these passages, even though justice done in righteousness is a positive experience for all parties at odds with one another. Also, everyone should be for the righteousness that trumps justice, especially via God's Holy spirit (the Holy spirit not being a separate entity, but rather God's force and power) in those called by Him. This, I contend, is Paul's real point for discussion in these verses. Righteousness by its greater authority fulfills and satisfies justice and goodness ("*For in righteousness Anointed finished The-Law*"). That righteousness comes from believing in God and in Christ's atonement sacrifice for us and is given as a gift to us from God through Christ; Paul is quite clear about this. There is a preponderance of "justice and goodness" done by man without righteousness. Justice is served (may I offer "atoned for"?) all the time, with plenty of innocent people paying for a crime or offense they did not commit but that is attributed to them with or without "evidence" or true concern and care, and often with an agenda.

    Paul would have already challenged the Ecclesiae and others to prove how the blood of bulls and goats would ever be equal or greater than a man's blood. He would have challenged all of them to prove that if The-Law and its ordinances were so pure, cleansing, and atoning, why did an Israelite need to continually perform the same ceremonies year in and year out? Nobody ever changed their actions so they could stop worrying about being sinful. Not only that, but the general population had to get tired of doing these things and putting themselves out. (I would have hated being one hundred years old and still going to the Temple to sacrifice. The only thing I would have gotten out of that is boasting about how long I had been "serving God.") Please be assured that this is being said facetiously, but there are plenty of people still today saying this. One would hopefully eventually realize that the demands of The-Law were senseless and worthless. The same goes for the Priesthood. They were all doing The-Law because they were "forced to." Also, nothing really hinted at or was openly evident that The-Law and all it encompassed would promise eternal life or a changed attitude, behavior, or approach for an individual. Christ hinted that that's what The Law was meant for when He answered the young man who wondered how he might have eternal life. No real justice and goodness were being served in The-Law, only the condemnation and sentencing of death which all people still serve today.

    The Greek words in these verses all are rooted in "being just, acting justly, justice, doing the noble and correct action, being good, having goodness" but do not properly mean "righteous" or its derivatives. It is possible for man to behave in such a manner apart from the righteousness of God, or not believe in God or The Savior as a man sent here to remove all sins. Paul says Israel was just going through the motions because they had to, not only for religious reasons but also societal. Society was enslaved as much to The-Law and the authority derived from it. That authority of enslavement within The-Law was granted to the Priesthood and the other governing entities for managing and controlling the population. (Who do you think really benefited from that control and authority?) It was "just" the way it was for all. No belief, no meaning, no repentance, no example, no expectations, no hope, no understanding.

10:5   The Greek word for "shall" offered in most translations is imperative and does convey the true sense. It is a direct commandment to perform and act with no room for error or mistakes. It is a "mandate," and I used this legal term in this verse.

10:6   Translating the second half of verse 6 ("That the-man doing them shall live by them"), one could understand that this is a fulfilled Scripture in the active tense now, as Christ is certainly not only alive as a living entity by "doing them" and being The-Man in Heaven today, but it is also how He lives (and lived) His life. This second statement is the only interpretation about this Scripture offered by all sources I consulted. Furthermore, we too will fulfill this verse at the Resurrection.

11:4   The word "appraisement" is meant as a divine reply, not determining the value of something.

11:5   The word "choice" is tied to a chance lottery (a roll of the dice) and not an arbitrary decision of one over another.

11:15   This is a rhetorical question that concludes that the receiving, or acceptance, of them is life from the dead. Most translations are as follows: "For if the casting away of them reconciles the world, what shall their acceptance be but life from the dead?"

13:3   The Greek word *proselabeto* translated as "taken" is rich in meaning. This is a type of possession of deep friendship and acceptance into one's soul and conscience, into one's heart. It is not a possession of ownership. It is to shelter someone, become a companion to.

14:4   The discussion about those serving or being slaves of a Christian believer in this passage is rather curious. The hinted message in a servant "standing or falling" is twofold, and potentially a third theme emerges. First is the idea of being in good or poor graces with one's master. Apparently, there was quite a bit of discussion stirring about what servants were or were not allowed to do, depending on who owned them.

Secondly, imagine two Christian slave owners discussing amongst themselves the balance between being a slave who believes and understands the message of not being under The-Law and doing their best to be independent and debtless. Owners understood that they themselves had "religious" as well "civic and societal freedoms" within God's Kingdom, but were these same freedoms not to be afforded to their servants? What a dilemma! It has all the foundational elements that slavery was not what God really intended for man but allowed the situation to occur for men to be "stuck in the middle," not knowing what to do about this moral dilemma.

Thirdly, what could also be implied in God making his presence known to both owner and slave is that God alone provided the opportunities, provided the strength and abilities for the slave and owner, and caused the situations to occur to serve his purposes. However, in the Resurrection both entities were to be in "good standing" with God at the Day of Judgment. In this situation both parties are sinless.

14:6   "The-Day" is referring to Sabbath observance and by inference all the Holy Days.

14:6   This "eating to The-Master" is a reference to taking and observing the Lord's Supper.

14:11 This passage from Isaiah stating every person will give honor and reverence to God does not mean by forced or oppressive actions. The passage is clear; this is a willing and open confession, a vowing by all as to who God is and His greatness. These actions are out of true acceptance and acknowledgment, without a hidden doubt or secret reservation in one's heart and mind.

ROMANS IN VERSE

ROMANS 1

1:1 Paul a slave of *Savior Anointed* [Christ], an apostle called and severed [cut out specifically, separated] for the well-message [gospel] of *GOD*

1:2 that *HE* promised before [in the past] in [through] the holy-writings through the-prophets of *HIM*

1:3 about *The-Son*-of-*HIM*, *The-One* coming out of the seed of David in flesh.

1:4 Designated [selected, designed to be] *The-Son-of-GOD* with unlimited-inherent-power according-to [with] the spirit-of-holiness out of [by, from, because of, due to] the Resurrection from the dead-ones. *Savior Anointed* [Christ] *The-Master* [Lord] of us

1:5 through whom we obtain grace and commissioned [apostleship] in faithful obedience to all The-Nations for the sake of *The-Name*-of-*Him*

1:6 among whom you are also the Called-Ones of *Savior Anointed*.

1:7 To all those in Rome loved-by-*GOD* and called Holy-Ones [saints] of *GOD*, grace and peace to you from *GOD* our *FATHER* and *Master* [Lord], *Savior Anointed*.

1:8 First indeed [in order] I-give-thanks *THE-GOD* of mine through *Savior Anointed* over all of you that the-belief of yours is announced in The-whole-System [world].

1:9 For *THE-GOD* is my witness whom I divinely serve in the-spirit of mine in the-well-message of *The-Son*-of-*HIM* how I unceasingly make mention of you always in my prayers.

1:10 Beseeching [pleading] at length somehow to find a way in the-will of *THE-GOD* to come to you.

1:11 I greatly desire to see you that I may share spiritual gifts with you so you will be established [standing firm],

Section I

1:12   that is together you and I will be encouraged and strengthened together by our belief.

1:13   For I am not willing for you to be ignorant, Brothers. Many times I have purposed to come to you and was forbidden until now so that I should have some fruit among you as among the-rest of the Nations [Gentiles].

1:14   To both Greeks and barbarians, both wise and foolish, I am an owner [obligated under gratitude for a favor received].

1:15   Thus I have eagerness in me to bring to you, The-Ones in Rome, to bring the well-message [gospel].

1:16   Because I am not ashamed of the-well-message-of-*The-Anointed*, for in it is *GOD'S* unlimited-inherent-power bringing salvation to everyone who believes. To Jews first before to Greeks.

1:17   For the justice [righteousness] of *GOD* is revealed in it from-not believing into believing as it has been written stating, **"The-Just shall-be be-living by believing."** [Hab 2:4]

1:18   For the indignation [anger] of *GOD* is revealed from heaven on all the irreverence [ungodliness] and injustice of men; The-Ones who hold down [suppress] *The-Truth* in injustice [unrighteousness].

1:19   Because that which is known about *THE-GOD* is apparent [clearly-made-visibly-apparent, openly-shown] among them for *GOD* has manifest [openly-shown] it to them.

1:20   For the-unseen-things of *HIM* from the creation of the System are still being apprehended [understood] and described by things that are made besides [along-with] his imperceptible unlimited-inherent-power and divinity. So they are defenseless because they knew *THE-GOD*.

1:21   They did not glorify him or thank him as *GOD*, but they became vain in their own reasoning, unintelligent and darkened in their hearts.

1:22   Alleging themselves to be wise, they are made stupid,

1:23   and they changed The-Glory-of-*THE-INCORRUPTIBLE-GOD* into the likeness and image of corruptible [subject to death and decay, being sinful] men, of flying creatures, four-footed beasts, and of reptiles.

1:24   Therefore *THE-GOD* has given up on them over [because of] the-uncleanliness-lusting of the-hearts of them and for the-dishonoring of their bodies among themselves.

1:25   Whom altering *The-Truth*-of-*THE-GOD* into a lie and revering [venerating, worshipping] and offering-divine-service to The-Creation rather than *THE-ONE CREATING*, who is to be blessed into The-Eons.

Amen.

ROMANS 2

1:26 Because of this *THE-GOD* has given them over to their vile passions; for even their females have changed their natural use against nature.

1:27 Likewise also the-males leaving the-natural use of a woman, burning in their craving for another man, males in males acting indecently, receiving the-reward of their deceptions in themselves as is due [only natural, fitting].

1:28 Accordingly they test *THE-GOD*, behaving like they have no knowledge of him. And *THE-GOD* gives over to them an unsound mind to be doing those things that are not fitting;

1:29 having been filled with every unjustness [unrighteousness], prostitution, wickedness, greed, extreme evil envy, murder, strife, fraud, depravity, whisperers,

1:30 backbiters, God haters [detesters], outrageous, proud, ostentatious, inventors of evil, disobedient to parents,

1:31 unintelligent, promise breakers [untrustworthy], unloving, truce breakers [unforgiving], unmerciful,

1:32 The-Ones who recognize The-Justice-of-*THE GOD*. The-Ones which commit such things deserve death not only doing the same, but also endorsing The-Ones-committing (them).

2:1 Therefore you are without any defenses [excuses], oh man! For everyone that judges, for that-which you are judging the-different-one, you condemn yourselves as the-one-judging [committing, practicing] the-same things.

2:2 For we are aware that The-Judgment-of-*THE-GOD* is according-to [executed with, accomplished with] truth on [opposed, against] the-ones who are practicing such things.

2:3 And you can count on this, oh man! The-one-judging those practicing such while you are doing the same will not escape The-Judgment-of-*THE-GOD*.

2:4 Do you despise the-riches of the-kindness-of-*HIM* and of the-forbearance [tolerance] and the-patience? Do you not know [comprehend] The-kindness-of-*THE-GOD* is leading you to repentance?

2:5 But in accordance with your hardened and unrepentant heart you are hoarding up indignation [righteous fury] for yourself when *THE-GOD* reveals *HIS* judgment in that Day-of-Indignation [wrath]

2:6 who will repay each one in accordance with his acts [deeds].

Section I

2:7   Indeed to the-ones who by patient endurance are doing acts of honor and glory and incorruption, eonian [age lasting, period lasting] life,

2:8   but to the-ones that are stubborn and full of strife, ignoring the-truth, committed [persuaded] to do the-injustice—fury and wrath,

2:9   affliction and distress on every soul of man that does evil. First to Jews and then Gentiles.

2:10   But glory and honor and peace to everyone that works well. To Jew first and then to Greek.

2:11   For there is no partiality with *THE-GOD*.

2:12   Because whoever has sinned without The-Law will-also perish without The-Law and for whoever has sinned in The-Law through The-Law shall be judged.

2:13   For listeners of The-Law are not just before *THE-GOD*, but the-doers of The-Law are being justified.

2:14   For whenever Nations not having The-Law by nature are doing The-Law, they are a law to themselves

2:15   who are displaying the-acts-of-the-Law written in their hearts. Their conscious is testifying as a witness by reasoning accusing or excusing themselves.

2:16   In That-Day *THE-GOD* will be judging the-hidden (things) of men according-to my well-message [gospel] through *Savior Anointed*.

2:17   Understand [recognize] you called a Jew and are resting [contently-relying] in The-Law and boasting about *THE-GOD*.

2:18   And note as well those who are testing the-things that are "most excellent" being instructed out of The-Law.

2:19   You have confidence that you are to be a leader of blind-ones, a light to the-ones in darkness,

2:20   a disciplining teacher of imprudent [the unbelieving foolish] ones, of minors, having a form of the-knowledge and of the-truth in The-Law.

2:21   The-one teaching another are you not teaching yourself? The-one proclaiming to not be stealing you are stealing!

2:22   The-one saying to not be committing adultery you are committing adultery! The-one hating idols you defile The-Sanctuary!

2:23   Whom are boasting in The-Law yet side stepping The-Law you are dishonoring *THE-GOD*!

2:24   For as it was written, **"*THE-NAME* of *THE-GOD* because of you is being blasphemed among the Nations."** [Ezek 16:27, Isa 52:5, Ezek 36:22]

2:25   Indeed circumcision is beneficial if you may be practicing The-Law, but if you are a transgressor of The-Law circumcision has become uncircumcision.

2:26   If ever then the-uncircumcised keeps the-just requirements of The-Law, shall not his uncircumcision be counted for circumcision?

2:27   And the-uncircumcision who is common [not set apart as holy, that of nature] accomplishes [meets the demands of] The-Law he shall be judging you, you of The-Letter and circumcision that transgresses The-Law.

2:28   For he is not The-Jew who is one outwardly, nor circumcised which is done outwardly on the-flesh,

2:29   but he is The-Jew inwardly and circumcised of the heart, in spirit, not in the Letter whose praise is not from men but from *THE-GOD*.

ROMANS 3

3:1   Where then is the-Jew's advantage, what benefit if any is in circumcision?

3:2   Great and in every manner [way]! For without argument first they believed and were entrusted with The-Oracles-of-*THE-GOD*.

3:3   So what if some disbelieved? Does their disbelief nullify [void] The-Belief in *THE-GOD*?

3:4   Never, no way, no how! *THE-GOD* is true and every man a liar just as it is written, **"So that YOU may be justified always in YOUR words,"** and, **"You should be a conqueror [over-comer] when you are to be judged."**   [Ps 51:4; 116:11]

3:5   For if the-injustice [unrighteousness] of us supports-and-maintains the-justice [righteousness] of *GOD*, what are we to argue? *THE-GOD* is unjust [unrighteous] who brings indignation [punishment, wrath]? (I speak [reason] as a man).

3:6   No! How else shall *THE-GOD* be judging The-System?

3:7   For if The-Truth-of-*THE GOD* is super-glorified through my lying why am I, also a sinner, still being judged {convicted, sentenced and punished as a criminal}?

3:8   And why not do evil so that good may come of it as we have been slanderously accused of and some claim that we have said? Their condemnation [judgment] is assured [fair, just].

3:9   What then are we privileged [better than them, different than them]? No without a doubt for we have charged both Jews and Greeks, all are under sin.

Section I

3:10 As it is written: **"There is no just one (righteous), not even one."**

3:11 **"There is no one who understands, there is no one who (is) seeking out THE-GOD."**

3:12 **"All avoid him simultaneously, they are useless." "There is not even one doing kindness."**

3:13 **"Their larynx has been opened like a sepulcher, their tongues they defraud with, the venom of asps under their lips;"** [Ps 5:9]

3:14 **"Their mouth is being crammed with execration (vile cursing) and bitterness."**

3:15 **Their feet fast to pour out blood;**

3:16 **crushing [bruising] and extreme callousness [wretchedness] is their way;**

3:17 **And the way of peace they know not.**

3:18 **There is no fear of GOD before their eyes."** [Ps 36:1]

3:19 For we are aware that whatever The-Law says, it is speaking to those under The-Law that every mouth may be being stopped and The-entire-System [world] is becoming guilty and subject to the just-verdict of *THE-GOD*.

3:20 Therefore by none of The-Law's acts [works, deeds] shall no flesh be justified at all in the sight of *HIM*, for through The-Law is knowledge [recognition, awareness] of sin.

3:21 But now apart from The-Law, the justice [righteousness] of *GOD* has been made to appear [manifested apparent, clearly understood] being witnessed [attested to] by The-Law and The-Prophets.

3:22 For *GOD'S* justice [righteousness] is through belief in *Savior Anointed* to all and on all The-Ones-Believing, for there is no distinction.

3:23 For all have missed [sinned] and come short of The-Esteem-of-*THE-GOD*.

3:24 Being gratuitously [unreservedly, wholeheartedly] justified by *HIS* grace through The-Deliverance of and in *Anointed Savior*

3:25 whom *THE-GOD* purposed [planned and intended] as a propitiation [conciliatory atonement offering] through The-Belief in *His* blood and showing [displaying] the-justice [righteousness] of *Him*. Because *THE-GOD* in mercy is passing over of the-penalties-of-sins that have previously occurred,

3:26 *THE-GOD* in his tolerance [mercy] at this time is displaying the-justice [righteousness] of *HIM* and a *JUSTIFYING-ONE* of the-one who has belief in *Savior*.

3:27 Where is the-boasting then? It is locked out [there is no place for it]! Through [Because of] which law? Or works? None! But through The-Law-of-Believing.

3:28   We logically conclude then a man is justified by believing apart from the-acts of The-Law.

3:29   Is *THE-GOD* only to Jews and not to the other Nations too? Yes, also to the other Nations

3:30   since it is *THE-ONE-GOD* who shall be justifying circumcision by belief and uncircumcision through believing.

3:31   Are we nullifying [voiding, claiming it has no authority or power] The-Law by [because of] believing? No way! No, we continue sustaining [to stand by the authority of] The-Law.

ROMANS 4

4:1   What shall we be declaring then of our Father Abraham having been found [to be seen] according-to [in] the flesh?

4:2   For if Abraham was justified out of works, he would be boasting but not toward [about, to] *THE-GOD*.

4:3   For what does the-writings say? "**Abraham believed *THE-GOD* and it is accounted to him for justice [righteousness].**"

4:4   Yet for the-one-working there is the-wage which is but a debt [payment due] which is not being accounted for grace.

4:5   For the-one who is not working yet believing on *THE-ONE-JUSTIFYING* the-irreverent [ungodly], his belief is accounted as just [righteousness].

4:6   Even as David has also said, "**Happy [blessed] is the-man whom from *THE-GOD* is accounted as just [righteous] apart from acts [works].**"

4:7   "**Happy are they who are pardoned from lawless acts and sins are covered over,**"

4:8   "**Happy is the-man whom the Lord will not be recognizing his sin.**"[Ps 32:1–2]

4:9   Does this blessing come on circumcision or only the-uncircumcision? We are stating that Abraham's righteousness is accounted to him by believing.

4:10   How then is it reckoned [this reasoned]? While being in circumcision or in uncircumcision? Not in circumcision, but in uncircumcision.

4:11   And the sign he obtained was circumcision, the seal of the-righteousness of (his) belief while-being in uncircumcision. That he is to be father of all the-ones-believing while uncircumcised that righteousness may be accounted [credited] to them also

4:12	and the father of those circumcised. And it not only to the-ones-of-circumcision, but the-ones-observing and walking in the-footprints of The-Belief-of-The-Father of us Abraham while he was in the-uncircumcision-condition.
4:13	For The-Law did not offer The-Promise for Abraham or his seed to be The-Enjoyer-of-the-Allotment of The-Coming-System but through righteousness by-believing.
4:14	For if they are Enjoyers-of-The-Allotment because of The-Law believing is voided and The-Promise has been nullified [voided].
4:15	The-Law is-producing anger-because-of-its-punishments. Also, where there is no law, neither are there transgressions.
4:16	For out of this believing by grace The-Promise is to be confirmed to the-entire-seed, not only for the-ones by The-Law but also to the-ones because of The-Belief-of-Abraham who is Father of all of us.
4:17	As it is written, while in the presence of GOD he believed *THE-ONE-MAKING-LIVE* the-dead-ones and *THE-ONE-CALLING* into existence those things which do not exist as though they are, **"I have appointed you the father of many nations,"** [Gen 17:6]
4:18	who beyond expectation [reason and understanding] believed with expectation [anticipated assurance] that he was to become the Father-of-Many-Nations according-to having been declared, **"So will your seed be."** [Gen 15:5]
4:19	With no weakness in believing, he did not consider his body as having already been dead when he was about one hundred years old or even Sara's womb dead.
4:20	He never doubted The-Promise-of-*THE-GOD* but was invigorated by believing giving esteem [glory] and honor to *THE-GOD*;
4:21	and being fully convinced for that which had been promised *HE* was able to do.
4:22	Therefore, **"It is accounted to him for righteousness."** [Gen 15:6]
4:23	Not only is it written because of him for his own accounting [credit],
4:24	but also because of us to whom it is being accounted [credited] as the-ones believing in *THE-ONE* who raised *Savior-The-Master* of us from the dead;
4:25	who was given up [sacrificed] because of the-offenses of us and was raised for The-Justification [deliverance from sin].
5:1	Being justified then by believing, we are having peace with *THE-GOD* through *The-Master* of us *Savior-Anointed*.

5:2 Through whom also we have access by-believing into The-Grace in which we have stood [remained] and in which we are boasting about The-Expectation-of-The-Glory-of-*THE-GOD*.

5:3 Not only that but we are boasting about The-Afflictions having perceived that The-Afflictions is producing endurance [patience],

5:4 by tested endurance and testing, The-Expectation.

ROMANS 5

5:5 Now The-Expectation is not mortifying, seeing [knowing] that the-Godly-love of *THE-GOD* has been poured out in the-hearts of us through the-Holy-spirit being given to us.

5:6 Still for us, the infirmed [strength-less], *Anointed* according-to the appointed season died for-the-sake-of the irreverent [ungodly].

5:7 For hardly for-the-sake-of a just [righteous] man shall anyone die, perhaps for-a-good-man would one even be daring [willing] to die.

5:8 Yet *GOD* is demonstrating *HIS* Godly-love for us that while we were still sinners, *Anointed* died for-the-sake-of us.

5:9 Much more than being justified now by the-blood of *Him*, we shall be saved through *Him* from The-Indignation [Judgment] (wrath).

5:10 For when being enemies we were reconciled to *THE-GOD*, through the-death of *HIS* Son we shall be saved in The-Life-of-*Him*.

5:11 Not only that, but also boasting [glorying] in *THE-GOD* through *The-Master* of us *Savior-Anointed* through whom now we have obtained The-Conciliation [Atonement, paid/purchase of the debt].

5:12 Because of this, even as sin entered into The-System [world] through one man and through sin entered The-Death and therefore death is passed through into all men for all have sinned.

5:13 Before The-Law sin was in the System, but sin was not being imputed [accounted, charged, associated with] with no existence to The-Law.

5:14 Still The-Death reigned from Adam to Moses and over the-ones that had not sinned as in the-likeness of Adam's transgression who is a type of *The-One* that was coming.

5:15 But the-gracious [free] gift (is) not as [like] the-offense. For if the-offense of one causes many to die, much rather the-grace [gift] of *THE-GOD* and by the-grace of *The-One-Man, Savior Anointed* super-abounds in the-many.

Section I

5:16 And not as the-one sinning comes the-gift. Indeed, out of that one is The-Judgment-of-Condemnation, for that gift is out of the many offenses resulting in its just effect [award].

5:17 For if by The-One-Man's offense The-Death reigns [dominates], how much more for The-Ones through *The-One* super-abounds grace and the-gift of obtaining the-justice [righteousness] of life and shall be reigning through *The-One-Savior-Anointed*?

5:18 Consequently [reasoning, by logic] then, since through one offense all men are condemned [to death], thus also through *The Just-One* is justification [gift, reward] of life for all men.

5:19 Just as through the-disobedience of one man many sinners were constituted [made, created, caused], also through the-obedience of *The One* shall the-many be made just.

5:20 For the Law crept in, increasing the-offenses and increasing the-sins, and-yet the-grace super-exceeds in domination.

5:21 For even as The-Death reigns through The-Sin, even greater the-grace is to be reigning through justice into life eonian through *Savior Anointed*, *The-Master* of us.

ROMANS 6

6:1 What shall we declare then? Shall we be remaining in sin that grace should be more abundant?

6:2 NO! How may it be becoming [What message does that send]? We who have died in sin shall still be living in her (it)?

6:3 Or are you being ignorant [unaware, do not realize] that as many of us that are baptized [immersed] into [with] *Anointed Savior* are baptized in the-death of *Him*?

6:4 We were together then entombed by baptism into [with] the-death with *Him*. Further even as *Christ* was roused [revived] up-out-of the dead-ones through The-Glory of *THE-FATHER* and so we should be walking in newness of life.

6:5 For not-only-have we have become planted [a planted seed, injected semen] together in the-likeness of The-Death-of-*Him*, but also in The-Standing-Up [Resurrection] shall we also be (like *Him*).

6:6 Knowing this, that the-old-man in us was impaled [crucified] (with *Him*) so-that The-Body-of-The-Sin may be nullified [destroyed], then by no means should we still be-slaving [serving] to The-Sin.

6:7	For the-one-dying from sin has been justified [pardoned and released, freed].
6:8	Yet if we died together with *Christ*, we are believing that we shall be living together also to [for, with] *Him*.
6:9	Having perceived [knowing, knowledge] that *Anointed* being roused [was awaken, rose up, is arisen] out of the dead-ones is no-longer dying, Death is no longer being-a-master [ruler, lord, ruling over, lording over].
6:10	For who *He* died, *He* died once for sin, but for who *He* is living; *He* is living for *THE-GOD*.
6:11	Thus also you be indeed accounting [recognizing] yourself dead to The-Sin yet alive for *THE-GOD* and *Anointed Savior, The-Master* of us.
6:12	Do not let The-Sin be reigning in your mortal body and obeying her, in the-lusts of it.
6:13	Nor yet be presenting your members as implements of unjustness [unrighteousness] for sin, but present yourselves to *THE-GOD* as living out of the dead and your members as implements of justice [righteousness] for *THE-GOD*.
6:14	For sin shall not be mastering over you for you are not under the Law but under grace.
6:15	What-then? Shall we be [continue] sinning then seeing that we are not under the Law but under grace? NO WAY!
6:16	Are you not aware that to whom you are presenting yourselves you are slaves to obey? You are slaves to whom you are obeying whether of sin for death or to obedience into [for] justice [righteousness].
6:17	But thanks [grace] be to *THE-GOD* that while you were slaves to sin, you out of the heart obeyed the teaching [doctrine] that was given to you.
6:18	Being freed from The-Sin, you are enslaved [a slave, a servant] to justice [righteousness].
6:19	As a man I am saying this because of the-unfirmness [weakness] of your flesh for you present your members as slaves for uncleanliness and to lawlessness into (greater, more) lawlessness. Now present yourself and your members as slaves into [for] justice [righteousness], into [for] holiness.
6:20	For when you were slaves to sin, you were free from [not associated with, no portion of, no knowledge of, with no way to perform or become] justice [righteousness].
6:21	What fruit, then, did you have on which you are now being ashamed [feeling guilty about]? For the-complete-finish of those things is death.

SECTION I

6:22　And now being freed from The-Sin, being enslaved [a slave, a servant] to *THE-GOD* you are having your fruit in holiness and also ending in life eonian [for the ages].

6:23　For the-purchased-provisions [rations, bought affect, wages] of sin—death, but the-gracious-effect [gift] of *THE-GOD* is life eonian in *Anointed Savior, The-Master* of us.

7:1　Or are you being ignorant, Brothers? For I am speaking to the ones with-knowledge about the Law that The-Law is mastering [dominating] the-man for as much time as he-is-living,

7:2　just-as a woman by The-Law is in-servitude-and-shackled-to to-the-living-man. She is exempt from the-law of her husband if he is dead.

7:3　Consequently [therefore, this is why] she shall be called an adulterous if the-man (husband) is yet living and she ever came to [lives with, establishes a marital-relationship with] a different man. But if her man may be dead, she is free from The-Law; she is not an adulteress if she comes to [lives with, establishes a marital relationship with] a different man.

7:4　So now, my Brothers, you also were caused to die in The-Law through The-Body-of-*The Anointed* that you should come [be married] to a different one who is raised from the dead-ones. That we should be bearing fruit to *THE-GOD*

7:5　for when we were in the-flesh, the-passions-of-The-Sins through The-Law operated [worked] inside our members to bear fruit for The-Death.

7:6　But we were exempted from The-Law in which we were retained [held captive] for dying [death] so that in the newness of spirit we are to be serving and not to the oldness [passing-away] of The-Writings.

ROMANS 7

7:7　What shall we declare then? Is The-Law sin? No way! I would not know The-Sin but for the Law; I would not have been aware of coveting if The-Law had not said, "You shall not be coveting."

7:8　But The-Sin taking the advantage [gaining a strategic position] through The-Commandment produces in me all manner of coveting for apart-from [without] the Law sin is dead.

7:9　Now I was-once-alive not-having-the Law, but when The-Commandment came, sin revived-and-came alive [gained strength and dominating control] and I died.

7:10	And I found [realized, discovered, was given understanding] The-Commandment made for life really delivers death.
7:11	For Sin rushed in through The-Commandment seducing me, and through it [the commandment] kills [slays, murders] me.
7:12	So The-Law indeed is holy, and The-Commandment holy and just and good.
7:13	Then "being-good" has become death for me? No way! But The-Sin that it may-be-appearing [so that it is disclosed, made to be recognized as] as sin by "being-good" is producing [sentencing] me in [to] death. That The-Sin through The-Commandment has-one-become-overwhelmingly [makes infinitely one a greater] a sinner.
7:14	For we are aware that The-Law is spiritual, but I am of-the-flesh, having been disposed of [sold and discarded, scrapped for trash] under sin.
7:15	For that which I am affecting [doing] I am not knowing [don't understand] because that which I am willing [want, desire] to do; this I am not practicing but which I hate this I am doing.
7:16	But if I am doing this which I-am-not-willing [desire not], I am positively-confirming that The-Law is ideal.
7:17	For it is still no longer I doing it but Sin making its home in me.
7:18	I am aware that nothing good is making its home in me, this flesh of mine. For to be doing-good is accompanying [inside] me, but how to do the-ideal I am not finding.
7:19	For I am willing [desire] to do good, but I do not. I am not willing [do not desire] to do that which is evil, and this I am practicing.
7:20	But if I am doing that which I am not willing [not wanting to do], it is no longer I doing it but Sin that is making its home in me.
7:21	Consequently, I am finding The-Law in me willing to be doing the-ideal but finding the-evil is lying beside me [in bed with, present with me].
7:22	Now I am gratified about The-Law-of-*THE GOD* according-to [concerning] the-inward-man,
7:23	but I am observing a different law in my members warring against The-Law-of-My-Mind and leading me into captivity to The-Law-of-Sin which is in my members.
7:24	I am a wretched man! Who shall-deliver [rescue, is the Deliverer of] me from The-Death in the-body?

SECTION I

7:25   I am thankful to *THE-GOD* through *Savior Anointed The-Master* of us. Consequently then, I am indeed in my mind slaving to [serving] the Law-of-*GOD*, but in the-flesh the Law-of-Sin.

ROMANS 8

8:1   In conclusion, nothing condemns the-ones in *Anointed Savior*. They are not walking according-to the flesh but according-to the spirit.

8:2   For The-Law-of-The-Spirit-of-The-Life in *Anointed Savior* frees me from The-Law-of-Sin and of The-Death.

8:3   For it is impossible for The-Law (to do) because it was infirmed [hindered] through the-flesh. *THE-GOD* sending *HIS* own *Son* in the likeness of sinful flesh, and concerning [about, for] Sin, condemns Sin in the-flesh.

8:4   That the-just effect [requirements/righteousness] of The-Law may be fulfilled and the-ones are not trotting [passing their life] about in accordance with the flesh but with the spirit.

8:5   For the-ones being according-to [in] the-flesh are being disposed [think of, think about] of the fleshly things, but the-ones in accord [agreement, union, concurrence] with the spirit, the things of the-spirit.

8:6   For the nature of the-flesh—death, yet the nature of the-spirit—life and peace.

8:7   For the-nature of the-flesh is hatred toward God, for it is not subject to The-Law-of-*THE-GOD* for it is unable to.

8:8   So the-ones being in the-flesh are not able to please *GOD*.

8:9   But you are not of flesh but of spirit if it so be that [that is if] the spirit of *GOD* is making its home in you. Yet if anyone is not having the spirit of *Anointed*, this one is not [an associate of, in partnership with] of *Him*.

8:10   For indeed if *Anointed* is in you, the body is dead because of sin, but the-spirit-is alive because of justification.

8:11   For if The-Spirit that roused up *Savior* out of dead-ones is making its home in you, *THE-ONE-ROUSING The-Anointed* out of the dead-ones shall be making alive your mortal bodies because of *HIS* spirit making its home in you.

8:12   Therefore, Brothers, we are debtors not to the-flesh or to live according-to flesh

8:13   for if you are living according-to the flesh you shall die. Yet if the spirit is causing-the-practices of-the-body to die, you shall be living.

8:14   For whoever is being led by the Spirit-of-*GOD*, these are Sons-of-*GOD*.

8:15	For you have not gotten a spirit-of-slavery again to fear, but you got [have] the spirit-of-Sonship in which we are calling aloud [scream, exclaim, implore] ABBA, *THE-FATHER*.
8:16	The-spirit itself is together witnessing with our spirit that we are offspring [children] of *GOD*
8:17	and since offspring, also Enjoyers-of-the-Allotment. Without-a-doubt Enjoyers-of-the-Allotment-of-*GOD* and joint Enjoyers-of-The-Allotment-of-*Anointed*, if it be that we are suffering together that also we should be being glorified together.
8:18	For I am accounting that the-emotions [sufferings] of the-current-season [time, era] are not worthy of the esteem [glory] to be revealed in us
8:19	for the-premonition [desire, expectation] of The-Creation is waiting for the-unveiling of The-Sons-of-*THE-GOD*.
8:20	For Creation was not voluntarily subjugated to vanity [decay] but through The-One-Subjecting her on [in] expectations.
8:21	And that same Creation shall be freed from the-slavery-of-corruption into the-glorious-freedom by The-Offspring-of-*THE-GOD*.
8:22	We are aware that The-entire-Creation is groaning together and travailing [with birthing pains] together even now.
8:23	But not only this, but we ourselves also The-First-Fruits-of-The-Spirit. We ourselves also are groaning waiting for our sonship and from the-loosening [unchaining, deliverance] from our body.
8:24	We were saved for The-Expectation by expectation. For expecting what is being observed is not expectation. Why? For what one sees why does he need to expect it?
8:25	But through endurance [patience] we are waiting, expecting what we do not see.
8:26	Similarly also the-spirit is together supporting the-unfirmness [weakness] of us and for what? Because we are not aware of what we should be praying according-to that which must be. But this-same-spirit is pleading [exceedingly, over the top] for-the-sake-of us with inarticulate [unspeakable] groaning.
8:27	Yet *THE-ONE-SEARCHING* the-hearts is aware of the-disposition [the way, manner something works] of-the-spirit that in accordance [union, oneness] with *GOD* is pleading for-the-sake-of the Holy-Ones [saints].
8:28	We are aware that all are working together for good for The-Ones-Godly-Loving *THE GOD*, for the-ones being called according for-this purpose.

Section I

8:29 That whom *HE* before knew [already had knowledge of] and also designated before [predetermined] to be conformed into the-image of *The-Son* of-*HIM*, *Firstborn* among many brethren.

8:30 For whom *HE* designated before [predetermined] these *HE* also calls, these also *HE* justifies, whom *HE* justifies these *HE* also glorifies.

8:31 What if anything-more shall we declare toward these things? If *THE-GOD* is over [protects, rules] us who is against us?

8:32 Who surely [truly] did not spare *HIS* own *Son* but gave *Him* up [delivered *Him* up, sacrificed *Him*] for all our sakes. How not also together with *Him* for us shall *HE* be graciously granting all things?

8:33 Who shall be indicting [prosecuting, accusing] against The Chosen-Ones [elect] of *GOD*? *GOD* is THE ONE-JUSTIFYING.

8:34 Who is the-one condemning *Anointed* who died? Even better who is roused awake [risen] and is in [at] the right hand of *THE-GOD* who also is pleading [interceding] for-the-sake-of us?

8:35 What shall be separating us from the-Godly-love of *The-Anointed*? Affliction or distress or persecution or famine or nakedness or danger or sword?

8:36 As it is written: **"That on account of you, we are being put to death [slaughtered] the-whole-day; we are counted as sheep for the slaughter."** [Ps 44:24]

8:37 No, in all these things we are more than conquering through THE-ONE GODLY-*loving* us.

8:38 For I have been persuaded that neither death, nor life, nor messengers [angels], nor sovereignties, nor powers, nor anything present, nor anything about to come,

8:39 nor height, nor depth, nor any different creation shall be able to separate us from the-Godly-love of *THE-GOD* in *Anointed Savior, The-Master* of us.

9:1 I am telling the truth in Christ; I am not lying. My conscience together with Holy spirit is a witness for me

9:2 that in me is great sorrow and unceasing pain in my heart.

9:3 Wishing this about myself that I was specifically-set-aside-away from *The-Anointed* for my brothers, my relatives by birth.

9:4 Any who are Israelites to whom was given The-Sonship and The-Glory and The-Covenants and The-Legislations [laws] and The-Divine-Service and The-Promises.

9:5 By whom out of The-Fathers came *The Anointed*, in the flesh, *The One-Being-On* [over] all.

GOD be blessed into The-Eons.

Amen.

FIRST ADD TO THE ORIGINAL LETTER CIRCULATED ~ 65 C.E.

The Relationship of Jew and Gentile within THE REVELATION OF THE-SECRET

ROMANS 9

9:6   At no time has the-saying [word] of *THE-GOD* fallen short [lapsed]. For not all of The-Ones out of Israel are Israelites

9:7   neither are they all that are seed of Abraham offspring but, "in Isaac shall your seed be called."

9:8   Meaning not the-offspring of the-flesh. These (are) not the children of *THE-GOD* but The-Offspring-of-The-Promise is accounted as the Seed.

9:9   For this is *The-Word-of-Promise*, according-to this, "I shall be coming in the-season and there shall be a son for Sarah."

9:10 And not only this, but also out of Rebecca, the-one having bedded [had sex] with Isaac, The-Father of us

9:11 for [those] of us not being born yet nor yet practicing anything good or evil that according-to the-purposeful-choice of *THE-GOD* may be-remaining [permanent-and-accomplished]. Not by acts [works] but out of *THE-ONE-CALLING*.

9:12 It was declared to her: **"That the-greater [elder] shall be slaving [a servant] to the-inferior [younger]."** [Gen 25:23]

9:13 Further as it has been written, **"The-Jacob I love yet, The-Esau I hate."** [Mal 1:2, 3]

9:14 What shall we be declaring then, there is only injustice [unrighteousness] with *THE-GOD*? NO WAY!

9:15 For to Moses *HE* is saying: **"I shall be having mercy to whomever I may be merciful,"** and,

"I shall have pity [compassion] on whomever I may be pitying [have compassion]." [Exod 33:19]

9:16 Consequently then (it is) not the-one-willing [choosing] or the-one-racing [trying to perform] but out of *GOD* being merciful.

Section I

9:17 For the writings [Scripture] says about The-Pharaoh, **"That for this same (purpose, cause) I roused [created and prepared] you up so that I should be displaying in you my ability [power],"** and, **"So that my name should be being messaged [known, published, declared] everywhere in the-land [on earth]."** [Gal 3:8; Exod 9:16]

9:18 Consequently [so], then to whom *HE* is willing [chooses] *HE* is being merciful, to whom *HE* is willing [chooses] *HE* hardens.

9:19 Why then are you protesting [claiming, complaining] to me that *HE* is still blaming [finding fault with] me? For who has withstood [can comprehend, understand] the-council [intention and reasoning] of *HIM*?

9:20 Then surely indeed oh man are any of you the-one to answer [challenge, oppose in debate, open a legal claim] instead [against] *THE-GOD*? Shall the-one-which-is-molded say to *THE-ONE-MOLDING* [forming it], "Why have you made me so [this way]?

9:21 Does not the-potter have all-authority over the-mud [clay]? Out of the same kneading [clay lump] to make one instrument [vessel] which indeed has value [honor] but to another no value [dishonor]?

9:22 For if *THE-GOD* is willing to show indignation [anger] and to make known *HIS* the-ability [unlimited-inherent-power] of *HIM* and carries in much [great] patience instruments-[vessels]-of-indignation having been adapted for destruction

9:23 then also *HE* should be making known the-riches of *HIS* esteem [glory] on instruments-of-mercy which *HE* had prepared before for glory.

9:24 Us whom *HE* calls. Not only out of Jews but also out of Nations.

9:25 And as *HE* is also saying in Hosee [Hosea]: **"I will call them my people who were not people of mine,"** and, **"her beloved who was not beloved."** [Hos 2:23]

9:26 and, **"It will come to pass in the-place where it was declared to them; "You are not my people," There they will be being called Sons-of-Living-God."** [Hos 1:10]

9:27 For Isaiah is crying over Israel: **"If ever it may be that the-number of The-Sons-of-Israel are as the-sand-of-the-sea, The-Remnant will be saved."**

9:28 **"For in justice [righteousness] He will concisely finish accounting," "Master [Lord] on the-land [Earth] will cut short that accounting [work]."** [Isa 10:23, 28:22]

9:29 And according as Isaiah has declared before, **"Unless (the) Master of Sabaoth [Host, Armies] had not abandoned [left remaining] to us a Seed," "We have forever become like Sodom and forever likened as Gomorrah."** [Isa 1:9, 13:19]

ROMANS 10

9:30   What shall we be declaring [are we claiming] then? That The-Nations not chasing justice [righteousness] have gotten [overtook, secured] justice [righteousness], even righteousness without-believing?

9:31   but Israel, chasing [pursuing] the Law-of-Justice has not attained the Law-of-Justice [Righteousness]?

9:32   Why not [How is this to be understood]? Because of not through [seeking] or out of [by] any believing [faith] but as out of [by] acts of [works, only going through the motions of doing] the Law, for they stumble at *The-Stumbling-Stone*.

9:33   Recall as it has been written, **"Perceive! I am placing in Sion [Jerusalem] a stone of stumbling and a rock of snare [entrapment],"** and, **"Everyone believing on *Him* shall not be disgraced."** [Ps 118:22; Isa 28:16]

10:1   Brothers, it is the-delight of my heart and the-petition toward *THE GOD* for The-Israel to be saved

10:2   and testifying for them. They are having a boiling [zeal] of God but not according-to knowledge [recognition, understanding].

10:3   For they unknowing [being ignorant of] The-Justice-[goodness, righteousness]-of-*THE-GOD* and seeking to establish their own justice [righteousness] they were not set under [submitting themselves to] The-Justice-[righteousness]-of-*THE-GOD*.

10:4   For in justice *Anointed* finished [consummated, completed, ended] the Law for everyone believing.

10:5   For Moses is writing of-the-justice [righteousness] out of The-Law, **"That the-man doing them shall [be mandated to] live by them."** [Lev 18:5]

10:6   For from believing comes righteousness that is said in this manner, **"In the-heart of you do not be asking who shall be ascending into The-Heaven."** [Deut 30:12–1]

That is [meaning who is] to be leading *Anointed* down [from above].

10:7   Or, *"Who shall be descending into The-Abyss?"* This is [that is who] to be leading *Anointed* up out of dead-ones [from the dead]?

10:8   But what does it say? *"The-declaration [word] is near you, in your mouth and in the-heart of you."* This is *The-Declaration [Word]* of-belief we are proclaiming [heralding].

Section I

10:9   That you always should ever be [continually] vowing [confessing, claiming] with your mouth (the) *Master* (is the) *Savior* and should be believing in your heart that *THE-GOD* roused [raised] Him out of dead-ones shall be saving you.

10:10   For it is a believing heart into [bestows, imparts, grants, makes available] righteousness and a confessing mouth that saves.

10:11   For The-Writings say this, "Everyone believing on Him shall not be disgraced [down-viled]."

10:12   For there is no distinction between Jew and Greek for the-same *Master-of-All* is rich [generous] to all of The-Ones-calling on *Him*.

10:13   For everyone, whoever should be calling on *The-Name-of-The-Master* shall be saved.

10:14   Then how shall they be called to whom they do not believe? Further how shall they believe about whom they have not heard? And apart from proclaiming [heralding, preaching] (how) shall they be hearing?

10:15   Now how shall they be proclaimed to [heralded to, preached to] if no one is being commissioned [sent]? As it is written, **"How beautiful are the-feet of the-ones-bringing-the-message of-peace, of the-ones-bringing-the-good-message of good (things)!"** [Isa 52:7]

10:16   For not all have obeyed [accepted, followed] The-Good-Message [Gospel]. Isaiah is saying, **"Lord! Who believes our tidings [report]?"** [Isaiah 53:1]

10:17   Consequently, believing out of [comes from] hearing and hearing through the-declaration [preaching, word] of God.

10:18   But I am asking, "Do they not hear [understand what was said]?" Indeed, most assuredly, **"Into [From] every land comes an utterance [sound] from them,"** and, **"to The-Ends of the-inhabited earth by the-declarations [words] of them."** [Ps 19:4; I Kgs 18:10]

10:19   But I am asking, "How could Israel not know?" First Moses said, **"I shall be provoking you to jealousy by a no [insignificant, are not of a] Nation; I shall be vexing [angering] you (by a) unintelligent [foolish] Nation."** [Deut 32:21]

10:20   And Isaiah said very daringly [boldly without fear], **"I was found by the-ones that were not seeking me, I became in appearance [available] to-the-ones that were not inquiring of [asking for] me."** [Isa 65:1]

10:21   Further about Israel *HE* said, **"I have expanded [stretched out] my hands toward an un-persuading [stubborn] and contradicting [belligerent] people."** [Isa 65:2]

ROMANS 11

11:1 Am I not saying [proposing, suggesting] then *THE-GOD* has thrust [pushed, cast] away His people? No way! For I am an Israelite coming out of the seed of Abraham of the Tribe of Benjamin.

11:2 *THE-GOD* has not thrust away *HIS* people whom *HE* knew before [had foreknowledge of], or have you not perceived [understood] what Elijah is saying by this writing [scripture] to *THE-GOD* as he is pleading against Israel saying,

11:3 **"Master! They have killed your prophets and the-sacrifice-places [altars] of yours they are digging down [undermining],"** and, **"I was reserved alone and they are seeking the-soul of me."** [I Kgs 19:10, 14]

11:4 But what is the-appraisement {implies divine reply} saying to him? **"I have reserved for myself 7000 men who have not now bent the knee to The-Baal."** [I Kgs 19:18]

11:5 Thus also then [Even today], there has come to be a remnant according-to the lottery by grace in this season now [current era].

11:6 Now if by grace, (it is) no longer out of acts [works] or else grace no longer becomes grace. And if out of acts [works], it is still not grace or else the act [work] is no longer an act [work].

11:7 Why then is Israel still seeking this which she has not encountered but The-Lottery [elected] has happened on it [encountered it]? Because the remaining were calloused [scaling over the eyes, blinded].

11:8 Just as it has been written, **"*THE-GOD* gives to them a spirit-of-stupor, eyes to not be observing and ears to not be hearing to this very day,"** [Isa 29:10, 13; 29:3, 4]

11:9 and David is saying, **"Let their table become [be turned] into a trap and into a mesh and into a snare and into a repayment to them."** [Ps 69:22]

11:10 **"Let the-eyes of them become darkened that they not may not be looking [observing] and continually bowing together the-backs of them."** [Ps 60:23]

11:11 I ask then, have they tripped [stumbled] that they should fall [not rise, be unable to return]? No way! For by those that offended, saving [salvation] has come to The-Nations to provoke a boil [jealousy] in them.

11:12 For if the-offense [sin, deviation] of them enriches [benefits] The-System [world] and their diminishing [waning, losing ground, being abandoned] enriches of [benefits] the Nations, how much-greater The-Filling [Return, Complement, Restoration] of them?

Section I

11:13   For I am saying to you, to The-Nations [you Gentiles], that I am indeed commissioned [an apostle] for the Nations [Gentiles] and through my service I am esteemed [honored]

11:14   if somehow through my flesh I should provoke (them {the Jews}) to jealousy and should be saving any of them.

11:15   For if the-casting-away of them (be) conciliation [legally resolves the situation] for the System [world], what is the-taking-back of them [how do they return] if there is no life from the dead-ones?

11:16   Because if *The-First-Fruit* is *Holy* so-also the kneading [dough lump] and if *The-Root* is *Holy* so also The-Boughs [branches].

11:17   For if some of The-Boughs are broken out [pruned out] and you being wild olives grafted in among them and Joint-Participants-of-*The-Root*, you become the-fatness of the-olive [become the tree and bear ripened fruit].

11:18   You do not boast [taunt and consider yourself better than] against The-Bough. For if you are boasting, you are not bearing [reflecting, imitating, duplicating] *The-Root*; you are your own root.

11:19   Shall you be declaring that *The-Boughs* are broken out [pruned out] that I may be grafted in?

11:20   Ideally [For a purpose] they are broken [pruned] by disbelief and you have stood [remained] by faith? Do not be highly disposed [extremely haughty]! For you should be [in great] fear!

11:21   For if *THE-GOD* did not spare the natural branches, be aware *HE* should not be sparing you.

11:22   Be aware then of the kindness and cutting [harshness] of *GOD*! Indeed, on those falling—harshness. Yet on you kindness if you may always be remaining in (*HIS*) kindness or else you shall be stricken out [hewn out].

11:23   Also those that may yet to be ever [for those that continue] remaining in disbelief shall be able to be grafted in for *THE-GOD* is able to again graft them.

11:24   For if you are of the wild olive according by nature and stricken [hewn] out and grafted in to a cultivated olive, how much easier these the-natural-ones shall be grafted back into their own olive tree?

11:25   For I am not willing for you to be ignorant, Brothers, of The-Secret so that in your prudence [wisdom] you may not be beside yourselves [arrogantly haughty]! That in part the callousness [blindness, cataracts] to Israel has come (to them) until the-full-complement [all of] of The-Nations [Gentiles] has come to be [is completed].

11:26 And therefore all Israel shall be saved just it has been written, **"Out of Sion The-One-Rescuing [Deliverer] shall be arriving,"** and, **"HE shall be turning away the irreverence [ungodliness] from Jacob"** [Isa 59:20, 21]

11:27 and, **"This to them is MY covenant, at-a-time I should be lifting [eliminating] them from their sins."** [Isa 27:9]

11:28 Indeed according-to the-good-message [gospel] enemies because of you but according-to The-Selection [drawing, lottery] beloved because of The-Fathers.

11:29 For the-gracious-gifts [effects] and The-Calling-of-*THE GOD* are unregrettable [not to be repented of].

11:30 For even as you also were once stubborn [unpersuaded, disobedient, did not believe in] to *THE-GOD,* but now you have been shown mercy through their stubbornness [unbelief].

11:31 Therefore, these now unbelieving, through mercy given to you, that they also may be getting [receiving, obtain mercy].

11:32 For *THE-GOD* has The-All locked up together into disbelief that *HE* should be being merciful to The-All.

11:33 OH, the depth of riches and wisdom and knowledge of God! How unsearchable The-Judgments of *HIM* and how untraceable are *HIS* ways!

11:34 **"For who knew the mind of *The MASTER* [The Lord]?"** **"Who has become *HIS* counselor [adviser]?"** [Isa 40:13; Jer 23:18]

11:35 or, **"Who has given to *HIM* first and it shall be repaid by *HIM*?"** [Job 41:11]

11:36 Seeing that out of *HIM* and through *HIM* and in *HIM* all!

To *HIM* is The-Glory into The-Eons.

Amen.

SECOND ADD: THE CLOSING OF PAUL'S CAREER ~ 66–68 C.E.

A Call to Remain Loyal and True as One Entity, Be Self-Governing in Behavior and Selfless Toward Others

ROMANS 12

12:1 I am entreating you now, Brothers, by the-pities [mercies] of *THE-GOD* that you present your bodies a living sacrifice, holy, well pleasing to *THE-GOD* which is the-logical divine-service of you.

Section I

12:2 And you do not be configured to this eon [age, present period] but be renewing the-mind of yours. Testing what is the-good and well-pleasing and mature [perfect] will of THE-GOD.

12:3 For I am saying through the-grace being given to me for every being [person] among you to not be over disposed [feeling great, think highly] (about yourself) beyond which is binding [limiting] (your) being disposed [thinking, of who you suppose you are] but be sanely disposed [think soberly] as the measure of belief as THE-GOD imparts to each.

12:4 For even as we have many members in one body, yet not every member has the-same practice [function].

12:5 Though many, we are one body in Christ, and yet we are one of another member [with each member operating independently]

12:6 but having gracious-diverse-gifts according-to the-grace being given to us. Whether excelling in prophecies according-to the-analogy [equivalent, proportion] of belief

12:7 or through service [ministry] in ministering, or the teacher in teaching,

12:8 or the-one-calling [exhorting] in calling [admonishing, encouraging, comforting], or the-one-giving in generosity, the-one-presiding [managing, leading] in diligence or the one being merciful in glee [cheerfulness].

12:9 (Let) Godly-love be un-hypocritical, detesting-utterly [abhorring] the-wicked clinging to-the-good.

12:10 (Let) brotherly affection be a natural fond affection for each other, value [honor] another one first.

12:11 In diligence do not be slothful; being fervent in the-spirit slaving [serving] *The-Master*;

12:12 rejoicing in The-Expectation, enduring The-Affliction [tribulation], persevering in prayer,

12:13 contributing to the needs of The-Holy-Ones [Saints], pursuing hospitableness.

12:14 Be blessing the-ones-persecuting you; be blessing and not cursing!

12:15 Be rejoicing with the-ones-rejoicing and lament [weep] with the-ones-lamenting.

12:16 [Be] disposed [think of] the-same about one another, not the-high-minded but the-humble, not being led away with becoming disposed [thinking only, conceited in] of yourselves.

12:17 Render to no one evil for evil, making it ideal provisions [be honest] in-the-sight-of all men.

12:18 If able, as much as is in you, with all men be at peace.

12:19 Beloved do not avenge yourself but be giving place to [set aside] anger. As it is written says the Lord, **"Vengeance is mine, I shall be repaying."** [Lev 19:18, Deut 32:35]

12:20 **"If ever your enemy may be hungering be-giving-him-the-morsel [food], If he maybe thirsting, be-getting-him-the-drink. For doing this you will be heaping embers of fire on his head."** [Prov 25:21, 22]

12:21 Do not be conquered by the-evil but be you conquering the-evil with the-good.

ROMANS 13

13:1 Let every soul be subject to superior authorities. For there is no authority that is not from *GOD*. The-ones in authority have been set there by *THE-GOD*.

13:2 So then the-one-[an individual]-resisting the-authority has withstood the mandate of *THE-GOD* for the-ones having withstood [resisted] shall-be-getting [receiving] judgment on themselves.

13:3 For The-Chiefs [magistrates] are not in fear of the-good acts but of the-evil ones. But do not be fearful of The-Authority. Do good! Then by you doing the-good you shall be having praise out of her [it].

13:4 For God's servant is for you for the-good. Yet if you may be doing evil, you be fearful! For the servant of God is not wearing the-sword feignedly [for show, in vain], it is for avenging [punishing] indignation [in anger] to the-ones-practicing [committing] the-evil.

13:5 Therefore be subject out-of necessity, not only because of The-Indignation [wrath] but also because of the-conscience.

13:6 Because of this you also supply the taxes, for they are officials [ministers] of GOD preserving this same (thing).

13:7 Be then giving to-the-one all which is owed [obligated], the-taxes to the-one taxing, the-tribute [custom] to the-one's tribute [custom], the-fear [respect] to-the-ones of fear [respect], value [honor] to-the-one of value [honor].

13:8 To no one owe anything! Be loving to one another for the-one Godly-loving a different one has fulfilled the Law.

13:9 For you shall not be committing adultery, you shall not be murdering, you shall not be stealing, you shall not be testifying falsely [a false witness], you shall not be coveting and if any other different precept [direction] it is summed up in this saying as: "You shall Godly-love the-near-one [associate, neighbor, stranger] as yourself."

Section I

13:10 The-Godly-love is not acting evil to the-one near [associate, neighbor, stranger]; it complements [fulfills, is the fullness, completion of] then of The-Law-of-Godly-Love.

13:11 Also be aware of this, the-season, that hour is already now for us to-be aroused out of sleep for our salvation, is nearer for us than we believe.

13:12 The-night progresses, but The-Day has drawn near, and we should be putting off the-acts of the-darkness, and we should be slipping on [outfitting] The-Implements-[battle armor] of-Light.

13:13 We should be walking respectfully as in The-Day, not in revelries and drunkenness, not in chambering [fornication] and wantonness [lewdness, vices], not in strife and jealousy.

13:14 But you put on *The-Master Savior Anointed* and be making no provision for lusts of the-flesh.

ROMANS 14

14:1 Yet for the-infirmed [weak] in The-Belief, gather them to you not by discriminating [prejudged, already in opposition, prejudicial] reasoning.

14:2 Indeed, one believes all things can be eaten and the-one-infirmed [weak] eats greens [herbs],

14:3 the-one that eats is not-to-be scorning the-one not eating, and the-one who is not eating, do-not-be judging the-one that eats for *THE-GOD* has taken [accepted, become a close companion to] them for *HIMSELF*.

14:4 Who are you to be judging another's domestic [servant]? He is standing or he is falling to his own master, but he is able to stand, for it is *THE-GOD* to stand him.

14:5 Who indeed is deciding this day over that day? Who yet is deciding every day? Let each one be fully assured in his own mind.

14:6 The-one-convinced The-Day is for *Master* is disposed to that; the one convinced The-Day is not *Master's* is disposed to that. And the-one eating to *Master*, he-is-thanking *THE-GOD*, and the-one not eating to *Master* is thanking *THE-GOD*.

14:7 Understand not one of us lives to himself, and no one dies to himself.

14:8 If ever we may be living for *The-Anointed*, we are living; if ever we may be dying for *The-Master*, we are dying, for whether we are living or dying we are *The-Master's*.

14:9 For into this [this purpose] *Anointed* died and rose and revives and that for the living-ones and the dead-ones *He* should be *Master*.

14:10 So why are you judging your brother? Or why are you also scorning your brother? We shall all be standing [presented] at The-Platform-[judgment stand]-of-*The-Anointed*.

14:11 For it has been written, **"As I am living says the LORD, every knee shall be bowing to me,"** and, **"every tongue shall be avowing [confessing] to THE-GOD."** [Isa 45:23]

14:12 Consequently then each of us will be giving an account concerning himself to *THE-GOD*.

14:13 Then by no means still should we be judging one another, but rather you decide this, to not put in place a stumbling-block or snare toward the-brother.

14:14 I have been persuaded [taught] and I know according-to [personally from] the *Master Savior* that nothing of itself is common [contaminated, unclean]. But if the-one-that-accounts [reckons, reasons] anything as common, to that one it is common.

14:15 Yet if over food you have sorrowed [offended, not considered] your brother, you are no longer walking according-to Godly-love. Do not be destroying him for whose sake *Anointed* died because of your food.

14:16 Do not let your good be spoken as if evil.

14:17 For The-Kingdom-of-*THE-GOD* is not food and drink but of justice [righteousness] and peace and joy in the Holy-spirit.

14:18 For the-one slaving [serving] in these things to *The-Anointed* well pleases *THE-GOD* and attested [is approved] by men.

14:19 Consequently we should then be pursuing peace and the-edification of one another.

14:20 There should be no demolishing [destroying] the-work of *THE-GOD* because of food. Indeed, all is clean, but evil to the-man through eating stumbling [causes to fall] the-one.

14:21 Ideally do not be eating meats or be drinking wine in which your brother stumbles, is snared, or is being weakened.

14:22 Do you have belief [faith]? You should be having it [practicing, living in it] to yourself in view of [as seen by] *THE-GOD*. Happy is the-one who does not judge himself in which he is attesting [allowing].

14:23 Yet the-one doubting whatever he eats is condemned seeing that it is not out of believing, for whatsoever is not out of believing is sin.

Section I

ROMANS 15

15:1   For we ought to be able to bear the-infirmities of the-impotent [weak] and not to be pleasing ourselves.

15:2   For each of us let him be pleasing the-near one [associate, neighbor] toward good edification.

15:3   For also *The-Anointed* pleased not himself but according as it has been written, **"The-reproaches of The-Ones reproaching YOU fell on Me."** [Ps 69:7, 9, 20]

15:4   For whatever was written before was written ahead of our time for our teaching, that through the-endurance and through the-consolation [support] of The-Scriptures we may be given The-Expectation.

15:5   Yet may THE-GOD of endurance [patience] and consolation [comfort, support, relief] be granting you the-same-disposition [mind, approach] to one another just as *Anointed Savior*.

15:6   That with one accord [mind] in one mouth [in one sound, unison] glorifying THE-GOD and FATHER of *The-Master* of us *Savior Anointed*.

15:7   Therefore be talking to one another according and also as *The-Anointed* took [firmly locked-grasped] us to himself for the glory of GOD.

15:8   Now I am saying *Savior Anointed* had to become a servant of The-Circumcision for-the-sake-of the truth [The-Promise made] by GOD [to fulfill God's oath] to confirm The-Promises to The-Fathers

15:9   and for The-Nations [Gentiles] to glorify THE-GOD for-the-sake-of (*HIS*) mercy. According it has been written, **"Because of this *I* shall be acclaiming YOUR name among the Nations,"** and, **"To *YOUR* name I shall play music [sing, praise],"** [II Sam 22:50; Ps 18:49]

15:10   and elsewhere, **"You be gladdened [be making merry, rejoice] Nations along with his people."**

15:11   And again be-praising, **"The Nations [Gentiles] be praising *Him, The-Master*! All you peoples be lauding *Him*!"** [Ps 117:1]

15:12   And also Isaiah says, **"There shall be *The-Root-of-Jesse, The-One* rising up being-Chief [leading] of the Nations, on *Him* the Nations shall be relying [trusting, have hope]."** [Isa 11:10]

15:13   Now may *THE-GOD-of-The-Expectation* be filling you with all joy and peace in believing, that you be super-abounding in The-Expectation by the unlimited-ability-and-power of the Holy-spirit.

15:14   Now I have been persuaded, my Brothers, about you also myself, that you are bulging full [distended] of goodness having been filled of every knowledge [having the full truth and understanding] also being able to be admonishing [watching over, caring and preserving] one another.

15:15 But more daringly [openly and boldly] have I written to you Brothers as a part (of) reminding [prompting] you because of the-grace [gift of divine service] being given under to [authority] me by *THE-GOD*.

15:16 To me as The-Official [minister] of *Savior Anointed* to The-Nations acting as a priest of The-Well-Message of *THE-GOD* that it may be carried toward The-Nations. Properly received having-been-made-holy by the Holy-spirit.

15:17 Through *The-Anointed Savior* I then have boasting about *GOD*.

15:18 For I dare not be speaking of any other acts which *The Anointed* has not said [spoken] or worked [performed] through me into the [for the] obedience [training and teaching] of the Nations.

15:19 In mighty-overwhelming-undisputable-power of signs and of miracles and the unlimited-ability-and-power of the spirit of *GOD* from Jerusalem and all around to The-Illyricum by me has The-Well-Message of *The-Anointed* been filled [completely-preached].

15:20 Thus being ambitious to-not-be-bringing-the-well-message to where *Anointed* is named [already known] so that I am not building on another's foundation.

15:21 But as it is written, **"To whom it was not informed concerning *Him* they shall not be seeing,"** and **"of *whom* they have not heard, they shall understand."** [Isa 59:15]

15:22 For which [this reason] I was greatly hindered from coming to you.

15:23 While still not having a place in the-regions [area] but having had a longing to-be-coming to you for many years

15:24 and if I ever may be going to Spain, I will come to you first. For I am expecting to gaze upon you as I am going through and by you being first filled by your hospitality, (then) part from (there) being filled [satisfied, provided for],

15:25 but now I am going into Jerusalem serving The-Holy-Ones [Saints].

15:26 For Macedonia and Achaia delighted to make some contribution to-the-poor-ones of The-Holy-Ones in Jerusalem.

15:27 They are delighted and debtors to them. For if The-Nations are able to participate in their spiritual things, they also owe [have a duty to] them to minister in the-needs-of-the-flesh.

15:28 After finishing this and sealing this fruit [finish this blessing] to them, I will be coming through you into Spain.

SECTION I

15:29 I have perceived that when coming to you I shall be coming with the-full-blessing of *The-Anointed* for The-Well-Message.

15:30 I am entreating you Brothers through *The-Master* of us *Savior Anointed*, through the-Godly-love of the-spirit struggle-together with me in the-prayers over-the-sake-of me toward THE-GOD

15:31 that I should be rescued from The-Stubborn-and-Unpersuaded [unbelievers] in Judea and that through my service for them in Jerusalem it may be well received by The-Holy-Ones,

15:32 that I may be coming to you in joy through the will of *GOD* and with you should be together refreshed.

15:33 Now THE GOD-OF-PEACE (be) with all of you.
Amen.

POST SCRIPT: CLOSING GOODBYES, ACKNOWLEDGMENTS, AND LAST WARNINGS AND BLESSINGS

ROMANS 16

16:1 Also I am commending to you Phoebe, the-sister of us, being a server of the Ecclesia [called-out] in Cenchrea.

16:2 You should be receiving her in the *Master*, worthy of The-Holy-Ones and they would be standing by her in whatever matter she may be needing from you. For she has become a patroness to many and to me myself.

16:3 You welcome Priscilla and Aquila, fellow workers of mine in *Anointed Savior*.

16:4 Who for the-sake-of my soul [life] jeopardized their necks, whom not only I am thanking but also all of The-Called-Out of The-Nations

16:5 and also The-Out-Called from their home. You welcome Epanetus [On praise], my beloved, who is The-First-Fruit of Achaia in *Anointed*.

16:6 Greet you Mary, who toiled greatly over us.

16:7 You welcome Andronicus and Junia, the-relatives of mine. Also my fellow captives, who are the Notable-Ones among The-Commissioners [apostles] who were also in *Anointed* before me.

16:8 Greet you Amplias, my beloved in *Master*.

16:9 Salute Urbanas, our fellow worker in *Anointed* and Stachys, my beloved.

16:10   Salute Apelles, tested in *Anointed*. Salute the-ones of the-ones from Aristobulus.

16:11   Greet Herodian, my relative. Greet you the-ones of the-ones of Narcissus, the-ones being in *Master*.

16:12   Salute Tryphena and Tryphosa, the-ones toiling in *Master*. Salute Persis, the-beloved who toils much in *Master*.

16:13   Salute Rufus, the-one-called by *Master*, and his mother and mine.

16:14   Welcome Asyncritus, Phlegon, Hermas, Patrobas, Hermes, and the-brothers with them.

16:15   Salute Philologus, and Julia, Nereus and his sister and Olympas, and together with all Holy ones with them.

16:16   Greet one another with a holy brotherly-kiss. The-Called-Outs of *The-Anointed* are greeting you.

16:17   Now am I entreating you Brothers to take note of The-Ones of Dissensions and the-snares against the-teaching which you learned and avoid them!

16:18   For they are not slaving such to *The-Master* of us *Savior Anointed* but for their own bowel [belly] through complements [pretend, theatrics] and adulations [empty-pretentious-praise], they are seducing the-hearts of the-innocent [simple].

16:19   I am rejoicing over all of you for your obedience has reached far to all, yet I am willing [desiring] that you would indeed be wise to that which is good yet artless [uncontrived, guileless, simple] to evil,

16:20   and *THE-GOD-of-Peace* shall-be-crushing under your feet The-Adversary [Satan] in swiftness [quite soon].

The-grace of *The-Master* of us *Savior Anointed* (be) with you.

Amen.

16:21   Greeting you are Timotheus my fellow worker with Lucius and Jason and Sosipater [Save Father], my relatives.

16:22   I, Tertius, the-one-writing the-letter in *Master*, am greeting you.

16:23   Gaius, the-lodger [host] of me and of all The-Called-Out [Ecclesia], greet you. Erastus, The-Administrator of The-City, and Quartus his brother are greeting you.

16:24   The-Grace of *The-Master* of us *Savior Anointed* (be) with all of you.

Amen.

16:25   Now for *THE-ONE* being able to establish you in accordance with the-well-message of mine and The-Proclamation of *Savior Anointed* in accordance with

Section I

The-Revelation of The-Secret having been hushed [kept silent, unknown] from time eonian [time began]

16:26 but is now-being-made-to-appear [understood, known] through prophetic scriptures according-to the injunction [court order, commandment, royal decree] of *THE-EONIAN-GOD* being made known to all The-Nations into obedience by-believing.

16:27 To the *ONLY-WISE-GOD* through *Savior Anointed* (be) the-glory into The-Eons.

Amen.

(Written to the Romans from Corinth; delivered by Phoebe the servant of the Cenchrea Ecclesia)

I CORINTHIANS COMMENTARY

Paul, in his second letter within the sacred order, wastes no time in establishing his credentials and heads right into the order of business at this "Stockholders Meeting." We are reading the minutes of that meeting. As much as Romans sets the tone by being a legal document, I Corinthians follows the same pattern of legal opinions, legal briefs, and executive ordered actions (because these are the divine instructions from the "President and CEO," Christ himself, to the corporation, "The-Body, The-Ecclesia"). It's a series of lectures and debates of why and why not, and it provides answers to questions submitted from the "floor" to the attorney Paul. This is clearly a letter of corrective action to a divisive body not even close to acting like the rest of The-Chosen-Ones.

I have opened I Corinthians by making it sound like a board meeting because it has all the elements of one. The reader should understand that there is legality going on in heaven—even to this day—with title and deed transfers taking place, property being reclaimed, and repossession. These and a host of other activities all are leading you to take possession of and manage your portions of the Kingdom/Government of God (serving as a trustee or commissioner). You are expected to do the same in the future, just as any lawyer, trustee, power of attorney, or notary should do. In addition, you will have the credentials of being divine royalty with power. The portions of the Kingdom/Government you will be managing will certainly pay attention to you.

We are receiving a primer in all the letters and books showing how things are being done in heaven and what we will be doing in the heavenlies. We are receiving instruction on not only what to do but how to do it—and why it is not just in a group setting, but also a personal, one-to-one interface. Paul's letters are the foundation of your behavior and actions in the future, and his training and background as a rhetorician, debater and legal counsel benefits you and me directly. He is passing on his training, education, direct information, and instructions. This is one of the reasons he was uniquely qualified to be used by Christ for His purposes. Paul is not creating theology or a religion; instead he is directly relating his instructions.

Objectifying Paul as a theologian is foundationally a misrepresentation, and therefore using his material as theology forces one to immediately course down a path that creates misrepresentative intentions, purposes, instructions, and errant tenets. Paul actually adds clarity to many social activities, historical events, and defense of

Section I

beliefs and practices. He is dealing with daily ordinary living, not something called religion or the business of theology.

The same analogy could be said concerning the Abrahamic Covenant. It was not God's intention to turn his promise to Abraham into a religion, but rather a daily walk in life where one treats others with respect, dignity, honor, and aids as and when needed in addition to the one-on-one relationship with the Creator. All of Paul's letters, instructions, and directions appear to follow the same approach and intentions.

There is not much religion in all the texts of the Bible other than possibly the sacrificial and Temple activities. But even those have legal undertones and intentions. The sacrificial system would have probably never occurred either, other than due to God's wisdom in arranging such to insure that no created being would ever boast, glorify, or think to make themselves greater or in dominion of God or Christ. It's also to ensure that we understand God's and Christ's unbounded and unexplainable Godly–love for us in those past temple rituals, rehearsals, and past (and limited future also) practices.

Religion is just another contrivance of The-System, a slight-of-hand device used by Satan as ruler of this current era to keep everyone peering in the wrong direction in fear and bondage. Religion is a false substitute for simple living for God and your fellow man. But I have digressed, so let's get back to Corinthians as a letter and the board meeting at hand.

Beginning in verse 1:1, Paul immediately establishes his credentials as the trustee of that body of Christ called the Ecclesia, specifically for the nations outside of the Jews. It is obvious in the next few verses that the Corinthians were in-fighting over who had what authority and who had what value or no value. Paul is really calling out anyone who thought they had greater authority and bravado than him. Step forward, you can hear him demanding. Challenge my authority. Who do you think you are?

In verses 1:4–6, Paul briefly rehearses the fact the Corinthians know The-Secret (see verses 5–6, where it is inferred and then clearly spoken about in 4:1) and indicts them (1:12–16) for not being unified or acting correctly with this full knowledge of God in which they know they are to judge and rule. One can only imagine the megalomaniacs from the Ecclesia running around with no sensibility about the public-relations or internal nightmare they are causing (the same attitude and actions can be found also in Romans, and Paul corrects the same problem there too). This is a complete disaster for the Ecclesia in Corinth. Thus, beginning in verse 17, as a corporate attorney, Paul begins setting out his series of accusations, arguments, debates, and proofs to begin the rethinking process about this "freedom and authority" afforded the Corinthians. They are far out in the ocean without any life preserver. Paul's statement is not without a purposeful, serious declaration. He is getting ready to "circumcise" a brother in the Ecclesia who, as a son is having open sexual relations with his mother. Paul is furious, ready to "hand them over personally and directly to 'The-Satan!'"

Hence, beginning with verse 17, this letter builds in greater fury to a crescendo of the highest order until I Corinthians 5:1, when Paul brings all this to a screaming, screeching halt. It is a major crash and disaster of the highest order. The son having sex with his mother is even an outrage in the world's view. Somehow it is now acceptable by the Ecclesia because, "all things are lawful for me?" Paul immediately orders the excommunication and expulsion of both in order to save their lives, in mercy, at the later resurrection. Paul thunders and roars in this passage as he accuses all the leaders and members for allowing this to occur and rebukes them for having no shame, courage, or correct understanding and actions (this is all a backdrop against The-Secret). They all are charged with this sinful crime; it's death to all so they may all be saved later. They all are guilty and deserve the same excommunications and loss of the first estate, the First Resurrection.

If that was not a wake-up call for them and did not cause them to shudder to their very core, one can only imagine the correction Christ would take (and was taking) with them: many were killed, sick and debilitated for not honoring the Lord's Supper. This is beyond a woe to all. It is also meant as a lesson and a warning for us to guard our actions and attitudes and protect Christ's Body if we truly understand the sweeping majesty and reward of the first resurrection and the fact that we had already been given salvation from the moment of creation. Any words produced would still fail to make one understand the enormity of this.

Paul's next accusation is in judging (I Corinthians 6:1–20), which is a by-product of them letting this activity occur for so long. If they can't even take care of their own internal problems, how are they going to manage and judge what is being held in reserve for them?

So, from I Corinthians 1:1 through 6:20, Paul tears into the Corinthians and demands that they adopt a new set of values and actions, all done with great passion and the desire to live from hearts desiring to serve God and Christ.

Starting in Chapter 7, Paul—sounding very matter of fact and nearly blunt—provides legal advice and instructions for his clients on a series of questions the Ecclesia has forwarded to him. These are:

- 7:1–40: Marriage, husband-and-wife relations, keeping the promise of marriage with the virgins
- 8:1–13: Foods intended for idols but now found on the open market for retail sale
- 9:1–27: Paul's credentials and the fact that he is acting as the notary public for the Ecclesia
- 11:1–15: Women in authority over men in general, preaching and leading the Ecclesia
- 11:16–34: Disservice of the Lord's Supper and gathering together

Section I

- 12:1–31: The many different talents and abilities as supplied by God for His purpose but all equal, no matter what gift has been given
- 13:1—14:40: Speaking a foreign language (a recognizable and current language, not an ancient and unrecognizable one)
- 15:1–58: A review of The-Belief and the First Resurrection
- 16:1– 4: Gifting and giving

Paul then ends with a series of desires, wishes, requests, and quick, one-line reviews so typical of many of his letters. Everything is designed to strengthen, upgrade, encourage, and remain believing, ready to teach, and ready to serve in Godly-love.

What a tremendous amount of information and instructions to take in all at once! Additionally, here is an apostle with all the power and authority to create miracles as well as to execute whatever demands or instructions he provides backed by the authority of The-Christ. Paul was quite displeased with all. So, the next question arises, was he able to turn this shipwreck around in time? Hopefully II Corinthians gives us an answer or clue.

Of all of Paul's letters, I Corinthians sweeps across a panorama of living principles and protocol for the Ecclesia like none other. Few letters should be studied so intently and so often, and yet I know of no other letter that is ignored more by those calling themselves Christians. I fear too many are Corinthians still to this day.

I CORINTHIANS AS A LETTER

PAUL, CALLED-TO-THE-OFFICE OF COMMISSIONER of *Savior-Anointed*, by the will of *GOD* and The-Brother Sosthenes to the Ecclesia of *THE-GOD*, the-ones being in Corinth, to-the-ones-having-been-hallowed in *Anointed-Savior,* called Holy-Ones, together with all the-ones in every place calling on the name of *The-Master* of us *Savior-Anointed*, they with us. Loving-kindness to you and peace from *GOD, FATHER* of us and *Master-Savior-Anointed*.

I-am-thanking *THE-GOD* of mine always about you for The-Grace-of-*THE-GOD* being given to you in *Anointed-Savior.* So that in all you-are-richly-furnished by *Him* in all doctrine-and-instruction and all knowledge according-to the proclamation of *The-Anointed* confirmed among you so that you are not deficient in any gracious-gift patiently-waiting-for the-unveiling-and-appearance of *The-Master* of us *Savior-Anointed. Who* also at the end shall-be-making-good-the-promise you are-to-be-unblameable at The-Day of *The-Master* of us *Savior-Anointed*.

Believe *THE-GOD*! Through *WHOM* you-were-called into an intimate-fellowship with *The-Son* of *HIM, Savior-Anointed, The-Master* of us.

Now I am imploring you Brothers in the name of *The-Master* of us, *Savior-Anointed,* that you are all speaking the same and may-have no schisms and you may be restored to the same mind and in the same opinion-and-purpose. It-has-been-made-clearly-understandable to me about you, my Brothers, by the-ones of Chloe, that there is strife-and-fighting among you.

Further I am asking this for each of you claiming, "I am certainly of Paul," or "I am of Apollo," or "I am of Cephas," or "I am of *Anointed.*" Has *The-Anointed* been-divided? Paul was not crucified for your sake nor are you immersed in the name of Paul. I-am-thanking *THE-GOD* that not one of you I baptized other than Crispus and Gaius so that no one may say that I baptized in my name. I also did baptize the household of Stephanas but I-do-not-remember any others I baptized.

For *Anointed* did not commission me to-be-baptizing but to-be-bringing-the-Well-Message. Not with words of wisdom depriving-the-force-{and}-making-appear-false-and-hollow The-Pale-of-*The-Anointed.* For *The-Word*-of-The-Pale is indeed foolish to-the-ones-that-must-be-put-to-death. But it is for us, inherent-unlimited-power from *GOD,* the-ones-being-saved. For it is written, "I shall be destroying the wisdom of the wise-ones and I will frustrate-and-nullify the understanding of the

Section I

intelligent-ones." Where, where is the wise-one? Where is the writer? The scholar-and-debater of this eon? Does THE-GOD not make the wisdom of The-System prove-to-be-foolish?

For since-in-fact by the-wisdom of *THE-GOD,* The-System's wisdom cannot know *THE-GOD*. For the Jews are demanding-and-passionately-calling for a sign and the Greeks are seeking wisdom.

Yet we are proclaiming *Anointed* as-having-been-crucified for the Jews, indeed an impediment and to the Greeks stupidity. But of these, the-ones-called both Jew and Greek, *Anointed* is *The-Unlimited-Inherent-Power-of-GOD* and *The-Wisdom-of-GOD*. For the stupidity of *THE-GOD* is wiser than men and the weakness of *THE-GOD* is exponentially-and-infinitely-stronger than men.

So understand your calling, Brothers. There are not many wise in the-flesh, not many powerful and well-bred. But *THE-GOD* has picked-out-and-chosen for office the-stupid of The-System that *HE*-may-be-disgracing the-wise, and *THE-GOD* has chosen the-weakest of The-System that *HE*-may-be-disgracing the-mighty. For the low-born and contemptible *THE-GOD* has chosen so that the-ones with-no-influence-and-no-value *HE*-should-cause to-cease-and-render-inoperative those with influence so that no one of-flesh will-be-boasting-and-claim to have value in *HIS* presence.

Yet you are generated by *HIM*, through *Anointed-Savior Who* has become wisdom for us from GOD with righteousness and holiness and deliverance. So that as it is written, "He that claims glory, let him be claiming glory in the *Master.*"

For when I came to you Brothers, I came not with distinguished-elegance of speech or wisdom preaching to you The-Testimony-of-*THE-GOD*. For I had decided-and-determined while with you to not teach anything but *Savior-Anointed, The-One* having-been-crucified because I was unskilled-in-speaking and in fear of public speaking and very-scared to come to you. Yet my persuasive speaking and my preaching was not by wisdom of men, but by-the-demonstration-and-manifesting-of spirit and Godly-power that The-Belief of you is-not-to-be in the wisdom of men, but in the unlimited-inherent-power of *GOD*.

Yet the-wisdom we are speaking among the-mature-ones is not the wisdom of this eon, neither of The-Chiefs-of-The-Eon; this and these-are-becoming-inoperative-and-replaced.

But we speak of the wisdom of *GOD*, held in secret, having been concealed but foreordained-and-decreed-before-the beginning-of-the Eons, to-give-a-most-exalted-state-to us which not-a-one of The-Chiefs-of-this-Eon had known. For if they had known, they would have never-ever-impaled *The-Master-of-The-Glory*.

Just as it-has-been-written, "For no eye has seen and ear has-not-heard," "nor yet ascended on the heart of men what *THE-GOD* makes-ready for the-ones Godly-loving *HIM!*"

Yet *THE-GOD* revealed it to us through *HIS* spirit, for the spirit is searching all, even the-depths of *THE-GOD*. For if not for the-spirit of a man that is in him, what would men know about a man? Most certainly no-one would be-acquainted-with *THE-GOD* if not for The-Spirit-of-*THE-GOD*. Yet we have not received The-Spirit-of-The-System but the-spirit which is out of *THE-GOD* that we may know what is being-given-graciously to us by *THE-GOD* which we also are teaching. Not as-is taught by man's wisdom but taught by the Holy-spirit comparing spiritual to spiritual.

But the soul of man is not receiving that from The-spirit-of-*THE-GOD*, for to him it is stupid and he is not able to investigate-and-determine and know what is spiritual. Yet the-spiritual-one is-indeed examining all, but he is-being-examined by no-one for who has-known the mind of *Master*, who is instructing *Him*? Yet we are-given the mind of *Anointed*.

For I, Brothers, was not able to teach you as spiritual-ones but with-fleshly-intellect as toddlers in *Anointed*. I have given you milk to drink and not food for you were then not as yet able, and even now you are still not able, for you are still under-the-control-of-the-flesh for there is jealously and strife and dissension among you. Are you not carnal and behaving as men? For indeed whenever anyone may-be-saying I am of Paul or a different-one I am of Apollos, are you not carnal? Is not then Paul or further Apollos but servants through whom you believe and as *The-Master* has-given to each? I plant, Apollos irrigates, but *THE-GOD* makes-it-grow. So that neither the one-planting, nor is it any one-irrigating, but *THE-ONE-GOD* making it grow up.

For the one-planting and the-one-irrigating are ones having-the-same-purpose-and-mind, and each shall collect their own wage according-to their own labor. For we are fellow-workers of *GOD*; you are a-cultivated-field of *GOD*, of *GOD's* growth-and-development.

By The-grace-of-*THE-GOD* being granted to me as a wise master-builder, I have laid the foundation, and another has built on it. But let him be carefully-examining on what he is building on. For no-one is-able-to lay any another foundation other-than *The One-Being-Laid*, which is *The-Anointed-Savior*.

For if anyone is building on *The-Foundation* that of gold, silver, precious stones, wood, grass, or straw, each of the-work will become apparent. For The-Day shall be making it shown, that by fire it is being-revealed and what is the kind of work of each one The-Fire shall be testing. If anyone's work shall-be-remaining which he has built on, he shall receive his wage. If anyone's work shall-be-consumed-by-fire, he-shall-be-suffering-loss, yet he shall-be-being-saved and in the same manner through fire.

Do you not understand that you are the-Temple-of-*GOD* and The-spirit-of-*THE-GOD* is residing-and-fixed-and-operating in you?

If anyone is defiling The-Temple-of-*THE-GOD*, this-one *THE-GOD* shall-be-leading-away-from-that-state-of-knowledge-and-holiness. For The-Temple-of-*The-GOD* is holy which is what you are. Let no-one be-deluding himself! If anyone is of-the opinion-and-seems-to-think to be wise among you in this eon, let him become the fool so that he may-be-becoming wise. For the wisdom of The-System is foolishness next to *GOD*. It has been written, "*THE-ONE* manages the-wise by their own craftiness," and also, "*The-Master* knows the inward-thoughts-purpose-design-and-deliberations of the wise that they are useless-and-purposeless." So let no-one be boasting about men which you all are. Whether Paul or Apollos or Cephas or the world or life or death or that present or that impending, it-all-belongs-to you. And you belong to *Anointed*, and *Anointed* belongs to *GOD*.

Therefore, let men be recognizing us as subservient to *Anointed* and a manager-of-the-house of The-secret-of-*GOD*. And further it is being sought in a steward that a certain one may be found being loyal-and-true. For me it is the least-concern that I am being examined by you or in This-Day-of-Man, for I neither judge myself. For my conscience has-no-guilt, for I have not been justified because-of-this; that *The-One* examining me is *Master*. Therefore, do not be judging anything before its season until *The-Master* may come bringing-into-the-light that hidden in-the-darkness and shall cause-to appear the purposes-and-reasoning of the hearts and then shall-bring-to-existence to each The-praise from *THE-GOD*.

For, Brothers, I mirrored myself with Apollos because of you. That through us you-may-be-learning nothing more than which has been written, that no one thinks one is over another and being-exalted against the other.

Just who is making you to cause-separation? Just what is missing you have not obtained? Why are you boasting as if not receiving it? Are you already satisfied-to-the-fullest? How are you rich apart from us? If only that you should-be reigning so that we also would be reigning together with you! Because I am of-the-opinion that *THE-GOD* has appointed us last to demonstrate in The-Theater-of-The-System and of angels and of men we are doomed-for-death. Because of *Anointed* we are fools, but in *Anointed* you are wise; we are infirmed, yet you are strong; you are honored and we dishonored? Even at this present hour we both are hungering and are thirsting and are naked and being-treated-violently and with no permanent home. We work with using our own hands being-reviled, we-are-blessing while carrying-the-burden-of being-chased, we comfort while being spoken-evil-of, refuse-and-filth-and-the-most-abject-and-despicable of The-System becoming tossed-plate-scraps, scum in all things at the present.

I write these to you not to bash you, but as my Beloved Offspring I am admonishing you. For if you had myriads of tutors in *Anointed*, there are not many fathers, for in *Anointed Savior* through the well-message I generated-and-fathered you. I am pleading you then to become imitators of me. Because of this I send to you Timotheus who is my beloved offspring, a believer in *Master* who shall be reminding you of the ways of mine in *Anointed* just-as on every-soil I am teaching the Ecclesiae.

In your vanity some would desire that I not come to you. But I shall be coming to you swiftly when the *Master* wills it and I shall not be speaking as the-ones in-flowery-elegance-and-empty philosophy-and-teaching-and-self-importance but the-Godly-power. For the Kingdom-of-*THE-GOD* is not a-make-believe-story, but in unlimited-inherent-power!

What is your will, I come with a beating-rod or in the spirit of Godly-love to you with gentleness?

Actually being reported about you is prostitution, such sexual-immorality not even openly-spoken about among the-Nations that someone is having an-unlawful-relationship-with the wife of his father! But instead in your pride-arrogance-and-vanity, you are not wailing-and-lamenting! This one doing the act is to be expelled from the midst of you. Even though as I am absent from this Body but present in the-spirit have judged as being present this-one doing this disgraceful-deed.

In the name of *The-Master* of us *Savior-Anointed*, when you are gathered together along with the spirit of mine, together by-the Godly-power of *The-Master* of us *Savior-Anointed*, give-over the-individuals to The-Satan for the complete-destruction of the flesh that the-spirit may be saved in The-Day-of-*The-Master-Savior*.

Your boasting is very-dangerous! Do you not know that a little ferment leavens the entire kneading? Completely-expel it out! That this old leaven may become the fresh kneading because you are unleavened. For *Anointed* was sacrificed as The-Passover for the-sake-of us so that we may keep The-Festival not as old leaven, not the leaven of evil and wickedness, but unleavened in sincerity and truth.

I write to you in this letter to-not-be-being-mixed up with fornicators-and-worldly-lovers and not ally with the paramours of this The-System, or the greedy, or extortionists, or idol-worshippers since you intentionally-should-be-coming out of The-System.

And now I write to you to not be-mixed-up with any Brother if he is identified-and-known-to be as a worldly-lover-and-fornicator, or greedy, or idolater, or abusive-criticizing-language, or a drunk, or extortionist. Do not even be eating together with such-ones. For what have I to do with judging those outside-the-Ecclesia-and-outside-the-body-of-Christ? You are not even judging the-ones within.

For the-ones without THE-GOD are judging and will-expel the wicked-ones from out of you.

How daring is anyone of you having a matter of law against another-Brother to go the unjust and not to the Holy-ones? Do you not know the Holy-ones shall be judging The-System? Because if The-System is being judged by you, are you unfit-for the bench of a judge in the least-trivial of cases? Do you not comprehend-and-understand we shall be judging angels? For sure then things pertaining to this life. Certainly then as judges in life's affairs. Bring-before-the-judgment-seat those you have that treat-with-contempt against the Ecclesia.

I say this to your shame. Is there not-even one among you wise? Not even one who is able to adjudicate between him and the Brothers? Instead a Brother is suing another Brother and doing-this using an unbeliever!

There is absolutely no doubt a defect is with you. What is it you have that there are lawsuits among yourselves? Why not rather accept the injury? Why not rather be

Section I

cheated-robbed-and-defrauded? Instead you are injuring and are cheating and this to Brothers!

Are you ignorant about the unjust-ones that shall-not-be-enjoying The-Allotment-of-The-Kingdom-of-*GOD*? Don't fool yourselves! Neither fornicators, nor idolaters, nor adulterers, nor the effeminate, nor sodomites, neither thieves, nor a greed to have more, nor drunkards, nor abusive language and talkers, nor extortionists shall-be-enjoying The-Allotment-of-The-Kingdom of *GOD*. And anyone of these you were, but you are bathed-off and you are dedicated-to-God and you are declared righteous in the name of *The-Master-Savior* and in the-spirit-of-*THE-GOD* of us.

Everything is permitted for me, but not all is expedient-profitable-and-helpful. Everything is allowed for me, but I shall-not-be-under-the-power-and-influence-of anything. Food for the belly and the belly for the food. Yet *THE-GOD* shall-be-throwing-away this and that. For the body is not for illicit-sexual-intercourse but for *The-Master* and *The-Master* for the body. For *THE-GOD* raised-up *The-Master* and shall-be-raising-up us through *HIS* unlimited-inherent-power. Do you not know your bodies are members of *Anointed*? Should I then take the-members of *The-Anointed* and make them prostitutes? No way! Do you not understand that the one-being-joined to the prostitute is one body? *HE* has declared, "The two shall become one flesh." For the-one joined to *The-Master* is one spirit.

Flee sexual-immorality! Whichever other sin men commit it is external to the body. Yet the one committing sexual-immorality is sinning against his own body! Or do you not understand that your body is the Temple for the Holy-spirit in you which you have from *GOD* and you are not your own? You are bought by an extravagant-fixed price. Immediately praise-worship-and-honor *THE-GOD* with your body and in your spirit which is from *THE-GOD*!

Now to address which you wrote to me. It is not honorable for a man to cohabit with a woman. But because of the sexual-immorality, let each man have his own wife and each woman have her own husband. For the wife, the man is to in happiness-and-willingly-in honor-and-respect provide as promised-under-oath his conjugal duty and likewise the wife to the man. The wife does not have jurisdiction of her own body but her husband does, and neither does the husband have jurisdiction over his own body but the wife has. Do not deprive one or the other unless it is out of agreement for a season so that you may have leisure for the-fasting and for the-prayer. And doing the same coming together again that The-Satan may not be trying you because of your lack of self-control. And I am saying this as an acknowledgement not as a command, for I wish all men are as resolved as I am, but each is given his own gracious-gift from *GOD*, one with this and one with that.

And I say this to the unmarried and the widows it is best if they, in case they remain such, to be as I. But if they cannot control themselves, then let them marry! For it is better to marry than to be purged by fire. And to the ones having married, I am charging, not I but *The-Master*, the wife to not leave her husband. And if she does depart, let her remain unmarried or repair the damage with the husband and the husband not abandon-and-divorce his wife.

Speaking to the rest I say, not *The-Master*, if a brother's wife is unbelieving and she approves to make a home with him, do not let her leave. Also, the woman who has an unbelieving husband and he is agreeable to make a home with her, do not leave him. For the unbelieving husband is made holy by the woman, and the unbelieving wife is made holy by the husband or else the children of yours are unclean but are now holy. But if the unbelieving departs, let them go! The brother or the sister in-this-condition is not in-obligated service, for THE-GOD has called us to peace. For how do you know, wives, if you shall-be-saving the husband and if the husband shall-be-saving the wife? For THE-GOD has not divided each, and as *The-Master* has called each, so should they walk. I am therefore publishing-and-announcing-this in the Ecclesiae.

Has anyone been called having-been-circumcised? Let him remain circumcised. Was anyone called being uncircumcised? Let him remain uncircumcised. The-circumcision means nothing and the-uncircumcision is nothing but keeping the precepts of God do. Let him not depart from The-Calling to which he was called.

Do you carry the title slave? Do not let it cause you to worry. But if you are to become free, rather use it. For the-one in *Master* being called slave is the *Master's* freeman, likewise the-one free is being-called slave of *Anointed*. You are a very-highly-valuable-purchase; do not become slaves to men. Brothers, in whatever-condition you-are-called, let-each-of-you-be-remaining in this with THE-GOD.

Now for the virgins, I do not have a command from *Master*, but as one-having-obtained-mercy through *Master*, I offer this advice: be-faithful.

I am inferring, then, it is best to be, because of this present calamity, that it is best for a man to be in this condition. Have you-been-bound to a wife? Do not divorce her. If you are divorced from the wife, do not seek a wife. Yet if you do marry, you have not sinned. And if ever the-virgin-should-marry, she has not sinned. For I am trying to spare you from such stress-and-affliction you shall be having in the flesh. For I am saying this Brothers, that the season has-been-limited, and for the remaining-time that the-ones having wives may be as not having one, and the-ones lamenting as if not lamenting, and the-ones rejoicing as with no joy, and the-ones buying as if not in-possession-of, for the-ones using The-System to not use it. For this manner of life of The-System is disappearing. I desire that you be without worry. To the-one-unmarried, care for those things of *The-Master*, how you may-be-pleasing *The-Master*. For how can the-one married caring about the-things of The-System be-pleasing the wife?

The difference between a wife and a virgin is the unmarried cares about the-things of *The-Master* that she may be holy in body and spirit. For how can a wife caring about the-things of The-System be-pleasing the husband? Now I speak to you for your own profitability, not to place a noose on you but that I should-produce the honorable and without distraction devoted to *The-Master*.

Section I

But if a father is worried about not acting honorably about his engagement obligations with the-virgin of him and is concerned that she is passing her prime and owes it to-marry and he-is willing, he is not sinning. Let them marry. But if a father is settled in the heart, having no need of the dowry, and has authority over his own household and has firmly-decided in his heart to keep his virgin is-doing acceptable. So that the one giving her is doing the proper, but the one not giving her in marriage is doing better. The wife is bound by law as long as her husband is living, but when the husband is dead, she is free to-be-married to whom she will, only in *Master*. However, I presume she would be happier about staying as she is and to be having the spirit of GOD as I.

Now concerning the idol sacrifices. We know that we all have the knowledge but that knowledge creates pride, but Godly-love holiness. And if any presumes to be knowledgeable, he knows nothing about what is needed to be known, for if any Godly-loves *THE-GOD*, this-one is known by *HIM*.

Concerning the food used in idol sacrifices. We know an idol is empty-and-man-made in the System and that there are no other gods but *ONE*. Even though there are those claiming to be gods, whether in heaven or on the earth, and there are many gods and many masters but for all-of-us *ONE-GOD*, *THE-FATHER* through whom we and all are from *HIM*.

How is it there is not this knowledge in some? Their conscience is weak and polluted about idols, eating still now idol sacrifices. Food does not give-us-a-standing-with *THE-GOD*. For whatever we eat or not, what we wear or not, we still are in need. But you beware about your liberty-to-do-as-you-please by not becoming a stumbling-block to the-ones-being-weak. Suppose anyone having knowledge sees you eating-at-the-table at idol-shrines, will his weak conscience be encouraged and eat at the idol-sacrifices? Or shall the weak Brother for who *Anointed* died perish because of your knowledge? For when you are sinning against the Brother and beating their weak conscience, you are sinning against *Anointed*. Therefore, if food is an-offense for my Brother, I will eat no meat for the eon that no Brother of mine is offended.

Am I not a Commissioner? Am I not free, have I not seen *Savior-Anointed*, *The-Master* of us? Are you not my work in *Master*? If I am not a Commissioner to others, no doubt I am to you. For you are the seal of my commission in *Master*.

My defenses to-the-ones examining me are this: Do we not have the power of choice-and-right-and-freedom-and-permission-and-authority to eat and drink? Do we not have the authority to lead a sister, a wife and also the rest of the Commissioners and the Brothers of *The-Master* and Cephas? Or is it only Barnabas and I that do not have the authority to not be working?

Who at war provides their own provisions on their own? Who plants a vineyard and does not eat the fruit from it? Who shepherds a flock and does not eat the milk of the flock? Am I not speaking with-the-reasoning-of-men or does not the Law also say this? For it is written in the Law of Moses, "You shall not muzzle ox threshing."

Is *THE-GOD* caring only-for the oxen or is it really for our benefit? Undoubtedly it is said because of us, for it was written that in expectation needs the-one plowing to-be-plowing and for the-one threshing in his expectation to be sharing in expectation.

For we sow the spiritual with you. Is it a great matter if we reap from you with things needed for sustenance? If others having-the-authority over you are taking, not also we? However, we have not used this authority, but we have in all kept silent that no hindrance may-be-preventing the Well-Message-of-*The-Anointed*. Do you not understand that the-ones servicing the-holy-things eat from the Temple? The-ones working the altar get a portion of the altar. Even *The-Master* has also arranged for the-ones announcing the Well-Message to-be living from the Well-Message.

But I have used nothing of these, and I do not write this that it will be done. For me it is better to die than anyone should make my boasting mean nothing. For even though I may-be-bringing the Well-Message, it is not for me to boast. This was placed on me intentionally, and woe to me if I do not bring the Well-Message! For I am committed to this voluntarily, and I have my wages, and if I involuntarily administer with what I have been entrusted, what then is my compensation? I offer the Well-Message-of-*The-Anointed* with no expenses, freely, that I do not abuse my authority in the Well-Message.

For I am free from all, I have enslaved myself to all that I should be gaining the greater. With the Jews, as a Jew, that I should gain those Jews. To the-ones under the Law, as under the law, that I should gain the-ones under the Law. To the-ones without the Law, as without the Law, while not forsaking the Law-of-*GOD* and aided by *Anointed* that I should gain the-ones without the Law. For the weak, I become the weak that I should win over the weak. I become all to all that I should save some by all means. I am doing this because of the Well-Message so that I may become of it a joint-participant. Do you not understand all the-ones running in the stadium are racing? But only one obtains the game-prize. So, race that you may take-firm-possession-of-it! For every one competing disciplines himself in all things. Certainly they compete for that corruptible wreath, but we an incorruptible (one). I too am running not with doubt and I am boxing but not as-if punching air. I discipline my body and lead it into slavery unless somehow preaching to others I may disqualify myself.

Now I do not want you to be ignorant, Brothers! That all the Fathers of us were under the cloud and passed-over the sea and all with Moses were baptized in the cloud and by the sea. Also all ate the same spiritual food. And all drank the same spiritual drink. For they drank from the-spiritual rock following them, for *The-Rock* is *The-Anointed*. But THE-GOD was not delighted with the majority of them for they were strewn-along in the wilderness. Now these examples are for us to not crave evils as also those lusted. So don't become idolaters as some of them. For it is written, "The people sat to eat and to drink and they rose up for an orgy." So don't commit idolatry-and-sexual immorality as some of them and fell in one day twenty-three thousand. And do not put *The-Anointed* to the trial as also some of them tried *Him* and were

Section I

killed by the snakes. And do not secretly grumble-and-cause division as some of them murmured and were destroyed by The-Destroyer.

For all these examples happened to them, and it was written for our admonition for *Whom* is arriving, *The-Finisher-of-The-Eons*. So be careful believing you have strong-character and not fail-to-condemnation.

For no trial has taken to you that is not-uncommon to man. But THE-GOD is believable who shall not leave you while being tested above which you are able but shall making-together with the trial also the exit to enable you to endure it. Therefore, beloved, flee from idolatry.

For the prudent-ones, weigh-and-make-a-decision what I claim!

The Cup-of-Blessing which we bless, is it not the sharing of the blood of *The-Anointed*? The Bread that we break, is it not the sharing of The-Body-of-*The-Anointed*? For one bread, one body, we the many are. For we are all out of *The-One-Bread* we share.

Watch Israel of the flesh, are not the ones eating the sacrifices sharing it from the altar? What am I claiming? The idol is of-value-to-be-honored? Or that the idol-sacrifice is something? What about that which is sacrificed to demons by the-Nations and not to *GOD*? I do not want you to become a companion with the demons. You are not allowed to-be-drinking from The-Master's Cup and the Cup-of-Demons. Neither are you allowed to share the Master's Table and the Table-of-Demons.

Do we-provoke *The-Master* to jealousy? Are we the stronger than *Him*? I am legally-able to do all things, but not all things are profitable. All for me is allowed. But not all is-beneficial. Let no-one desire-exclusively-about himself but for the needs of each other. Everything being sold in the meat-market eat. Don't ask because of conscience sake. For the earth is *The-Master*'s and all-that-is-in-it. And if any invites you that are not believers and you are willing to go, everything that has been placed before you eat! Do not ask-about it for conscience sake. But if anytime any says to you this is an idol-sacrifice, do not eat it because it has been divulged and for conscience sake. For the earth and all that is in it is *The-Master*'s. When I said conscience, I did not mean yours but the other ones. For why should my liberty be decided by another's conscience? For if I participate with gratitude, why would I be slandered for which I give thanks? Whenever you are eating or drinking or anything, be doing it all for the glory of GOD. Do not become an offense to anyone, of Jews, of Greeks and the Ecclesia of *THE-GOD*. As I also try to please all, not seeking for myself, but being-of-profit to the many that they may be saved. Become my imitators as I of *Anointed*.

Now I applaud you, Brothers, that you have remembered me in all and the instructions you are holding fast to I gave to you. But I want you to know that the head of every man is *The-Anointed* and of the woman the man is the head, and of *Anointed*, THE-GOD.

Every man praying or moved-to-speak veiling his head is dishonoring his head, but every woman praying or prophesying uncovering the head disgraces her head for it is the same as having her head shaved. For the woman that is not covered, let her be shorn. For it is a filthy-disgrace for a woman to be shorn or to be shaven. Let her be covered. For indeed a man is not to be covering the head being-created in the image and glory of *GOD*, but a woman's glory is the man. For a man is not from a woman but a woman out of man. Neither was man created because of the woman but the woman because of the man. Because of the Angels the woman must wear the-authority-to-show-the-man-has-the-authority on the head. However, neither is man not apart from a woman or the woman apart from man in *Master*. As much as a woman is out of man also *The-Man* came through *The-Woman*, but everything out of *THE-GOD*. Evaluate for yourself, does it serve a woman to pray uncovered to *THE-GOD*? Does not nature itself teach you that if a man indeed has tresses, it is his disgrace? But if a woman has tresses, it is her glory, for tresses instead of clothing was given her.

Now if anyone has-a-reputation-for-being divisive-and-contentious, we have no such custom, neither has the Ecclesia-of-*THE-GOD*. Concerning this I declare that I am not in approval of your coming together. It is not advantageous but for the worse. First, for sure when-coming-together I am hearing of schisms in the Ecclesia to be existing with you, and I in some part believe. There must also be selective-groups within you for-you-require that it must be apparent the-ones are accepted by you. Then when you come to the same-place to eat, it is not *Master*'s dinner? For each-one is getting their own dinner first. And who indeed is left starving, and who is getting drunk? Do you not have homes to eat and drink in, or do you hate and are-disgraced-by the Ecclesia, the-ones having nothing? What am I to say to you? Shall I approve you in this? I do not approve. For what I was instructed from *The-Master* is that which I pass-on to you, that *The-Master-Savior* on the night which *He* was-handed-over took bread and gave thanks, broke it and said, *"You take this and eat it. It is me. This body is being violently-killed for your sake. Do this in the remembrance of me."* Also, the same for the cup taking a sip said, *"This drinking vessel is the new compact by my blood. This you do, as often as you may be drinking in my remembrance. For as many times you may-be-eating this bread and may-be-drinking this cup, you are making-known the death of The-Master until whenever He comes."* Therefore, whoever may eat this bread or drink this Cup-of-*The-Master* in an-unworthy-manner shall-carry-the-penalty of the body and blood of *The-Master*. So let each man test himself and then eat from the bread and drink out of the cup. For the-one eating and drinking unworthily condemns himself not honoring the Body-of-*The-Master* by eating and drinking. For this reason, many among you are infirmed and sick and a considerable number are dead.

For if we examined ourselves, we would not be judged. For when we are examined by *Master*, we-are-being-disciplined so that we are not condemned together with The-System. So now, my Brothers, when coming together to eat, be waiting for one-another. And if any may-be-hungry, let-him-eat at home so you may not come together into that judgment-and-punishment. As for the rest, I shall give orders when I arrive.

Section I

Now I do not want you to be ignorant of the spiritual, Brothers. For you know that you were-led-away from the-Nations, from worshipping and being-led and joined to those voiceless idols. I am making known to you clearly that no-one speaking by *GOD*'s spirit speaks cursing the *Savior* and no-one is able to say the *Savior* is the *Master* but by the-Holy-spirit and divine-gifts are not-given-equally-to-all but it-is still the same spirit. Also the-offices are not-given-equally-to-all, but the same *Master*. And as for responsibility they-are not-given-equally-to-all, but it is the same *GOD* who is *THE-ONE* operating the all in all.

But being given to each is the-materialization of the-spirit for that-which-is-profitable. Indeed, for through the same spirit the-spirit is giving to some words of wisdom and for others words of knowledge. To a different-one belief but by the same spirit, for others divine-gifts of healing by the same spirit. For another working of miracles and for others prophecy, for others distinguishing spirit, to others types of languages, for others to translate languages. Yet all of these operate by the one and same spirit, distributing to each own as it-is-intended. Even as the body is singular and has many members, and all the-members are of that body, *The-One* consisting of many is a Body, it is *The-Anointed*.

For also by one spirit we are dipped into one body, whether Jews or Greeks, whether slaves or free and are-saturated-and-permeated by one spirit.

Also, the body is not one member but many. For what if the foot said, "See I am not a hand, I am not from that body"? Yet is it not part of the body? What if the ear said, "See I am not an eye, I am not from that body"? Yet is it not part of the body? If the entire body was an eye, where is the hearing? What about the sense of smelling?

Most assuredly *THE-GOD* placed each one of the members in the body as *HE*-wills, and if it was only one member, where is the body? Now indeed are many members, but one body and the eye cannot say to the hand, "I have no need for you!" Or again the head to the feet, "I have no need for you!" Oddly, rather the members of the body seeming less-attractive-and-little-value are the most necessary. And that of the body we think less-attractive we invest with the special honor and the most-indecent with even greater-respectability. For the good-looking has no need for covering. But *THE-GOD* has put together the body so that the-one with deficiencies are given the greatest honor. So there is no divisions in the body and each member is anxious to take care of one-another. And if one member is suffering, all feel-it-together, all the members. Or if one member is being honored, all the members should-rejoice-together.

You are the body of *Anointed* and members of the whole. Indeed, *THE-GOD* has placed those first in the Ecclesia commissioners, second prophets, third teachers, then miracles, then divine-gifts of healing, supporters, wise counselors, and types of languages. Not all commissioners, not all prophets, not all teachers, not all miracle workers, not all divine-gifts of healing, not all linguists, not all speakers. But crave for the greater divine-gifts. For I-am-showing you through-out a preeminent-and-superior way.

I CORINTHIANS AS A LETTER

Now if I speak all the languages of men and of the Angels but have not Godly-love, I have the sound of copper or a clanging-noisy cymbal. For if I could foretell-the-future and understand all of the secrets and every-bit of knowledge or have all of the-belief to-be-able to transplant mountains, but if I do not have Godly-love, I am no-one. Or if I feed all and give up all of my possessions or give up my body so I-should-be-burned, still if I do not have Godly-love it has not benefitted me anything.

For Godly-love is patient, is kind. Godly-love is not jealous-and-envious. Godly-love does not brag, not self-inflating. It is not indecent-behaving, does not demand-something for itself, does not keep count of evil, does not rejoice in injustice, but it rejoices together in *The-Truth*. Conceals-the-errors-and-faults-of all, believes all, expects all, and is enduring in the Godly-love, never lapses whether prophesies are caused-to-cease-and-rendered inactive or languages end or knowledge has-vanished. For we know only-a-little, and we prophesize a little. But whenever the-maturing is completed, then the parts shall-disappear-due-to-having-been-done.

When I was a minor, I spoke as a minor. I behaved and reasoned as a minor, but when I became a man, I discarded that of the minor. For we are gazing-and-staring presently into a dark-and-mysterious viewer. For the present I understand a little, but then I shall know in full even as I am also completely recognized when seen face-to-face.

For these three now are to remain: believing, trust, and Godly-love. But of these, the-Godly-love is the greater.

Chase Godly-love with a boiling fury and the spiritual and also that you may prophesize. For *THE-ONE* speaks in a language no man speaks, only *THE-GOD*. For no one understands except *HE* reveals secrets by the spirit. But the-one prophesying to men speaks edification and exhortation and comfort. *THE-ONE* speaking *HIS* own-native language is building-a-home, but the-one prophesying builds up the Ecclesia.

I wish all could speak a language, but much greater I would have you prophesying. For the-one prophesying is higher-on-the-scale than anyone speaking a language. For the one prophesying, other than the-one translating a language is to be strengthening the Ecclesia.

And now, Brothers, if I were to come to you speaking a foreign-language, how would I profit you? How should I teach-and-instruct to you? Using revelation or from knowledge or using prophecy or by teaching? Just as inanimate-objects make sounds such as flute or lyre, how is it known what is the flute or the lyre unless they give distinctive sounds? Also, who can prepare for battle with an unsure trumpet sound? So it is with you. Unless the language is intelligibly spoken how can it be understood? What you say is emptied into the air. For there are many types of languages in The-System and not-one is without its-own-power. For if I do not understand the intent-and-meaning of the language, I would be like one speaking to a barbarian and the-one speaking as a barbarian to me. Same with you. Since you seek the spiritual things be super-abounding in zeal for the edification of the Ecclesia. Therefore let-him-pray the-one speaking in a language that it may be translated. For if I pray in a foreign-language, my spirit is praying but my understanding is gaining nothing. How is it then I would pray? I will pray in the spirit and with the-understanding rejoicing and with the spirit playing-music also in understanding.

How can it be when you are giving-thanks in the spirit that-one not in a position of understanding can declare an "amen" since in fact he does not understand what you are saying? You indeed give thanks well, but no one is gaining edification. I thank *THE-GOD* of mine I speak more languages than all of you, but in the Ecclesia I-am-willing to say only five words with understanding and also be instructing others than to speak a myriad of words in a foreign-language.

Brothers, do not be little-boys in your thinking, for you are minors with evils and think you have become mature!

In the Law it is written, "With different languages and with different mouths I will speak this to the-people," and, "Yet they shall still not be understanding-and-comprehending me says *MASTER*." So languages are not a sign for the-ones-believing but for the unbelievers, and prophecy is not for unbelievers but for the-ones-believing. Now if the entire Ecclesia would gather in one place and all were speaking languages and an ordinary-person or an unbeliever entered in, will they not declare you are insane-and-raving lunatics!

But what if all were prophesying and some unbeliever entered or an ordinary-person plainly-understands all and as he examines all and in doing so that hidden in his heart becomes plain-and-apparent and there falls on his-face in-his-worship to *THE-GOD* declaring that *THE-GOD* in truth-and-unquestionably is among you?

But how is it, then, Brothers, that when you come together each of you has your psalm, your doctrine, has a language, has a revelation, and has an interpretation? Let-it-all-become for edification! If any is speaking a language, allow two or the most three and done in succession, also let-one-be-interpreting. But if there is no interpreter, keep-him-silent in the Ecclesia and he-is-to-speak to himself and to *THE-GOD*.

And prophets, let two or three speak, and let the others test-and-determine. And if it is revealed to one sitting next to him, this first be silent! For you can all prophesy one by one that all may learn and all-may-be encouraged-and-instructed. For the spirit of the prophets are controlled by prophets. For *THE-GOD* is not the state of disorder but peace as in all the Ecclesiae of the Holy-Ones.

Let the-women in the Ecclesiae be silent, for it-has-not-been-permitted for them to be speaking but in-subject-to also as the Law says. And if any are determined-and-desire to be informed, let them interrogate-and-question in the home of their husbands for it is a dishonor for women to-be-speaking in the Ecclesiae. For did *The-Word* of *THE-GOD* come from you or did it only come to you?

If any presumes to-be a prophet or spiritual, let him acknowledge that what I am writing to you, they-are directions from *The-Master*. If any chooses to be wrong, let them be wrong! But you Brothers have-a-boiling-passion to be prophesying and do not forbid the speaking in languages. Let it all occur in respectability and with order.

Again I remind you, Brothers, the Well-Message I instructed to you which you accepted and also are-established-by through which you are also-being-saved. That is, if you remember the Well-Message I brought to you unless you faked your belief. For I delivered to you that which I was taught and accepted; that *Anointed* died for the sake of the-sins of us according-to The-Writings, that *He* was-entombed and that *He* has-been-raised on the third day according-to the Writings and that *He* was seen by Cephas and thereafter by the twelve. After that *He* was seen by over five-hundred brothers at the same time of whom the majority are still alive with also some now in death. Then *He* was seen by James, thereafter to all the Commissioners and last of all as if a premature-birth *He* was also seen with me. For I am the-so-far-beyond-least-in-rank-and-excellence of the Commissioners who is not worthy to be called a Commissioner because I persecuted the Ecclesiae-of-*THE-GOD*.

But by the grace of *GOD*, for I am what I am, that *HIS* grace has not become meaningless-purposeless-and-pointless with me. For I have toiled much more than all of them, but it is not I but The-Grace-of-*THE-GOD* which is with me. Therefore, whether I or they are proclaiming, you also believe. For if *Anointed* is-being-declared that He has risen from out of the-dead-ones, how can some of those among you claim there is no resurrection from the dead? Because if there is no resurrection from the dead-ones then neither has *Anointed* risen. And if *Anointed* has not risen then conclusively-without-argument our proclamation is a lie, a scam, and also your belief.

Yes, if we are determined-to-being false witnesses of *THE-GOD*, seeing we testify accordingly from *THE-GOD* that *HE* raised *The-Anointed*, *Whom*, if-it-is-true *HE* did not raise-up, then the dead-ones are not being-brought-back-to-life. And if the dead-ones do not rise, then neither is *Anointed* alive, and if *Anointed* is not alive your belief is worthless, and you are still in your sins. Consequently, also the-ones being dead in *Anointed* are lost-never-to-return. For if in this life we have an expectation in *Anointed*, then we are the most without-mercy-without-hope-and-miserable of all.

But now *Anointed* is alive from the dead-ones, becoming *The-First-Fruit* of the-dead. For it is a fact through man—The-Death, just as by man, The-Resurrection from the dead-ones. For it is a fact that by Adam all are-dying just as by *The-Anointed* all will-be-made-alive. But each individual in their own set-and-order-of-appointed-time, *Anointed The-First-Fruit*, afterwards the-ones in *Anointed* at the return of *Him*. Then The-Finishing when *He*-has-conquered-abolished-and-deprived the force of all sovereignties and all authority and powers and *He*-gives-over The-Kingdom to *THE-GOD* and *FATHER*. For *He* is to reign until all of *His* enemies are placed under *His* power-and-authority abolishing the last enemy The-Death.

For *HE* has subjugated all under *His* feet. However, when all has been subjugated under *Him*, this is outside of *THE-ONE* giving *Him* the authority over the all, once all is subjugated under *Him* then *The-Son Himself* shall-be-subjugated to *THE-ONE* setting all under *HIM* that *THE-GOD* may be all in all.

Section I

For what else are the-ones-baptized to do for the sake of the dead-ones if the-dead are absolutely not being-brought-back-to-life? Why are-you-being-baptized for the sake of the-dead and why do we place ourselves in danger every hour?

It kills me every day because of your boasting in *Anointed Savior The-Master* of us! If as a man I-fight-the-wild-beasts in Ephesus, what benefit is it for me if the dead-ones do not rise-up? Let us just eat and drink for tomorrow we die!

Do not be deceived, evil conversation corrupts character. Come out of your stupor! Be just and do not sin! For some have ignorance about *GOD*! I state this to your dishonor.

Now some may ask how do the dead arise? What type of a body are they coming with? You senseless ones! That which is sown does not come to life unless it dies. And what are you sowing? What you are sowing is not for this body like a-single-kernel may produce a wheat plant or something other. For *THE-GOD* gives to him a body as *HE* wills and for each of the seeds their own body. Not all skin is the same skin, for there is indeed the skin of men and the skin of beasts, another for fish and another for flyers. There are bodies in the heavens and bodies of land and indeed differences in the glory in the heavenlies and in the terrestrial. Another glory of the sun, a glory of the moon, another glory of the stars, even stars differ in glory. Thus, so is The-Resurrection of the dead-ones. Being sown in corruption to rise-up in incorruption; it is sown in dishonor, being raised with the-highest-honor; it is sown in weakness, being raised in unlimited-power. It is sown a soul-requiring-a-breathing body, being raised a spiritual body. There is a soulish body and a spiritual body. For as it is written, "The first man Adam a living soul." *The-Last-Adam* is a living spirit. Why was the-first not the-spiritual but the-soulish, secondly-then the-spiritual? Out of soil of the earth was the first man. The second man, *The-Master*, is out of heaven. From such The-Soilish-One are also the soilish-ones and as-is *The-Heavenly-One* also are they heavenly-ones. As we wear the likeness of The-Soilish-One, we shall wear the likeness of *The-Heavenly-One*.

Now I state this, Brothers, that flesh and blood are not able to enjoy The-Allotment-of-*GOD*'s-Kingdom neither can the-corrupt enjoy The-Allotment-of-The-Incorrupt.

Pay attention, I am telling you a secret, it is certain we-all-shall-not-die and we-shall-all-be-changed! In an instant! In-the-blink of an eye! At The-Last-Trumpet *He*-shall-trumpet for the dead-ones to be raised incorruptible and we-shall-be-transformed. For the-corrupt is-by-necessity to put on the-incorruptible and mortal-and-temporary is to-be-putting-on immortality-and-permanence. And when the corrupted becomes this incorruptible and the mortal becomes this immortal, then shall-be-completed these words, "The-Death is devoured in victory! Where are you Death, The-Piercer? Where are the prizes in your graves for The-Piercer, The-Death, The-Sin?" For the gripping-power of sins is in the Law. But by the Grace-of-*THE-GOD*, *THE-ONE-GIVING* us the victory it is through *The-Master* of us, *Savior-Anointed*. Therefore, my beloved Brothers, you are to be firm, firmly-persistent, super-abounding in the work of *The-Master*. That your strenuous-and-difficult-labor is not worthless-and-wasted for *Master*.

Now concerning the collection for the Holy-ones. As I directed the Ecclesiae of Galatia, so also you do. On one of the Sabbaths, each of you by yourself place in storage that, if anything, you may-have-been prospered with so that I, when I come, no collections has to occur. And when I come to you, I will send those selected-and-chosen with letters-of-commendation to transport your gracious-gifts to Jerusalem. And if it is worthwhile I go also, they-shall-go together with me.

I am coming to you when I pass through Macedonia, for I am passing through Macedonia. And I might abide with you or also be wintering so that you can send me forward wherever I may be going. I will not see you this-time on the way but I am expecting to stay some time with you if the *Master* permits it. For now I will remain in Ephesus until Pentecost for a great opportunity has been opened to me and actively-attacking are many adversaries.

Now, if Timotheus may come, make sure that he comes not having to fear about you, for he is working as I for *Master*. And make sure none utterly-looks-down-on him. But send him forward in-safe-and-secure to me for I am waiting for him with the Brothers.

Now concerning the-Brother Apollo, I earnestly asked him to come to you with The-Brothers, and it was clearly not his will that he come now, but he will come when he-has-the-opportunity.

Be attentive! Stand firm in The-Belief. Be a-stronghold. Let everything be done in Godly-love.

I plead with you, Brothers, become acquainted with the house of Stephanas, the first-fruits of Achaia and their-having-devoted themselves to the service of the Holy-Ones. That you may also set-things-in-order to do the same and with everyone that labors and works-with-us. And I rejoice about the company of Stephanas and Fortunatus and Achaicus for they added-to-complete the meager-contribution from you. For they have restored my spirit and that of-yours. Credit them then for doing this.

The Ecclesiae of Asia greet you in *Master*. Aquila and Priscilla especially greet you with the Ecclesia in their home. All of the Brothers greet you. Greet each in a holy fraternal-kiss.

My greetings from my hand, Paul.

If anyone is not in-admiration-of-and-loves-from-believing *The-Master, Savior-Anointed*, let them be-put-under-a curse. Our Lord will come!

The Grace of *The-Master Savior-Anointed* be with you.

My Godly-love is with all of you in *Anointed-Savior*.

Amen.

(Written to the Corinthians from Philippi)

I CORINTHIANS STUDY NOTES

Note: Through my many translations, I have come to believe that the phrase or associated phrasing of "inheritance" [ex: Col 1:12] accurately translated as "the-allotment" in Scripture is not a good or proper translation (i.e., inheritance). Paul makes it clear that we are to be family members (I state: royal and godly) destined to be with HIM and HE with us and we in Christ and He in us. Inheritance has an implied connotation, an accepted concept that someone has died. THE-GOD is certainly not dead, and Christ has risen to life eonian (there are times of times of times) as well. I see this as a watering down of the intent and meaning of the Scriptures and have dropped using the word *inheritance* when speaking of THE-GOD's plan and purpose for us. We are to take rulership in an active kingdom with Christ at the head of the realm and we under Him, with THE-GOD over all of us.

Note   The Greek word *agapen* translated as "love" in most translations is missing that this is Godly in nature and not of men or any other such creature. I have therefore carried the adjective to add clarity to the meaning of this word throughout this translation.

Note: In my research, nearly all translations have dropped "the" as a modifier, but the Greek word for "the" is in every text and not meant to be ignored or deleted. It is often specifically singular, and when attached to the noun, it is describing that noun as unique, one of a kind, a specific thing, the original, the one and only. It is for this reason that I carry "the" everywhere it appears in all translations. Whether of God, Jesus, Satan or any other entity, concept, or idea, the modifier "the" clears up a lot of generalized words, ideas, concepts, and entities.

Note: The root of the word *pnuemia*, translated as "spirit, wind, or breath," has no gender identity since this is a word that is neuter in gender. *Pnuemia* is an "it." The Greeks, as we of English language, often fix a gender to objects and things— for example: cars, boats, the moon, the sun. For the Greeks, *pnuemia* at times has a male gender affixed to it. *Pnuemia* in the Scriptures is never capitalized or designated as a standalone being, entity, principality, or sovereignty when used as the word "spirit." It is simply the power inherent in the

being, whether of man, or God, or Christ, or any other entity. If anything is living, "it" possesses a spirit. The "Holy-spirit" is simply the power from and of The-God, giving and renewing life and performing The-God's will.

Note: Paul constantly claims and mentions "principles, powers, authorities, sovereignties not of our world." He quite clearly claims that these beings are the ones that certainly influence and control (predominately in a negative way) the systems of this world, people of the nations, and as individuals directly. You can find this concept also contained in The Old Testament through the implications of the first commandment. This claim and the concept of the warring factions in heaven makes a fascinating study.

Note: Time periods, eons, ages, millennia, eons, and eons—I stayed true to the Greek words associated with time and what we still use today in our common language. A study of time periods is fascinating but is also an area that can cause confusion. The-God always works on some kind of a timetable, but understanding which is which and when is when is a bit of a mystery. Some timetables are only known to The-God and made clear to man at God's will.

Note What is the difference between "expectation" and "hope?" Nearly all translations adopt the word "hope" for "expectation," but Paul uses almost exclusively the word "expectation." Here is why I constantly use "expectation." Having an expectation means you have no doubt at all. It is sure and certain with no ambiguity or doubt. Having a hope means you are not 100 percent convinced and convicted. I can tell you that Paul is undeniably convinced and convicted in what he delivers and talks about. Using "hope" sends a message that there is some possibility for "wiggle room," doubt, error, or excuses.

Even worse, much of the use of the word "expectation" in Paul's writings has the modifier "the" attached to "expectation," thus forming the proper translation and singular concept of "The-Expectation." This makes "The-Expectation" an event, not a philosophy or theological premise. Not recognizing "The-Expectation" as an event will lead the reader immediately down an incorrect understanding of what is being offered or discussed.

1:4 *"So that in all you-are-richly-furnished"* by Him in all speech [doctrine, teaching, instruction] and all knowledge." This "richly-furnished" is intended to mean in spiritual matters and "all knowledge" about Christian life.

1:6 Take notice of "'The-Day' of *The-Master.*" Paul is telling his audience that this is a specific day in the future of Christ's return.

1:9 Many translations offer the following to open up this verse: "Faithful (is) God"; God (is) faithful." The Greek word *pistos* is properly translated as "belief, believe," and by inference "faith." *Pistos* is found in the first position of

Section I

this verse; the word "is" does not belong in the Greek which allows *pistos* to be interpreted as a declaration. As such this verse is better stated as: "Believe! Believe GOD!" This is not a matter of God's faithfulness.

1:10 From the Greek word *schismata* we get directly the English word "schism."

1:17 The phrase "not with words of wisdom" implies worldly-wisdom, not from God. This is wisdom that cannot comprehend and is in opposition to Godly-wisdom. Worldly-wisdom only "voids" the crucifixion and sacrifice of Christ.

1:18 Take note I have translated the Greek as "The-Word" and identified it to mean The-Christ as identified by the Apostle John in John 1:1. This is not in keeping with any translations. All translations I conferred with ignored the modifier "the" in front of "Word." But once the proper translation of "the-Word" is used and the rest of the sentence structure is completed, it is obvious Paul is identifying Christ as "The-Word" along with His crucifixion. In my research, I could have also rendered this sentence as: "For indeed the crucifixion of Christ (The-Word) is foolishness to the ones being put to death. But for us, the ones being saved, it is demonstrating the unlimited inherent power of God." This then adds validity and harmonizes the translation with the Gospel of John.

1:20 "The-System" Paul is referring to is more than the "world." He is referring to the-system and powers and authorities (actual entities) in the heavens as well as on earth.

2:1 So just what is "The-Testimony-of-THE-GOD" versus the "Witness-of-The-Christ" or "Testimony-of-The-Christ" or what the other translations offer in verse one of chapter 2? First, my translation of "The Testimony of The-God" is not in keeping with other translations simply because "the" is ignored in every translation I conferred with. Many offer: "the testimony about God," which redirects the reader from what is being talked about. Several translations also offer: "the testimony of God's secret," "God's secret plan," or "God's mystery." None of the words "mystery," "secret," or "secret plan" are in the original Greek. But I agree with this interpretation that Paul is clearly referencing "The-Secret" that was revealed to the Ecclesiae concerning the admission of Gentiles to the family of God and that they are to take possession of the starry-heavens and universes. This would then make this writing to the Corinthians somewhere at or after AD 63 versus some traditional dates of AD 54–58. This, however, still does not answer my original question.

In its simplest explanations:

a. The testimony of Christ was to introduce The-Father and reintroduce His kingdom and prepare for it as well as open the way for the spirit-of-God (God's Holy-spirit). Christ was originally sent to the Jews only. This includes the Holy-spirit that was poured out on those Jews in the Temple on Pentecost. That is, until Peter received his visions concerning meats and Gentiles and the original Apostles came to understand God was doing something more than with just the Jews. This was a point of great confusion and uncertainty about what they had been taught or at least what they thought was taught and was going to happen for a long period of time with all of them. What I mean by that is that the Apostles and Jews were only thinking in terms of their specific physical nationalism and the Jews coming into dominance and power over the entire world. There was nothing spiritual in nature at all associated with their thinking, belief, and expectations. Imagine the complete head-turn that occurred with the introduction of Gentiles being directly injected into the Body of Christ. We know this is true from the raging and heated debating going on within the Apostles and the Ecclesiae until the Gentiles were handled by Paul. The book of Acts records this historic event and turning point for the Body of Christ.

b. The witness of Christ is Christ's fulfillment of the Scripture as a man in the flesh, including his death and resurrection and with Godly enthronement at the right side of The-Father.

c. The Testimony of God is that all of mankind, every being who has ever lived or yet to come to life, is to become his family member in Christ as a spirit being to help manage and rule all of His Creation, from the terrestrial to the heavenlies. This makes you today a Godly-royal family member with all the power, authority, and esteem of God-The-Father and also sitting to the right of The-Father in Christ. While we have not yet received this ordained state, it is imminent.

2:8 "The-Chiefs" includes the heavens and the earth. "The-Chiefs" also implies the rulers of the world who knew The-God has always been, but have replaced God's kingdom with their own.

2:9 ***"nor yet ascended on the heart [entered the mind] of men what THE-GOD makes-ready for the-ones Godly-loving HIM!"***

Isaiah 65:17 is what Paul had in mind when he wrote this sentence. Isaiah 65:17 directly mentions a "new heaven and new earth." Paul is indirectly reiterating what was revealed to the Corinthians about what man is to inherit, and he wanted his audience to think and reflect on what the implications of ruling such new creations meant.

2:25 "The-Belief [faith]" requires some expansion from my studies. Using "faith" almost covers up the need to first believe before exercising faith. Both actions are in tandem with each other, but Paul's use of the word "belief" at times stands alone in meaning, and where this occurs, I have not provided the alternate translation "faith."

Section I

3:11   "The-One-Being-Laid" is a direct reference to Christ and in the Greek, represented by a singular word *keimenon*. With this knowledge, I have translated this as one of Christ's titles and certainly a fulfillment of his testimony.

3:13   "each of the work will become apparent for *The-Day* shall be making it exposed" (underline and italics mine). This is in fact referring to a specific event and day. My studies offer Christ's return to claim his promise and legal property and holdings. I pulled this portion of the verse out because it is easy to read over a verse and not grab a pregnant idea nestled inside it.

4:1   Here Paul directly mentions "The-Secret."

4:7   "Just what is missing you have not obtained [received, claimed, laid hold of]?" Paul is challenging the Corinthians about their disbelief in "The-Secret" that was revealed to them. Their future as intimate God-members was already sure and certain, even though not yet completely handed to them. (The receiving of God's Holy-spirit is your down payment, however.) Essentially Paul is asking, "Is this world and its systems really worth putting in front of your heavenly allotment and giving up on the rewards of the First Resurrection? You have been given everything by God The-Father. No one will get anything more than the next."

4:8   The questions in this verse are really implying: "Are you already enjoying the promises and benefits of God's kingdom? Filled fully with all eternal blessings and riches?" "Reigning as kings, for we certainly wish you were because we would be doing the same!" This was a direct reference to "The-Secret."

5:6   Paul is alluding to the Passover week and the removing of all leavening out of the households during the "Week of Unleavened Bread."

5:8   The festival referred to is the Festival (Week) of Unleavened Bread (*Chag Hamatzot*), of which the Passover is one of the high days within this week; it begins the Festival (Week) of Unleavened Bread. This is rich in meaning and symbolism for those following God through Christ.

6:7   The Greek word translated as "defect" has its root in and origin in coin making and the acceptance or rejection of any coin having any defect.

7:5   Paul is referring to coming together to have marital sex with your mate.

7:39   The interesting premise about this verse is that this does not seem to apply to a man, which in that era would have been allowable since a man could have had more than one wife. However, the woman is held captive and trapped, and Paul also discusses this matter in his other letters. The analogy for the audience is that she is trapped in the marriage as man is trapped by the Law of Moses. It is also interesting to think about the first/old covenant with Israel's marriage to God: even though they abandoned the covenant several times, they still always belonged to God. To release a woman from this "marriage," one had to become a widow or widower. One cannot pause to think about Christ's death as Israel's release to be on her own, free to enter into a new relationship.

9:5   When pausing to reflect on this verse, Paul identifies some interesting relationships. Paul identifies Jesus as having at least two half-brothers, while tradition and other translations indicate four half-brothers as well as two half-sisters.

9:5–6   Paul is questioning those who are questioning him about his authority over the original remaining apostles. One senses that the apostles were struggling with what Paul was revealing, especially "The-Secret," which would have been quite controversial to Jewish thinking, understanding, and supposition.

9:11   Paul is really asking, "Is this that big of a deal if we ask for help for our own physical needs from you?"

10:7   The Hebrew word Paul uses is very improperly translated as "play" in the King James Version. The Hebrew word is an idiom understood to mean "adultery and fornication." More directly, an orgy was going on, and I have kept that word as the proper translation.

10:8   This verse refers to Numbers 29 and the seduction of the Israelite men at Peor. Paul says the number of men killed was 23,000 but Numbers 29:5 says 24,000. Which is correct? Both! Paul did not include the mandatory slaughter of 1,000 men ordered by God through Moses. The 23,000 was strictly the plague number.

10:9   See Num 21:6–9.

10:10   See Exod 12:33; 16:2; Num 14:37.

10:18   Paul is referring to the Jewish Priesthood not having God's spirit.

11:10   The "covering" of a woman demonstrates to the angels that it is a man who has the authority for her. But this same word by inference also shows the angels that she is wearing a crown of authority regarding events to occur in the future.

14:1–5   Many translations use the word "tongue," which from a pure translation is the root concept—that is, the "use of the tongue." But these passages are clear that this is talking about regional dialects and known languages common in the day. If a guest speaker was present from a foreign country and spoke his native language, then someone was needed to be able to properly translate his speaking for the Ecclesia. It is not referring to a strange and unknown language able to be interpreted by only one other "inspired" individual. This

Section I

	interpreting also included the witnessing or verification of at least to two more separate individuals.
14:6	"by knowledge" implies in this phrase what Paul was taught in his face-to-face encounter with Christ.
15:3–4	"Christ died for our sins" (see Ps 16:10–11; Isa 53:10).
15:7	Jacobus, Jesus' half-brother, better known as James.
15:8	Many translations use the word "by," but the Greek word implies a wider audience. Therefore, I have used the word "with" to convey more than a private, singular audience or series of meetings.
15:9	"persecuted,"—Paul is reminding the audience that he was once a hired assassin intending to exterminate this new "Christian uprising and movement" by killing off its leadership as well as its members.
15:23	The Greek word translated "class" is a direct military term, not meant as a caste system, such as peasant instead of elite. It is meant more like a graduating class from high school or a class, band, or troop of soldiers.
15:44	(verses 44–49) Be sure to catch Paul's play on words using "soilish" and "soulish" in these verses and in the teaching he is presenting.
15:52	Paul directly says two things in the words "The-Last-Trumpet." It is a direct reference to the Jewish festival Rosh Hashanah, and he is telling us specifically what day the change will happen in the plan of God (just as Christ's physical birth was prophesied to occur on Rosh Hashanah [in -3 BC] which has and is changing the civilization of man and Satan's rule). A study of the Jewish feast reflects the overall intent of God in the same way as the encampment of Israel with the zodiacal symbols attached to each tribe and the constellations in heaven (now corrupted by astrology and governments). God has witnessed to man with at least three distinct methods what His intentions are.
15:54	Here Paul has given a short and terse interpretation of Hosea 13:14.
16:8	Paul is recognizing this "Holy-Day" not so much as out of religious observance but rather to mark a point in time. When it served the purpose, Paul would observe the Jewish festival days, and when it did not, he ignored them. To a Jew, he was a Jew; to a Greek, he was a Greek to win them over to the Messiah.
16:15	The word translated "plead" has more of a legal sense, such as a defense attorney making a closing argument to persuade the jury in his favor.

I CORINTHIANS IN VERSE

I CORINTHIANS 1

1:1 Paul, called-to-the-office of Commissioner [apostle] of *Jesus-[Savior]-Anointed*, by the will of *GOD* and *The-Brother Sosthenes* (Safe in Strength),

1:2 to the Called-Out [Ecclesia] of *THE-GOD*, the-ones being in Corinth, to-the-ones-having-been-hallowed in *Anointed-Savior*, called Holy-Ones [saints], together with all the-ones in every place invoking [calling on] the name of *The-Master* [Lord] of us *Savior-Anointed*, they besides [with] us.

1:3 Grace [favor, loving-kindness] to you and peace from *GOD*, *FATHER* of us and *Master-Savior-Anointed*.

1:4 I-am-thanking *THE-GOD* of mine always about you for The-Grace-of-*THE-GOD* being given to you in [through, by] *Anointed-Savior*.

1:5 So that in all you-are-richly-furnished by *HIM* in all speech [doctrine, teaching, instruction] and all knowledge

1:6 according-to the witness [testimony, proclamation] of *The-Anointed* established [confirmed] among you

1:7 so that you are not deficient [wanting, lacking] in any gracious-gift patiently-waiting-for the-unveiling [appearance, manifestation] of *The-Master* of us *Savior-Anointed*.

1:8 *Who* also at the end shall-be-confirming [making-sure, establishing, anchoring, making good the promise] you are-to-be-unblameable in [at] The-Day of *The-Master* of us *Savior-Anointed*.

1:9 Believe *THE-GOD*! Through *WHOM* you-were-called into communion [intimate-fellowship, joint-participation] with *The-Son* of *HIM*, *Savior-Anointed*, *The-Master* of us.

1:10 Now I am entreating [implore, beg, plead] you, Brothers, in the name of *The-Master* of us, *Savior-Anointed*, that you are all speaking the same and may-have no schisms [divisions, dissensions] and you may be in order [repair and

Section I

arrange, adjust to, mend, restored to], in the same mind and in the same view [opinion, judgment, purpose].

1:11 It-has-been-made-clearly-understandable to me about you, my Brothers, by the-ones of Chloe [Verdant, Blooming], that there is contention [strife, wrangling, fighting] among you.

1:12 Further I am asking this for each of you claiming, "I am certainly of Paul [Place of Rest]," or "I am of Apollos [Strength, Sun God]," or "I am of Cephas [Rock, Peter]," or "I am of *Christ* [Anointed]."

1:13 Has *The-Anointed* been-parted [divided]? Paul was not crucified for your sake nor are you baptized in the name of Paul.

1:14 I-am-thanking THE-GOD that not one of you I baptized other than Crispus [Curly-haired] and Gaius [Happy, Rejoice]

1:15 so that no one may say that I baptized in my name.

1:16 I also did baptize the household of Stephanas [Crown, Garland], but I am not aware of [do not remember] any others I baptized.

1:17 For *Anointed* [Christ] did not commission me to-be-baptizing but to-be-bringing-The-Well-Message [gospel]. Not with words of wisdom depriving-the-force [voiding the effect, make appear false or hollow] of The-Pale [stake, crucifixion] of *The-Anointed*.

1:18 For *The-Word*-of-*The-Pale* [crucifixion] is indeed foolish to the ones-being-destroyed [those that must be put to death]. But it is for us, inherent-unlimited-power from [of] *GOD*, the-ones-being-saved.

1:19 For it is written, **"I shall be destroying the wisdom of the wise-ones and I will thwart [frustrate, nullify] the understanding of the intelligent-ones [learned]"** [Isa 29:14]

1:20 Where, where (is) the wise-one? Where (is) the writer [scribe, recorder, secretary]? The sophist [theoretician, scholar, nit-picker, debater, obscurantist] of this eon? Does THE-GOD not make the wisdom of The-System [world] prove-to-be-foolish?

1:21 For since-in-fact by the-wisdom of THE-GOD, The-System's [world's] wisdom cannot know THE-GOD.

1:22 For the Jews are requiring [demand, call for, crave] a sign and the Greeks are seeking wisdom.

1:23 Yet we are heralding [proclaiming] *Anointed* [Christ] as-having-been-crucified for the Jews, indeed an impediment [trigger-stick, snare, stumbling-block] and to the Greeks stupidity [foolishness].

I CORINTHIANS IN VERSE

1:24 But of these, the-ones-called both Jew and Greek, *Anointed* [Christ] (is) the unlimited-inherent-power-of-*GOD* and (the) Wisdom-of-*GOD*.

1:25 For the stupidity [foolishness] of *THE-GOD* is wiser than men, and the weakness [infirmity] of *THE-GOD* is exponentially-and-infinitely-stronger than men.

1:26 So observe [understand] your calling, Brothers! There are not many wise in the-flesh, not many powerful and well-bred [noble families, noble-minded].

1:27 But *THE-GOD* has chosen [hand-picked, picked-out, chosen for office] the stupid [foolish] of The-System [world] that *HE*-may-be-disgracing the-wise and *THE-GOD* has chosen the weakest of The-System [world] that *HE*-may-disgracing the-strong [mighty].

1:28 For the low-born [of no name or reputation, not of noble-birth] and contemptible *THE-GOD* has chosen so that the-ones with-no-influence [have-no-value, no account] *HE*-should-be-discarding [cause to cease, render inoperative] those with influence [considered having value]

1:29 so that no one [all of those (made)] of flesh will-be-boasting [bragging, claim to have glory, claim to have value] in *HIS* sight [presence].

1:30 Yet you are out of [created by, generated by] *HIM* in [through] Anointed-Savior who has become wisdom for us from GOD with justice [righteousness] and holiness and deliverance.

1:31 So that as it is written, **"He that boasts [claims glory], let him be claiming glory in (the) *Master*."** [Jer 9:23, 24]

I CORINTHIANS 2

2:1 For when I came to you Brothers, (I) came not with superiority [distinguished elegance] of speech or wisdom preaching to you The-Testimony-of-*THE-GOD*.

2:2 For I had judged [decided, resolved, an opinion, determined] among [while with] you to not teach any (thing) but *Savior-Anointed, The-One* having-been-crucified

2:3 because I was in weak [unskilled in speaking] and in fear [of public speaking] and in great-trembling [very-scared] to come to you.

2:4 Yet my persuasive speaking and my preaching (was) not by (the) wisdom of men, but by proof [demonstrating, manifesting of] by (the) spirit and Godly-power (with me)

2:5 that The-Belief of you may-not-be [is-not-to-be] in the wisdom of men, but in the unlimited-inherent-power of *GOD*.

Section I

2:6   Yet the-wisdom we are speaking among the-mature-ones is not the wisdom of this eon, neither of The-Chiefs- [rulers, leaders]-of-The-Eon, this and these-are-being-discarded [becoming inoperative, have no power or influence, being replaced].

2:7   But we speak of the wisdom of *GOD*, held in secret, having been concealed but designated-before [foreordained, predetermined, appointed, decreed before the beginning of] the eons to glorify [give a most exalted state to] us

2:8   which not-a-one of The-Chiefs- [rulers, leaders]-of-this-Eon had known. For if they had known they would have never-ever impaled *The-Master-of-The-Glory*.

2:9   Just as it-has-been-written, **"For no eye has seen and ear has-not heard," "Nor yet ascended on the heart [entered the mind] of men what THE-GOD makes-ready for the-ones Godly-loving HIM!"** [Isa 65:17]

2:10 Yet *THE-GOD* revealed (this, it) to us through *HIS* spirit, for the spirit is searching all, even the-depths [deep things] of *THE-GOD*.

2:11 For if not for the-spirit of a man that is in him what would men know about a man? Most certainly no-one would know of [be-acquainted with] *THE-GOD* if not for The-Spirit-of-*THE-GOD*.

2:12 Yet we have not received The-Spirit-of-The-System [world] but the-spirit which is out of *THE-GOD* that we may know what is being-given-graciously to us by *THE-GOD* which we also are teaching.

2:13 Not as-is taught by man's wisdom but taught by the Holy-spirit judging together [comparing] spiritual (things) to spiritual (things).

2:14 But the soul [sensuous nature, subject to appetite and passions, (natural)] of man is not receiving that from The-Spirit-of-*THE-GOD*, for to him it is stupid and he is not able to examine [investigate, determine] and know what is spiritual.

2:15 Yet the-spiritual-one is-indeed-examining all and he is-being-examined by no-one

2:16 for who has-known the mind of *Master*, who is instructing *Him*? Yet we are-given [possess, hold in our hand, joined in marriage with] the mind of *Anointed*.

I CORINTHIANS 3

3:1   For I, Brothers, was not able to teach you as spiritual-ones but as carnal [by fleshy nature, with fleshly intellect] as toddlers [an infant, little child] in *Anointed*.

3:2	I have given you milk to drink and not food, for you were then not as yet able, and even now you are still not able,
3:3	for you are still fleshly [under the control of the flesh], for there is jealously and strife and dissension among you. Are you not carnal and walking [behaving] as men?
3:4	For indeed whenever anyone may-be-saying I am of Paul or a different-one I am of Apollos, are you not fleshly [carnal]?
3:5	Is not then Paul or further Apollos but servants through whom you believe and as *The-Master* has-given to each?
3:6	I plant, Apollos irrigates, but THE-GOD makes-it-grow.
3:7	So that neither the one-planting nor is it any one-irrigating, but *THE-ONE-GOD* making it grow up.
3:8	For the one-planting and the one-irrigating are one [have the same purpose and mind] and each shall collect their own wages [reward] according-to their own labor.
3:9	For we are fellow-workers of *GOD*, you are tillage [a cultivated field] of *GOD*, of *GOD's* building [growth and development, body of Christians].
3:10	By The-Grace-of-*THE-GOD* being granted to me as a wise chief-artisan [master builder], I have laid the foundation another has built on it. But let him be carefully-examining on what he is building on.
3:11	For no-one can [is-able-to] lay any another foundation other-than *The One-Being-Laid* which is *Savior-[Messiah]-The-Anointed*.
3:12	For if anyone is building on *The-Foundation* that of gold, silver, precious stones, wood, grass, (or) straw
3:13	each of the-work will become apparent, for The-Day shall be making it exposed [shown], that by fire it is being-revealed and what is the kind of work of each one the-fire shall be testing.
3:14	If anyone's work shall-be-remaining which he has built on, he shall receive his wage [reward].
3:15	If anyone's work shall-be-consumed-by-fire, he-shall-be-forfeiting [suffering loss], yet he shall-be-being-saved and as-it-were [even-as, in the same manner] through fire.
3:16	Do you not understand [perceive, know, are aware] that you are the Temple-of-*GOD* and the-spirit-of-*THE-GOD* is making-its-home [residing, dwelling, fixed and operating] in you?

SECTION I

3:17   If anyone is corrupting [defiling, neglecting one's duties] The-Temple-of-*THE-GOD*, this-one *THE-GOD* shall-be-corrupting [lead away from that state of knowledge and holiness, be destroyed]. For The-Temple-of-*The-GOD* is holy which is what you are.

3:18   Let no-one be-deluding himself! If anyone is presuming [of the opinion, reputed, seems to think] to be wise among you in this eon, let him become the fool so that he may-be-becoming wise.

3:19   For the wisdom of The-System [world] is foolishness next to *GOD*. It has been written, **"THE-ONE takes-hold [catches, controls, manages] the-wise by their own craftiness."** [Job 5:13]

3:20   and also, **"THE-MASTER knows the reasoning [inward thoughts, purpose, design, deliberations] of the wise that they are vain [useless, devoid of truth, purposeless]."** [Ps 94:11]

3:21   So, let no-one be boasting about men which you all are.

3:22   Whether Paul or Apollos or Cephas or the world or life or death or that present or that impending, all is [it all belongs to] yours.

3:23   And you are of [belong to] *Anointed* [Christ's], and *Anointed* of [belongs to] *GOD* [is GOD's].

I CORINTHIANS 4

4:1   Therefore let men be recognizing us as subservient [an assistant, rendering a service, as a preacher of] to *Anointed* and a steward [manager of the house or business, overseer, superintendent] of The-Secret-of-*GOD*.

4:2   And further it is being sought in a steward that a certain one [the man] may be found being loyal-and-true.

4:3   For me it is the least (matter, concern, care] that I am being examined [cross-examined and judged] by you or in This-Day-of-Man for I neither examine [judge] myself.

4:4   For my conscience has nothing [is clear, has no guilt], for I have not been justified by this [because of this] for *The-One* examining me is *Master*.

4:5   Therefore do not be judging anything before (its) season [time] until *The-Master* may come who shall-be-illuminating [bringing into the light] that hidden in the-darkness and shall be making [cause to] appear the counseling's [purposes and reasoning] of the hearts and then shall-be-coming [bring to existence, make happen] to each The-Praise from *THE-GOD*.

4:6	For, Brothers, I mirrored myself with Apollos because of you. That through us you-may-be-learning nothing more than which has been written, that no one thinks [is disposed, believes, has the mind of] one is over another and being-exalted [inflated, puffed-up] against the other.
4:7	Just who is making you to judge [discriminate, cause separation]? Just what is missing you have not obtained [received, claimed, laid hold of]? Why are you boasting as if not receiving it?
4:8	Are you already sated? How are you rich apart from us? If only that you should-be [were] reigning so that we also would be reigning together with you!
4:9	Because I am supposing [of the opinion, think, postulate] that *THE-GOD* has commissioned [appointed] us last to show [demonstrate] in the Gazing-Place-[theater]-of-The-System [world] and of messengers [Angels] and of men we are doomed-for [to]-death.
4:10	Because of *Anointed* [Christ] we (are) fools, but in *Anointed* you are wise; we are infirmed, yet you are strong; you are glorified [honored] and we despised [dishonored]?
4:11	Even at this present hour we both are hungering and are thirsting and are naked and being-chastened [struck with fists, treated violently] and are un-settled [no certain abode, stroll about, with no permanent home].
4:12	We work with using our own hands, being-speared [abused, reviled], we-are-blessing [offer, sending, give] while bearing [suffering, carrying the burden of] being-chased [persecuted],
4:13	we comfort [exhort, instruct, beg, pray] (while) being blasphemed [spoken evil of, falsely accused]; refuse [filth, the most abject and despicable] of The-System [world]; becoming scrapings [tossed plate scraps, scum] in all things at the present.
4:14	I write these to you not to bash [shame] you, but as my Beloved Offspring I am admonishing (you)
4:15	for if you had myriads [innumerable, countless] of tutors [guides, guardians] in *Anointed* there is not many fathers, for in *Anointed Savior* through the Well-Message I generated [converted, fathered] you.
4:16	I am pleading [calling on] you, then, to become imitators [followers] of me.
4:17	Because of this I send to you Timotheus, who is my beloved offspring (son), a believer in *Master* who shall be reminding you of the ways of mine in *Anointed* just-as on every-soil [everywhere] I am teaching (the) Ecclesiae.
4:18	In your vanity, some would [desire, hope] (that) I not come to you.

SECTION I

4:19 But I shall be coming to you swiftly [quickly] when the *Master* wills it, and I shall not be speaking as the-ones being-inflated [in flowery elegance, empty philosophy and teaching and self-importance] but the-Godly-power.

4:20 For The-Kingdom-of-*THE-GOD* is not in word [a fairy-tale, a make-believe story] but in unlimited-inherent-power!

4:21 What is your will, I come with a beating-rod or in the spirit of Godly-love to you with meekness [gentleness]?

I CORINTHIANS 5

5:1 Actually, being heard [reported, told] about you is prostitution, such prostitution not even mentioned [openly-spoken about, unheard of] among the-Nations [Gentiles] that someone is having [in an unlawful relationship with] the wife of the [his] father!

5:2 But instead in your inflatedness [pride, arrogance, vanity], you are not mourning [wailing, lamenting]! This one doing the act is to be expelled from the midst of you.

5:3 Even though as I am absent [not present] from this Body [Ecclesia] but present in the-spirit have judged as being present this-one doing this disgraceful-deed.

5:4 In the name of *The-Master* of us *Savior-Anointed*, when you are gathered together along with the spirit of mine, together by-the Godly-power of *The-Master* of us *Savior-Anointed*

5:5 give-over the-such [individuals, ones who are of such a character] to The-Satan for the complete-destruction of the flesh that the-spirit may be saved in The-Day-of-*The-Master-Savior*.

5:6 Your boasting is not ideal [very-dangerous]! Do you not know that a little ferment [leaven] leavens the entire kneading [dough]?

5:7 Clean [purge, completely expel] it out! That this old leaven may become the fresh kneading because you are unleavened. For *Anointed* was sacrificed as The-Passover for-the-sake-of us

5:8 so that we may keep The-Festival, not as old leaven, not the leaven of evil and wickedness, but unleavened in sincerity and truth.

5:9 I write to you in this letter to-not-be-being-mixed up [to avoid, stay away from] with paramours [fornicators, worldly-lovers]

5:10 and not ally [by all means, in no wise] with the paramours [lovers] of this The-System, or the greedy, or extortionists, or idol-worshippers since you intentionally-should-be-coming out of The-System.

5:11 And now I write to you to not be-mixed-up with any Brother if he is being-named [identified, known to be] as a paramour [worldly-lover, fornicator] or greedy, or idolater, or abusive language [constantly criticizing], or a drunk, or extortionist. Do not even be eating together with such-ones.

5:12 For what have I to do with judging those not of the-ones [outside the ecclesia, outside the body of Christ]? You are not even judging the-ones within.

5:13 For the-ones without *THE-GOD* are judging and will-expel [condemn, push-out, take out] the wicked-ones from out of you.

I CORINTHIANS 6

6:1 How daring is anyone of you having a matter (of law) against a different-one [another (Brother)] to go the unjust and not to the Holy-ones?

6:2 Do you not know the Holy-ones shall be judging The-System? Because if The-System is being judged by you, are you unworthy [unfit for] the bench of a judge [deciding, judging] in the most-inferior [least, trivial] of cases?

6:3 Do you not understand we shall be judging Angels? For sure then things pertaining to this life.

6:4 Certainly then as judges in life's affairs. Sit them down [bring before the judgment seat] those you have that have no regard [utterly despise, treat with contempt] for the Called-Out [Ecclesia].

6:5 I say this to your shame. Is there not-even one among you wise? Not even one who is able to adjudicate [decide a dispute] between him and the brothers?

6:6 Instead a brother is suing another brother and doing-this using an unbeliever!

6:7 There is absolutely no doubt a defect [fault] is with you. What is it you have that there are lawsuits among yourselves? Why not rather accept the injury? Why not rather be deprived [cheated, robbed, defrauded]?

6:8 Instead you are injuring and are cheating and this to Brothers!

6:9 Are you ignorant about the unjust-ones [unrighteous] that shall-not-be-enjoying The-Allotment-of-The-Kingdom-of-*GOD*? Don't fool [deceive] yourselves! Neither paramours [worldly-lovers, fornicators], nor idolaters, nor adulterers [one who is faithless to GOD], nor soft-ones [the effeminate, homosexual relationships], nor sodomites,

Section I

6:10 neither thieves, nor covetous-ones [a greed to have more], nor drunkards, nor revilers [abusive language and talkers], nor extortionists shall-be-enjoying The-Allotment-of-The-Kingdom-of-*GOD*.

6:11 And anyone of these you were, but you are bathed-off [washed, cleansed] and you are holy [dedicated to God] and you are justified [declared righteous] in the name of *The-Master-Savior* and in the-spirit-of-*THE-GOD* of us.

6:12 All is allowed for me, but not all is beneficial [expedient, profitable, helpful]. All is allowed for me, but I shall-not-be-held-in-authority [be under the power and influence of] by anything.

6:13 Food for the belly and the belly for the food. Yet *THE-GOD* shall-be-throwing-away this and that. For the body is not for fornication [illicit sexual intercourse, vices, earthly-pleasure] but for *The-Master* and *The-Master* for the body.

6:14 For *THE-GOD* roused [awoken from a dead sleep, raised up, resurrected] *The-Master* and shall-be-rousing [raising up, resurrecting] us through *HIS* unlimited-inherent-power.

6:15 Do you not know your bodies are members of *Anointed*? Should I then lift-away [remove, take] the members of *The-Anointed* and make them prostitutes (harlots)? No way!

6:16 Do you not understand that the one-being-joined to the prostitute is one body? *HE* has declared, **"The two shall become one flesh."** [Gen2:24]

6:17 For the-one joined to *The-Master* is one spirit.

6:18 Flee prostitution [fornication, sexual immorality]! Whichever other sin men commit it is external to the body. Yet the one committing sexual immorality is sinning in [against] (his) own body!

6:19 Or do you not understand that your body is the Temple for the Holy-spirit in you which you have from *GOD* and you are not your own?

6:20 You are bought by an extravagant-fixed price. Immediately glorify [praise, worship, highly-esteem, honor the most] *THE-GOD* with your body and in your spirit which is of [from] *THE-GOD*!

I CORINTHIANS 7

7:1 Now to address which you wrote to me. It is not honorable for a man to cohabit [without being married and have carnal intercourse] with a woman.

7:2 But because of the prostitution, let each man have his own wife and each woman have her own husband.

7:3	For the wife, the man is to in kindness [happily and willingly in honor and respect] provide [what is properly due, promised under oath] his conjugal duty [having sex, use of the marriage bed] and likewise the wife to the man.
7:4	The wife does not have jurisdiction of her own body but her husband does and neither does the husband have jurisdiction over his own body but the wife has.
7:5	Do not deprive one or the other unless it is out of agreement for a season [period of time] so that you may have leisure for the-fasting and for the-prayer. And doing the same coming together again that The-Satan may not be trying you because of your lack of self-control.
7:6	And I am saying this as an acknowledgment, not as a command,
7:7	for I wish all men are as resolved as I am, but each is given his own gracious-gift out-of [from] *GOD*, one with this and one with that.
7:8	And I say this to the unmarried and the widows: it is best if they, in case they remain such, to be as I.
7:9	But if they cannot control themselves, then let them marry! For it is better to marry than to be purged by fire.
7:10	And to the ones having married, I am charging, not I but *The-Master*, the wife to not separate [leave] (her) husband.
7:11	And if she does depart let her remain unmarried or repair the damage with the husband and the husband not send-away [neglect, abandon, divorce] his wife.
7:12	Speaking to the rest, I say, not *The-Master*, if a brother's wife is unbelieving and she is agreeable [approves] to make a home [to dwell] with him, do not let her leave [divorce her].
7:13	Also the woman who has an unbelieving husband and he is agreeable to make a home with her, do not leave him.
7:14	For the unbelieving husband is made holy in [by] the woman and the unbelieving wife is made holy in [by] the husband, or else the children of yours (are) unclean but are now holy.
7:15	But if the unbelieving departs, let them go! The brother or the sister such in this [in this condition] is not enslaved [in bondage, in obligated service] for *THE-GOD* has called us for [to] peace.
7:16	For how do you know wives if you shall-be-saving the husband and if the husband shall-be-saving the wife?

Section I

7:17 For *THE-GOD* has not divided each and as *The-Master* has called each, so should they walk. I am therefore carrying-[publishing, announcing]-this in the Ecclesiae.

7:18 Has anyone been called having-been-circumcised? Let him remain circumcised. Was anyone called being uncircumcised? Let him remain uncircumcised.

7:19 The-circumcision is [means] nothing and the-uncircumcision is nothing but keeping the precepts of God (do).

7:20 Let him be remaining [not depart, hold sure to] in the-calling to which he was called.

7:21 Do you carry the title slave? Do not let it cause you to worry. But if you are to become free, rather use (it).

7:22 For the-one in *Master* being called slave is the *Master's* free(man); likewise the-one free is being-called slave of *Anointed*.

7:23 You are a very-highly-valuable-purchase; do not become slaves to [of] men.

7:24 Brothers, in what you-are-called, let-each-of-you-be-remaining in this with *THE-GOD*.

7:25 Now for the chaste [virgins (both male and female)], I do not have an injunction [command] from *Master*, but as one-having-obtained-mercy through *Master* I offer this opinion [view, advice], be-believing [faithful].

7:26 I am inferring then it is best to be, because of this present calamity, that (it is) best for a man to be thus [in this state, condition].

7:27 Have you been-bound to a wife? Do not divorce her. If you are divorced from the wife, do not seek a wife.

7:28 Yet if you do marry, you have not sinned. And if ever the-virgin-should-marry, she has not sinned. For I am trying to spare you from such pressure [stress, affliction] you shall be having in the flesh.

7:29 For I am saying this, Brothers, that the season [era] has-been-limited and for the-rest [remaining time] that the-ones having wives may be as not having (one).

7:30 And the-ones lamenting as if not lamenting, and the-ones rejoicing as with no joy, and the-ones buying as if not in-possession-of,

7:31 for the-ones using The-System to not use (it), for this manner of life of The-System is passing-by [departing, disappearing].

7:32 I desire that you be without worry. To the-one-unmarried, be-anxious [care for] for those [the things] of *The-Master*, how you may-be-pleasing *The-Master*.

7:33 For how can the-one married [husband] caring about the-(things) of The-System be-pleasing the wife?

7:34 The difference between a wife and a virgin is the unmarried cares about the-things of *The-Master* that she may be holy in body and spirit. For how can a wife caring about the-things of The-System be-pleasing the husband?

7:35 Now I speak to you for your own profitability [well-being, advantage] not to cast [create, place] a noose [snare, hanging knot] on you, but that I should-cast [create, produce] the honorable and without distraction devoted to *The-Master*.

7:36 But if any(one) (a father) is worried about not acting honorably [about his engagement obligations] with the-virgin of him and is concerned that she is passing her prime [getting beyond the usual marrying age] and owes it (to marry) and he-is willing, he is not sinning. Let them marry.

7:37 But who (if a father) is settled in the heart, having no need (of the dowry) and has authority over his own will (household) and has firmly-decided in his heart to keep his virgin is doing acceptable.

7:38 So that the one giving (her) is doing the proper, but the one not giving (her) in marriage is doing better.

7:39 The wife is bound by law as long as her husband is living, but when the husband is dead, she is free to-be-married to whom she will, only in *Master*.

7:40 However, I presume she would be happier about staying as she is and to be having the spirit of GOD as I.

I CORINTHIANS 8

8:1 Now concerning the idol sacrifices. We know that we all have the knowledge but that knowledge creates pride [self-loftiness], but Godly-love piety [holiness].

8:2 And if any presumes to be knowledgeable, he knows nothing about what is needed to be known,

8:3 for if any Godly-loves THE-GOD, this-one is known by *HIM*.

8:4 Concerning the food used in idol sacrifices. We know an idol (is) nothing [make-believe, empty, man-made] in (the)-System and that there are no other gods but *ONE*.

SECTION I

8:5 Even though there are those claiming to be gods, whether in heaven or on the earth, and there are many gods and many masters [lords]

8:6 but for all-of-us ONE-GOD, THE-FATHER through whom we and all (are) from HIM.

8:7 How is it there is not this knowledge in some? Their conscience is still weak and polluted now about eating idol sacrifices.

8:8 Food does not give-us-a-standing-with THE-GOD. For whatever we eat or not, what we wear or not, we still are lacking [in need].

8:9 But you beware about your authority [liberty to do as you please] by not becoming a stumbling-block to the-ones-being-weak.

8:10 Suppose anyone having knowledge sees you recline [eat at the table] at idol-shrines; will his weak conscience be encouraged and eat at the idol-sacrifices?

8:11 Or shall the weak Brother for whom *Anointed* died perish because of your knowledge?

8:12 For when you are sinning against the Brother and beating [unease, unseat, create calamity in] their weak conscience, you are sinning against *Anointed*.

8:13 Therefore if food is a snare [is an offense] for my Brother, I will eat no meat for the eon [time] that no Brother of mine is snared [offended].

I CORINTHIANS 9

9:1 Am I not a Commissioner [apostle]? Am I not free, have I not seen *Savior-[Messiah]-Anointed, The-Master* of us? Are you not my work in *Master*?

9:2 If I am not a Commissioner to others, no doubt I am to you. For you are the seal of my commission in *Master*.

9:3 My defenses to-the-ones examining me are this:

9:4 Do we not have the liberty [power of choice, right, freedom, permission, authority] to eat and drink?

9:5 Do we not have the authority to lead a sister, a wife and also the rest (remaining, of the) Commissioners and the Brothers of *The-Master* and Cephas?

9:6 Or (is it) only Barnabas and I (that) do not have the authority to not be working?

9:7 Who at war provides their own provisions on their own? Who plants a vineyard and does not eat the fruit from it? Who shepherds a flock and does not eat the milk of the flock?

9:8	Am I not speaking as a man [with the reasoning of men] or does not the Law (of Moses) also say this?
9:9	For it is written in the Law of Moses, **"You shall not muzzle ox threshing."** Is *THE-GOD* caring only-for the oxen or (is it) not because of us? [Deut 25:4]
9:10	Undoubtedly it is said because of us, for it was written that in expectation [hope] needs the-one plowing to-be-plowing and for the-one threshing in his expectation [hope] to be sharing in expectation [hope]?
9:11	For we sow the spiritual with you. Is it a great matter if we reap [are rewarded] from you pertaining-to-the-flesh [with things needed for sustenance]?
9:12	If others having-the-authority over you are taking, not also we? However, we have not used this authority, but we have in all (matters) kept silent that no hindrance may-be-preventing the Well-Message-of-*The-Anointed*.
9:13	Do you not understand that the-ones servicing the-holy-things eat from the Temple? The-ones working the altar get a portion of the altar.
9:14	Even *The-Master* has also arranged for the-ones announcing the Well-Message to-be living from the Well-Message.
9:15	But I have used nothing of these and I do not write this that it will be done. For me it is better to die than any (one) should make my boasting useless [false, hollow, mean nothing].
9:16	For even though I may be bringing the Well-Message, it is not for me to boast. This was placed on me intentionally, and woe to me if I do not bring the Well-Message!
9:17	For I am committed to this voluntarily, and I have my wages, and if I involuntarily administer with what I have been entrusted, what then are my wages [reward, compensation]?
9:18	I offer the Well-Message-of-*The-Anointed* with no expenses [freely] that I do not abuse my authority in the Well-Message.
9:19	For I am free from all; I have enslaved myself to all that I should be gaining the greater.
9:20	With the Jew, as a Jew, that I should gain those Jews. To the-ones under the Law, as under the Law that I should gain the-ones under the Law.
9:21	To the-ones without the Law, as without the Law, while not forsaking the Law-of-*GOD* and aided by *Anointed,* that I should gain the-ones without the Law.
9:22	For the weak, I become the weak that I should win over the weak. I become all to all that I should save some by all means.

9:23 I am doing this because of the Well-Message so that I may become of it a joint-participant [be with you, be your companion].

9:24 Do you not understand all the-ones running in the stadium are racing? But only one obtains the game-prize. So race that you may grasp it [take firm possession of it]!

9:25 For every one contending [competing] masters [disciplines] himself in all things. Certainly they contend [compete] for that corruptible wreath, but we an incorruptible.

9:26 I too am running not with uncertainty [doubt], and I am boxing but not as-if punching air.

9:27 I discipline my body and lead it into slavery unless somehow proclaiming [preaching, heralding] to others I may not-stand-the-test [test coins, disqualify] myself.

I CORINTHIANS 10

10:1 Now I do not want you to be ignorant, Brothers! That all the Fathers of us were under the cloud and passed-over the sea

10:2 and all with Moses were baptized in the cloud and by the sea.

10:3 Also all ate the same spiritual food.

10:4 And all drank the same spiritual drink. For they drank from the spiritual rock following (them), and *The-Rock* is *The-Anointed*.

10:5 But THE-GOD was not delighted with the majority of them for they were strewn-along in the wilderness.

10:6 Now these examples are for us to not become eager for [crave] evils as also those lusted.

10:7 So don't become idolaters as some of them. For it is written, **"The people sat to eat and to drink and they rose up for an orgy."** [Exod 32:6]

10:8 So don't commit prostitution [fornication, idolatry, sexual immorality] as some of them and fell in one day twenty-three thousand.

10:9 And do not put *The-Anointed* to the-trial as also some of them tried *HIM* and were killed by snakes.

10:10 And do not secretly complain [grumble, cause division] as some of them murmured and were destroyed by The-Destroyer [Exterminator].

10:11 For all these examples happened to them and it was written for our admonition [exhortation] for whom is arriving, *The-Finisher-of-The-Eons*.

10:12 So be careful believing you have strength [ability, force, strong-character] (and) not fall-out [fall to judgment, fall to condemnation].

10:13 For no trial has taken to you not of (known, uncommon to) man. But *THE-GOD* is believable [faithful] *WHO* shall not leave you being tried [while testing the quality of, proving the character and faith of] above which you are able but shall with the trial provide also the step-out [egress, exit] to enable you to carry [endure] (it).

10:14 Therefore beloved flee from idolatry.

10:15 For the prudent-ones [ones-so-disposed], judge [weigh and make a decision] what I claim!

10:16 The-Cup-of-Blessing which we bless, is (it) not the sharing of the blood of *The-Anointed*? The bread that we break is (it) not the sharing of the Body-of-*The-Anointed*?

10:17 For one bread, one body, we the many are. For we are all out of *The-One-Bread* we share.

10:18 Watch Israel of the flesh, are not the ones eating the sacrifices sharing (it) from the altar?

10:19 What am I claiming? The idol is something [of value, to be honored]? Or that the idol-sacrifice is something?

10:20 What about (that) which is sacrificed to demons (by) the-Nations [Gentiles] and not to *GOD*? I do not want you to become a companion [an associate] with the demons.

10:21 You are not able [permitted, allowed] to-be-drinking from *The-Master's*-Cup and the Cup-of-Demons. Neither are you able [permitted, allowed] to share the *Master's*-Table and the Table-of-Demons.

10:22 Do we-provoke *The-Master* to jealousy? Are we the stronger than *Him*?

10:23 I am permitted [have the authority, legally able] to do all things but not all things are profitable. All for me is permitted [allowed]. But not all edifies [is beneficial, is good, promotes the best].

10:24 Let no-one crave [think of, desire exclusively about] for himself but for the (needs) of each other.

10:25 Everything being sold in the meat-market eat. Don't ask because of conscience sake.

10:26 For the earth is *The-Master's* and its fullness [all that is in it].

Section I

10:27 And if any invites you that are not believers and you are willing to go, everything that has been placed before you eat! Do not examine [question, ask about] it for conscience sake.

10:28 But if anytime any says to you this is an idol-sacrifice, do not eat it because it has been divulged and for conscience sake. For the earth and all that is in it is *The-Master*'s.

10:29 When I said conscience, I did not mean yours but the other ones. For why should my freedom [liberty] be decided by another's conscience?

10:30 For if I participate with gratitude, why would I be slandered for which I give thanks?

10:31 Whenever you are eating or drinking or any(thing), be doing it all for the glory of GOD.

10:32 Do not become a stumbling-block [offense] to anyone, of Jews, of Greeks and the Ecclesia of *THE-GOD*.

10:33 As I also try to please all, not seeking for myself, but being-of-benefit [profitable] to the many that they may be saved.

11:1 Become my imitators as I of *Anointed*.

I CORINTHIANS 11

11:2 Now I applaud you, Brothers, that you have remembered me in all and the instructions you are holding fast to I gave to you.

11:3 But I want you to know that the head of every man is *The-Anointed* and of the woman the man is the head, and *Anointed*, *THE-GOD*.

11:4 Every man praying or prophesying [moved to speak, instruct, comfort, encourage, foretell the future] veiling his head is disgracing [dishonors] his head,

11:5 but every woman praying or prophesying uncovering the head disgraces her head for it is the same as having her head shaved.

11:6 For the woman that is not covered, let her be shorn. For it is a shame [filthy-disgrace] for a woman to be shorn or to be shaven. Let her be covered.

11:7 For indeed a man is not to be covering the head being-created in the image and honor [glory] of *GOD*, but a woman's glory is the man.

11:8 For a man is not from a woman but a woman out of man.

11:9 Neither was man created because of the woman but the woman because of the man.

11:10	Because of the Angels the woman must wear the-authority [to show the man has the authority, the-crown] on the head.
11:11	However neither is man not apart from a woman or the woman apart from man in *Master*.
11:12	As much as is a woman out of man also *The-Man* came through The-Woman, but all [everything] out of THE-GOD.
11:13	Evaluate for yourself, does it serve a woman to pray uncovered to THE-GOD?
11:14	Does not nature itself teach you that if a man indeed has tresses [lets the hair grow long] it is his dishonor[disgrace]?
11:15	But if a woman has tresses, it is her glory for tresses instead of clothing [mantle, veil] was given her.
11:16	Now if anyone is reputed [a reputation for being] divisive [fond of strife, contentious], we have no such custom, neither has the Ecclesia-of-*THE-GOD*.
11:17	Concerning this, I declare that I am not in approval. Your coming together it is not advantageous but for the worse.
11:18	First for sure, when-coming-together I am hearing of schisms [splits, divisions] in the Ecclesia to be existing with you, and I in some part believe.
11:19	There must also be dissentions [selective groups] within you for-you-require that it must be plain [apparent, clear] the-ones are qualified [tested, accepted] by you.
11:20	Then when you come to the same-place to eat, it is not *Master*'s dinner [supper] for each-one is first getting their own dinner.
11:21	And who indeed is left starving and who is getting drunk?
11:22	Do you not have homes to eat and drink in or do you despise [disdain, hate] and are-ashamed of [disgraced by] the Ecclesia, the-ones having nothing? What am I to say to you? Shall I approve you in this? I do not approve.
11:23	For what I was instructed from *The-Master* is that which I pass-on to you, that *The-Master-Savior-[Messiah]* on the night which *He* was-given-up [handed-over, betrayed] took bread
11:24	and gave thanks, broke it and said, *"You take this and eat it. It is me. This body is being violently-killed for your sake. Do this in the remembrance of me."*
11:25	Also the same for the cup taking a sip said, *"This drinking vessel [cup] is the new compact [testament, covenant] by my blood. This you do, as often as you may be drinking in my remembrance."*

Section I

11:26 *"For as many times you may-be-eating this bread and may-be-drinking this cup, you are announcing [declare, make known] the death of The-Master until whenever He comes."*

11:27 Therefore whoever may eat this bread or drink this Cup-of-*The-Master* in an-unworthy-manner shall-carry-the-penalty of the body and blood of *The-Master*.

11:28 So let each man test himself and then eat from the bread and drink out of the cup.

11:29 For the-one eating and drinking unworthily sentences [condemns] himself not honoring the body of *The-Master* by eating and drinking.

11:30 For this reason many among you are infirmed [weak] and ailing [sick] and a considerable (number) are reposing [dead].

11:31 For if we examined ourselves, we would not be judged.

11:32 For when we are examined by *Master*, we-are-being-disciplined so that we are not condemned together with The-System.

11:33 So now, my Brothers, when coming together to eat, be waiting for one-another.

11:34 And if any may-be-hungry, let-him-eat at home so you may not come to-gether into that judgment [sentencing, condemnation, decree, punishment]. As for the rest, I shall arrange-it [give orders] when I may-be-coming [arrive].

I CORINTHIANS 12

12:1 Now I do not want you to be ignorant of the spiritual, Brothers.

12:2 For you know that you were-led-away from the-Nations [Gentiles], from falling-forward [worshipping] and being-led and joined to those voiceless [no speaking ability, silent] idols.

12:3 I am making known to you clearly that no-one speaking by *GOD*'s spirit speaks vehemently-denouncing [cursing] *Savior* and no-one is able to say *Savior [Messiah]* (is) *Master* but by the Holy-spirit

12:4 and divine-gifts are distributed-differently [not given equally to all] but it-is still the same spirit.

12:5 Also the-servicing [ministry, offices] are not-given-equally-to-all, but the same *Master*.

12:6 And as for works they-are not-given-equally-to-all, but it is the same *GOD* who is *THE-ONE* working [operating] the all in all.

12:7 But being given to each is the-materialization [sign, expression, appearance] of-the-spirit for that-which-is-profitable.

12:8	Indeed, for through by the same spirit, the-spirit is giving to some words of wisdom, and for others words of knowledge.
12:9	To a different-one belief [faith] by the same spirit, for others divine-gifts of health [healing] by the same spirit.
12:10	For another working of miracles, and for others prophecy, for others judging [recognize, differentiate, distinguish] spirits, to others breeds [types] of languages, for others to translate [interpret] languages.
12:11	Yet all of these operate by the one and same spirit, distributing to each (their) own as it-is-intended.
12:12	Even as the body is singular and has many members, and all the members are of that body, *The-One* consisting of many is a *Body*, it is *The-Anointed*.
12:13	For also by one spirit we are dipped [baptized] into one body, whether Jews or Greeks, whether slaves or free, and are-watered [saturated, permeated, filled] by one spirit.
12:14	Also the body is not one member but many.
12:15	For what if the foot said, "See, I am not a hand; I am not from that body"? Yet is it not part of the body?
12:16	What if the ear said, "See I am not an eye, I am not from that body"? Yet is it not part of the body?
12:17	If the entire body was an eye, where is the hearing? What about the sense of smelling?
12:18	Most assuredly *THE-GOD* placed each one of the members in the body as *HE*-wills
12:19	and if (it was) only one member, where (is) the body?
12:20	Now indeed (are) many members, but one body,
12:21	and the eye cannot say to the hand, "I have no need for you!" Or again the head to the feet, "I have no need for you!"
12:22	Oddly rather, the members of the body seeming weaker [inferior, less attractive, little value] are the most necessary.
12:23	And that of the body we think less-honorable [unvalued, less attractive], we invest [bestow, confer, present] with the most [special] reverence [honor] and the most-indecent with even greater-respectability [are made to be more presentable].
12:24	For the shapely [good-looking] has no need for covering. But *THE-GOD* has put together the body so that the-one with deficiencies are given the greatest honor.

Section I

12:25 So there are no divisions in the body, and each member is anxious to take care of one-another.

12:26 And if one member is suffering, all feel-it-together, all the members. Or if one member is being honored, all the members should-rejoice-together.

12:27 You are the body of *Anointed* and members of the part [lot, destiny, in regard to this, of the whole].

12:28 Indeed, *THE-GOD* has placed those first in the Ecclesia commissioners [apostles], second prophets, third teachers, then miracles, then divine-gifts of healing, help [supporters], wise counselors, types of languages.

12:29 Not all commissioners, not all prophets [moved to speak, instruct, comfort, encourage, foretell the future], not all teachers, not all miracle (workers),

12:30 not all divine-gifts of healing, not all linguists, not all speakers.

12:31 But be zealous [covet, crave] for the better [greater] divine-gifts. For I-am-showing you through-out a preeminent [superior] way.

I CORINTHIANS 13

13:1 Now if I speak all the languages of men and of the Angels but have not Godly-[divine]-love, I have the sound of copper or a clamoring [clanging, noisy] cymbal.

13:3 And if I could prophesize [foretell the future] and understand all of the secrets and every-bit of knowledge or have all of the-belief to be able to transplant mountains, but if I do not have Godly-love, I am no-one [nothing]. Or if I feed all and give up all of my possessions or give up my body so I-should-be-burned, still if I do not have Godly-love, it has not benefitted me anything.

13:4 For Godly-love is patient, is kind. Godly-love is not jealous [envious]. Godly-love does not brag, not vain [self-inflating].

13:5 It is not indecent-behaving [acts disgraceful], does not seek [demand something, crave] for itself, does not keep count of evil,

13:6 does not rejoice in injustice but it rejoices together in *The-Truth*

13:7 excluding [conceals the errors and faults of, protect, preserve] all, believes all, expects all, is enduring (in) the Godly-love,

13:8 never lapses [fails]; but whether prophesies are discarded [caused to cease, abolished, rendered inactive] or languages end or knowledge is-discarded [vanishes].

13:9 For we know in part, and we prophesize a little.

13:10 But whenever the-maturing is completed, then the parts shall-be-discarded [vanish, disappear due to having been done, completed in entirety].

13:11 When I was a minor [little child, not of age], I spoke as a minor. I behaved and reasoned as a minor, but when I became a man, I discarded that of the minor.

13:12 For we are observing [gazing, staring] presently into an enigmatic [dark and mysterious] viewer. For the present I understand a little, but then I shall know completely [in full] even as I am also completely recognized when seen face to face.

13:13 For these three now are to remain: belief [faith], expectation [trust, hope], Godly-love. But of these the-Godly-love is the greater.

I CORINTHIANS 14

14:1 Chase Godly-love with a boiling fury [zeal] and the spiritual and also that you may prophesize.

14:2 For *THE-ONE* speaks in a language no man speaks only *THE-GOD*. For no one hears [understands] except *HE* speaks [reveals] secrets by the spirit.

14:3 But the-one prophesying [moved to speak, instruct, comfort, encourage] to men speaks edification and exhortation and comfort.

14:4 *THE-ONE* speaking *HIS* own [native] language is building-a-home [repairing or restoring a building, growing in wisdom and holiness, promoting growth (in Christian virtues)] but the-one prophesying builds up the Ecclesia.

14:5 I wish all could speak a language, but much greater I would have you prophesying. For the-one prophesying is greater [having more rank, higher on the scale, more exalted] than anyone speaking a language. For the one prophesying, other than the-one translating a language, is to be building up [strengthening] the Ecclesia.

14:6 And now, Brothers, if I were to come to you speaking a (foreign)-language, how would I profit you? How should I speak [teach, instruct] to you? By revelation, or from knowledge, or using prophecy [moved to speak, instruct, comfort, encourage, foretell the future], or by teaching?

14:7 Just as soulless [inanimate objects] items give [make] sounds [noises], such as flute or lyre, how is it known what is the flute or the lyre unless they give distinctive sounds?

14:8 Also, who can prepare for battle with an unclear [dubious] trumpet sound?

Section I

14:9 So it is with you. Unless the language is intelligibly [clearly, obviously] spoken [expressed], how can it be understood? What you say is spoken [emptied] into the air.

14:10 For there are many types of sound [languages] in The-System and not-one is without a voice [each language has its own power].

14:11 For if I do not understand the power [significance, intent, meaning] of the language, I would be like one speaking to a barbarian and the-one speaking as a barbarian to me.

14:12 Same as you. Since you seek the spiritual (things), be super-abounding in zeal [desire, strive] for the edification of the Ecclesia.

14:13 Therefore let-him-pray the-one speaking in a language that it may be translated [interpreted, made understandable].

14:14 For if I pray in a (unknown, foreign) language, my spirit is praying but my mind [understanding] is barren [gaining nothing to the improvement of].

14:15 How is it then I would pray? I will pray in the spirit and with the-mind [understanding], playing-music [rejoicing] and with the spirit playing-music [rejoicing] also in mind [understanding].

14:16 How can it be when you are blessing [giving thanks] in the spirit that-one not in a position of understanding can declare an "amen" since in fact he does not understand what you are saying?

14:17 You indeed give thanks well, but no one is gaining edification.

14:18 I thank *THE-GOD* of mine I speak more languages than all of you,

14:19 but in the Ecclesia I-am-willing to say only five words with understanding and also be instructing others than to speak a myriad of words in a (foreign) language.

14:20 Brothers, do not be little-boys in your thinking, for you are minors with evils [trouble, wickedness, malice] and think you have become mature!

14:21 In the Law it is written, **"With different languages and with different lips [mouths]** *I* **will speak this to the-people,"** and**, "yet they shall still not be hearing [understanding, comprehending] me says** *Master***."** [Isa 28:11, 12]

14:22 So languages are not a sign for the-ones-believing but for the unbelievers, and prophecy is not for unbelievers but for the-ones-believing.

14:23 Now if the entire Ecclesia would gather in one place and all were speaking languages and an ordinary (one, person) or an unbeliever entered in, will they not declare you are mad [insane, raving lunatics, babblers, beside one's self, out of your minds]!

14:24 But if all were prophesying and some unbeliever entered or an ordinary (one, person) is exposed to [plainly understands] all and he examines [sifts, judges and decides] all

14:25 and in doing so that hidden in his heart becomes plain [apparent, exposed] and there falls on (his) face in-his-worship to *THE-GOD* reports [proclaims, heralds, declares] that *THE-GOD* is really [in truth, unquestionably] among you.

14:26 But how is it then, Brothers, that when you come together each of you has your psalm, your teaching [doctrine], has a language, has a revelation, has a translation [interpretation]? Let-it-all-become for edification!

14:27 If any is speaking a language, allow two or the most three and done in part [one after another, in succession]; also let-one-be-interpreting.

14:28 But if there is no interpreter, keep-him-hushed [silent] in the Ecclesia, and he-is-to-speak to himself and to *THE-GOD*.

14:29 And prophets [foretelling the future, moved to speak], let two or three speak and let the others examine [judge, test and determine].

14:30 And if it is revealed to one sitting next to (him), this first be silent!

14:31 For you can all prophesy one by one that all may learn and all-may-be-consoled [comforted, encouraged, instructed, strengthened].

14:32 For the spirit of the prophets are subjugated [controlled, arranged under the] by prophets.

14:33 For *THE-GOD* is not turbulent [unstable, the state of disorder, a state of confusion] but peace as in all the called-outs [Ecclesiae] of the Holy-Ones.

14:34 Let the-women in the Ecclesiae be silent, for it-has-not-been-permitted for them to be speaking but be set-under [arranged, in subject to] also as the Law says.

14:35 And if any are willing [determined, desire, wish] to be informed [learn, increase in knowledge] let them inquire [diligently interrogate, demand by asking, question] in the home of their husbands, for it is a dishonor for women to-be-speaking in the Ecclesiae.

14:36 For did *The-Word* of *THE-GOD* come from you or did it only come to you?

14:37 If any presumes to-be a prophet [moved to speak, instruct, comfort, encourage, foretell the future] or spiritual, let him acknowledge that what I am writing to you, they-are directions [orders, charges, commanded] from *The-Master*.

14:38 If any chooses ignorance [to sin, to be wrong], let them be ignorant!

Section I

14:39   But you, Brothers, have-a-boiling-passion [be zealous] to be prophesying and do not forbid the speaking in languages.

14:40   Let it all occur in respectability and with order.

I CORINTHIANS 15

15:1   Again I remind you, Brothers, the Well-Message I instructed [preached, taught] to you which you accepted and also stand [are established by] through which you are also-being-saved.

15:2   That is if you remember the Well-Message I brought to you unless you faked your belief.

15:3   For I delivered to you that which I was taught and accepted, that *Anointed* died for the sake of the-sins of us according-to the Writings [scriptures],

15:4   that *He* was-entombed and that *He* has-been-raised on the third day according-to the Writings

15:5   and that *He* was seen by Cephas and thereafter by the twelve.

15:6   After that *He* was seen by over five-hundred brothers at the same time of whom the majority are still present [alive] with also some now in repose [dead].

15:7   Then *He* was seen by Jacobus [James], thereafter to all the Commissioners

15:8   and last of all as if a premature-birth [untimely birth], *He* was also seen with me.

15:9   For I am the-most-inferior [least in rank and excellence, in importance, an unfit and unhealthy child] of the Commissioners [apostles] who is not fit [worthy, suited, proper, appropriate] to be called a Commissioner because I persecuted the Ecclesiae-of-*THE-GOD*.

15:10   But by the-Grace-of-*GOD*, for I am what I am, that *HIS* grace has not become empty [meaningless, purposeless, pointless] with me. For I have toiled over and above [more remarkably, much more than, super-exceeded] all of them, but it is not I but The-Grace-of-*THE-GOD* which is with me.

15:11   Therefore whether I or they are proclaiming [preaching, announcing, instructing], you also believe.

15:12   For if A*nointed* is-being-proclaimed [declared] that *He* has risen from out of the-dead-ones, how can some of those among you claim there is no resurrection from the dead?

15:13 Because if there is no resurrection from the dead-ones, then neither has *Anointed* risen.

15:14 And if *Anointed* has not risen, then conclusively [decisively, without argument] our proclamation is empty [a lie, a scam] and also your belief.

15:15 Yes, if we are found [discovered, determined to be] false witnesses of THE-GOD, seeing we testify accordingly from THE-GOD that HE raised *The-Anointed*, Whom, if-it-is-true HE did not raise-up, then (the) dead-ones are not being raised [awakened, brought back to life].

15:16 And if the dead-ones do not rise, then neither is *Anointed* raised-up [alive].

15:17 and if *Anointed* is not alive, your belief is worthless and you are still in your sins.

15:18 Consequently also the-ones being reposed [dying, dead] in *Anointed* are perished [lost, never to return].

15:19 For if in this life we have an expectation in *Anointed*, then we are the most forlorn [without mercy, without hope, miserable] of all.

15:20 But now *Anointed* is alive from the dead-ones, becoming *The-First-Fruit* of the-dead.

15:21 For it is a fact through man—The-Death, just as by man The-Resurrection from the dead-ones.

15:22 For it is a fact that by Adam all are-dying, just as by *The-Anointed* all will-be-made-alive.

15:23 But each individual in their own class [set-and-order-of-appointed-time], *Anointed The-First-Fruit*, afterwards the-ones in *Anointed* at the presence [coming, return] of *Him*.

15:24 Then The-Finishing [end of all] when *He*-has-put-to-an-end [conquered, abolished, deprived the force of] all sovereignties and all authority and powers and *He*-gives-over The-Kingdom to THE-GOD and FATHER.

15:25 For *He* is to reign until all of *His* enemies are placed under *His* feet [power and authority].

15:26 Abolishing (the) last enemy The-Death.

15:27 For HE has subjugated all under His feet. However, when all has been subjugated under *Him*, this is outside of THE-ONE giving *Him* the authority over the all,

15:28 once all is subjugated under *Him*, then *The-Son Himself* shall-be-subjugated to THE-ONE setting all under HIM that THE-GOD may be all [complete,

Section I

totally integrated with, satisfy all intent and reasoning, aspects] in all [God's will, purpose and pleasure].

15:29 For what else are the-ones-baptized to do for the sake of the dead-ones if the-dead are absolutely not rising [being brought back to life]? Why are-you-being-baptized for the sake of the-dead

15:30 and why do we place ourselves in danger every hour?

15:31 It kills me every day because of your boasting in *Anointed Savior The-Master* of us!

15:32 If as a man I-fight-the-wild-beasts in Ephesus, what benefit is it for me if the dead-ones do not rise-up? Let us just eat and drink, for tomorrow we die!

15:33 Do not be deceived; evil conversation corrupts character.

15:34 Sober-up [come out of your stupor]! Be just [righteous] and do not sin! For some have ignorance about *GOD*! I state this to your shame [dishonor].

15:35 Now some may ask how do the dead arise? What type of a body are they coming with?

15:36 You senseless ones! That which is sown does not come to life unless it dies.

15:37 And what are you sowing? What you are sowing is not for this body like a-single-kernel may produce (a) wheat (plant) or some(thing) other.

15:38 For *THE-GOD* gives to him a body as *HE* wills and for each of the seeds their own body.

15:39 Not all skin is the same skin, for there is indeed the skin of men and the skin of beasts, another for fish and another for flyers [birds].

15:40 There are bodies in the heavens and bodies of land and indeed differences in the glory in the heavenlies and in the terrestrial.

15:41 Another glory of the sun, a glory of the moon, another glory of the stars, even stars differ in glory.

15:42 Thus so The-Resurrection of the dead-ones. Being sown in corruption to rise-up in incorruption;

15:43 it is sown in dishonor, being risen with glory [highest-esteem, highest-honor]; it is sown in weakness, being raised in unlimited-power.

15:44 It is sown a soulish [requiring breath as animal life, fleshly] body, being raised a spiritual body. There is a soulish body and is a spiritual body.

15:45 For as it is written, **"The first man Adam a living soul."** *The-Last-Adam* a living spirit. [Gen 2:7]

15:46 Why was the-first not the-spiritual but the-soulish, secondly-then the-spiritual?

15:47	Out of soil of the earth the first man. The second man, *The-Master*, out of heaven.
15:48	From such The-Soilish-One are also the soilish-ones and as-is *The-Heavenly-One* also are they heavenly-ones.
15:49	As we wear the image [likeness] of The-Soilish-One we shall wear the image of *The-Heavenly-One*.
15:50	Now I state this, Brothers, that flesh and blood are not able to enjoy The-Allotment-of-*GOD*'s-Kingdom; neither can the-corrupt enjoy The-Allotment-of-The-Incorrupt.
15:51	Pay attention, I am telling you a secret: it is certain we-all-shall-not-die and we-shall-all-be-changed!
15:52	In an instant! In the-blink of an eye! At The-Last-Trumpet *He*-shall-trumpet for the dead-ones to be raised incorruptible and we-shall-be-transformed.
15:53	For the-corrupt is-required [compelled, obliged, by necessity] to put on the-incorruptible and the-death [mortal, temporary] to-be-putting-on un-death [immortality, permanence].
15:54	And when the corrupted becomes this incorruptible and the mortal becomes this immortal, then shall-be-completed these words, **"The-Death is swallowed [devoured, destroyed] in conquest [victory]!"** [Hos 13:14]
15:55	Where are you Death, The-Piercer? Where is the victory [prizes, tokens, booty] in your graves
15:56	for The-Piercer, The-Death, The-Sin? For the power [holding power, gripping-power] of sins (is in) the Law.
15:57	But by the Grace-of-*THE-GOD*, *THE-ONE-GIVING* us the victory (is) through *The-Master* of us, *Savior-Anointed*.
15:58	Therefore, my beloved Brothers, you are to be firm, unstirred [firmly-persistent], super-abounding in the work of *The-Master*. That your toil [strenuous, difficult labor] is not empty [worthless, wasted] for *Master*.

I CORINTHIANS 16

16:1	Now concerning the collection for the Holy-ones. As I directed the Ecclesiae of Galatia, so also you do.
16:2	On one of the Sabbaths each of you by yourself place in storage that, if any(thing), you may-have-been prospered with so that I, when I come, no collections has to occur.

Section I

16:3 And when I come to you, I will send those tested [deemed worthy, selected, chosen by] with letters-of-commendation to transport your gracious-gifts to Jerusalem.

16:4 And if it is worthwhile I go also, they-shall-go together with me.

16:5 I am coming to you when I pass through Macedonia, for I am passing through Macedonia.

16:6 And I might abide with you or also be wintering so that you can send me forward wherever I may be going.

16:7 I will not see you this-time on the way, but I am expecting to stay some time with you if the *Master* permits it.

16:8 For now I will remain in Ephesus until Pentecost,

16:9 for a great door [opportunity] has been opened to me and in-operation [actively attacking] is many opposing [adversaries].

16:10 Now if Timotheus may come, make sure that he comes not having to fear about you, for he-is working as I for *Master*.

16:11 And make sure none utterly despises [looks down on, derides] him. But send him forward in-peace [safe and secure] to me for I am waiting for him with the Brothers.

16:12 Now concerning the-brother Apollos. I earnestly asked him to come to you with The-Brothers, and it was clearly not his will that he come now, but he will come when he-has-the-opportunity.

16:13 Be attentive! Stand firm in The-Belief [faith]. Be brave [be a stronghold].

16:14 Let everything be done in Godly-love.

16:15 I plead with you, Brothers, become acquainted with the house of Stephanas (Crowned), the first-fruits of Achaia and their-having-devoted themselves to the service of the Holy-Ones.

16:16 That you may also arrange [set things in order] to do the same and with everyone that labors and works-with-us.

16:17 And I rejoice about the presence [company] of Stephanas and Fortunatus [Lucky, Fortunate] and Achaicus [From Achaia] for they filled-up [added to complete] the deficiency [meager contribution] from you.

16:18 For they have restored my spirit and that of-yours. Credit them then for doing this.

16:19 The Ecclesiae of Asia greet you in *Master*. Aquila [Eagle] and Priscilla [Ancient] especially greet you with the Ecclesia in their home.

16:20 All of the Brothers greet you. Greet each in a holy fraternal-kiss [brotherly-kiss].

16:21 My greetings from my hand, Paul.

16:22 If anyone is not friendly-to [in admiration of, longs for, loves from believing] *The-Master Savior-Anointed*, let them be-put-under-a curse. Our Lord will come!

16:23 The Grace of *The-Master, Savior-[Messiah]-Anointed* be with you.

16:24 My Godly-love (is) with all of you in *Anointed-Savior-[Messiah]*.

Amen.
(Written to the Corinthians from Philippi)

II CORINTHIANS COMMENTARY

II Corinthians is a follow-on to I Corinthians, but in reality, it is at least the third letter and possibly the fourth with direct contact by Paul if one counts the physical appearance he made at Corinth. In some aspect, we could relabel these as II and III Corinthians. I mention this because it sets the stage for Paul's red-hot, blistering, scathing accusations roughly two-thirds of the way into the letter that catches all the Corinthians still in lies, still pretending to live the principles Paul laid down and expected carried out. After reaching out to them this fourth time, he has had enough! Very few members changed and truly repented; the two least expected to change but did was the mother and son having sex with each other! Paul instructs the Ecclesia to allow them back into The Body.

This letter is an interesting one because Paul offers peace and godly-love, extending the "right hand of fellowship" if I may borrow such a phrase, but in his left hand is a dagger to "circumcise" the unchangeable, those still not repenting of their lifestyle. So, Paul starts out in verse 1:13 with a velvet mitten, drawing in the Corinthians for things which on the surface have been corrected. This includes starting off with words of encouragement and instructions about the mother and son to maintain unity and prevent Satan from getting a bigger foothold in The Body. Paul readdresses briefly his equal authority with the other Commissioners (apostles) and how their listening and following those Jews claiming circumcision plus the Law of Moses is the only way to God's Kingdom and life eonian.

Chapter 5:11–21 is a quick review and reminder of The-Secret for the members with Chapters 6—9 providing more proof and instructions on a wide variety subject matters, such as The Law, circumcision, treatment of others, and more.

Chapter 10 begins drawing the circumcision knife ever so slowly by Paul first humbling himself as a fool before the Corinthians but with the knowledge that he is going to slice and dice this group in blazing fury before the letter is finished. Paul continues to write more openly, boldly, and bluntly, and the reader can see him setting up the audience. Paul had sent Titus and Timothy specifically to find out the real situation of what was going on there without the Corinthians suspecting a thing. Paul finally snaps like a dry, dead tree limb—and the cracking and snapping is startling! This occurs between Chapter 12:16—13:10, where Paul, in an over-the-top, boiling fury, excoriates the members, telling them he is on his way to clean up this infected part of the Body of

Christ and intends to spare no one! He will cut it all off and out (notice the play on words throughout this letter referencing circumcision). Wow! Lastly, note how enraged Paul is by the way he ends this letter. No blessings and no "amen." Paul does, however, for the Corinthians' sake call upon the Savior to have grace poured out on them.

Now, the reader must answer for himself at least two questions, since all that is written is for our edification, and this includes II Corinthians. The number one question is: "Who if anyone survived Paul's housecleaning when he showed up again with Titus and Timothy?" These two are the "two witnesses" he brought back with him to be able to accuse and render a judgment to all, for these two "spies" had acquired knowledge and "befriended" people while in the company of the Corinthians. The second question is directed to you and me personally.

Corinth had the reputation for all the best of lusts and passions offered in that era. We may relate it to our "Las Vegas," the adult playground of today's world. If there was any kind of vice that you had an interest in or wanted to experience, Corinth was the place to go. And unlike today in our supposed "righteousness" society, it was all out in the open, with no restrictions or repercussions. Prostitution, gambling, the idol temples, bustling crowds, the selling of daughters and sons, slavery—you name it, it was there for the taking. With this newfound "freedom" offered in Christ, every person had become a law unto themselves, and anyone who stopped you from doing what you wanted be damned. So, the second question is: "Are you a law unto yourself without regard to your actions or to the Body of Christ?"

II Corinthians is really a study in freedom, and quite frankly, all the other books of the Bible have the same underlying theme. But this is the freedom in Christ, not what we imagine to be freedom as peddled or preached in today's society, and certainly not what will happen in God's Kingdom. What Paul is teaching is the standard and norm of life eonian in the Kingdom of God when it comes to behavior and practice. Paul uses the phrase "Ruler (measuring stick) of God," and II Corinthians presents a picture that is about as far off that scale as one can get. That is not the freedom we are to live by and promote. This true freedom is explained everywhere, but most curiously one of the smallest of books of the Bible follows Corinthians in the sacred order and explains that lifestyle and freedom in a simple and direct way. Galatians follows the order of Corinthians logically, although this may not be obvious to those who just read the Bible.

Within this letter, Paul, the corporate attorney, must once again address a member of "The Corporate Body" about what is and is not permitted; he must readdress what freedom in Christ really means and returns in person to clean house. Most likely a "change in management" occurred, and this Ecclesia was redirected, reeducated, and retrained in all corporate matters by Paul, with Titus and Timothy acting as his witnesses and accusers.

This letter serves as a warning to all those "called-out" by God to protect and guard the gifts they have been given.

II CORINTHIANS AS A LETTER

PAUL A COMMISSIONER OF *Savior-Anointed* through the will of *GOD* with Timotheus, The-Brother. To the Ecclesia of *THE-GOD*, The-Ones in Corinth together with the Holy-Ones all the ones-being in the whole of Achaia.

Grace to you and peace from *GOD* and *FATHER* of our *Master, Savior-Anointed*. Bless *THE-GOD* and *THE-FATHER* of *The-Master* of us *Savior-Anointed*, *The-Father-of-The-Mercies* and *GOD* of all consolation, *THE-ONE CONSOLING* us in our every distress. To be enabling us to be comforting the-ones in every distress through the comforting which we ourselves are comforted by *THE-GOD* since the trials-and-oppressions of *The-Anointed* super-abounds in us. Thus, also through *Anointed* is the consolation of us super-abounding. When for your sake we-are-being-afflicted, it is for your consolation and salvation, all-of-us are experiencing suffering with the same endurance. For we are comforted, and our expectation is in the knowledge about you. That even as participants in your distress, you also have comfort.

For we are not willing for you to be ignorant, Brothers, concerning our afflictions that came to us in the province of Asia. That we-were-severely-persecuted above our ability so-much that we desired to die, having lost all expectation. But-the-same-answer came to us about The-Death in our-death-sentence that we are to have no confidence in ourselves but in *THE-GOD, THE-ONE-RAISING* the dead-ones *WHO* rescued us from such-a-horrendous death and is-a-*RESCUING-DELIVERER* in *WHOM* we continue to rely on to rescue. For our sake, you assisted in praying for us. That from the many people came many gracious-gifts for us. May *HE* be-thanked because of us. For our boasting is this, the witness of our conscience, that in heartfelt-generosity and sincerity, *GOD*, not with worldly wisdom but in *GOD*'s loving-kindness, we conducted ourselves in The-System yet more-superabundantly for you.

Now we write to you about nothing more than what you have-read or also acknowledged. For I am hoping you will read to the end with also acknowledgment of our boasting about you in-this-respect, as even you also about us in The-Day-of-*The-Master Savior*. And with this confidence I intend to come to you as before that you may have a second benefit that through you to pass into Macedonia and from Macedonia come back to you and by you to-be-sent-forward to Judea.

Was this planning done as-if in casual thought? Or is this planning for selfish motives? Do I intend to say yes-yes or no-no at the same time? For as *THE-GOD* is believable, our word to you was not double-talk. For *The-Son-of-THE-GOD, Savior Anointed, The-One* preached among you by us, Silvanus and Timotheus and by me, was not yes and no, but in *Him* has become yes. For all the promises of GOD are about *Him* and yes, also in *Him*. AMEN and glory to *THE-GOD* from us!

Now THE-ONE-CONFORMING us together with you in *Anointed* and THE-ONE-ANOINTING us, THE-ONE-GOD, is also THE ONE-SEALING us and gave the-spirit as the down-payment in our hearts. Moreover, I invoke THE-GOD as a witness for my soul that I did not come to Corinth to spare you. Not that we-are-lording over your belief, but we are fellow-workers of your joy for you stand by believing.

For I decided by myself to not come again in mourning to you, for if I am making you to sorrow, who is the-one-to-gladden me but me by the-ones I made sorrowful? And I write this again that if I come, I may have not sorrow from whom I should be rejoicing and have confidence in. That is all of you; my joy is all of you. For out of great affliction and anguish of heart I wrote to you with many tears to not make you sorrowful but that you may deeply-understand the Godly-love I have for you in super-abundance. However, if anyone has-caused-sorrow, he has not sorrowed me, but to-some-degree-to-all of you. I do not want to press-too-heavily on you. The punishment was sufficient about this as done by the majority. So-that rather continuing-the-punishment you should deal graciously and console unless even more-excessive grief may-overwhelm the-individuals.

Therefore, I entreat you to confirm-publicly-and-return him in Godly-love. For in this I wrote to you that I may know with testing if you are obedient in all things. And to whom or anything you are forgiving also I, and if I for anything have-dealt-graciously-with, I have-forgiven because of you before-the-presence of *Anointed* so that we-should-not-be-taken-advantage-of by The-Satan. For we are not ignorant about his evil-purposes.

While coming into Troas with the Well-Message-of-*The-Anointed*, a door had been opened to me by *Master*. I had no ease in my spirit not finding Titus my brother, but taking leave from them I came into Macedonia. But thanks to *THE-GOD*, to THE-ONE-ALWAYS-TRIUMPHING us in *The-Anointed* and manifesting the odor-of-life-giving Knowledge-of-*HIM* for us in every place.

For indeed we are the fragrant-odor of *Anointed* for *THE-GOD* as the-ones being saved and for the-ones perishing, for who indeed is the odor of death in dying; yet the odor of life in life. Has enough been said about this? For we are not the majority of the-ones peddling the-word of *THE-GOD* but out of sincerity, rather from GOD in the sight of *THE-GOD* in *Anointed* we speak.

Do we need to again reintroduce ourselves? Do we need letters of introductions as some for you or from you introductions? You are our letters written in our hearts known and being read by all men. You are that letter of *Anointed* being displayed and distributed by us. Engraved not with ink but by the spirit-of-*THE-LIVING-GOD*, not on tablets of stone, but on the fleshy tablets of the heart. For we have such confidence

Section I

through *The-Anointed* about *THE-GOD*. We have no confidence in ourselves, to count ourselves as something among ourselves. But the-confidence of us is from *THE-GOD* who also equips us as ministers of the New Testament, not with Sacred-Writings-and-the Law, for the Letter is killing, but the spirit causes to live-and-begets-alive.

For if the administration of death is in the Writings having-been-chiseled in stones was so glorious, so-glorious that none of the-Sons-of-Israel was able to look at the face of Moses, how is it that glory on his face vanished? How much greater then shall be the glory through the assistance-and-advantage of the-spirit? For if the administration of sentencing-and-carrying-out-death is so glorious, how much exceedingly-greater is the administration of justice in glory? For even though that which has glory has no glory for this particular reason, because of the glory which exceeds-it-and-casts-its-shadow-over-it. For if that glory has vanished, how much greater is the-one-remaining in glory?

Having then this great expectation, we use openness in speaking. Not as Moses did placing a veil on his face so that the Sons-of-Israel could not stare-intently-gaze-and-observe to watch the-vanishing come to an end. For their minds were blinded. And even up to this day this same covering is remaining not-being-removed when reading of the Old Covenant which has-vanished-disappeared-and-was removed in *Anointed*. Even this day whenever Moses is read the heart is buried under The-Covering. And at-such-time should one turn back to *Master* the Covering will be lifted.

The Master, He-is now spirit, and where the spirit-of-*Master* is, freedom is there. And we all will mirror the glorified uncovered face of *Master*, transformed into the same likeness, from a-most-glorious-condition to a-most-exalted state just-like from the spirit of *Master*.

Since we have this service and we have-received this mercy we do not lose courage and renounce those concealed vile-things, not participating in cleverness-and-false-wisdom or mingling-divine-truth-with-wrong-notions with the *Word*-of-*THE-GOD*, but to clearly show *The-Truth*, standing-together with a clear conscience in the sight of every man and *THE-GOD*. For if our Well-Message is-being-veiled, it is being veiled on the-ones perishing in whom The-God-of-This-Eon blinds the understanding of The-Unbelieving to not be-bright-and-shine-forth bringing-to-light-and-exposure the Well-Message of The-Glory-of-*The-Anointed* who is the-nature-and-form-of *THE-GOD*.

For we are not calling-attention-to us but *Anointed Savior* and you are slaves because of *Savior*. For *THE-GOD*, *THE-ONE* commanded out of darkness light to shine, *WHO* shines in the hearts of us to illuminate the Knowledge-of-the-Glory-of-*THE-GOD* in-the-presence of *Savior Anointed*.

And we have placed-in-the-marrow, these earthenware vessels, this far-beyond-all-measure power which-is-from *THE-GOD* and not out of us. Being-oppressed in all but not distressed, not knowing how to decide but not renouncing all expectation, being-persecuted but not abandoned, being-thrown-to-the-ground but not destroyed, always carrying the-death of *Master Savior* in the body, to-show also The-Life-of-*The-Savior* may-be-made-manifested in the body of us.

For we which are living are being-handed-over to Death because of *Savior* so-that the Life-of-*The-Savior* may-be-made-to-appear in the dying-mortal flesh of us. Yes indeed, The-Death displays-its-activity on us, but *The-Life* is in you.

Having the same spirit of The-Belief with what has been written I believe, by which I speak, by which we also believe do declare knowing that THE-ONE-ROUSING *The-Master Savior* and we through *Savior* together with you shall be-resurrected and be-standing-beside-each-other. For all of this is because of you that The-Grace may be increasingly greater, thanksgiving should-be-super-abounding for the glory of THE-GOD. Therefore we-are-absolutely-not-without-any-hope. For even though the outward man is rotting-and-corrupted, nevertheless the-one inwardly is being-made-into a new kind of life day by day. For the moment the oppression of us is delicate-to-the-touch producing an exceeding-greatness beyond exceeding-greatness of a vast-and-transcendent eonian glory. Let us not consider-and-worry about that being-observed but not being-seen, that observed in-this-period-of-time but not being seen eonian.

We are aware that if ever our terrestrial House-of-the-Booth may-be-utterly-destroyed, we are to have from GOD a building, a dwelling-and-a-family not made with hands, eonian in the-starry-heavens-and-where-God-dwells. For we-are-groaning in this body of ours, desiring-craving to be clothed from out of Heaven since-surely we-shall-not-be-found naked and undressed. For we are also groaning as the-ones being weighted down in this booth. Not because we are-willing-to-be-unclothed but because we want to be dressed, that mortality may-be-swallowed-up by *The-Life*.

Now THE-ONE-is-PRODUCING this same in us, this GOD, THE-ONE is giving us the down payment which is the spirit. Always have courage then and be aware that while-living in this body we are still separated from the *Master*. By believing we walk, not by sight and yet we have confidence and desire-and-crave to-be-separated from the body and dwell with *The-Master*. And we also make it our honorable-pursuit to greatly-be-pleased by *Him* whether present or absent. For all of us are-obligated-to appear in-front-of the Judgment-Platform-of-*The-Anointed* where everyone is to receive upon the body for that which he-practices, whether committing good or evil.

Now knowing of the terror of *The-Master*, we are persuading men. For we have been made to appear before GOD, and I expect this also has-been-made-known in your conscience. Again, we are not recommending ourselves to you but offer you a reason to boast about us so you may be boasting to the-ones in their presence and not from the heart. For whether we-are-insane or are sane to you, we represent *GOD*. For the Godly-love of *The-Anointed* presses us decreeing this; that if for the sake of one all died, by reasoning all are dead. For *He* died for the sake of all that the-ones living should no more live for themselves but for *The-One* who died for the-sake-of them and is now-alive. So from this day we are not acquainted with anyone made of the

Section I

flesh, even though we knew *Anointed* in-physical-fleshy-form nevertheless no longer this way.

So, understand this, if any is in *Anointed*, a new creation! The-Originals have passed; all is becoming an-unheard-of-new kind! And all came-from *THE-GOD*, *THE-ONE-CONCILIATING* us to *HIM* through *Savior Anointed* and giving us The Ministry-of-the-Peace-Making-and-Healing, how that *GOD* was in *Anointed*, resolving to bring to *HIMSELF* the System deciding to not count the sins of them and placing in us The-Doctrine-of-The-Conciliation.

Now then we are ambassadors for *Anointed* as *THE-GOD* called for us. We are pleading on-behalf of *Anointed* for you to-become one-and-be-at-peace with *THE-GOD*. For *The-One* not knowing sin was made sin for our sakes that we may become just with *GOD* in *Him*.

Now we, working together, also entreat you to not receive the Grace-of-*THE-GOD* empty-handed. For *HE* says, "I am replying to you in the consecrated-appointed season and in the Day-of-Salvation I bring-aid to you. Be aware, now is the accepted season! Behold now is the day of salvation!"

Give no one a cause to stumble, that no mocking-and-faults are with the ministry but in everything stand with us as servants of *GOD* in great patience-and-perseverance, in oppression, in calamity, in extreme anguish, in stripes-whippings-lashings, in jails, during states-of-instability-and-confusion, in labors, in vigils, in fasts, in uprightness-of-life, in knowledge, in patience, in kindness, in Hoy-spirit, in Godly-love without-hypocrisy. In the word of truth, in the unlimited-inherent-power of GOD through the weapons of the-just to the right and the left. Through glory and disgrace, through defamation and good praise, by imposters or truthful, as unknowns or recognized, as dead and yet know we are living! Being disciplined and not put to death, with sorrow yet always rejoicing, destitute yet enriching many, as having nothing yet possessing all.

We have spoken-frank-and-openly to you Corinthians. Our hearts have em-braced-you-in-Godly-love. You are not being stressed by us, but by your own distresses have left us no place in your heart. As a fair exchange, I speak to you as my children requesting you also to be opening your hearts.

Do not be equally-yoked to unbelievers. For what partnership has justice with lawlessness? And what association light with darkness? And what agreement-unity-or-pact-or-business-arrangement-or-legal-matter does *Anointed* with Belial? Or what part a believer with an unbeliever? And what association-or-purpose-or-service does The-Temple-of-*GOD* have with idol-worship? For you are the Temple-of-GOD. As *THE-LIIVING-GOD* said, "That-*I*-shall-be-making-*MY*-home in them," and, "*I*-shall-be-walking-with-them," and "*I*-will-be their *GOD*," and "they will-be *MY* people." Therefore "Come out from the midst of them and be-cut-and-completely-removed says *Master*. "Do not touch the unclean and I shall-kindly-receive-and-treat you with favor," and "*I*-will-be to you a father," and "You shall-be to *ME* sons and daughters says *MASTER ALMIGHTY*."

Now having these promises, Beloved, we-should-be-cleansing ourselves from every defilement of flesh and by spirit perfecting holiness in fear of *GOD*. Make room for us we have injured no one; we have not forced-to-fall-away anyone, we have not taken advantage of anyone. I speak to not condemn you for I-declared-before you are in our hearts and with you to-be-dying-together and to-be-living-together. My great confidence is in you; my boasting is great over you. I-have-been-completely-filled with encouragement and with super-abundant joy with every distress we have, for even after our entering Macedonia no one had taken care of us, for everywhere all around is distress, terrors within. But *THE-ONE-CALLING* the-low-and-down-cast encouraged us, *THE-GOD*, with the presence of Titus and not only with the presence of him but also by the encouragement by which he was encouraged by you telling him about your vehemently-desiring and lamenting-and-mourning over us, your zeal over me and so that I would find-favor-with-everyone-again-for-doing-the-correct-things. Even though I am sorry for the letter I do not regret-it even though I did regret-it for I perceive that this letter threw you into sorrow even if at the point-in-time. Now I am rejoicing not because I made you sorrowful, but that you-were-sorrowful to re-pentance. For according-to *GOD* you should not-suffer-loss-over nothing by us as the sorrow of *THE-GOD* produces a-changed-mind for salvation not-to-be-repented-of, yet The-System's sorrow produces death.

Understand this, this same sorrow by *THE-GOD* causing you to be sorry, how great was the striving-to-accomplish in you, not in-defending-one's-self, not in-indignation, not fearing, with vehement-desire with zeal, not in vengeance. You have shown yourselves to-be pure in everything in this matter. For this reason I wrote to you. Not to be the one injuring neither as the one injured but because we wanted to show our earnestness over you in the sight of *THE-GOD* for you. Because of this we have-been-encouraged in the cheer-coming-from you, and even greater have we rejoiced in the joy of Titus that his spirit has-been-soothed-and-calmed by all of you. And if in anything I-have-boasted to him about you I was not disgraced. For in all truth we spoke openly-sharing-all-the-information and also to you the-boasting concerning Titus was done in truth. And his compassions for you is greatly-deepened and in remembering all of your compliance-and-submission receiving him having fear and trembling. I-am-certainly-rejoicing having confidence in everything about you.

Further we-are-making-known to you, Brothers, The-Grace-of-*THE-GOD* having-been-given by the Ecclesiae of Macedonia. During a great trial of persecution with a super-abundance of the-joy in them and while in their deep poverty gave abundantly of their possessions. I-am-bearing-record about that ability and their going-above-and-beyond their own ability with great insisting and pleading for us to receive the-gracious-gifts in fellowship and service for the Holy-Ones. And not as we expected but giving themselves first to *The-Master* and to us by the will of *GOD*. So we encouraged Titus that what he started, this he should also complete with you with this gracious-gifting.

Section I

For as you are super-abounding in all belief and doctrine and knowledge and all diligence and out of your Godly-love for us that also in this you may super-abound in The-Grace. I do not speak this as a legal decision-or-command but because of the accomplishment of others and to-examine if your Godly-love is genuine.

For you know The-Grace-of-*The-Master* of us *Savior Anointed* being "rich" but because of you became-reduced-to-nothing that *The-One* in poverty should be making you rich. Now I am giving this opinion for this is profitable for you who has not only started but was willing to do this from a year ago, that you also do this and complete it with even the same eagerness and willingness and also bring it to an end with what you have. For if the willingness is there, what anyone has is acceptable, not what he does not have. Not to relieve others and make-it-difficult-for you but out of fairness for the current season from your excess for those in need. Then also the excess of those may come to the needs for you, in this it becomes fair. As it is written, "The-one with much does not have anything left over and the-one with little is not lacking."

But thanks to THE-GOD, THE-ONE-GIVING this same care-and-diligence over you is in the heart of Titus. For indeed he in-great-eagerness accepted this request and out of his own willingness he came to you. And with him we sent together The-Brother who is praised through-out all the Ecclesiae for the Well-Message. Not only that, but also appointed-by-vote by the Ecclesiae to travel with us with the-gracious-gifts. This being administered by us for *The-Master* with this same glory and readiness-of-mind in you taking care of that no flaws should be found in anyone of us for this bountiful-collection being carried-and-supplied through us. Being-careful-to-do the honorable not only in the sight of *Master* but also the-sight-of men. And we-have-sent-them-with The-Brother whom we tested often watching intently-and-scrutinizing in many things and now with greater-diligence and greater confidence in you. Whether for the sake of my partner Titus and in your fellow-workers or our Brothers the Commissioners-of-The-Ecclesiae, the Glory-of-*Anointed*. Display to them then the-Godly-love of you and about our boasting over you; show this before the Ecclesiae.

Concerning the service to the Holy-Ones, there is no need to write more to you. I am aware of your eagerness. I have boasted about you to the Macedonians that Achaia was prepared over a year ago, and because of that your zeal provokes many. Still I have sent The-Brothers that our boasting over you is considered empty for this reason, that as I said you-may-be-ready unless somehow the Macedonians may get together with me and find you unprepared. Therefore I-deemed it necessary to prepare The-Brothers coming into your presence and have-made-adjustments-beforehand for these stated blessings of yours out of your bounty and not as-a-matter-of-giving-expecting-something-greater-back.

However, the-one sowing sparingly, sparingly shall also reap and the-one sowing bountifully with bountifulness shall also reap. Each as he-has-purposed from the heart, not with a grudge or out of compulsion for THE-GOD Godly-loves the hilarious-joyous giver. For *THE-GOD* is able to lavish all rewards-and-benefits on you that in every and all having contentment to super-abound in every good action.

As it is written, "*HE* scatters, *HE*-gives to the poor, the justice of *HIM* remains into the eons." For *THE-ONE* supplying the *Seed* to the sower and *THE-ONE* furnishing food and bread and multiplying the-seed of you and may-*HE*-grow the produce of virtue. Being-enriched in every and all which produces through us thanksgiving to *THE-GOD*. For this administration of service is not only replenishing the needs of the Holy-Ones but also increases-in-its-blessings by giving many thanks to *THE-GOD*. By the-proof of this service, praising-and-extolling *THE-GOD*, and defending your vow of the Well-Message-of-*The-Anointed* by generosity with the-contribution to them and to all. Also by their prayers over you, out-of-Godly-love for you because of the exceeding-and-surpassing grace of *THE-GOD* on you. And grace to *THE-GOD* for the where-words-fail gift from *HIM*.

Now I, Paul, personally call-on you in the meekness and gentleness of *The-Anointed*, who when present am indeed the lowest-rank among you but in absence with directness-and-bluntness to you. Still I-desire to not have to rely on this directness-and-bluntness when present, for I am thinking to challenge any of the-ones believing us as walking according-to our-passions-and-lusts. Even though we walk in flesh, we are not warring against flesh. For the implements of the-warfare of us are not of-the-flesh but *THE-GOD*, powerfully-able to pull-down bulwarks, pulling-down logic and every elevated-thing thrust against The-Knowledge-of-*THE-GOD* and taking captive every thought into obedience for *The-Anointed* and being-prepared to avenge every disobedience whenever your obedience is fulfilled.

Are-you-judging based on the-physical-appearance? If any has-confidence about himself belonging to *Anointed*, let him-consider-this again about himself! That as he is of *Anointed*, so also we *Anointed's*. For although I could boast more-excessively concerning our authority for which I-will-not-be-shamed that *The-Master* gives us for edification and not to demolish you. I do not want you to think I am trying-throw-you-into-a-violent-fright with the letters. Indeed, they-are-saying the letters are stern and carry-great-force even though when seen his body is weak but his speaking is forcibly-sure. Let such a one think this that-as sure-as writing by letters and while absent, we are also able to perform-and-deliver while present. For we are not daring to be judged by or be compared to some of the-ones giving-credit-to themselves. For they themselves measure themselves and compare themselves to themselves with no understanding. For we are not without being-beyond-measure but boast with the-measure of The-Ruler-of-*THE-GOD* which divides-and-imparts and measures each-of us, a ruler able-to-reach as-far-as you also. For we are not over-stretching out-reaching ourselves, for we have come as-far-as you out-reaching others in the Well-Message-of-*The-Anointed*. Not in the immeasurable boasting of other's toils but having expectation of growing-up in The-Belief of you, to be highly-esteemed among you according-to the Principles-of-Living in super-abundance. To

Section I

bring-The-Well-Message out-and-beyond you, not by another's measured already-prepared boastings. Yet the-one boasting, let-him-be-boasting in *Master*! For the-one boasting about himself, that-one is not accepted only whom *The-Master* approves.

Please bear with me in but a little foolishness and tolerating me, for I have-a-jealousy for you, a Godly-jealousy, for I committed-for-marriage you to *One-Man* presenting a chaste virgin to *The-Anointed*. But I am fearful that as The-Serpent deceived Eve with its craftiness also to-be-corrupting the sincerity of your mind about *The-Anointed*. Indeed, for if the-one-coming proclaimed a different savior that we did not teach or you obtained a spirit that was not given or different well-message which you did not receive, you have-willingly listened-and-considered. For I know I am not lacking in anything behind the most-eminent Commissioners.

For though spoken in plain language it-is not without knowledge, for we were up-front-and-hid-nothing about everything before you. Have I sinned in-humbling myself that you may-be-being-exalted since I brought the Well-Message-of-*THE-GOD* to you for-free-without-payment? I plundered other Ecclesiae to purchase-provisions toward the service of you. And when present with you and in need, I did not become-a-burden-to anyone. For my needs were supplied by The-Brother coming from Macedonia. In all things I have-not-burdened you and I shall keep on keeping myself.

In me is the-Truth-of-*Anointed*. This self-proclaimed-fact shall-not-be-silenced by me in the regions of The-Achaia. Why is that? Because I do not have Godly-love for you? *THE-GOD* knows!

That which I am doing I will continue to do. For I-will-remove-by-the-roots getting-an-opportunity-with the-ones willing to, if-the-opportunity-arises, declaring their glory to see if they are as we. For they are false commissioners, fraudulent workers, transforming themselves into commissioners of *Anointed*. And this is not an astounding-and-astonishing thing, for The-Satan himself is transformed into a messenger-of-light. Then this is not a great thing if also his servants are transformed as dispensers of justice whose complete-destruction shall be according-to their actions.

I again say, do not let anyone to-be thinking I am a fool, yet receive me as a fool as I am boasting about myself a little. For that which I-am-speaking, I am not speaking in-agreement-with *Master* but as a fool in this confidence of boasting. Since so many boast according-to their-accomplishments I also will-boast. For you put-up-with the foolish with-great-pleasure deeming-yourself-as-a-wise-one! For you-tolerate anyone enslaving you and anyone stripping-your-goods or anyone frauding, anyone exalting himself or anyone insulting-you. I'm ashamed to admit it that we (Timothy and I) don't have the strength to do those things to you. Whatever other people dare to be-fools-about I also speak in confidence.

Are they also Israelites as I? Are they also the seed of Abraham as I? Are they servants of *Anointed* as I? (I speak insanely). Am I so-far-beyond them in laboring, in beatings beyond count, jails many-more times, left dead many-times. From the Jews five times I got forty lashes minus one, three-times flogged-with-rods, stoned once, three-times shipwrecked, a day and a night in the-deep-sea, many journeys, the perils of rivers, the perils of robbers, the perils from my own countrymen, perils of swarms-of men and beasts, perils in cities, perils in the wilderness, perils in the sea, perils among false-brothers. In intense-labor-with-trouble-and-toil, many sleepless-nights, in starvation and thirst, in many fasts, left cold and naked. Apart from these external things, a troublesome-throng-of-people-are-seeking me besides the daily care-and-worry of all the Ecclesiae. Who is weak and I am not supposed to-be weak? Who is offended and I am not supposed to be-thoroughly-offended. If there-is-to-be-boasting I will out-of-necessity boast in my sickness-and-health-of-the-body. *THE-GOD* and *FATHER* of *The-Master* of us, *Savior Anointed* knows that I am not lying, *THE-ONE-BEING-BLESSED* into the eons! In Damascus, the Ethnarch of the King Aretas, garrisoned the city of Damascene desiring to arrest me and in a wicker-basket through a window I was lowered escaping the hands of him.

By-all-means let-me-continue to boast although nothing is gained, but I will now come to visions and divine-instructions of *Master*. I-knew a man in *Anointed* more than fourteen years ago, whether in the living-body or outside of the body I could not tell, *THE-GOD* knows about the-such-one being-snatched into the third Heaven. And I know this man, whether in the living-body or outside of the body I cannot tell, but *THE-GOD* knows; but he-was-snatched into Heaven and hears the-unspeakable-because-of-its-sacred declarations which no man is allowed to speak-about-and-reveal. Over such-a-one as this I-shall-boast but not about me will I-boast except about my physically-poor-conditions. If ever I-would-be-willing-to boast, I-would-not-be-a-fool, for this I state in truth but I hesitate unless anyone thinks more of me than what he sees or hears out of me. And because of the abundance of revelations so that I would not think of my being-special, there was given to me a splinter in my flesh for Satan's messenger to violently-prick-and-to also-verbally-abuse me so I-will-not-get-lifted-up. Three times I begged *The-Master* about this to withdraw-these from me. And *He* stated to me, "*My* merciful-kindness has-enough-strength for you because my power is being-perfected in weakness." With great gratification then I-shall-be-glorifying with these infirmities of mine that the-unlimited-mighty-power of *The-Anointed* may-be-tabernacling-with me. Therefore I-take-great-pleasure in infirmities, in injuries-inflicted-by-violence, in being-forced, in persecutions, in distresses for the-sake-of *Anointed* for whenever I am weakest then I am strongest.

You have-forced me to become a fool in boasting, for you are obligated to speak well of me for I am lacking nothing over the highest Commissioners, even though I am nothing.

Truly the identifying-signs of the Commissioners was performed among you with great patience, with signs and miracles and powerful-deeds. For was there anything you-were-lacking from the rest of the Ecclesiae other than I did not make-myself-a-burden on you? Deal-mercifully-with me over this injustice! Look, this is the third time I have to come to you and I will not be a burden to you, nor am I looking-for what is yours. But for you the children are not obligated to store in reserve for the parents but the parents for the children. For I would greatly-be-satisfied to spend and go-bankrupt over the souls of you even with the greater I Godly-love and I am loved less by you.

So-be-it! Still I did not burden you but since-I-am cunning I caught you in deceit! Did I take-advantage of anyone through him whom I dispatched to you? I asked Titus and sent with him The-Brother. Did Titus take advantage of you? Do we not walk-around with-the-same spirit, not in the same footprints? Again, do you think we-are-defending ourselves in front of you? We speak before *THE-GOD* through *Anointed* for all of you Beloved! For your edification! I am fearful that somehow when I come I will not be finding you as I-would-desire and you will not find me as you-are-desiring fearing-there-is still strife, jealousies, fighting, factions, obscene defamation, gossiping-and-back-biting, huge-egos, and turbulences only to come again to have *THE-GOD* humbling me in front of you. For I-shall-be-greatly-weeping for many, the-ones-having-sinned-before and not repenting for the-lusty-impure-lifestyle and prostitution and fornication which they practice.

This third time when I come it will be with the mouths of two or three witnesses with every statement being-firmly-confirmed. I-have-declared-before and I am predicting just as when I was with you the second time and being-absent, I am now writing to the-ones-having-sinned-before and to all the rest that when I come again, I will not hold-back. Since you demand proof of *Anointed* is speaking to me, *He* is not being-weak but is being-powerful among you. Even as He-was-crucified in weakness, now *He*-is-living by the unlimited-inherent-power of *GOD*. For we are also weak in *Him*, but we-shall-be-living together with-*Him* by the unlimited-inherent-power of *GOD* for you.

Examine yourselves if you are in The-Belief. Prove it! Do you not recognize yourselves that *Savior Anointed* is in you unless any of you are rejected? But I-am-hoping that you-shall-know we are not rejected.

Now I pray to *THE-GOD* you do no evil so we do-not appear to be part-of-the-same-activities. But you do the commendable-and-honorable even if we may-be as rejects. For we-are-not-able to do anything against *The-Truth* but for-the-sake-of *The-Truth*. For we-are-in-joy whenever we are-being-weak and you may-be with power. We also pray for your perfectioning. Therefore, I write these being absent so when present I should not be-chopping-off-and-removing according-to the authority *The-Master* gives to me for edification and not for demolition.

Finally, Brothers, be-rejoicing, be-perfected, be-encouraged, have the same unity-in-purpose-and-practice, be-peaceful and *THE-GOD* of the-Godly-love and of Godly-peace shall-be-with-you. Greet one another with a holy kiss. All the Holy-Ones greet you.

The-Grace of *The-Master Savior Anointed* and the Godly-love of *THE-GOD* in association of the Holy-spirit be with all of you.

II CORINTHIANS STUDY NOTES

Note: Through my many translations, I have come to believe that the phrase or associated phrasing of "inheritance" [ex: Col 1:12] accurately translated as "the-allotment" in Scripture is not a good or proper translation (i.e., inheritance). Paul makes it clear that we are to be family members (I state: royal and godly) destined to be with HIM and HE with us and we in Christ and He in us. Inheritance has an implied connotation, an accepted concept that someone has died. THE-GOD is certainly not dead, and Christ has risen to life eonian (there are times of times of times) as well. I see this as a watering down of the intent and meaning of the Scriptures and have dropped using the word *inheritance* when speaking of THE-GOD's plan and purpose for us. We are to take rulership in an active kingdom with Christ at the head of the realm and we under Him, with THE-GOD over all of us.

Note   The Greek word *agapen* translated as "love" in most translations is missing that this is Godly in nature and not of men or any other such creature. I have therefore carried the adjective to add clarity to the meaning of this word throughout this translation.

Note: In my research, nearly all translations have dropped "the" as a modifier, but the Greek word for "the" is in every text and not meant to be ignored or deleted. It is often specifically singular, and when attached to the noun, it is describing that noun as unique, one of a kind, a specific thing, the original, the one and only. It is for this reason that I carry "the" everywhere it appears in all translations. Whether of God, Jesus, Satan or any other entity, concept, or idea, the modifier "the" clears up a lot of generalized words, ideas, concepts, and entities.

Note: The root of the word *pnuemia*, translated as "spirit, wind, or breath," has no gender identity since this is a word that is neuter in gender. *Pnuemia* is an "it." The Greeks, as we of English language, often fix a gender to objects and things— for example: cars, boats, the moon, the sun. For the Greeks, *pnuemia* at times has a male gender affixed to it. *Pnuemia* in the Scriptures is never capitalized or designated as a standalone being, entity, principality, or sovereignty when used as the word "spirit." It is simply the power inherent in the

Section I

being, whether of man, or God, or Christ, or any other entity. If anything is living, "it" possesses a spirit. The "Holy-spirit" is simply the power from and of The-God, giving and renewing life and performing The-God's will.

Note: Paul constantly claims and mentions "principles, powers, authorities, sovereignties not of our world." He quite clearly claims that these beings are the ones that certainly influence and control (predominately in a negative way) the systems of this world, people of the nations, and as individuals directly. You can find this concept also contained in The Old Testament through the implications of the first commandment. This claim and the concept of the warring factions in heaven makes a fascinating study.

Note: Time periods, eons, ages, millennia, eons, and eons—I stayed true to the Greek words associated with time and what we still use today in our common language. A study of time periods is fascinating but is also an area that can cause confusion. The-God always works on some kind of a timetable, but understanding which is which and when is when is a bit of a mystery. Some timetables are only known to The-God and made clear to man at God's will.

Note What is the difference between "expectation" and "hope?" Nearly all translations adopt the word "hope" for "expectation," but Paul uses almost exclusively the word "expectation." Here is why I constantly use "expectation." Having an expectation means you have no doubt at all. It is sure and certain with no ambiguity or doubt. Having a hope means you are not 100 percent convinced and convicted. I can tell you that Paul is undeniably convinced and convicted in what he delivers and talks about. Using "hope" sends a message that there is some possibility for "wiggle room," doubt, error, or excuses.

Even worse, much of the use of the word "expectation" in Paul's writings has the modifier "the" attached to "expectation," thus forming the proper translation and singular concept of "The-Expectation." This makes "The-Expectation" an event, not a philosophy or theological premise. Not recognizing "The-Expectation" as an event will lead the reader immediately down an incorrect understanding of what is being offered or discussed.

1:8 The Greek word *thilipseos*, translated as "pressed," refers to the forging and stamping of coins, which requires great force and power to melt metal into a liquid and as much force to shape, stamp an impression, and polish for use.

1:8–10 This passage is quite a declaration of belief and trust by Paul and those in prison with him. They were fulfilling a death sentence imposed on them; they were prepared for martyrdom. They were so scared and confused that they were ready to return back to the world to avoid torturing and death until they received this divine message about God being able to resurrect them. Speculation in the passage would imply they allowed themselves to be killed

II CORINTHIANS STUDY NOTES

and left for dead only to be revived back to life. If true, what a shock and witness for the jailers, magistrates, and the entire city who would have believed them dead and gone! How far would that report have spread into the area and country concerning Paul and the others being "resurrected"?

1:10 "WHO *rescued us from such-and-so-great [such a horrendous] death and is-rescuing [a Deliverer]*" (underline mine). "*Is-rescuing*" in the Greek (*ruetai*) has a tense which includes past, present, and future. This word can properly and accurately also be translated as "deliverer, a deliver, the deliverer." One cannot avoid using "the deliverer" as a double entendre in place of "is-rescuing" to see Paul pointing his audience back to God's omnipotence, acting out His will, and letting nothing stand in the way of His purposes. I have carried "The Deliverer" into the letter formats intentionally with this knowledge.

1:14 "The-Day" refers to the specific date of Christ's return.

1:20 Paul states here that the entire "old covenant promises with its rituals, celebrations and services" were all about Christ as The Savior, The Suffering Servant, King of Kings and Lord of Lords, and all was completed by him. But notice in this verse that Paul is really giving credit, glory, and honor to God The-Father while acknowledging the preeminence of Christ.

2:7 This verse makes it clear that there were already many false preachers turning the message of God's Kingdom and the resurrection of Christ into a business for personal profit.

2:14–16 The "life giving odor" Paul is referencing would be the odors with which God found favor in the animal sacrifices. God recognized that an animal was giving up its life as a type of messiah and therefore found some comfort in the odor it was giving up in death. Just as God recognized that this "sweet life giving odor" was offered to temporarily remove sins (no Israelite just sacrificed once and was done; this was a lifelong event for all of them), we should be daily offering ourselves as a sweet fragrance and odor pleasing to God. There is an odor in life, such as the smell of a newborn child, and an odor in death and dying that is repulsive to those that have experienced such.

4:1 This "the-image of The-God" is more than physical appearance. It includes oneness in God's purpose, mind, actions, power, and *divinity* (italics mine) which you already have, recognizing and claiming Christ as your Messiah and Savior and receiving your new form/image at your resurrection. Your divinity and your "allotment" to restore the galaxies and universes was part of "The-Secret" revealed to Paul. It means that you are one in Christ, and as God looks to His right to see and talk to Christ, He is seeing and doing so with you. Those of us that are Gentiles have the same status, character, and essences of God as Christ today. We are gods, but we have not received the full measure

Section I

of this status. This is why we should fall to our knees in worship and adoration to The-God.

4:15   The translation of "increasingly greater" would be meant in mathematical terms "exponentially," off the charts, to infinity and beyond. This would also be true for verse 17.

5:1   I stayed with using "The House of Booth" and did not substitute tabernacle or temple. It should be clear from the text that your body is the temple of God. God's spirit is active and resides in you. You are therefore holy since God is holy and His spirit is holy.

5:1   Paul is setting up his audience with a prophetic statement. If not prophetic, it is certainly seeding the thought or reminding the audience that not only the physical Temple in Jerusalem was to be destroyed but our physical bodies as well, thus creating an analogy between both and the work of God with both.

5:1   Note at the end of the verse that "heavens" is plural. It implies that you will have more than one dwelling place to enjoy and use in different locations. I look forward to those "getaways" wherever they may be located.

5:2–3 Paul is reminding the audience of "The-Secret" and its consequences.

5:17   This is a verse to "hold on to your seat" for. The Greek is poorly translated in nearly all translations I conferred with and compared. And I state also poorly transposed because it also does not provide the reader with an opportunity to grasp and understand the full breadth of what is being discussed. This verse talks about beings, systems, creation, mankind, and all. You will notice I have stayed true to the Greek, keeping the modifier "The" in front of the word "Originals." They are joined and meant to be singular, an exclusive concept just as The-God, The-Death, The-Christ, the-ones.

5:17   "The-Originals have passed [perished]" is quite profound. "The-Originals" identification is multilayered and includes but is not limited to powers, principalities, entities as beings or as social groups, organizations, systems, creation, mankind (of the past) and that which man has not been made aware of. An entire series of books could be developed on this subject. All of it is perishing, to be replaced purely and in entirety by God's Kingdom as stated by Paul.

5:19   The translation of "make an account" is meant as an actual physical count. As an example, one either does or does not have actual money in a bank account.

5:21   "that we may become just [righteous with, in a condition acceptable to] with GOD in Him." Both equivalencies should cause you to pause and think. Nothing could be clearer about what God's divine will and intent is for you,

6:9 "being *disciplined* and not put to death (italics mine)." The Greek word translated as "disciplined" is *paideuomenoi*. Strong's offers as its third definition a disciplining as a father to his son, and many translations follow this line of thought in their commentaries. However, this concept is awkward and weak because "being disciplined by "a loving father," whether corporeal or by God, would not commonly be associated with "but not to death." So, what is meant in this verse? The better and more logical line of thinking is clearly being tortured and not put to death and is supported in terms of Paul's constant abusive treatment. Within verses 1–9, Paul, while directing his comments to his audience, is transposing them into his experiences. Essentially their treatment was or was to become much like Paul's. In support of this line of thinking, the following commentary by Andrew Womack Ministry[1] is quoted directly:

2 Corinthians 6:9

As unknown, and [yet] well known; as dying, and, behold, we live; as chastened, and not killed;

Note 21 at 2 Cor. 6:9: Paul was unknown, possibly in the sense of being ignored or not being acknowledged. In today's English, he might say, "I'm a nobody to some, but I'm a somebody to God" (2 Cor. 3:2; 2 Tim. 2:19). He was at the point of death many times, yet he was still alive (2 Cor. 1:8–9). He was beaten (chastened), yet miraculously preserved by God (2 Cor. 11:24–25).

The idea of Paul being neglected, abused, and beaten is as much a metaphor for us today and is in parallel with the experience of the Corinthians and all those called by God. While I have retained "disciplined," my sensibilities lean toward the concept of being tortured, not the chastening and disciplining of a caring father. We are all in a sense being "tortured but not killed" by The System in this life.

9:7 The Greek word translated as "gleeful" is the Greek *hilaros* from which we get the English "hilarious." Note that "hilarious" is a word meant to be very, very funny and ridiculous. Paul often uses the superlative sense in concepts and in his description of ideas and words.

10:15 "not by another's ruler already-prepared boastings." This obscure translation is referring to the Ecclesiae already founded and operating as well as those getting ready to be created by others, but not by Paul and his entourage.

---

1. Andrew Womack Ministry, http://www.awmi.net/bible/2co_06_09, italics added by AW Ministry.

Section I

Paul wanted nothing to do with those area ministers, given the actions of the people. He was focused intently on what he was given to care and nurture.

11:28 The Greek word *episustasis* has two distinct concepts attached to the translation. The classical rendering is "a troublesome mob seeking help, counsel, comfort," which I understand to mean a group of people incapable of making decision, frozen by fear, or lacking the mental capacity and acumen to think and act. This is brutal and brutish. I stayed with this concept in the translation. The second concept is less offensive, meaning having oversight of, paying attention to, or having care of. My reasoning for using the first is Paul is being quite blunt and direct with the Corinthians throughout Chapters 10 and 11 about their arrogance, practices, and egos. I did not interpret him as suddenly having a change of heart, a warm and fuzzy feel-good moment with the Ecclesia. These people still had huge issues.

11:33 For those who are curious, since the city of Damascene was garrisoned, there were somewhere between three hundred to one thousand soldiers hunting for Paul in order to apprehend him. His being hunted was not a casual incident at all—soldiers entered homes and businesses without asking permission, looking for him. These home and business invasions could not have endeared him to the citizenry. Yet even in his escape, the buzzing and talking that must have occurred afterward would have surely spread the reason for his being there, and thereby many became acquainted with Christ.

13:4 The Greek word *astheneias* simply translated as "weakness" in many translations misses that this is also a natural weakness inherent in the body as well as that caused by the brutal beating and stoning absorbed when being crucified. Is it a possibility Christ was not a regular robust and healthy individual during the prime of his manhood, but someone with inherent health issues before he suffered crucifixion? It is open for debate.

13:5–7 The use of the words translated as "disqualified" or "rejects" is based in the striking and making of coins. It was widely known many coins were "shaved," not having a true value in weight and materials.

II CORINTHIANS IN VERSE

II CORINTHIANS 1

1:1   Paul a Commissioner of *Savior-Anointed* through the will of *GOD* with Timotheus [God's Honor] The-Brother. To the Ecclesia of *THE-GOD*, The-Ones in Corinth together with the Holy-Ones, all the ones-being in the whole of Achaia.

1:2   Grace to you and peace from *GOD* and *FATHER* of our *Master, Savior-Anointed*.

1:3   Bless *THE-GOD* and *THE-FATHER* of *The-Master* of us *Savior-Anointed*, *The-Father*-of-*The*-Pities [Mercies] and *GOD* of all consolation,

1:4   *THE-ONE CONSOLING* us in every pressure [distress, oppression] of ours. To be enabling us to be comforting the-ones in every distress through the comforting which we ourselves are comforted by *THE-GOD*

1:5   since the sufferings [trials, oppressions] of *The-Anointed* super-abounds in us. Thus also, through *Anointed* is the consolation of us super-abounding.

1:6   When for your sake we-are-being-afflicted, it is for your consolation and salvation, we [all of us] are in-operation [experiencing] suffering with the same endurance.

1:7   For we are comforted and our expectation is in the knowledge about you. That even as participants in your distress you also have comfort.

1:8   For we are not willing for you to be ignorant, Brothers, concerning our afflictions that came to us in the (province of) Asia. That we-were-heavily-pressed [severely-persecuted] above (our) ability so-much that we had despaired hope also to be of the living [we desired to die having lost all expectation].

1:9   But the-same-answer came to us about The-Death in us [our sentence of death, our death sentence], that we are to have no confidence in ourselves but in *THE-GOD, THE-ONE-RAISING* the dead-ones.

Section I

1:10   WHO rescued us from such-and-so-great [such-a-horrendous] death and is-rescuing [a-deliverer] in WHOM we continue to rely on to rescue [deliver, is a Rescuing-Deliverer].

1:11   For our sake you assisted in petitioning [praying] for us. That from the many faces [people] came many gracious-gifts for us. May HE be-thanked because of us.

1:12   For our boasting is this, the witness of our conscience that in singleness [heartfelt-generosity] and sincerity, GOD, not with fleshly [worldly] wisdom but in GOD's grace [loving-kindness] we conducted ourselves in The-System yet more-superabundantly for you.

1:13   Now we write to you about nothing more than what you have-read or also acknowledged. For I am hoping you will read to the end

1:14   with also recognition [acknowledgment] of our boasting about you in-this-respect, as even you also about us in The-Day-of-*The-Master Savior*.

1:15   And with this confidence I intend to come to you as before that you may have a second benefit

1:16   that through you to pass into Macedonia and from Macedonia come back to you and by you to-be-sent-forward to Judea.

1:17   Was this planning done as-if in casual thought? Or is this planning for the flesh [selfish motives]? Do I intend to say yes-yes or no-no at the same time [Am I speaking out of both sides of my mouth]?

1:18   For *THE-GOD* (is) believable [faithful], our word to you was not yes and no [double-talk].

1:19   For *The-Son* of THE-GOD, *Savior Anointed*, *The-One* preached among you by us, Silvanus [Woods] and Timotheus and by me was not yes and no, but in *Him* has become yes.

1:20   For all the promises of GOD (are) about *Him* and yes, also in *Him*. AMEN and glory to *THE-GOD* from us!

1:21   Now THE-ONE-CONFORMING [uniting] us together with you in *Anointed* and THE-ONE-ANOINTING us, THE-ONE-GOD, is also (THE)-ONE-SEALING us and gave the-spirit as the down-payment in our hearts.

1:22   Moreover I invoke THE-GOD as a witness for my soul that I did not come to Corinth to spare you.

1:23   Not that we-are-mastering [lording] over your belief [faith], but we are fellow-workers of your joy for you stand by believing [faith].

II CORINTHIANS 2

2:1 For I decided by myself to not come again in sorrow [mourning, grief] to you,

2:2 for if I am making you to sorrow, who is the-one-to-gladden me but me by the-ones I made sorrowful?

2:3 And I write this again that if I come, I may have not sorrow from which I should be rejoicing and have confidence in. That is all of you; my joy is all of you.

2:4 For out of great affliction [difficulty, suffering, pain, misery] and pressure [anguish, distress] of heart I wrote to you with many tears to not make you sorrowful but that you may know the [feel the, deeply-understand the] Godly-love I have for you in super-abundance.

2:5 However, if anyone has-caused-sorrow, he has not sorrowed me, but to-some-degree-to-all (of you). I do not want to press-too-heavily on you.

2:6 The rebuke [punishment] was sufficient about this as done by the majority.

2:7 So-that rather to the contrary [continuing-the-punishment], you should deal graciously and console unless even more-excessive grief [pain, oppression] may-be-swallowed-up [overwhelm] the-such [individuals].

2:8 Therefore I entreat you to sanction [confirm publicly, make valid, return] him in Godly-love.

2:9 For in this I wrote to you that I may know with testing if you are obedient in all things.

2:10 And to whom or anything you are dealing-graciously [forgiving] also I and if I for anything have-dealt-graciously-with [forgive], I have-dealt-graciously [forgive] because of you, in face [before-the-presence] of *Anointed*

2:11 so that we-should-not-be-had [be taken advantage of] by The-Satan. For we are not ignorant about his evil-purposes.

2:12 While coming into Troas with the Well-Message-of-*The-Anointed*, a door had been opened to me by *Master*.

2:13 I had no ease in my spirit not finding Titus my brother, but taking leave from them I came into Macedonia.

2:14 But thanks to THE-GOD, to THE-ONE-ALWAYS-TRIUMPHING [granting complete success] us in *The-Anointed* and manifesting the odor [life-emitting, life-giving] Knowledge-of-*HIM* for us in every place.

2:15 For indeed we are the fragrant-odor of *Anointed* for THE-GOD as the-ones being saved and for the-ones perishing,

2:16	for who indeed is the odor of death in dying; yet the odor of life in life. Has enough been said about this?
2:17	For we are not the majority of the-ones peddling [making money selling] *The-Word*-of-*THE-GOD* but out of sincerity, rather from GOD in the sight of *THE-GOD* in *Anointed* we speak.

II CORINTHIANS 3

3:1	Do we need to again reintroduce ourselves? Do we need letters of introductions as some for you or from you introductions?
3:2	You are our letters written in our hearts known and being read by all men.
3:3	You are that letter of *Anointed* being displayed and distributed by us. Engraved not with ink but by (the) spirit of (*THE-*) *LIVING-GOD*, not on tablets of stone but on the fleshy tablets of the heart.
3:4	For we have such confidence through *The-Anointed* about *THE-GOD*.
3:5	We have no confidence in ourselves, to count ourselves as something among ourselves. But the-confidence of us is from *THE-GOD*
3:6	who also equips us as ministers of the New Covenant [compact, testament] not with letters [documents, Sacred Writings, the Law], for the Letter is killing, but the spirit gives life [causes to live, begets alive].
3:7	For if the administration of death is in the Writings having-been-chiseled in stones is so glorious, so-glorious that none of The-Sons-of-Israel was able to look at the face of Moses, how is it that glory on his face vanished?
3:8	How much greater then shall be the glory through the service [assistance, help, advantage] of-the-spirit?
3:9	For if the administration of condemnation [sentencing and carrying out of death] is glorious, how much exceedingly-greater is the administration of justice [righteousness] in glory?
3:10	For even though that which has glory, has no glory for this particular reason, because of the glory which transcends it [exceeds it, casts its shadow over it].
3:11	For if that glory has vanished, how much greater is the-one-remaining in glory?
3:12	Having then this great expectation, we use openness in speaking.
3:13	Not as Moses did, placing a veil on [by hiding, concealing] his face so that The-Sons-of-Israel could not stare-intently [gaze-and-observe] to watch the vanishing come to an end.

3:14 For their minds were blinded. And even up to this day this same covering [veil] is remaining not-being-uncovered [removed] when reading of the Old Covenant, which has-vanished [disappeared, was removed] in *Anointed*.

3:15 Even this day whenever Moses is read The-Covering [veil] is lying [buried, set] on the heart [the heart is buried under The-Covering].

3:16 And at-such-time should (one) turn back to *Master* the Covering will be lifted.

3:17 *The Master, He*-is now spirit and where the Spirit-of-*Master* (is), freedom (is) there.

3:18 And we all will mirror the glorified uncovered face of *Master*, transformed into the same likeness, from glory [a-most-glorious-condition] to glory [a-most-exalted state] just-like from the Spirit-of-*Master*.

II CORINTHIANS 4

4:1 Since we have this ministry [service] and we have-received this mercy, we do not lose courage

4:2 and spurn [renounce] those concealed vile-things [disgraceful, dishonorable], not treading [walking, participating] in cleverness [cunningness, false-wisdom], nor with deceitfulness [mingling-divine-truth-with-wrong-notions] with *The Word*-of-*THE-GOD* but to clearly show *The-Truth*, standing-together with a clear conscience in the sight of every man and THE-GOD.

4:3 For if our Well-Message is-being-covered [veiled, being-hidden], it is being veiled on the-ones perishing

4:4 on whom The-God-of-this-Eon blinds the understanding of The-Unbelieving to not radiate [be bright and shine forth] with the illumination [light, bringing to light-and-exposure] of the Well-Message of The-Glory-of-*The-Anointed* who is the-image [likeness-of-one-seen, nature and form] of THE-GOD.

4:5 For we are not heralding [preaching, announcing, calling-attention-to] us but *Anointed Savior*, and you are slaves because of *Savior*.

4:6 For THE-GOD, THE-ONE commanded out of darkness light to shine, WHO shines in the hearts of us to illuminate the Knowledge-of-The-Glory-of-*THE-GOD* in the-face [in-the-presence] of *Savior Anointed*.

4:7 And we have placed-in-the-marrow [stored deep within, as a treasury] these earthenware vessels [clay potteries], that this most-superior [far-beyond-all-measure, excellence of] power is-from THE-GOD and not out of us.

4:8	Being-afflicted [oppressed] in all but not distressed, not knowing how to decide [perplexed] but not renouncing all expectation,
4:9	being-chased [persecuted] but not abandoned, being-thrown-to-the-ground but not destroyed,
4:10	always carrying The-Death of *Master Savior* in the body, so [to show] also The-Life of *The-Savior* may-be-made-manifested in the body of us.
4:11	For we which are living are being-handed-over to Death because of *Savior* so-that the Life-of-*The-Savior* may-be-made-to-appear in the dying [mortal] flesh of us.
4:12	Yes indeed The-Death works [displays-its-activity, is-at-work] on us, but *The-Life* is in you.
4:13	Having the same spirit of The-Belief [faith] with what has been written I believe, by which I speak, by which we also believe do state [declare]
4:14	knowing that THE-ONE-ROUSING *The-Master Savior* and we through *Savior* together with you shall be-raised [resurrected] and presented [be-standing-beside-each-other, brought-into-an-intimate-fellowship].
4:15	For all of this is because of you that the-grace may be increasingly greater, thanksgiving should-be-super-abounding for the glory of THE-GOD.
4:16	Therefore we-are-not-utterly-spiritless [with-absolutely-no hope]. For even though the outward man is decaying [rotting, corrupted], nevertheless the-one inwardly is being-made-new [into a new kind of life] day by day.
4:17	For the moment the oppression of us is a light [easy, delicate to the touch] producing an exceeding-greatness beyond exceeding-greatness a weight of [vast and transcendent, an authority] of eonian [age to age, to never cease] glory.
4:18	Let us not take-note of [consider, worry about, reflect on] that being-observed but not being-seen; that observed for-the-season [temporarily, in-this-period-of-time] but not being seen eonian [in-the-future-time, the-lasting-time].

II CORINTHIANS 5

5:1	We are aware that if ever our terrestrial House-of-the-Booth [temporary dwelling, Tabernacle, The Temple] may-be-demolished [utterly-destroyed], we are to have from GOD a building, a home [dwelling, a family] not made with hands, eonian [ages to ages, age-lasting to age-lasting] in The-Heavens [starry-heavens-and-where-God-dwells].

5:2 For we-are-groaning in this habitation [body] of ours, longing [desiring, craving] to be clothed from out of heaven

5:3 since-surely we-shall-not-be-found naked [without a body] and undressed.

5:4 For we are also groaning as the-ones being weighted down in this booth [tabernacle, temple]. Not because we are-willing-to-be-unclothed but because we want to be dressed, that mortality may-be-swallowed-up by *The-Life*.

5:5 Now THE-ONE-is-PRODUCING this same in us, this GOD, THE-ONE is giving us the down payment which is the spirit.

5:6 Always have courage then and be aware that being-at-home [while-living] in this body we are away [living abroad, not in the presence, still separated] from the *Master*.

5:7 By belief [faith] we walk, not by sight

5:8 and yet we have confidence [are confidently hopeful] and prefer [desire, crave] to-be-separated from the body and dwell with *The-Master*.

5:9 And we also make it our aim [honorable duty, honorable pursuit] to greatly-be-pleased by *Him* whether present or absent.

5:10 For all of us must [are-obligated-to] appear in-front-of the Judgment-Platform-of-*The-Anointed* where everyone is to receive upon the body [glory or dishonor] for that which he-practices, whether committing good or evil.

5:11 Now knowing of the terror of *The-Master* we are persuading men. For we have been made to appear before GOD and I expect [hope] (this) also has-been-made-known in your consciences.

5:12 Again, we are not recommending ourselves to you but give [offer] you a base [resource, reason, incentive, an occasion] to boast about us so you may be boasting to the-ones in appearance [their presence] and not from the heart.

5:13 For whether we-are-besides-ourselves [insane] or are sane to you, to [we represent] *GOD*.

5:14 For the Godly-love of *The-Anointed* presses us judging [decreeing] this; that if for the sake of one all died, by reasoning all are dead.

5:15 For *He* died for the sake of all that the-ones living should no more live for themselves but for *The-One* who died for the sake-of them and is raised [arisen, now-alive].

5:16 So from the now [this day] we are not acquainted with anyone made of the flesh even though we knew *Anointed* in the flesh [in physical fleshy form], nevertheless no longer known (this way).

Section I

5:17 So understand this, if any is in *Anointed*, a new creation! The-Originals have passed [perished]; all is becoming new [a new kind, novel, unheard of]!

5:18 And all (are) out of [came-from] *THE-GOD, THE-ONE-CONCILIATING* [resolving-the-difference, making-peace] us to *HIM* through *Savior Anointed* and giving us The Service-[office of ministry]-of-The-Conciliation [making-peace and healing],

5:19 how that *GOD* was in *Anointed* resolving to bring to *HIMSELF* (the) System [world] not making-an-account [deciding to not count] the offenses [sins] of them and placing in us The-Saying-[teaching, doctrine]-of-The Conciliation.

5:20 Now then we are ambassadors for *Anointed* as *THE-GOD* called for us. We are pleading [desire, long for] on-behalf of *Anointed* for you to-be-conciliated [become one, be at peace] with *THE-GOD*.

5:21 For *The-One* not knowing [not conscious of having committed] sin was made sin for our sakes that we may become just [righteous with, in a condition acceptable to] of *GOD* in *Him*.

II CORINTHIANS 6

6:1 Now we working together also entreat you to not receive the Grace-of-*THE-GOD* for nothing [empty handed].

6:2 For *HE* says, **"I on hearing [heard, am replying] you in the acceptable [blessed, consecrated, appointed] season [time] and in The Day of Salvation, I help [bring-aid] you. Be aware, now is the accepted season [era, time-period]! Behold now is The Day of Salvation!"** [Isa 49:8]

6:3 Give no one a cause to stumble, that no flaws [blame, mocking, faults] are with the service [ministry]

6:4 but in everything stand with us as servants of *GOD* in great endurance [patience-and-perseverance], in afflictions [oppression, persecution], in distress [calamity], in extreme anguish,

6:5 in blows [stripes, whippings, lashings], in jails, during states-of disorder [instability, commotion, confusion], in labors, in vigils [watching, vigilance], in fasts,

6:6 in pureness [uprightness-of-life], in knowledge, in patience, in kindness, in Hoy-spirit, in Godly-love without-hypocrisy [sincerity].

6:7 In the word of truth, in (the) unlimited-inherent-power of GOD through the weapons [armor, warfare implements] of-the-just [righteousness] to the right and the left.

6:8	Through glory and disgrace, through defamation and good praise, by deceivers [corrupters, imposters] or true [truthful],
6:9	as unknowns or recognized, as dead and yet know we are living! Being disciplined [tortured] and not put to death,
6:10	with sorrow yet always rejoicing, destitute yet enriching many, as having nothing yet possessing all.
6:11	We have opened our mouths [spoken frank and openly] to you Corinthians! Our hearts have been enlarged [embraced you in Godly-love].
6:12	You are not being stressed by us, but you are distressed in your bowels [your own distresses have left us no place in your heart].
6:13	As a fair exchange [In return], I speak as to offspring [my children], I speak [ask, request] you also to be broadened [open your hearts].
6:14	Do not be equally-yoked to unbelievers. For what partnership has justice [righteousness] with lawlessness? And what communion [association] light with darkness?
6:15	And what agreement [unity, harmony, treaty, pact, business arrangement, legal matter] does *Anointed* with Belial [Without a Master, Yokeless, Worthless]? Or what part a believer with an unbeliever?
6:16	And what agreement [association, purpose, service] does The-Temple-of-GOD [Godly-worship] have with idols [idol-worship]? For you are the Temple-of-GOD. As *THE-Living-GOD* said, **"That-I-shall-be-making-*MY*-home in them"** and **"*I*-shall-be-walking-with-them"** and **"*I*-will-be their *GOD*,"** and **"they will-be *MY* people."** [Ezek 37:26, 27; Jer 32:38; Lev 26:12; Jer 31:33]
6:17	Therefore, **"Come out from the midst of them and be-severed [cut and completely removed] says *Master*. "Do not touch the unclean and I shall-be-admitting [receive kindly, treat with favor] you,"** [Isa 52:11]
6:18	and **"*I*-will-be to you a father,"** and, **"You shall-be to *ME* sons and daughters says *MASTER ALMIGHTY* [Ruler of All]."** [Jer 31:1, 9]

II CORINTHIANS 7

7:1	Now having these promises, Beloved, we-should-be-cleansing ourselves from every pollution [defilement] of flesh and by spirit completing [perfecting, executing, accomplishing] holiness in fear of *GOD*.
7:2	Make room for us; we have injured no one, we have not corrupted [forced to fall away] anyone, we have not taken advantage of anyone.

Section I

7:3   I speak to not condemn you, for I-declared-before you are in our hearts and with you to-be-dying-together and to-be-living-together.

7:4   My great boldness [confidence, assurance] is in you; my boasting is great over you. I-have-been-completely-filled with consolation [comfort, encouragement] and with super-abundant joy with every distress on us [we have]

7:5   for even after our entering Macedonia no one had eased our flesh [taken care of us] for everywhere on-the-outside [all around] is affliction [distress], fears [dreads, terrors] within.

7:6   But THE-ONE-CALLING [comforting, encouraging] the-low [humbled, discouraged, down-cast] encouraged us, THE-GOD, with the presence of Titus,

7:7   and not only with the presence of him but also by the encouragement by which he was encouraged by you telling him about your vehemently-desiring and wailing [lamenting, mourning] over us, your boiling [zeal] over me and so that I would rejoice [find favor with everyone again for doing the correct things].

7:8   Even though I am sorry for the letter, I do not care [repent, regret-it] even though I did regret-it, for I perceive that this letter threw you into sorrow even if at the point-in-time.

7:9   Now I am rejoicing, not because I made you sorrowful, but that you-were-sorrowful to repentance. For according-to GOD you should not-be-being-fined for [sustain-damage, suffer-loss-over] nothing by us

7:10   as the sorrow of THE-GOD produces a-changed-mind for salvation not-to-be-repented-of, yet The-System's sorrow produces death.

7:11   Understand this, this same (sorrow) by THE-GOD causing you to be sorry, how great was the earnestness [striving-to-accomplish] in you, not arguing [in-defense-of-one-self], not resenting [in-indignation], not fearing, with vehement-desire with zeal, not in vengeance. You have shown yourselves to-be pure in everything in this matter.

7:12   For this reason I wrote to you. Not to be the one injuring neither as the one injured but because we wanted to show our earnestness over you in the sight of THE-GOD for you.

7:13   Because of this we have-been-encouraged [strengthened] in the cheer-coming-from you, and even greater have we rejoiced in the joy of Titus that his spirit has-been-refreshed [soothed, calmed] by all of you.

7:14   And if in anything I-have-boasted to him about you, I was not disgraced. For in all truth we spoke about you [openly-shared-all-the-information] and also to you the-boasting concerning Titus was done in truth.

7:15 And his compassions for you is greatly-deepened and in remembering all of your obedience [compliance, submission] receiving him having fear and trembling.

7:16 I-am-certainly-rejoicing having confidence in everything about you.

II CORINTHIANS 8

8:1 Further we-are-making-known to you, Brothers, The-Grace-of-*THE-GOD* having-been-given by the Ecclesiae of Macedonia.

8:2 During a great test [trial] of persecution with a super-abundance of the-joy in them and while in their deep poverty gave generously [abundantly] of their riches [possessions].

8:3 I-am-testifying [bearing record] about that ability and going-above-and-beyond their own ability

8:4 with great insisting and pleading for us to receive the-gracious-gifts in fellowship and service for the Holy-Ones [saints].

8:5 And not as we expected but giving themselves first to *The-Master* and to us by the will of *GOD*.

8:6 So we encouraged Titus that what he started, this he should also complete with you with this gracious-gifting [loving-kindness, favor].

8:7 For as you are super-abounding in all, belief [faith] and doctrine [teaching] and knowledge and all diligence and out of your Godly-love for us that also in this you may super-abound in The-Grace.

8:8 I do not speak this as an injunction [legal decision, order, command] but because of the accomplishment of others and to-examine if your Godly-love is genuine.

8:9 For you know The-Grace-of-*The-Master* of us *Savior Anointed* being rich [wealthy in material resources] but because of you became-afflicted [was-a-beggar, was-poor, reduced-to-nothing] that *The-One* in poverty should be making you rich [wealthy in virtue and eternal possessions].

8:10 Now I am giving this opinion for this is profitable for you who has not only started but was willing to do this from a year ago

8:11 that you also do (this) and complete (it) with even the same eagerness and willingness and also bring it to an end with what you have.

8:12 For if the willingness is there, what anyone has is acceptable, not what he does not have.

Section I

8:13　Not to ease [relieve, omit, discharge] others and afflict [burden, make-it-difficult-for] you but out of equity [fairness] for the current season [because of the current time, situation] from your excess for those in want [need].

8:14　Then also the excess of those may come to the needs for you, in this it becomes equal [fair].

8:15　As it is written, **"The-one with much does not increase [has nothing left over] and the-one with less [little] is not-inferior [is not lacking]."** [Exod 16:18]

8:16　But thanks to *THE-GOD*, *THE-ONE*-GIVING this same earnestness [care and diligence] over you is in the heart of Titus.

8:17　For indeed, he in-great-eagerness received [accepted] this request and out of his own willingness he came to you.

8:18　And with him we sent together The-Brother who is praised through-out all the Ecclesiae for the Well-Message.

8:19　Not only that, but also selected [appointed by vote] by the Ecclesiae to travel with us with the-grace [gracious-gifts]. This being administered [carried] by us for *The-Master* with this same glory and eagerness [readiness-of-mind] in you

8:20　taking care of that no flaws [no mocking, blame] should be found in anyone of us for this bountiful-collection being served [carried and supplied] through us.

8:21　Taking-thought-for [being careful to do] the ideal [honorable] not only in the sight of *Master* but also the-sight-of men.

8:22　And we-have-sent-them-with The-Brother whom we tested often diligently [watching intently, scrutinizing] in many things and now with greater-diligence and greater confidence in you.

8:23　Whether for the sake of my partner Titus and in your fellow-workers or our Brothers the Commissioners [apostles] of The Ecclesiae, the Glory-of-*Anointed*.

8:24　Display [Show, demonstrate, prove] to them then the-Godly-love of you and about our boasting over you; show this before the Ecclesiae.

II CORINTHIANS 9

9:1　Concerning the service to the Holy-Ones, there is no need to write more to you.

II CORINTHIANS IN VERSE

9:2   I am aware of your eagerness. I have boasted about you to the Macedonians that Achaia was prepared over a year ago, and because of that your zeal provokes many.

9:3   Still I have sent The-Brothers that our boasting over you is considered empty for this reason, that as I said you-may-be-ready

9:4   unless somehow the Macedonians may get together with me and find you unprepared.

9:5   Therefore I-deemed it necessary to prepare The-Brothers coming into your presence and have-made-adjustments-beforehand for these stated blessings of yours out of your bounty and not as-a-matter-of-covetousness [giving expecting something greater back].

9:6   However, the-one sowing sparingly, sparingly shall also reap, and the-one sowing bountifully with bountifulness shall also reap.

9:7   Each as he-has-purposed from the heart, not with a grudge [a-soured-mind] or out of compulsion [out-of-being-shamed] for *THE-GOD* Godly-loves the gleeful [hilarious, joyous] giver.

9:8   For *THE-GOD* is able to lavish all grace [favors, rewards, benefits] on you that in every and all having contentment to super-abound in every good action.

9:9   As it is written: **"<u>HE scatters, HE-gives to the poor, the righteousness of HIM remains into the eons."</u>** [Ps 12:9]

9:10   For *THE-ONE* supplying the seed to the sower and *THE-ONE* furnishing food and bread and multiplying the-seed of you and may-*HE*-grow the produce of virtue [righteousness producing benefits, integrity, acceptable to God].

9:11   Being-enriched in every and all which produces through us thanksgiving to *THE-GOD*.

9:12   For this administration of service is not only replenishing the needs of the Holy-ones but also super-abounds [increases-in-its-blessings] by giving many thanks to *THE-GOD*.

9:13   By the-proof-[demonstration]-of this service, glorifying [praising, extolling] *THE-GOD* and defending your vow of the Well-Message of *The-Anointed* by generosity with the-contribution to them and to all [everyone].

9:14   Also by their prayers over you, longing [out-of-godly-love] for you because of the over-casting [exceeding, surpassing] grace of *THE-GOD* on you.

9:15   And grace [thanks] to *THE-GOD* for the un-detailed [unspeakable, indescribable, where-words-fail] gift from *HIM*.

Section I
II CORINTHIANS 10

10:1 Now I, Paul, personally call-on you in the meekness and gentleness of *The-Anointed* who when present am indeed the least [lowest-rank] among you but in absence with courage [directness and bluntness] to you.

10:2 Still I-long [desire] to not have to rely on this courage [directness and bluntness] when present for I am thinking to challenge any of the-ones believing us as walking according-to [after] the flesh [our-passions-and-lusts].

10:3 Even though we walk in flesh, we are not warring against flesh.

10:4 For the implements of the-warfare of us (are) not of-the-flesh but *THE-GOD*, powerfully-able to pull-down bulwarks [fortresses, strongholds],

10:5 pulling-down logic [argument] and every elevated-thing [offensive-rampart, highly–opinionated-thing, arrogant-obstacle] elevated [raised-up, thrust] against The-knowledge-of-*THE-GOD* and taking captive every thought into obedience for *The-Anointed*

10:6 and have in readiness [being-prepared] to avenge [vindicate-protect-defend] every disobedience [unwillingness to listen] whenever your obedience is fulfilled.

10:7 Are-you-looking [judging] as at [based-on] the-face [external surface, physical appearance]? If any has-confidence about himself belonging to *Anointed*, let him-consider-this again about himself! That as he is of *Anointed*, so also we *Anointed's*.

10:8 For although I could boast more-excessively concerning our authority, for that I-will-not-be-shamed which *The-Master* gives us for edification and not to pull [demolish, extinguish] you down.

10:9 I do not want to think I am trying-throw-you-into-a-violent-fright with the letters.

10:10 Indeed, they-are-saying the letters are heavy [stern] and powerful [carry-great-force] even though when seen his body is weak but his speaking is forcibly-sure.

10:11 Let such a one think this that sure-as writing by letters and while absent we are also able to act [do-so, perform, deliver] while present.

10:12 For we are not daring to be judged by or be compared to some of the-ones introducing [recommending, accrediting, giving-credit-to] themselves. For they themselves measure themselves and compare themselves to themselves with no understanding.

10:13 For we are not without being-beyond-measure but boast with the-measure of The-Ruler-of-*THE-GOD* which distributes [divides, imparts] and measures for [each of] us, a measure [ruler] able-to-reach as-far-as also you.

10:14 For we are not over-stretching out-reaching ourselves, for we have come as-far-as you out-reaching others in the Well-Message-of-*The-Anointed*.

10:15 Not in the immeasurable boasting of other's toils but having expectation [hope] of growing-up in The-Belief [faith] of you, to be highly-esteemed among you according-to the Rule [standard, living, principles-of-living, "Golden Rule"] in super-abundance.

10:16 To bring the Well-Message out-and-beyond [areas, regions] you, not by an-other's ruler already-prepared boastings.

10:17 Yet the-one boasting, let-him-be-boasting in *Master*!

10:18 For the-one accrediting [boasting about] himself, that-one is not accepted only whom *The-Master* approves.

II CORINTHIANS 11

11:1 Please bear with me in but a little foolishness and tolerating me,

11:2 for I have-a-jealousy for you, a Godly jealousy, for I betrothed [committed-for-marriage] you to *One-Man* presenting a chaste virgin to *The-Anointed*.

11:3 But I am fearful that as The-Serpent beguiled [deceived] Eve with its craftiness also to-be-corrupting the sincerity of your mind about *The-Anointed*.

11:4 Indeed, for if the-one-coming proclaimed a different savior that we did not teach or you obtained a spirit that was not given or different well-message which you did not receive, you have-willingly put-up-with-it [listened, considered].

11:5 For I know I am not lacking in anything behind the most-eminent Commissioners [apostles].

11:6 For though spoken in plain language [as if literate] it-is not without knowledge for we were in plain-view [up-front, hid-nothing] about everything before you.

11:7 HaveIsinnedin-humblingmyselfthatyoumay-be-being-exaltedsinceIbrought the Well-Message-of-*THE-GOD* to you freely [for-free-without-payment]?

11:8 I despoiled [plundered, robbed] other Ecclesiae to purchase-provisions toward the service of you.

Section I

11:9 And when present with you and in need, I did not encumber [become-a-burden-to] anyone. For my needs were supplied by The-Brother coming from Macedonia. In all things I have-not-burdened you and I shall keep on keeping myself.

11:10 In me is The-Truth-of-*Anointed*. This boast [self-proclaimed-fact] shall-not-be-silenced by me in the regions of The-Achaia.

11:11 Why is that? Because I do not have Godly-love for you? *THE-GOD* knows!

11:12 That which I am doing I will continue to do. For I-will-hewn-down [remove-by-the-roots] finding-the-occasion [getting-an-opportunity-with] of the-ones willing to, upon the occasion [if-the-opportunity-arises], declaring their glory (to see) if they are as we.

11:13 For they are false commissioners, fraudulent workers, transforming themselves into commissioners of *Anointed*.

11:14 And this is not a marvelous [astounding, astonishing] thing for The-Satan himself is transformed into a messenger of light.

11:15 Then this is not a great thing if also his servants are transformed as dispensers of justice [righteousness] whose finish [demise, end-of-life, complete-destruction] shall be according-to their actions [works].

11:16 I again say, do not let anyone to-be thinking I am a fool, yet receive me as a fool as I am boasting about myself a little.

11:17 For that which I-am-speaking, I am not speaking in-agreement-with *Master* but as a fool in this confidence of boasting.

11:18 Since so many boast according-to the-flesh [their-accomplishments] I also will-boast.

11:19 For you put-up-with the foolish with-relish [great-pleasure] deeming-yourself-as-a-wise-one!

11:20 For you-tolerate anyone enslaving you and anyone devouring [stripping-your-goods] or anyone frauding [swindling, running-a-deceitful-scam-or-hoax], anyone exalting (himself) or anyone slapping your face [insulting-you].

11:21 I'm ashamed to admit it that we (Timothy and I) don't have the strength to do those things to you. Whatever other people dare to be-fools-about [brag-about] I also speak in confidence.

11:22 Are they also Israelites as I? Are they also the seed of Abraham as I?

11:23 Are they servants of *Anointed* as I? (I speak insanely). Am I so-far-beyond them in laboring, in beatings beyond count, jails many-more times, left dead many-times.

11:24	From the Jews five times I got forty (lashes) minus one,
11:25	three-times flogged-with-rods, stoned once, three-times shipwrecked, a day and a night in-the-deep-sea,
11:26	many journeys, the perils of rivers, the perils of robbers, the perils from (my) breed [own countrymen], perils of swarms-of men and beasts, perils in cities, perils in the wilderness, perils in the sea, perils among false-brothers.
11:27	In intense-labor-with-trouble-and-toil, many vigils [sleepless-nights], in famine [starvation] and thirst, in many fasts, left cold and naked.
11:28	Apart from these external, a troublesome-throng-of-people-seeking me besides the daily anxiety [care, worry] of all the Ecclesiae.
11:29	Who is weak and I am not (suppose) to-be weak? Who is offended and I am not (suppose) to be-on-fire [thoroughly-offended, thoroughly-mad-and-disgusted]?
11:30	If there-is-to-be-boasting I will bind-it [out-of-necessity] boast in my infirmities [sickness-and-health-of-the-body].
11:31	*THE-GOD* and *FATHER* of *The-Master* of us, *Savior Anointed* knows that I am not lying, *THE-ONE-BEING-BLESSED* into the eons!
11:32	In Damascus the Ethnarch [governor] of the King Aretas [Agreeable, Virtuous] garrisoned the city of Damascene desiring to arrest me
11:33	and in a wicker-basket through a window I was lowered escaping the hands of him.

II CORINTHIANS 12

12:1	By-all-means let-me-continue to boast although nothing is gained but I will now come to visions and revelations [divine-instructions] of *Master*.
12:2	I-knew a man in *Anointed* more than fourteen years ago, whether in the living-body or outside of the body I could not tell, *THE-GOD* knows about the-such-one being-snatched into the third Heaven.
12:3	And I know this man, whether in the living-body or outside of the body I cannot tell, but *THE-GOD* knows
12:4	but he-was-snatched into The-Park [pleasure ground, Heaven, Eden] and hears un-declarable [the-unspeakable-because-of-its-sacredness] declarations which no man is allowed to discuss [tell, speak-about, reveal].
12:5	Over such-a-one as this I-shall-boast but not about me will I-boast except about my weaknesses [physically-poor-conditions].

Section I

12:6   If ever I-would-be-willing-to boast I-would-not-be-a-fool, for this I state in truth [fact] but I abstain [hesitate] unless anyone thinks more of me than what he sees or hears out of me.

12:7   And because of the abundance of revelations so that I would not think of my being-special, there was given to me a splinter in my flesh for Satan's messenger to violently-prick-and-to also-verbally-abuse me so I-will-not-get-lifted-up.

12:8   Three times I begged *The-Master* about this to withdraw-these from me.

12:9   And *He* stated to me, "*My* grace [favor, merciful-kindness] is-sufficient [has-enough-strength] for you because my power is being-perfected in weakness." With great gratification then I-shall-be-glorifying with these infirmities of mine that the-unlimited-mighty-power of *The-Anointed* may-be-tabernacling-with me.

12:10   Therefore I-take-great-pleasure in infirmities, in injuries-inflicted-by-violence, in being-forced, in persecutions, in distresses for-the-sake-of *Anointed* for whenever I am weakest then I am strongest.

12:11   You have-forced me to become a fool in boasting, for it-is-owed by you [you are obligated] to stand-with [speak well of, laud] me for I am lacking nothing over the highest [chief] Commissioners [apostles], even though I am nothing.

12:12   Truly the identifying-signs of the Commissioners was performed among you with great patience, with signs and miracles and powerful-deeds.

12:13   For was there anything you-were-lacking from the rest of the Ecclesiae other than I did not make-myself-a-burden on you. Deal-mercifully-with me over this injustice!

12:14   Look, this is the third time I have to come to you and I will not be a burden to you, nor am I looking-for (what is) yours. But for you the children are not obligated to be hoarding [accumulating riches, store in reserve] for the parents but the parents for the children.

12:15   For I would greatly-be-satisfied to spend and go-bankrupt over the souls of you even with the greater I Godly-love and I am loved less by you.

12:16   So-be-it! Still I did not burden you but since-I-am cunning, I caught you in deceit!

12:17   Did I gain [take-advantage-of] of anyone through him whom I dispatched to you?

12:18   I asked Titus and sent with him The-Brother. Did Titus take advantage of you? Do we not walk-around with-the-same spirit, not in the same footprints?

12:19   Again, do you think we-are-defending ourselves in front of you? We speak before *THE-GOD* through *Anointed* for all of you Beloved! For your edification!

12:20   I am fearful that somehow when I come, I will not be finding you as I-would-desire and you will not find me as you-are-desiring fearing-there-is still strife, jealousies, fighting, factions, obscene defamation, whispering [gossiping, back-biting], huge-egos (and) turbulences

12:21   only to come again to have THE-GOD humbling me in front of you. For I-shall-be-greatly-weeping for many, the-ones-having-sinned-before and not repenting for the-uncleanliness [lusty-impure-lifestyle] and prostitution and fornication which they practice.

II CORINTHIANS 13

13:1   This third time when I come, it will be with the mouths of two or three witnesses with every statement being-firmly-confirmed [established, ratified].

13:2   I-have-declared-before and I am predicting just as when I was with you the second time and being-absent, I am now writing to the-ones-having-sinned-before and to all the rest that when I come again I will not spare [hold-back].

13:3   Since you demand proof of *Anointed* is speaking to me, *He* is not being-weak but is being-powerful among you.

13:4   Even as He-was-crucified in weakness now *He*-is-living by the unlimited-inherent-power of *GOD*. For we are also weak in *Him*, but we-shall-be-living together with-*Him* by the unlimited-inherent-power of *GOD* for you.

13:5   Examine yourselves if you are in The-Belief [faith]. Prove it! Do you not recognize yourselves that *Savior Anointed* is in you unless any of you are disqualified [rejected]?

13:6   But I-am-hoping that you-shall-know we are not rejected.

13:7   Now I pray to THE-GOD you do no evil so we do not appear to be accepted [part of the same activities]. But you do the excellent [commendable, honorable] even if (we) may-be as rejects.

13:8   For we-are-not-able to do anything against *The-Truth* but for-the-sake-of *The-Truth*.

13:9   For we-are-in-joy whenever we are-being-weak and you may-be able [have strength, with power]. We also pray for your perfectioning.

13:10   Therefore I write these being absent so when present I should not be-severing [cutting off, removing, chopping off] according-to the authority *The-Master* gives to me for edification and not for destruction [demolition].

Section I

13:11 Finally, Brothers, be-rejoicing, be-perfected, be-encouraged, have the same mind [unity-in-purpose-and-practice], be-peaceful and *THE-GOD* of the-Godly-love and of Godly-peace shall-be-with-you.

13:12 Greet one another with a holy kiss.

13:13 All the Holy-ones greet you.

13:14 The-Grace of *The-Master Savior Anointed* and the Godly-love of *THE-GOD* in association of the Holy-spirit (be) with all of you.

(This second letter was written to the Corinthians, written from Philippi in Macedonia through Titus and Lucas)

GALATIANS COMMENTARY

GALATIANS, THE FOURTH BOOK in the Sacred Order, is a most monumental letter. This letter, while still corrective in nature, continues the theme of being a legal brief by summarizing all three of the first letters by Paul. Paul plainly explains in simplest terms the best and most direct reasons, causes, and instructions for the Body of Christ concerning your rights, behavior, expectations, and defense of The-Belief, Christ as the Savior. In a court of law this letter would be called an affidavit, a printed statement under oath, a case law or legal precedent. You can consider it a review of the Galatians' contract (and yours) with God.

Galatians, however, is monumental for other purposes, and it directly affects you because this letter is *the* letter of Declaration of Independence and Freedom-in-Christ. It is akin to the United States Declaration of Independence, only it is founded in justice and righteousness through Christ and God. It is stated so directly. Freedom has been the underlying theme in Romans and Corinthians. Freedom—you, a son or daughter of God, are not chained to the institutions and empty practices of the Systems of this world and its Rulers. They are dead and being removed. This includes all legal and religious restrictions; claims of ownership whether of souls or physical body; demands of obedience and forced or expected payments; restricted privileges and rights; the captivity, removal, and control over the lusts of the flesh; and perhaps greatest of all, the captivity and overpowering of The-Death and his death grip on you while in the flesh. They all are being removed "off the books" along with the replacement of the governing entities and Beings (seen and unseen) today. They have no authority over you and have been replaced in authority and dominion by The Just and Righteous High Priest and Messiah, Anointed Savior, The-Master, and The-God Himself—and all of this as a divine-gift from God The-Father. You cannot earn it or deserve it, but this divine-gift of freedom through God's spirit has been given to you. It is staggering to reflect and meditate on. You are alive and free only because of Christ's sacrifice and Godly-love, and you and I owe all praise, honor, and glory to God for having created Him for us within God's purpose and will. Paul claims you have "Diplomatic Immunity" and represent another Kingdom and Government, even though you dwell in your time and place in the current System in which God has placed you. Because you still exist in the flesh, however, you cannot do anything you please since

Section I

you still do represent another Kingdom, another government. Even diplomatic immunity only goes so far.

Galatians is monumental for at least another equal reason: freedom, as staggering and stupendous as it may be, does not compare to the second divine-gift being handed to you freely by God in his will and purpose. Paul has told us we will have the very divine nature and character of God! Think about this. This is what gives you that freedom. This would be a pale comparison to the Constitution of the United States defining your rights, freedoms, responsibilities, and expected behavior. For anyone who has read Galatians 5:22–23, Paul could not state any more plainly or simply what is contained within these two verses. Paul defines for us the very nature and behavior of God and what we are to be like in His Kingdom; we are to practice and live by these "Principles of Living," our "Constitution," while in the flesh. We are certain to be and do so as spirit beings.

Galatians is the defining letter of the highest order of basic principles and what the ABCs of the Gospel are all about. It explains freedom from the restrictions in and of this life and your eventual nature, what your behavior should and will be, and your rank and purpose within God's Kingdom. In five short chapters Paul sweeps across all the topics of Romans and Corinthians and sums up all four books' purpose in Galatians 5:14. Everything in Galatians in one way or another supports this Scripture and what it intends. All of us are called and commanded to do this; Galatians 5:14 is our oath and allegiance to God within His Kingdom.

As a general review, Galatians, after the general introduction, presents the following themes that can be found in Romans and Corinthians. Each topic is a legal review with supporting facts and arguments being addressed.

- Paul's credentials and authority. He respects no man including Peter's or John's or James' position in the Ecclesia, or for that matter, anyone coming out of Jerusalem claiming the Law and circumcision.
- Salvation by believing (this is the contract we accept as sons and daughters of God) as Abraham did, not by works, not by circumcision and not by The Law of Moses.
- The sacrifice of Christ as a man in the flesh today, now resurrected, and what that does and means for you.
- True freedom comes by believing, and in this freedom, you can control and conquer the desires of the flesh and stand as equals in The Kingdom (the "Declaration of Independence").
- The promise of becoming an Enjoyer of The Allotment of The Kingdom of God
- The spirit and nature of God and eventually yours (your "Constitutional" nature, behavior, and rights). [/BL 1–6]

Few books in the Bible offer such clarity, directness, and the best points of arguments and facts defending and supporting the doctrines of Christ as the Savior; The-Belief; the Coming Kingdom, how to treat one another; and so plainly the nature, character, quality, and behavior of God, The-One we should all mimic. This is a book that cannot be examined, reviewed, and studied enough, in my opinion. I hope you see this letter with a completely new and astonishing perspective, a new point of view, and a deeper appreciation for where it belongs in the Sacred Order, for what it tells you, and for its deep profoundness.

So closes the first principles of the foundations of Paul's ministry and teachings for the Nations. These are the arguments and debates we should be able exercise and use as called on by God to support and defend His causes and purposes. Mathematically we are moving out of simple addition, subtraction, multiplication, and division and have been given the elements of algebra and geometry in preparation for calculus. But God is not stagnant, and neither is the Body of Christ. We move on to the next phase of the Gospel in the most mature teachings provided to the Ecclesiae and the next letters in the Sacred Order.

GALATIANS AS A LETTER

PAUL, COMMISSIONER, NOT FROM men or through men but through *Savior-Anointed* and *FATHER GOD, THE-ONE-ROUSING Him* out of the dead-ones and all Brothers, the-ones together with me, to The-Called-Outs of Galatia.

Grace to you and peace from *FATHER GOD* and *Master* of us *Savior-Anointed*. *The-One-Giving* himself for the-sake-of our sins so that *He-May-Be-Extricating* us out of the present wicked eon according-to the-will of *THE-GOD* and *FATHER* of us to *WHOM* be the-esteem into the-eons of the-eons.

Amen.

I-am bewildered-by how swiftly you-are-being-transferred from *THE-ONE-CALLING* you in the grace of *Anointed* into a different well-message which is really-nothing-new-or-different. For not few are the ones-agitating-and-creating-distress with you and desiring to reclaim you from the Well-Message-of-the-*Anointed*. Pay attention, if ever we or an angel out of heaven should-be-bringing-a well-message to you from what we-brought to you, let him be bound-under-a-curse! As we-have-declared-before and repeating again I-am-pronouncing if anyone is-bringing-a-well message to you different from what you accepted let him be bound-under-a-curse!

For whom am I currently trying to persuade? Men or *THE-GOD*? For if I am seeking to be accommodating-other-men's-desires, then I never pleased or was I a slave of *Anointed*. But I am certifying-and-declaring to you, Brothers, the Well-Message that was preached to me, that it is not from men. For I neither accepted it nor was taught from men but by divine-instructions from *Savior-Anointed*. For you heard of my deeds-and-actions when I was in Judaism how that I persecuted beyond-reason-and-beyond-measure The-Ecclesia-of-*THE-GOD* and ravaged her. Because of this I was progressing in The-Judaism beyond many of the contemporaries in the-lineage of mine having an above-and-beyond zealousness in the "inherited traditions" of The-Fathers of mine.

But when it-was-the-correct-time-for *THE-GOD, THE-ONE-SEVERING* me out of the womb of my mother and calling through the grace of *HIM*, to reveal *The-Son*-of-*HIM* to me that I may-be-bringing-The-Well-Message-of-*Him* among The-Nations. Immediately I did not consult-or-conference with flesh and blood, neither went I back to Jerusalem to The-Ones, the Commissioners prior to me, but I went to Arabia and again I returned to Damascus. Once there, after three years I came back to Jerusalem to relate my story to Peter, and I stayed with him fifteen days. But I did not get-introduced-to any different Commissioners except James, the-brother-of-*The-Master*.

Pay attention to what I am writing to you! As-a-witness-before *THE-GOD* that I am not lying! After that I came to the regions of Syria and Cilicia. And since I was unknown by appearance to The-Called-Outs of Judea in *The-Master* but only by-what-was-being-told, that the one-persecuting us at-one-time now is-bringing the Well-Message-of-The-Belief where once he-ravaged. And they glorified with me *THE-GOD*.

Then after fourteen years I went up again to Jerusalem with Barnabas, taking along with me also Titus. And I went up in acknowledgment-of a divine-instruction and presented-before them the Well-Message which I am proclaiming to The-Nations on my own privately, to The-ones-of-Reputation, unless somehow I may be racing or ran for nothing. For not even Titus who was with me, a Greek, was not compelled to be circumcised.

But because of the-false-Brothers who-smuggled-in, who crept in to spy out The-Freedom of ours which we have in *Anointed-Savior* so-that they should be bringing-us-back-into-bondage. To whom we did not even for one hour yielded to demanded-obedience that the truth of the Well-Message should be continuing with you. But for ones-believing-they-had-some-kind-of-reputation, whoever they once were, they were nothing of any consequence to me. *GOD* has no regard for men. For the ones-thinking-they-were-someone, added nothing to me but seeing to the contrary that I-have-been-entrusted with the Well-Message to The-Uncircumcision as Peter is to The-Circumcision. For *THE-ONE-OPERATING* in Peter with the commission to The-Circumcision operates also in me for The-Nations. And knowing The-Grace being given to me, James and Cephas and John, The-Ones-considered-as pillars, gave to me and Barnabas the-right-hand of fellowship that us to The-Nations and them to The-Circumcision with-only that we-may-be-remembering the poor which I also endeavor to do this same thing.

However, when Peter came to Antioch, I confronted him, personally finding fault with him. For before the-appearance of some from James, he ate together with The-Nations and after those coming from James, he in-fear-disavowed and cut-off himself fearing the-ones of Circumcision. And playing the hypocrite was the-rest of the Jews with him so-that even Barnabas also was submitting-one's-self-to-the-lowly-conditions of those of The-Hypocrisy! For when I realized that they-were-not acting uprightly about the truth of the Well-Message, I said to Peter in front of all, "If you being-born-and-reared-as a Jew are living like The-Nations and not as a Jew, why are you compelling The-Nations to be living like a Jew? We are Jews by birth and not sinners from The Nations. We-know that a man is not being justified by works nor even by the Law but through belief in *Savior-Anointed*. Also, we believe in *Anointed-Savior* that we-may-be-justified by The-Belief of *Anointed* and not by works of the Law because no flesh shall-be-justified out of the works of the Law. For if we were found seeking to

Section I

be justified in *Anointed* and we-ourselves were-discovered-and-examined as sinners, is the-conclusion-that *Anointed* is a dispenser of sins? No Way! For if I utterly-raze what I am building, I am proving-and-establishing myself a transgressor. For through the Law I am dead in the Law that I-should-be-living to *GOD*. I-have-been-crucified-together with *Anointed* and I am no longer living but *Anointed* in me. Even though now I am living in the flesh, I-am-living by belief in *The-Son*-of-*THE-GOD*, *The-One-Loving* me and giving *Himself* up for the sake of me. I am not denying-or-refusing the-Grace-of-*THE-GOD* for if righteousness is through the Law the-conclusion-is *Anointed* unnecessarily-and-without-a-cause has died."

Oh, foolish Galatians! Who put-a spell-on you that are not to-be-being-confident-about-the-truth? Before you it has been clearly and openly demonstrated what was-written-before for you of *Savior-Anointed* having-been-crucified. I am willing to-be-taught only this from you. Did you get the-spirit from works of the Law or by believing after hearing it? How foolish that you started-off-with the spirit, now you-are-being-made-whole-and-sinless by the flesh!? Did you suffer so much without-cause-or-purpose if surely it was for nothing? *THE-ONE* then supplying you the-spirit and operating in inherent-divine-mighty-power among you, is it done by the works of the Law or by believing by hearing? Even Abraham believes *THE-GOD* and it is accounted to him as righteousness.

Therefore understand-and-realize that The-Ones by-believing, these are the Sons-of-Abraham and The-Scripture knew-before that *THE-GOD-IS-JUSTIFYING* The-Nations by-believing by delivering The-Well-Message to The-Abraham "that in you shall-be-being-blessed all The-Nations." So that The-Ones by-believing are-being-blessed together with The-Believing-Abraham. For those who are out of works of the Law are exposed-to-penalty-of-a-curse. As it has been written that, "Everyone is cursed who is not keeping-and-faithful in all having-been-written in The-Scrolls-of-the-Law and to do them."

For in the Law no-one is-being-justified with *THE-GOD*. It is evident that "The-just-one shall-be-living by-believing."

Now The-Law is not out of believing but in performing-works but those men doing them shall-be-living in them.

Anointed buys-back us out of the Curse-of-The-Law becoming for-the-sake-of us The-Curse. For as-it-is-written, "cursed is everyone hanging on the tree," so-that the blessing of Abraham may-be-becoming to The-Nations through *Anointed-Savior* that we-may-be-obtaining The-Promise-of-The-Spirit through The-Belief.

Brothers, I am reasoning as a man, that a covenant having-been-ratified-and-legally-agreed-to-and-publically-accepted no-one can annul-and-reject or modify it for to Abraham and to the Seed of him were declared The-Promises. And *HE* is-not-saying "of the Seeds," as in just-anyone but through *The-One-Seed* of *HIM* which is *Anointed*. And I am saying this covenant was first-in-order having-been-ratified by *THE-GOD* in *Anointed*. Then the Law arrived after four-hundred and thirty years which cannot invalidate-and-eradicate The-Promise. For if The-Enjoyment-of-The-Allotment is due-to the Law it is no longer due-to the Promise for to Abraham *THE-GOD* has-graciously-granted The-Promise.

What is the purpose of The-Law? It was added on behalf of the transgressions until *The-Seed* may-be-coming to whom *He*-was-promised being told-about-prior to through messengers. For *The-Mediator* does not represents-only-one-party yet *THE-GOD-IS-ONE*.

Does The-Law rival-and-oppose The-Promises of *THE-GOD*? There is no way! For if the Law was designed-and-intended to being-able-to-give life was justice really ever delivered-by the Law? For The-Scripture securely-concludes all are under The-Sin, that The-Promise by-believing in *Savior-Anointed* may-be-being-given to The-Ones-Believing.

For before The-Belief came to be we-were-garrisoned under the Law having-been-chained-and-shackled until the Belief came to-be revealed. Now The-Law became our boy-leader to *Anointed* that by-believing we-may-be-being-justified. Now The-Belief is here we are no longer under the boy-leader. For you are all *Sons*-of-*GOD* through The-Belief in *Anointed-Savior*. For as many of you are baptized in *Anointed* you have put on *Anointed*. There is no Jew or either Greek, there is no slave or yet freeman, there is no male and female, for you are all one in *Anointed-Savior*. And if you are of-*Anointed*, then you are The-Seed-of-Abraham and Enjoyers-of-The-Allotment according-to the Promise.

Now I say this, as much as a child is the-enjoyer-of-an-allotment even-though-he-is master of all, he is as the same as a slave as long as he is under guardians and administrators until the-appointed-time by-the-father. Even we, as we were minors, we-were-enslaved under The-Elements of the world. But when The-Filling-of-The-Time came, *THE-GOD* from out of a woman birthed *HIS Son* to come under the Law that for us, the-ones under the Law, *He-is-a-Reclaimer*, that we-may-be-recovering the place-of-a-son. Seeing that you are now Sons, *THE-GOD* sends The-spirit-of-*The-Son* in your hearts crying-out-with-a-loud-voice *ABBA, THE-FATHER*. Therefore, you are no longer slaves but a son and if a son also an Enjoyer-of-the-Allotment-of-*GOD* through *Anointed*.

How is it indeed then when you did not know *GOD*? You slaved to ones that are not gods by nature. And now knowing *GOD*, rather yet being-known by *GOD*, how is it you are turning your back again to those weak and wasteful Elements? Are you willing to be-being enslaved once again? You are observing days and months and season and years. I fear for you that somehow I have toiled in waste over you.

Brothers, I beseech that you are to become as I am, for I am also as you, and you have not in any way injured me because you are aware that during the infirmity of the flesh that I brought the Well-Message to you first. With this trial of mine in my flesh, you did not utterly-despise neither rejected me, but as an angel of God you received me as *Anointed-Savior*. Do you remember your happiness? I-am-claiming that if possible, you would have gouged your eyes so I could have them forever.

Have I become the enemy because I am being true with you? They are not being honorable or passionately-concerned over you but to have-control-of-you that you may-be-passionately-concerned over them. Yet to be always in genuine zealousness is ideal for you and just not in my presence.

My little children whom again I-am-travailing over until *Anointed* is formed in you for I desire to be present with you right now and to change my language for I-don't-know-what-to-decide about you.

You tell me about The-Ones intending-and-determined to be under the Law! Do you really understand what the Law is all about? For it-has-been-written that Abraham had two sons, one out of the-female-slave and one out of the-free-woman. For the-one indeed out of the-female-slave has-been-begotten by the flesh but the-one of the-free is through The-Promise which is comparing-in-parallel these women for the two are covenants. One indeed from Mount Sinai for causing slavery, which is Hagar. For The-Hagar is Mount Sinai in Arabia and represents what is now Jerusalem, for she-is-being-in-slavery with her children.

But The-Jerusalem above is free who is the mother of all of us. For it-has-been-written, "You be glad Sterile-One, The-One not bringing forth! Burst forth you! Implore The-One not travailing! For the neglected has many more children, more than The-Woman having The-Husband." But we Brothers are offspring according-to the Promise as Isaac. For even as the-one generated from the flesh persecuted the-one with the spirit, and now so it is. Now what does The-Writing say? "You-be-casting out the-female-slave and her son! For the-son of the-female-slave should-not-be-enjoying the *Allotment* with the-son of the-free-woman." In conclusion, Brothers, we are not of the female-slave but of the free-woman.

Now The-Freedom-of-*The-Anointed* frees us. You-be-standing-firm and not yoked and ensnared in bondage again! Listen up! I am Paul telling you those circumcising Christ is not making you better. I am with-authority-issuing-a-judgment again that every man circumcising is duty-bound to do The-Law in entirety. For you became cut-loose from *The-Anointed* any who are being-justified in the Law, you have fallen out of grace. We through (the) spirit, by believing, are waiting with joyful-confident-expectation justice. For in *Anointed-Savior* neither circumcision nor uncircumcision has-the-strength-and-ability-to-overcome only by believing displaying Godly-love.

You were running great. Who has cut into you to not be persuaded in *Truth*? This treacherous-deception is not by THE-ONE-CALLING you. A little leaven is-leavening the-entire-kneading.

I have confidence in you in *Master* that in none other teaching you-shall-be-believing. But the-one-causing-dissension shall be bearing The-Judgment whoever he may be. For Brothers if I was still supporting circumcision why am-I-being-persecuted? Does that mean the-stumbling-block at The-Pale has-been-voided-and-removed?

Indeed, would these, the-ones-raising-insurrection also be-cutting themselves off from you!

For you were-called to freedom, Brothers. Not only The-Freedom to attack the flesh, but in the Godly-love in-willing-divine-bondage to one another for The-Law in entirety is-being-fulfilled in one statement, "You-shall-be-Godly-loving the-one near you as yourself." Now if you-are cannibalizing one another, beware so you are not consumed by one another!

I am saying that you are to be walking in spirit and you-should-not-be-executing-and-performing the lust of the flesh. For The-Flesh rivals-and-desires for control of The-Spirit and also The-Spirit against The-Flesh. And these are opposing one another so that you are not able to do what you desire to do. Still if you-are-being-led in spirit, you are not under the Law.

Now the acts of the-flesh are obvious which is: adultery, prostitution, impure motives, excessive lust, idolatry, enchantments, hatred, contentious arguing, envious rivalries, passionate angers, self-seeking an office, causing division and sedition, preferences, envies, murders, drunkenness, riotous drunken and sexual parties, and the likes of these. As I was saying before to you and as such I also say to you again that The-One committing-one-self-to such shall-not-be-enjoying The-Allotment-of-The-Kingdom of-*GOD*.

But the-effect of The-Spirit is Godly-love, gladness, peace, endurance-with-perseverance-and-slow-to-avenge, kindness, uprightness of heart, faithfulness, gentleness-and-mildness, self-control; against such there is no law. For The-Ones of *The-Anointed* crucify the-flesh together with the-passions and the-lusts. If we-may-be-living by spirit in spirit, we-may-be-observing-these-fundamentals. Also, may-we-not-appear-in-history-having-empty conceit challenging-and-provoking one another, to envy one another.

Brothers, if ever a man may-be-being-overtaken in some offense, you the-ones spiritual, you put-in-order-and-repair making one what he ought to be in the spirit of meekness examining-and-observing yourself so you also may-not-be-being-tried. You be supporting the burdens-and-troubles of one another and that is how you fully satisfy The-Law-of-*The-Anointed*.

Yet if anyone is supposed to be of eminence, being he is nothing, he-is-subject-to-fantasies. But let him-be-testing the actions of himself, each one, and then alone to himself have self-praise and not to the remaining. For each one shall-be-carrying their own faults-and-condemning-conscience.

And the-one-being-instructed in The-Scripture let-him-be a sharer with the one-instructing in all good. And do not be deceived, *GOD* is not to be sneered at! For whatever a man may be planting, this he shall also be rewarded with. For the-one sowing for the flesh to himself from the flesh shall-be-cut-off-and-gather The-Corruption, and the-one sowing to the spirit, from the spirit shall-be-reaping life eonian. And we should not be despondent by doing the correct-and-praiseworthy. In season

Section I

if we do not weaken, we-will-be-reaping our own. So when then, as we have the time-and-opportunity, we are to be working for the good for all and especially toward The Family-Members-of The-Belief.

See how large I write the individual-characters to you by my own hand. For all those who desire-and-intend to please-and-placate to the flesh, those who are compelling you to be circumcised, it is not for The-Pale-of-*The-Anointed* but to-not-be-being-persecuted. For not even the-ones demanding being-circumcised are not maintaining the Law. But they are willing for you to-be-being-circumcised that they-should-be-boasting about your obedience-and-being controlled.

Yet may it not be so with me to-be-boasting except in The-Pale-of-*The-Lord* of us *Savior-Anointed* through whom to me the System is crucified and I to the System. For in *Anointed-Savior* neither circumcision nor uncircumcision has any value but is-a new creation. And whoever shall-be-following-the-fundamentals of this rule, peace on them and mercy also to The-Israel-of-*THE-GOD*. Of the-remaining burdensome-laws let no-one be-challenging me. For I can-show the branding-marks of *The-Lord* on my body. The-Grace of *The-Lord* of us *Savior-Anointed* be with your spirit, Brothers.

Amen.

GALATIANS STUDY NOTES

Note: Through my many translations, I have come to believe that the phrase or associated phrasing of "inheritance" [ex: Col 1:12] accurately translated as "the-allotment" in Scripture is not a good or proper translation (i.e., inheritance). Paul makes it clear that we are to be family members (I state: royal and godly) destined to be with HIM and HE with us and we in Christ and He in us. Inheritance has an implied connotation, an accepted concept that someone has died. THE-GOD is certainly not dead, and Christ has risen to life eonian (there are times of times of times) as well. I see this as a watering down of the intent and meaning of the Scriptures and have dropped using the word *inheritance* when speaking of THE-GOD's plan and purpose for us. We are to take rulership in an active kingdom with Christ at the head of the realm and we under Him, with THE-GOD over all of us.

Note The Greek word *agapen* translated as "love" in most translations is missing that this is Godly in nature and not of men or any other such creature. I have therefore carried the adjective to add clarity to the meaning of this word throughout this translation.

Note: In my research, nearly all translations have dropped "the" as a modifier, but the Greek word for "the" is in every text and not meant to be ignored or deleted. It is often specifically singular, and when attached to the noun, it is describing that noun as unique, one of a kind, a specific thing, the original, the one and only. It is for this reason that I carry "the" everywhere it appears in all translations. Whether of God, Jesus, Satan or any other entity, concept, or idea, the modifier "the" clears up a lot of generalized words, ideas, concepts, and entities.

Note: The root of the word *pnuemia*, translated as "spirit, wind, or breath," has no gender identity since this is a word that is neuter in gender. *Pnuemia* is an "it." The Greeks, as we of English language, often fix a gender to objects and things— for example: cars, boats, the moon, the sun. For the Greeks, *pnuemia* at times has a male gender affixed to it. *Pnuemia* in the Scriptures is never capitalized or designated as a standalone being, entity, principality, or sovereignty when used as the word "spirit." It is simply the power inherent in the

being, whether of man, or God, or Christ, or any other entity. If anything is living, "it" possesses a spirit. The "Holy-spirit" is simply the power from and of The-God, giving and renewing life and performing The-God's will.

Note: Paul constantly claims and mentions "principles, powers, authorities, sovereignties not of our world." He quite clearly claims that these beings are the ones that certainly influence and control (predominately in a negative way) the systems of this world, people of the nations, and as individuals directly. You can find this concept also contained in The Old Testament through the implications of the first commandment. This claim and the concept of the warring factions in heaven makes a fascinating study.

Note: Time periods, eons, ages, millennia, eons, and eons—I stayed true to the Greek words associated with time and what we still use today in our common language. A study of time periods is fascinating but is also an area that can cause confusion. The-God always works on some kind of a timetable, but understanding which is which and when is when is a bit of a mystery. Some timetables are only known to The-God and made clear to man at God's will.

Note   What is the difference between "expectation" and "hope?" Nearly all translations adopt the word "hope" for "expectation," but Paul uses almost exclusively the word "expectation." Here is why I constantly use "expectation." Having an expectation means you have no doubt at all. It is sure and certain with no ambiguity or doubt. Having a hope means you are not 100 percent convinced and convicted. I can tell you that Paul is undeniably convinced and convicted in what he delivers and talks about. Using "hope" sends a message that there is some possibility for "wiggle room," doubt, error, or excuses.

Even worse, much of the use of the word "expectation" in Paul's writings has the modifier "the" attached to "expectation," thus forming the proper translation and singular concept of "The-Expectation." This makes "The-Expectation" an event, not a philosophy or theological premise. Not recognizing "The-Expectation" as an event will lead the reader immediately down an incorrect understanding of what is being offered or discussed.

1:4   "so that He-May-Be-*Extricating*" (italics mine). Notice that this is direct legal term, and Paul is stating quickly in this dissertation that what is happening on a spiritual level is executed within the realm of mankind. This extricating is meant not only to pull-out, displace, and remove from a physical position but also to include a release from all personal debts and obligations. If you read Galatians as a legal reference, you will realize the freedom and responsibilities you have in Christ.

GALATIANS STUDY NOTES

1:4   "The-One-Giving Himself" is multilayered in meaning. I found *Strong's Concordance* offering the following ideas, and I'll allow the reader to reflect on the implications:

a. To give something of one's own accord, to his advantage

b. To grant, let have

c. To give over, to reach out

d. To give what is due or obligatory, to pay: wages or reward

Strong's offers other definitions that one can explore, but I see these applying at several levels.

1:6   The beginning of the first verse starts as: "I-am *wondering* [amazed, trying to understand in astonishment, bewildered by] how swiftly you" (italics mine). My examination of the Greek word *thaumazo*, translated in many texts as "amazed," most often is intended in the Greek positively, as one held in great admiration and respect, not out of suspicion and concern. Clearly the intent of the opening line is in the negative sense. Then the complimentary antonym or anti-idea attached to all of this is a marveling, with the concepts of being bewildered or bewitched. It is not a stretch to supplement either of these two words in the appropriate position of the sentence since Paul will directly use the word "bewitch" in Galatians 3:1. Thus he maintains from beginning to end a theme of the Galatians being enchanted with a different message of the gospel from what he delivered and being taken away to be possessed by another.

1:6   The Greek *metatithesthe* or "displaced" means "to transfer." This is meant as being a transference such as a legal transfer of property, and more specifically as a transference of souls, which Paul often alludes to when discussing the current reign of dominions, principalities, and powers. It also can be understood to "desert or fall away from," which is the common translation provided by most translators.

1:7   The Greek *tarassontes* translated as "ones-disturbing." In addition to the alternate concepts offered in [brackets], I was struck by this offering and pulled it out separately for discussion: "to perplex the mind of one by suggesting scruples or doubts."

Causing doubts has been discussed in theological circles as The-Adversary's greatest weapon. The Galatians were apparently being bombarded with nice-sounding philosophies, but they were not going back into the Scriptures to verify and be re-grounded in the teachings delivered by Paul. Many were in doubt and apparently being swayed away from the well-message. Verse 7 appears to set the intent for the rest of the letter and Paul's discourse.

Section I

1:14   "And I was progressing in The-Judaism." I was struck by the phrasing of "The-Judaism," for it sounded like "The-Judaism" was a business piranha or some uncaring and self-serving corporate entity, not a benefit for the people or in honored humbled service to THE-GOD of Israel or Judah. One can only come to the conclusion that the whole institution of the scribes and priesthood was corrupt back then, in addition to Saul (Paul) as an individual. If it was then, would it not still be so today?

1:14   "in the inherited traditions of The-Fathers" is an immense statement and not to be overlooked. Paul was stating then, just as much as the Jews today do, that being a Jew was all about "tradition." It was simply a going through the motions and emotions of the culture and all the systems associated with it. There was nothing real or sincere in correct or proper understanding about the events or relationships toward God or their fellow man. It was all show with no substance in what was being done or why, often done in misguided sincerity and fervor because of centuries of always being on the wrong path. This also included a self-serving superiority belief. "The world was meant for the Jews, not the Jews for the world." "The Jews are the superior race destined to rule the world." This "in the inherited traditions" also carries a racial philosophy. That was exactly what Paul was doing in his day while he was working his way "up the corporate ladder" before his conversion. Take some time to meditate on this in your own life as well. All cultures and people are surrounded with tradition that blinds and binds them against what should be done. Paul was what we would call today a type "AA" personality, a super-jingoist.

1:16   I discussed Paul's super-patriotism to Judaism in verse 14, and in this verse, he demonstrates his immediate super-loyalty and belief in The Savior and God the Father.

2:2   "The-ones-of-Reputation" was a group larger than the apostles alone as a group of twelve. Christ had many followers, and the reader must realize that after receiving the Holy-spirit on the Day of Pentecost, many would have attached themselves to the apostles as associates and members and stayed to work and be associated with "The Twelve." Out of that group came Matthias to replace Judas. Also, recall that Jesus always had a contingency of men surrounding him nearly twenty-four hours a day and hanging on to his every word. They would have repented and come back to be part of the "headquarters," and in verse 6 Paul lets us know that not one of those men, not even the apostles, had anything to rebut, change, or say to him concerning what Paul relayed to them. These people were Jewish elders and leaders within the Ecclesiae, with nothing further to offer other than to remember to help the destitute and struggling Jewish Ecclesiae. The "Ones of Reputation" is a term

Paul clearly is using as a slander in verse 6, and he infers that even the apostles may have had "ego concerns." This theme shows up later when Paul publicly calls out Peter and the Jewish Jerusalem contingency that persuaded Peter to separate himself from the Gentiles.

On a positive note and to offer a postulate concerning "The-Ones-of-Reputation," these may have also been the men with John at the end of the first century and after the deaths of Peter and Paul that helped to canonize and complete the New Testament as we have received it today. Many would have still been contemporaries and alive with John and with the skills and knowledge to assemble, and to complete assembling the Second Testament which was well within their capabilities and under John's God given authority.

Let the reader also pause on Paul's statements in verses 2–15 because he is giving us something else to positively reflect on for our times. In moments of deep despondency, we berate ourselves for giving in to the flesh and its lusts and, like Paul, cry out to God, "When will this ever end?" because we just can't seem to stop our negative actions on our own, even though we know in our hearts and mind what is correct. But even the great Apostles—and I say this with all the deepest and most passionate sincerity and respect, were still men overcoming traditions, culture, and preconceived ideas; they, too, were still tied to the flesh. All of us who have the spirit of God living in us still get drawn into the weaknesses of the flesh, pleading to our Father for His Kingdom to come and to be released from the bondage of the flesh. This is only one of the areas of the everyday part of life where Christ stands preeminently above us as our Brother and High Priest. Take hope, for the time is coming when the flesh will disappear, and we will take on completely God's and Jesus' character and nature.

2:3   The word "cut" here is meant to have a harsh, brutal, torturous connotation to it.

2:6   "believing-they-had-some-kind-of-reputation" should be questioned: Who were these men? I propose that they were leaders from the Jerusalem Ecclesia secretly not in the agreement of with the Apostle's compact. These were men associated with the "Pillar" apostles, and because of some kind of relationship with them, used that to create false authority and power to influence and manipulate. What a dangerous assumption these individuals had taken on, believing they had the authority and could force a dead doctrine! Even more accusatory, they knew that none of the Mosaic Law had any compulsory requirements on the Nations. These men were not without that knowledge; they were there when Paul presented the gospel, and probably never accepted it but kept quiet. They could not give up their "Judaism," the same disease Paul had in his life before his conversion. They came seeking power and control,

Section I

believing the Nations were to be "slaves" to the Jews since the Jews were being preserved by God to "save the world."

2:6   "God is not taken up with men." When I translated this, I could not but pause at the profundity of this verse. It seems to add definition to what The-God is not, what man is not, and the relationship between both. It shows what perspective The-God could have about us as His creation; these verses reveal what The-God is desiring, providing, and going to do for us because of His love for us.

3:1   In order for Paul to show from the "writings" the crucifixion of Christ, he had to use the Old Testament Scriptures, thus bridging the Old Covenant (Testament) to the New Covenant (Testament) epistles, letters, and teachings.

3:2   "I am willing to-be-learning [be taught] only this from you. Did you get the-spirit from works of the Law or by believing after hearing it?" When examining this verse, I was struck by two thoughts concerning "the-spirit" ("the" is a definite article here and is in the original Greek). Was Paul really asking them, "Which spirit did you get?" Was it a spirit of some other enchantment or divination or was it the Holy-spirit? Especially since in the first verse he uses the word "bewitch." The Greek does not have the word "holy" anywhere associated with "spirit" in the original, and some texts have added the word "holy" in an effort to emphasize an apparent agenda. I think Paul is inferring they have a spirit for sure, but it is not the one they need or should have.

3:3   "How foolish that you are undertaking [began in, started off with] the spirit, now you-are-being-completed [being perfected, made whole and sinless] in the flesh!" An examination of the Greek word translated as "undertaking" may be a pun used by Paul to indicate that the spirit the Galatians were following was a spirit for the "dead." And we know an "Undertaker" handles the dead.

Of interest though, is the topic of Circumcision, which has been a running theme in this discourse; Paul is still debating and proving that it is meaningless and void. So Paul now asks in this second half of the verse ("are-being-completed [being perfected, made whole and sinless] in the flesh!"), are you who are mature in Christ and who will receive all the benefits provided by Christ because you are a man with missing foreskin versus being a spiritual man living by spiritual laws? To be forced to perform circumcision in order to "perfect the flesh," to receive salvation that everyone already knew was spiritual in nature? I would be asking, if I were there, just what does that mean and how does that work? That I can have salvation because I cut off my foreskin? My "perfected flesh" is due to my missing foreskin being required in addition to the crucifixion and resurrection of Christ? God and Christ need my foreskin? Christ's life and sacrifice fall short, so you, or rather the Deities, need my foreskin? Severing my foreskin plus Christ's sacrifice can earn me salvation? Or is it just by me lacerating myself? Because God or Christ is certainly not performing this act for me; I realize that I am the only one who can give up my foreskin. The whole argument to that is so illogical it makes the brain freeze. Take note also that Paul uses the word "mature" many more times than "perfect," so if you "mature" your flesh (I am not even sure I know what it means to "mature my flesh" expressed this way) by cutting off your foreskin, would this give you salvation too? There is no logic in using this word or what is understood by its definitions either in this posed question. Salvation could never be produced by simply cutting the flesh, and Paul reiterated this to Peter and the Jewish Jerusalem contingency in his debate with them.

3:5   "THE-ONE then supplying you *The-spirit*" (italics mine). Here Paul is referring to God's Holy-spirit.

3:17   Paul is emphasizing the extreme length of time between The Promise to Abraham and the delivery of The Law. The preeminent position belonged to Abraham's promise because it was in first in rank, position, and status and thus holding the greater prestige and purpose. God offers the best first, not last.

3:21   "Was righteousness really ever out of The Law?" How profound! We recognize the Mosaic Laws (especially the Ten Commandments) are righteous, and we need to live by them, but we never can perfectly! We can never achieve or secure righteousness, and therefore our salvation through them. We need something else. Paul calls it The-Belief in Christ, The-(one and only)-Anointed-Messiah and The-(one and only)-God, The-Father.

4:3   "we-were-enslaved under *The-Elements* of the world." (italics mine). The-Elements mentioned here are the unseen and invisible principalities, sovereignties, and powers as well as the laws of nature and those physical beings in control and governing this world. Those living in the flesh are clearly still being "garrisoned" and "led" by these influences.

4:4   "But when *The-Filling-of-[appointed, completion of]-The-Time* came THE-GOD from out of a woman put-out" (italics mine). I capitalized this because this is an event, just as New Year's is an annual event and is capitalized. When viewed as such, the meaning and intent of what is being offered to the Sons of God is immense.

4:17   The translation of "but-to-lock-you-out" for me can be understood on two levels. The first is the fleshly level; that is, to prevent the individual from enjoying the same treatment or life or power as the one who is doing the locking out. The second is the spiritual arena; that is, to prevent you from the "enjoyment of the allotment." Paul is not short on discoursing about the spiritual realm and The-Adversary who would love nothing more than prevent you from receiving any sort of reward or grace from The-God. I might also add here that I think this phrase means to lock-out the mind into spiritual blindness so you are prevented from understanding the purpose and will of The-God.

4:19   According-to *Thayer's Lexicon*, the following is quoted for the Greek word *morpho* (*Strong's* G3445): "οὗ μορφωθῇ Χριστός ἐν ὑμῖν i.e., literally, until a mind and life in complete harmony with the mind and life of Christ shall have been formed in you, Gal. iv. 19."

4:20   The Greek word for "sound" (voice, tone) is φωνή (*Strong's* g5456) transliterated as "phone" pronounced as *fona* (long "o" and long "a").

4:23   My first translation for Galatians 4:23 was:

"For the-one indeed out-of-the-maid [female-slave] has-been-begotten *through* (kata) the flesh . . ." (italics mine).

I recognize I could have also used the word "by," but using the word "through" spun me into the thought that while out of duty and common cultural practice at the request of his wife, his willingness to do this had another motive, that is "happy to do this" for the lust of a younger woman (not out of true love, hence through the "lust of the flesh"). This would turn the verse into a double negative (in the witness of two) of the comparison taking place in the verse and theme. After all, the request and activity were done using "the reasoning of men."

4:27   "You be glad Sterile-One, The-One *not bringing forth! Burst forth* you! Implore The-One not paining [travailing]!" (italics mine). This portion of the translated verse bears thinking about. Sarah, having not yet had Isaac, is the same as the Sons of God not having yet received the Kingdom. But at Christ's return, there will truly be a "bursting forth of children." This is a prophecy with future implications. This Second Covenant has yet to burst forth with Sons of God.

4:27   The Greek word translated as "desolate" misses the richness and deeper and usage. *Strong's* has several definitions for *eremou* fitting the way Hagar was treated by Abraham and Sarah when tossed out of their sight. All of these are the associated definitions: she certainly became "of the wilderness, was forced into uncultivated regions not fit for pasture, was deserted and forced into a lonely region." "Deprived of protection and aid especially of friends and acquaintances and her kindred, a woman neglected by her husband." Also, we know Hagar generated many more children than Sarah, fulfilling this prophecy and lament precisely.

5:4   Paul uses the Greek word *katergethete*, which is translated commonly as "exempted" but better rendered as "severed or cut-off"—and in this lies the idea of circumcision. What the reader misses here is the play on words with a double meaning in the Greek. Paul is just as easily saying this also: "For you became exempted [terminated, severed, loosed] from *The-Anointed*, any who are being-justified in the Law, you have fallen out of grace." "For you became severed from The-Anointed, any who are being-justified in The Law, you have fallen out of grace."

This is the clearer rendition editing "fallen-out" with the equivalent concept(s) cut-off, thrown-off: "For you became circumcised from The-Anointed any who are being-justified in the Law, you have been cut-off from grace."

5:7   I cannot help but smile at Paul's use of the Greek word *anekopsen*, often translated as "hindered" but is much more accurate using the alternate definition of "cut-off." See my discussion concerning 5:4. When you place "cut-off" back in the sentence, you can see Paul using a phrase against those insisting that one must still be obeying the Mosaic Law, which included circumcision. It's a perfect example of Paul being facetious while condemning those that insist on the practice of "cutting the flesh" to be a "fleshly" Jew to receive the promised blessings. In the letter, I always reassemble after translating; I translated the verses using "circumcise" and dropping the word "hindered." Paul is quite effective at "turning a phrase" in defense or attack in an argument or refuting errant and demonic doctrine. Hence:

"You were running great. Who has hindered [cut into, cut off] you to not be persuaded in the truth?" becomes: "You were running great. Who has circumcised you to not be persuaded in the truth?"

Note: If the audience hadn't gotten the message concerning believing versus The Law and circumcision, would they ever? Paul was certainly "boxing them about the ears and head," using their own offensive arguments and claims against them at every chance.

5:11   The "stumbling block" was actually nothing more than a street curb the multitudinous holy day crowds in Jerusalem would literally have tripped over as they were pressing into the city and the Temple precinct. It was most likely at the foot (base) of the crucifixion site where the Passover crowd could see the "treacherous King of The Jews," including the two thieves' fate and theirs if they caused sedition while going in and out of the city. No one missed this sight; it was prominent and a commonly known location by everyone.

This was the same curb The-Adversary asked Jesus to literally step down from or walk off from the sidewalk to the street pavement (maybe three to six inches high). It was part of the temple complex, therefore "Holy-Ground." The-Adversary did not need to have Christ truly perform a miracle to step off the curb, and in fact he knew it was not really necessary to have any angels there to "catch" Jesus when taking a step

Section I

down. That was simply for dramatic effect and to badger Christ into such a simple task. The-Adversary knew exactly who Christ was (and is today). Satan only needed Christ to obey him in the simplest of tasks to disqualify Jesus. How much more is Satan's desire for our "obedience" to him?

Anyone who knew anything about Jerusalem knew about this "problem" entering the city, and this included the Gentiles at the time of the letter. They knew it was still there as much as Paul. So, on two levels (witnesses), Paul reiterates that there is no need for the Mosaic Law and circumcision. However, soon the curb, the road, and all of Jerusalem became completely razed and disappeared with the destruction of the city along with the temple in 70 C.E. With the stumbling stone and the Temple's disappearance, they both became (then and now) a certain, sure "sign" to all that all of the "law and circumcision and practices" are no longer in effect; they have been done away with.

6:17 "Of the rest [In the future, {of the Mosaic Law}]." I requote this portion of this verse to offer a different understanding for the phrase "of the rest." All the translations I conferred with interpret this as timing issues; as such I have placed in first position "In the future" honoring tradition. My offering is completely different but in line with the discussion and treatment of circumcision and the Mosaic Law. I interpret the word "rest" to mean to put an end to, close-out, or cease, and this fits in quite well with the discussion of putting an end to practicing the Mosaic Laws. My sense is that Paul is telling his audience with an underlying message to cease all the other Mosaic Laws too. I have therefore added my sense in {parenthesis} to distinguish it from all other translations.

GALATIANS IN VERSE

GALATIANS 1

1:1 Paul, Commissioner, not from men or through men but through *Savior-Anointed* and *FATHER GOD, THE-ONE-ROUSING Him* out of the dead-ones

1:2 and all brothers, the-ones together with me, to The-Called-Outs [Ecclesiae] of Galatia.

1:3 Grace to you and peace from *FATHER GOD* and *Master* of us *Savior-Anointed*.

1:4 *The-One-Giving* himself for the-sake-of our sins so that *He-May-Be-Extricating* [pluck-out, rescue, choose-out, select] us out of the present wicked eon according-to the-will of *THE-GOD* and *FATHER* of us

1:5 to *WHOM* (is, be) The-Esteem [Glory] into The-Eons of The-Eons.
Amen.

1:6 I-am wondering [amazed, trying to understand, bewildered by] how swiftly you-are-being-displaced [transferred] from *THE-ONE-CALLING* you in the grace of *Anointed* into a different well-message

1:7 which is not another [really nothing new or different]. For not few are the ones-disturbing [agitating, stirring up, troubling, create distress and anxiousness with] you and willing [desiring] to turn [distort, reclaim, turn around, transmute, corrupt, pervert] (you) after [from] the Well-Message-of-*The Anointed*.

1:8 But also [Pay attention], if ever we or a messenger [Angel] out of heaven should-be-bringing-the well-message to you from what we-messaged [brought] to you, let him be anathema [bound under a curse]!

1:9 As we-have-declared-before and repeating again I-am-saying [pronouncing] if anyone is-bringing-a-well message to you different from what you accepted let him be anathema [bound under a curse]!

Section I

1:10   For whom am I presently persuading [currently trying to persuade]? Men or *THE-GOD*? For if I am seeking to be pleasing [accommodate others desires] men, then I never pleased or was I a slave [bound by divine duty] of *Anointed*.

1:11   But I am making it known [testifying, certify, declare] to you, Brothers, the Well-Message that was preached to me that it is not from men.

1:12   For I neither accepted it nor was taught from men but by revelations [divine-instructions, disclosure of truths] from *Savior-Anointed*.

1:13   For you heard of my behavior [deeds and actions] when (I) was in Judaism how that I persecuted inordinately [beyond reason, exceedingly, beyond measure] The-Ecclesia-of-*THE-GOD* and ravaged her [it].

1:14   Because of this I was progressing in The-Judaism above [over, beyond] many of the contemporaries in the-breed [race, lineage] of mine having a more exceeding [above and beyond] boiling [zealousness] in the "inherited traditions" of The-Fathers [Abraham, Isaac, and Jacob] of mine.

1:15   But when it-was-the-correct-time-for *THE-GOD*, *THE-ONE-SEVERING* [separating for divine purpose] me out of the womb of my mother and calling (me) through the grace of *HIM*,

1:16   to reveal *The-Son-of-HIM* in [to] me that I may-be-bringing the Well-Message-of-*HIM* among The-Nations. Immediately I submitted not to [consulted, communicated, conference with] flesh and blood [any man]

1:17   neither came [went] I up [back] to Jerusalem to The-Ones, the Commissioners [apostles] prior to me, but I came-away [went] to Arabia and again I returned to Damascus.

1:18   Once there, after three years I came up [back] to Jerusalem to relate my story to Peter, and I stayed with him fifteen days.

1:19   But I did not become acquainted [get introduced to, did not associate] with any different Commissioners except James, the-brother-of-*The-Master*.

1:20   Be-perceiving [Pay attention] to what I am writing to you! In sight of [in full view, as a witness before] *THE-GOD* that I am not falsifying [lying]!

1:21   After that I came to the regions of Syria and Cilicia.

1:22   And since I was unknown by face [appearance] to The-Called-Outs [Ecclesiae] of Judea in *The-Master*

1:23   but only having heard [by only what was being told], that the one-persecuting us once [at one time] now is-bringing the Well-Message-of-The-Belief [faith] where once he-ravaged.

1:24   And they glorified with me *THE-GOD*.

GALATIANS 2

2:1 Then after fourteen years I went up again to Jerusalem with Barnabas, taking along with me also Titus.

2:2 And I went up in accordance with [acknowledgment of] a revelation [divine instruction] and submitted to [presented before] them the Well-Message which I am proclaiming [heralding] to The-Nations on my own only [privately], to The-Ones-of-Reputation, unless somehow I may be racing or ran for emptiness [in vain, for nothing].

2:3 For not even Titus who was with me, a Greek, was not compelled to be cut [circumcised].

2:4 But because of the-false-Brothers who-smuggled-in, who crept in to spy out The-Freedom of ours which we have in *Anointed-Savior* so-that they should be enslaving us [bringing back into bondage].

2:5 To whom we did not even for one hour yielded to (their) subjection [demanded obedience] that the truth of the Well-Message should be continuing with you.

2:6 But for the ones-believing-they-had-some-kind-of-reputation [self-reputation, self-promotion, a name with supposed authority] whoever they once were, they were nothing of any consequence to me. *GOD* is not taken-up [has no regard for] with men. For the ones-having-a-reputation [thinking they were someone] submitted [added] nothing to me

2:7 but seeing to the contrary that I-have-been-entrusted with the Well-Message to The-Uncircumcision as Peter is to The-Circumcision.

2:8 For *THE-ONE-OPERATING* in Peter with the commission [apostleship] to the-Circumcision operates also in me for the-Nations.

2:9 And knowing The-Grace being given to me, James and Cephas and John, The-Ones-considered-as pillars, gave to me and Barnabas the-right-hand of communion [fellowship] that we to The-Nations and them to The-Circumcision

2:10 with-only that we-may-be-remembering the poor which I also endeavor to do this same thing.

2:11 However, when Peter came to Antioch, I withstood [confronted] him to his face [personally] censuring [finding fault with, accusing] him.

2:12 For before the-coming [appearance] of some from James, he ate together with the-Nations and after those coming from James, he shrank back [timidly withdrew, in fear disavowing] and severed [separated, excluded, cut off, {circumcised}] himself fearing the-ones of Circumcision.

SECTION I

2:13   And playing the hypocrite was The-Rest of the Jews with him so-that even Barnabas also was-led-away-with [submitting one's self to the lowly conditions] of those of The-Hypocrisy!

2:14   For when I perceived [realized] that they-were-not-in-a-correct attitude [walking a straight course, acting uprightly] about the truth of the Well-Message, I said to Peter in front of all, "If you are inherently [being born and reared as] a Jew are living like the-Nations and not as a Jew, why are you compelling the-Nations to be living like a Jew?

2:15   We are Jews by nature [birth] and not sinners from The Nations [as gentiles].

2:16   We-know that a man is not being justified out of [by] [acts] works nor even by the Law but through belief [faith] in *Savior-Anointed*. Also, we believe in *Anointed-Savior* that we-may-be-justified out of [by] The-Belief-[faith]-of-*Anointed* and not out of [by] works of the Law because no flesh shall-be-justified out of the works of the Law.

2:17   For if we were found seeking to be justified in *Anointed* and we-ourselves were-found [discovered, examined] as sinners, (is) consequently [the conclusion that] *Anointed* is a dispenser of sins? No Way!!

2:18   For if I demolish [utterly raze] what I am building, I am commending [presenting, proving, establishing] myself a side-stepper [transgressor, sinner].

2:19   For through the Law I am dead in the Law that I-should-be-living to *GOD*.

2:20   I-have-been-crucified-together with *Anointed* and I am no longer living but (it is) *Anointed* in me. Even though now I am living in the flesh, I-am-living by belief [faith] in *The-Son*-of-*THE-GOD*, *The-One-Loving* me and giving *Himself* up for the sake of me.

2:21   I am not repudiating [denying, disregard, reject, refusing] The-Grace-of-*THE-GOD* for if righteousness is through the Law consequently [the conclusion is] *Anointed* gratuitously [unnecessarily, without a cause, in vain] has died."

GALATIANS 3

3:1   Oh, foolish Galatians! Who bewitches [put a spell on, charmed by wicked arts] you that are not to-be-being-persuaded-to [confident about] *The-Truth*? That according-to your eyes it [Before you it has been clearly and openly demonstrated] what was-written-before [designated before-hand, described, portrayed] for you of *Savior-Anointed* having-been-crucified.

3:2   I am willing to-be-learning [be taught] only this from you. Did you get the-spirit from works of the Law or by believing after hearing it?

3:3 How foolish that you are undertaking [began in, started off with] the spirit, now you-are-being-completed [being perfected, made whole and sinless] in the flesh!?

3:4 Did you suffer so much in vain [without cause or purpose, nothing] if surely it was for nothing?

3:5 *THE-ONE* then supplying you the-spirit and operating in inherent-divine-mighty-power (working miracles) among you, is it done by the works of the Law or by believing [faith] out of [by] hearing?

3:6 Even Abraham *believes THE-GOD and it is accounted to him as righteousness.*

3:7 Consequently [Therefore] be-you-knowing [understand, realize] that The-Ones out of [by]-believing [faith], these are the Sons-of-Abraham

3:8 and The-Scripture knew-before that *THE-GOD-IS-JUSTIFYING* The-Nations out of [by]-believing [faith] by delivering-the-well-message to The-Abraham *"that in you shall-be-being-blessed all The-Nations."*

3:9 So that The-Ones out of [by]-believing [faith] are-being-blessed together with The-Believing-Abraham.

3:10 For those who are out of [by] works of the Law are under execration [exposed to penalty of a curse]. As it has been written that, **"Everyone is cursed who is not remaining [being true, keeping, is faithful] in all (things, instructions, commands, practices, purposes, intent) having-been-written in The-Scrolls-of-the-Law and to do them."** [Deut 27:26]

3:11 For in the Law no-one is-being-justified with *THE-GOD*. It Is evident that **"The-just-one shall-be-living by-believing [by faith]."** [Hab 2:4]

3:12 Now The-Law is not out of believing [faith] but in doing [acting rightly, do well, performing, works, actions] but those men doing them shall-be-living in them.

3:13 *Anointed* [Christ] reclaims [buys-back] us out of the Curse-of-The-Law becoming for the-sake-of us The-Execration [Curse]. For as-it-is-written, **"cursed is everyone hanging on the wood [tree],"**

3:14 so-that the blessing of Abraham may-be-becoming to The-Nations through *Anointed-Savior* that we-may-be-obtaining The-Promise-of-The-Spirit through The-Belief. [Deut 21:23]

3:15 Brothers, I am saying [reasoning] as a man, that a covenant having-been-ratified [legally agreed to, publicly accepted] no-one can repudiate [disavowing, annulling, disregard, reject] or modify it

Section I

3:16   for to Abraham and to the Seed of him were declared The-Promises. And *HE* is-not-saying "of the Seeds," as in just-anyone but through *The-One-Seed* of him which is *Anointed* [Christ].

3:17   And I am saying this covenant was first-in-order having-been-ratified by *THE-GOD* in *Anointed*. Then the Law arrived after four-hundred and thirty years which cannot un-sanction [invalidate, nullify, eradicate] The-Promise.

3:18   For if The-Enjoyment-of-The-Allotment is out of [from, due to] the Law it is no longer out of [from, due to] the Promise, for to Abraham *THE-GOD* has-graciously-granted The-Promise.

3:19   Why then [What is the purpose of] The-Law? It was added on behalf of the transgressions until *The-Seed* may-be-coming to whom *He*-was-promised being prescribed [told about prior to, ordained, appointed, arranged] through messengers [envoys, a messenger from GOD, prophets, angel].

3:20   For *The-Mediator* is not of-one [represents only one party], yet *THE-GOD-IS-ONE*.

3:21   Then (is) [does] The-Law against [rivaling, opposing] The-Promises of *THE-GOD*? There is no way! For if the Law was given [designed, meant, intended to] being-able to-make-alive [give life] was justice [righteousness] really ever out of [delivered by] the Law?

3:22   For The-Writing [Scripture] locks-up-together [securely concludes] all are under The-Sin, that The-Promise out of [by]-believing [faith] in *Savior-Anointed* may-be-being-given to The-Ones-Believing.

3:23   For before The-Belief [faith] came to be we-were-garrisoned under the Law having-been-locked-together [chained, shackled] until Belief [faith] came to-be revealed.

3:24   Now The-Law became our boy-leader [tutor, guardian, schoolmaster, escort] to *Anointed* that out of [by]-believing [faith] we-may-be-being-justified.

3:25   Now The-Belief [faith] is here we are no longer under the schoolmaster.

3:26   For you are all *Sons-of-GOD* through The-Belief [faith] in *Anointed-Savior*.

3:27   For as many of you are baptized in *Anointed*, you have put on *Anointed*.

3:28   There is no Jew or either Greek, there is no slave or yet free (man), there is no male and female; for you are all one in *Anointed-Savior*.

3:29   And if you are of-*Anointed*, then you are The-Seed-of-Abraham and Enjoyers-of-The-Allotment according-to the Promise.

GALATIANS 4

4:1 Now I say this, as much as a child is the-enjoyer-of-an-allotment [as an heir] being [even though he is] master of all, he is as the same as a slave

4:2 as long as he is under guardians and administrators until the-placement [appointed time] by the-father.

4:3 Even we, as we were minors, we-were-enslaved under The-Elements-of-the-World.

4:4 But when The-Filling-of [appointed, completion of]-The-Time came, *THE-GOD* from out of a woman put-out [birthed, sent-out, delegated, assigned, purposefully sent] *HIS* Son to come under the Law

4:5 that for us, the-ones under the Law, *He-is-a-Reclaimer* that we-may-be-getting [receiving, take back, recover] the place-of-a-son.

4:6 Seeing that you are now Sons, *THE-GOD* puts-out [assigns, purposefully sends] The-Spirit-of-*The-Son* in your hearts crying-out-with-a-loud-voice *ABBA, THE-FATHER*.

4:7 Therefore you are no longer slaves but a son and if a son also an Enjoyer-of-the-Allotment-of-*GOD* through *Anointed*.

4:8 How is it indeed then when you did not know *GOD*? You slaved to ones that are not gods by nature.

4:9 And now knowing *GOD*, rather yet being-known by *GOD*, how is it you are turning your back again to those infirmed [weak] and poor [wasteful] Elements [practices, principles, dominions, powers, false-gods]? Are you willing to be-being enslaved once again?

4:10 You are keeping [observing] Days {Holy-days} and months and season {weekly and seasonal religious practices} and Years {sabbatical, jubilee}.

4:11 I fear for you that somehow I have toiled in waste over you.

4:12 Brothers, I beseech that you are to become as I am, for I am also as you and you have not in any way injured me

4:13 because you are aware that during the infirmity of the flesh that I brought the Well-Message to you first.

4:14 With this trial of mine in my flesh you did not scorn [took no account, ignored, utterly despise], neither loathed [rejected, spurn, spit-out] (me), but as a messenger [angel] of God you received me as *Anointed-Savior*.

4:15 What then was [Do you remember] your happiness? I-am-witnessing [claiming] that if possible, you would have gouged your eyes to be ever giving them to me [so I could have them forever].

Section I

4:16   Have I become the enemy because I am being true with you?

4:17   They are not being ideally [honorable] boiling [zealous, honorable, passionately concerned] over you but to lock you out [have control of you] that you may-be-being-zealously [passionately concerned] over them.

4:18   Yet to be always in ideal [genuine, morally noble, honorable] boiling [zealous, passion, good] is ideal for you and just not in my presence.

4:19   My little children whom again I-am-paining [travailing] over until *Anointed* is formed [morphed, transformed, have the mind and life of *Christ*] in you

4:20   for I will [desire] to be present with you right now and to change my sound [voice, language] for I-am-being-perplexed [embarrassed for, in doubt, at a loss, don't know what to decide] about you.

4:21   You tell me (about) The-Ones willing [intending, determined, purposing, wishing, loving, taking delight in] to be under the Law! Are you not hearing The-Law? [Do you really understand what the Law is all about?]

4:22   For it-has-been-written that Abraham had two sons, one out of the-maid [female slave] and one out of the-free-woman [freeborn, free from the Mosaic Law].

4:23   For the-one indeed out of the-maid has-been-begotten by the flesh, but the-one of the-free is through The-Promise

4:24   which is allegorizing [metaphor, symbol, comparing in parallel] these women for the two are covenants. One indeed from Mount Sinai for generating [causing, creating, birthing] slavery [bondage], which is Hagar.

4:25   For The-Hagar is Mount Sinai in Arabia and is-rowing-together [standing or marching in the same row and file as a soldier, resembles, represents] what is now Jerusalem for she-is-being-in-slavery with her children.

4:26   But The-Jerusalem above is free who is the mother of all of us.

4:27   For it-has-been-written, **"You be glad Sterile-One, The-One not bringing forth! Burst forth you! Implore The-One not paining [travailing]! For the desolate [deserted, neglected, the wilderness] has many more children, more than The-Woman having The-Husband."** [Isa 54:1]

4:28   But we, Brothers, are offspring [children] according-to the Promise as Isaac.

4:29   For even as the-one generated from the flesh chased [persecuted] the-one with the spirit and now so it is.

4:30   Now what does The-Writing say? **You-be-casting out [get rid of] the-maid and her son! For the-son of the-maid should-not-be-enjoying the-*Allotment* with the-son of the-free-woman.** [Gen 21:10]

4:31   In conclusion, Brothers, we are not of the maid but of the free-woman.

GALATIANS 5

5:1 Now The-Freedom- [true liberty, license, from the Mosaic Law]-of-*The-Anointed* frees [from the dominion of sin, delivers] us. You-be-standing-firm and not yoked and ensnared in slavery [bondage] again!

5:2 Listen up! I am Paul telling you those circumcising Christ is not benefitting [profiting, making better] you.

5:3 I am testifying [with authority issuing a judgment] again that every man circumcising is an owner [is obligated to perform, duty bound, a sinner to] to do The-Law in entirety.

5:4 For you became exempted [terminated, severed, cut-loose, circumcised] from *The-Anointed* any who are being-justified in the Law, you have fallen out of grace.

5:5 We by spirit out of [by] Belief [by faith] are waiting with joyful-confident-expectation justice [righteousness].

5:6 For in *Anointed-Savior* neither circumcision nor un-circumcision is-being-strong [has power, has the strength and ability to overcome] only believing [faith] acting [operating, displaying] in Godly-love.

5:7 You were running great. Who has hindered [cut into, cut off] you to not be persuaded in *Truth*?

5:8 This persuasion [treacherous deception] is not out of [by] THE-ONE-CALLING you.

5:9 A little leaven is-leavening the-entire-kneading [dough lump].

5:10 I have confidence in you in *Master* that in none other (teaching) you-shall-be-being-disposed [believe, have a like mind]. Yet the-one-disturbing [causing dissension] shall be bearing The-Judgment whoever he may be.

5:11 For, Brothers, if I was still heralding [supporting, teaching, claiming] circumcision, why am-I-being-persecuted? Does that mean the-snare [offense, stumbling block] at The-Pale [Crucifixion] has-been-nullified [voided, dismissed, removed]?

5:12 Indeed would these, the-ones-raising-insurrection, also be-cutting [circumcised] themselves off from you!

5:13 For you were-called to freedom, Brothers. Not only The-Freedom to rush [a place to attack from, as an incentive, as a resource, driven away] from the flesh, but in the Godly-love slaving [in willing-divine-bondage] to one another,

Section I

5:14 for The-Law in entirety is-being-fulfilled in one statement, "You-shall-be-Godly-loving the-one near you as yourself."

5:15 Now if you-are biting [wounding the soul] and devouring [destroying, utterly consuming, cannibalizing] one another, beware so you are not consumed by one another!

5:16 I am saying that you are to be walking in spirit and you-should-not-be-consummating [a last act that completes, executing, performing, conjoined in marriage to] the lust of the flesh.

5:17 For The-Flesh is lusting against [turning on, rivals and desires for control of] The-Spirit and also The-Spirit against The-Flesh. And these are opposing one another so that you are not able [to purpose, to resolve, to wish] to do what you are willing [desire to do, to produce, to bear forth, to do].

5:18 Still if you-are-being-led in spirit, you are not under the Law.

5:19 Now the acts of the-flesh are apparent [obvious] which is; adultery, prostitution [illicit sexual intercourse of all manners], uncleanness [impure motives, lustful impurity], unbridled lust [shamelessness, insolence, excess licentiousness],

5:20 idolatry [and its vices], enchantment [use of drugs, sorcery and black magic, the seduction of idolatry], enmities [hatred, hatred to God], strife [contentious arguing], jealousies [envious rivalries], furies [passionate angers], factions [self-seeking an office, electioneering, office intrigue, politics], dissensions [causing division, sedition], preferences [ones following their own tenets, sects, choosing one [thing/person] over another],

5:21 envies, murders [slaughters], drunkenness, revelries [riotous drunken and sexual parties and behavior], and the likes of these. As I was saying before to you and as such I also say to you again, that the-ones practicing [commit oneself to] such shall-not-be-enjoying The-Allotment-of-The-Kingdom-of-*GOD*.

5:22 But the-fruit [affect, result, utility, advantage, profit] of the-spirit is Godly-love, joy [gladness], peace [harmony, tranquility (of the soul), security, safety], patience [endurance, perseverance, slow to avenge, far-feeling], kindness [benign, gentleness, moral integrity], goodness [uprightness of heart, beneficence], faithfulness [conviction in relationships [of God and man]], trustworthy,[reliable character],

5:23 meekness [gentleness, mildness], self-control [master of desire and passions, temperance]; against such there is not law.

5:24 For The-Ones of *The-Anointed* crucify the-flesh together with the-passions and the-lusts.

5:25   If we-may-be-living [to live, pass life, active, among the living, efficient] by spirit, in spirit we-may-be-observing-these-fundamentals [the basic instructions, first teachings] also.

5:26   May-we-not-become [appear in history, come on the stage, finished, be made] empty-esteemed [(with) empty conceit, vain glory], calling-out [challenging, provoke, irritate] one another, to envy one another.

GALATIANS 6

6:1   Brothers, if ever a man may-be-being-overtaken in some offense, you the-ones spiritual, you be down-equipping [mend, adjust, strengthen, put in order, repair, make one what he ought to be] the-such (an one, an individual, the-one) in the spirit of meekness, take notice [contemplate on, examine, observe, watch] of yourself so you also may-not-be-being-tried [test one's faith, enticed to sin, be tempted, in wicked conduct to test God's justice and patience, challenge to test God].

6:2   You be bearing [carry, support, uphold] the heaves [burdens, heaviness, trouble] of one another and thus (in this manner, that is how) you-fill-up [fully satisfy, observe perfectly] The-Law-of-*The-Anointed*.

6:3   Yet if anyone is supposing (himself) to be anything [someone, of prominence, important, of eminence] being himself nothing, he-is-imposing-on [deceived in his mind, subject to fantasies].

6:4   But let him-be-testing the acts of himself, each one, and then alone to himself be he-be-having the-boast [self-glory, self-praise] and not to the different-one [remaining, your neighbor, the rest (of everyone)].

6:5   For each one shall-be-bearing [carrying] their own load [burden, faults, oppressive [condemning] consciousness].

6:6   And the-one-being-instructed in The-Saying [Scriptures, word, gospel] let-him-be-in-fellowship [a partner, a sharer, an associate] with the one-instructing in [about] all good (things).

6:7   And do not be deceived, *GOD* is not to be sneered at [derided, mocked, ridiculed, scoffed, scorned]! For whatever a man may be sowing [planting], this he shall also reap [be rewarded with, be securing].

6:8   For the-one sowing for the flesh for himself, from the flesh shall-be-reaping [cut-off, destroy, to sickle, gather] The-Corruption [perishable] and the-one sowing to the spirit, from the spirit shall-be-reaping life eonian [into the ages].

6:9	And we should not be despondent [exhausted, be weary, grow tired] in [by] doing the ideal [genuine, correct, praiseworthy, honorable] (thing). In season if we do not lose-out [faint, relax, weaken, grow-weary] we-will-be-reaping our own.
6:10	So when then as we have the season [time, opportunity, occurrence], we are to be working for the good for all and especially toward The Family-Members-of The-Belief [faith].
6:11	See how large I write the (individual) letters [individual characters {as in a, b, c, d, e}] to you by my own hand.
6:12	For all those who are willing [desire, intend, be fond of, purposed, wish, resolved] to-put-on-a-fair-face [to please, placate, appease, conciliate, beautify, enhance] to the flesh, those who are compelling you to be circumcised, it is not for The-Pale-[Crucifixion]-of-*The-Anointed* but to-not-be-being-persecuted.
6:13	For not even the-ones about [the subject of, lifestyle of, preaching, instructing, demanding] being-circumcised are not maintaining the Law. But they are willing for you to-be-being-circumcised that they-should-be-boasting [receive glory from] in [about] your flesh [obedience, being controlled].
6:14	Yet may it not be so with me to-be-boasting if it is not [except] in The-Pale-[Crucifixion]-of-*The-Lord* of us *Savior-Anointed*, through whom to me the System [world] is crucified and I to the System [world].
6:15	For in *Anointed-Savior* neither circumcision nor un-circumcision has any value [avails, prospers] but is-a new creation.
6:16	And whoever shall-be-observing-[following]-the-fundamentals of this rule, peace on them and mercy also to The-Israel-of-*THE-GOD*.
6:17	Of the-remaining toils [works, of laboring, burdensome laws {related institutions of the Mosaic Law}], let no-one be-tendering [render, give, supply, challenging] me. For I am bearing [carrying, sustain, can show] the branding-marks [whips, scourging, imprisonments, stoning] of *The-Lord* on my body.
6:18	The-Grace of *The-Lord* of us *Savior-Anointed*, (be) with your spirit, Brothers. Amen.

(Written to the Galatians from Rome)

Section II

A MERGER, AN AFFIRMATION
OF ENTITLEMENT
and Authority of the Out-Called Announcement
and Explanation of the Revelation of the-Secret
Advanced Instructions as a Unified Body

The Letters of
EPHESIAN, COLOSSIANS, and PHILIPPIANS

EPHESIANS COMMENTARY

THE LETTERS OF EPHESIANS, Philippians, and Colossians stand unique against the backdrop of the Romans and Corinthians letters. While it is true that The-Secret is mentioned in Romans and Corinthians, those letters were sent out originally to provide the Believers with the formula, the method, and the means to defend their Belief—meaning how to reason, argue, and counter-argue to defend The-Belief. That Belief being that Christ came in the flesh as "The-Son."

He is defined as the one and only unique such individual, now with all the power, authority, and nature of THE-GOD. He was resurrected on the third day as a man and now rules at the right side of GOD The-Father. We are to be the same—to literally be one in Him through the spirit of GOD. Also, that salvation comes from believing only, not by works or actions or through the Law of Moses and any of its ordinances (including clean and unclean foods). All these had passed away, disappearing completely and forever into the eons. That gift comes to you on behalf of GOD providing it for and to you. Circumcision as a requirement for salvation is a perversion. As a Chosen-One, you are to receive a legal part of an allotment of the Kingdom, I prefer government of GOD, with rank and role in the government and provided with GOD's nature, character, and quality.

This is quite a list to study and to know, defend, and memorize by heart, but something further has been revealed to several members—not just Paul, but also to the Apostles and others in the Ecclesiae. This is the revelation of "The-Secret." The Father has always had the intention to grant salvation to all created beings that can acknowledge Him. This is *universal salvation* for all—past, present, and future. Nothing in the First Contracts or the Second initiated by Christ even hinted at such a thing. It was shocking to be taught this. Why? No longer was the original Ecclesia now the "only Chosen" along with a select few of the past as those new converts understood. (They would have understood the principle of the firstborn being equivalent to being a first-fruit and being the "first in line" to receive the double portion or greater and prime gifts and blessings.) Now that rulership, divinity, judgeship, and management was being spread and offered to billions and billions of more entities—entities including those called "The Originals and a host of other "demonic" entities, unknown or acknowledged (see Eph 3:6–7). This Secret also answered the question of what about those lost or never hearing the name of Jesus or the Christ or the plan of God. God in His will and pleasure is allowing Christ to become Lord and Master of *The-All*, bringing all back to life or restoration, all beings, and all creation in unison, only to have Christ hand that unified Kingdom back to God! This is quite mind-boggling, and many members of The-Body had a hard time accepting this. Actually, all but a handful would abandon Paul as he writes in I Timothy about this. Why would they not accept this greater and better news?

I offer a possible cause for this based on my initial study of Corinthians and Romans. I suggest that tremendous numbers of the Ecclesiae were enamored with this newfound freedom, power, authority, and nature. They expected GOD's Kingdom in their time frame and expected to be invested with rulership and masterdom over those that were oppressing them in their day. Their "empires" were now being distilled and thinned out. Also, the megalomaniacs were still bustling around Corinth and other regions corrupting the teachings and instructions of Paul, and Rome was not far behind with their dissidents and corruptors.

I could extrapolate that this was occurring in every Ecclesia based on the evidence in several of the apostle's writings. I think those abandoning The-Belief, which now included The-Secret, missed the point of being servants, not lords and masters. The "supposed bottom fell out" when they realized that this promised glory and power of theirs was not going to be in their time frames. Further, these promises were to be distilled even more exponentially. This means that they would miss the chance to turn the table on those brutes oppressing them now since "the brutes" (I use this term in a rhetorical sense) were accepted (in the sense that a buy-out of a company took place and the two organizations were being merged) into The Body of Christ (I speak in a corporate sense). "The-Chosen" were probably just salivating over the thought of sitting in judgment and passing sentence over the oppressors. They now took a soured approach and reasoned they had enough of what appeared to be empty promises of a return and "fantasy stories" of a risen Savior; this was in addition to the persecutions taking place, not to mention Paul's "brutal verbal" treatment and probably physical winnowing of a most deserving group in Corinth. I believe word of that would have spread among the Ecclesiae, making people stop to wonder if this was really "worth it."

And so begins a new era, an expanded corporation of the Body of Christ in the Ecclesiae where everyone is, in fact, a son or daughter of The-God and all will have equal status, power, and authority as Christ finishes the plan of God. You, as the first of such sons and daughters, need to walk in a higher and more worthy manner than the Corinthians or Galatians who were giving up on The-Belief.

Ephesians is a compact letter expounding this "Secret" (1:9), but I must caution the reader. While this "Secret" is revealed, it is done so by showing its legality within what has already been established in the principles of Romans, Corinthians, and Galatians. Hence Paul has still not deviated from his original teachings, advice, and instructions as the Ecclesiae General Council and Lawyer for The Nations. Paul is, however, presenting and explaining a new expanded legal merger and contract whereby he defends upholding and approving this change over the original contract with the Ecclesiae. If read carefully, it expands the duties, responsibilities, and rewards of the Chosen-Ones. If I could borrow a poor analogy, The-Chosen, the First-Fruits, are in some respect being moved up the corporate ladder with more responsibilities and duties and better rewards, but few at that time see it in this manner. Especially keep in mind that Paul said God is no respecter of man, and I can with high confidence say the same of any of His creation. All are equal in God's sight other than Christ, The-Messiah, having preeminence, which is only logical and proper.

As you read Ephesians, be sensitive to some of these legal terms—will, grant, management, lot, purchased deliverance, sponsorship, sonship, authority—and how they intertwine with the foundational teachings Paul has already established for the Ecclesia.

I am also going to suggest for the more spiritually sensitive that this letter is also intended to have been written and reviewed for those Beings and Entities in the Heavens (plural intended since Paul uses it in plurality meaning the starry sky and universe in addition to the Heaven where the Temple and Throne of God is currently located) in Ephesians 3:10. This Secret has legal implications, too, now for them as "individuals" to the amended contract.

You need to be aware that nearly all of Paul's letters carry a message to those spirit beings and other entities that also read and study the Scriptures. Their future and past history is contained within the Writings as ours. Paul's letters often carry parallel discussions, meanings, concepts, and messages. This is all throughout his material, but it takes time to research and study it since we are not accustomed to thinking with a spiritual reference as we read. This is really another theme Paul wished he could have spent time teaching to the Ecclesiae; however, of all letters, Hebrews in my opinion is the most apparent about spiritual matters and just as much intended for a spiritual audience as physical one. I have not chosen to discuss that theme within this material, but it needs to be noted that the reader should spend some time studying Paul's letters with this understanding in mind. You will also see hints of this in my Study Notes throughout.

The letter of Ephesians, like all of Paul's writings, opens by first establishing his legal authority to his audience and follows with praise and worship of God the Father and Christ the Savior.

Paul then immediately reassures his audience that they have not lost anything with this new information and announces that the purpose of this letter is to provide a mini-overview of The-Secret, what it is about, who has originated this change in understanding, and what impact it has on the creation of God. (I see this as an initial letter to stockholders explaining a company's intentions to acquire a new business unit and giving the details of the why and how it is to be done and when it is to take place).

Ephesians 1:12—2:12 reiterates The-Chosen's first lien position in the plan and purpose of God. It encourages such a one to recognize that they have been given a

Section II

great gift to have been called first; first public and prime stock options would be a good analogy here. This will have its own rewards for your loyalty and trust in God's promises.

Beginning in verse 2:13, Paul begins setting the introduction and explains the purpose for the changes coming. It will demonstrate God's great mercy and His love for all His creation, which He wishes to be present with Him into the eons. As a side note, Paul really does "get it." He understands the greater impact this change brings. Realizing this, by confession to the Ekklesia stated the physical beatings and trials which took place over the years and this "gift" (my euphemistic remark) from Christ with his eye plus the Demon that accompanied him were considered even more as nothing. He is more accepting of the past events, even though in his early letters he was sharing his infirmities and trials. He is all for this greater opportunity since it benefits everyone greater. This is quite a confession, and one can sense Paul's excitement about the impact of this change with its greater glorious implications than he once understood, thought, or imagined. All those chosen first should be even more ecstatic than before. Paul is promoting this change with excitement and enthusiasm.

Ephesians 4 is a call to hold ourselves in even higher esteem and act like the divine and royal family members we are. It's a "higher calling" than previously understood or taught, and it reiterates the higher "Principles of Living" and behavior we are to maintain. All of these actions are grounded, founded, and based on Godly-loving God first, the one near us next, and ourselves.

In closing out Ephesians in 6:10 Paul exhorts and calls his audience to stand firm over the fight to remove them as The-Chosen ones from this preeminent position, a battle to recapture their souls and thinking and to re-enslave them, to be replaced by others with improper intentions. He exhorts them to review, answer, and rebut any arguments and accusations being charged and prosecuted against them (this word fits not only a legal theme but also fighting a war or battle).

And so opens the new information, arrangement, order of business, and change in the business plans of the Ecclesia, with Philippians and Colossians following to supplement and complete the new revelation.

EPHESIANS AS A LETTER

Paul, Commissioner of *Savior-Anointed* through the will of *GOD* to The-Holy-Ones, The-Ones being in Ephesus and believing in *Anointed-Savior*. Grace to you and peace from *GOD, FATHER* of us and *Master-Savior-Anointed*.

Bless *THE-GOD* and *FATHER* of *The-Master* of us *Savior-Anointed*, *THE-ONE-BLESSING* us in every spiritual blessing in The-Heavens in *Anointed* according as *HE* chose us in *Him* before the disruption of the System. We are Holy-Ones and flawless before *HIM* in Godly-love. Unbreakably-gripping us prior-to-time with the status of a son through *Savior-Anointed* into *Him* in unison-and-purpose with the-delight in the-will of *HIM* for praising in glory about The-Grace-of-*HIM* in which *HE* honors us with blessings in *The-One-having-been-Loved*. In whom we are having The-Deliverance through the-blood of *Him* for the-forgiveness of the-offenses according-to the-riches of the-loving-kindness of *HIM* which he lavishes into us in every wisdom and understanding. Making known to us The-Secret-of-the-Will-of-*HIM* according-to the-delight of *HIM* which *HE* before purposed-and-determined in *HIMSELF* for the management-of-household-affairs of The-Completion-of-The-Eras to gather-into-one, The-All, in *The-Anointed* both in The-Heavens and that on The-Earth in *Him* with *Who* also our lot was cast being designated before according for the purpose of *THE-ONE*; The-All, operating in unison-and-purpose with the-counsel of-the-will of *HIM*.

We are for the praise of The-Glory-of-*HIM*, The-One's having-a-prior-expectancy in *The-Anointed*. In *Whom* you also hearing the-word of the-truth, The-Well-Message-of-The-Salvation about you in *Whom* you also believing are sealed by the-spirit-of-The-Holy-Promise which is a down-payment of our Allotment-of-Enjoyment by The-Purchased-Deliverance for praise and the-glory of *Him*.

Because of this I am hearing about your belief about *The-Master-Savior* and the-Godly-love to The-All, The-Holy-Ones. I am not ceasing giving thanks for your sake mentioning of you in my prayers, that *THE-GOD* of *The-Master* of us *Savior-Anointed*, *THE-FATHER-of-THE-GLORY*, may be giving to you the spirit of wisdom and revelation in the knowledge of *HIM*. That through the-eyes of your mind having been opened to know-the-fact what is The-Expectation of The-Calling-of-*HIM* and the-riches of-the-glory of *HIS* Enjoyment-of-the-Allotment among *HIS* Holy-Ones. To-know what is the-transcendental-greatness of-the-unlimited-inherent-power-and-majesty of *HIM* for us, The-One's-Believing in unison with the-operation of the-mighty-strength of *HIM*. In which *HE* operates in *The-Anointed* rousing *Him* out of the dead-ones and seats to the right of *HIM* among The-Heavenlies over every sovereignty and authority and power and lordship and every name being named, not only this eon, but also in The-One-Impending and all subjects under the-feet of *Him* and gives *Him* supreme-authority over all The-Called-Out which is The-Body-of-*Him*, the-full-complement of The-All and is completed by All.

And you being dead to the-offenses and the-sins in which you once tread about according-to The-Eon-of-The-System, this in agreement-and-unison with The-Chief-of-The-Authority-of-The-Spirit-of-The-Air that now operates in The-Sons-of-The-Stubbornness in whom we all also behaved once in the-lusts of our flesh, doing the-desires of the-flesh and of the-mind and were offspring by nature of glaring-stubbornness as even The-Remaining. Yet *THE-GOD* being rich in mercy because of the-vast-Godly-love of *HIM* in which *HE* loves us and us being dead in the-offenses, *HE* makes us together with *The-Anointed* alive. By grace you are the-ones having been saved.

And *HE* together gathers and together seats us among The-Heavenlies in *Anointed Savior* that *HE* should be displaying in The-Eons-Coming the-transcendental riches of The-Grace-of-*HIM* in kindness on us in *Anointed-Savior*.

For by grace you are the ones having been saved through The-Belief and this not coming from you but The-Gift of *GOD*. Not out of acts that anyone should be boasting.

For we are *HIS* workmanship being created in *Anointed-Savior* for good acts which *THE-GOD* ordained that we should be walking in them. Therefore, be remembering you were once The-Nations of flesh, The-Ones being called Uncircumcised by The-Ones called Circumcised of flesh done-by-hands. That you were in The-Season without *Anointed* having been alienated from the-citizenship of Israel and foreigners of The-Covenants of The-Promise having no expectation and without *GOD* in The-System.

Now yet in *Anointed-Savior*, you who once being far off have become near-by the-blood of *The-Anointed*. For He is our peace, *The-One* making both one and has utterly-destroyed The-Central-Barrier-Wall having abolished in *His* flesh the-conflict of The-Law-of-The-Directions with decrees that-from the two, *He* should be creating in *Himself* into one new man making peace, and *He* should be unifying the-both in one body to *THE-GOD* through The-Pale slaying the-conflict in it and came bringing The-Well-Message-of-Peace to you, The-Ones being far and to The-Ones near. That through *Him* we both are having the-access in one spirit toward *THE-FATHER*.

Recognize-and-realize then you are no longer guests and foreigners but fellow citizens of The-Holy-Ones and Family Members of *THE-GOD* being built on the-foundation of The-Commissioners and Prophets. *Savior-Anointed* being The-Capstone-of-The-Corner in *Whom* the-entire-building being connected together is growing into the Holy-Temple in *Master* in *Whom* also you are being built together into the dwelling place of *THE-GOD* in spirit.

Of this grace, I, Paul, the-bound-one of *The-Anointed-Savior* over you The-Nations, since surely you understand the-special-consideration of The-Grace-of-*THE-GOD, THE-ONE-BEING* giving me for you that according-to the divine-instruction *He*-made-known to me, The-Secret as I wrote before in brief, to which you are able to read to apprehend the-understanding of mine about The-Secret of *The-Anointed*. Which was not made known in different generations to the-sons-of-men, but it is now revealed to The-Holy-Commissioners and Prophets of *Him* by spirit that The-Nations are equal-in-status-having-the-same-privileges-and-holds-title-to-and-of Enjoyers-of-an-Allotment and enjoined to The-Promise-of-*HIM* in *The-Anointed* through the-Well-Message for which I became a server according-to The-Gift-of-The-Grace-of-*THE-GOD. THE-BEING* granting-this to me according-to the-divine-supreme-planning of *HIS* unlimited-and-inherent-power.

To me, the-greatest-of-the-most-inferior of all The-Holy-Ones, was granted grace to bring the Well-Message among The-Nations of the-untraceable riches of *The-Anointed* and to enlighten all about the-fellowship of The-Secret having been concealed from The-Eons in THE-GOD, THE-ONE-CREATING The-All for *Savior Anointed*. That now being made known to The-Originals and The-Authorities among The-Celestial-Ones through The-Ecclesia the great variety of ways of wisdom of *THE-GOD* according-to creating The-Eons which HE made for *Anointed-Savior-The-Master* for us, in *Whom* we are having the boldness and the access in confidence through The-Belief of *Him*.

Therefore, I am requesting to not be despondent by the-afflictions of me for your sake which is your glory. Of this gift, I bow my knees to *THE-FATHER* of *The-Master* of us *Savior-Anointed* out of *Whom* every lineage in heaven and on earth is named. That HE may be giving you according-to the-riches of The-Glory-of-*HIM*, to be made to grow strong through the-spirit of *HIM* into the-internal-inner man to dwell *The-Anointed* through The-Belief in your hearts having been rooted and grounded in Godly-love. That you should be unbreakably-grasping together with all The-Holy-Ones what is the-breadth and length and depth and height. To also know about the-Godly-love of *The-Anointed* which transcends knowledge that you may be completely filled in the-entire-fullness-with-the-divinity of *THE-GOD*. Yet to *THE-ONE-BEING-ABLE* to do above all exceedingly, extravagantly, above we are requesting or are thinking according-to the-power operating in us, to *HIM* be the-glory in The-Called-Out in *Anointed-Savior* into all the generations of The-Eons of The-Eons.

Amen.

I am entreating you then, I the-bounded one in *Master*, to walk in-the-highest-value of The-Calling which you were called with all humility and meekness, with patience bearing with one another in Godly-love, endeavoring to be keeping the-oneness of-the-spirit together in the-bond of peace. One body and one spirit, according even as you were called in one Expectation with your Calling, *One-Master*, one belief, one

Section II

baptism, *ONE-GOD* and *FATHER* of all, *THE-ONE* in-dominance-of all and through all and in all you.

Yet to each one of us was given The-Grace according-to the measure of The-Gift-of-*The-Anointed*. Through which *HE* is saying, "When *He* ascended to high, *He* captured Captivity and gives gifts to men." Yet what does "When *He* ascended" mean but that *He* first descended into the lower parts of the earth? *The-One* descending is also *The-One* in-authority-of all The-Heavens that He should be finishing all.

This same *One* gives ones commissioners and prophets and the-ones evangelists and the-ones as shepherds and teachers for the perfecting of The-Holy-Ones for acts of service into edification of The-Body-of-*The-Anointed* until we all should be attaining the oneness of The-Belief and the-precise-and-correct-knowledge of *The-Son-of-THE-GOD* as a perfect man in the state-of-adulthood, in the complete-divinity of *The-Anointed*. That we should by no means still be minors surging here and there and being carried about by every wind of teaching taking a losing bet in men in craftiness with a method to deceive. But being true in Godly-love we, The-All, should be growing into *Him* who is *The-Ruler, The-Anointed*. Out of *Whom* the-entire-body being articulated and fitted-as-one together through every supplied joint according-to the measured action of each part of the growing body is making and building itself in Godly-love.

I am saying this then and am witnessing for *Master* that by no means are you to be walking as the-remaining of the Nations are walking devoid-of-truth in their mind, with comprehension been darkened, being separated from *The-Life-of-THE-GOD*. This ignorance is in them because of the-callousness of their heart who are-past-having-feelings-and-emotions give themselves over to The-Debauchery to act in impure-motives in greediness.

But you are a disciple of *The-Anointed* if truly you hear *Him* and in *Him* you were taught. The-Truth is in *The-Savior*. That you are to be completely-removing the-former-behavior of the old man, the-one being corrupted according-to The-Seduction-of-The-Desires and be rejuvenated by the-spirit in your mind and let-slipping-in the-new-man according-to *THE-GOD* being created in justice and true holiness.

Therefore, putting away lying, each of you be-speaking truth with the-near-one! We are members of one another. "Be angry but do not sin," "Do not let the sun go down your vexation" nor giving place to The-Adversary! The-one-stealing, by no means let him be stealing! Rather let him be toiling, working the-hands for the-good that he may be having a share in giving to the-one having a need. Do not be issuing at all rotten words out of your mouth, but good if any, for edification of the-need that it may be giving grace to the-ones-hearing. And do not be suppressing-and-ignoring the-spirit-of-*THE-HOLY-GOD* in which you are sealed for The-Day-of-Deliverance. Let all bitterness and fury and anger and clamor and slander, let it all be taken away from you! Together with all malice and you become kind, tenderly compassionate to one another, dealing graciously among yourselves also as THE-GOD in *Anointed* deals graciously with you.

You then become imitators of *THE-GOD* as beloved offspring and you be walking in Godly-love just as *The-Anointed* Godly-loves us and has given *Himself* as an offering on behalf of us as a fragrant-odor sacrifice to *THE-GOD*. And do not let it be found among you prostitution and all uncleanness or greediness as you have become to be Holy-Ones. Nor obscenity and stupid speaking or improper insinuations but rather be thankful about this, you know that every male prostitute or unclean or greedy one who is an idolater is not having an Enjoyment-of-The-Allotment in The-Kingdom of *The-Anointed* and *GOD*. Let no one be seducing you with empty teaching because of this the anger of *THE-GOD* is coming on The-Sons-of-Stubbornness. Do not then become associates with them!

For you were once in darkness, now a light in *Master*, walk as offspring of light! For the-effect of the-spirit is in every goodness and righteousness and truth. Prove what is well pleasing to *The-Master* and you do not be joint-participants associated with the acts of The-Unfruitful-Darkness but rather expose them. For it is a shame to even speak of the things being done in hiding by them.

For all those things are being exposed by the light, for the light exposes everything. Therefore HE says, "Be aroused The-Lounging-One! Stand up you out of the-dead-ones," and, "The Anointed shall be appearing." Be observing then how accurately you are walking not unwise but as wise reclaiming The-Season because the-days are wicked.

Because of this do not become stupid but be ones understanding the-desires of *The-Master*. And do not be drunk with wine which is wastefulness-and-reckless but you be filled in the-spirit. Speak-in-devotion-in psalms and hymns and spiritual songs to yourselves singing and playing music in your heart to *The-Master*. Give thanks always for all in the name of *The-Master* of us Savior-Anointed to *THE-GOD* and *FATHER*, being subject to one another in awe-and-respect of *GOD*.

Wives be-willing-subjects-to your own husbands as if *The-Master*. For the-husband has-the-prominent-position-of-the-wife even as *The-Anointed* is the head of The-Called-Outs and *He* is the *Savior* of The-Body. Even as The-Ecclesia is subject to *The-Anointed* therefore also the-women to their own men in all.

Husbands, you be Godly-loving the-wives as also *The-Anointed* Godly-loves The-Ecclesia and gave *Himself* up for-the-sake of her. That *He* should be making-her-holy and cleansing with the bathing of the water by declaration that *He* should be presenting her to *Himself*, glorious, The-Ecclesia, having no spot or wrinkle or any of the-such but that it is holy and flawless. So the husbands are to-be-Godly-regarding-the-welfare-of their own wives as their own bodies. The one Godly-loving his wife is highly-guarding-the-welfare-of himself. For no one at any time hates his flesh but is nurturing and cherishing her even as also *The-Master* The-Ecclesia.

Section II

For we are members of The-Body-of-*Him*, out of *His* flesh and from *His* marrow. This is the reason why a man shall be leaving his father and mother and shall be joined to his wife and the-two are-to become one flesh. Still I am saying this is a great mystery of *Anointed* and in The-Ecclesia. Nevertheless, each one of you be Godly-loving your wife as himself and the wife that she may be having-a-reverence-for the-husband.

Children be-obeying your parents in *Master*; this is of virtue. Be honoring your father and mother, which is the first precept with-a promise "that it may be well with you and you should be living a long time on the earth."

And you Fathers, do not be vexing your offspring but be nurturing them in upright education and training and the-lessons of *Master*.

Slaves, be obeying your Masters of the flesh with fear and trembling in the-sincerity of your heart as to *The-Anointed*. Not under-the-scrutiny-of-the-Master-to-be-as men-pleasers, but as slaves of *The-Anointed* doing the-will of THE-GOD out of the soul, with good humor slaving as to *The-Master* and not to men, knowing that whatever good one should be doing this he shall be paid-back by *The-Master* whether slave or free.

And Masters, you be doing the same thing toward them, omitting your threats to them, being aware that your *Master* is in the Heavens and there is no partiality with *Him*.

Lastly, Brothers, be you invigorated in *Master* and in the force and ability-over-external-things by *Him*. You put on every battle-armor of THE-GOD for you to be enabled to stand to the-stratagems of The-Adversary. We are not wrestling against flesh and blood, but against The-Originals against The-Authorities against The-System-Holders of The-Darkness-of-The-Eon, against The-Spirits-of-The-Wickedness among The-Heavenlies.

Because of this be fully-dressed-in the-full-array-of-battle-armor of THE-GOD that you may be enabled to withstand in The-Wicked-Day, having done all to stand. You be standing then girded about your loin in truth and placing-on The-Breastplate-of-Justice and sandal the-feet in preparation of The-Well-Message-of-Peace. Above all take up The-Large-Shield-of-Belief in which you shall be able to extinguish the-arrows being fiery of The-Wicked-One and The-Helmet-of-Salvation. You receive The-Sword-of-The-Spirit which is *The-Word* of GOD during every prayer and long petitioning pleas at every occasion in spirit and this being the same for vigilance, in all perseverance and pleading-and-requests concerning all The-Holy-Ones.

And for my sake, that for me, may it be granted that I may open my mouth expressing in boldness making known The-Secret-of-The-Well-Message for which I am being an ambassador in bonds that in it I should be being bold as it is right-and-proper for me to speak.

So that you may be acquainted with my affairs, I am engaging and shall be introducing you to Tychicus the-beloved and faithful Brother and believing servant in

Master whom I send to you for this same thing, that you may know the concerns of us and he should be consoling your hearts.

Peace to The-Brothers and Godly-love with belief from *FATHER GOD* and *Master-Savior-Anointed*.

The-Grace to all The-Ones-Godly-loving *The-Master* of us *Savior-Anointed* in sincere-never-diminishing Godly-love.

(Written to the Ephesians from Rome through Tychicus)

EPHESIANS STUDY NOTES

Note: Through my many translations, I have come to believe that the phrase or associated phrasing of "inheritance" [ex: Col 1:12] accurately translated as "the-allotment" in Scripture is not a good or proper translation (i.e., inheritance). Paul makes it clear that we are to be family members (I state: royal and godly) destined to be with HIM and HE with us and we in Christ and He in us. Inheritance has an implied connotation, an accepted concept that someone has died. THE-GOD is certainly not dead, and Christ has risen to life eonian (there are times of times of times) as well. I see this as a watering down of the intent and meaning of the Scriptures and have dropped using the word *inheritance* when speaking of THE-GOD's plan and purpose for us. We are to take rulership in an active kingdom with Christ at the head of the realm and we under Him, with THE-GOD over all of us.

Note The Greek word *agapen* translated as "love" in most translations is missing that this is Godly in nature and not of men or any other such creature. I have therefore carried the adjective to add clarity to the meaning of this word throughout this translation.

Note: In my research, nearly all translations have dropped "the" as a modifier, but the Greek word for "the" is in every text and not meant to be ignored or deleted. It is often specifically singular, and when attached to the noun, it is describing that noun as unique, one of a kind, a specific thing, the original, the one and only. It is for this reason that I carry "the" everywhere it appears in all translations. Whether of God, Jesus, Satan or any other entity, concept, or idea, the modifier "the" clears up a lot of generalized words, ideas, concepts, and entities.

Note: The root of the word *pnuemia*, translated as "spirit, wind, or breath," has no gender identity since this is a word that is neuter in gender. *Pnuemia* is an "it." The Greeks, as we of English language, often fix a gender to objects and things— for example: cars, boats, the moon, the sun. For the Greeks, *pnuemia* at times has a male gender affixed to it. *Pnuemia* in the Scriptures is never capitalized or designated as a standalone being, entity, principality, or sovereignty when used as the word "spirit." It is simply the power inherent in the

being, whether of man, or God, or Christ, or any other entity. If anything is living, "it" possesses a spirit. The "Holy-spirit" is simply the power from and of The-God, giving and renewing life and performing The-God's will.

Note: Paul constantly claims and mentions "principles, powers, authorities, sovereignties not of our world." He quite clearly claims that these beings are the ones that certainly influence and control (predominately in a negative way) the systems of this world, people of the nations, and as individuals directly. You can find this concept also contained in The Old Testament through the implications of the first commandment. This claim and the concept of the warring factions in heaven makes a fascinating study.

Note: Time periods, eons, ages, millennia, eons, and eons—I stayed true to the Greek words associated with time and what we still use today in our common language. A study of time periods is fascinating but is also an area that can cause confusion. The-God always works on some kind of a timetable, but understanding which is which and when is when is a bit of a mystery. Some timetables are only known to The-God and made clear to man at God's will.

Note What is the difference between "expectation" and "hope?" Nearly all translations adopt the word "hope" for "expectation," but Paul uses almost exclusively the word "expectation." Here is why I constantly use "expectation." Having an expectation means you have no doubt at all. It is sure and certain with no ambiguity or doubt. Having a hope means you are not 100 percent convinced and convicted. I can tell you that Paul is undeniably convinced and convicted in what he delivers and talks about. Using "hope" sends a message that there is some possibility for "wiggle room," doubt, error, or excuses.

Even worse, much of the use of the word "expectation" in Paul's writings has the modifier "the" attached to "expectation," thus forming the proper translation and singular concept of "The-Expectation." This makes "The-Expectation" an event, not a philosophy or theological premise. Not recognizing "The-Expectation" as an event will lead the reader immediately down an incorrect understanding of what is being offered or discussed.

1:13 My understanding of the placement of the adjective "holy" calls the promise of salvation "Holy"; it is not attributed to the word spirit. Hence, while the sentence would transcribe in many translations as "in Whom you also hearing the word of the truth, the well-message [gospel] of your saving [salvation] in Who you also believing are sealed in (the) *Holy* spirit of the promise," my understanding is "in *Whom* you also believing are sealed in (the) spirit of the "*holy* promise." Most translations relate the word holy with "Holy Spirit," not holy promise.

Section II

1:14   The Greek word *arrabon* translated as "earnest" is a term to do with a legal contract where money is paid as a pledge, a down payment toward the purchase of an item. This also clears up any confusion about the "spirit" being an entity or third person of the trinity doctrine. The word "earnest" does carry a masculine sense but is still an object, much like we would attribute the name of a man or woman to a car. The spirit is referred to as a pledge in this sentence, not an entity or being. If the "Holy spirit" was a third person, to call "him" a "pledge" would certainly be blasphemy as if it could be bought or sold.

1:22   The word *subject* is open-ended and implies any and everything from man to animals, the earthly creation, and all beings, entities, and power in the heavenlies. As a side note, the word "heavenlies" is a plural translation implying other worlds, kingdoms, powers, sovereignties as well as where God-The-Father and Christ are at this time. It provides a sense that what we know of creation as men is limited.

1:23   The Greek word *pleroma* translated as "filling or compliment" has a nautical basis referring to the manning of the sailors of a ship, also laden fully with cargo and material.

2:6   Verses 2:6–8; 2:10 signify OUR destiny. It is the most profound and clearest declaration of The-God to us, about us through The-Christ as taught and revealed by Paul.

3:1   This entire chapter discusses and explains the "Secret" that was withheld and how it affects all things. This chapter is the entire reason Paul wrote to the Ephesians Ecclesia.

Note: Church verses ecclesia—which? The etymology of the word *church* is the same as "circle," "coven," and "circuit." These words all have one thing in common: they all come around and return to themselves—a closed group, property, or organization. The etymology of the word *ecclesia* is directly translated as "called-out ones." That is removed from a closed-in group, property, or organization. God is not a closed-in being. I have stayed with the original that describes God's elect at this eon.

3:8   *Untraceable* would also imply "unsearchable." Because God's way is described as both, only HE can reveal them to us.

3:7   The Greek word *energeian* translated as "operation" and "effectual working" does not grasp or demonstrate the "superhuman" power to make every part fit and operate in unison as one. Hence a better translation is "supreme working," "divine master planning," or "divine supreme planning."

3:7   The Greek word *dunameos* translated as "power" misses the strength meant within the word. The root of this Greek word is where we get "dynamite," and hence we should translate this as "explosive" or "ultimate power." It also means that this "ultimate power" is inherent within the person or thing. Our inherent power is limited compared to God and those in heaven.

3:9 "through Savior-Anointed," or "by Jesus Christ" often seen at the end of verse 9 in many translations is not in any of the original manuscripts, and as such I have excluded them. Any translations including these are a corruption of the verse, surely added by scribes within the KJV and other late translations to support the errant philosophy of the trinity.

3:9 Paul reveals to the Ecclesia that the sovereignties and authorities in heavens (notice this is plural and not singular suggesting worlds, universes, or kingdoms we have not been aware of) have only come to know about this secret, this "mystery," since it has come through the apostles and revealed to The-God's called-out ones. The-God is using his earthly "instruments" to instruct and teach those in the heavens as much as we are often taught from above. One reason the angels and those in heaven follow closely the affairs of mankind might be because they do not have all knowledge when it comes to the affairs of men or themselves in heaven.

Many translations use the word "mystery" over "secret," but mystery implies there is a hidden or undiscovered knowledge in an act or thing. "Secret" is the clearer and proper translation. This new knowledge was not a "mystery"; Paul explains clearly what it is. It was simply a held secret until it was revealed. No other beings had any hint such intent existed in God's plans, purposes, or will at all.

4:8 "He captured Captivity" is a clear reference to Jesus seizing Death and placing it under His control and authority.

4:9 "Yet what does "When He ascended" mean but that He first descended into the lower parts of the earth." When researching this verse, and reading various translations, all were quite awkward and left uncertainty about what was being discussed. But Paul is not complex in his writing, even though his subjects are deep and complex upon reflection. This passage is talking about Christ being in the grave before He ascended and seized Death's authority and power after His resurrection.

4:12 The Greek word translated as "home-building" is better understood as "edification" and can also imply to repair and improve the condition of.

4:14 Are you "gambling" away your calling based on the cleverness and errant teaching of men?

4:15 The Greek word *agape* is Godly love, not the love that men or other creatures and beings have or produce, and I have included this adjective to give complete meaning of the word often only translated as "love."

Section II

5:2   The Greek word *euodias* translated commonly as "sweet smelling" or "fragrant" is better understood as an odor of satisfaction or of acceptance. As the animal sacrifices' "odor" (this was a sweet, life-giving odor) pleased God, how much more the "sweet life-giving odor sacrifice" of Jesus was found to be "exceedingly acceptable" by The-God?

5:2   The Greek word *osme* translated commonly as "odor" also means smell. One of the specific uses has to do with the smell that is diffused or emitted by life, and in itself imparts life. This is the sense that Paul is telling his audience, and I added the word "life" to better clarify the intent glossed over in many translations.

5:3   The Greek word *porneia* translated commonly as "fornication"—normally understood to be sexual impropriety in its many forms—also refers to eating the sacrifices offered to idols. Paul talks extensively in Romans concerning eating meat and addresses directly meat offered to idols and offending others by serving it (as a meal) if another's belief was not strong enough to understand that all food was now acceptable as sustenance. The side concern or issue about idol sacrifices was properly draining the blood out of the animal when slaughtered. The use of the word "uncleanness" therefore implies meat in addition to sexual impropriety.

Concerning sexual impropriety; historical records of the period often mention the "ease and amount" of times people were having illicit relations with another's mate, whether in marriage or those divorced. It was a normal part of and accepted lifestyle among the Gentiles. Paul was telling his audience to stop that lifestyle and walk in righteousness.

5:5   From the Greek word *pornos* directly translated as male prostitute, as *Strong's Concordance* says of the word "G4205—*pornos*:"

       1) a man who prostitutes his body for another's lust for hire
       2) a male prostitute
       3) a man who indulges in unlawful sexual intercourse, a fornicator[/NL 1–3]

5:6   From the root of the Greek word *apeitheias* we would recognize one of our words, "apathy." This is an "I don't care attitude" that always implies a certain amount of stubbornness and haughtiness.

5:22   The Greek word *hypotassesthe* translated as "subject." *Strong's Concordance* says the following about being "under the subject": "This word was a Greek military term meaning 'to arrange [troop divisions] in a military fashion under the command of a leader.' *In non-military use, it was 'a voluntary attitude of giving in, cooperating, assuming responsibility, and carrying a burden.'*" (italics mine).

EPHESIANS STUDY NOTES

While husbands and men may be under the impression the first definition is intended to mean having supreme control, Paul clearly means the second. Therefore, as a husband, you should be aware that the wife is willingly allowing the subjection to occur as we (men) should be doing with our Master. Be aware that she is imitating what you as a man should do in Christ. As the head goes, so follows the body. This same concept applies to Ephesians 5:21.

5:25   The Greek word *autes* is directly translated as "he, she, and it" and all associated derivatives. But I am reminded that Christ is to "marry" the Ecclesia, and therefore the pronoun is given a feminine association, hence translated as "her." In a broader sense, that which is in heaven is here on earth. Is there in heaven an entity equivalent that the Ecclesia represents or vice versa? Is "the one in heaven being prepared" for marriage as the Ecclesia is "being prepared" for Christ's return and marriage?

5:32   Verses 32 and 33 should cause us to pause. Paul reveals a great mystery that he was given but cannot offer an explanation or any details of how it worked or what it meant or what was to be made of it. He appears to not have anything to offer beyond the fact he knew it was revealed to him. His response in verse 33 is as if he just shrugged his shoulders and admitted ignorance after posing the enigma, dropping the subject, and moving on to reiterating how the relationship between a husband and wife needed to be.

EPHESIANS IN VERSE

EPHESIANS 1

1:1 Paul, Commissioner [apostle] of *Savior-Anointed* through the will of *GOD* to The-Holy-Ones [saints], The-Ones being in Ephesus and believing in *Anointed-Savior*.

1:2 Grace to you and peace from *GOD*, *FATHER* of us and *Master-Savior-Anointed*.

1:3 Bless *THE-GOD* and *FATHER* of *The-Master* of us *Savior-Anointed*, *THE-ONE-BLESSING* us in every spiritual blessing in The-Heavens [abode of God and angels, the stars] in *Anointed* [Christ]

1:4 according as *HE* chose us in *Him* before the disruption of the System [world]. We are Holy-Ones and flawless [un-blamable] in sight of [before] *HIM* in Godly-love.

1:5 Seizing [securely/unbreakably-gripping, with a wrestling hold] us before [prior to time] with the place [position, status] of a son through *Savior-Anointed* into *Him* in accord [unison, purpose] with the-delight in the-will of *HIM*

1:6 for praising in glory about The-Grace-of-*HIM* in which *HE* honors us with blessings [graces us] in *The-One-having-been-Loved*.

1:7 In whom we are having The-Deliverance through the-blood of *Him* for the-forgiveness of the-offenses [sins] according-to the-riches of the-loving-kindness [grace] of *Him*

1:8 which he lavishes into us in every wisdom and prudence [understanding].

1:9 Making known to us The-Secret-[hidden thing]-of-The-Will-of-*HIM* according-to the-delight of *HIM* which *HE* before placed [purposed, determined] in *HIM (SELF)*

1:10 into [for] the administration [management of household affairs, stewardship] of The-Filling-[completion]-of-The-Seasons [eras] to head up [gather into one, to sum up into one] The-All in *The-Anointed* both in The-Heavens and that on The-Land [earth]

1:11   in *Him* with *Who* also our lot was cast [a divine lottery] being designated before [predetermined] according-to [by, for] the purpose of THE-ONE, The-All, operating in accordance [unison, purpose] with the-counsel of the-will of *HIM*.

1:12   That us [we] are for the praise of The-Glory-of-*HIM*, The-One's having-a-prior-expectancy [having trusted first, believing, belief] in *The-Anointed*.

1:13   In *Whom* you also hearing *The-Word* of *The-Truth*, The-Well-Message-[gospel]-of-The-Salvation about you in *Whom* you also believing are sealed by The-Spirit-of-The-holy-Promise

1:14   which [that] is an-earnest [the pledge, a down payment] of our Allotment-of-Enjoyment by The-Procured-[Purchased]-Deliverance for praise and the-glory of *Him*.

1:15   Because of this I am hearing about your belief [faith] according-to [about] *The-Master-Savior* and the-Godly-love to The-All, The-Holy-Ones.

1:16   I am not ceasing giving thanks for your sake, making reminders [mentioning] of you in my prayers,

1:17   that THE-GOD of *The-Master* of us *Savior-Anointed*, THE-FATHER-of-THE-GLORY, may be giving to you the spirit of wisdom and revelation in the knowledge of *HIM*.

1:18   That through the-eyes of your mind having been enlightened [opened] to perceive [know the fact] what is The-Expectation of The-Calling-of-*HIM* and the-riches of the-glory of *HIS* Enjoyment-of-the-Allotment among *HIS* Holy-Ones.

1:19   {To know} what is the-transcendental-greatness of the-unlimited-inherent-power-and-majesty of *HIM* for us, The-One's-Believing in accord [unison] with the-action [operation] of the-mighty-strength of *HIM*.

1:20   In which *HE* acts [operates] in *The-Anointed* rousing *Him* out of the dead-ones and seats to the right of *HIM* among The-Heavenlies [region, sanctuary, temple, stars, angels]

1:21   over every sovereignty and authority and power and lordship [master, dominion] and every name being named, not only this eon but also in The-One-Impending

1:22   and all subjects under the-feet of *Him* and gives *Him* head [supreme authority] over all The-Called-Out [Ecclesia]

1:23   which is The-Body of *Him*, the-full-compliment of The-All and is completed by All.

Section II

EPHESIANS 2

2:1 And you being dead to the-offenses and the-misses [sins]

2:2 in which you once tread about according-to The-Eon-[age]-of-The-System [world], this in accord [agreement, unison] with The-Chief-of-The-Authority-[jurisdiction]-of-The-Spirit-of-The-Air that now operates in The-Sons-of-The-Stubbornness

2:3 in whom we all also behaved once in the-lusts of our flesh, doing the-wills [desires] of-the-flesh and of the-mind and were offspring [children] by nature of indignation [glaring stubbornness, impudence] as even The-Remaining.

2:4 Yet *THE-GOD* being rich in mercy because of the-vast-Godly-love of *HIM* in which *HE* loves us

2:5 and us being dead in the-offenses [sins], *HE* makes (us) together with *The-Anointed* alive. By grace you are the-ones having been saved.

2:6 And *HE* together rouses [gathers] and together seats (us) among The-Heavenlies in *Anointed Savior*

2:7 that *HE* should be displaying in The-Eons-Coming the-transcendental riches of The-Grace-of-*HIM* in kindness on us in *Anointed-Savior*.

2:8 For by grace you are (the) ones having been saved through The-Belief [faith] and this not coming from you, (but) The-Oblation [Gift] of *GOD*.

2:9 Not out of [by] acts [works] that anyone should be boasting.

2:10 For we are *HIS* achievement [workmanship] being created in *Anointed-Savior* for good acts which *THE-GOD* made ready before-hand [ordained] that we should be walking in them.

2:11 Therefore be remembering you were once The-Nations in [of] flesh, The-Ones being called Uncircumcised by The-Ones called Circumcised of flesh done-by-hands.

2:12 That you were in The-Season apart from [without] *Anointed* having been alienated from the-citizenship of Israel and guests [foreigners] of The-Covenants of The-Promise having no expectation and without *GOD* in The-System [world].

2:13 Now yet in *Anointed-Savior*, you who once being far off have become near by the-blood of *The-Anointed*.

2:14 For He is our peace, *The-One* making both one and has razed [utterly-destroyed] The-Central-Barrier-Wall

2:15 having abolished in *His* flesh the-enmity [antagonism, conflict] of The-Law-of-The-Directions [commandments] (contained) with decrees [ordinances]

	that-from the two, *He* should be creating in *Himself* into one new man making peace
2:16	and *He* should be reconciling [unifying] the-both in one body to *THE-GOD* through The-Pale [Crucifixion, cross] killing [slaying, putting to death] the-enmity [conflict] in it
2:17	and came bringing The-Well-Message-of-Peace to you, The-Ones being far and to The-Ones near.
2:18	That through *Him* we both are having the-access in one spirit toward *THE-FATHER*.
2:19	Consequently [recognize, realize, understand] then you are no longer guests and sojourners [foreigners] but fellow citizens of The-Holy-Ones and Family Members of *THE-GOD*
2:20	being built on the-foundation of The-Commissioners [apostles] and Prophets. *Savior-Anointed* being The-Capstone-of-The-Corner [chief cornerstone]
2:21	in *Whom* the-entire-building being connected together is growing into the Holy-Temple in *Master*
2:22	in *Whom* also you are being built together into the dwelling place of *THE-GOD* in spirit.

EPHESIANS 3

3:1	Of this grace, I Paul the-bound-one of *The-Anointed-Savior* over you The-Nations [gentiles]
3:2	since surely you hear [understand] the-administration [dispensation, special consideration] of The-Grace-of-*THE-GOD*, *THE-ONE-BEING* giving me for you
3:3	that according-to the revelation [divine-instruction] *He*-made-known to me, The-Secret as I wrote before in brief,
3:4	to which you are able to read to apprehend the-understanding of mine about The-Secret of *The-Anointed*.
3:5	Which was not made known in different generations to the-sons-of-men but it is now revealed to The-Holy-Commissioners and Prophets of *Him* by spirit
3:6	that The-Nations are joint [are equal in status, have the same privileges, is an equal owner of, holds title to and of] Enjoyers-of-an-Allotment and bodied together [the same body, partakers, enjoined] of The-Promise-of-*HIM* in *The-Anointed* through The-Well-Message

Section II

3:7   for which I became a server [minister] according-to The-Gift-of-The-Grace-of-*THE-GOD*. *THE-BEING* granting-this to me according-to the-operation [effectual working, supreme working, divine supreme planning] of *HIS* power [unlimited and inherent].

3:8   To me the-greatest-of-the-most-inferior [absolute worst, inferior-of-the-least] of all The-Holy-Ones, was given [granted] grace to bring the Well-Message among The-Nations of the-untraceable riches of *The-Anointed*

3:9   and to enlighten all about the-fellowship of The-Secret having been concealed from The-Eons in *THE-GOD, THE-ONE-CREATING* The-All.

3:10   That now being made known to The-Originals and The-Authorities among The-Celestial-Ones through The-Ecclesia the great variety of forms [ways, manifold] of wisdom of *THE-GOD*

3:11   according-to before placing The-Eons [before creating time periods] which *HE* made in [for] *Anointed-Savior-The-Master* for us

3:12   in *Whom* we are having the boldness and the access in confidence through The-Belief of *Him*.

3:13   Therefore I am requesting to not be despondent [spiritless, wearied out, exhausted] by the-afflictions of me for your sake which is your glory.

3:14   Of this gift [grace] I bow my knees to *THE-FATHER* of *The-Master* of us *Savior-Anointed*

3:15   out of *Whom* every fatherhood [family, lineage] in heaven and on earth is named.

3:16   That *HE* may be giving you according-to the-riches of The-Glory-of-*HIM*, to be made to grow strong through the-spirit of *HIM* into the-internal-inner man

3:17   to dwell *The-Anointed* through The-Belief in your hearts having been rooted and grounded in Godly-love.

3:18   That you should be strongly [unbreakably]-grasping together with all The-Holy-Ones what is the-breadth and length and depth and height.

3:19   To also know about the-Godly-love of *The-Anointed* which transcends knowledge that you may be completely filled with the-entire-compliment [fullness with complete divinity] of *THE-GOD*.

3:20   Yet to *THE-ONE-BEING-ABLE* to do above all exceedingly, extravagantly, which we are requesting or are thinking according-to the-power operating [acting] in us,

3:21   to *HIM* (be) the-glory in The-Called-Out [Ecclesia] in *Anointed-Savior* into all the generations of The-Eons of The-Eons.

Amen.

EPHESIANS 4

4:1 I am entreating you then, I the-bounded one in *Master*, to walk worthily [in highest value] of The-Calling which you were called

4:2 with all humility and meekness, with patience bearing with one another in Godly-love,

4:3 endeavoring to be keeping the-unity [oneness] of the-spirit together in the-bond of peace.

4:4 One body and one spirit, according and [even] as you were called in one Expectation [hope] with your Calling,

4:5 *One-Master*, one belief, one baptism,

4:6 ONE-GOD and FATHER of all, THE-ONE over [above, in dominance of] all and through all and in all you.

4:7 Yet to each one of us was given The-Grace according-to the measure of The-Gift-of-*The-Anointed*.

4:8 Through which HE is saying, **"When *He* ascended to high, *He* captured Captivity and gives gifts to men."** [Ps 66:18]

4:9 Yet what does "When *He* ascended" mean but that *He* first descended into the lower parts of the earth.

4:10 *The-One* descending is also *The-One* ascending up-over [in authority of] all The-Heavens that He should be completing [finishing] all.

4:11 Indeed and (this) same *One* gives ones commissioners and prophets and the-ones evangelists and the-ones as shepherds [pastors] and teachers

4:12 for the adjusting [perfecting] of The-Holy-Ones for acts of service into home-building [edification, improvement] of the-body of *The-Anointed*

4:13 until we all should be attaining the oneness [unity] of The-Belief [faith] and the-full-realization [precise and correct knowledge] of *The-Son-of-THE-GOD* as a mature [perfect] man in the prime measure [state of adulthood, as an adult], in the complete fullness [divinity] of *The-Anointed*.

4:14 That we should by no means still be minors surging here and there and being carried about by every wind of teaching in the-cube of men [as dice gambling with men, taking a risk with, taking a losing bet] in [of] cleverness [craftiness] with a way [method] to deceive.

4:15 But being true in Godly-love we, The-All, should be growing into *Him* who is *The-Head-*[ruler, master]-*The-Anointed*.

Section II

4:16 Out of *Whom* the-entire-body being articulated and united [fitted-as-one] together through every supplied touch [joint] according-to the measured action of each part of the growing body is making and building itself in Godly-love.

4:17 I am saying this then and am witnessing for *Master* [Christ] that by no means are you to be walking as the-remaining of the Nations are walking in the vanity of [devoid of truth in] their mind,

4:18 with comprehension been darkened, being alienated [estranged, separated] from *The-Life-of-THE-GOD*. This ignorance is in them because of the-callousness [cataracts, blindness, hardness] of their heart

4:19 who feeling no grief [are past having feelings and emotions] give themselves over to The-Debauchery to act in uncleanness [impure motives] in greediness.

4:20 But you have not so learned [are not taught this by, but you are a pupil of; a disciple of] *The-Anointed*

4:21 if surely [truly] you hear *Him* and in *Him* you were taught. The-Truth is in *The-Savior*.

4:22 That you are to be putting off concerning [throwing away, discard, completely remove] the-former-behavior of the old man, the-one being corrupted according-to The-Seduction-of-The-Desires

4:23 and be rejuvenated [spiritually renewed in] by the-spirit in your mind

4:24 and be putting on [let slipping in] the-new-man according-to *THE-GOD* being created in justice [righteousness] and true holiness.

4:25 Therefore, putting away falsehood [lying], each of you be-speaking truth with the-near-one [associate, neighbor, stranger]! We are members of one another.

4:26 **_"Be angry but do not sin," "Do not let the sun go down your vexation [anger],"_**

4:27: nor giving place to The-Adversary! [Ps 4:4, 37:8]

4:28 The-one-stealing by no means let him be stealing! Rather let him be toiling, working the-hands (for) the-good that he may be having a share in giving to the-one having a need.

4:29 Do not be issuing at all rotten [tainted, corrupted] words out of your mouth, but good if any, for edification of the-need that it may be giving grace to the-ones-hearing.

4:30 And do not be causing sorrow to [suppressing, ignoring] the-spirit-of-*THE-HOLY-GOD* in which you are sealed for The-Day-of-Deliverance.

4:31 Let all bitterness and fury and anger and clamor and slander, let it all be taken away from you! Together with all malice

4:32	and you become kind, tenderly compassionate to one another, dealing graciously among yourselves also as *THE-GOD* in *Anointed* deals graciously with you.

EPHESIANS 5

5:1	You then become imitators of *THE-GOD* as beloved offspring
5:2	and you be walking in Godly-love just as *The-Anointed* Godly-loves us and has given *Himself* as an offering on behalf of us as a fragrant-{life}-odor [savor] sacrifice to *THE-GOD*.
5:3	And do not let it be named [found] among you prostitution and all uncleanness or greediness as you have become to be Holy-Ones.
5:4	Nor obscenity and stupid speaking [foolish talking] or improper insinuations but rather be thankful (about) this,
5:5	you know that every male prostitute or unclean or greedy one who is an idolater is not having an Enjoyment-of-The-Allotment in The-Kingdom of *The-Anointed* and *GOD*.
5:6	Let no one be seducing you with empty saying [teaching, doctrine] because of this the anger of *THE-GOD* is coming on The-Sons-of-Stubbornness.
5:7	Do not then become joint-partakers [associates] with them!
5:8	For you were once in darkness, now a light in *Master*, walk as offspring [children] of light!
5:9	For the-fruit [affect, result] of the-sprit is in every goodness and righteousness and truth.
5:10	Test [prove] what is well pleasing to *The-Master*
5:11	and you do not be joint-participants associated with the acts of The-Unfruitful-Darkness but rather expose them.
5:12	For it is a shame to even speak of the things being done in hiding by them.
5:13	But all those things are being exposed by the light, for the light exposes everything.
5:14	Therefore *HE* says, "**Be aroused The-Lounging-[sleeping, drowsing]-One! Stand up you out of the-dead-ones,**" and, "**The Anointed shall be appearing (to you).**" [Isa 26:19, 60:11]
5:15	Be observing then how accurately you are walking not unwise but as wise
5:16	reclaiming The-Season [era] because the-days are wicked [evil].

Section II

5:17 Because of this do not become imprudent [foolish, stupid] but be ones understanding the-will [desires] of *The-Master*.

5:18 And do not be drunk with wine which is profligacy [wastefulness, reckless] but you be filled in the-spirit.

5:19 Talking [Speak in devotion in] psalms and hymns and spiritual songs to yourselves, singing and playing music in your heart to *The-Master*.

5:20 Give thanks always for all in the name of *The-Master* of us *Savior-Anointed* to THE-GOD and FATHER,

5:21 being subject to one another in fear [awe and respect] of *GOD*.

5:22 Wives, set yourselves under [be willing subjects to] your own husbands as if *The-Master*.

5:23 For the-husband is head [has the prominent position] of-the-wife even as *The-Anointed* is the head of The-Called-Outs [Ecclesiae] and *He* is the *Savior* [Preserver] of The-Body.

5:24 Even as The-Ecclesia is set under [subject] to *The-Anointed* therefore also the-women [wives] to their own men [husbands] in all.

5:25 Husbands, you be Godly-loving [Godly regarding the welfare of] the-wives as also *The-Anointed* Godly-loves The-Ecclesia and gave *Himself* up for-the-sake of her [it].

5:26 That *He* should be making-her-holy and cleansing with the bathing of the water in [by] declaration [that thing spoken of, the declared word]

5:27 that *He* should be presenting her to *Himself*, glorious, The-Ecclesia, having no spot or wrinkle or any of the-such but that it is holy and flawless.

5:28 So the husbands are to-be-Godly-loving [Godly regarding the welfare of] their own wives as their own bodies. The one Godly-loving [with Godly regard for the welfare of] his wife is Godly-loving [highly guarding the welfare of] himself.

5:29 For no one at any time hates his flesh but is nurturing and cherishing her [it] even as also *The-Master* The-Ecclesia.

5:30 For we are members of The-Body of *Him*, out of *His* flesh and out of the-bones of [from *His* marrow] *Him*.

5:31 Correspondingly to this [This is the reason why] a man shall be leaving his father and mother and shall be joined to his wife and the-two are-to become one flesh.

5:32 Still I am saying this is a great secret [mystery] in [of] *Anointed* and in The-Ecclesia.

5:33 Nevertheless, each one of you be Godly-loving your wife as himself and the wife that she may be having-a-reverence-for the-husband.

EPHESIANS 6

6:1 Children, be obeying your parents in *Master*, of this is just [acceptable of God, right, of virtue].

6:2 Be honoring your father and mother, which is the first precept with-a promise

6:3 *that it may be well with you and you should be living a long time on the earth.*

6:4 And you Fathers, do not be vexing your offspring but be nurturing them in upright education and training and the-admonition [warning, lessons] of *Master*.

6:5 Slaves, be obeying your Masters of the flesh with fear and trembling in singleness [the sincerity] of your heart as to *The-Anointed*.

6:6 Not with the eye-slavery [under the scrutiny of the Master to be a] as men-pleasers, but as slaves of *The-Anointed* doing the-will of *THE-GOD* out of the soul [from the heart],

6:7 with good humor [good-will, kindness] slaving [serving] as to *The-Master* and not to men,

6:8 being aware [knowing] that whatever good one should be doing this he shall be requited [paid back] by *The-Master* whether slave or free.

6:9 And Masters, you be doing the same thing toward them, omitting your threats to them being aware that your *Master* is in the Heavens and there is no partiality with *Him*.

6:10 Lastly, Brothers, be you invigorated [be strengthened] in *Master* and in the might [force] and strength [ability over external things] by *Him*.

6:11 You put on every implement [panoply, full array, full battle armor] of *THE-GOD* for you to be enabled to stand to the-stratagems of The-Adversary.

6:12 We are not wrestling [putting our hands on the neck holding in submission] against flesh and blood, but against The-Originals [sovereignties, angels, and demons] against The-Authorities [authority over mankind] against The-System-Holders [lords of the world, princes of this age, devil and his demons] of The-Darkness-of-The-Eon, against The-Spirits-of-The-Wickedness among The-Heavenlies.

Section II

6:13   Because of this be fully-dressed-in the-full-array-of-battle-armor of *THE-GOD* that you may be enabled to withstand [after having gone through every struggle] in The-Wicked-Day, having done all to stand.

6:14   You be standing then girded about your loin in truth and placing-on The-Breastplate-of-Justice [righteousness]

6:15   and sandal the-feet in readiness [preparation] of The-Well-Message-of-Peace.

6:16   Above all take up The-Large-Shield-of-Belief in which you shall be able to extinguish the-arrows [missile, javelin] being fiery of The-Wicked-One

6:17   and The-Helmet-of-Salvation. You receive The-Sword-of-The-Spirit which is *The-Word* of *GOD*

6:18   during every prayer and long petitioning pleas in [at] every season [occasion] in spirit and this being the same for vigilance, in all perseverance and entreating [pleading and requests] concerning all The-Holy-Ones.

6:19   And for my sake, that for me, may it be granted that I may open my mouth expressing in boldness making known The-Secret-of-The-Well-Message

6:20   for which I am being an ambassador in chains [bonds] that in it I should be being bold as it is binding [right and proper for] me to speak.

6:21   So that you may be acquainted with my affairs, I am engaging and shall be introducing you to Tychicus, the-beloved and faithful Brother and believing servant in *Master*

6:22   whom I send to you for this same thing that you may be know the concerns of us and he should be consoling [comforting] your hearts.

6:23   Peace to The-Brothers and Godly-love with belief from *FATHER GOD* and *Master-Savior-Anointed.*

6:24   The-Grace to all The-Ones-Godly-loving *The-Master* of us *Savior-Anointed* in incorruption [sincerity, never diminishing love].

(Written to the Ephesians from Rome through Tychicus)

PHILIPPIANS COMMENTARY

Philippians is placed second in order containing more developed instructions and added clarification concerning The-Secret. Even with the background of his current imprisonment and persecution, Paul demonstrates that his goal is to continue representing Christ as his legal representative and send The Well-Message of The-Savior to all Nations in any circumstance. He welcomes even those not spreading the truth about the Messiah but at least spreading Jesus' name, as if this is a great marketing achievement for the Body of Christ. To use a marketing concept, the "brand name and product" was getting out there, and people were bound to investigate and determine for themselves what this movement and lifestyle was all about. A media "buzz" was happening all around. God would certainly use even the corrupted messages and errant purposes of others to call The-Chosen through Christ using whatever material and campaign was in use for the time period. (Today God still uses the Bible with its obscure, archaic language, lost or misunderstood idioms, plus many other methods to call those whom He has chosen before the creation of all things through Christ). Paul saw this as a win in either circumstance. Whether in truth or in a lie, the "brand name" was getting out.

Paul talks about Christ giving up his "entitlement" (2:1–13) as the first purpose of creation of God and as His Son for us to be in God's Kingdom and how He was able to understand that this was not a loss to do this. How did Jesus come to this conclusion and then willingly divest all to become a pauper, vagrant, a pariah, a man? Books could be written exploring and explaining what Christ understood doing this. When reading these verses using this legal term "entitlement," the godly-love Jesus has for us is staggering in comparison to what I admittedly fall short of when it comes to my fellow man. This is quite a profound passage in Philippians to meditate on and clearly a mature theme, unlike anything else in any of Paul's other letters. The reader should keep this discussion in mind because Paul is going to again come back to the theme of titles, entitlement, and possessions. If Christ gave up the greatest of all titles, entitlements, and possession, what would make us "treasure" ours so much? Keep this in mind when reading the rest of Philippians.

Entitlement should be expounded concerning Christ. He was in line as the King of the Jews via his father Joseph, a direct descendant of King David and a firstborn via God's actions impregnating Mary who also had status. Christ had royal endowment

Section II

but never claimed it. The Romans were very aware of his heritage as well as the rulers, elite and royalty of the nation and Satan himself with his hordes. Satan offered Christ a substitute kingship of the world. He directly admitted it to Pontius Pilate he was born as King of the Jews hence Pilate's order for the nameplate at Jesus' crucifixion. That is what he gave up while aware of his purpose in God's overall plan to redeem mankind. Not any pre-divinity life form as many claim to become a man then return as a god again. That would have defeated the purpose and reason for a man to serve as a pure sacrifice. All the Apostles called Jesus a man, and a man to this day.

Paul also in this letter has started to hint that his time as the primary counsel and leader of The Nations was drawing nearer to an end, and he has started preparing Timothy to replace him at the helm. Essentially Paul was training his replacement and passing on his authority little by little to Timothy, whom he sees as his "junior legal representative" (starting in 2:14). This will be abundantly clear later in the letters to Timothy.

Paul next acknowledges his legal representative Epaphroditus and the work he performed among the Philippians, giving him his due credit.

Paul again returns to two themes that have "dogged" (3:2) him from the beginning of his ministry: 1) Jews still claiming circumcision and 2) those Jews, with their "preeminent title and authority," demanding that the observance of the Law of Moses be practiced. Paul then again challenges any one of those men to step forward and prove they can compare to the premier credentials he brings to their "dog and pony show." Their claims make them look like a group of kindergarteners debating with an eminent, multi-degreed scholar, professor, and teacher. Paul again attacks the Philippians for listening to such trash and allowing it to be in their presence.

Paul then closes the letter with a lecture using military analysis about studying and being prepared for the greater onslaught of false teachers, prophets, and messiahs sure to come after him. He knows he has only been able to hold back the tidal wave temporarily. Paul's fame was quite recognized and known everywhere within the Roman Empire—and likely well outside the reaches of the empire since he was the one sent to "The-Nations"; geographically this was much larger than tiny Israel and the Palestine area. The name of Christ was being spread everywhere like wildfire, and certainly the names of the "Pillar Apostles" which included Paul by this time, were carrying the message.

The book of Philippians discusses Christ's divesture of title and entitlements, given up willingly for you and me. The name of Jesus, The-Christ, continues to be carried everywhere, and whether in perversion or truth, God's will in calling and executing his purpose and plan for salvation will be accomplished. The Law of Moses has no legal enforcement or power, no forced "physical" cutting, actions, or works to save us; we are saved by believing. Do not glory in or chase titles or entitlements to satisfy the drives and passion of the flesh; do not think that in the Kingdom you will have more recognition than anyone else since Christ is the Preeminent One and Head of The Body. Lastly, we are called to serve others just as our Master who claimed no title while here the first time in the flesh did. Christ admitted to several people those titles and rights were his but it was not the time to exercise or call upon the power and authority He had. This is a mature teaching to reflect on also.

PHILIPPIANS AS A LETTER

PAUL AND TIMOTHEUS, SLAVES of *Savior-Anointed* to all The-Holy-Ones in *Anointed-Savior*, to The-Ones being in Philippi together with supervisors and servants. Grace to you, peace from *GOD, FATHER* of us and *Master-Savior-Anointed*.

I am thanking to *THE-GOD* of mine at every remembrance of you always in every petition of mine for-the-sake-of all of you with joy while in prayers for your contribution to The-Well-Message from the first day until now, having this same confidence that *THE-ONE-UNDERTAKING* a good work in you shall-be-continuing it until the Day-of-*Savior-Anointed*.

Just as it is appointed to me to-be-thinking-and-caring over all of you because in me is to-be-having the-heart for you in both my imprisonment and the defense-and-confirmation of The-Well-Message being joint participants of The-Grace with all you. For *THE-GOD* is my witness how I am longing for you in all deep-compassions as *Savior-Anointed*.

And this I am praying, that the-Godly-love of you still continue-to-increase-beyond-measure and even-greater may be super-abounding in the knowledge and every-moral-and-ethical-discernment that you are to be testing with the results that you may be found-pure-when-examined and without-offense in the Day-of-*Anointed* in-complete-entirety with the-fruits-of-justice through *The-Savior-Anointed* for the glory and highest-praise of *GOD*.

But you are to have-understanding-about what I am intending Brothers. That what-has-happened-to-me has actually-by-far served to advance The-Well-Message so that the-imprisonment of mine in *Anointed* became plainly-recognized in The-whole-Praetorian and to all the-remaining and to the-majority of The-Brothers in *Master* causing greater confidence through my imprisonment to be daringly, in-supreme-boldness speaking *The-Word*. Indeed, some are heralding *The-Anointed* out of envy and strife and some because of choice-and-will.

For The-Ones with Godly-love understand that for the defense of The-Well-message I am located here. The-Ones out of self-promotion are announcing *The-Anointed* not out-of-sincere-intentions (but) plotting-and-believing to be increasing afflictions to me in imprisonment. Does it matter? For either way, whether in pretense or in truth, *Anointed* is being made known. And in this I am rejoicing and will-not-stop continuing rejoicing. For I am aware of this, that to me eventually shall be salvation through your prayer and a supply of *the-spirit-of-Savior-Anointed* along with my watchfulness-and-anxiousness and assured-confidence that in nothing I shall be being put-to shame but in all boldness, as always, also even-now I continue-to magnify *Anointed* in my body whether through life or through death. For to me to be living is-for *Anointed* and to die—gain.

For if I am to continue-to-live in this flesh, fruit for my work! What do I prefer? I do not know. For I am pressed between the-two having a yearning to die and be together with *Anointed* which is far more-better, or the-continuing in the-flesh which-is more necessary because of you. And having this self-confidence, I am aware that I shall be remaining and staying-longer with all of you in your progress and joy of The-Belief with me, that your glory may be super-abounding in *Anointed-Savior* through my coming again to you. Only continue being worthy citizens of The-Well-Message-of-The-Anointed! Whether I come and see you or being absent that I should be hearing about you that you are standing unmovable in one spirit, one soul, assisting-together for The-Belief-of-The-Well-Message and not being frightened by anything by The-Ones-Opposing which to them is indeed proof of your ruin-and-loss-of-life, but to you is salvation and this from *GOD*. That to you is graciously-granted for-the-sake-of *The-Anointed* to not only be believing in *Him* but also to be suffering for-the-sake-of *Him* having the-same struggle such as you see me having and you are now hearing about me.

If any consolation then in *Anointed*, if any comfort of Godly-love, if any fellowship-and-intimacy of the spirit, if any tender-mercies and pities fill yourself full-of-these! That my joy may be the-same, in like-mindedness, the-same Godly-love having joined together in souls with the-same knowledge-and-understanding. Let nothing be-done in self-promotion or empty glory but in humility, valuing the other being superior to yourself. Let each one be nothing to themselves but for the-interests-of-different-ones. Let this perspective-and-approach be among you which was also in *Anointed-Savior*. *Who* in the-substance-and-form of *GOD* determined-and-decided it not a stolen-or-lost-privilege-or-entitlement to-not-be an-equal with *GOD* for *He* emptied *Himself* becoming modeled-to-be a slave and identical-as-any man and being found in full-representation-and-entire-in-all-ways a man, became obedient to Death even dying on The-Pale.

Therefore, also *THE-GOD* preeminently-exalted *Him* and divinely-gifts *Him* an-exclusive-title in-domination-of every name that in The-Name of *Savior* every knee should be bowing, of The-Celestial-Ones and of Terrestrial-Ones and of Subterranean-Ones and every language should be confessing-openly-and-in-honor that *Master-Savior-is-the-Anointed* to the-supreme-honor-and-recognition of *FATHER GOD*.

So, Beloved, as you have always obeyed me, not only as in my presence but now much more in the-absence of me, with fear and trembling accomplishing your salvation for *THE-GOD* is *THE-ONE-OPERATING* in you and resolutely-intends-and-resolved-to and is acting for-the-sake-of *HIS* benevolence-and-desire.

Section II

All you do, do it without secretive-displeasure and disputing so you may-be-becoming not-guilty and innocent children of *GOD*, without-blemish in the midst of a crooked and generation having been perverted among whom you are appearing as luminaries in the System attending-to the *Word-of-Life* so I may glory in the Day-of-*Anointed* that I neither raced or toiled for nothing. But if I am even being poured-out-and-my-blood-is-spilled for the-sacrifice and the-officiating of your Belief I am rejoicing, and I am rejoicing together with all of you! And for the-same purpose-and-cause, you also are rejoicing and you be rejoicing and rejoicing with me! For I am expecting in *Master Savior* to swiftly send Timotheus to you that I also may be satisfied-in-my-soul knowing the-state-of-affairs of you. For I have no one of equal sensitivity and genuine care-and-concern over the-care of you. For all are seeking for their own selves not that of *The-Anointed Savior*. Yet you have-the-full-knowledge-of the-proof of him that as a father to his child, together with me he slaves for The-Well-Message. This one then I am expecting to send so I may be seeing how things will be concerning me soon.

For I have confidence in *Master* that also myself shall be swiftly coming, but I deem it necessary to send to you my brother Epaphroditus, a fellow worker and warrior of yours and yet a commissioner and minister of my needs. It is a fact he was longing for all of you and was depressed because he heard how you heard he is sick. For he was also very near death in his sickness, but *THE-GOD* is merciful to him, but not only him but also to me that I should not be having sorrow over sorrow. I then send him more purposefully so that seeing him again you may be rejoicing and I may be sorrow free. Then you be receiving him in *Master* with all joy and holding in such high honor. Because for The-Work-of-*The-Anointed* he drew near to death not regarding the-soul that he should be fully taking care of me because of your lack of ministry toward me.

To the-remaining of the Brothers of mine, be you rejoicing in *Master*! To be writing the-same to you indeed is to me not irksome; you are secure. You be aware about Those-Dogs! You be aware about the-evil-workers and you be aware about The-Maimcision! For we are of The-Circumcision, The-Ones-in-spirit offering-divine-service to *GOD* and glorying in *Anointed-Savior* and not having a claim to a title because-of pedigree for even I also have a-pedigree in the flesh and if anyone is presuming he thinks-their-pedigree-is-the-finest, mine is of a far greater degree. Circumcised on the eight day out of the breed of Israel, Tribe-of-Benjamin, a preeminent-lineage of Hebrew out of Hebrews according-to the Law, a Pharisee filled with the-upmost-zeal persecuting The-Ecclesia according-to the justice in The-Law without blamelessness. But what if anything was that of gain for me because I have decided-and-determined it freely-given-up for *The-Anointed*.

But be assured, I have also determined all to be forfeited to have the-highest-degree of The-Knowledge-of-*Anointed Savior*, *The-Master* within me because of *Whom* I have freely-given-up it all and I understand it is refuse-garbage-animal excrement-dung so-that I should be gaining *Anointed*. And may I be found in *Him* not of my own righteousness out of The-Law but through The-Belief of *Anointed* by the Justice-of-*GOD* which is in The-Belief.

That I know all about *Him* and the-mighty-divine-power of The-Resurrection of *Him* and The-Intimate-Participation of *His* sufferings being conformed to the-death-of-*Him*, if somehow I should be participating in The-Resurrection-of-The-Dead-Ones.

Not that I have already obtained or already-have-been-perfected, for I am chasing-it-at-all-cost and I also am-trying-to-be-locked-grasped onto which I was locking-grasped by, *The-Anointed Savior*. Brothers, I myself have not understood fully to-figure-out-how-to-release and forget the past and claim the future. I am chasing both the goal and The-Prize-of-the-High-Calling-of-*THE-GOD* in *Anointed Savior*.

As many then as are in-adult-state about this, that we may be believing-and-acting the same and if in anything you are differently in-doubt-and-not-understanding *THE-GOD* shall be revealing this to you. Nevertheless, for we that are more mature, we ought to be observing the-same fundamentals and rules being of-the-same mind.

Brothers, be you mimics of me and taking-notice-of The-Ones living-their-lives imitating me, for you have us for a model. For many are now-walking-about of whom I often have told you and I am now lamenting telling you The-Ones are enemies of The-Pale-of-*The-Anointed* on whom is the-consummate-destruction whose god is the-belly and glory is their shame, The-Ones taking-care-of The-Terrestrial.

For our Realm-and-Kingdom is the possession of Heavens from which we are also awaiting our *Savior, Master Savior Anointed Who* shall be changing-the-form our low-estate-and-contemptible body into it having-the-identical-form-of The-glorious-Body-of-*Him* according-to the-divine-master-planning enabling *Him* to even conquer-and-control The-All for *Himself*.

So that my Godly-beloved and longed-for Brothers, my joy and crown-prize-and-honor be loyal-and-true in the *GODLY-BELOVED-Master*!

I am pleading-and-begging Euodia and Syntyche to be of-the-same belief-and-practice about *Master*, and I am entreating you also fellow-yoked be genuine! Be helping them who in The-Well-Message are striving-and-laboring together with me as-also Clement and the-remaining of the fellow-workers whose names are-in the Scrolls-of-Life.

Always be rejoicing in the *Master*, again I am declaring be rejoicing! Allow the-fairness-and-moderation of you be known to all men. *The-Master* is near! Do not be worrying about anything but in everything by the-prayer and the-petitioning with thanksgiving let it be being made known to *THE-GOD* your requests and The-Peace-of-*THE-GOD* being far-superior to all-understanding-and-intellectual-capacity shall be preventing-a-hostile-invasion-of the-hearts of you and your thoughts-and-fears in *Anointed-Savior*.

Finally, Brothers, whatever is true, whatever is honorable-and-revered, whatever is pure, whatever is pleasing-and-acceptable, whatever is sounding-proper, anything

Section II

of virtue and if any praising you be reflecting-and-practicing these which you learned and accepted and heard and seen in me. These be practicing! And The-Peace-of-*THE-GOD* shall be with you. For I rejoiced in *Master* greatly and at length that when you flourished-again-and-provided-for me knowing you did care but lacked the opportunity. Not that I am saying that I-am having a need for I have learned to be content whatever-condition-or-state I am. I know to be humbled, and I know how to be super-abounding in everything, and among all I have-an-intimate-acquaintance in being filled-and-full and to be hungering and to be super-abounding and to be deeply-suffering. I am being all powerful in *The-One-Abling* me, *Anointed*. Moreover, you are-doing-correctly contributing together for me in The-Affliction.

And you Philippians are also knowledgeable that at the beginning of The-Well-Message when I came out from Macedonia not one of the Ecclesiae participated in the matter of giving and receiving, only you. For even in Thessalonica you sent once and then twice for my need and not because I-wanted-or-sought-personally-for-me a donation. For I am searching through the-fruit of the-increased giving of yours for I am collecting everything and I am super-abounding now having been filled full receiving from Epaphroditus this from you, a sweet-fragrant-sacrificial-odor, extremely-accepted-pleasing to *THE-GOD*.

For *THE*-GOD of mine shall be filling your every need purposefully-and-willfully with The-Riches-of-*HIM* in glory in *Anointed-Savior*. And to *THE-GOD* and *FATHER* of us The-Glory into the-eons of the-eons.

Amen.

Greet you every Holy-One in *Anointed Savior*, those Brothers with me are greeting you. All the Holy-ones are greeting you especially The-Ones of out of The-Caesar's-household.

The-Grace-of-*The-Master* of us *Savior-Anointed* be with all you.

Amen.

(Written to the Philippians from Rome through Epaphroditus)

PHILIPPIANS STUDY NOTES

Note: Through my many translations, I have come to believe that the phrase or associated phrasing of "inheritance" [ex: Col 1:12] accurately translated as "the-allotment" in Scripture is not a good or proper translation (i.e., inheritance). Paul makes it clear that we are to be family members (I state: royal and godly) destined to be with HIM and HE with us and we in Christ and He in us. Inheritance has an implied connotation, an accepted concept that someone has died. THE-GOD is certainly not dead, and Christ has risen to life eonian (there are times of times of times) as well. I see this as a watering down of the intent and meaning of the Scriptures and have dropped using the word *inheritance* when speaking of THE-GOD's plan and purpose for us. We are to take rulership in an active kingdom with Christ at the head of the realm and we under Him, with THE-GOD over all of us.

Note   The Greek word *agapen* translated as "love" in most translations is missing that this is Godly in nature and not of men or any other such creature. I have therefore carried the adjective to add clarity to the meaning of this word throughout this translation.

Note: In my research, nearly all translations have dropped "the" as a modifier, but the Greek word for "the" is in every text and not meant to be ignored or deleted. It is often specifically singular, and when attached to the noun, it is describing that noun as unique, one of a kind, a specific thing, the original, the one and only. It is for this reason that I carry "the" everywhere it appears in all translations. Whether of God, Jesus, Satan or any other entity, concept, or idea, the modifier "the" clears up a lot of generalized words, ideas, concepts, and entities.

Note: The root of the word *pnuemia*, translated as "spirit, wind, or breath," has no gender identity since this is a word that is neuter in gender. *Pnuemia* is an "it." The Greeks, as we of English language, often fix a gender to objects and things— for example: cars, boats, the moon, the sun. For the Greeks, *pnuemia* at times has a male gender affixed to it. *Pnuemia* in the Scriptures is never capitalized or designated as a standalone being, entity, principality, or sovereignty when used as the word "spirit." It is simply the power inherent in the

Section II

being, whether of man, or God, or Christ, or any other entity. If anything is living, "it" possesses a spirit. The "Holy-spirit" is simply the power from and of The-God, giving and renewing life and performing The-God's will.

Note: Paul constantly claims and mentions "principles, powers, authorities, sovereignties not of our world." He quite clearly claims that these beings are the ones that certainly influence and control (predominately in a negative way) the systems of this world, people of the nations, and as individuals directly. You can find this concept also contained in The Old Testament through the implications of the first commandment. This claim and the concept of the warring factions in heaven makes a fascinating study.

Note: Time periods, eons, ages, millennia, eons, and eons—I stayed true to the Greek words associated with time and what we still use today in our common language. A study of time periods is fascinating but is also an area that can cause confusion. The-God always works on some kind of a timetable, but understanding which is which and when is when is a bit of a mystery. Some timetables are only known to The-God and made clear to man at God's will.

Note What is the difference between "expectation" and "hope?" Nearly all translations adopt the word "hope" for "expectation," but Paul uses almost exclusively the word "expectation." Here is why I constantly use "expectation." Having an expectation means you have no doubt at all. It is sure and certain with no ambiguity or doubt. Having a hope means you are not 100 percent convinced and convicted. I can tell you that Paul is undeniably convinced and convicted in what he delivers and talks about. Using "hope" sends a message that there is some possibility for "wiggle room," doubt, error, or excuses.

Even worse, much of the use of the word "expectation" in Paul's writings has the modifier "the" attached to "expectation," thus forming the proper translation and singular concept of "The-Expectation." This makes "The-Expectation" an event, not a philosophy or theological premise. Not recognizing "The-Expectation" as an event will lead the reader immediately down an incorrect understanding of what is being offered or discussed.

1:13 The Praetorian. See http://en.wikipedia.org/wiki/Praetorian_prefecture_of_Illyricum for a beginning discussion of the judgment hall often attached to a royal palace. See also http://www.padfield.com/2001/praetorian.html for an excellent discussion concerning Paul's imprisonment and http://www.answers.com/topic/praetorian-guard to understand what it meant to be the elite guard, much like those that protect the Tomb of The Unknown Soldier in Arlington Cemetery outside Washington, DC.

2:1 "Bowels" is better understood according to *Strong's* as (see b):

1. bowels, intestines, (the heart, lungs, liver, etc.)

a. bowels

b. the bowels were regarded as the seat of the more violent passions, such as anger and love; but by the Hebrews as the seat of the tenderest affections, esp. kindness, benevolence, compassion; hence our heart (tender mercies, affections, etc.)

c. a heart in which mercy resides

2:6 This verse is profound. There are two clear and distinctive ideologies occurring. First, all translations hide the fact the Greek word *huparchon,* nearly always translated simply as "being," has as its primary definition "created below" or "created lower." Hence the verse often reads as "being [i.e.: belonging, being inherently] in the form of," which misses completely that Christ was created not like THE-GOD, but in a "lower form"; he was man. Christ was created in a form lower than GOD and angels, but he had the external appearance of GOD just as many a son reflects his corporal parent in appearance. So it is with Christ's "external" physical and, dare I say, spiritual appearance. This first half of the verse is stating and declaring that Christ was born as a man.

However, the bigger discussion here may be the second half of the verse, often translated as "thought it not robbery to be equal to GOD." The first interesting discussion within this verse is the word "robbery." I can interpret this to be accusatory, charging THE-GOD of not being fair or being intentionally evil in intent because HE has not automatically given some or all of the same status, power, and dominion that HE has. One could explore some other themes within the concept of robbery. The second is the word "equal." It is absolute sheer folly and fantastic bravado, taking a supreme egoist to conceive that one could ever become or be THE-GOD. Christ was well aware of this and of what he was and is as a created being. He does not desire to be above or have the same status and power and divinity of THE-GOD, although THE-GOD has filled Christ with fullness of HIS deity and divinity. This is unlike some of the other of THE-GOD's creatures and creation, who think and crave themselves to be exactly like or above THE-GOD. This is one of many sub-themes threaded throughout the Bible.

2:9–10 "*and graces [divinely gifts] Him a* name *over [in domination of] every name*" (emphasis mine). The concept of "name" is more than providing a label or tag in these verses. This should be thought of as being "titled," or to use a medieval concept, being "knighted." With this is also meant a legal transfer of a "title (hence 'name') deed" taking ownership and possession of something such as a car, a boat, or the creation. This verse is telling us that Christ is not only given a preeminent label to be worshiped and revered, but that with this, comes a title deed that supersedes any "claim of ownership" by any other entity, sovereignty, or being other than Father God Himself. Reading these verses with the knowledge of this dynamic will give the reader a completely new understanding of Christ's emptying his himself for us and his crucifixion.

3:2 "Maimcision" according-to http://www.concordant.org/expohtml/StudiesIn-Philippians/Philippianso8.html is discussed in the following article:

THE MAIMCISION

This is the epithet which reveals what the Circumcision really was and is in this era when the flesh has lost all standing before God. Circumcision was once a token of covenant relationship with the Deity. It entailed many precious privileges. It will have a great place in the future again, when the physical seed of Abraham will be restored to divine favor. But now circumcision has lost all virtue and has degenerated into a mere mutilation of the flesh. The right to the rite is a physical one. Descent from Abraham is essential, except for proselytes. This term may be applied to all who give it a place in service today, whether they are actual sons of Israel, or take this rite upon themselves in order to share in the blessings which it is supposed to bring.

> Circumcision is a *cutting off* of the flesh, and was intended to set forth its futility. Had the Circumcisionists fully realized what the sign signified, they would have lost all confidence in the flesh. Instead they gave the flesh the highest place, and sought to make it the basis of all blessing. As we, who place no confidence in the flesh whatever, really carry out the true significance of the sign (even if we do not possess it) *we are the genuine Circumcision*. We have no ritual, no priesthood, no temple in which to go through the outward forms and ceremonies of the divine service, but, in spirit, we offer to God that essential worship which the temple service only shadowed. Too often, alas, the substance was lacking. We need no physical symbol. We dare not be circumcised. It has become a badge of apostasy. Beware of the maimcision!

Strong's discussion is much more interesting and novel: "Phil. iii. 2, where Paul sarcastically alludes to the word εργατας which follows verse 3; as though he would say, keep your eye on that boasted circumcision, or to call it by its true name 'concision' or 'mutilation.' Cf. the similar passage, Gal v. 12."

3:12 The second half of this sentence, where Paul says he is grasping Christ, reminds me of the same thing Jacob did with the angel in the wilderness before the angel changed his name to Israel. It is a real struggle to the end and after being defeated, still not giving up for the blessing which was (and is) to follow.

PHILIPPIANS IN VERSE

PHILLIPIANS 1

1:1 Paul and Timotheus, slaves of *Savior-Anointed*, to all The-Holy-Ones [saints] in *Anointed-Savior*, to The-Ones being in Philippi together with supervisors and servants.

1:2 Grace to you, peace from GOD, FATHER of us and *Master-Savior-Anointed*.

1:3 I am thanking to *THE-GOD* of mine at every remembrance of you

1:4 always in every petition [request, prayer, supplication] of mine for-the-sake-of all of you with joy in making the-petitions [while in prayers]

1:5 for your contribution to The-Well-Message [gospel] from the first day until now,

1:6 having this same confidence [trust] that THE-ONE-UNDERTAKING a good work in you shall-be-performing [continue] (it) until the Day-of-*Savior-Anointed*.

1:7 Just as it is appointed to me to be being disposed [thinking, caring, with a deep interest, confidently assured] over all of you because in me is to be having the-heart for you in both my bonds [imprisonment] and the defense-and-confirmation of The-Well-Message being joint participants of The-Grace with all you.

1:8 For *THE-GOD* is my witness how I am longing for you in all compassions [deep within the bowels] as *Savior-Anointed*.

1:9 And this I am praying, that the-Godly-love of you still rather more [continue-to-increase-beyond-measure] and more [even-greater] may be super-abounding in the knowledge and to every sensibility [not only of the senses but also the intellect, moral and ethical discernment]

1:10 that you are to be testing with the consequences [results, {whether: good or evil, lawful or unlawful}] of things that you may be sincere [found pure when examined] and not stumbling [without offense] in the Day-of-*Anointed*

SECTION II

1:11   having being filled [in complete entirety] with the-fruits-of-righteousness through *The-Savior-Anointed* for the glory and laud [highest-praise] of *GOD*.

1:12   But you are to be knowing [have understanding about] what I am intending [what I have chosen], Brothers. That the-affairs of mine [what has happened to me] have actually [rather, by far] served to progress [advance] The-Well-Message

1:13   so that the-bonds [imprisonment] of mine in *Anointed* became apparent [plainly recognized] in The-whole-Praetorian [Governor's palace, hall of judgment] and to all the-remaining

1:14   and to the-majority [very many] of The-Brothers in *Master* causing greater confidence through my bonds to be daringly [with absolute confidence and no fear], fearlessly [supreme boldness] speaking The-Word.

1:15   Indeed, some are heralding *The-Anointed* out of envy and strife and some because of delight [by choice, by good will].

1:16   For The-Ones with Godly-love understand that for the defense of The-Well-message I am located here.

1:17   The-Ones out of faction [self-promotion, seeking an office] are announcing [preaching] *The-Anointed* not purest [out of sincere intentions, with a hidden agenda, spinning yarns (tales and stories)] surmising [thinking, plotting, believing] to be bringing on more [adding, increasing] afflictions to me in bondage [while in bonds].

1:18   What then (does it matter)? For either method [way, approach], whether in pretense [a pretended cause] or in truth, *Anointed* is being announced [introduced, made known]. And in this I am rejoicing and will-not-stop continuing rejoicing.

1:19   For I am aware of this, that to me eventually shall be salvation through your prayer and a supply of *the-spirit-of-Savior-Anointed*

1:20   along with my premonition [watchfulness and anxiousness] and expectation [assured confidence] that in nothing I shall be being in [put to] shame but in all boldness, as always, also even-now (I) continue-to magnify *Anointed* in my body whether through life or through death.

1:21   For to me to be living (is for) *Anointed* and to die—gain.

1:22   For if (I) am to be living [continue to live] in this flesh, fruit for my work! What do I prefer? I do not know.

1:23   For I am pressed between the-two having a yearning to be loosed [depart, to die] and be together (with) *Anointed* which is much [far] more-better,

1:24	or the-remaining [continuing] in the-flesh which-is more necessary [required by the condition of things] because [on account, for the sake] of you.
1:25	And having this confidence, I am aware that I shall be remaining and abiding [staying longer] with all of you in your progress and joy of The-Belief [faith]
1:26	with me, that your glory may be super-abounding in *Anointed-Savior* through my presence [coming] again to you.
1:27	Only continue being worthy citizens of The-Well-Message-of *The-Anointed*! Whether I come and see you or being absent that I should be hearing about you that you are standing firm [unmovable] in one spirit, one soul, competing-together [assisting together] for The-Belief-[faith]-of-The-Well-Message
1:28	and not being startled [frightened] by anything by The-Ones-Opposing [The Adversaries] which to them is indeed proof of your destruction [ruin, loss of {eternal} life, exclusion to the Kingdom of God], but to you is salvation and this from *GOD*.
1:29	That to you is graciously-granted for-the-sake-of *The-Anointed* to not only believe in *Him* but also to be suffering for-the-sake-of *Him*
1:30	having the-same struggle [obstacles or dangers standing in the way to believe, holiness and a desire to spread the gospel] such as you see in me [see me having] and you are now hearing about me.

PHILIPPIANS 2

2:1	If any consolation [comfort, refreshing solace] then in *Anointed*, if any comfort of Godly-love, if any communion [fellowship, intimacy] of the spirit, if any bowels [tender mercies] and pities,
2:2	fill yourself full (of these)! That my joy may be the-same, in like-mindedness, the-same Godly-love, having joined together in souls with the-same minds [the same knowledge and understanding].
2:3	Let nothing be-done in strife [self-promotion, factious spirit], or empty glory but in humility deeming [esteeming, valuing] the other being superior to yourself.
2:4	Let each one be nothing to themselves [one's view] but for the-(interests of)-different-ones [others].
2:5	Let this mind [view, perspective, approach] be among you which was also in *Anointed-Savior*.
2:6	*Who* in form [external appearance, reflection, substance and form] of *GOD* deemed [determined and decided] it not snatching [a pillaging, to seize, lost

Section II

prize, lost booty, stolen or lost privilege or entitlement, removed against the will, as a robbery, an insult, lost valuable taken by force against one's will] to be equal to *GOD*,

2:7 for *He* emptied *Himself* becoming in form [modeled to be] of a slave and figure [identically as any, image, likeness] of man

2:8 and being found in fashion [full representation, entire in all ways] a man, became obedient to Death even dying on The-Pale [crucifixion].

2:9 Therefore also *THE-GOD* over-heightens [preeminently exalted, highly exalts] *Him* and graces [divinely gifts] *Him* a name over [in domination of] every name [whether individuals or collection of beings having heritage or rank, with authority, of sovereignties or masterdoms or kingdoms].

2:10 That in The-Name of *Savior* every knee should be bowing of The-Celestial-Ones and of Terrestrial-Ones and of Subterranean-Ones

2:11 and every tongue [language] should be acclaiming [confessing openly, profess in honor] that *Master-Savior-(is)-the-Anointed* to the-glory [supreme honor and recognition] of *FATHER GOD*.

2:12 So, Beloved, as you have always obeyed me, not only as in my presence but now much more in the-absence of me, with fear and trembling affecting [accomplishing, achieving] your salvation

2:13 for *THE-GOD* is *THE-ONE-OPERATING* in you and wills [resolutely intends, is resolved to] and is acting [operates] for-the-sake-of *HIS* delight [pleasure, benevolence, desire].

2:14 All you do, do it without murmuring [secretive displeasure] and reasoning [arguing, disputing]

2:15 so you may be becoming blameless [not guilty] and pure [innocent] children of *GOD*, flawless [without blemish] in the midst of a crooked and generation having been perverted among whom you are appearing as luminaries [shining beacons] in the System [world]

2:16 holding on [attending to] the *Word-of-Life* so I may glory in the Day-Of-*Anointed* that I neither ran [raced] or toiled [worked, labored] for nothing [in vain].

2:17 But if I am even being offered [poured out, my blood is spilled] for the-sacrifice and the-officiating of your belief [faith] I am rejoicing, and I am rejoicing together with all of you!

2:18 And for the-same reason [purpose, cause] you also are rejoicing and you be rejoicing and rejoicing with me!

2:19	For I am expecting in *Master Savior* to swiftly [in haste, great speed] send Timotheus to you that I also may be of good cheer [satisfied in my soul] knowing the-concerns [state of affairs] of you.
2:20	For I have no one of equal sensitivity and genuine anxiousness [care, concern] over the-care of you.
2:21	For all are seeking for their own selves not that of *The-Anointed Savior*.
2:22	Yet you are knowing [have the full knowledge of] the-proof of him, that as a father to his child, together with me he slaves for The-Well-Message.
2:23	This one then I am expecting to send so I may be seeing how things will be concerning me soon.
2:24	For I have confidence in *Master* that also myself shall be swiftly coming,
2:25	but I deem it necessary to send to you my brother Epaphroditus, a fellow worker and warrior [soldier] of yours and yet a commissioner [apostle] and minister of my needs.
2:26	It is a fact he was longing for all of you and was depressed because he heard how you heard he is sick.
2:27	For he was also very near death in his sickness, but THE-GOD is merciful to him, but not only him but also to me that I should not be having sorrow over sorrow.
2:28	I then send him more diligently [purposefully] so that seeing him again you may be rejoicing and I may be sorrow free.
2:29	Then you be receiving him in *Master* with all joy and holding in such high honor.
2:30	Because for The-Work-of-*The-Anointed* he drew near to death not regarding the-soul [his life] that he should be fully filling [taking care (of me)] because of your lack of ministry [officiating] toward me.

PHILIPPIANS 3

3:1	To the-remaining of the Brothers of mine, be you rejoicing in *Master*! To be writing the-same to you indeed is to me not irksome [exasperating, infuriating], you are secure [safe, secure].
3:2	You be aware about those-Dogs! You be aware about the-evil-workers and you be aware about The-Maimcision!
3:3	For we are of The-Circumcision, The-Ones-in-spirit offering divine service to [ministering to, offer gifts, worship, serving] GOD and glorying in

Section II

Anointed-Savior and not having confidence [trusting in what or where one comes from, a claim to a title because of one's pedigree] in the flesh

3:4 for even I also have confidence in the flesh [I have a pedigree], and if anyone is presuming he has confidence of the flesh [thinks their pedigree is the finest], mine is of a far greater degree.

3:5 Being cut [circumcised] on the eighth day out of the breed of Israel, Tribe-of-Benjamin, a Hebrew out of Hebrews [preeminent lineage] according-to the Law, a Pharisee

3:6 filled with boiling [the upmost zeal] persecuting The-Ecclesia according-to the justice [righteousness] in The-Law without blamelessness.

3:7 But what if anything was that of gain for me because I have deemed [decided and determined] it forfeited [freely given up] for *The-Anointed* [Christ].

3:8 But be assured, I am also deeming [determining it] all to be forfeited because of [to come, to have] the-superiority [highest degree] of The-Knowledge-of-*Anointed* [Christ] *Savior, The-Master* [Lord] of me because of whom I have forfeited it all and I am deeming [counted and understand] it refuse [trash, garbage, animal excrement, dung] that I should be gaining *Anointed*.

3:9 And may I be found in *Him* not of my own righteousness out of The-Law but through The-Belief of *Anointed* out of the [by the] Justice-[Righteousness]-of-*GOD* which is in The-Belief.

3:10 That I know all about *Him* and the-mighty-divine-power of The-Resurrection of *Him* and The-Communion [intimate participation, sharing in intimacy] of *His* sufferings being conformed [identical in image] to The-Death-of-*Him*

3:11 if somehow I should be attaining [participating in] to The-Resurrection-of-The-Dead-Ones.

3:12 Not that I have already obtained perfection. I am pursuing [chasing at all cost] (it) and I also am-trying-to-be grasped to which I was grasped by, *The-Anointed Savior* [that I am wrapping [as in a locked-wrestling hold not letting go of an opponent] myself around *The-Anointed* as *He* has a locked-wrestled held *Himself* around me].

3:13 Brothers, I myself have not understood fully to have grasped this yet [to fully figure out how to] to forget that behind and stretch out to that in front [forget the past and claim the future].

3:14 I am chasing both the goal and The-Prize-of-the-High-Calling-of-*THE-GOD* in *Anointed Savior*.

3:15 As many then as are mature [in adulthood, an adult state or condition] about this that we may be thinking [believing and acting] the same, and if

PHILIPPIANS IN VERSE

in anything you are differently thinking [in doubt, not understanding] *THE-GOD* shall be revealing this to you.

3:16   Nevertheless for we that are more mature, we ought to be observing the-same fundamentals and rules being of the-same mind.

3:17   Brothers, be you becoming like [imitators, mimics] me and be noting [taking notice of] The-Ones-treading [living their lives] according as [imitating] me for you have us for a model.

3:18   For many are treading about [now walking about] of whom I often have told you and I am now lamenting [weeping, crying, in sorrow] telling you The-Ones are enemies of The-Pale-[Crucifixion]-of-*The-Anointed*

3:19   on whom is the-consummate-destruction whose god (is) the-bowel [belly] and glory is the shame of them [their shame], The-Ones minding [tending to, taking care of] The-Terrestrial [earthy things].

3:20   For our Realm [citizenship, administration of civil affairs, kingdom] is belonging in [occupies, is the possession of] (the) Heavens from which we are also awaiting our *Savior, Master Savior Anointed*

3:21   *Who* shall be transfiguring [changing the form, morphing, metamorphing] our humiliating [low estate, contemptible] body into it be-becoming conformed to [having the identical form of] The-glorious-Body-of-*Him* according-to the-divine-master-planning enabling *Him* to even subject [have dominion of, conquer and control] The-All [all things, everything and anything, all kingdoms and principalities and authorities] to [for] *Himself*.

PHILIPPIANS 4

4:1   So that my Godly-Beloved and longed-for Brothers, my joy and wreath [crown, prize, honor] be standing firm [remain loyal and true] in the *godly-beloved-Master*!

4:2   I am entreating [pleading, begging] Euodia and Syntyche to be of the-same mind [belief, practice] of [about] *Master*,

4:3   and I am entreating you also fellow-yoked [bonded by marriage, fellow laborers, colleagues], be genuine [true]! Be helping them who in The-Well-Message are competing [striving, laboring] together with me as-also Clement and the-remaining of the fellow-workers whose names are-in the Scrolls-of-Life.

4:4   Always be rejoicing in the *Master*; again I am declaring be rejoicing!

4:5   Allow the-leniency [mildness, fairness, moderation] of you be known to all men. *The-Master* is near!

Section II

4:6 Do not be worrying about anything but in everything by the-prayer and the-petitioning [supplication, pleading, earnest requesting] with thanksgiving let it be being made known to *THE-GOD* your requests

4:7 and The-Peace-of-*THE-GOD* being superior [rising prominently above, goes so far beyond] to every mind [all understanding, all intellectual capacity] shall be garrisoning [guarding, preventing a hostile invasion of] the-hearts of you and your apprehensions [thoughts and purposes, fears] in *Anointed-Savior*.

4:8 Finally, Brothers, as much as [whatever] is true, whatever is grave [honorable, venerated, revered], whatever is pure, whatever is agreeable [pleasing, lovely, acceptable], whatever is renowned [sounding proper, spoken auspiciously], anything of virtue and if any praising you be taking into account [reflecting, practicing] these

4:9 which you learned and accepted and heard and seen in me. These be practicing! And The-Peace-of-*THE-GOD* shall be with you.

4:10 For I rejoiced in *Master* greatly and at length that when you blossomed again [re-sprouted, flourished again, provided for] over me, knowing you did care but lacked the occasion [opportunity].

4:11 Not that I am saying that (I am) having a want [need], for I have learned to be content [sufficient] wherever [whatever condition or state] I am.

4:12 I know to be humbled and I know how to be super-abounding in everything and among all I have been initiated [have an intimate acquaintance] in being satisfied [filled and full] and to be hungering and to be super-abounding and to be deeply-wanting [suffering].

4:13 I am being all strong [powerful] in *The-One-Abling* me, *Anointed*.

4:14 Moreover you do ideally [are doing correctly] communing [contributing] together for me in The-Affliction.

4:15 And you Philippians are also knowledgeable that at the beginning of The-Well-Message when I came out from Macedonia, not one of the Ecclesia participated in the matter of giving and receiving, only you.

4:16 For even in Thessalonica you sent once and then twice for my need

4:17 not because I was seeking [I wanted or sought personally for me] for the-gift [a donation]. For I am searching through the-fruit of the-increased account [giving] of yours

4:18 for I am collecting all [everything] and I am super-abounding now having been filled full receiving from Epaphroditus this from you, a sweet-fragrant-sacrificial-odor, extremely-accepted-pleasing to *THE-GOD*.

4:19	For *THE*-GOD of mine shall be filling your every need according [purposefully, willfully] with The-Riches-of-*HIM* in glory in *Anointed-Savior*.
4:20	Yet to THE-GOD and FATHER of us The-Glory into The-Eons of The-Eons. Amen.
4:21	Greet you every Holy-One in *Anointed Savior*, those Brothers with me are greeting you.
4:22	All the Holy-Ones are greeting you especially The-Ones of out of The-Caesar's-house (hold).
4:23	The-Grace-of-*The-Master* of us *Savior-Anointed* (be) with all you. Amen.

(Written to the Philippians from Rome through Epaphroditus)

COLOSSIANS COMMENTARY

Colossians wraps up the three letters on the final teachings and Revelation of The-Secret before a completely different topic is introduced in the Thessalonians' letters. This letter has four chapters and seventeen verses, and one may ask how such a short letter can truly address the complete teachings and doctrines associated with it and what the legal implications are. Does Colossians really reflect the other letters of Paul?

The purpose of this letter is to identify the articles of incorporation and merger associated with the new contract within The-Secret's knowledge, completing the final doctrines and leaving it to the readers and listeners to research and develop the entire teachings associated with each topic.

What do I mean by articles of incorporation? Identification of the principles involved with the business/Kingdom; the purpose of the business; proper registrations of business ownership; the operating principles and tenets as required by law to be followed within the corporation.

The-Secret (or revealed mystery as translated by some) is that you have the same divinity as Christ and God The-Father since you are in Christ and as Christ while still being human. The implication is that you are to be worshipped (future event); you also are destined to inherit the universes and galaxies to repair and make whole as intended originally.

Being introduced by Paul, these are the articles you should know and be able to discuss, defend, or reject in the order presented within Colossians:

The-Belief	1:4
The-Expectation being reserved for you	1:5
The-Truth of The-Well-Message	1:5
The-Grace-of-THE-GOD-in-Truth	1:6
Having the Fullest-of-the-Knowledge-of-The-Will-of-GOD	1:9
The-Glory-of-THE-GOD	1:11
GOD-THE-FATHER	1:12
The-Allotment-of-The-Holy-Ones-of-The-Light	1:12
The-Kingdom-of-the-Son	1:13
The-Deliverance through the-blood of Christ	1:14
The-Pardoning-of-The-Sins	1:14

Christ the image and nature of THE-UNSEEN-GOD	1:15
Christ Firstborn of every Creation	1:15
Christ is the cause of creation "all is attributed to and through Him"	1:16–17
Christ is the Cohesion of all and any	1:16–17
Christ is the Head of The-Body, The-Ecclesia	1:18
Christ is The-Beginning of and The Firstborn from the Dead	1:18
Christ delights and permits the full divinity of GOD to live in and through Him	1:19–20
Christ is the one that makes Peace with all through his blood and sacrifice	1:20
In Christ you are holy, unflawed, blameless, innocent, and unimpeachable	1:21
You can be moved and removed from The Expectation (First Resurrection)	1:23
The Nations were given to Paul by the will and purpose of GOD	1:25
The Secret, The-Glory-of-The-Secret, The-Anointed is already in you	1:27–28
GOD is THE-TREASURY of all wisdom and knowledge, known or unknown	2:3
The seduction of The-Traditions-of-Men	2:8
The Original Rulers of The-System	2:8
The full Deity-of-GOD is in Christ therefore you since Christ is in you today	2:9
Christ is The-Head over any and every Sovereignty and Authority	2:10
The Circumcision-of-The-Anointed is also your circumcision	2:11
Christ's Circumcision is the Cutting out of The-Body The-Sins-of-The-Flesh	2:11
You were entombed in Christ's Baptism and rose out of it with Him alive	2:12
You were forever committed to death by your sins but now alive In Christ	2:13
The-Decrees (Law of Moses, et al) are completely gone, erased off the books	2:14
Do not get caught up in dead traditions and practices (food, Sabbaths)	2:16
Avoid spiritual cowardice	2:18
Avoid playing with or invoking The Spirits or the Spirit world	2:18
Your life is laid up into The-Anointed	3:3
As Christ is, so are you to the right of THE-FATHER	3:1
At Christ's return, you will be made to appear in Glory (First Resurrection)	3:4
The-Indignation-of-The-God	3:6
Imitate Christ and Paul in proper and pleasing behavior	3:5–11
You are The-Chosen-of-The-God	3:12
Practice and live in Godly-love	3:14
The-Peace-of-The-God	3:15
You are called into One Body and to be the Thankful Ones	3:15
The Word of The-Anointed is to dwell in you	3:16
Family Relationships	3:18–21
Business Relationships	3:22–4:1
Prayer and Thankfulness	4:2
For Paul's word to reach into the ages to come	4:4
Be able to encourage and defend any of the teachings and doctrines	4:6
Warn others when they are not properly serving in their accepted roles	4:16–17

Section II

Listed here are fifty-one topics that represent the statutory requirements associated with the final teachings of the Ecclesia once The-Secret was revealed and what anyone belonging to The Kingdom of God needs to defend and live by. What is more fascinating is that all of this is written on your heart and in your mind as The-Chosen, and all of these can be easily managed and fulfilled if you Godly-love God first, your fellow man as yourself second, knowing that your fellow mankind consists of God's sons and daughters too. All the items in this list are accomplished within that seemingly simple order and direction.

Colossians certainly looks like any other letter executed by Paul. You can comprehend how this letter is also a giant among Paul's letters. It copies Galatians as a letter that summarizes not only the ABCs but the XYZs of your life in Christ and the coming Kingdom and is placed in this third position. It still follows a legal format and is in complete harmony from start to finish with all the other previous letters to the other five Ecclesia, each one building on the next, with the seventh Ecclesia to follow.

To further demonstrate that this book is in the correct position in the Sacred Order, realize that there is the Ecclesia of Romans, Corinthians, and Galatians (a total of three locations), followed by Ephesians, Philippians, then Colossians for a total of six—a number representing "man" or "pertaining to man" in biblical numerology. What we have here is a set of letters for men established divinely by God. As Galatians finishes the basics, Colossians finishes the mature teachings—three plus three equaling six. But there is a "double witness" in what was intended by God. Corinthians was sent two letters, making the count four plus three, totaling seven. Seven is attributed to the idea "of completeness" or "of God." Not only has God told us that these letters are intended for mankind, but they are complete in His purpose for mankind. Talk about one stopping in their tracks in amazement! Here we have a double divine witness in the order and the material.

The message of The-Secret is clear. Christ is already in you and has been since you took your first breath of life, and you were in Him during his first appearance as a man on earth. As Christ sits at the right hand with the full divinity and quality of God, the same is being developed in you. Legally if Christ has possession of this Divinity and Godhead, so also do you since you are in Christ. This is a free gift, given to you by Father God at his pleasure, purpose, and will. See that you use this freedom and divinity and authority wisely—don't abuse it! With you being divine, The Godhead is actually FATHER GOD, Christ, you, me, and others. That is the great message, promise, and intent of God, and let all glory, boasting, and honor be to God for such an indiscernible and indescribable gift and opportunity! God surely is holding the lottery of all lottery tickets, meant for you and me and all creation, and He through Christ is preparing to cash it in for all of us.

What a fantastic message about you being a direct family member of the Godhead and restoring the Heavens and Earth. To restore all of creation and return it back to Christ and then to God! All will share in that divinity, and all have it already. How can one not spread such a great message, promise, joy, and expectation of God's will and purpose? Any words I might offer concerning God in His divine master plan, purpose, and will are shallow and cannot come close to His magnificence and to the gratefulness I have for Him. I hope you can also grasp this and understand what God has done for you from the foundations of the world.

What an ending to The Revelation of the Secret and the mature teachings of God and His Kingdom—your promised sonship and intimate relationship with God! Shout AMEN and fall to your knees in worship and adoration to God in the name of Christ over the Revelation of The Secret that is yours!

COLOSSIANS AS A LETTER

PAUL, COMMISSIONER OF *SAVIOR-ANOINTED* through the will of *GOD*, and The-Brother Timotheus to The-Holy and believing Brothers in Colossae in *Anointed*, grace and peace to you from *FATHER-GOD* of us and *Master-Savior-Anointed*.

To *THE-GOD* and *FATHER* of *The-Master* of us *Savior-Anointed*, we are thanking always praying about you upon hearing of The-Belief of you in *Anointed-Savior* and the Godly-love to The-All, The-Holy-Ones because of The-Expectation, the-one-being-reserved for you in The-Heavens which you heard before in the-teaching of The-Truth-of-The-Well-Message. This being-present in you also throughout The-entire-System and is bearing-fruit also in you from the day that you heard and recognized The-Grace-of-*THE-GOD* in truth as also you learned from Epaphras the-beloved fellow-slave of us who is a believing servant of *The-Anointed* over you and the-one showing to us of your Godly-love in spirit.

Because of this we also from the day which we heard are not ceasing in praying over you and requesting that you may be being filled with The-Fullest-of-The-Knowledge-of-the-Will-of-*HIM* in every wisdom and spiritual understanding. You are to walk in-the-highest-regard of *The-Master*, in everything pleasing, in every good action bearing fruit and growing into The-Knowledge-of-*THE-GOD* being-exceedingly-strengthened in all the-mighty-power in The-Glory-of-*HIM* in all endurance and patience with joy giving thanks to *THE-FATHER, THE-ONE-MODELING* us into the-part of The-Allotment-of-The-Holy-Ones-of-The-Light. *WHO* rescues us out of The-Jurisdiction-of-The-Darkness and transports us into The-Kingdom-of-*The-Son* for the Godly-love of *Him* in *Whom* we are having The-Deliverance through the-blood of *Him*, The-Pardoning-of-The-Sins.

Who is an identical-and-exact-image-and-nature of *THE-UNSEEN-GOD*, *Firstborn* of every creation. That for *Him* is created The-All, in The-Heavens and on The-Earth the visible and invisible, whether thrones or masterdoms or Originals that The-All for *Him* and in *Him* has been created. And *He* is before all and The-All in *Him* is-in-proper-place-and-staying-together.

And *He* is The Head-of-The-Body, The-Ecclesia, *Who* is *The-Beginning-Firstborn-of-The-Dead-Ones* that in all *He* has the preeminence. That *He* in-a-willful-choice-to-allow the-entire-divinity dwelling-in and through *Him* to reunite-and-repair The-All into *Him* making peace through the-blood of The-Pale-of-*Him*, through *Him*, whether that of The-Earth or that in The-Heavens.

Now you once were omitted-separated-and-alienated and enemies knowingly by the-wicked-acts. But now *HE* pardons-and-unites in the-body, in the-flesh of *Him* through The-Death to present you holy and blameless-and-innocent and unimpeachable in the sight of *HIM* if surely you are persistently-persevering-and-continuing in The-Belief having been established and immoveable and not being forced from The-Expectation-of-The-Well-Message which you hear, *The-One-Being-Proclaimed* in The-entire-Creation under The-Heaven of which I Paul became a server. Who I am now rejoicing over this-suffering of mine for the sake of you and I am instead filling the-deficiencies of the-affliction in my flesh from *The-Anointed* for the sake of The-Body-of-*Him* which is The-Ecclesia; of which I became a minister as the-household-trustee of THE-GOD, THE-ONE-GIVING you to me to complete The-Teaching-of-*THE-GOD*. Even The-Secret having been concealed from The-Eons and from the-generations and is given now to The-Holy-Ones-of-*Him*. To whom THE-GOD-WILLS to make know what the-riches-of-the-glory-of-The-Secret, this Secret among The-Nations which is *Anointed* is in you, *The-Expectation-of-The-Glory Whom* we are announcing, admonishing every man, and teaching every man in all wisdom that we should be presenting every man perfected in *Anointed-Savior* to which also I am toiling, struggling, according-to the-every-single-part of *Him* in divine-power operating in me.

I am willing for you to know how great the struggling-contest I am having concerning you and The-Ones in Laodicea and whomever has not seen me-personally. That the-hearts of them may be consoled and be united in Godly-love and into all the riches of the-full-assurance of the-understanding-of-The-Knowledge-of-The-Secret-of-*THE-GOD* and FATHER of *The-Anointed*, in WHOM, secretly-hidden IS THE TREASURY of all the-wisdom and the-knowledge.

And I say this, that no man should be deluding any of you in persuasive words for even if I am absent in the-flesh, together you and I am in the-spirit rejoicing and managing-to the orderly-presentation of you as when you accepted *The-Anointed-Savior*. *The-Master*, in *Him* you be walking having been already-thoroughly-grounded-and-affixed and continually-growing in The-Belief as you were taught super-abounding in it with thanksgiving!

You beware! Let not anyone become the-one of-the-booty-of-war put under the persuasive-power of empty-truthless philosophy and seduction with The-Tradition-of-Men along with The-Original-Rulers-of-The-System and not according-to *Anointed*. For in *Him* is dwelling all-of-and-the-complete-fullness-and-state-of-*THE-DEITY* in-body.

And in *Him* you have been filled to-the-very-cup-brim *Who* is *The-Head* of every sovereignty and authority in *Whom* you were circumcised by a circumcision not done by hands, in cutting-out-of The-Body The-Sins-of-The-Flesh. In

Section II

The-Circumcision-of-*The-Anointed* being entombed together with *Him*, in The-Baptism in which you also were roused together through The-Belief of The-Divine-Master-Planning-of-*THE-GOD*, *THE-ONE-ROUSING Him* out of the-dead-ones. You also being dead in the-offenses and the-uncircumcision of your flesh, *HE* has made you alive together with *Him* freely-forgiving you all the-offenses. Rubbing-out the handwriting of The-Ordinances which was hostile to us and has completely-removed-them nailing it to The-Pale disarming The-Originals and in-fearless-confidence openly-disgracing The-Spiritual-Potentates with-entire-and-complete-subjugation-and-dominion-over them in it.

Then do not let any of you be judging concerning food or in drinking or particular festivals or The-New-Moon or of Sabbaths which is a shadow of The-Impending and is The-Body-of-*The-Anointed*.

Let no man defraud-you-in-arbitration-of-the-prize-of-the-victory by willing submissive-spiritual-cowardice or rituals of The-Angels which not he has not seen, or with-wrong-intent playing-with-the-spirits, being puffed up in his judgment-and-thinking of-the-flesh and not retaining-and-acknowledging *The-Head* out of whom The-entire-Body through the-joints and ligaments being supplied and united is increasing in the-development-and-purpose of *THE-GOD*.

If then you died together with *Anointed* from The-Elements-of-The-System, why, as though living in The-System do you subjugate yourselves to The-Decrees? You should not be touching, nor should be-tasting or not coming into contact with all things from use which is corroding-away such-as The-Directions and teachings-of-men which indeed appears-to-have some wisdom in The-Expressions in valueless worship with false-and-empty humility and not neglecting the-body which-does-not-have any lasting-value toward satiating-the-desires-of the-flesh.

If then you being roused together to *The-Anointed*, be seeking that above where *The-Anointed* is sitting to the right of *THE-GOD*. You be thinking-and-reflecting on that above, not of that of The-Land. For you have died and the-life of yours has been kept-laid-up-and-secured together with *The-Anointed* in *THE-GOD*. Whenever *The-Anointed* may be made to appear, *The-Life-of-Us*, then you also together with *Him* shall be made to appear in glory.

Put to death then the-members of yours which are of the-earth; prostitution, uncleanliness, lusty-passionate desires, evil and never-ending-covetousness which is idolatry. Because of this The-Indignation of *THE-GOD* is coming on The-Sons-of-the-Stubbornness in whom you also lived-the-lifestyle-of when you lived among them. But now you also be putting away all of anger, fury, malice, blasphemy, obscenity out of your mouth, not lying to one another, cutting off the-old-man and the-practices of him and be putting on the-young, being renewed in knowledge in all-respects after the-divine-nature of *THE-ONE-CREATING Him*. For there is neither Greek nor Jew, circumcised or uncircumcised, barbarian, Scythian, slave, free, but The-All and All in *Anointed*.

Then as The-Chosen-of-*THE-GOD*, Holy-Ones and having-been-Godly-loved, put you on compassions of unbounded-and-unending-mercy, kindness, humility, meekness, patience, bearing one another and dealing graciously among yourselves. If ever anyone may be having a complaint toward anyone as also *The-Anointed* deals graciously with you, do you also. Yet over all of these, The-Godly-Love which is the uniting-bond of state-of-perfection and let The-Peace-of-*THE-GOD* be directing-and-controlling in the-hearts of you in which you also were called in One-Body and you-become The-Thankful-Ones. Let the word of *The-Anointed* be dwelling inside him, in abundance, in every wisdom teaching and encouraging yourselves in psalms and hymns and spiritual songs in joy-pleasure-and-sweetness singing in your heart to *The-Master*. And in everything you may be doing in word or actions, do all in The-Name-of-*Master-Savior* giving thanks to THE-GOD and FATHER through *Him*.

The-wives, be-a-willing-subject-to your own husbands as is proper in *Master*. Husbands, be-Godly-loving the-wives and do not be bitterly-irritating-and-rendering-anger toward them. Children, be obeying your parents in all things, for this is well-pleasing to *The-Master*. Fathers, do not be provoking your children so that they may not be broken-in-spirit-disheartened-and-uncaring.

Slaves, you be obeying in all The-Masters-of-the-flesh not in distrust, not as men-pleasers, but in sincerity of the heart fearing THE-GOD. And in all which you are doing, work out of the soul as to *The-Master* and not to men. Be aware that from *Master* you shall be getting the repayment-of-The-Enjoyment-of-The-Allotment for you are slaves to *The-Master-Anointed*. And the-one-injuring shall be paid back for which he causes injury for there is no partiality. The-Masters, be-exhibiting being just and equitable to the slaves! Being aware you also having a *Master* in Heaven.

Remain-constant in prayer taking-care in her to-be-thankful praying in unison also concerning us that *THE-GOD* should be opening to us a door for The-Word to speak The-Secret-of-*The-Anointed*. Because of this I am out-of-honor-and-duty-bound that I should be clearly showing what-is-right-and-proper-for me to speak. You be walking in wisdom with the-ones not-of-The-Ecclesia making-wise-and-sacred-use-of-every-opportunity-to-do-good-in the season. Let your words always be in grace as seasoning salt to understand-and-know how to answer each one in what-is-right-and-proper.

All of my affairs shall be made known to you by Tychicus, The-Beloved-Brother and faithful servant and fellow-slave in *Master* whom I send to you that with this same thing that he may be knowing the-concerns of you and he should be consoling your hearts with Onesimus-The-Faithful and beloved-brother who is one-of-your-own making known all things here for you.

Aristarchus, my fellow-captive, greets you and Mark, the-cousin-of-Barnabas, from whom you obtained the-proper-understanding-of-The-Commandments. If he ever returns to you, be you receiving him along with Jesus which is the-one called

Section II

Justus. Only these born-of The-Circumcision, these fellow-workers of The-Kingdom-of-*THE-GOD* have come-to-be any solace for me.

Epaphras, who is one of you, greets you, a slave of *Anointed* always in-great-concern-and-care over you in the-prayer that you may be an-adult standing and having been filled beyond-being-able-to-be-held in every will of *THE-GOD*, for I am testifying for him that he is having a boiling zeal for you and the-ones in Laodicea and the-ones in Hierapolis. Luke-The-Beloved-Healer is greeting you and Demas.

You greet the Brothers in Laodicea and Nymphas with The-Ecclesia in the home of him and wherever you should be make-sure-to-be reading from this letter. Also to The-Ecclesia of the Laodicea it should be being read and beyond Laodicea may you be reading.

And you be warning Archippus about the-service which he accepted in *Master* that you may be fulfilling her.

Be remembering the-greeting from my hand Paul. Be remembering my bonds.

Grace to you.

Amen.

(This was written through Tychicus and Onesimus from Rome to the Colossians)

COLOSSIANS STUDY NOTES

Note: Through my many translations, I have come to believe that the phrase or associated phrasing of "inheritance" [ex: Col 1:12] accurately translated as "the-allotment" in Scripture is not a good or proper translation (i.e., inheritance). Paul makes it clear that we are to be family members (I state: royal and godly) destined to be with HIM and HE with us and we in Christ and He in us. Inheritance has an implied connotation, an accepted concept that someone has died. THE-GOD is certainly not dead, and Christ has risen to life eonian (there are times of times of times) as well. I see this as a watering down of the intent and meaning of the Scriptures and have dropped using the word *inheritance* when speaking of THE-GOD's plan and purpose for us. We are to take rulership in an active kingdom with Christ at the head of the realm and we under Him, with THE-GOD over all of us.

Note The Greek word *agapen* translated as "love" in most translations is missing that this is Godly in nature and not of men or any other such creature. I have therefore carried the adjective to add clarity to the meaning of this word throughout this translation.

Note: In my research, nearly all translations have dropped "the" as a modifier, but the Greek word for "the" is in every text and not meant to be ignored or deleted. It is often specifically singular, and when attached to the noun, it is describing that noun as unique, one of a kind, a specific thing, the original, the one and only. It is for this reason that I carry "the" everywhere it appears in all translations. Whether of God, Jesus, Satan or any other entity, concept, or idea, the modifier "the" clears up a lot of generalized words, ideas, concepts, and entities.

Note: The root of the word *pnuemia*, translated as "spirit, wind, or breath," has no gender identity since this is a word that is neuter in gender. *Pnuemia* is an "it." The Greeks, as we of English language, often fix a gender to objects and things— for example: cars, boats, the moon, the sun. For the Greeks, *pnuemia* at times has a male gender affixed to it. *Pnuemia* in the Scriptures is never capitalized or designated as a standalone being, entity, principality, or sovereignty when used as the word "spirit." It is simply the power inherent in the

Section II

being, whether of man, or God, or Christ, or any other entity. If anything is living, "it" possesses a spirit. The "Holy-spirit" is simply the power from and of The-God, giving and renewing life and performing The-God's will.

Note: Paul constantly claims and mentions "principles, powers, authorities, sovereignties not of our world." He quite clearly claims that these beings are the ones that certainly influence and control (predominately in a negative way) the systems of this world, people of the nations, and as individuals directly. You can find this concept also contained in The Old Testament through the implications of the first commandment. This claim and the concept of the warring factions in heaven makes a fascinating study.

Note: Time periods, eons, ages, millennia, eons, and eons—I stayed true to the Greek words associated with time and what we still use today in our common language. A study of time periods is fascinating but is also an area that can cause confusion. The-God always works on some kind of a timetable, but understanding which is which and when is when is a bit of a mystery. Some timetables are only known to The-God and made clear to man at God's will.

Note What is the difference between "expectation" and "hope?" Nearly all translations adopt the word "hope" for "expectation," but Paul uses almost exclusively the word "expectation." Here is why I constantly use "expectation." Having an expectation means you have no doubt at all. It is sure and certain with no ambiguity or doubt. Having a hope means you are not 100 percent convinced and convicted. I can tell you that Paul is undeniably convinced and convicted in what he delivers and talks about. Using "hope" sends a message that there is some possibility for "wiggle room," doubt, error, or excuses.

Even worse, much of the use of the word "expectation" in Paul's writings has the modifier "the" attached to "expectation," thus forming the proper translation and singular concept of "The-Expectation." This makes "The-Expectation" an event, not a philosophy or theological premise. Not recognizing "The-Expectation" as an event will lead the reader immediately down an incorrect understanding of what is being offered or discussed.

1:11 According to *Strong's*, the Greek word *hypomone[n]* and translated as "steadfastness, endurance, and constancy" has inherent in its meaning "the characteristic of a man who is unswerved from his deliberate purpose and loyalty to faith and piety by even the greatest of trials and sufferings."

1:13 Note that "The-Darkness" is capitalized and is in keeping with one of Paul's themes: that of us fighting with spiritual powers, authorities, being, and entities.

COLOSSIANS STUDY NOTES

1:16–17   These verses in most translations make it appear that Christ is the creator. Nothing could be further from the truth, but he is certainly the cause and force behind all things created by the Father, and it is therefore attributed or ascribed to him. (Legally a son is an inheritor and the reason or cause for a father passing on an inheritance. It all belongs to the son, and he is the full authority with ownership and custody.) Hebrews is the public legal transference of all titling, authority, power, and ownership of all creation to Christ from God.

1:16   Paul uses the word "originals" [Greek: *archai*] often throughout his writings and is clearly telling the group of a preexisting kingdom before man. While the explanation for us is not complete, the audience must have clearly understood what he meant. After all, Colossae was one of the centers of pagan god worship where the demons and demigods were known to manifest themselves or their power, and tales and stories had permeated the culture for centuries. Paul also uses this word "originals" in his letter to the Ephesians and is a bit more detailed about this theme in that epistle.

1:22   Two legal terms used in the court of law in this sentence caught my attention: "unflawed" [without blame, innocent] and "impeachable." In Romans Paul talks about standing in front of the "pediment," a clearly technical term in court meaning to be before the bench of a judge. Those of us in Christ are certainly going to stand before the judgment bench of THE-GOD, but by only by the grace of THE-GOD through the blood of Christ and His resurrection will we be found innocent when asked to take an accounting of our actions, words, and works. Only Jesus-The-Christ [The-Anointed-Savior] saves and Paul makes this clear.

1:24   Paul talks about the affliction he is carrying in his flesh from Christ, but the depth of that affliction is not what we might think or fully understand as only a grievous and halting symptom. While it is surely all of that, *Strong's Concordance* offers the following concept while carrying that affliction: *thlipsis* [*Strong's* G2347] translated as: "affliction, distress, oppression, tribulation, or strait." *Strong's* adds the following editorial explanation of these terms: "the afflictions which Christ had to undergo and which, therefore, his followers must not shrink from." We may be missing the fact that we must follow our *Brother's* footsteps and acts as we suffer in or with afflictions also.

2:3   The equivalent concept of "is the treasury" is the physical location where national treasures are held under the strictest guard and protection. This is the same way Fort Knox in the United States is said to house the nation's gold, a physical storage location and stronghold. It's not just in a philosophical sense, even though THE-GOD is and has the sum of all knowledge, wisdom, and understanding.

Section II

2:8 The Greek word *sulagogon*, translated as "despoiled," is a direct military reference of the battle victor coming in and taking plunder and treasures. The more philosophical or theological implication is of one carried away from the truth and becoming attached to another's doctrine, with the collection of souls as booty. The Ecclesia of the time in Colossae hopefully must have recognized this to be a spiritual fight over their souls with the introduction of foreign teachings and doctrines (not the doctrines delivered by Paul). Any student of the Bible would also recognize the Ecclesia of Laodicea as a group in trouble of losing its divine gifts and promises if not being convinced of and staying with the well-message delivered to them. As Paul often references in his letters, we fight (wrestle is not really as accurate and dramatic as what we are in the midst of) with spiritual authorities, dominions, principalities, and beings.

Note The study of Greco-Roman wrestling is interesting. The Greek term is actually translated as "to put your opponent down hard and hold his neck and take rulership over him." One promised to serve the one who won. This is an extremely high, dominating position—including control of your mind since all flows from the head through the neck. You swap your ownership (and soul, so to speak) and become the slave of the one you've lost to. By whom are you dominated?

2:9 It took me a while to digest this, but I understand and now am convinced that this means his actual body (spirit as it may be now and when he walked in the flesh as you and I do). He possesses all the authority and power of GOD (as power of attorney, legal representative) and yet takes his direction and honors and glorifies his (and our) FATHER.

2:18 "Let no man be beguile [defraud you of the prize of the victory, depriving salvation, swindle] in willing humility [submissive spiritual cowardice, pusillanimity, lacking manly strength and trust in God], and ritual of the angels which he has not seen, making hostile incursion [going into curious and subtle speculations about things seen in visions, playing with the spirits], in vain being puffed up in his by the mind [judgment and thinking] of the flesh."

I've quoted the entire Scripture here for the word "pusillanimity." When I had first translated this verse, I was not clear about what was being said about "willing humility." I sensed that Paul was not saying that this was a positive attribute. *Strong's Concordance*, after supplying a fuller explanation of the definition of the word "humility," did not identify any of these definitions with verse 2:23. What was offered in *Strong's* was a side commentary that what this verse hinted at was a negative humility. The excerpted quote from *Strong's* is: "used of an affected and ostentatious humility in Col. ii. 18, 23. (The word occurs in neither the O.T., nor in prof. auth. {professional authorities, brackets mine}—[but in Joseph. {Josephus} b. j. 4, 9, 2 in the sense of pusillanimity; also Epictet. {Epictetius} diss. {discussions} 3, 24, 56 in a bad sense. See Trench..."

The word "pusillanimity" was unknown to me. A word search on Google sent me to the website http://www.struggler.org/pusillanimity.htm, which discusses this word and its doctrinal heresy[1]. The definition of pusillanimity is quite clear, and I confess that I have been guilty of this and still at times not manly enough to stand up and not compromise when it comes to my understanding and knowledge of The-God's directions and instructions.

Here are some direct paragraphs from the website:

> Pusillanimity, a virtually obsolete word, is the name of a heresy rampant in the world today. Most people have never heard of it, but it has some important thought elements which make it useful in identifying a common spiritual disorder. Therefore, Orthodox Christians should consider it carefully. Pusillanimity denotes *spiritual cowardice, lack of "manly" strength, spiritual inertia, a certain diminution of faith and trust in God"* (italics mine).
>
> Why is pusillanimity a heresy? It is a heresy because it denies the continuous and continuing presence and operation of the Holy Spirit in the Church. It minimizes the Holy Spirit, and minimizes Jesus Christ Who sent the Holy Spirit upon the Church to keep it from error. Pusillanimity is the belief that one cannot obey the Gospel as did people of old. It is the claim that there are no spiritual fathers left in the world today. It is the belief that the Church of Christ has not yet been established, but awaits the concurrence of world religions, many of which deny the divinity of Christ and other basic Orthodox dogmas.

4:3 Paul often talks about being bound or chained. At first blush this sounds harsh, as if one is forced against one's will or purpose. But a further study of the word "bound" reveals that it also means "out of duty and honor," of the law, or as a husband and wife are bound to each other. This latter concept is clearly what Paul is telling his audience—that this is a willing binding and honor to serve THE-ONLY-GOD and The-Anointed. He tells us plainly in plenty of Scriptures that he has calculated the cost of his sufferings—that it would have no value in comparison to his Belief and Expectation-of-the-Allotment being reserved for him and GOD's own. We also should have the same mindset.

---

1. Note: website is no longer active.

COLOSSIANS IN VERSE

COLOSSIANS 1

1:1 Paul, Commissioner [apostle] of *Savior-Anointed* through the will of *GOD*, and The-Brother Timotheus

1:2 to The-Holy and believing Brothers in Colossae in *Anointed*, grace and peace to you from *FATHER-GOD* of us and *Master-Savior-Anointed*.

1:3 To *THE-GOD* and *FATHER* of *The-Master* of us *Savior-Anointed* we are thanking always praying about you

1:4 upon hearing of The-Belief of you in *Anointed-Savior* and the-Godly-love to The-All, The-Holy-Ones [saints]

1:5 because of The-Expectation, the-one-being-reserved for you in The-Heavens which you heard before in the-saying [preaching, teaching] of The-Truth-of-The-Well-Message [gospel].

1:6 This being-present in you as also throughout The-entire-System [world] and is bearing-fruit also in you from the day that you heard and realized [understood, recognized, knew of] The-Grace-of-*THE-GOD*-in-*Truth*

1:7 as also you learned from Epaphras, the beloved fellow-slave of us, who is a believing servant [minister] of *The-Anointed* over you

1:8 and the-one making-evident [showing, demonstrating] to us of your Godly-love in spirit.

1:9 Because of this we also from the day which we heard are not ceasing in praying over you and requesting that you may be being filled with The-fullest-of-The-Knowledge-of-the-Will-of-*HIM* in every wisdom and spiritual understanding.

1:10 You are to tread [walk] worthily [in the highest regard] of *The-Master*, in every-(thing) pleasing, in every good action [work] bearing fruit and growing into The-Knowledge-of-*THE-GOD*

1:11 being endued [being exceedingly strengthened] in all the-mighty-power in The-Glory-of-*HIM* in all endurance [steadfastness, constancy {under the greatest trial and sufferings}] and patience with joy

1:12 giving thanks to THE-FATHER, THE-ONE-MAKING [rendering, modeling] us into the-part of The-Allotment-of-The-Holy-Ones-of-The-Light.

1:13 *WHO* rescues us out of The-Authority-[jurisdiction]-of-The-Darkness and transports us into The-Kingdom-of-*The-Son* for the Godly-love of *Him*

1:14 in *Whom* we are having The-Deliverance through the-blood of *Him*, The-Pardoning-of-The-Sins [misses].

1:15 *Who* is (the) image [identical, exact in appearance and nature] of THE-UN-SEEN-GOD, *Firstborn* of every Creation.

1:16 That for *Him* is created The-All, in The-Heavens and on The-Earth the visible and invisible, whether thrones or masterdoms [lordships, dominions] or Originals [demons, angels, sons of God] that The-All through *Him* and in *Him* has been created.

1:17 And *He* is before All and The-All in *Him* has cohesion [is-in-proper-place-and-staying-together].

1:18 And *He* is the Head-of-The-Body, The-Ecclesia, *Who* is *The-Beginning-Firstborn-of-The-Dead-Ones* that in all *He* may be-becoming being first [has the preeminence].

1:19 That *He* delights in [in a willful choice to allow] the-entire-fullness [divinity] dwelling-in

1:20 and through *Him* to reconcile [reunites and repairs] The-All into *Him* making peace through the-blood of The-Pale-[crucifixion, cross]-of-*Him*, through *Him*, whether that of The-Earth or that in The-Heavens.

1:21 Now you were once estranged [separated, omitted, alienated] and enemies in comprehension [in knowledge] in [by, with] the-wicked-acts. But now HE reconciles [pardons and unites, enjoins]

1:22 in the-body in the-flesh of *Him* through The-Death to present you holy and unflawed [blameless, innocent] and unindictable [unimpeachable] in the sight of *HIM*.

1:23 if surely you are persistently-remaining [staying true, persevering, continuing] in The-Belief [in faith] having been grounded [established, made stable] and settled [immoveable, firm, steadfast] and not being removed [forced from, taken away] from The-Expectation-of-The-Well-Message [gospel] which you hear, *The-One-Being-Proclaimed [Heralded]* in The-entire-Creation under The-Heaven of which I, Paul, became a server [dispenser, proclaimer, minister].

Section II

1:24 Who I am now rejoicing over this-suffering of mine for the sake of you and I am instead filling the-wants [deficiencies] of the-constriction [affliction] in my flesh of [for, from] *The-Anointed* for the sake of The-Body-of-*Him* which is The-Ecclesia;

1:25 of which I became a minister as the-household-administration [a trustee, an administrator] of *THE-GOD, THE-ONE-GIVING* you to me to complete The-Saying- [word, knowledge, teaching]-of-*THE-GOD*.

1:26 Even The-Secret having been concealed from The-Eons and from the-generations and now was made to appear [is given now] to The-Holy-Ones-of-*Him*.

1:27 To whom *THE-GOD-WILLS* to make known what is the-riches-of-the-glory-of-The-Secret, this Secret among The-Nations which is *Anointed* is in you, *The-Expectation-of-The-Glory*

1:28 *Whom* we are announcing. Admonishing every man and teaching every man in all wisdom that we should be presenting every man mature [perfected] in *Anointed-Savior*

1:29 to which also I am toiling, struggling, according-to the-operation [every single part] of *Him* in divine-power operating in me.

COLOSSIANS 2

2:1 I am willing for you to know how great the struggling-contest I am having concerning you and The-Ones in Laodicea and whomever has not seen my face in the flesh [me personally].

2:2 That the-hearts of them may be consoled [comforted in faith, piety and hope, assured, instructed, exhorted, encouraged] and be united in Godly-love and into all the riches of the-full-assurance of the-understanding-of-the-knowledge-of-The-Secret-of-*THE GOD* and *FATHER* of *The-Anointed*,

2:3 in *WHOM*, stored up [secretly hidden] are treasures [*IS THE TREASURY*] of all the-wisdom and the-knowledge.

2:4 And I say this, that no man should be deceiving [deluding] any of you in persuasive words

2:5 for even if I am absent in the-flesh, together you and I am in the-spirit rejoicing and observing [considering, contemplating, taking heed to, managing] the orderly-condition [orderly array, military presentation and array] of you

2:6 as when you accepted *The-Anointed-Savior. The-Master* in *Him* you be walking

2:7	having been rooted [already thoroughly grounded and affixed] and being built up [continually growing] in The-Belief as you were taught super-abounding in her [it] with thanksgiving!
2:8	You beware! Let not any one of you shall be [become] the-one-being-spoiled [the booty of war] [led away from the truth] put under the sway [persuasive-power] of empty [devoid of truth, fruitless, a vessel which contains nothing, truthless] philosophy and seduction with The-Tradition-of-Men in according [along] with The-Elements [Original Rulers] of The-System [world] and not according-to *Anointed*.
2:9	For in *Him* is dwelling the-entire-compliment-[all of and the complete fullness and state of]-of-*THE-DEITY* [state of being GOD] in-body.
2:10	And in *Him* you have been fully filled [in full abundant measure, to the very cup brim] *Who* is *The-Head* of every sovereignty and authority
2:11	in *Whom* you were circumcised by a circumcision not done by hands, in stripping [cutting, slipping, laying aside] out-of The-Body The-Sins-of-The-Flesh.
2:12	In The-Circumcision-of-*The-Anointed* being entombed together with *Him*, in The-Baptism in which you also were roused [rose] together through The-Belief [faith] of The-Operation-[divine-master-planning]-of-*THE-GOD*, *THE-ONE-ROUSING Him* out of the-dead-ones.
2:13	You also being dead in the-offenses and the-uncircumcision of your flesh. *HE* has made (you) alive together with *Him* gracing [freely forgiving] you all the-offenses [sins].
2:14	Erasing [rubbing out] the handwriting of The-Decrees [ordinances, doctrine] which was hostile to us and has taken it away out of the midst [completely removed them] nailing it to The-Pale [crucifixion, stake],
2:15	stripping off [disarming] The-Originals [sovereignties, principalities] and boldly [in fearless confidence] disgracing [openly] The-Authorities [spiritual potentates] triumphing [with entire and completely subjugation and dominion] over them in it.
2:16	Then do not let any of you be judging concerning food or in drinking or particular festivals or The-New-Moon (festival) or of Sabbaths
2:17	which is a shadow of The-Impending and is The-Body-of-*The-Anointed*.
2:18	Let no man be arbitrating-away [defraud you of the prize of the victory, depriving salvation, swindle] by willing humility [submissive spiritual cowardice, pusillanimity, lacking manly strength and trust in God] and [or] rituals of The-Angels which he has not seen making hostile [with wrong intent, purpose] incursion [going into curious and subtle speculations about things seen

	in visions, playing with the spirits] in vain being puffed up in his by the-mind [judgment and thinking] of-the-flesh
2:19	and not holding [retaining, acknowledging] *The-Head* out of whom The-entire-Body through the-joints and ligaments being supplied and united is growing[increasing] in the-growth [development, purpose] of *THE-GOD*.
2:20	If then you died together with *Anointed* from The-Elements-[spiritual powers, authorities, bonds]-of-The-System, why, as though living in The-System, do you subjugate yourselves to The-Decrees [ordinances, practices]?
2:21	You should not be touching nor should be-tasting or not coming into contact
2:22	with all things from use which is perishing [is corroding-away] as to [such as] The-Directions [commandments, ordinances] and teachings of men
2:23	which indeed is having [appears to have] some wisdom in The-Saying [its expressions] in arbitrary [valueless] worship and (falseness, emptiness) humility and not sparing [neglecting] the-body not in [which does not have] any lasting-value toward satisfying [satiating the desires of] the-flesh.

COLOSSIANS 3

3:1	If then you being roused together to *The-Anointed*, be seeking that above where *The-Anointed* is sitting in [at, to] the right of *THE-GOD*.
3:2	You be disposed [thinking, reflecting] on that above not of that of The-Land [earth].
3:3	For you have died, and the-life of yours has been hidden [secured, certain, kept laid up] together with *The-Anointed* in *THE-GOD*.
3:4	Whenever *The-Anointed* may be made to appear, *The-Life of Us*, then you also together with *Him* shall be made to appear in glory.
3:5	Put to death then the-members of yours which are of the-land [earth]: prostitution, uncleanliness, lusty-passionate desires, evil, and greediness [never-ending covetousness] which is idolatry.
3:6	Because of this The-Indignation-of-*THE-GOD* is coming on The-Sons-of-the-Stubbornness
3:7	in whom you also tread about in once [were active participants, lived the lifestyle of] when you lived among them.
3:8	But now you also be putting away all of anger, fury, malice, blasphemy, obscenity out of your mouth,

3:9	not lying [falsifying] to one another, slipping [cutting, stripping] off the-old-man and the-practices [deeds, actions] of him
3:10	and be putting on the-young (new man), being renewed in recognition [knowledge] in accord [all respects] with [after] the-image [blessed, holy, morale, of divine nature] of *THE-ONE-CREATING Him.*
3:11	For there is neither Greek nor Jew, circumcised or uncircumcised, barbarian, Scythian, slave, free, but The-All and All in *Anointed.*
3:12	Then as The-Chosen-of-*THE-GOD*, Holy-Ones and having-been-Godly-loved, put you on compassions of pities [unbounded and unending mercy], kindness, humility, meekness, patience,
3:13	bearing one another and dealing graciously among yourselves. If ever anyone may be having a complaint [quarrel, dispute] toward anyone as also *The-Anointed* deals graciously with you, do you also.
3:14	Yet over all of these, The-Godly-Love which is the uniting-bond of maturity [state of adulthood, perfection]
3:15	and let The-Peace-of-*THE-GOD* be arbitrating [directing, controlling] in the-hearts of you in which you also were called in One-Body and you-become The-Thankful-Ones.
3:16	Let the *Word* of *The-Anointed* be dwelling inside him, richly [in abundance] in every wisdom teaching and admonishing [encouraging] yourselves in psalms and hymns and spiritual songs in grace [joy, pleasure, delight, sweetness] singing in your heart to *The-Master.*
3:17	And in everything you may be doing in word or action [deed], (do) all in The-Name-of-*Master-Savior* giving thanks to *THE-GOD* and *FATHER* through *Him.*
3:18	The-women [wives], set yourselves under [be a willing subject to] your own men [husbands] as is proper in *Master.*
3:19	Men [Husbands], be-Godly-loving the-women [wives] and do not be bitter [exasperating, irritating, render anger] toward them.
3:20	Children, be obeying your parents in all things, for this is well-pleasing to *The-Master.*
3:21	Fathers, do not be provoking your children so that they may not be being unfeeling [broken in spirit, become callous, disheartened and disinterested, uncaring].
3:22	Slaves, you be obeying in all The-Masters-of-the-flesh not under the eye scrutiny [in distrust], not as men-pleasers, but in singular [sincerity] of the heart fearing *THE-GOD.*

Section II

3:23   And in all which you are doing, work out of the soul [from the heart] as to *The-Master* and not to men.

3:24   Be aware that from *Master* you shall be getting the repayment-of-The-Enjoyment-of-The-Allotment for you are slaves [serving] to *The-Master-Anointed*.

3:25   And the-one-injuring [wronging] shall be paid back for which he causes injury [wrong] for there is no partiality.

4:1   The-Masters, be tendering [afford, offer, exhibit] being just and equitable to the slaves! Being aware you also having a *Master* in heaven.

COLOSSIANS 4

4:2   Persevere [remain-constant] in prayer watching [keeping, taking care] in her [it] to-be-thankful

4:3   praying in unison also concerning us that THE-GOD should be opening to us a door for The-Word to speak The-Secret-of-*The-Anointed*.

4:4   Because of this I have also been bound [out of honor and duty] that I should be clearly showing as is binding [right and proper for] for me to speak.

4:5   You be walking in wisdom with the-ones out [not of The Ecclesia] reclaiming [making wise and sacred use of every opportunity to do good in] the season [era].

4:6   Let your words always be in grace as seasoning [salving, healing] salt to perceive [understand, know] how to answer each one in binding [what is right and proper].

4:7   All of my affairs shall be made known to you by Tychicus, The-Beloved-Brother and faithful servant and fellow-slave in *Master*

4:8   whom I send to you that with this same thing that he may be knowing the-concerns of you and he should be consoling [comforting] your hearts

4:9   with Onesimus-The-Faithful and beloved-brother who is out [from, one] of you [one of your own] making known all things here to [for] you.

4:10   Aristarchus, my fellow-captive, greets you and Mark the-cousin-of-Barnabas from whom you obtained Directions [the proper understanding of The-Commandments]. If he ever returns to you, be you receiving him

4:11   along with Jesus which is the-one called Justus. Only these being-of [born of] The-Circumcision [these Jews], these fellow-workers of The-Kingdom-of-*THE-GOD* have come-to-be any solace [comfort, relief, consolation] for me.

4:12 Epaphras, who is one of you, greets you, a slave of *Anointed* always struggling [in great concern, in care, fervently] over you in the-prayer that you may be in maturity [adulthood, an adult] standing and having been filled entirely [beyond being able to be held] in every will of THE-GOD

4:13 for I am testifying for him that he is having a boiling zeal for you and the-ones in Laodicea and the-ones in Hierapolis [Sacred-City].

4:14 Luke, The-Beloved-Healer [physician], is greeting you and Demas.

4:15 You greet the Brothers in Laodicea and Nymphas with The-Ecclesia in the home of him

4:16 and wherever you should be cause [make sure to be] the reading of this letter. Also to The-Ecclesia of the Laodicea it should be being read and beyond Laodicea may you be reading.

4:17 And you be warning Archippus about the-service [ministry] which he accepted in *Master* that you may be fulfilling her [it].

4:18 Be remembering the-greeting [salutation] from my hand Paul. Be remembering my bonds.

Grace to you.
Amen.

(This was written through Tychicus and Onesimus from Rome to the Colossians)

Section III

AN EXTRACT AND A REBUTTAL

Additional Instructions and a Prophecy
of the End of an Eon

The Letters of
I and II THESSALONIANS

I THESSALONIANS COMMENTARY

We now have come to the seventh Ecclesia on the ancient mail route: Thessalonica. Thessalonians not only completes the instructions, advice, rebuttals, and arguments associated with The-Belief, but it also foretells the end of an eon and the ushering in of the Kingdom of The Christ—as well as Paul's service ending as General Council and Attorney for The-Nations. The way Timothy is presented hints of Paul's stepping aside, and Paul's more detailed information concerning the order of the First Resurrection also attests to how the close of this current eon of man will end with another and completely different "new world order" that is to begin.

I Thessalonians is sitting in the seventh position in the Holy Order, thus providing a clue to the reader that it completes all instruction necessary until Christ returns to set up His Kingdom, at which time something new and completely different is to occur. As mentioned that as Colossians ends the XYZs of the finalized instructions, the number seven within the Theory of Numerology stands for completeness of a subject, of perfection, and "of God." Tiny I Thessalonians neatly fits both these roles, nestling in its position in the letters.

The letter is short, and if read simply without some knowledge of the information and knowledge from Romans to Colossians, it appears empty of any real relevance other than to treat others well, defend The-Belief, remain true and loyal, Timothy is coming to see you, and oh yes, some event appearing to be a raising from the dead and with that, certain ones still alive are going to experience the same occurrence. As generic as the letter would read to any unknowledgeable person, those having the full knowledge of all the teachings of Paul see this as a much different letter. It is the case summary of the legal proceedings of Paul's teachings concerning Christ and the Coming Kingdom. It is much more profound than just a simple generic letter.

This letter truly brings to close the letters to all the Ecclesiae as a whole and serves as a summation of a legal decision for the charge associated with who has right to the ownership and rulership of all Creation. It's a review of the complete and full knowledge and information needed about Christ as The-legal-Head of The-Body (legal owner of the corporation), The-Body of Christ (as an organization and business entity and what is and is not permitted for that organization), and your role and expected behavior within this framework. It also contains the forecasted end of this current reign of The-Originals, Elements, Sovereignties, and Powers of the world. It is

Section III

not hard to analyze the letter to understand why it ends the first seven letters to The Nations and also serves as a prophetic letter showing the end of an eon.

I Thessalonians opens with the feel of tender love, happiness, and concern by the aging and worn trustee Paul as he thanks this Ecclesia for its continued loyalty to the Ecclesiae as a whole and to The-Belief they continue to defend. Paul provides a gentle reminder to avoid shaming The-Body of Christ and offending anyone they come in contact with, but instead to be "Sons-of-Light," the correct and positive example to all (1:1—4:12). This is, if you will, the legal review of all of Paul's effort over the years. This is a court summation that is short and to the point, and the letter assumes you are filled with the full knowledge of the case and its activities by following it all along its proceedings over the time of the case trial.

You have been involved as a jurist (and as one of the possessions associated with this case) from the beginnings of Romans until Colossians with the court case about who has legal right of ownership and leadership of this corporation, Body of Believers. There has been an attempted hostile takeover, and your future has been hanging in the balance of that court decision. The good news for you is that the case has been overwhelmingly and clearly proven beyond a shadow of a doubt, with undeniable and irrefutable proofs by the witness of thousands, and unanimously judged in favor of The Messiah and Anointed Savior, The-Man. The Son of The God is the clear owner and has the full legal right of ownership and leadership of The-Body. But will you accept this or claim loyalty to someone or something else?

It is the court case of the eons, and nothing set beside it stands in comparison to what it means for the future as it also reaches back into the past. As a reader, if you take the time now to go back and reread the first seven letters of Paul in order, you'll see the opening of the case, the debates and arguments preceding back and forth, the presentation and building up of the proofs, and the logical and overwhelming conclusion of who has ownership and full authority over all. It is Jesus The-Christ. So ends the summation of the case.

Starting in 4:13 Paul transitions the discussion of legal ownership, what that decision means and begins turning more specifically to the future, a prophetic series of events. Described is the end of this eon, detailing how it will end, the ordering of events culminating in the First Resurrection. The Trumpet of God sounds, Christ descends with his army of beings, the dead are brought back to life to meet him, followed by those remaining still alive. Paul tells us that the reign of Christ is now officially taking place, and he is to come back to claim his legal possessions. But be aware, between then and now there will be plenty of false and fraudulent attempted takeovers, claims of false possession, and countersuits. Even The-Satan is predicted to stage a spectacular event to reclaim, repossess, fool, and remove the very Chosen from believing, meant to have you give up your "birthright," (As Adam did) becoming a spoil of a spiritual battle. Don't get caught in those counterclaims and false "divine" events; don't give up your allotment in The Kingdom being prepared for you.

Paul's declaration that "The-One-Calling you is also The-One that shall be doing it" (5:24) is really the conclusion of the entire matter. It is Paul's short, sweet, and to-the-point review of the entire legal matter and the carrying out of the judgments.

I Thessalonians is not so tiny a letter after all, and it is the perfect ending for the Ecclesiae of God and Christ not only then, but also throughout the ages.

I THESSALONIANS AS A LETTER

PAUL AND SILVANUS AND Timothy to the Out-Called of Thessalonica in *FATHER GOD* and *Master Savior Anointed*. Grace to you and peace from *GOD, FATHER* of us and of *Master Jesus Anointed*.

We are thanking *THE-GOD* always concerning all of you, making mentioning of you in the-prayers of ours. Remembering unceasingly your work in The-Belief and the-toil with the-Godly-love and the endurance in The-Expectation in *The-Master* of us *Savior Anointed*, in the presence of *THE-GOD* and *FATHER* of us. Knowing, Brothers, you are The-Choice having been loved by *GOD*. For the Well-Message by us came not to you by only the-word but also in powerful strength and in the Holy-spirit and in full-abundant-assurance as you know what we did among you for your sake. For you had become imitators of us receiving from *The-Lord* the-word in great affliction with joy by the Holy spirit so that you became models to all the ones-believing in the-Macedonia and the-Achaia. For from you has been sounded forth The-Word-of-*The-Master* not only in Macedonia and Achaia, but also in every place of The-Belief of yours toward *THE-GOD* has become known so that there was found no need for us to speak about anything. For they are reporting to us how we came and were accepted by you and how you turned back to *THE-GOD* from the idols to-be-in-divine-service to *THE-LIVING-AND-TRUE-GOD* and to be waiting for *The-Son-of-HIM* out of the Heavens whom *HE-ROUSES* out of dead-ones, *Savior, The-One-Rescuing* us from the coming angered-punishment.

You yourselves know, Brothers, our coming to you, that it has not become for nothing. For even the sufferings before and being shamefully treated as you know about at Philippi, we were bold about *THE-GOD* of ours to speak to you the Well-Message-of-*THE-GOD* in an immense struggle. For the calling by us is not for private gain, nor out of impure motives, nor as a lure. But as we have been tested by *THE-GOD* to be entrusted with The-Well-Message, therefore we are speaking not to please men but *THE-GOD, THE-ONE-TESTING* the hearts of us. For not at any time as you are aware did we come in expressions of flattery, neither in hidden purpose for greed as *GOD* is witness neither seeking glory from men, neither from you, nor from others, nor to be a burden being since we are Commissioners-of-*Anointed*. But we were coming gently in the midst of you, as a nursing-woman is-to-be-cherishing the children of her. Thus, being ardently attached to you we are delighting to share with you not only the Well-Message-of-*THE-GOD* but also for our own souls because that you have become beloved to us.

Brothers, for you remember the hard work of us and the laboring and working night and day to not be burdensome to any of you. We proclaimed the Well-Message-of-*THE-GOD* to you. You are witnesses and *THE-GOD* too how with piety and innocence and blamelessly to you, the-ones-believing we acted. Even as you know how each one of you as a father consoles and comforts his children we did with you and witnessed to you in The-Worthy-Walk-of-*THE-GOD*, *THE-ONE-CALLING* you into The-Kingdom of *HIS* and glory. Because of this we are also thanking *THE-GOD* unceasingly that by accepting the word by hearing about *THE-GOD* from us you did not accept the saying of men but as *The-True-Word*-of-*GOD* which is also operating in you, the ones-believing.

For you, Brothers, were becoming imitators of The-Ecclesia-of-*THE-GOD* as the-ones living in Judea in *Anointed Savior* for even you suffered the same by your own fellow-countrymen as those persecuted by the Jews, the-ones also having killed *The-Master-Savior* and their own prophets. For they banished us and are not pleasing to *GOD* and are adversarial-and-antagonistic to all men, forbidding us to speak to the Nations so that they-may-not-be-being-saved, to increase their sins to the-fullest so that on them will be full and complete anger.

Yet, Brothers, we were bereaved when we were gone from you for an hour period and not face-to-face and were persistently in great desire to see your face. Therefore we were coming to you, even I Paul, even once, even twice but hindering us was The-Adversary. For whom of us has any expectation or joy or crown of rejoicing? Will not you even be in the presence of *The-Lord* of us *Savior Anointed* at the-coming of *Him*? You are the-glory and joy of us.

Since continuing to be held back, it seemed well for us to be left in Athens alone and we sent Timotheus, The-Brother of us and servant of *THE-GOD* and fellow-worker of us in the Well-Message-of-*The-Anointed*, for the establishment of you and to console you concerning The-Belief of you so that no-one is to-give up-and-be-removed in the tribulations. For these you yourselves are aware that to this we are being appointed-by-*GOD*'s-purpose. Even about this to you, which we predicted to you and it happened that we are to be afflicted all about and you know this. For this reason, when I continued to be restrained, I sent to know The-Belief of you lest somehow the tempting-and-trials of The-One-Trying resulted in the toils of us may become for nothing.

But now the returning of Timothy to us from you and bringing the good news to us of The-Belief and the Godly-love of you and that you are always having a good remembrance of us and a great desire to be seeing us and also us of you. Because of this we were consoled, Brothers, by you in all the afflictions and distresses of ours through The-Belief of you that now we are alive if you continue standing firm in *Master*. What thanksgiving are we able to repay to *THE-GOD* concerning you for all the

Section III

joy in which we are rejoicing because of you in front of *THE-GOD* of us! Night and day over-exceedingly beseeching to be seeing the face of you and to complete the understanding of The-Belief of you!

Yet *THE-GOD HIMSELF* and the *FATHER* of us and *The-Lord* of us *Savior-Anointed* may be directing the way of us to you. And may *The-Lord* of you, may *He* be increasing and may *He* be super-abounding in you the-Godly-love to one another and to all as even we also to you. To establish in your hearts unblameable in holiness in front of *THE-GOD* and *FATHER* of us in the presence of *The-Master* of us *Savior-Anointed* with all the Holy-Ones of *Him*.

To the rest of the Brothers, we are asking and pleading-and-begging you in *Master-Savior* just as you accepted from us how you must be walking and to be pleasing to *GOD* that you may be even more super-abounding. For you are aware of the charges we gave to you through *The-Master-Savior*. For this is the will of *THE-GOD, THE-ONE-MAKING* you holy that you are to be abstaining from the fornications, that each of you are to know how to be managing and controlling his sexual organ in holiness and honor, not in passions of lust as also even the Nations do which have-no-knowledge-of *THE-GOD*. To not be causing sin and taking advantage of the brother of him as a practice because the *The-Master* is an *Avenger* concerning all these things as we have said before and certify to you. For *THE-GOD* has not called us for uncleanliness but in holiness. Surely in consequences then the-one-with-disregard is not rejecting men but *THE-GOD, THE-ONE-GIVING* the Holy spirit of *HIM* to us.

Concerning brotherly-affection I have no need to be writing about this for you are taught-by-*GOD* to be Godly-loving to one another as also you are doing it to all the Brothers in the whole of Macedonia. But we are entreating with you to give even more in super-abundance and to be making it one's purpose to lead a quiet life and engaged in your own business and to be working with your own hands according as we have charged you. That you may be walking respectably with the-ones not of the Ecclesia and that you should not have a need for anything.

But, Brothers, I am not willing for you to be ignorant concerning those in death that no one may sorrow unlike the-rest, those having no hope. For if we are believing *The-Savior* died and rose, then through *Savior*, *THE-GOD* shall be resurrecting the-ones in death with *Him*. For this we are saying to you by the instruction of the *Master*, that we the living surviving-ones until *The-Master's* return will not precede the-ones-being-put-to-repose. For *The-Master Himself*, in the shout of a command, in a voice of *The-Chief-Messenger* and with The-Trumpet-of-*GOD* shall be descending from Heaven, and the-dead-ones in *Anointed* shall be rising first. Secondly, we the living surviving-ones together with them shall be being carried-off-by-divine-force in the clouds to meet *The-Master* in the air and thus we shall always be together with *Master*. Therefore, be encouraging-and-comforting one another with these words.

You have no need for me to write to you concerning the times and seasons for you are accurately aware that The-Day-of-the-*Master*. It is coming as a thief in the night for whenever they may be saying, "Peace and Security," then unawares to them is standing by utter extermination even as having pangs inside of the belly and no, not one of them may be escaping.

Yet you, Brothers, are not in darkness that The-Day may be catching you as a thief. You are all Sons-of-Light and are The-Sons-of-The-Day, and we are neither of the night nor darkness. Consequently then, we should not be asleep as even the-rest, but we should be watching and keeping sober, for the-ones drowsing in the night remain sleeping and the ones being drunk in the night remain drunk. Yet we of The-Day may be sober, putting on the Breastplate-of-Belief and Godly-love and a helmet of expectation and salvation. For *THE-GOD* has not appointed us to divine anger but salvation by the purchase through *The-Master* of us *Savior-Anointed, The-Resurrected-One* who for the sake of us, that whether we may be alive or may be dead, at the same time together with *Him* we should be living. Therefore you be comforting-and-encouraging one another and be edifying-and-esteeming one another according as you are doing.

And we are asking of you, Brothers, to know that the ones-toiling among you and caring-and-protecting over you and admonishing you in the *Master* to be considering them in above-extravagant Godly-love because of their work and you be at peace among yourselves.

Now we are entreating you, Brothers, be warning the-disorderly. You be comforting the feebleminded, upholding the weak, and be patient with all! Be certain not anyone is giving vindicating evil with evil but always be pursuing the-good to one another and to all.

Always be rejoicing! You be praying unceasingly. In everything you be giving thanks for this is will of *GOD* in *Anointed-Savior* for you.

Do not be putting-out the-spirit. Do not consider as nothing prophecies. Be you testing all things and take possession of the genuine-morally-good-and-that-which-is-accurate.

Abstain from every perception of wicked things and *THE-GOD-OF-THE-PEACE HIMSELF* may be making you holy in completeness and entirely faultless. And may your spirit and the soul and the body be-held in reserve with-no-condemnation-and-denouncement in the presence of *The-Lord* of us *Savior-Anointed.*

THE-ONE-CALLING you is also *THE-ONE* that shall be doing it.

Brothers, be praying for us. You greet all the Brothers with a holy kiss. I want you to promise by *The-Master* that this letter is to be read to all the Holy Brothers.

The Grace of *The-Master* of us *Savior-Anointed* be with you.

(Written from Athens to the Thessalonians)

I THESSALONIANS STUDY NOTES

Note: Through my many translations, I have come to believe that the phrase or associated phrasing of "inheritance" [ex: Col 1:12] accurately translated as "the-allotment" in Scripture is not a good or proper translation (i.e., inheritance). Paul makes it clear that we are to be family members (I state: royal and godly) destined to be with HIM and HE with us and we in Christ and He in us. Inheritance has an implied connotation, an accepted concept that someone has died. THE-GOD is certainly not dead, and Christ has risen to life eonian (there are times of times of times) as well. I see this as a watering down of the intent and meaning of the Scriptures and have dropped using the word *inheritance* when speaking of THE-GOD's plan and purpose for us. We are to take rulership in an active kingdom with Christ at the head of the realm and we under Him, with THE-GOD over all of us.

Note The Greek word *agapen* translated as "love" in most translations is missing that this is Godly in nature and not of men or any other such creature. I have therefore carried the adjective to add clarity to the meaning of this word throughout this translation.

Note: In my research, nearly all translations have dropped "the" as a modifier, but the Greek word for "the" is in every text and not meant to be ignored or deleted. It is often specifically singular, and when attached to the noun, it is describing that noun as unique, one of a kind, a specific thing, the original, the one and only. It is for this reason that I carry "the" everywhere it appears in all translations. Whether of God, Jesus, Satan or any other entity, concept, or idea, the modifier "the" clears up a lot of generalized words, ideas, concepts, and entities.

Note: The root of the word *pnuemia*, translated as "spirit, wind, or breath," has no gender identity since this is a word that is neuter in gender. *Pnuemia* is an "it." The Greeks, as we of English language, often fix a gender to objects and things— for example: cars, boats, the moon, the sun. For the Greeks, *pnuemia* at times has a male gender affixed to it. *Pnuemia* in the Scriptures is never capitalized or designated as a standalone being, entity, principality, or sovereignty when used as the word "spirit." It is simply the power inherent in the

being, whether of man, or God, or Christ, or any other entity. If anything is living, "it" possesses a spirit. The "Holy-spirit" is simply the power from and of The-God, giving and renewing life and performing The-God's will.

Note: Paul constantly claims and mentions "principles, powers, authorities, sovereignties not of our world." He quite clearly claims that these beings are the ones that certainly influence and control (predominately in a negative way) the systems of this world, people of the nations, and as individuals directly. You can find this concept also contained in The Old Testament through the implications of the first commandment. This claim and the concept of the warring factions in heaven makes a fascinating study.

Note: Time periods, eons, ages, millennia, eons, and eons—I stayed true to the Greek words associated with time and what we still use today in our common language. A study of time periods is fascinating but is also an area that can cause confusion. The-God always works on some kind of a timetable, but understanding which is which and when is when is a bit of a mystery. Some timetables are only known to The-God and made clear to man at God's will.

Note What is the difference between "expectation" and "hope?" Nearly all translations adopt the word "hope" for "expectation," but Paul uses almost exclusively the word "expectation." Here is why I constantly use "expectation." Having an expectation means you have no doubt at all. It is sure and certain with no ambiguity or doubt. Having a hope means you are not 100 percent convinced and convicted. I can tell you that Paul is undeniably convinced and convicted in what he delivers and talks about. Using "hope" sends a message that there is some possibility for "wiggle room," doubt, error, or excuses.

Even worse, much of the use of the word "expectation" in Paul's writings has the modifier "the" attached to "expectation," thus forming the proper translation and singular concept of "The-Expectation." This makes "The-Expectation" an event, not a philosophy or theological premise. Not recognizing "The-Expectation" as an event will lead the reader immediately down an incorrect understanding of what is being offered or discussed.

1:3 "The-Expectation" Paul is referring to is to the promise of your resurrection and becoming a spirit being with position and rank as a son or daughter of God as he restores His Kingdom at Christ's return. This includes *His* divine character and deity. See my discussion on the-allotment verses inheritance.

1:4 The Greek word *egapemenoi* is a divine love since it has rooted within this word "agape" which is godly-love, and I have carried it into the translation as "having-been-godly-loved."

Section III

1:4   "having-been-Godly-loved by God" is both the past active and present active verb tense. The message within this verse is that you were already known and being loved with a Godly love by God before the beginning of all things.

1:8   Paul is telling his audience that they needed no additional teaching for their understanding and practice in the community or toward one another.

1:9   The concept of "to-be-slaving" in the Greek is a bit thought-provoking since the concept of slavery is used. A study of a variety of sources for this concept infers this to mean that as a husband and wife willingly submit in love to each other, they become slaves to each other. They both would be in divine-service to each other.

2:7   "Nurse" is meant as a nursing woman with a child clinging to her breast.

2:8   "Being ardently attached" is a euphemism for the deep bonding that takes place between both the nursing mother and her child.

2:17   "Bereavement" in this verse refers to the loss of a parent and their child's deep lament, lost love, and broken heart.

2:19   Notice that Paul tells his audience they are already standing in God's presence; there is no period of waiting for their place in God's Kingdom, and they will stand with Christ at his return.

4:12   "To the-ones outside" is speaking about the general public, not the Ecclesia.

4:13–15   "Being-put-to-repose" is the proper Greek translation meaning "being dead" or "put to death." Paul, however, describes death in this phrase as a deep, unconscious sleep. Notice that there is no mention of "going to heaven" in this verse, which would have been a prime opportunity to say such if it were true. Nothing could be clearer: you are dead when you die, facing death as all men have and will. Paul is telling everyone that when you die, you are dead until the return of Christ (or within a person's own season and time, for there are multiple times of resurrections mentioned in the Bible). By Christ's returning, he is laying the groundwork to bring "Heaven" here on earth.

4:16   "The-Trumpet" is referring to the "Day of Trumpets," one of the seven annual Jewish Holy Days. Paul has told us during which festival Christ is scheduled to return in the future. This is apparently "The-Day" Paul refers to often throughout his letter to the Thessalonians and others.

5:1   "The times and seasons" Paul is referring to here are the observances of the Jewish holy days which the Thessalonians understood to have passed away as they were fulfilled by the life and death of the Messiah Jesus.

5:14   To the phrase "the-disorderly" many texts add "about ungodly pleasures," which is not in the original but certainly appears to clear up any ambiguity and doubt about what "the-disorderly" were doing. Thessalonica was like any other Gentile city with its temples and services, general prostitution, and rampant adultery, and within this Ecclesia there were still some individuals needing maturing and perfecting. But I offer this alternate, which is that there was even inside this Ecclesia those beginning to teach doctrines and instructions contrary to what Paul gave them. My support for this is found in II Timothy where Paul tells Timothy that all the Ecclesiae have abandoned him.

5:20 I find this warning for the Ecclesia concerning ignoring and not placing credence on prophecy interesting, especially since Paul eventually will state that "all have left him" (see note 5:14). For all the maturity in this group, apparently they chose to leave and abandon the teachings and instructions of Paul.

I THESSALONIANS IN VERSE

I THESSALONIANS 1

1:1 Paulos [Paul] and Silouanos [Silvanus] and Timotheus [Timothy] to the Out-Called [Ecclesia] of Thessalonica in *FATHER GOD* and *Master* [Lord] *Jesus* [Jehovah Is Salvation] *Anointed* [Christ]. Grace to you and peace from *GOD, FATHER* of us and of *Master Jesus Anointed.*

1:2 We are thanking *THE-GOD* always concerning all of you, making mentioning of you in the-prayers of ours.

1:3 Remembering un-intermittently [unceasingly] your work in The-Belief [faith] and the-toil with the-Godly-love and endurance in The-Expectation in *The-Master* of us *Savior Anointed*, in the place toward [in front of, in the presence of] *THE-GOD* and *FATHER* of us.

1:4 Having perceived [Knowing], Brothers, you are The-Choice [hand selected] having been loved by *GOD*.

1:5 For the Well-Message of ours [by us] came not to you by only the-word but also in powerful strength and in (the) Holy spirit and in full-abundant-assurance as you have perceived [know] such-as we-were-becoming [what we did] among you because of you [for your sake].

1:6 For you had become imitators of us receiving from *The-Lord* the-saying [word] in great affliction with joy by (the) Holy spirit

1:7 so that you became models to all (the) ones-believing in the-Macedonia and the-Achaia.

1:8 For from you has been sounded forth The-Word-of-*The-Master* not only in Macedonia and Achaia, but also in every place of The-Belief [faith] of yours toward *THE-GOD* has-come-out [become known] so that there was found no need for us to be having to be speaking [to speak about] anything.

1:9 For they are reporting to us what kind of an entrance [how one arrives and is accepted by, to administer an office] we have had toward you and how you turned back to *THE-GOD* from the idols to-be-slaving [in-divine-service] to *THE-LIVING-AND-TRUE-GOD*

1:10 and to be waiting for *The-Son* of *HIM* out of the Heavens whom *HE-ROUSES* out of dead-ones, *Savior, The-One-Rescuing* us from the coming indignation [angered punishment].

I THESSALONIANS 2

2:1 You yourselves are aware [know], Brothers, the-entrance of us toward [how we administered to, our coming to] you that (it) has not become empty [for nothing, wasted].

2:2 For even (the) sufferings before and being outraged [shamefully treated] as you are aware [you know about] at Philippi, we were bold about *THE-GOD* of ours to speak to you the Well-Message-of-*THE-GOD* in (a) vast [immense] struggle.

2:3 For the calling by us is not out of deception [acting for private gain], nor out of uncleanliness [impure motives], nor in guile [as a lure].

2:4 But as we have been tested by *THE-GOD* to be entrusted (with) The-Well-Message, therefore we are speaking not to please men but *THE-GOD, THE-ONE-TESTING* the hearts of us.

2:5 For not at any time, as you are aware, did we come in expressions of flattery, neither in pretense [the false motive, hidden purpose] for greed (as) *GOD* is witness

2:6 neither seeking glory from men, neither from you, nor from others, (nor) to be a burden being as [since we are] Commissioners-[apostles]-of-*Anointed*.

2:7 But we were coming gently in the midst of you, as a nurse [nursing-woman] is-to-be-cherishing the children of her.

2:8 Thus being ardently attached to you, we are delighting to share with you not only the Well-Message-of-*THE-GOD* but also for our own souls because that you have become beloved to us.

2:9 Brothers, for you remember the toil [hard work] of us and the laboring and working night and day to not be burdensome to any of you. We proclaimed [heralded] the Well-Message of *THE-GOD* to you.

2:10 You (are) witnesses and *THE-GOD* (too) how benignly [with piety] and justly [innocence] and blamelessly [without guilt] to you, the-ones-believing, we became [behaved, acted].

Section III

2:11   Even as you know how each one of you as a father consoles and comforts his children, we did with you

2:12   and witnessed to you in The-Worthy-Walk-of-*THE-GOD*, *THE-ONE-CALL-ING* you into The-Kingdom of *HIS* and glory.

2:13   Because of this we are also thanking *THE-GOD* unceasingly that in accepting (the) word [sayings] by hearing about *THE-GOD* from us you did not receive [take up, accept] (as the) saying of men but as *The-True-Word-of-GOD* which is also operating in you, the ones-believing.

2:14   For you Brothers were becoming imitators of The-Ecclesia-of-*THE-GOD* (as) the-ones being [living] in the Judea in *Anointed Savior* for even you suffered the same by your own fellow-tribesman [countrymen, kinfolk] as those under [persecuted by] the Jews,

2:15   the-ones also having killed *The-Master-Savior* and their own prophets. For they banished us and (are) not pleasing to *GOD* and (are) contrary [adversarial, antagonistic] to all men

2:16   forbidding us to speak to the Nations [Gentiles] so that they-may-not-be-being-saved, to increase their sins to the-full [the brim, overflowing] so that on them will be full and complete anger [indignation].

2:17   Yet, Brothers, we were bereaved [lamenting as over a parent] when we were gone from you for an hour period and not face-to-face and were persistently [ever-trying] in great yearning [desire] to see your face.

2:18   Therefore we were coming to you, even I Paul, even once, even twice [repeatedly, many times] but hindering us was The-Adversary [Satan].

2:19   For who of us has any expectation or joy or wreath [crown] of glorying [rejoicing]? Or [Are] not even you in the front of [presence] of *The-Lord* of us *Savior Anointed* at the presence of *Him* [at *His* return]?

2:20   You are the-glory and joy of us.

I THESSALONIANS 3

3:1   Since continuing to be refrained [held back], it seemed well for us to be left in Athens alone,

3:2   and we sent Timotheus, The-Brother of us and servant of *THE-GOD* and fellow-worker of us in the Well-Message-of-*The-Anointed* for the establishment of you and to console you concerning The-Belief [faith] of you

3:3	so that no-one is to-be-being-swayed [give up, be removed] in the constrictions [afflictions, tribulations]. For these you yourselves are aware that to this we are being located [appointed by God's purpose, destined].
3:4	Even about this to you, which we predicted to you and it became [happened] that we are to be afflicted all about and you know (it, this).
3:5	For this reason when I continued to be restrained, I sent to know The-Belief [faith] of you lest somehow the tries [tempting, trials] of The-One-Trying [The-Tempter] resulted in the toils of us may becoming for nothing.
3:6	But now the coming [returning] of Timotheus to us from you and bringing the well-message [good news] to us (of) The-Belief [faith] and the Godly-love (charity) of you and that you are always having a good remembrance of us and longing [a great desire] to be seeing us and also we of you.
3:7	Because of this we were consoled, Brothers, by you in all the afflictions and distresses of ours through The-Belief [faith] of you
3:8	that now we are alive if you continue standing firm in *Master*.
3:9	What thanksgiving are we able to repay to *THE-GOD* concerning you for all the joy in which we are rejoicing because of you in front of *THE-GOD* of us!
3:10	Night and day over-exceedingly beseeching to be seeing the face of you and to adjust the deficiencies [complete the understanding] of The-Belief [faith] of you!
3:11	Yet *THE-GOD HIMSELF* and (the) *FATHER* of us and *The-Lord* of us *Savior-Anointed* may be directing the way of us to you.
3:12	And may *The-Lord* of you, may *He* be increasing and may *He* be super-abounding in you the-Godly-love to one another and to all as even we also to you.
3:13	To establish in your hearts unblameable in holiness in front of *THE-GOD* and *FATHER* of us in the presence of *The-Master [Lord]* of us *Savior-Anointed* with all the Holy-Ones of *Him*.

I THESSALONIANS 4

4:1	To the rest of the Brothers, we are asking and entreating [pleading, begging] you in *Master-Savior* just as you accepted from us how you must be walking and to be pleasing to *GOD* that you may be even more super-abounding.
4:2	For you are aware of the charges [command, message] we gave to you through *The-Master-Savior*.

Section III

4:3   For this is the will of THE-GOD, THE-ONE-MAKING you holy that you are to be abstaining from the fornications,

4:4   that each of you are to be aware of [know how to] to be acquiring [managing and controlling] his instrument [vessel, sexual organ] in holiness and honor,

4:5   not in passions of lust as also even the Nations (do) which are-not-being-acquainted (with) [have-no-knowledge-of] THE-GOD.

4:6   To not be overstepping [defrauding, causing sin] and overreaching [taking advantage of] the brother of him as a practice [in business affairs] because the *The-Master* is an *Avenger* [Vindicator] concerning all these things as we have said before [warned] and witness [certify, claim] to you.

4:7   For THE-GOD has not called us for uncleanliness but in holiness.

4:8   Surely in consequences then the-one-repudiating [with disregard, rejecting] is not repudiating [rejecting] men but THE-GOD, THE-ONE-GIVING the Holy spirit of *HIM* to us.

4:9   Concerning brotherly-affection I have no need to be writing about this for you are taught-by-*GOD* to be Godly-loving to one another

4:10   as also you are doing it to all the Brothers in the whole of Macedonia. But we are entreating [pleading] with you to give even more in super-abundance

4:11   and to be ambitious [make it one's aim] in being quiet [lead a quiet life] and engaged in your own (things, business) and to be working with your own hands according as we have charged you.

4:12   That you may be walking respectably with the-ones outside [not of the Ecclesia, not of Christ] and that you should not have a need for anything.

4:13   But, Brothers, I am not willing for you to be ignorant concerning those having-been-reposed [asleep, in death] that no one may sorrow unlike the-rest, those having no expectation [hope].

4:14   For if we are believing *The-Savior* died and rose, then through *Savior* THE-GOD shall be leading [raising, resurrecting] the-one being-reposed [in death] with *Him*.

4:15   For this we are saying to you by the word [instruction, command] of (the) *Master*, that we the living surviving-ones until *The-Master's* presence [coming, return], should [will] not be outstripping [come before, precede, obtain the fellowship of Christ before] the-ones-being-put-to-repose.

4:16   That (for) *The-Master Himself*, in the shout of a command, in a voice of *The-Chief-Messenger* [Highest Ranking Being, Leader of all Beings] and with *The-Trumpet-of-GOD* shall be descending from Heaven, and the-dead-ones in *Anointed* shall be rising first.

4:17	Thereupon [secondly] we the living surviving-ones together with them shall be being snatched [carried off by divine force] in the clouds to meet *The-Master* in the air, and thus we shall always be together with *Master*.
4:18	Therefore be exhorting, [encouraging, reminding, comforting] one another with these words.

I THESSALONIANS 5

5:1	You have no need for me to write to you concerning the times and seasons
5:2	for you are accurately aware that The-Day-of-(the)-*Master*. It is coming as a thief in the night,
5:3	for whenever they may be saying, "Peace and Security," then unawares to them is standing by whole ruin [utter extermination] even as having pangs inside of the belly [a woman's travail and birthing] and no, not one of them may be escaping.
5:4	Yet you, Brothers, are not in darkness that The-Day may be overtaking you [catch not ready, unprepared, not vigilant] as a thief.
5:5	You are all Sons-of-Light and are The-Sons-of-The-Day, and we are neither of the night nor darkness.
5:6	Consequently then we should not be drowsing [asleep] as even the-rest but we should be watching and keeping sober
5:7	for the-ones drowsing in the night remain sleeping and the ones being drunk in the night remain drunk.
5:8	Yet we of The-Day may be sober, putting on the cuirass-[corselet, breastplate]-of-Belief [faith] and Godly-love and a helmet of expectation and salvation.
5:9	For *THE-GOD* has not appointed us to divine anger [indignation, wrath] but salvation into procuring [by the purchase of, an obtaining of] through *The-Master* of us *Savior-Anointed,*
5:10	*The-One-From-Dying* [*The-Resurrected-One*] (*Who*) for the sake of us, that whether we may be watching [alive] or may be sleeping [dead], at the same time [simultaneously] together with *Him* we should be living.
5:11	Therefore you be comforting [consoling, encouraging] one another and be home-building [edifying, esteeming] one another according as you are doing.
5:12	And we are asking of you, Brothers, to know that the ones-toiling among you and presiding [superintending, caring, protecting] over you and admonishing you in (the) *Master*,

Section III

5:13 to be deeming [considering] them in above-extravagant Godly-love because of their work and you be at peace among yourselves.

5:14 Now we are entreating you, Brothers, be admonishing [warning] the-disorderly. You be comforting the fainthearted [feebleminded], upholding the infirmed [weak] and be patient with all!

5:15 Be certain not anyone is giving [rendering, repaying, vindicating] evil with evil but always be chasing [pursuing] the-good to one another and to all.

5:16 Always be rejoicing!

5:17 You be praying unceasingly.

5:18 In everything you be giving thanks for this is will of *GOD* in *Anointed-Savior* for you.

5:19 Do not be extinguishing [putting out, stifle, suppress] the-spirit.

5:20 Do not be scorning [despise utterly, consider as nothing, hold in contempt] prophecies.

5:21 Be you testing all (things) and be retaining [take possession of] the ideal [genuine-morally-good, that which is accurate].

5:22 Abstain from every perception of wicked things

5:23 and *THE-GOD-OF-THE-PEACE HIMSELF* may be making you holy in whole [completeness] and unimpaired [totally free from sin, entirely faultless]. And may your spirit and the soul and the body be-being-kept [guarded, held in reserve] blameless [so that there is no call for censure, criticism, condemnation, denouncement] in the presence of *The-Lord* of us, *Savior-Anointed*

5:24 *THE-ONE-CALLING* you is also *THE-ONE* that shall be doing it.

5:25 Brothers, be praying for us.

5:26 You greet all the Brothers with a holy kiss.

5:27 I am oathing you [solemnly imploring, want you to take an oath] by *The-Master* that this letter is to be read to all the Holy brothers.

5:28 The Grace of *The-Master* of us *Savior-Anointed* (be) with you.

(Written from Athens to the Thessalonians)

II THESSALONIANS COMMENTARY

II Thessalonians is a follow-on letter to the first one sent and continues the themes of justice verses injustice. It provides an explanation for the next and nearly last—but certainly the most fierce and devastating attempted takeover yet of The-Body of Christ for control and ownership of that group and individuals within in it (there is a third additional period after the Resurrection where Satan will be allowed a short time to try this again). It also includes general living principles within The Ecclesia. Even shorter than I Thessalonians and still in keeping with its theme of the ending of the eon of man as we know it, Paul provides greater detail about the final events leading to the reclamation of Christ's possessions.

The "lawyering" is on Satan's strategy versus God, prosecution versus defendant. Can Satan win such a mock debate and trial? In reality no; God does know the beginning from the end. But God in his wisdom and divine purpose still needs to draw out, "trap," and humble before His presence any final "trump or wild" cards in the deck for all to honor, worship, and acknowledge His greater divinity, majesty, power, influence, creativity, and authority over any of His creation at any time, whether past, present or future. This is worth pausing over, for it seems that Father God has something even greater in mind and purpose to be executed into the eons. Nothing will ever really be able to compare to God, although He will instill in us His nature, and this is something we need to know and understand—not doubt or for a moment think that we can truly duplicate or replace God.

II Thessalonians is placed in the eighth position in Paul's writings, and I understand it to add greater detail of the events leading directly to Christ's return. It is a letter, however, that seems to point the reader forward, beyond everyday living and the mature teachings of Godly-love and defending The Belief. Out attentions are being pulled outward to another cause and purpose, that which is clearly intended to be more Heavenly: Christ's Kingdom.

While I see this letter serving the immediate prophetic purpose of the events leading to Christ's return and living a life serving others, it also has as an undertone, a sense of "a set of higher order of things to come and reflect on" but not mentioned directly. It's not just focusing on The-Lawless One and the events surrounding him, but something beyond that. While Paul is graciously retelling his audience what must happen, you can hear him really saying, "Focus on the future; be prepared for today but stay focused on the future." If I have read too much into this, I apologize, but behind this letter is Hebrews, and if any letter by Paul is a transition or bridge letter between the physical to the spiritual, I do not know where it is. There is no other letter like it, other than Job, that approaches the Supreme Court of the Heavens in such a manner. I also contend that Hebrews is the highest order of legal discourse and intended to set the legal rhetorical arguments associated with and prevent this hostile takeover and is meant for a wider audience than one may be prepared to think of.

So II Thessalonians begins to set the stage for the letter of Hebrews and the higher order of things that I contend are the tasks you and I need to understand and be able to explain and exercise: rulership, just judgments and sentencing, being the suffering servant for others as Christ still today is serving us, exercising Godly-love and wisdom, and understanding how to handle relationship issues in Christ's Kingdom. These topics are legal in nature, but they are also of a higher order, a higher purpose, a higher path of living and ruling principles. The next set of letters from Paul begins laying the foundation of these principles. Hebrews sets the stage for authority, birthrights, legal purchases and ownership, rulership, judgeship, and priesthood. Timothy's letters show us how to serve groups and divisions of beings, and the three last letters show how to approach and be humble before others in consideration of the principles of Godly-love. After all, we will be dealing far more with individuals one-on-one in the future, and we need more care and attention in how to do this. We have been provided with three letters to study, meditate, reflect, and put into practice now. Three letters, not one, as a point of emphasis for the completion of our character, demeanor, and way to deal with God's creation. I think this is a point for discussion and will accept counterpoint.

II Thessalonians starts then in praise and glory to God the Father and recognition of Christ and the Ecclesia, as is typical of Paul's letter. Following this (1:3) Paul acknowledges the tremendous persecution the Ecclesia is dealing with and recognizes this as a sign that they are doing something correct; in doing good they are being persecuted just as Christ was. They are following His example.

In chapter 1, verses 7–12 talk about an event called eonian extermination. The Greek word means "extermination," not hell, not purgatory, not even a grave to come back from. This is not just a sentencing; it is the carrying out of that sentencing—capital punishment God's way. This is total and lasting destruction; it is forever and a "never to be returned from" for rejecting God despite recognizing God for who He is and what He does.

There is universal reconciliation in this, but we still have a choice to fully accept God's way of life gratefully, humbly, and wholeheartedly wanting and desiring to live in it—or accept a different choice. Do not confuse your will by thinking it will prevent God from doing His. This is one of the items that makes God who He is and unlike you and me. While you may in fact accept something as true and correct does not mean that you will incorporate it into your life, attitude, and actions. Many know that smoking cigarettes is not healthy but continue to smoke anyway. Jonah, too, tried to do his "own thing," knowing fully well what to do and who God was. He even had a "direct connection" to God, so to speak. Jonah is not the only example in this area, by the way. God ruled his day, however in the end, also let Jonah walk away from Him despite God reaching out to Jonah in mercy several times. Jonah fully acknowledged and knew God. Will Jonah be in that First Resurrection? I could argue against it. But in comparison, offering universal salvation does not mean that all will accept it. Not all will "buy that horse," to borrow a phrase. I believe God desires to lose none, but we still have been given a choice. If this is incorrect, I accept proof to correct my current understanding. I pray that all see and understand that this is still an ultimate divine-free-gift and one for you to willingly and joyfully accept. There is no work assigned to you with this gift.

Following the discourse on crime and punishment Paul started in 2:1–12, he informs us of the next attempt at the hostile takeover of Christ's Body and ownership. These passages talk about The-Revelation-of-The-Man-of-Sin, his purpose, where his power and authority come from, and where he stands in the order of sequenced events before Christ's return. This is a return to I Thessalonians, briefly pulling it "forward" into II Thessalonians and adding more detail to what has been taught in that previous letter.

Paul then turns the audience's attention to their role of the "elected office" for which God has chosen them. In these passages Paul begins to draw the attention away from the physical events occurring prior to The-Chosen's anticipation of and participation in the future. Beginning in 2:13—3:12, Paul wants the Thessalonians to start thinking ahead and preparing for this activity and therefore pointing their focus to the future. This provides the opening lead for next letter, Hebrews.

Tiny II Thessalonians starts out as a "mustard seed," but what is to grow out of it will look like a carpet of woven gold across the fields when in bloom. II Thessalonians sets the stage for your role and the defense of your birthright in The Kingdom; your dealing with peoples and individuals as a new creation in that Kingdom; your duty of being a servant to others while empowered fully with God's divinity, royalty, and power; and your reconciliation and mediation in and for Christ. All these are legal topics and in keeping with Paul's themed letters.

II THESSALONIANS AS A LETTER

PAUL AND SILVANUS AND Timothy to the Ecclesia of the Thessalonians in *GOD, FATHER* of us and *Master Savior Anointed*. Grace to you and peace from *GOD, FATHER* of us and *Master-Savior-Anointed*.

We are divinely-obligated-to-give thanksgiving to T*HE-GOD* always about you, Brothers, as it is justly-deserved that The-Belief of yours is greatly-flourishing and is increasing in the Godly-love in each one of all of you to one another. So that we ourselves are to be boasting about you in the Ecclesia of *THE-GOD* for the sake of the endurance of you and believing during all the-persecutions of yours and the tribulations which you are enduring in displaying the-justice-and-observation-of-divine-laws of *THE-GOD, WHO-IS-DEEMING* you worthy for The-Kingdom-of-*THE-GOD* for which is the reason you are suffering. Understand that it is *GOD* to justly repay afflictions to the ones afflicting you.

And to you, the-ones being afflicted, be-assured by us about The-Return-and-Revealing-of-The-Truth-of-*The-Master-Savior* from Heaven with Angels and *His* mighty-divine-power. In a flame of fire dealing out vengeance to the-ones not being-acquainted with *GOD* and to the-ones that are not obeying the Well-Message-of-*The-Master* of us *Savior-Anointed*. Who shall be carrying-out-the-sentencing-of justice by eonian extermination from the face of *The-Master* and from the glory of the might-and-ability of *Him* whenever *He* may-be-coming to be glorified by the Holy-Ones-of-*Him* and to be admired in all the-ones-believing in That-Day that believed the testimony of us to you. For which we are also praying always concerning you that you should-be-counted-worthy of the calling of *THE-GOD* of us and should-be-fulfilling every delight of goodness and work of-belief in *HIS* divine-mighty-power so that the name of *The-Master* of us, *Savior-Anointed*, may be glorified in you and you in *Him* according-to the divine-influence of *THE-GOD* of us and *Master-Savior-Anointed*.

Now we are asking you, Brothers, for the sake of The-Return-of-*The-Master* of us *Savior-Anointed* and for our assembling in *Him* that you are not to be shaken quickly from the-mind nor to-be-alarmed either through spirits or through words or through letters as from us as that The-Day-of-*The-Anointed* is impending-and-close-at-hand. Nor should anyone be deluding you by any manner about that there may-not-be-a-coming for first-in-order there is a falling away and be a revealing of The-Man-of-The-Sin, The-Son-of-The-Destruction, The-One-Opposing and lifting himself up over all The-Beings called god or objects of worship even seating himself into the Holy-of-Holies of *THE-GOD* as a god himself, demonstrating-and-exhibiting he is god. Do you not remember these things I told you when still with you? And now you have knowledge about the-holding-back of *Him* and the-revelation of *His* season.

For The-Secret-of-The-Lawlessness is already in operation at present but The-One-Detaining, when he arrives, it is then he shall be revealed. And when The-Lawless-One is to be revealed, it is whom *The-Master* shall be consuming by the spirit of *His* mouth and shall-be-causing-to-cease-and-terminating him at the appearance of *His* return. Whose coming is in accordance with the plans and purposes of The-Adversary with all "divine-power and signs" and magician's miracles and in every seduction of The-Injustice by the-ones perishing not receiving a love of *The-Truth* for them to be saved. And because of this *THE-GOD* shall be sending them The-Operation-of-Deception for them to be-believing a lie that all may be judged, the-ones not believing *The-Truth*, but delighting in The-Injustice.

But we are in-grateful-obligation thanksgiving to *THE-GOD* always concerning you, Brothers, beloved by *Master*. Seeing that *THE-GOD* from the beginning has chosen-and-selected-to-an-office you for saving by the holiness of the spirit and belief of truth into which *HE-CALLS* you through The-Well-Message of us in procuring the glory of *The-Master* of us *Savior-Anointed*. Consequently then, Brothers, be standing unmoved-and-firmly-anchored and be holding to the traditions which you were taught whether through word or through the letter of us. Now *The-Master-Himself*, *Savior-Anointed* and *THE-GOD* and *FATHER* of us, *THE-ONE-LOVING* us and giving eonian Messianic-salvation with-a divinely-blessed gift because of divine-forgiveness, may-*HE*-be-consoling the hearts of you and may *HE* anchor you in every word and good act.

And furthermore, you be praying, Brothers, about us that The-Word-of-*The-Master* may be rapidly-propagated, may-be-being-glorified as also in you, also we-should-be-being-delivered from the-unrighteous-and-harmful and wicked men for not all of them have The-Belief. Yet believable is *The-Master* who-shall-be-establishing and shall-be-guarding you from The-Wicked-One. Yet we have confidence in *Master* about you, that also in which we-are-charging, you also shall-be-doing. And may *The-Lord*, may-*He-Be-Straightening* your hearts in the-Godly-love of *THE-GOD* and be-steadfast-in-piety-and-purpose in *The-Anointed*.

We are charging you, Brothers, in the Name-of-*The-Master* of us *Savior-Anointed* to withdraw yourselves from every deviating brother and not practicing in the tradition which they-accepted from us. For you yourselves know how you are obligated for you to be imitating us that we did not impose on you, neither did we eat gratuitously bread from anyone but in toil and labor, night and day, worked so we would not be burdensome to any of you. Not because we did not have any right to do so but that of ourselves we might be giving you a model to be imitating us. For even when we were with you, this we charged you that if anyone is not willing to be working neither let-him-be-eating! For we are hearing some are walking about among you disorderly not working but are meddling and to those we are charging and command through *The-Lord* of us *Savior-Anointed* that with no complaining work providing for themselves by their own effort.

But you, Brothers, should-not-be-being-despondent in doing ideally. And if any is not obeying the-instructions of us through this letter let this be a sign to you! You are not to be mixed-up-together with him that he may ashamed. Not counting him as an enemy but be encouraging him as a brother. Yet *The-Master Himself*, may *He* be giving you peace, The-Peace in all, in every way.

The-Master be with all of you.

This salutation is by my hand, of Paul, which is the distinguishing-mark of every letter; this is how I end-my-letters.

The-Grace of *The-Master* of us *Savior-Anointed* be with all of you.

Amen.

(Written to the Thessalonians from Athens)

II THESSALONIANS STUDY NOTES

Note: Through my many translations, I have come to believe that the phrase or associated phrasing of "inheritance" [ex: Col 1:12] accurately translated as "the-allotment" in Scripture is not a good or proper translation (i.e., inheritance). Paul makes it clear that we are to be family members (I state: royal and godly) destined to be with HIM and HE with us and we in Christ and He in us. Inheritance has an implied connotation, an accepted concept that someone has died. THE-GOD is certainly not dead, and Christ has risen to life eonian (there are times of times of times) as well. I see this as a watering down of the intent and meaning of the Scriptures and have dropped using the word *inheritance* when speaking of THE-GOD's plan and purpose for us. We are to take rulership in an active kingdom with Christ at the head of the realm and we under Him, with THE-GOD over all of us.

Note   The Greek word *agapen* translated as "love" in most translations is missing that this is Godly in nature and not of men or any other such creature. I have therefore carried the adjective to add clarity to the meaning of this word throughout this translation.

Note: In my research, nearly all translations have dropped "the" as a modifier, but the Greek word for "the" is in every text and not meant to be ignored or deleted. It is often specifically singular, and when attached to the noun, it is describing that noun as unique, one of a kind, a specific thing, the original, the one and only. It is for this reason that I carry "the" everywhere it appears in all translations. Whether of God, Jesus, Satan or any other entity, concept, or idea, the modifier "the" clears up a lot of generalized words, ideas, concepts, and entities.

Note: The root of the word *pnuemia*, translated as "spirit, wind, or breath," has no gender identity since this is a word that is neuter in gender. *Pnuemia* is an "it." The Greeks, as we of English language, often fix a gender to objects and things— for example: cars, boats, the moon, the sun. For the Greeks, *pnuemia* at times has a male gender affixed to it. *Pnuemia* in the Scriptures is never capitalized or designated as a standalone being, entity, principality, or sovereignty when used as the word "spirit." It is simply the power inherent in the

Section III

being, whether of man, or God, or Christ, or any other entity. If anything is living, "it" possesses a spirit. The "Holy-spirit" is simply the power from and of The-God, giving and renewing life and performing The-God's will.

Note: Paul constantly claims and mentions "principles, powers, authorities, sovereignties not of our world." He quite clearly claims that these beings are the ones that certainly influence and control (predominately in a negative way) the systems of this world, people of the nations, and as individuals directly. You can find this concept also contained in The Old Testament through the implications of the first commandment. This claim and the concept of the warring factions in heaven makes a fascinating study.

Note: Time periods, eons, ages, millennia, eons, and eons—I stayed true to the Greek words associated with time and what we still use today in our common language. A study of time periods is fascinating but is also an area that can cause confusion. The-God always works on some kind of a timetable, but understanding which is which and when is when is a bit of a mystery. Some timetables are only known to The-God and made clear to man at God's will.

Note: What is the difference between "expectation" and "hope?" Nearly all translations adopt the word "hope" for "expectation," but Paul uses almost exclusively the word "expectation." Here is why I constantly use "expectation." Having an expectation means you have no doubt at all. It is sure and certain with no ambiguity or doubt. Having a hope means you are not 100 percent convinced and convicted. I can tell you that Paul is undeniably convinced and convicted in what he delivers and talks about. Using "hope" sends a message that there is some possibility for "wiggle room," doubt, error, or excuses.

Even worse, much of the use of the word "expectation" in Paul's writings has the modifier "the" attached to "expectation," thus forming the proper translation and singular concept of "The-Expectation." This makes "The-Expectation" an event, not a philosophy or theological premise. Not recognizing "The-Expectation" as an event will lead the reader immediately down an incorrect understanding of what is being offered or discussed.

1:5 "The-just" has several thesauri equivalents, but the most intriguing is "observing-the-divine-laws." This equivalent would be a direct reference to Galatians 5:22 where Paul gives the characteristics of the divine law of love for "which there is no law against." I have chosen to retain this equivalent "observing-the-divine-laws" within II Thessalonians.

1:5 For those with God's holy-spirit, this is a verse to take comfort in.

1:10 "That-Day" is referring to "The-Day" of Christ's return to this earth to claim his kingdom and the resurrection of the dead holy-ones and those still alive in "That-Day." Paul has stated in his other letters that "That-Day" is the Jewish feast known as The Day of Trumpets.

2:1 "Assembling" is not just pulling together an organization or company but also a machine, or rather, as stated by Paul often, the actual body of Christ in spirit.

2:3 "That-there-may-not-be-a-coming" is a direct reference to Christ's return.

2:3 It is interesting the Greek word *apoleias*, translated as "destruction" in most translations, has its root in banking, trading, bartering, buying, and selling. This is why I placed it first in order for alternate concepts along with "utter-ruin" and "doomed to misery."

2:7 This is a difficult verse to interpret, since Paul does not accurately identify who "the-one-detaining" is, and several proposals exist. For a fascinating discussion on those theories about who "the-one-detaining" is, read the entire article at http://www.bibletruth.cc/the_restrainer.htm so you can decide for yourself who or what that entity may be.

2:8 This verse reminds me a of a chess game in which a player is trying to remove a queen or entrap and conquer an opponent's king. What is the opponent's next move? What is his strategy?

2:9 *Dunamei* is a Greek word I have consistently translated as "divine-inherent-power" and is used by Paul in a "tongue-in-cheek" manner. He is really saying that Satan's power still does not equal THE-GOD, but with more than enough mighty ability to deceive men.

2:9 *Pseudous,* translated often as "lying" ("lying miracles") in many texts, is better translated as "of-falsehood," meaning sleight of hand, not true, a false thing. It's much like the way a magician can fool his audience with his signs, "miracles," and actions using his sleight of hand. I have retained "magician" as a thesauri equivalent.

2:16 "Now *The-Master-Himself*, *Savior-Anointed* and THE-GOD and FATHER of us, THE-ONE-LOVING us and giving eonian consolation [Messianic salvation] and [with-a] good [divinely-blessed] expectation [gift, reward, of salvation, hope] in [because of, by] grace [divine forgiveness]." Most translations have substituted the word "expectation" with the word "hope," but this is not a passage about hope. Paul is reviewing the scope of salvation in this verse with his audience, and a portion of that sweeping panorama is your allotment in the heavens. That is the "expectation" Paul is reconfirming because it is truly a "divinely blessed gift." In nearly all of his other letters, especially after The-Secret was revealed, Paul talks about receiving the gift of life eonian with

Section III

divinity, rulership, and power in Christ and an allotment in the heavens from God.

3:6 The instruction referred to was given in I Thessalonians 4:11 to lead a quiet and peaceable life helping others. Apparently an individual commonly known in the Ecclesia by all was obviously not following those instructions.

II THESSALONIANS IN VERSE

II THESSALONIANS 1

1:1   Paulos [Paul, Place of Comfort] and Silouanos [Silvanus, Woods] and Timotheus [Timothy, Respect for God] to the Ecclesia [Out-Called] of the Thessalonians in *GOD, FATHER* of us and *Master Savior Anointed.*

1:2   Grace to you and peace from *GOD, FATHER* of us and *Master-Savior-Anointed.*

1:3   We are owing [divinely-obligated-to-give] thanksgiving to T*HE-GOD* always about you, Brothers, as it is worthy [justly-deserved, befitting] that The-Belief [faith] of yours is growing–up [greatly-flourishing] and is increasing in the Godly-love in each one of all of you to one another.

1:4   So that we ourselves are to be boasting about you in the Ecclesia of *THE-GOD* for the sake of the endurance of you and believing during all the-persecutions of yours and the constrictions [afflictions, tribulations] which you are tolerating [bearing, carrying the load, enduring] with

1:5   in showing [displaying] the-justice [upright, virtuous, observation-of-divine-laws] judging [selection, justice] of *THE-GOD, WHO-IS-DEEMING* you worthy for The-Kingdom-of-*THE-GOD* for which is the reason you are suffering.

1:6   Seeing [understand, realize] that it is *GOD* to justly repay [take vengeance, penalize] afflictions to the ones afflicting you.

1:7   And to you the-ones being afflicted, ease [take rest, be assured, be satisfied] with us about The-Unveiling-[revealing the truth, appearance, return]-of-*The-Master-Savior* from Heaven with messengers [Angels] and *His* mighty-divine-power.

1:8   In a flame of fire dealing out vengeance to the-ones not being-acquainted (with) *GOD* and to the-ones that are not obeying the Well-Message-of-*The-Master* of us *Savior-Anointed.*

Section III

1:9 Who shall be incurring [executing, carrying-out the sentencing of] justice (with) eonian extermination [destruction, fleshly destruction and subjection] from the face of *The-Master* and from the esteem [glory] of the strength [might, ability] of *Him*

1:10 whenever *He* may-be-coming to be glorified by the Holy-Ones-of-*Him* and to be marveled [have in admiration, admired] in all the-ones-believing in That-Day that believed the testimony of us to you.

1:11 For which we are also praying always concerning you that you should-be-counted-worthy of the calling of *THE-GOD* of us and should-be-fulfilling every delight of goodness and work of-belief [faith] in (*HIS*) divine-mighty-power

1:12 so that the name of *The-Master* of us, *Savior-Anointed*, may be glorified in you and you in *Him* according-to the grace [divine influence, divine forgiveness] of *THE-GOD* of us and *Master-Savior-Anointed*.

II THESSALONIANS 2

2:1 Now we are asking you, Brothers, for the sake of the presence [return, coming] of *The-Master* of us *Savior-Anointed* and for our assembling in *Him*

2:2 that you are not to be shaken quickly from the-mind [understanding] nor to be alarmed either through spirits or through words or through letters [epistles] as from us as that (realize) The-Day of *The-Anointed* is present [impending, close at hand, coming].

2:3 Nor should anyone be deluding you by any manner about that there may-not-be-a-coming for before-most [first in order] there be an apostasy [defection, a falling away] and be an uncovering of [revelation, revealing] The-Man-of-The-Sin, The-Son-of-The-Destruction [perishing or ruin of money, utter ruin, doomed to misery],

2:4 The-One-Opposing and lifting himself up over all The-Beings called god or objects of veneration [worship] even seating himself into the temple [sanctuary, Holy of Holies] of *THE-GOD* as a god himself, showing [demonstrating, displaying, exhibiting] he is god.

2:5 Do you not remember these things I told you when still with you?

2:6 And now you have knowledge about the-detaining [hindering, holding back] of *Him* and the-uncovering [revelation] of *His* season [time period].

2:7 For The-Secret-of-the-Lawlessness is already in action [operation] at present but The-One-Detaining [holding back (*Christ's* return) {The-Lawless-One}]

until he may be coming out [arrives] out of the midst [it is then he shall be revealed].

2:8 And when The-Lawless-One is to be revealed, it is whom *The-Master* shall be consuming by the spirit of *His* mouth and shall be discarding [terminating, causing to cease, abolishing] him at the appearance of (*His*) presence [return, coming]

2:9 whose {The-Lawless-One} coming is in accordance with the operation [plans and purposes] of The-Adversary [Satan] with all "divine-power and signs" and lying [false, magician's] miracles

2:10 and in every seduction of The-Injustice [unrighteousness] in the-ones perishing, not receiving a love of T*he-Truth* for them to be saved.

2:11 And because of this THE-GOD shall be sending them The-Operation-of-Deception for them to-be-believing a lie

2:12 that all may be judged, the-ones not believing *The-Truth*, but delighting in the-injustice [unrighteousness].

2:13 But we are owing [in grateful obligation] thanksgiving to THE-GOD always concerning you Brothers, beloved [preferred, most fond of] by *Master*. Seeing that THE-GOD from the beginning has preferred [chosen, elected to an office] you for saving [salvation] by the holiness-of-the-spirit and Belief-of-(the)-Truth

2:14 into which HE-CALLS you through The-Well-Message of us in procuring [preserving, obtaining] the glory of *The-Master* of us *Savior-Anointed*.

2:15 Consequently then, Brothers, be standing firm [unmoved, firmly anchored] and be holding to the traditions which you were taught whether through word [hearing] or through the letter of us.

2:16 Now *The-Master-Himself*, *Savior-Anointed* and THE-GOD and FATHER of us, THE-ONE-LOVING us and giving eonian consolation [Messianic salvation] and [with-a] good [divinely-blessed] expectation [gift, reward, of salvation, hope] in [because of, by] grace [divine forgiveness],

2:17 may-*HE*-be-consoling the hearts of you and may *HE* establish [anchor] you in every word and good act.

II THESSALONIANS 3

3:1 And furthermore, you be praying, Brothers, about us that The-Word of *The-Master* may be racing [rapidly propagated], may-be-being-glorified as also in you,

Section III

3:2 also we-should-be-being-rescued [delivered] from the-abnormal [unrighteous, harmful] and wicked men for not all of them have The-Belief.

3:3 Yet believable [faithful] is *The-Master* who-shall-be-establishing and shall-be-guarding you from The-Wicked-One.

3:4 Yet we have confidence in *Master* about you, that also in which we-are-charging, you also shall-be-doing.

3:5 And may *The-Lord*, may-*He*-*Be*-*Straightening* [directing] your hearts in the Godly-love of *THE-GOD* and in the endurance [be steadfast in piety and purpose] in *The-Anointed*.

3:6 We are charging you, Brothers, in the-Name-of-*The-Master* of us *Savior-Anointed* to be putting [cease, withdraw, depart] yourselves from every disorderly [deviating] brother and not walking [tracing, treading, practicing] in the tradition which they-accepted from us.

3:7 For you yourselves know how it-is-binding [you are obligated] for you to be imitating us that we were not disorderly [did not impose on] among you,

3:8 neither did we eat gratuitously [free of charge, expected free because of status] bread from anyone but in toil and labor, night and day, worked so we would not be burdensome to any of you.

3:9 Not because we did not have any right to do (so) but that of ourselves we might be giving you a model to be imitating us.

3:10 For even when we were with you, this we charged you that if anyone is not willing to be working neither let-him-be-eating!

3:11 For we are hearing some are walking about among you disorderly not working but are meddling [busy-bodies in other's affairs].

3:12 and to those we are charging and entreating [exhort, command] through *The-Lord* of us *Savior-Anointed* that with quietness [no complaining] work for themselves they may be eating the-bread [feeding themselves by their own effort, provide their own needs themselves].

3:13 But you, Brothers, should-not-be-being-despondent in doing ideally.

3:14 And if any is not obeying The-Word [instructions] of [by] us through this letter, let this be a sign to you! You are not to be mixed-up-together with him that he may ashamed.

3:15 Not counting (him) as an enemy but be encouraging [admonishing, exhorting] him as a brother.

3:16 Yet *The-Master Himself*, may *He* be giving you peace, The-Peace during [in] all, in every means [way].

The-Master (be) with all of you.

3:17 This greeting [salutation] is by my (own) hand, of Paul, which is the sign [distinguishing mark] of every letter (of mine); this is how I am writing [end all my letters].

3:18 The-Grace of *The-Master* of us *Savior-Anointed* (be) with all of you.

Amen.
(Written to the Thessalonians from Athens)

Section IV

PROOF OF CHRIST'S ENTITLEMENT AND AUTHORITY

Prophecy of the Temple Destruction Along with the Law of Moses

Temple Symbolisms and Teachings

The Legal Challenge and Claim for Transfer of
Titles, Authorities, Ownership, and Property Rights

The Letter of HEBREWS

PROOF OF CHRIST'S UNLIMITED AUTHORITY

HEBREWS COMMENTARY

Hebrews is tenth in the sacred order of the letters of Paul and is a transition letter from ecclesiastical to spiritual matters. It is also the one letter that a not few scholars contend was not written by Paul. I am not of that persuasion or opinion, for to me this is clearly Paul's work. My initial defense for this statement is that Paul is and was the preeminent debater and Jewish scholar. It was Paul that engaged in debate the greatest minds of Greek intelligentsia at Mars Hills within their "Court of Reason and Natural Law."

I have been demonstrating throughout this entire book that Paul has been the general counsel and lawyer for Christ to the Nations and to the Ecclesia as a whole. Hebrews, in my opinion, is the highest form of legal argument and rhetorical debate within the entire Bible next to the Book of Job. This is exactly what Paul has provided for us. There is much to be said concerning the letter of Hebrews and Paul's themes. Not the least is its structure as prose and poetry, its content, the historical information, and the associated doctrinal material it contains. My purpose in this commentary is not to write an entire book dedicated only to a complete study of Hebrews.

However, I do intend to prove and demonstrate by reasoning and contextual support that this letter continues to focus on legal issues that establish the ownership and title with associated authority, defending or clarifying misunderstood application of gifts and freedoms, how gifts and freedoms can be lost, the future, and what you need to do to keep and prepare for what Paul calls "The-Expectation" and also the "Allotment of The Kingdom of God." These terms and themes are clearly constant in all of Paul's letters. But this letter in particular has a completely different nuance; it is written as if being argued before a Supreme Court, and it is the highest bench of justice in any land and in Heaven. This is a man bringing a spiritual lawsuit before the Court in Heaven against those in Heaven, a reverse of Job where the Heavenly Prosecutor has Job on the witness stand. Paul has the Originals and Angels on the witness stand, demanding that they prove their claims along with the spiritual potentates challenging Christ's authenticity and claims of ownership of all.

Hebrews is spiritual; it closes out the letters on the physical and opens spiritual matters. All letters to follow are rooted in spiritual matters and concerns, even though on the surface they appear physical.

Section IV

Additionally, I am proposing two radical purposes and reasons for this letter occurring and sitting in the position it is. These are: 1) Hebrews is the first prophetic piece written after the revelation of The-Secret, and 2) it is a spiritual legal lawsuit, an open challenge brought against the Hosts in the Heavens for fraud and murder while they are still trying to lay legal claim and keep Creation and your soul as booty of war (essentially a hostile takeover of a family or privately owned business or corporation). The Hosts in the Heavens are on trial here. You and I are off to the side, sitting either in the Jury Box or as court spectators. Expect Paul to stand in front of us as he accuses the "Plaintiffs" at the Judgment Platform behind him. I have not found or been able to research anyone else that has forwarded these propositions associated with this letter, and I challenge the reader to disprove me in my claims.

I see Hebrews as a prophecy because this letter was written before the fall of the temple in 70 C.E. It proves the failure of The-Law, but even greater how the pact was fulfilled by a man, and this is why The Law of Moses is no longer in force or effective. All associated with it must go and will disappear. The-Law as delivered by The Messengers of God was a substituted fraudulent pact despite being "good" and "holy." Those were merely words designed to have us looking in the other direction, a magician's sleight of hand. I will also leave the reader with the thought that what was truly intended was "hijacked" by The Originals and replaced, as if sneaking through a series of last-minute laws late at night when no one was aware of what was taking place. Examples of this can be found all the time in the way the Senate and Congress of the United States or other governments, for that matter, pass laws filled with "earmarks"—that is, specialty interest laws designed to benefit only those passing the law or a legislator's benefactor all under the guise for the "benefit of the whole." The-Law was actually designed and sold to an ignorant people as if to give life but was really intended to enslave and kill all men. Why and how? The real purpose was to prevent a Messiah, a man of flesh, from coming to fulfill the demands of The-Law and therefore never allow the return of any legal holdings back to God. But a man, right in front and known to those Originals and every Host in Heaven, did complete the contract, and not only completed it but went above and beyond the contract to add value; in doing so he ended that death and destruction policy and thus legally returned all of God's creation and personal property. Hebrews therefore becomes a prophecy for the destruction of the Temple, The Priesthood, and all related services associated with the Temple. Christ has taken the control out of the hands of those Originals and associated liars, thieves, and thugs. This letter is direct in explaining the failure of The-Law and all things associated with The Law and why it now is permanently removed from the legal books. This includes the Order of Melchizedek as a priesthood, which one would have logically fallen back on if not for the introduction of Christ as the new order of High Priest. With no Law, there is no longer a need for a Temple structure or anything to support it. The second associated reason Hebrews is prophetic is that it relates our role and purpose in the future. Both of these topics that will be discussed briefly within the body of this commentary, but the reader is advised to research this claim and decide for themselves.

With this knowledge, Hebrews also becomes a logical, progressive letter explaining why another "Man of Sin" (see II Thessalonians), another fake substitute, is to come along in order to re-enslave and kill all those associated with God and why Hebrews states there is an "eonian destruction" coming. While universal salvation is to take place, apparently not all will accept that choice. As Nero, will you choose a thumbs up or down using a free and clear conscience about that choice? For you, choices still have direct consequences.

My second proposal that this letter is not actually a dissertation and lecture meant for men still fleshly in nature. This lecture is actually a charge, a legal demand and lawsuit by Paul against The-Originals, Sovereigns, Principalities, Powers, Elements, Angels, and all The Host in the Heavens. This is a spiritual letter, a lawsuit demanding them to prove, show, or demonstrate which, if any, can make a legal claim to the position, rank, title, and authority that Christ can, does, and now has, or how they themselves have fulfilled the first compact. Which of them came as a son of man and The Son of The God? This is a legal lawsuit to end all legal claims of what and who has possession. Do you understand what I claim? This letter is intended for those who have been opposing you. You are watching and involved with a direct spiritual matter; call it a spiritual legal res (for the definitions of a "re/res," see http://legaldictionary.thefreedictionary.com/RES). See this as a lawsuit in which legal proceedings are taking place. This is what makes Hebrews so unique—and for some so confusing and "deep." This is written by a man inspired from above who is calling to court those in The Heavenlies. We are truly "in the spirit" ourselves in this court proceeding. You, as a Son or Daughter of God, benefits from the information and instruction associated with this letter, including but not limited to the legal charge and proof who is the one and only and true legal possessor, to understanding the symbolism of the Temple furnishings and how they relate to Christ, the Heavenly Temple, why The Law is a failure and is fraudulent and yet has been fulfilled to the letter and beyond by a man called Savior-Anointed, the introduction of Christ as the High Priest and why he is superior to Melchizedek and Moses, two references to The-Secret, your legal position within the Body of Christ, and a warning to not forsake or harm the Family of God.

Hebrews is a historic piece of literature sitting directly in the middle of Paul's work. It is the apex of his letters. It transitions from the physical Ecclesia and the day-to-day activities and the issues and behaviors associated with that and those "worldly matters" to matters much larger, universal and spiritual in scope, purpose, and need. Our understanding and perspectives are going directly from the physical to the spiritual. You are in the spirit here, evaluating and deciding the fate of those subversives, bribers and kidnappers, murderers, thieves, and liars, and you are asked to also judge your own intentions and purposes. Are you with them or against them? No one other than Paul could have been responsible for such matters and used to create this letter.

Section IV

No one has his background to perform and execute such a legal proceeding in an effective and conclusive manner. This is also why it is Paul's finest piece of literature. It is not meant for man as much as intended for the Spirit Kingdom. A man charging The-Spirits in a legal claim! Unheard of! It requires a different tone and approach and one so different from all the rest that Paul writes. This is why many scholars and laymen get confused and lost about the author of this letter. Without viewing the whole, the minutia becomes the whole, and all else is forgotten or unrecognized. The obverted becomes the inverted.

While I believe these are the primary purposes for the letter of Hebrews, I contend as further proof that the language and the structure belong to Paul because this is in a language written for legal debate and rhetorical arguing, just like all of Paul's letters. Again, this letter can and does include man, but it is first written to The-Spirits. Within the debating, Paul provides irrefutable and clinching proof for the positions that he offers before the reader and to The-Spirits. Once again, as a reader you find yourself sitting in the juror's box listening to Paul's claims and proofs concerning the first and ultimate right of ownership and legal possession. Supporting and proving his claim include:

A review of The Secret	1:2
What Christ is today	1:3–4
The law suit and charge against The-Spirits	1:5–7
Why Christ legally holds the position of title as The-King and The-Ruler surpassing all and in no comparison to any	1:8—2:18
God The Father's declarations and legal requirements	1:8–14

Paul's Defense and Offensive Arguments

Christ came in the flesh as a man	2:14
Moses was faithful over his household but his" household" was not loyal and true, breaking immediately the contract	3:5–11
Salvation is only from believing, it is free divine-gift given for you, legally owned by God but for you to take care of	3:6
A review of the first resurrection	4:1–6
There is "another day." Referring to at least a second resurrection	4:8
You will stand before The Judgment Platform of Christ and God for your actions (Spirits and you)	4:13
The declaration that Christ is our high Priest, a priesthood greater than Melchizedek or Moses and why	8:1–5
It was God who predicted and declared the death of and the dissolving of the first compact or contract	8:13
An explanation of the true temple, not a physical one	9:1–28
An explanation of how the Spirit of God, His Holy spirit, has come to be provided for man	9:8–10

The failed and fraudulent pact called The Law of Moses and all associated services and activities related to it	9:13—10:21
The Law is actually a counterfeit for what was intended	9:13—10:26
A discussion of the "Suffering Servant"	9:27–28
You can lose out as Sons and Daughters and can be destroyed into eonian extermination	10:38–39; 10:26
Why believing is superior to any law	11:1–40
God is merciful and will forgive more than once	6:10; 12:5–29
The final death is by fire	12:18

This is quite an extensive list, but it is not all. An even more thorough read reveals more (see George Wesley Buchanan's book, *The Book of Hebrews: Its Challenge from Zion*, Wipf & Stock, 2006).

The letter of Hebrews starts in chapter 1, verses 1–7 with The-Secret, the quality and nature of God, and the declaration of who and what Christ is now. Moving into 1:8—3:19, Paul begins with the accusation and proofs that only Christ has met all the requirements as demanded by God. Paul's proofs that no other Beings can claim are:

- A son verses an angel
- Called a son
- Appointed to be worshiped, no angel or others have
- Born directly from God Himself, carrying the nature and quality of God
- The Creator (cause of) of the Angels
- Appointed to "The-Throne"
- Sovereign rulership is appointed to Christ
- Divinely consecrated with and given the spirit of God
- Creator (cause of) of The Originals, Earth and the Heavens
- Everlasting before and after the ages.
- Already had an intimate association with God
- Is not a servant of God
- God provided heavenly signs and wonders as proof of whom Christ is and the pouring out of His Holy spirit
- Christ is appointed to rule the coming Kingdom
- Predicted to be a man and lower than the angels
- Christ is the man that legally meets all physical requirements
- Meets the prophecy of the Suffering Servant
- Came in the flesh

Section IV

- Is found blameless and unimpeachable
- Came to destroy The-Death and The-Satan
- Created to become the high priest for man.
- Has saved the mankind family

Next comes Paul's transition of Christ being the Savior of Mankind to becoming the High Priest for all mankind and all of God's creation. Can any such creatures other than Christ prove themselves to fit these requirements? Chapter 4:1through Chapter 8:13 starts the discourse of the new priesthood with Christ as The Chief High Priest. Christ has superiority over The Order of Melchizedek, Aaron, or any other priesthood for the following reasons:

- Was tried as all men and found guiltless
- Not able to not get caught up in errant emotions due to people's ignorance and weaknesses
- Does not have to make continual atonements for sin because he is the sin offering and he has already died once
- Perfected through obedience
- Brings a better and new atoning sacrifice
- By prophecy, the order of Melchizedek was to disappear and be replaced
- Failure of Melchizedek to understand the failures or have sympathy for men
- Melchizedek continues to serve but under Christ
- By prophecy, also the Order of The Aaronic priesthood is to disappear and replaced
- By prophecy, following the Order of Melchizedek must be of a greater priesthood
- Christ's priesthood unable to be passed on, not only in title and authority, but also by progeny to a successor since he has no direct offspring; it is His forever
- Christ called the Guarantor of The Greater Compact by being the high priest
- With no physical priesthood and the law abolished and removed, the temple in Jerusalem also to be destroyed
- Our new high priest able to save in entirety and completely
- Our new high priest sits directly to the right of God The-Father
- Christ not just our high Priest, also called The Mediator
- God has no need to have anything physically inscribed to tell everyone how to live in godly love; places this in and on their hearts

Following Paul's challenges and proofs there is only one logical man to assume the permanent priesthood in the affairs of the operation and purpose of the Heavenly Temple, The Law of Moses, the sacrifices and washings, tithes and offerings, and other "man-inspired" (were these really men inspired?) ordinances and decrees. In this section Paul again accuses the Hosts of The Heavens for putting in place a law that was designed and supposed to give life but instead was given a faux front, a false covering and enslaved, kidnapped, murdered, and prevented men from gaining salvation. In addition, The Law Of Moses never offered salvation in its decrees, ordinances, and commandments. The only commandment with a promise was to obey your parents so that one could have a long life, but not live into the eons or guarantee being fully just and righteous. The Law never brought light, changing and curing the darkness and blackened soul of a man. Paul's accusation in this section is that The Originals which delivered the Ten Commandments and the laws and decrees and had ownership (or at least legal representation) of this current estate had placed a covering over what was really intended, bringing death to mankind in order for The-Originals to keep their sphere of influence, power, dominion, and estate.

How can I make such a statement? Moving into his third accusation (9:1—10:39), Paul presents the following proofs of a fraudulent compact knowing men would never be able to complete the requirements, insuring no man could justify himself by works or actions, and forcing something greater that "no man or God" could overcome. But the Originals were wrong, as witnessed by the resurrection and acceptance of Christ fulfilling The-Law and beyond and by what has been placed in Christ. This fraudulent compact, with its built-in snares and entrapments, included:

- The High Priest's blood or any ordinary man would never be pure enough to enter and stand before God.
- The High Priest's conscience would never be pure enough for all men having a built-in hatred for God
- The Law prevented God's Holy spirit from entering permanently into the Holy of Holies.
- God's spirit was captured in the blood of men and could not be freed.
- The blood of bulls and goats was a substitute for man's blood, further preventing the spirit of God to enter The-System.
- No man could ever serve as Executor for the will and testament; a last will and testament implies that one has died and an inheritor can claim legal possession.
- Blood initiated the first compact, and the pure blood of a man was required to end it.
- In the new compact, it is the spirit that initiates the contract.
- The Law required a Suffering Servant.

Section IV

- The Law only cast a shadow, a false covering, of what is to come.

- The defect in The Law is that it required blood; logically and conclusively the blood of animals is not the blood of men.

- Bringing the Law to the end required a new body, a special body; that body belonged to Christ.

- That body of Christ was designed to be holy and be the sacrifice as a man, not an animal or any other inanimate object.

- The sacrifice of Christ giving himself in godly-love for creation is only needed to be accomplished once in a one-of-a-kind act, never to be repeated.

- It was never God's great desire to see anything sacrificed or killed in place of something or someone else, and yet the sacrifices forced this issue.

- The Law commanded the Levites to rob their own brothers.

- If any law is ever required and demands something to be or done, then the individual, society, clan, nation, culture, system is already defective and is immediately heading down the path of failure.

Once again, Paul shows conclusively that it was Christ, Savior Anointed, The Man, The Only Firstborn Son Of God, who was destined and prepared to be such a sacrifice and to end this forced and fraudulent contract upon men and trap The-Originals at their own game and scheme. The hunters become the hunted and are now doomed.

Paul's next major discourse is an accusation of what The Originals never had. This is believing, which begins in chapter 11. Believing The-God is the only true God. The only One above and in dominion of, so infinitely extended out and beyond any Being or creature that thinks they can be or should be equal to The-God. Not believing only God alone has the divinity, the inherent unlimited mighty power, that wills and purposes to accomplish whatever He desires. Believing they can oppose Him, or stand in His way. Paul begins to ask The Originals who has ever believed that The-God is their true benefactor, Father and is The-Only-God. Which Original (clearly some spiritual being) has ever:

- Made such a promise to Abraham and his descendants

- Made such a sacrifice as Abel's

- Transplanted a man from one location to another because of that man's love for his God

- Provides true and lasting rewards for those seeking them

- Made a woman pregnant decades after her menstrual cycle was closed and eliminated

- Promised men a new city, a new body, a role and position and rank within their government
- Provided an abundance of witnesses willing to sacrifice everything in their life in the most demeaning and horrible way for the future of The Originals' kingdoms
- Promised that all will receive salvation

In closing this letter to the Hebrews, starting with 12:7 Paul begins his exhortation and admonition to The Spirits and to any of us still be uncertain of God's love for us and the free gift of salvation. Paul also reiterates for the ones called, the ones believing, that there is a kingdom and a city with a preeminent and high-ranking Brother preparing for his return and our acceptance into that Body of Christ. Paul exhorts us to continue being faithful, meaning true and loyal, to continue believing, and to not turn our backs on Christ or God.

Paul, in typical fashion, closes by calling for those needing to repent to turn their hearts and souls back to God; he continues to show his great, passionate desire for all to become one in The Body of Christ, whether in the heavens or on the earth or in the earth.

No other letter of Paul is so dynamic, so structured, so clear, and so accusatory as Hebrews. No other letter presents such a discourse, lecture, purposefully planned and crafted series of legal accusations, proposals, debates, and arguments. No other letter not only defends The Truth, The Word, The King of Kings and Lord of Lords, The Savior Anointed, The Messiah, The Lord and Master, The Name above all Names, Jesus The Christ, but also puts all other beings on the defense, declaring their time has come to an end.

Truly the apex of all of Paul's writings, the most mysterious to some, but to the crowd intended for, crystal clear. This is not a letter to the Hebrews or for the Hebrews, though it may carry the name. This is for The-Originals and the Spirits, all opposing God and Christ. None of those Beings can oppose, or claim to have, fulfilled any of Paul's demands and accusations. None but *One*!

I hope this letter provides a new perspective on the Commissioner given to us, The Nations, and really inspires new insight to your understanding, research, and belief in Christ and in The-God for what they have been doing all along for you since you have been in Christ before the eons were made.

HEBREWS AS A LETTER

THE-GOD SPEAKING TO THE-FATHERS of old at many times and in many methods by the-prophets speaks to us in the last of these days by *HIS Son* whom *HE* ordained *Enjoyer-of-The-Allotment-of-All*, the-means-for whom also *HE-MAKES* The-Eons. Who is a shining luminous body reflecting the-majesty of *GOD* and the-exact-precise-image-and-reproduction-in-every-aspect of the-nature-and-quality of *HIM*. And is holding-up-and-preserving all things by-the-declaration-of-*HIS*-mind-made-in-words through the unlimited-inherent-power in *HIM*. He in-a-singular-one-of-a-kind-not-to-be-duplicated-act provides a purifying-and-removing-of our sins, is exalted to the right of *THE-MAJESTY* in The-Heights.

Exalted such that-there-is-absolutely-no-comparison-with The-Angels and because *He* is so much more excellent than them, *He* has received The-Allotment in-dominion-and-rulership-over them.

For when at any time to whom did *HE* say to The-Angels, "You are my son, today I have born you?" And again, "I shall be to him a Father and he shall be my son." Furthermore, when *GOD* having brought *The-Firstborn* into the world *HE* said, "Let them worship *Him*, all angels of *GOD!*" More indeed to The-Angels *HE* asks, "Who is the-one-making his angels as spirits and his ministers blazing fires?" But to *The-Son*, "*Your* throne, *The-God* is into the eon of the eon. *Yours* is a scepter of impartiality-and-righteousness, *The-Scepter of The-Kingdom*. *You* dearly-love justice and detest lawlessness." "Because of this THE-GOD, your *GOD*, anoints you with divine oil of exaltation exalted over your partners."

And, "You *Master* are-the-active-cause-as-the-leader-of-the Originals. Creating the-earth and the-heavens are the works of *Your* hands. They shall-be-being destroyed yet *You* are remaining." And, "All as an outer-garment is deteriorating," and, "*You* shall roll them up like a-wrap and they shall be transformed." "Yet *You* are the same and *Your* years will never stop." But to which of The-Angels has *HE* declared at any time, "Sit to the right of *ME* until *I* place *Your* enemies under *Your* feet like *Your* footstool"? Are they not all serving spirits being commissioned for-the-service for-the-ones being about to-be-enjoying The-Allotment-of-Salvation?

Because of this it is right and proper we be exceedingly attached-and-devoted to the things being heard lest at some time we may be drifting away. For if through The-Angels the-word that was spoken became valid-and-unbreakable and every transgression and disobedience obtained a fair-and-proper payment due of the-sentence-of-death, how would we be escaping? By neglecting such and so great a salvation which was obtained through *The-Master* and told-to-us by the-ones hearing him and was proved-by-truth-and-divinity to us? *THE-GOD* is also corroborating with signs, miracles and many powerful deeds and the distribution of the-Holy-spirit according-to The-Will-of-*HIM*.

For *HE* has not given control of The-Impending-Home to The-Angels which we are talking about. But where did someone solemnly-testify saying, "What is man that *YOU* care about him or *The-Son* of man that *YOU* are taking notice of him? *YOU* made him a bit inferior than any Angels. *YOU* crowned *Him* with glory and honor and set-*Him*-in-charge over the works of *YOUR* hand subjecting all under the feet of *Him*." For in setting all under *Him*, nothing is left to be controlled. Presently for now we are not seeing all the things having been subjected to *Him*. And *The-One* having been made a bit inferior than The-Angels we know is *Savior*. That for everyone for the pardoning-of-their-offenses from *GOD He* was to experience the-suffering of The-Death and became crowned with glory and honor. For it was necessary for *Him*, in whom all and through all is, to be perfected through sufferings leading many sons to their glory as *The-Prince-of-Salvation*. For *THE-ONE-HALLOWING* and the-ones being hallowed are all out of *The-One* for *He* is not ashamed to-be-calling them Brothers. Affirming, "I shall make-openly-known-avow-and-praising your name to my Brothers in the midst of The-Called-Out. I shall be singing hymns to *YOU*." And again, "I shall have complete-belief-in in *HIM*" and again, "Look! I and the little boys and girls *THE-GOD* gives to me."

Since the little boys and girls are-in-fellowship by flesh and blood, *He* also has in the same way become the same. That through The-Death *He* should cease-and-abolish The-One having the-dominion-and-power over The-Death. This is The-Adversary and should be releasing these whoever fears death over their entire lifetime, shackled in slavery. Most certainly not to rescue-for-eternal-life angels, but to rescue the-seed of Abraham. For this reason, *He* was-imposed-by-special-consideration-and-duty to all to be made like the-Brothers, so-that *He* would become merciful and faithful, *The-High-Priest* for *THE-GOD* as the-salvation-offering for the-sins-of-the-people for which *He* experienced-and-performed. Being tried *He* is able to help the-ones being tried.

Therefore, Brothers of the-Holy-calling, Heavenly Partners, you fix your eyes on who we profess to-be *The-Apostle* and *High Priest* of us, *Anointed-Savior*. Being loyal-and-true to *THE-ONE-MAKING Him* as also Moses in all the household of him. For *This-One*, *He* has been counted worthy with even greater glory and honor than Moses, saving the-family of *THE-ONE-CONSTRUCTING Him*. For every house is built by someone, yet *THE-ONE-CONSTRUCTING* all—*GOD*! Moses indeed was faithful and his entire household; a servant of God testifying about the things which were to-be-spoken. Yet *Anointed* is a son over *HIS* household. We are *HIS* household if only we

Section IV

are holding-fast in fearless-confidence and The-Glory of The-sure-Expectation until all is finished in entirety. Through which the-Holy-spirit is saying today if you are listening to its sound, "Do not be hardening your hearts as in The-Provocation, in The-Day of The-Temptation in The-Wilderness when your fathers were trying *ME*. They tested *ME* and saw with their eyes *MY* works for forty years. Therefore, *I* am disgusted with that generation, and *I* said they are always straying in their heart and still they have not known *MY* ways so *I* swore in *MY* anger that they shall-not-be-coming into The-Rest-of-*MINE*."

So you beware, Brothers, that if at some time anyone of you with a wicked heart of disbelief withdraw from the *LIVING-GOD*. But you be encouraging-and-exhorting yourselves each day while it is still being called today, that not a one of you may be hardened by the-lusty-deceitfulness of sins. For we have become partners of *The-Anointed* if we commit to holding on to our first confidence to The-End.

Listen to what is being said, "Today if you hear the-sound of *HIM* do not harden your heart as like The-Provocation." For some of the-ones hearing had bitterness but not all of the-ones coming out of Egypt with Moses. And yet to who was *HE* disgusted with for forty years? Not all the-ones had sinned whose carcasses fell in the wilderness. But to whom swore *HE* that-would not be entering into The-Rest of *HIM*? Was it not the-ones not believing? So we are seeing that they could not be entering because of disbelief.

Then we should be afraid that The-Promise leaves of entering into The-Rest-of-*HIM* anyone of you being found lacking. Also we have preached the Well-Message to you and also them. But *The-Word* of the-news has no benefit for them, not having been united-and-mixed with The-Belief as the-ones hearing. For we, the-ones believing, are coming into The-Rest. As *HE* has declared, "As *I* swear in *MY* anger, if—they (decide to) enter into *MY* Rest, even though the-works were completed when The-System came to be." And where is it *HE* has declared the same about a rest on the-seventh? "*THE-GOD* on the-seventh day rested from all of *HIS* works." And again, in this, "if—they shall enter in The-Rest-of-*MINE*?" Therefore it is being left open for any to enter into it and for those to not enter because of disbelief who once received the Well-Message.

Yet today *HE* is decreeing-and-ordaining a certain day through David saying, "After a certain time," and today has been declaring, "Should you hear *HIS* voice, you should not be hardening your hearts." For if *Savior* had given them rest, He would not have spoken about this "another day." By-logic-and-by-reasoning there is left a Sabbath for The-People-of-*THE-GOD*.

For *The-One* coming into *His* Rest has also ceased from *His* acts even as *GOD* from (*HIS*) own. We should be endeavoring to be entering into that Rest so that no one should be falling in the same example of disbelief. For living is *The-Word-of-THE-GOD* and powerful and cuts-keener beyond every two-edged sword and going-straight-through until cleaving-asunder both spirit and soul, joints and marrow and skilled-in-judging feelings and thoughts of the-heart. And there is not anything created that is hidden from *HIS* sight-and-presence for all is naked and exposed to *HIS* eyes; to *WHOM* we must give an account.

Then having a *Great-High-Priest*, *The-One* having passed into The-Heavens, *Savior*, *The-Son*-of-*THE-GOD*—may we keep carefully and faithfully this Statement-of-Belief. For we are not having a high priest unable to feel-and-have-compassion with the weaknesses-trials-and-troubles of the-soul of us but having-*One*-been-tried in all likeness without sin. May we in-agreement-as-one-approach-and-present-ourselves with boldness then to The-Throne-of-*THE-GRACE* that we may be receiving mercy and may-be-finding grace and timely help.

For every high priest from men being-used-and-selected for the sake of men is appointed from *THE-GOD* that he may be bringing-and-presenting both honorable-gifts-and-offerings and sacrifices for the sake of sins; able to be not caught up-in-and-overwhelmed in emotion because of the-ones being ignorant and straying since he is also by-nature-of-being-a-man with weaknesses. And because of this he is bound-by-also-being-only-a-man for himself as also with the-people, to be making atoning sacrifices for the sake of sins. And no one chooses-and-selects this honor for himself, but being the-one called by *THE-GOD*, just as Aaron. So also, *The-Anointed* did not think about himself to be-made the-high-priest but *THE-ONE-SPEAKING* to *Him* said, "*You* are *MY* son; today *I* have begotten *You*." And also in another place *HE* says, "*You* Priest into the-eon like the-order of Melchisedek." Who in the days of *His* flesh offering both petitions and supplications with strong distressful wailing and tears to *THE-ONE-BEING-ABLE-TO-BE-SAVING Him* out of death and was heard because-of Godly-reverence. And being a son, *He* also learned obedience from which *He* suffered, and being perfected *He* became *The-Author-of-Eonian-Salvation* for all the-ones obeying *Him*. Addressed *High Priest* by *THE-GOD*, "like the-order of Melchisedek," about whom we have much to say but is hard to present and difficult to explain since you have become dull to instruction. For also as the-ones that ought to be teachers by this time again you need to be taught what are the-first-principals of the-beginnings-of-the-oracles of *THE-GOD* and have become needing to have nursing-milk and not solid nourishment.

For everyone feeding-on nursing-milk is unskilled in the-word of justice for he is an infant. For solid nourishment is for the mature-ones, the-ones because of the use of the mind have been striving-earnestly-to-become-Godly by judging-discerning-and-distinguishing between the-ideal and evil.

Leave therefore the beginning instructions of *The-Anointed* behind; we should move-on-to perfection, not again laying the foundation of repentance from dead works and of-Belief in *GOD*, of the teachings of baptism, the laying on of hands, the resurrection of dead ones and of eonian judgment. But this we shall do, that is if *THE-GOD* may allow.

Section IV

For it's impossible for the-ones once being enlightened, tasting The-Gift-of-The-Heaven and becoming partakers of the-Holy-spirit and have tasted The-perfect-Message-of-*GOD's* inherent-unlimited-power in The-coming-Eon to indeed fall away then repeat the-renewing of repentance by crucifying for himself again *The-Son*-of-*THE-GOD* and making *The-Son* a public disgrace. For the land drinks showers that come on her as often as it comes and brings forth herbage fit for those from whom also farm it, blessings from *THE-GOD*. Yet bringing forth thorns and star-thistles is a disqualification and are a curse, whose total-consummation is burning.

Yet we have been persuaded about you Godly-Beloved about the better and having salvation, although we are speaking in this manner. For *THE-GOD* is not unjust to be forgetting your acts and the-act of Godly-love which you display in the-name of *HIM* when serving the-Holy-ones and are serving. Yet we a have a great desire for each one of you, displaying the same diligence in the Surety of-*The-Expectation* until The-End that you may not become indolent-and-lethargic but become imitators of the-ones through believing and patience to enjoy The-Allotment-of-The-Promises.

For The-Promise to Abraham by *THE-GOD*, since *HE* had no one greater to swear by, *HE* swore by *HIMSELF* saying, "Truly in blessing *I* shall be blessing you and in increasing, *I* shall multiply you." So by being patient he obtained The-Promise. Indeed, men swear by the-greater and the-oath as a confirmation putting to an end contradiction for all of them. *THE-GOD* deliberately-intentionally-and-purposed to show superabundantly-beyond-any-doubt-or-uncertainty to The-Enjoyers-of-The-Allotment-of-The-Promise *HIS* fixed-unalterable-divine-will-and-plan pledging-himself with an oath. Because of these two fixed-and-unalterable facts-and-matter-of-laws it is impossible for *GOD* to break-*HIS*-pledge. May we continue having sure encouragement The-Ones fleeing for refuge, seize-and-faithfully-retain The-Expectation appointed-and-destined which we have as an anchor of-the-soul. Both secure and certain and be received beyond The-Interior-of-The-Curtain where *Savior* entered for our sake as *The-Forerunner*, becoming *The-Chief-High Priest* like the-order of Melchisedek.

For it was this Melchisedek, The-King-of-Salem, High-Priest of *THE-MOST-HIGH-GOD* who met Abraham returning from the-combat-slaughter of The-Kings and blessed him, and to whom Abraham divided a tenth out of all. Principally understood commonly as King-of-Justice, and also as King-of-Salem, or as King-of-Peace. Fatherless, motherless, without a genealogy, having neither beginning of days nor end of life. A copy as *The-Son*-of-*THE-GOD* and remains a priest into the-continuous.

Now you think about this-Eminent-One and to whom The-Patriarch Abraham gave a tenth from the best of the-booty. Now truly the-ones out of Levi, the sons of the-priestly-office are-ordered-and-ethically-commanded to not-refuse-reject-and-collect tithes from the people according-to The-Law, this is from their brothers including those having come out of the-loins of Abraham. But This-One is not in the genealogy of those of The-Abraham having received the tenth part and blessed him

The-One having The-Promise and beyond opposition-and-argument the inferior is being blessed by the better. Indeed, today men receiving tithes do die, yet *The-One* being affirmed-by-being-seen-and-heard *He* is living. And let me declare this so it is clear, even Levi, the-one receiving tithes, had been tithing through Abraham for he was still in the-loin of The-Father when he met together with Melchisedek.

By reasoning then, if perfection came through the Leviticus priesthood—for by it the-people had been placed under The-Law—what is the purpose-and-role to rise up a different Order-of-Melchisedek or why is it not being said, "Like the Order-of-Aaron?"

Now the priesthood is transferred out of necessity, causing also a change to The-Law. For *Who* these things are being said belongs to a different tribe and about that-Altar about which no one devoted-thought-and-service to. For it is openly evident that out of Judah has risen *The-Master* of us from which tribe Moses speaks nothing concerning the priesthood. And still it is more-superabundantly evident-and-clear just as the-likeness of Melchisedek, now-in-place is a different priest who has appeared-publicly in the flesh, not in the manner of the Mosaic priesthood-rule-of-lineage-law but due-to-his-own-nature not subject to death. For *HE* is witnessing that, "*You* are a Sacred-Priest into The-Eon like The-Order-of-Melchisedek."

Certainly-and-surely to come is an abolishment of the Commandments because of its weakness and being without benefit. For The-Law perfects no-one, yet a better expectation was brought to which we are drawing nearer to *THE-GOD*. And not compared like the-ones swearing an oath, for indeed without-taking a sworn oath has become a priest. For *The-One* received the-sworn-oath through *THE-ONE-SAYING* to *Him*, "*MASTER* swears and will not regret it, *You* are a Sacred-Priest into The-Eon like The-Order-of-Melchisedek." With this greater compact *Savior* has become *The-Guarantor*. Indeed, there have been several ones becoming priests and were prevented to continue-in-service because of death. But because of *Him*, *The-One* to be remaining into The-Eon, has the unchangeable-and-not-able-to-pass-to-a-successor priesthood.

And also, *He* is able to save in-entirety-and-completely the-ones coming through *Him* to *THE-ALWAYS-LIVING-GOD* to be pleading for the sake of them. For such a man became *High Priest* for us, holy-without-sin, innocent, undefiled, having been separated from the-sinners and became honored-exalted-eminent in The-Heavens. Who does not need to daily as those high priests to be offering-up sacrifices for their own sins then next for the-people; this *He* did all at once offering *Himself* up. For The-Law appoints men as chief priests having weaknesses. Yet *The-Word* of *The-Sworn-Oath*, *The-Son* in-fellowship-with The-Law, has been perfected into the-eon.

The central point being spoken of is this; we have a high priest who is seated at the right of The-Throne of *THE-GREAT-TOGETHERNESS* in The-Heavens and being *The-Holiest-Minister* and of *The-True-Temple* which *The-Master* fastens-together and not men. For every high priest is to-administer-the-office-of to be-offering both the-gifts and sacrifices which also is necessary for this-*One* that *He* may have something

Section IV

to offer. Indeed, for if *He* was on earth, he would never be a high priest, knowing the priests are the-ones offering the gifts according-to The-Law who are a representation-and-imitation and an outline-and-sketch of offering-divine-service in The-Heavenlies just as Moses had been divinely instructed about The-Tabernacle to be created. *HE* declared, "Insure-and-make-certain you complete all just as the-image-and-pattern, the-one having-been-shown to you in the mountain."

And now *He* has become *Master* of a surpassing ministry, and a far greater *Mediator* of a more excellent covenant which is sanctioned by a-legally-resolved-matter because of greater promises. For if that first-one was not without defect, a second-one would not be required-and-demanded to replace it. The fault was found with them.

HE says, "Look! The days are coming says the *MASTER* that *I*-shall be ending-one-and-begin a new covenant with The-House of Israel and The-House of Judah." "Not like the Covenant which *I* made with The-Fathers in that Day by taking hold of their hand and leading them out of the land of Egypt. Because they did not remain true-to-and-did-not-mean-what-they-pledged about *MY* covenant and *I* took-no-care-for them says the *MASTER*." "Here is the covenant which *I*-shall-be-covenanting with The-House of Israel after those days says *MASTER*. By-committing-and-bestowing-as-a-gift by inscribing-and-fixing *MY* laws in their mind and also in their hearts and *I* shall be their *GOD* and they shall be *MY* people." "And they shall not teach to the-one near him and saying to each of his brothers, "Become acquainted with *THE-MASTER*" for all shall-have-knowledge of *ME*, from the least to the greatest of them." "For *I* shall be merciful and *I* will no longer recall to mind their unjustness and their sins and their lawlessness."

This means *HE* has declared the former outdated by being obsolete and deprived-of-force-and-authority from age and is near destruction.

Truly the first Covenant also had the-ordinances of divine service and an earthly holy place. For The-Temple is constructed such that in the front section is The-Lamp-Stand also The-Table, displaying The-Showbread which is called The-Sanctuary. And after the-second-curtain, the tabernacle is called the Holy-of-Holies, having The-Golden Censor instrument and The-Ark-of-The-Covenant covered entirely in gold, with The-Golden Urn having The-Manna and The-Rod of Aaron the-one sprouting forth leaves, and The-Tablets of The-Covenant. And up-over The-Ark The-Cherubim-of-Glory cover which shades The-Mercy-Place about which now there is not a particular thing to be teaching.

Now indeed making things ready continually, entering in the-front of The-Tabernacle, working the-divine-service are The-Priests. Now only once a year only The-High-Priest goes into the-second, never without blood which he offers for the sake of himself and for the-sins of the-people. This signified the-spirit having not yet making a way known into The-Holy-of-Holies, still having to stand in front of The-Tabernacle, which is a parable for the-present period where both gifts and sacrifices being offered are not being able to perfect the conscience of The-One-offering-divine-services; only in-control-of foods and drinks with different washings and fleshly ordinances for the period placed on them until restored-to-their-natural-and-normal-condition.

Yet *Anointed* was-purposed to be the *High-Priest* of the good things to come, through the greater and more perfect Temple, not hand-made, that is, not of the-creation. Not using the-blood of goats and calves but by *His* own blood entering once for all eonian into the Holy-places, acquiring salvation.

For if the-blood of bulls and male goats and ashes of The-Heifer sprinkling the-ones-having-been-contaminated makes-holy purifying the-flesh, how much to-an-infinite degree the-blood of *The-Anointed* who through the-eonian-spirit, offered *Himself* unflawed to THE-GOD, cleansing your conscience from dead acts to be-offering-divine-service to THE-LIVNG-GOD. For this reason, *He-is-Mediator*. That by becoming dead removed flaws from the-first Will-and-Testament so the-ones-having-been called may-be-receiving The-Enjoyment-of-The-Allotment of The-Eonian. For where there is a will-and-testament it is necessary to bring death to the-covenant-taker. For a last-will-and-testament is executed after dying since at-no-time it has enforcement when the-covenant-victim is living. For this reason, the first Covenant was required to be using blood. For each-and-every direction of The-Law that was spoken by Moses to the-entire-people, he took the-blood of the-calves and he-goats and water and The-Scarlet-Wool and Hyssop and with them sprinkled both The-Scroll and the-entire people. Affirming-and-advising, "This is the blood of The-Covenant which THE-GOD commands with regard to you." Also in the same manner sprinkling The-Tabernacle and all the-instruments of the-ministry for almost all is being cleansed with blood by The-Law and without pouring out blood is no pardoning. Then it is indeed necessary by the-examples in The-Heavens for these to be purified, but in The-Heaven-Temple is a more excellent sacrifice than these.

For *The-Anointed* entered into the Holy-places of The-True-Type not made by hands, but into this same Heaven-Temple appearing to the face of THE-GOD now for the sake of us. And not to be continually offering *Himself* even as the-high-priest entering into the-Holiest place each year with other's blood. Since *His* continual suffering was necessary from The-Inception-of-The-System and now once for all abolishing-and-annulling sin through *His* appearance and sacrifice at The-Finish-of-The-Eons. And since it is reserved for men to die once then after this judgment, so then *The-Anointed* was offered-up once for all burdened-with the-sins for the-many, waiting to be seen by the-ones by *His* salvation.

For The-Law possesses a shadow of the good to come, not the-identical-image. The same for the-practices with a definite period of time, the same of sacrifices they are offering having a finality. Those never were able to bring the-ones to come being perfected. Why are they to ever cease being offered? Because the-ones-offering-divine-service have been purged from being guilty once and for all no longer having a conscious-desire for sins. For in the-practices-and-sacrifices is a remembrance-and-recollection of sins each year making-it-impossible for the-blood of bulls and he-goats

Section IV

to-be-eliminating sins. By entering into The-System *He* says, "Sacrifices and offerings *YOU* did-not-intend-wished-for-and-take-pleasure-in yet a body *YOU* arranged for me." "Whole burnt offerings and all things-and-activities-concerning sin *You* have no pleasure in." "Then *I* said: "Look, *I-Am* arriving, as the volume of The-Scroll has written about *Me* to do The-Will-of-*THE-GOD!*"" Repeating again, "That sacrifice and offering and whole-burnt-offerings and all-things-and-activities-concerning sin *YOU* do not take pleasure in, neither do *YOU* seem delighted with anything The-Law has been offering." Then *He* has declared, "Look, *I-Am* arriving to do The-Will-of-*THE-GOD*." For you *HE*-is-abolishing The-First that *HE* should be establishing The-Second. By *GOD*'s-choice-and-desire we having-been-made-holy by the-offering of The-Body-of-*The-Savior-Anointed* once for all. For certain, everyday priests stand officiating often the same offerings and sacrifices which can never be-taking-away sins. Yet *He* for the sake of sins offered one sacrifice for ever sitting at the-right by *THE-GOD* now waiting to place under the footstool of *His* feet The-Enemies. For in one offering *He*-has-perfected eonian the-ones being made-holy.

And testifying to us is also the-Holy-spirit. For it has been declared before as this, "This is The-Covenant which *I* shall covenant with them after those days is saying *MASTER, I* shall give-and-write my laws on their hearts, also inscribing them in their minds," and, "The sins of them and the iniquities-and-wickedness of them *I* should no longer be reminded." Meaning this, when pardoned-and-forgotten, there is no further offering for sin.

Then, Brothers, having boldness, make an entrance into the-Holiest-place by The-Blood-of-*Savior* which he initiated-and-consecrated a way for us through this curtain, that is *His* flesh recently slain but living, also a High Priest over the-house of *THE-GOD*.

May we come with a genuine-and-real heart in certain-and-sure-confidence of-believing, having the-hearts being cleansed by sprinkling from a wicked conscience and the-body-bathed with pure water. May we grasp-firmly-and-keep-secure the-confession of The-Expectation without wavering believing about *The-Promised-One*. And may we be considering one another, to incite in acts of Godly-love and ideal acts. Not forsaking the leading together of ourselves as the-custom of us but entreating and even greater in your watching for The-Day approaching. For if we voluntarily sin after receiving-and-understanding the knowledge of The-Truth, no further offering for sins remains. But certain terrible-and-formidable judgment and a fiery jealousy is about, waiting to be-cannibalizing The-Hostile-Ones.

Now anyone rejecting-refusing-and-thwarting The-Law of Moses with two to three witnesses is put to death without pity. How much more worthy of a greater punishment do you suppose shall be for the-one insulting-and-treating-with-rudeness-and-insulting-neglect *The-Son* of *THE-GOD* and considering-and-thinking the-blood of The-Covenant contaminated that hallowed *Him* and in despising-and-insulting the-spirit of *THE-GRACE*? For we are acquainted with *THE-ONE* saying, "Avenging is mine, *I* shall be repaying says *MASTER*," and also, "The *MASTER* shall be judging *HIS* people." To be falling into the hands of *THE-LIVNG-GOD*, fearful!!

But call to remembrance the former days when being enlightened you endured the-vast hard combats-and-struggles of afflictions-and-evil. So indeed, being publicly humiliated by both reproaches and afflictions and by this have become companions with the-ones-participating also in this same manner. You also sympathized with me in my bonds and with joy the-plundering of your possessions in anticipation knowing that in yourselves is in the Heavens a better property and is permanent. Then do not be casting away your boldness which has a great reward, for you have need of endurance that you should be obtaining The-Promised-Blessing doing The-Will-of-*THE-GOD*. "For in a very, very little while *The-One-Coming* shall-be-arriving and shall not be delaying," and, "The-just-one shall-be-living by believing and if ever he-should-withdraw *MY* soul is not delighted with him." But we are not shrinking back into utter-destruction but by-believing preserving the soul.

Now believing is a conviction of an accomplished feat not being observed. In this, The-Forefathers were witnesses. By-believing we have perfect understanding to declare The-Eons-of-*GOD* from that which is not apparently-seen to that which is to coming to be seen.

By believing Abel offered a better sacrifice than Cain to *THE-GOD* by which he was shown to-be-righteous by *THE-GOD*. Because of his honored-gifts and by them he is still speaking in death.

By believing Enoch was transplanted to avoid death and could not be found because before being transferred by *THE-GOD* he had been declared-and-affirmed to-have-been-favored-by *THE-GOD*. For without believing its impotent-and-impossible to-please-well for the-one must believe coming to *THE-GOD*, that *HE-IS*, and becoming to the-ones craving-begging-and-investigating *HIM* a *REWARDER*.

Noah by believing was divinely-instructed concerning things not-as-yet being observed. Being pious, constructs The-Ark saving his household by which he-condemned The-System and by believing became righteous, an Enjoyer-of-The-Allotment.

By believing, Abraham being called, obeyed coming out into the place he was about to obtain as a possession and came out not knowing where he was going. By believing he lived next to The-Land-of-Promise as a foreigner living in tents with Isaac and Jacob, The-Joint-Participants of The-same-Promise. For he waited for The-City, the-foundations whose craftsman and architect—*THE-GOD*.

By believing Sarah, she had strength to receive injected semen beyond her season of prime, gave birth since she believed *THE-ONE-PROMISING* believable. Though considered-unable-to-bear-a-child from one has many been born, just-as many as the multitude of constellations of The-Heaven and as the-innumerable-sand along the shoreline of the sea.

These all died believing not obtaining The-Promise but from a distance from them knew and were persuaded and welcomed and vowed they are strangers and expatriates on the earth. For such the-ones openly declared that they are clamoring-for-craving-and-wishing the *FATHER'S*-homeland. And if truly they remembered from where they came out of, they could have had the opportunity to return. But now they are craving a better place, this of heavenly origin. Where THE-GOD is not ashamed of them, to put the-name of GOD on them, for them HE-MAKES ready a city.

By believing, Abraham being tested presented-as-an-offering Isaac, indeed the-only-begotten. After having presented-the-offering received The-Promises. To whom was declared, "That in Isaac your seed shall be invited-named-and-titled," calculated-and-reasoned-and-was-convinced that out of the-dead-ones THE-GOD is able to rise-him-up and according-to-the-stories-and-legends recover the-risk.

By believing, Isaac blessed Jacob and Esau concerning what will come to pass. By believing, Jacob while dying blessed each of the sons of Joseph and worshiped while propping-himself-up on the top of his staff.

By believing, Joseph when dying called to remembrance concerning The-Exodus to The-Sons-of-Israel and ordered what to do with his bones.

By believing, Moses being born was hid three months by his parents because they saw the little boy was attractive and was not afraid of the mandate of The-King.

By believing, Moses already with power-and-rank abdicated-and-rejected being called The-Son-of-the-Daughter-of-Pharaoh preferring rather to be sharing persecution with The-People-of-*THE-GOD* than for temporarily to have pleasure born from sins believing-and-reasoning The-Reproach-of-*The-Anointed* was of greater riches than the-treasures in Egypt, steadfastly-gazing on that reward. By believing, he left Egypt not being afraid of the-fury of The-King, steadfastly paying-heed-to *THE-INVISIBLE-ONE*. By believing he carried out The-Passover and the-pouring of the-blood so that The-Exterminating-One of the firstborn would not injure them. By believing they crossed-over The-Red-Sea as if dry, which the-Egyptians while attempting to-recapture were-swallowed-up.

By believing, the-walls of Jericho fell after being surrounded seven days. By believing, Rahab the-prostitute received the-spies with peace and was not destroyed with the-ones not believing.

And further-more, my lacking time, I could speak relating the times concerning Gideon, Barak, also about Samson and Jephtha, David, also about Samuel and the-prophets. Who through believing brought down kingdoms, worked righteousness, received promises, barred the-mouths of lions, extinguished fire's strength, escaped the sword's edge, from cowardice became valiant in the line of battle routing foreigners.

Women received their dead-ones back to life and others were tortured not accepting-and-allowing deliverance so they-may-be getting-and-securing of that best Resurrection. Further other ones in trials of mockeries and scourging and still more in bonds and imprisonment. They were stoned, they were sawn, they were tried for murder, they died from the sword, and they wandered about in sheep and goatskins;

being destitute, afflicted and treated evilly. Of whom The-System was not worthy; wandering in the wildernesses and mountain and cave and the holes in the earth. And all of these were giving an honorable-testimony by believing not having received The-Promise. *THE-GOD* has something better to look forward to concerning us, that not without us they may be perfected.

Surely then since we also have such a vast and encompassing cloud of witnesses for us, put off every burden-and-weight and long-standing sins that we may racing with endurance the-contest before us. Turn your attention to *The-Origin* and *Leader* and *Perfecter* of The-Belief, *Savior*. Who instead of the joyful-appointed-state he-possessed-and-was-present-with *Him*, endured the-disgraceful-dishonor of the contemptible-and-hated Pale and is seated to the right of The-Throne of *THE-GOD*. Take this into account about *The-One* having endured such opposition by sinners against *Him* that you may not be faltering and your souls fainting. You have not as of yet battled by using blood to fight against sin.

And you have been oblivious to the pleading which was discussed with you as a son, "*MY* son, do not hate the nurturing-chastening of *MASTER*! Do not weaken being corrected by *HIM*." "Whom the *MASTER* loves he is disciplining and every son whom he acknowledges he scourges."

If you endure the disciplining as sons, *THE-GOD* will carry you. For what father is there who does not discipline his son? And if you go without disciplining, as all have become participants of, then you are bastards and not sons. Further, indeed if our fleshly fathers we have are discipliners and we give them reverence, how much more then shall we yield-to-the-admonition-of *THE-FATHER* of The-Spirits and we shall be living? Indeed, for few are the-days for the-ones which seems to them as chastising, yet profitable for the-ones that are-to-be-participating in the-holiness of *HIM*. For indeed all chastening in the-present is not seen to be as joy but painful and yet for the-ones being vigorously exercised through it, peaceable fruit of righteousness is given back. Therefore raise-and-elevate the exhausted hands and the feeble-and-weakened knees and make a straight path for your feet that no one lame be shunned-and-turned-aside but rather may be healed. Be earnestly-endeavoring-to-acquire peace with all and the-holy, apart from which no one shall be seeing *The-Master*. Watching carefully that not any fail-to-become-a-partner from The-Grace-of-*THE-GOD*. Nor any root of bitterness to grow where through this many are defiled-contaminated-and-stained. Nor any unlawful sexual intercourse or profanity or as Esau, who for one meal rejected his birthright. For you are aware that afterwards he repented of his rejection, seeking it out with even great tears, yet no place was found for him in The-Blessing to enjoy The-Allotment.

For you have not come to a high-ranking-preeminent-one that can be be-bought-off and motivated-by-enraged-anger and say-one-thing-but-do-another-intentionally and no-regard-for-an-action-or-damage-caused and impulsive-and-not-predictable and clamorous-and-confusing and a-booming-frightening-ominous-and-scary voice

Section IV

which the-ones hearing begged no more words be spoken any more. For they could not carry out the demand: "If at any time a wild beast may come into contact with The-Mountain it shall be stoned or shot down with an arrow." And so fearful was the event-and-demonstration even Moses said, "I am terrified and quaking!"

But you have come to Mount Zion and to The-City-of-the-*LIVING-GOD*, heavenly Jerusalem with innumerable multitudes of angels, to a universal assembly and brought forward first by *The-Called-Out* with a pedigree in Heaven; and to *GOD-JUDGE-OF-ALL* and to Spirits as Just-Ones having been perfected, and to *Savior*, *Mediator* of the-recently born compact, with blood appointed for purifying more excellent than spoken of Abel.

You beware! Do not be refusing-and-rejecting THE-ONE-REVEALING. For if they will not find-safety-and-escape rejecting *The-One-Revealed* on earth, how much greater we will not escape, the-ones rejecting-and-deserting *THE-ONE* from Heavens? Whose voice then violently-earth-quaked The-Earth but now *HE*-has-promised saying, "*I will still once again quake not only the earth, but also The-Heaven!*" And that being shaken once again is to make-clear-and-leave-no-doubt what should be remaining and should not be left-in-place so that we may receive a permanent Kingdom. May-we-have grace through which we-may-be-offering-well-pleasing-divine-service to *THE-GOD* with reverence and godly-veneration. For even *THE-GOD* also has a consuming-burning-passion for us.

Let the-brotherly-affection continue. Do not forget hospitality for in doing this we were oblivious we lodged some Angels. Keep being mindful of the-prisoners as being bound-together with them and the-ones being maltreated, for you are of the same Body. Marriage is honorable for all and the-undefiled-bed. Yet male prostitution shall be judged by *THE-GOD*. Do not love money; be satisfied with the present manner of life. *HE* has declared, "*I will not ever give-up-and-send-back nor will I ever abandon-and-desert you.*" With us have courage to say—"*THE MASTER is my helper and what shall I be afraid of that a man can do to me?*"

Be remembering the-ones before you who preach *The-Word*-of-*THE-GOD* to you. Consider along with their behavior you-being-imitators of their believing.

Savior Anointed, *The-Same-One* yesterday, today, and also into the-eons.

Do not be carried off with various and strange teachings. For a purified heart is established by *GODLY*-gifting, not by food which has no profitability for the-ones walking about. We have an Altar which the-ones offering divine service at The-Temple have no authority to be eating from. For the carcasses of those animals, whose blood for sins is carried into The-Holy-of Holies by The-High-Priest is burned-up outside The-Camp where *Savior* suffered, making-holy through his own blood the-people outside of The-Gate. Now then, may we come forward to *Him*, outside The-Camp, carrying *His* condemnation. For we do not have here a permanent city, but we are craving for The-One-Impending.

Through *Him* then may we be offering up continually sacrifices of praise to *THE-GOD*, this is fruit from the lips, declaring *THE-NAME* of *HIM*. And also, do not be forgetting gathering together and doing good to others for such sacrifices greatly-pleases *THE-GOD*. Be convinced to yield to the-ones leading you. For they are watching over your souls and will give an account. That with joy may they be doing this and not ones groaning for this is disadvantageous for you.

Pray concerning about us that we have confidence with a pure conscience that we are able to have in all honest behavior. And to a greater degree I am begging to do this that I may return to you very quickly.

Now *THE-GOD-of-THE-PEACE*, *THE-ONE-NAVIGATING* out of the-dead-ones *The-Great-Shepherd*-of-*The-Sheep*, through *The-Blood*-of-*The-Eonian-Covenant*, *The-Master*-of-us, *Savior*, that *HE* may equip you for every good act, in doing *The-Will*-of-*HIM*, working in you what is well-pleasing in *HIS* sight, through *Savior-Anointed* to who be glory into *The-Eons*.

And I am calling on you, Brothers, to endure in *The-Word* and with encouragement for I have written to you in few words. You know that Brother Timothy has been released, with whom, if ever he may come shortly, I will see you. Greet all the-ones leading you and all the-Holy-Ones are greeting you, the-ones from Italy.

The-grace to all of you.

Amen.

HEBREWS STUDY NOTES

Note: Through my many translations, I have come to believe that the phrase or associated phrasing of "inheritance" [ex: Col 1:12] accurately translated as "the-allotment" in Scripture is not a good or proper translation (i.e., inheritance). Paul makes it clear that we are to be family members (I state: royal and godly) destined to be with HIM and HE with us and we in Christ and He in us. Inheritance has an implied connotation, an accepted concept that someone has died. THE-GOD is certainly not dead, and Christ has risen to life eonian (there are times of times of times) as well. I see this as a watering down of the intent and meaning of the Scriptures and have dropped using the word *inheritance* when speaking of THE-GOD's plan and purpose for us. We are to take rulership in an active kingdom with Christ at the head of the realm and we under Him, with THE-GOD over all of us.

Note   The Greek word *agapen* translated as "love" in most translations is missing that this is Godly in nature and not of men or any other such creature. I have therefore carried the adjective to add clarity to the meaning of this word throughout this translation.

Note: In my research, nearly all translations have dropped "the" as a modifier, but the Greek word for "the" is in every text and not meant to be ignored or deleted. It is often specifically singular, and when attached to the noun, it is describing that noun as unique, one of a kind, a specific thing, the original, the one and only. It is for this reason that I carry "the" everywhere it appears in all translations. Whether of God, Jesus, Satan or any other entity, concept, or idea, the modifier "the" clears up a lot of generalized words, ideas, concepts, and entities.

Note: The root of the word *pnuemia*, translated as "spirit, wind, or breath," has no gender identity since this is a word that is neuter in gender. *Pnuemia* is an "it." The Greeks, as we of English language, often fix a gender to objects and things— for example: cars, boats, the moon, the sun. For the Greeks, *pnuemia* at times has a male gender affixed to it. *Pnuemia* in the Scriptures is never capitalized or designated as a standalone being, entity, principality, or sovereignty when used as the word "spirit." It is simply the power inherent in the

being, whether of man, or God, or Christ, or any other entity. If anything is living, "it" possesses a spirit. The "Holy-spirit" is simply the power from and of The-God, giving and renewing life and performing The-God's will.

Note: Paul constantly claims and mentions "principles, powers, authorities, sovereignties not of our world." He quite clearly claims that these beings are the ones that certainly influence and control (predominately in a negative way) the systems of this world, people of the nations, and as individuals directly. You can find this concept also contained in The Old Testament through the implications of the first commandment. This claim and the concept of the warring factions in heaven makes a fascinating study.

Note: Time periods, eons, ages, millennia, eons, and eons—I stayed true to the Greek words associated with time and what we still use today in our common language. A study of time periods is fascinating but is also an area that can cause confusion. The-God always works on some kind of a timetable, but understanding which is which and when is when is a bit of a mystery. Some timetables are only known to The-God and made clear to man at God's will.

Note What is the difference between "expectation" and "hope?" Nearly all translations adopt the word "hope" for "expectation," but Paul uses almost exclusively the word "expectation." Here is why I constantly use "expectation." Having an expectation means you have no doubt at all. It is sure and certain with no ambiguity or doubt. Having a hope means you are not 100 percent convinced and convicted. I can tell you that Paul is undeniably convinced and convicted in what he delivers and talks about. Using "hope" sends a message that there is some possibility for "wiggle room," doubt, error, or excuses.

Even worse, much of the use of the word "expectation" in Paul's writings has the modifier "the" attached to "expectation," thus forming the proper translation and singular concept of "The-Expectation." This makes "The-Expectation" an event, not a philosophy or theological premise. Not recognizing "The-Expectation" as an event will lead the reader immediately down an incorrect understanding of what is being offered or discussed.

PROPHETIC SCRIPTURES

The following are prophetic in nature indicating the elimination of the Aaronic Priesthood, the Temple's destruction, the elimination of the First Covenant, and Christ as the High Priest.7:8–28; 8:8–12; 8:13; 9:11–12; 10:1–4,1:1

Little about this letter is recognized that it is really about The-God throughout. This letter starts with Him and ends pointing back to Him at the closing and is the undercurrent throughout. While Christ becomes a subject within this letter, this letter

Section IV

demonstrates God's plans and purposes for Christ today and in the future and for those "called-out." Paul demonstrates in verses 1 and 2 how God has communicated to mankind even today and whom is the cause for creation, including the Heavenly Hosts—the created cause and purpose being Jesus.

1:2 "In these final days, though, he spoke to us through a Son. God made his Son the heir of everything and created the world through him" (Common English Bible, p. 1206). I quote this directly because the sentence leads one to believe that Christ is the Creator, not God The-Father. Nothing could be further from the truth, and the reason for this is twofold. The primary reason is that the translation of the Greek word *di* (see *Strong's* G1223) in this portion of the sentence that reads "and created the world through him" is a preposition and does not mean the force or action causing an event. The word is properly rooted in the definition of the means and purpose, the reason for. This portion of the verse reads correctly: "the means by whom HE-MAKES The-Eons." This translation still acknowledges God as the Creator and shows it was in God's purpose to make all things for His Son, Jesus. Jesus is the cause and means of creation, including you and me. Therefore, creation is attributed to Christ as it belongs to him, being the intent of God. As Christ honored and worshipped only God the-Father, that is where our attention needs to be as well. Nowhere are we told to worship Christ, but we are certainly told to honor him and imitate him.

Secondly, when originally translated, the word "through" allowed for the translators to support the concept of the trinity, making it appear that Christ was with God at the beginning of creation—a God turned into a man turned back into God. Nowhere in the Scripture is any of that supported or implied.

1:2 "The-means-by whom also *HE-MAKES* (*epoiesen*, Strong's G4160) the eons [cause life, the worlds, all things contained in time]." These three alternatives were not what I expected when I began to investigate the word translated as "eon" (see *Strong's* G165, *aionas*). Most often commonly understood and translated as "ages" or "ages of time," this word in this verse is rooted more in terms of the third concept offered by the *Blue Letter Lexicon*: "all things contained in time." This sentence then becomes quite an encompassing, sweeping, panoramic statement. It not only implies items, entities, and beings that, as mere men, we may or not be aware of, but it is also outside of time. Do any of us have any concept of what that may be? This is quite a ponderous statement made by Paul—if you take the time to really meditate and reflect on it.

1:3 This verse is so profound and pregnant in describing Christ—what He looks like, who he is, what He does, what He has done, and what He is doing. I struggle to think about how any other word in modern English captures the breadth of all these synonymous phrases and words. Without knowing all the majestic ideas captured in the lexical and thesauri equivalents, no one would grasp the breadth, profoundness, and awe of what is being said in these sentences. If anyone were to merely read any of the other translations without researching the Greek, what is said and intended to be taught and understood is sadly, wretchedly completely missed, almost completely hidden.

Also, overlooked in this verse is Paul telling us that Jesus creates for God, having that authority and ability given to him since he now sits at God's right hand. We of the English language understand that to be someone's "right-hand man" means to have the same authority and means as the true authority or person in charge.

1:3　The translation of the Greek word *rhemti* (*Strong's* G 4487) or "declaration" offers several meanings for this word, but I was stopped immediately at reading this first statement: "1) that which is or has been uttered by the *living voice*, thing spoken, [*word*]" [italics mine].

I was struck immediately by two words "living voice." I wonder if Paul meant to subtly say to his audience that Christ is the "Living-Voice," and or "The-Word" by using *rhemti*. First, think about what this is saying about Christ. Both fit, and Christ is attributed as the "word" (correctly understood in the Greek as the cause of, the purpose, plan, reason, or logic of, the program) directly by John (see John 1:1). ("The/The"-Word" is not in any of the traditional texts and was reconstructed as such to support the trinity. The original is simply "word.") Second, having done several translations of Paul, I have come to realize that he often layers in the deeper, or real, meaning just below the surface of what he writes. This is one of the reasons studying his letters is interesting, and it takes time to thoroughly investigate not just the pure definitions and equivalents but to view them in conjunction with the historical activity and setting in which he writes each letter.

1:3　"Through *Himself* cleansing [purifying, removing the guilt from sins]." The Greek word for cleansing is *katharismos* [*Strong's* G2512]. We would recognize the word "cauterize" meaning to "sear off, prevent, or burn" from the root of this word.

1:5　"For when at any time to whom" is accusatory in structure; it is not a rhetorical question. This begins the lawsuit Paul brings to any Beings of conscience. This is a demand for someone or something to present themselves as qualified for the demands, listed requirements, and actions to follow.

1:5–14　Paul might be talking to a group of men, but if reading these verses as if they are a narrative, you can clearly sense that Paul is directing this lecture to any angels that may have been present in the audience. The lessons being presented about Christ's superiority over the angels (and other beings) would have been of interest for their concern, curiosity, and understanding. After all, they also search and study the Scriptures, seeking out their fate in the eons and God's Kingdom, just as we do.

1:9   "anoints you with olive oil [divine] of exaltation." All the associated words relayed in this partial sentence have a reference for an activity at the Jewish feasts. This partial sentence can be translated as "anoints you with oil of gladness" and would refer back to Psalm 44 and Psalm 45:8. *Blue Letter Lexicon* says this for *Strong's* [G20] *agalliasis* (exultation, extreme joy, gladness): "At feasts, people were anointed with the "oil of gladness." Heb 1:9 alludes to this *inaugural ceremony* of anointing, and uses it as an emblem of the divine power and majesty to which the Son of God has been exalted" (italics mine).

1:9   The translation of the Greek word *metochous* as "partners" is interesting. Christ is not equated with a set of brothers, and the treatment of the word "partners" has more of a corporate sense, in a business setting versus a family environment. My initial read of this verse made me consider Christ and the Sons of God mentioned in Job and the Psalms as being more of business associates than a clan or close family situation. Or if it is a family situation, there exists quite a rift to not call those beings "Brothers" and is meant to be insulting. Whether intentional or not, meant as a minor or a major insult, I can certainly read this into what is quoted. It makes for interesting thinking and speculation. While this passage is more about angels, since this seems to be the primary area needing clarification, the reader should be able to see that a bigger set of spirit entities are being hinted at by using "partners" since partners imply some equivalent relationship, power, or authority.

1:10   Take note of use of the word "Originals." In many translations, this has been interpreted as the divinities, powers, angels, and sons of God who were present at the restoration of the earth mentioned in Genesis 1:2—2:2. However, in this sentence, *Strong's* G746 (*archas*) is translated as "beginnings" as well as "originals." The author appears to allude to the pre-creation of all things, and the Lord is the responsible reason/being for bringing all things into existence. This verse seems to tie directly and exclusively to Genesis 1:1.

1:8–12   If not careful, one might read these verses as if Christ were the creator. This is not correct, but what is being said in this passage is that Christ is the active cause for the Father's works. All creatures were made for Christ and now belong to him, and therefore Christ via divine appropriation, application, and assignment is attributed with the activity and action of creation.

1:14   "The-Allotment-of-Salvation" is an event, and I have identified it as such, just as a national holiday is for any country.

HEBREWS STUDY NOTES

2:1   The concept of "drifting" is to be removed from the shoreline without consciously being aware of it until it is too late.

2:3   The messengers (angels) in this passage were the ones who delivered the Ten Commandments to Moses on behalf of God at Mt. Sinai. Essentially they acted as agents or with the power of attorney to judge, decide, and enact in the place of God.

2:3   "Which was obtained through The-Master and spoken [told to us] by the-ones hearing him" is making a direct reference to the apostles and their witnessing and miracles.

2:5–18   Notice how this passage reads like a story, a drama, or a tragic play when words, instead of theological concepts, become characters of a story (because I've kept modifiers such as "the" in my translation as they are in the original Greek). These passages become alive with a new and richer meaning when shown that all things have a relationship with one another. To clarify my proposal, notice the construction of verse 14: "That through The-Death *He* should put to an end The-One having the dominion-and-power of [over] The-Death. This is The-Adversary." Here Paul clearly says The-One is Satan who controls the actions of a being called "Death," and Christ is to use Death against Satan to vanquish him. This has all the elements of a great drama. All that is missing are the details of how this is being done. This would also explain and re-verify why Death is the last being (or entity) to be vanquished by Christ, not Satan. Death will be, if I may borrow such a quote, "the last man standing" on the field of battle as an enemy.

3:2   It was Moses' household (meaning all relatives and direct family members) that remained faithful, for we know the Nation as a whole was left to perish in the wilderness for their disbelief.

4:3   This verse is translated as "For us, the-ones believing are coming into The-Rest. As HE has declared: "As I swear in MY anger, *if* they enter into my Rest, although the-works were completed when The-System [world] came to be [from the foundation of the world]" (bold and italics mine). "If" found in this sentence is not a conditional tense with a consequence of some kind (either good or unfortunate) but rather conveys a sense of questioning on God's part. This is a contemplative pause with pondering speculation by God in the middle of making a point for discussion. Will the-one called willingly enter into God's "*Rest*" or not? The remainder of this sentence says the-one called was already assured by God as far as God is concerned, but what final choice would the individual take?

Section IV

4:5   This verse reiterates a contemplative pause is occurring. That is, The-God is wondering out loud to the audience about what choice will be made on their part.

4:8   This other "Day" being referred to is the first resurrection and God eventually establishing the New Jerusalem and His Kingdom here on earth.

4:13   The Greek word *tetrachelismena* [*Strong's* G5136] translated as "exposed" has a much more violent primary definition. The following definitions all apply for this word:

1. to seize and twist the neck or throat
   a. of combatants who handle thus their antagonist
2. to bend back the neck of a victim to be slain, to lay bare or expose by bending back
3. to lay bare, uncover, expose
4. laid bare, laid open, made manifest to one

4:16   "May we *come* [in agreement as one approaches the presence of; present ourselves; in a courtly and stately manner, together unified] with boldness then to The-Throne of The-Grace that we may be receiving mercy and may-be-finding grace and well-seasoned [timely] help" (italics mine). Notice all the correct and profound equivalent substitutes for the word "come." A study of this Greek word *proserchometha* has the concept of unity and oneness, and you as a called-one and as one in Christ are understood in this verse to be in the very Holy-of-Holies, at the very front of and at the Throne of God. Since Paul has made it clear in several other letters and other passages in Hebrews that you are a son or daughter of God in Christ, you are in fact seeded with God's spirit with holiness and royalty as a prince or a princess. It is therefore proper to understand that each day as you talk to your Father in heaven, you are to be stately and royal when coming to His Throne and conduct yourself as such in the presence of others. This is where the boldness comes from, not by any of your effort or actions.

5:1   "For every chief-sacred-one [high priest] out of [from] men being-obtained [*marked*, used, *chosen, selected*] for the sake of men is *appointed from THE-GOD*" (italics mine) is a portion of a verse loaded with information if one is not familiar with how the selection of the High Priest (as well as many of the others serving in priestly roles were determined) was done by "casting lots." Essentially, a common act known today as "rolling the dice" is the way it was determined who served in what role and capacity and at what time of service for an individual or family. This "lottery" was directed through God's will and divinity in selecting who and where. The idea of a lottery, an allotment, a lot, and casting lots is mentioned everywhere in Paul's writings, and it is how before the inception of all of creation you were determined to be where you are and what you are in order to serve God's will, purpose, and pleasure. Done in an unbiased method, a lottery determined how we all will fulfill God's master plan. Because of that act of drawing "the lot" about and for you, there is of necessity (if I may be so bold to suggest that God has to do anything based on man's reasoning) a time and place for you to come to the knowledge of God and have an opportunity to participate in the future beyond your earthly experience. The idea of your salvation in your time and place is defendable from within the Scriptures.

5:10   Many translations open this verse with "Called by God," but the word translated as "called" is much too informal in presentation. The better translation is as one would address someone of importance in public by their title, such as Mr. President, Madam Speaker, or Pastor Brown. God is actually publicly acknowledging Christ by one of His titles: High Priest.

5:11   The Greek word *dusermeneutos* is a word sweeping in meaning—literally "hard to interpret, difficult to explain." Several translations gloss over the entire concept contained in this word and instead use such words as "uttered," "say," or "speak."[1]

6:4   The subject of "tasting The Gift of The Heaven" alludes to an individual having the knowledge of God's plans and purposes and of their calling.

6:8   "Yet bringing forth thorns and star-thistles is a disqualification" is meant as a metaphor for producing acts or behaving in a manner not honoring the role, position, and belief to which you have been called. You are forgiven and have been handed the spirit of God not because of any action or goodness done by you. Therefore, you are not to neglect that gift with callousness and a disregard for the belief in Christ.

6:8   "*Star-thistles*" may be a reference back to the crown of thorns thrust and pressed into Christ's head at the crucifixion.

6:8   "*is burning.*" Realize this is how God intends to purge and cleanse the earth the next time, not with water but with fire and burning.

6:13–18 The two immutable matters are both law and fact. There is not a greater being or thing to pledge by than The-God, and The-God is showing His divine counsel, will, and plan.

---

1. See www.blueletterbible.org/lang/lexicon/lexicon.cfm?Strongs=G1421&t=KJV >.

Section IV

6:14   This famous passage about God's promise to Abraham concerning "blessing" and "multiplying" reuses both these words within each concept redundantly, one after the other inside this quoted sentence. A careful review of the spellings of each word, however, reveals that there is a difference in this "redundancy" and implies the second time the word is being used, that there is more to be understood than a simple repeating of the words "blessing" and "multiplying." Further research implies that the second use of the word "blessing" in this phrase is both divine in nature as well as physical—a double blessing. The word "multiplying" is better translated the first time as "increasing," making the second word "multiplying" used mathematically in an exponential use—a much, much greater impact and intention.

6:17   The use of the word translated as "contradictory" per *Strong's* G485 implies that though an individual keeps his oath, it is not without strife while going through the process of honoring the pledge. Thinking this through makes sense, for while an individual "frets" or is anxiously waiting to receive the promise, the other individual commonly "frets" and is anxiously making sure the oath is fulfilled as intended and in entirety. Both are "strife-filled" conditions.

6:17   Notice the word "mediated"—a direct legal action involving an agreement or resolution of two parties.

6:18   Contained within in this verse are two distinct concepts. When Paul writes about the two immutable reasons, he is referring to verses 16 and 17. Reason one is the oath God made using His own name since there is nothing or no one greater to promise by, and reason two is God displaying His power to the ones He has called. The second concept in this verse is intended to encourage the audience by both reasons during this time of their fleeing persecution.

6:18   One of the interesting definitions for the word translated as "practices" is "that of a legal matter." When I came across this suitable definition, I spent time researching the concept of who or what is legally being retained or transferred. In several of his writings, Paul talks about Satan being the legal ruler in this current eon of this world and all its matters, customs, and practices during his rulership. Several verses discuss the transferring of souls in a legal sense between Christ and Satan, and Paul is often quick to mention about guarding one's promise and fate against Satan. This is a discussion too deep to delve into for the purposes of this material. It is a study about legality and how Adam transferred his legal rights to Satan to rule this world, Christ legally purchasing it back through his crucifixion, our role as individuals bought by the blood of Christ, and the purchase of Creation being returned to Christ. Few organizations discuss or really understand the impact of this "matter of law" occurring in heaven and affecting matters on earth and the universe. All I can comment is to say that it is immense, relevant, and directly affects you.

6:19 "and be received beyond the interior of the-curtain." This was (and is) about as clear as it can be for both Jewish and Gentile audiences. They (we) are to be received (as royalty and as a dignitary) and be directly in front of and at the throne of God, facing and seeing God. We know that the curtain to the entrance of the Holy of Holies was literally ripped down the middle, from top to bottom, un-repairable, and the doors of the Holy of Holies were miraculously flung open daily for anyone to see into the interior, and if bold enough, to walk inside, despite the lingering priestly and scribal practices. (It took four men to open one leaf of the double door due to its size and weight, so imagine the amazement to wake up each morning and see the doors swung wide open with all sacred items inside exposed to everyone!) A similar example exists today if you visit the royal temple of the Imperial Palace in Thailand; there you can enter the temple but only so far, while those called of God will be literally able touch His throne and hence Him once changed.

7:1–28 This entire chapter can (and probably should) be read as a prosecuting attorney arguing a case before a jury concerning priesthoods, laws, purpose, and intent. To read this with a legal mind adds depth and meaning to Christ's role and sacrifice.

7:4–11 This discussion is about Melchizedek. Hebrew tradition say Melchizedek was Seth who slew Nimrod. However, this is in opposition to these verses since Paul says Melchizedek is alive today, without father and genealogy, implying that he is a singular creation without a family lineage.

7:11 "By reasoning then, if perfection [completion and maturity] came through the Leviticus priesthood—for by her the-people *had been placed under* The-Law" (italics mine). The Greek word *nenomotheteto* translated as "had-been-placed-under" has the implied meaning of being forced against one's will and desires. It's not necessarily meant to restrict, redirect, or prevent something in the best interest of the individual(s) or their needs. This could be interpreted as a form of forced slavery, in fear and threat of punishment because a higher or stronger authority is in place, a negative action designed to make one understand what the better position to take is or be (in understanding, philosophy, legality, and action). The audience would have understood that this was not a positive and agreeable action being imposed on those living in or "under" The-Law. More importantly, the audience would have clearly understood that The-Law, while good and just, even by man's standards, still does not meet the demands, desire, and needs of salvation and is lacking in its ability to save anyone. As Paul writes in his other letters, The-Law captured man (not released him) and condemned him to death, not saving or providing anything that could save and not providing any rewards other than long life for obeying and honoring one's parents.

7:12 The word "now" is not intended to imply timing but rather is an emphatic declaration of condition, and therefore is but one of the prophetic indicators of the coming destruction of Aaronic priesthood and temple.

7:13 The reference to "that Altar" refers to the altar of the Red Heifer (*Parah Adumah*) that was just outside the camp of Israel and where Jesus is said to have been sacrificed (crucified). Read *The Secrets of Golgotha: The Lost History of the Crucifixion* (second edition) by Dr. Earnest L. Martin, PhD; Associates for Scriptural Knowledge, 1996. In parallel, the altar Abel and Cain sacrificed at was also "outside the camp" (outside of the Garden of Eden) where Melchizedek probably served as the priest, not only representing God but also serving as an example of the future coming "High Priest" taking (or in the case of Cain, rejecting) the offerings presented.

7:15 "Just as the-likeness of Melchizedek is standing up [now in place is] a different sacred-one [priest]" is a verse that took me a while to digest. My first line of understanding, which I have abandoned since it is not a defensible position, is that Melchizedek is still "standing up" today, meaning that this individual is still alive, resident in Heaven and serving still in a priestly capacity of some kind but clearly not as our mediator and not offering or accepting gifts or sacrifices anymore. Christ has replaced all of that, and this is made quite clear. That line of thinking, while awkward, for now may have some merit, but I am certain that is not what was intended in the discussion.

However, after further research, I believe my second line of reasoning is correct in identifying this phrase as a timing event. Currently today, as of this moment, Christ is The-One in place. Further, if "standing up" is intended also as a "double entendre," Christ is also "standing-up" for his called-out. This position is clearly defensible and most certainly fits both concepts of timing and authority.

7:18 "Indeed [Certainly-and-assuredly] to come is an abolishment" is a second emphatic statement and another prophetic precursor to the end of the Aaronic priesthood and temple.

7:20 The interesting idea to think about in this verse is that Paul has told his audience that Christ has taken the role of High Priest without having to have an oath or a swearing in ceremony of any kind, unlike all men before Him.

7:21 Regarding the translation of "master swears and will not regret it," many commentaries say that this statement infers a sense of remorse, or rather a regretful change in mind after the fact. Using the Mosaic system hardly seemed to lead to real and lasting repentance and true worship of The-God.

HEBREWS STUDY NOTES

The conclusion is that the institution of the Mosaic system was (and is) not as noble (although it is righteous and beneficial), not fulfilling the intent and purpose, as the replacement of Jesus as the High Priest and what His service and sacrifice does.

7:21　This sentence implies that since the Aaronic Priesthood received the ordination without an oath, God never intended for this activity to last into the eons.

7:26　"in the heavens." Notice that this is plural, telling you as the reader that something is occurring among the stars and galaxies as well as where God and Christ currently dwell.

7:27　"this *He* did all at once [once for all] offering *Himself* up" (bold mine). The words "all at once" are the proper translation and order of the Greek words. This implies that this is first an issue of timing, performing a series of collective acts in a span of time instead of, as most translators do, transposing the words, which leads the reader to understand this to be a singular act of finality meant for a collective group of beings and entities. If one uses "once for all," "all" is meant to be understood of people as well as heavenly beings or other beings with a conscience that can acknowledge God. It's not acknowledging or implying that any actions or events have occurred first. Christ's death and resurrection immediately abolished the former covenant, commandments, and laws. That act occurred first. While I agree that Christ's act is for "all," my "project engineering" background understands this to mean a series of events occurring first, leading to the act of salvation for "all." As the proverbs says, "timing is everything," and so sometimes is word order.

8:2　"And being *The-Holiest-Minister* and of *The-True-Booth* [Tabernacle, Temple]" is another indicator that the physical temple was not to last.

8:4　This verse is about as clear as it can be that if the Aaronic priesthood continued to exist, Christ would never have served as the High-Priest.

8:6　Therefore "sanctioned by law" is properly understood to have the matter legally dissolved or resolved.

8:13　This verse indicates that this letter was written just prior to the destruction of the temple in AD 69–70—i.e., "the old is ready to die" is another prophetic precursor.

9:1–28　This entire chapter provides a tour for the audience of what the physical arrangement was in the temple as well as some of the ceremonial activities that took place there. Paul then bridges the physical and spiritual—the intent and applications of the items with the services performed with an emphasis of

Section IV

the spiritual being exceedingly greater and complete for all of creation, both physical and spiritual creation.

9:1 "earthly sanctuary." Commentaries offer that being "earthly" is understood to have character flaws unlike that which is "heavenly" or that which comes from above.

9:8 My translation of this sentence is not in agreement with the many other texts I compared it to. All attach "holy" to spirit when clearly the topic is a discussion about entering the inner tabernacle or the "Holy" of Holies. The physical placement of the word "holy" in the sentence has it positioned closer as an adjective to assign it to the holiest part of the physical temple. It should also be noted the Greek word *pnuemia* is not capitalized and is quite common and nearly always translated as "spirit or wind" without any hint of holiness in it although it can be inferred as such.

The logical line of thought is that the high priest was also in front of the Holy of Holies, entering once a year, every year, but Christ needed to enter it only once, for all times (eons, the ages).

9:19 "For every (each) direction" means that Moses read and explained each separate command and ordinance. Also for each tenet, the people agreed to the terms and conditions. Moses performed the ritual sprinkling of the blood and water on both the scroll upon which The-Law was written and literally on the people, thus sealing each agreement.

9:19 "The Scroll" by allegory represented God, so not only were the people sprinkled with blood, but also God did "get wet" from the ceremony and was sealed to perform His part.

9:18–20 God, with the people, made a blood covenant. The only way to end the covenant was with a blood sacrifice by the death of one of the participants. Since God did not utterly destroy Israel and has kept a remnant alive despite their breaking every single promise they made, guess who it was for you and me?

9:20 See I Corinthians 11:23–26 for the nearly identical passage relayed to Paul by Christ during Paul's conversion.

9:26 "at The-Finish [conclusion] of The-Eons" suggests that "time" as well as anything that marks periods of ages will be features of the past and are to vanish. This verse could suggest the eventual disappearance of the moon and the sun, which are used to mark time.

10:21 "also a *Great-Sacred-One [High Priest]* over the-house of THE-GOD" (italics mine). Notice that this verse makes two points. First, you are called, labeled, and titled a High Priest, also meaning that you have rank and have obligations and duties to maintain, and second, you have every right and privilege to come face-to-face with The-God and Father of us through The-Messiah. I will add a third point in this verse: your duties and obligations are also "over the-house (or "household" or "family for all" are correct translations) of The-God. They are not just those today around you but into the future as well.

10:25 "[watching] for The-Day drawing near [approaching]." "The-Day" being referred to here is the Day of Trumpets, one of the eight traditional Jewish festivals. The sound of a trumpet has several symbolic meanings within this festival period, but certainly one interpretation is the announcement of the Messiah by the blowing of a horn or trumpet.

10:34 Take note of the word "property." This has physical implications, and for those of "The Secret" it implies possession of the galaxies and universes.

11:4 The Greek language assigns a gender to all concepts, nouns, and verbs. Without this knowledge, in English we would easily and properly substitute a word translated "her" with "it." Using "it" in this passage, it becomes clear "her," or rather "it," refers to the sacrificial gift.

11:4 The statement that "through Abel's sacrifice he is still heard" is intriguing. The ground was forced to swallow and accept his blood, something that was never intended to occur (The-God declared "the ground spoke to Him"), and yet his testimony of righteousness lives on through the Scriptures.

One also must wonder about the earth's need for restoration as part of the creation for all the blood spilled and the earth being forced to "swallow it." There must certainly be more to this than a simple allegory.

11:5 The Greek word *metetethe* translated as "transferred" and "transplanted" refers to a physical location, not a heavenly or ethereal place. With this knowledge, Enoch's being "transplanted" was not to heaven but to someplace else on the earth. One tradition and very plausible explanation is his being transplanted back into the Garden of Eden, where he died as "all men do." This move back into Eden was to avoid persecution, as this set of Scriptures clearly indicates that the "whole civilization" knew he was God's favorite, and they carried a jealousy with a desire to murder him. Enoch was transplanted from Nod into the Land of Eden for his own protection.

The temples built by Moses, Solomon, and others were all patterned after the Garden, the Land of Eden, and the Land of Nod. For an excellent discourse and study on this subject, read the book *The Temples That Jerusalem Forgot* by Dr. Earnest L. Martin, PhD; Associates for Scriptural Knowledge, 1994. Eden consisted of two parts, the Garden (Holy of Holies) and the Land of Eden (The Camp of Israel).

11:19 "that out of the-dead-ones THE-GOD is able to arouse [rise up, resurrect] him and *by parable*" (italics mine). Those familiar with the teachings conducted by Christ knew they were presented as parables, stories with a moral lesson or teaching. But that is not what parable is intended here within the structural context of the verse. "Parable" here means concerning the legends and stories passed down through the generations. These are the "campfire stories" where traditions, cultures, folklores, and teachings were passed on to each generation. Abraham and his household knew about and rehearsed these stories about a future King, Savior, Messianic figure. After all, he was a near contemporary of Noah (a tenth-generation grandson born three years after Noah's death), and surely both Noah and his sons had passed on their knowledge from the Ancients and beginning of man's time plus post-flood events. (Shem was still alive and lived for an additional 450 years after the birth of Abraham and could have directly given him thirdhand information about the Garden of Eden and firsthand information about the flood). By this time Abraham also had had some interaction with the Angels who were representatives for God. Make no mistake: it still took a tremendous amount of courage and belief on both father and son's part to offer each other's sacrifice. It is obvious by Isaac's actions that he also believed, though it is not mentioned directly in these passages. These men did not use faith. They did not hope for something to occur—they believed!

11:19 So what does "recover the risk" indicate? The reader should pause to think about what is clearly being implicated in this statement. If Abraham believed he was "recovering the risk," he also realized that "the-risk" could have been Isaac and that Isaac was that individual concerning the ancient legends and folklores about a Messiah. Having this "knowledge of a Messiah" implies there has always been someone with a presence, knowledge, or understanding of God and His purposes and plans from the beginning of man's time—a Messiah from the beginning of time. This statement also implies that all legends and stories of lore should be able to trace themselves back to Nebuchadnezzar's Kingdom and then straight back to Noah.

11:21 This verse has its parallel event in Genesis 48:12, where in order for Israel to keep his balance when he bowed his head to worship, he needed his staff to support him (I might add for thought and discussion as Christ supports us). The Genesis account does not mention the staff, but it is revealed in Hebrews. So why is it mentioned? One commentary quoted directly for discussion and thought (see paragraph three specifically) is *Jamieson-Fausset-Brown Bible Commentary*:[2]

> 21. both the sons-Greek, "each of the sons" (Ge 47:29; 48:8–20).

---

2. http://bible.cc/hebrews/11-21.htm.

He knew not Joseph's sons, and could not distinguish them by sight, yet he did distinguish them by faith, transposing his hands intentionally, so as to lay his right hand on the younger, Ephraim, whose posterity was to be greater than that of Manasseh: he also adopted these grandchildren as his own sons, after having transferred the right of primogeniture to Joseph (Ge 48:22).

and worshipped

This did not take place in immediate connection with the foregoing, but before it, when Jacob made Joseph swear that he would bury him with his fathers in Canaan, not in Egypt. The assurance that Joseph would do so filled him with pious gratitude to God, which he expressed by raising himself on his bed to an attitude of worship. His faith, as Joseph's (Heb 11:22), consisted in his so confidentially anticipating the fulfillment of God's promise of Canaan to his descendants, as to desire to be buried there as his proper possession.

leaning upon the top of his staff—Ge 47:31, Hebrew and English Version, "upon the bed's head."

> The Septuagint translates as Paul here. Jerome justly reprobates the notion of modern Rome, that Jacob worshipped the top of Joseph's staff, having on it an image of Joseph's power, to which Jacob bowed in recognition of the future sovereignty of his son's tribe, the father bowing to the son! The Hebrew, as translated in English Version, sets it aside: the bed is alluded to afterwards (Ge 48:2; 49:33), and it is likely that Jacob turned himself in his bed so as to have his face toward the pillow, Isa 38:2 (there were no bedsteads in the East). Paul by adopting the Septuagint version, brings out, under the Spirit, an additional fact, namely, that the aged patriarch used his own (not Joseph's) staff to lean on in worshipping on his bed. The staff, too, was the emblem of his pilgrim state here on his way to his heavenly city (Heb 11:13, 14), wherein God had so wonderfully supported him. Ge 32:10, "With my staff I passed over Jordan, and now I am become," &c. (compare Ex 12:11; Mark 6:8). In 1 Ki 1:47, the same thing is said of David's "bowing on his bed," an act of adoring thanksgiving to God for God's favor to his son before death. He omits the more leading blessing of the twelve sons of Jacob; because "he plucks only the flowers which stand by his way, and leaves the whole meadow full to his readers" [Delitzsch in Alford].

11:21   Note the acceptance of Joseph's two sons made for thirteen tribes or camps. Christ promised his twelve disciples that became apostles each a rulership over the tribes of Israel but the addition of Paul makes thirteen and fits nicely with number of the camps of Israel.

11:35   The Greek word *etupanisthesan* is translated as "tortured." A root word found inside the Greek is *tympanum*, which is a torture device. For those in the medical profession, it is the name given to the inner eardrum. Tympanum is found in other professions too.

11:35 The "best Resurrection" tells us there is more than one resurrection, but the first is the "best."

12:2 The Greek word *charas*, commonly translated as "joy," misses entirely that this is a state or condition of bliss due to being in God's presence. A better translation is "joyful-condition" or "joyful-state." It could also be interpreted as an appointed/destined condition or state.

12:6 The Greek word translated "disciplining" is meant as a father punishing for corrective actions with whippings and other forms of discipline—by extension to allow calamities and the use of evils. This same concept applies to the word "scourges."

12:13 "Lame" is understood to be anyone with damage, whether physical, mental, emotional, or spiritual.

12:17 Notice how Esau, once he fully understood what the value and meaning of "The-Blessing" and what "The-Allotment" was all about, became completely emotionally devastated.

12:18 The Greek word *pselaphomemo*, translated as "stroked-touch," is understood to mean "to buy-off," to handle someone for public relations purposes, or purchase a favor in return for a future promise.

12:18 The Greek word *orei*, translated properly as "mountain," is a metaphor for an official, particularly a very high-ranking one with power and authority. Of course, the passage here is describing what Christ is not and men are.

12:18 This verse is full of metaphors: to be "consumed by fire" means to motivate someone in their anger and have them do something for your purposes; "murkiness" would be to act in an underhanded way by deceit and unscrupulous means, saying one thing and doing another; "darkness" means to "turn a blind eye to," not seeing or caring about the collateral damage a decision has caused; "sudden storm" means an individual that is impulsive, not predictable.

12:21 Apparently, god (lower case intentional because this was an angel representing God) was not pleased by the rejected response of the people. While I do not claim to understand the purpose of eliminating animals off a mountain, reasoning as a man, one would ask what value or purpose would that have really served? Especially while a negotiation was occurring (because this is certainly understood within the context), this would have been a rejection of the request. What I find curious is that the Angel's response to being told "no" is almost like throwing a temper tantrum to force his will on the people. I need to clear up any misconception about using the word "God" in this discussion.

HEBREWS STUDY NOTES

The "god" delivering the commandments was an angel representing God and had the full capability and legal authority to enforce or demand whatever was permitted based upon whatever directions he received from The-God. Could this be only one of multiple reasons the angels are to be judged? This being seems to have overstepped the purpose and the directions provided to him by throwing a tantrum and showing off his power and authority. This is strictly speculation on my behalf.

12:23 "Brought forward first by the-called-out [ecclesia]" is telling the audience that this is the first event happening as Christ is returning from Heaven to take over the earth and to remove the remaining deities and earthly powers. Paul has reminded his audience they are part of that event if they continue to believe and not go back into the world.

12:24 Paul makes it clear that this second covenant is also a blood covenant with the use of Christ's blood.

12:24 The mention of the excellence of Abel's blood must have been a subject the audience was familiar with because the topic is not expounded in this lecture. Strictly speculating, it must have been understood to be of the "prime order." As pure as a man could have or be, "the standard" all other men were compared to was still woefully short of Christ.

13:12 "Suffered outside *The-Gate*" (italics mine) is referring to a specific location just "outside the camp of Israel." This location is where the stoning took place for those individuals who were called "traitors, enemies to the state, blasphemers of God" of Israel. Not only was Stephen murdered here by stoning, but so was Christ crucified here as an enemy of the state of Israel in addition to the crucifixion [the Gentile/worldly condemnation]. Christ was also stoned by those attending the Passover and passing by this site on the way to the temple (Israel also participated in the crucifixion, physically throwing stones at Christ as well as sitting in the seat of condemnation, much like those in the United State passing judgment from the jury box). This was also the place where the carcasses were burned for the Red Heifer offering. In *Secrets of Golgotha*, Dr. Earnest L. Martin, PhD, has more to say about this.

13:13 "outside the Camp." One of the interesting things about study and research is that such a statement can be easily read and overlooked. But this statement contains profound information. Outside the camp for Israel was the place where the State death sentences were carried out. It was also the location of the Red Heifer Altar where sacrificial carcasses and waste ash was burned in complete entirety. "The Camp" that included the temple as its center point was a 2,000-cubit circle. This is the physical location of Christ's death and occurred on the Mount of Olives. As much as Christ, Stephen would have been

Section IV

murdered in this area also. See http://www.askelm.com/Timeline/Timeline.pdf, pages 36 and 37, for a physical map and the last movements of Christ. Read *Secrets of Golgotha* for a full explanation of both ideas and how they relate back to the Garden of Eden.

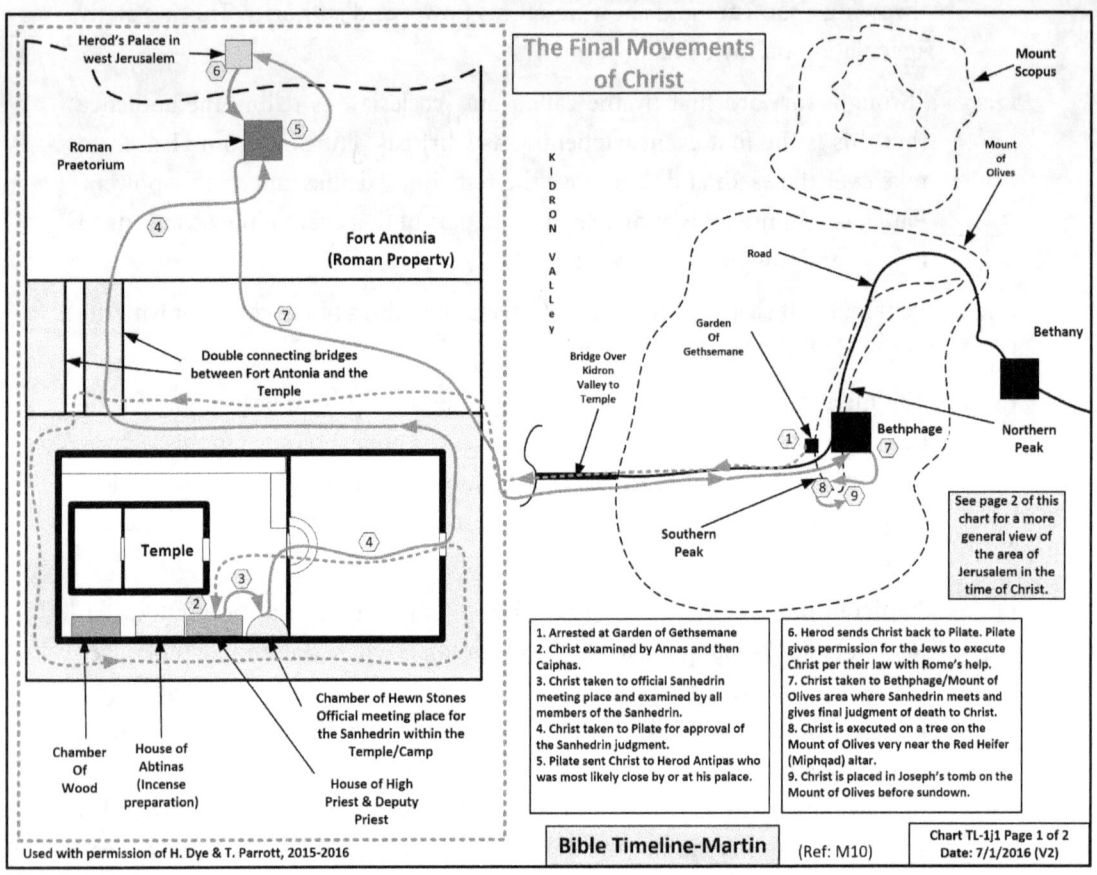

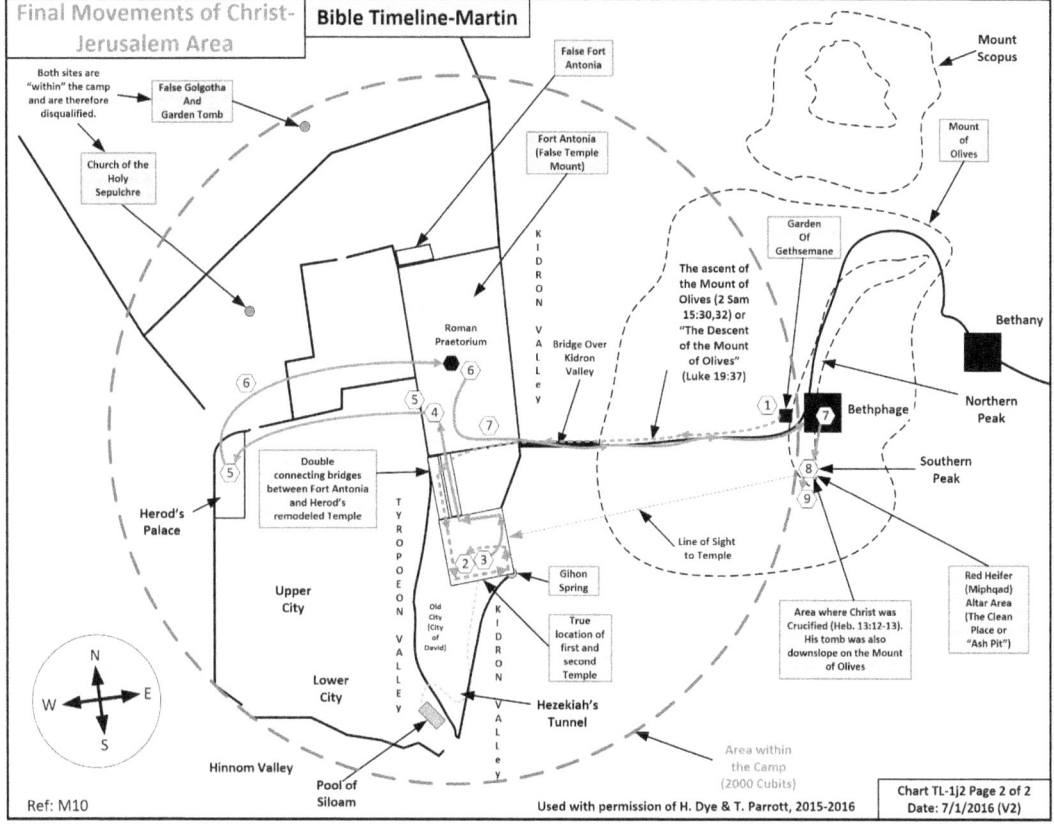

HEBREWS IN VERSE

HEBREWS 1

1:1 *THE-GOD* speaking to The-Fathers of old at many times and in many ways [methods] by the-prophets

1:2 speaks to us in the last of these days by (*HIS*) *Son* whom *HE* ordained *Enjoyer-of-The-Allotment-of-All*, the-means-for whom also *HE-Makes* The-Eons [causes life, the worlds, all things contained in time].

1:3 *Whom* is a shining luminous body reflecting the-majesty of *GOD* and carved [the-exact-precise-image-and-reproduction-in-every-aspect] of the nature [quality] of *HIM*. And brings forth [produces, is holding up, preserving] all things in declaration [uttered by the living voice, by the word, the command, by the declaration of one's mind made in words] by [through] the unlimited-inherent-power in *HIM*. Through [in-a-singular-one-of-a-kind-not-to-be-duplicated-act] *Himself* makes [render, provides] a cleansing [purifying, removing the guilt from sins] our sins, is seated [exalted to, made higher than the heavens] at [to] the right of *THE-MAJESTY* in the heights.

1:4 Becoming [Exalted as such] so much more excellent than [there is absolutely no comparison with] The-Messengers [angels] in as much as [and because] *He* is so much more excellent [Messianic title and divinity, rulership] than them *He* has received The-Allotment over [in dominion over] them.

1:5 For when at any time to whom did *HE* say to The-Angels, **"*YOU* are my son, today *I* have generated [begotten, born] *You*?"** And again, **"*I* shall be to *Him* a Father and *He* shall be *My* son."** [Ps 2:7, II Sam 7:14]

1:6 Furthermore when *GOD* having brought [in *HIS* time and place] *The-Firstborn* into the world *HE* said, **"Let them worship *Him*, all messengers [angels] of *GOD*!"** [Deut 32:43 {Septuagint}]

1:7 More indeed to The-Messengers *HE* asks, **"Who is *THE-ONE-making* his messengers [angels] as spirits and his ministers blazing fires?"** [Ps 104:4]

1:8 But to *The-Son*, "**Your divine throne (is) into the eon of the eons.**" [Ps 45:6]

1:9 "**Yours is a scepter of straightness [impartial and righteousness], *The-Scepter-of-The-Kingdom*. You dearly-love justice [righteousness] and hate [detest] lawlessness. Because of this *THE-GOD*, your *GOD*, anoints You with olive oil [divine] of exaltation [gladness] beyond [exalted above, over] your partners.**" [Ps 45:7; Isa 61:3]

1:10 And, "**You *Master* through [with the, are the active cause with, as the leader of the, commenced with the] Originals [the ones at the beginning of all things, at the beginning of all things spoken] founded [laid the foundation, creating] the earth and the heavens are the works of *Your* hands.**"

1:11 "**They shall-be-being destroyed [ruined, put to death, perish], yet *You* are remaining. And all as a cloak [outer garment] is aging [deteriorating],**"

1:12 and, "***You* shall roll them up like a mantle [a wrap, a covering] and they shall be changed [transformed]. Yet *You* are the same and *Your* years will never cease [stop].**" [Isa 34:4, 50:9, 51:6]

1:13 But to which of The-Messengers has *HE* declared at any time, "**Sit to the right of *ME* until *I* place *Your* enemies under *Your* feet like *Your* footstool**"? [Ps 110:1]

1:14 Are they not all serving [ministering] spirits being commissioned for the-service for the-ones being about to-be-enjoying The-Allotment-of-Salvation?

HEBREWS 2

2:1 Because of this it is right and proper we be exceedingly giving attention [attached, addicted, devoted] to the things being heard lest at some time we may be drifting away [carried away, allowed to escape, slips the mind].

2:2 For if through The-Messengers the word that was spoken became confirmed [valid-and-unbreakable] and every transgression and disobedience obtained a just [fair, proper, righteous] payment due of wages [reward, the sentence of death],

2:3 how would we be escaping? By neglecting such and so great a salvation which was obtained through *The-Master* and spoken [told to us] by the-ones hearing him [the apostles] and was confirmed [proved by truth and divinity] to us?

2:4 *THE-GOD* is also witnessing [corroborating] with signs, miracles and many powerful deeds and the distribution of the-Holy-spirit according-to The Will-of-*HIM*.

2:5 For *HE* has not given control [subjection] of the-impending [coming] home to The Messengers [angels] which we are talking about.

Section IV

2:6 But where did someone witness [state, solemnly testify] saying, **"What is man that *YOU* are reminded [have a remembrance in order to care about, have a concern or care for]] of him or The Son of man that *YOU* are taking notice of [choose, employ] *Him*?"**

2:7 **"*YOU* made him a bit inferior than any Messengers. *YOU* wreathed [crowned him] with glory and honor and appointed [to administer an office, set in charge] *Him* over the works of *YOUR* hand**

2:8 **subjecting all under the feet of him."** [Ps 8:4–6]

For in setting all under *Him* nothing is left to be subjected [controlled]. Presently for now we are not seeing all the things having been subjected to *Him*.

2:9 And *The-One* having been made a bit inferior than The-Messengers we observe [discern, understand to be, known by experience, know] is *Savior*. That for everyone by [for] the grace [favor, pardoning of their offenses] from *GOD* He was to be tasting [was to experience] the suffering of The-Death and became crowned with glory and honor.

2:10 For it was necessary for *Him* in whom all and through all is, to be perfected through sufferings leading many sons to their glory as *The-Chief-Leader-[Prince]-of-Salvation*.

2:11 For THE-ONE-HALLOWING and the-ones being hallowed are all out of *The-One* for *He* is not ashamed to be calling them Brothers.

2:12 Saying [affirm, teach, stating], **"I shall be proclaiming [declaring, make openly known, avow and praising] your name to my Brothers in the midst of The-Called-Out [ecclesia]. I shall be singing hymns to *YOU*."** [Ps 22:22]

2:13 And again, **"I shall have confidence [complete belief in] in *HIM*"** and again, **"Look! I and the little boys and girls *THE-GOD* gives to me."** [II Sam 22:3; Isa 8:17, Isa 8:18]

2:14 Since the little boys and girls are partners [sharers, are in fellowship] by flesh and blood, *He* also has in the same way become the same. That through The-Death *He* should cause to cease [annul, put to an end, abolish] The-One having the might [dominion, power] of [over] The-Death. This is The-Adversary

2:15 and should be freeing [releasing] these whomever fears death over their entire lifetime, bound [shackled, subjected, obligated, guilty and worthy of punishment] in slavery.

2:16 Most certainly not to aid [help, rescue for eternal life] messengers [angels], but to rescue the-seed of Abraham.

2:17 For this reason *He* owed [had an obligation, was imposed by special consideration, out of duty] to all to be made like the-Brothers, that [so-that] *He* would become merciful and faithful, *The-Chief-[High]-Priest* for *THE-GOD* as the propitiation [appeasing offering, peace-making offering, salvation offering] for the-sins of the-people

2:18   for which *He* suffered [experienced, underwent, performed]. Being tried *He* is able to help the-ones being tried.

HEBREWS 3

3:1   Therefore, Brothers of the-Holy-calling, Heavenly Partners, you fix your eyes on who we profess to-be *The-Apostle* and *High Priest* of us, *Anointed-Savior*.

3:2   Being faithful [loyal and true] to *THE-ONE-MAKING Him* as also Moses in all the household of him.

3:3   For *This-One, He* has been counted worthy with even greater glory and honor than Moses, saving the-household [family, [called-out]] of *THE-ONE-CONSTRUCTING Him*.

3:4   For every house is built by someone, yet *THE-ONE-CONSTRUCTING* [equipping with all things necessary] all—*GOD*!

3:5   Moses indeed was faithful and all of his [his entire] household; a servant of God testifying about [of, repeating] the things which were to-be-spoken.

3:6   Yet *Anointed* is a son over *HIS* household. We are *HIS* household if indeed [only] we are retaining [holding fast] in fearless-confidence and The-Glory of The-sure-Expectation until all is finished in entirety.

3:7   Through which the-Holy-spirit is saying today if you are listening to his [its] sound [voice],

3:8   "Do not be hardening your hearts as in The-Provocation, in The-Day of The-Temptation in The-Wilderness

3:9   when your fathers were trying *ME*. They tested *ME* and saw with their eyes *MY* works for forty years.

3:10   Therefore *I* am disgusted with that generation and *I* said they are always straying in their heart and still they have not known *MY* ways.

3:11   So *I* swore in *MY* anger that they shall-not-be-coming into The-Rest-of-*MINE*."

3:12   So you beware, Brothers, that if at some time anyone of you with a wicked heart of disbelief withdraw from (the) *LIVING-GOD*.

3:13   But you be entreating [encouraging, exhorting] yourselves each day while it is still being called today, that not a one of you may be hardened by the-seduction [lusty-deceitfulness] of sins.

Section IV

3:14   For we have become partners of *The-Anointed* if we commit to holding on to our first confidence to The-End.

3:15   While it [Listen to what] is being said, "Today if you hear the-sound [voice] of *HIM* do not harden your heart as like The-Provocation." [Ps 95:7, 8]

3:16   For some of the ones hearing had bitterness [provoked, roused indignation] but not all of the-ones coming out of Egypt with Moses.

3:17   And yet to whom was *HE* disgusted with for forty years? Not all the ones had sinned whose carcasses fell in the wilderness.

3:18   But to whom swore *HE* that-would not be entering into The-Rest of *HIM*? Was it not the-ones-being-stubborn [not believing]?

3:19   So we are seeing that they could not be entering because of disbelief.

4:1   Then we should be afraid that The-Promise leaves of entering into The-Rest-of-*HIM* anyone of you being found lacking.

4:2   Also we have preached the Well-Message to you and also them. But *The-Word* of the-tidings [news, reports] has no benefit for them, not having been blended together [united, mixed with, combined into an organic structure such as the body] with The-Belief as the-ones hearing.

4:3   For we, the-ones believing, are coming into The-Rest. As *HE* has declared, **"As I swear in *MY* anger, if—they enter into *MY* Rest, even though the-works were completed when The-System [world] came to be [from the foundation of the world]."** [Ps 95:11]

4:4   And where is it *HE* has declared the same about a rest on the-seventh (day)? "*THE-GOD* on the-seventh day rested from all of *HIS* works."

4:5   And again in this, "if—they shall enter in The-Rest of *MINE*."

4:6   Therefore it is being left open for any to enter into her [it] and for those to not enter because of stubbornness [disbelief] who once received the Well-Message.

HEBREWS 4

4:7   Yet today *HE* is declaring [decreeing, ordaining] a certain day through David saying, "After so [a certain] much time," and today has been declaring, **"Should you hear *HIS* voice, you should not be hardening your hearts."** [Ps 95:7, 8]

4:8   For if *Savior* [Joshua, Jehovah-Saves, Jehovah-is-Generous] had given them rest *He* would not have spoken about this "another day."

4:9 Consequently [By logic, by reasoning] there is left a Sabbath for The-People-of-*THE-GOD*.

4:10 For *The-One* coming into *His* Rest has also ceased from *His* acts [works] even as *GOD* from (*HIS*) own.

4:11 We should be endeavoring to be entering into that Rest so that no one should be falling in the same example of stubbornness [disbelief].

4:12 For living is *The-Word-of-THE-GOD* and powerful and cuts-keener more than [beyond] every two-edged sword and piercing [going-straight-through] until separating [cleaving asunder] both spirit and soul, joints and marrow and skilled-in-judging feelings and thoughts of the heart.

4:13 And there is not anything created that is hidden from *HIS* view [sight, presence] for all is naked and exposed to *HIS* eyes; to *WHOM* we must give an account.

4:14 Then having a *Great-Chief-Sacred-One* [High Priest], *The-One* having passed into the heavens, *Savior*, *The-Son-of-THE-GOD*—may we keep carefully and faithfully this confession [Statement of Belief].

4:15 For we are not having a sacred-chief-one [high priest] unable to sympathize [feel, have compassion] with the infirmities [weaknesses, trials, and troubles] of the soul of us but having-*One*-been-tried in all likeness apart from [without] sin.

4:16 May we come [in agreement as one, approach the presence of, present ourselves, in a courtly and stately manner, together unified] with boldness then to *The-Throne-of-THE-GRACE* that we may be receiving mercy and may-be-finding grace and well-seasoned [timely] help.

HEBREWS 5

5:1 For every chief-sacred-one [high priest] out of [from] men being-obtained [marked, used, chosen, selected] for the-sake-of men is appointed from *THE-GOD* that he may be carrying [bringing, presenting, handling] both oblations [honorable gifts, offerings] and sacrifices for the sake of sins;

5:2 able to be not unduly disturbed [overtaken, caught up in, engulfed, overwhelmed] in emotion because of the-ones being ignorant and straying since he is also laid-about [surrounded, by nature of being a man] with infirmities [weaknesses].

Section IV

5:3 And because of this he owes [is bound, by duty, by also being only a man] for himself as also with the-people, to be making atoning sacrifices for the sake of sins.

5:4 And no one takes [gains, chooses, selects] this honor for himself, but being the-one called by THE-GOD, just as Aaron.

5:5 So also *The-Anointed* did not think [have the opinion, regarded] of [about] himself to have become [be made] the chief-sacred-one [high priest] but THE-ONE-SPEAKING to *Him* said, **"You are MY son; today I have generated [begotten] you."** [Ps 2:7]

5:6 And also in another place HE says, **"You Sacred-One [Priest] into the-eon after [as, like] the-order of Melchisedek."** [Ps 110:4]

5:7 Who in the days of *His* flesh offering both petitions and supplications with strong distressful wailing and tears to THE-ONE-BEING-ABLE-TO-BE-SAVING *Him* out of death and was heard due to [because of] Godly-reverence.

5:8 And being a son *He* also learned obedience from [by] which *He* suffered,

5:9 and being perfected *He* became *The-Cause-[Author]-of-Eonian-Salvation* for all the-ones obeying *Him*.

5:10 Addressed *Chief-Sacred-One* [High Priest] by THE-GOD **"according-to [as, after, like] the-order of Melchisedek."** [Ps 110:4]

5:11 About whom we have much to say but is hard to present and difficult to explain since you have become dull to hearing [instruction].

5:12 For also as the-ones that ought to be teachers by this time, again you need to be taught what are the elements [first principals] of the originals [beginning] of-the-oracles-of-*THE-GOD* and have become needing to have milk [nursing milk, breast milk] and not solid nourishment.

5:13 For everyone using [feeding-on] milk [nursing milk, breast milk] is inexperienced [unskilled] in the-word of justice [righteousness] for he is an infant [childish, not of age]

5:14 for solid nourishment is for the mature-ones, the-ones because of the habit [use of] of the faculties [the mind] have been exercising [striving earnestly to become Godly] for [are, by] discriminating [judging, discerning, distinguishing] between the ideal [praiseworthy, noble, morally good] and evil [wrong, injurious, destructive].

HEBREWS 6

6:1 Leave therefore the original [primary, beginning [first grade]] saying [teachings, instructions] of *The-Anointed* behind, we should carry on to [bring in, move on to] perfection. Not again throwing down [laying] the foundation of repentance from dead works and of-belief in *GOD*.

6:2 Of the teachings of baptism, the laying on of hands, the resurrection of dead ones and of eonian judgment.

6:3 But this we shall do, that is if *THE-GOD* may allow.

6:4 For unable are [it's impossible for] the-ones once being enlightened, tasting The-Gift-of-The-Heaven and becoming partakers of the-Holy-spirit

6:5 and have tasted the perfect declaration [word, message] of *GOD's* inherent-unlimited-power in The-Coming-Eon

6:6 to indeed fall away then repeating the renewing of repentance by crucifying for himself again *The-Son-of-THE-GOD* and making (*Him, The-Son*) a public disgrace.

6:7 For the land drinks showers [rain] that come on her as often as it comes and brings forth herbage fit for those from who also farm it, blessings from *THE-GOD*.

6:8 Yet bringing forth thorns and star-thistles is a disqualification [are unfit, do not stand the test] and are a curse, whose finish [total-consummation] is burning.

6:9 Yet we have been persuaded about you, Godly-Beloved, about the better (things) and having salvation, although we are speaking as this [in this manner].

6:10 For *THE-GOD* is not unjust to be forgetting your acts and the-act of Godly-love which you display in the-name of *HIM* when serving the-Holy-ones and are serving.

6:11 Yet we a have a great desire for each one of you, displaying the same diligence in The-Assurance [confidence, Surety]-of-The-Expectation until The-End

6:12 that you may not become dull [indolent, lethargic, slothful] but become imitators of the-ones through believing [faith] and patience to enjoy The-Allotment-of-The-Promises.

6:13 For The-Promise to Abraham by *THE-GOD*, since *HE* had no one greater to swear by, *HE* swore by (*HIM*) *SELF*

SECTION IV

6:14 saying, "**Truly in blessing *I* shall be blessing [consecrate, prosper] you and in increasing, *I* shall multiply you.**"

6:15 So by being patient he attained [obtained] The-Promise.

6:16 Indeed men swear by the-greater and the-oath, as a confirmation puts to an end contradiction for all of them.

6:17 *THE-GOD* intending [deliberately, intentionally, purposed] to show super-abundantly-more [beyond any doubt or uncertainty] to The-Enjoyers-of-The-Allotment-of-The-Promise *HIS* fixed-unalterable counsel [divine will and plan (through Christ)], mediated [sponsored, pledging of himself] with an oath.

6:18 That through [on account of these, for these reasons, because of these] two immutable [fixed, unalterable] practices [facts, deeds, matter of law] it is impossible for *GOD* to falsify [lie] [break HIS pledge]. May we continue having sure [firm, strong] encouragement [consolation and comfort through the Messiah's salvation]. The-Ones fleeing for refuge, take hold [take master of, powerfully possess, seize, faithfully retain] of The-Expectation laying before [appointed, destined]

6:19 which we have as an anchor of the-soul. Both secure [true, can be relied on, confirmed] and certain [absolutely sure, firm, unshakeable] and be received beyond The-Interior-of-The-Curtain

6:20 where *Savior* entered for our sake as *The-Forerunner*, becoming *The-Chief-Sacred-One* [High Priest] according-to [like, as, after] the-order-of-Melchisedek.

HEBREWS 7

7:1 For it was this Melchisedek, The-King-of-Salem, High-Priest of *THE-MOST-HIGH-GOD* who met Abraham returning from the-combat-slaughter of The-Kings and blessed him

7:2 and to whom Abraham divided a tenth out of all. Indeed before most [truly first in rank, chief, principal, at the first] translated in the common as [understood commonly] as King-of-Justice [Righteousness] and also as King-of-Salem or as King-of-Peace.

7:3 Fatherless, motherless, without a genealogy, having neither beginning of days or end of life. Being pictured [modeled, made like, a copy, image] as *The-Son-of-THE-GOD* and remains a Sacred-one [priest] into the-continuous [finality, forever].

7:4 Now you consider [ponder about, think, meditate and reflect on] this-Eminent-One and to whom The-Patriarch Abraham gave a tenth from the best of the-spoils [booty].

7:5 Now truly the-ones out of Levi, the sons of the-priestly-office have direction [are ordered, ethically commanded] to take [carry away, not refuse and reject, collect (as a tribute)] tithes from the people according-to The-Law, this is from their brothers including those having come out of the-loins of Abraham.

7:6 But *This-One* is not in the genealogy of those of The-Abraham having received the tenth part and blessed him The-One having The-Promise

7:7 and beyond all contradiction [opposition, argument] the inferior is being blessed by the better [superior].

7:8 Indeed here [today] men receiving tithes do die, yet *The-One* being witnessed [being given a testimony for, affirmed by being seen and heard] *He* is living.

7:9 And let me declare this so it is clear, even Levi, the-one receiving tithes, had been tithing through Abraham

7:10 for he was still in the-loin of The-Father when he met together with Melchisedek.

7:11 By reasoning then, if perfection [completion and maturity] came through the Leviticus priesthood—for by her the-people had been placed under The-Law—what is the need [purpose, role] to rise up a different Order-of-Melchisedek or why is it not being said, [calling, maintaining] "according-to [just as, just like] the-Order-of-Aaron?"

7:12 Now the priesthood is-transferred out of necessity making [causing] also a transference [change] to The-Law.

7:13 For who these things are being said belongs to a different tribe of and [about] that-Altar which no one has paid attention [devoted thought and service] to.

7:14 For it is openly evident that out of Judah has risen [descended] *The-Master* of us from which tribe Moses speaks nothing concerning the priesthood.

7:15 And still it is more-superabundantly plain [evident, thoroughly clear] just as the-likeness of Melchisedek is standing up [now in place is] a different sacred-one [priest]

7:16 who has appeared [publicly] in the flesh, not in the manner of the Mosaic priesthood law [per the rule of lineage] but in inherent-power [due to his own nature] not subject to destruction [death].

7:17 For *HE* is witnessing that, **"You (are a) Sacred-One [Priest] into the Eon like The-Order-of-Melchisedek."** [Ps110:4]

Section IV

7:18 Indeed [certainly, surely] to come is an abolishment for the Commandments [lineage of priesthood, the Mosaic Law and Jewish traditions] because of her [its] weakness and being without benefit.

7:19 For *The-Law* matures [perfects] no-one, yet a better expectation [hope, desire] was brought to which we are drawing nearer [approaching, be joined to, become acquainted with, turn one's thoughts] to *THE-GOD*.

7:20 And not compared like the-ones swearing [taking] an oath for indeed apart from [without taking] a sworn oath had become a sacred-one [priest].

7:21 For *The-One* received the-sworn-oath through *THE-ONE-SAYING* to *Him*, **"*MASTER* swears and will not regret it, *You* Sacred-one [Priest] into The-Eon like The-Order-of-Melchisedek."** [Ps 110:4]

7:22 With this greater covenant [compact, testament] *Savior* has become *The-Sponsor* [*The Guarantor*].

7:23 Indeed, there has been several ones becoming sacred-ones [priests] and were prevented to be remaining [continue in service] because of death.

7:24 But because of *Him*, *The-One* to be remaining into The-Eon has the unchangeable-and-not-able-to-pass-to-a-successor priesthood.

7:25 And also *He* is able to save to the uttermost [in entirety and completely] the-ones coming through *Him* to *THE-ALWAYS-LIVING-GOD* to be pleading [praying, intercessions] for the sake of them.

7:26 Of this kind [For such a man] became High Priest for us, holy-pious [without sin], innocent, undefiled, having been separated from the-sinners and became honored-exalted-eminent in The-Heavens.

7:27 Who does not need to daily as those high priests to be offering-up sacrifices for their own sins then next for the-people; this *He* did all at once [once for all] offering *Himself* up.

7:28 For *The-Law* appoints [to administer the office [duties]] men as chief priests having weaknesses [body and soul]. Yet *The-Word-of-The-Sworn-Oath*, *The-Son* after [in fellowship with] The-Law has been perfected into the-eon.

HEBREWS 8

8:1 The central point being spoken of is this; we have a sacred-priest-one [high priest] who is seated at the right of The-Throne of *THE-GREAT-TOGETHERNESS [MAJESTY]* in The-Heavens

8:2 and being *The-Holiest-Minister* and of *The-True-Booth* [Tabernacle, Temple] which *The-Master* pitches [fastens together] and not men.

8:3 For every chief-sacred-one [high priest] is appointed [to administer the office of] to be-offering both the-gifts and sacrifices which also is necessary for this-One that *He* may have something to offer.

8:4 Indeed, for if *He* was on earth, he would never be a sacred-one being [knowing, seeing] the priests are the-ones offering the gifts according-to The-Law

8:5 who are a show [representation, copy, imitation] and shade [outline, image, sketch] of offering-divine-service in the heavenlies just as Moses had been divinely commanded [instructed] about The-Booth [Tabernacle, Temple] to be accomplished [made, created]. HE declared, **"Look to see [insure, make certain] you should do [complete] all just as the-image [print, model, pattern], the-one having-been-shown to you in the mountain."**

8:6 And now *He* has become *Master* of a more excellent [surpassing] ministry, and a far greater *Mediator* of a more excellent covenant which is sanctioned by law [a legally resolved matter, enacted, legislated, established] because of [for, on account of] greater promises.

8:7 For if that first-one was not without defect [fault, blameless] a second-one would not be sought [required, demanded] to replace it.

8:8 The fault was found with them. HE says, **"Look! The days are coming says (the) MASTER that *I*-shall be ending-one-and-begin a new covenant with The-House of Israel and The-House of Judah."**

8:9 **"Not like the Covenant which *I* made with The-Fathers in that day by taking hold of their hand and leading them out of the land of Egypt. Because they did not remain [be true to, continued, keep, persevere in anything, [made light of, did not mean what they pledged]] in [about] *MY* covenant and *I* neglected [took no care for, ignored] them says the *MASTER*."**

8:10 **"Here is the covenant which *I*-shall-be-covenanting with The-House of Israel after those days says *MASTER*. Furnishing [give, impart, commit, bestow as a gift, furnish, grant, commission] by writing [inscribing, fix, and be present] *MY* laws in their mind [the faculty of understanding, feelings and desires] and also in their hearts [center and seat of spiritual life] and I shall be their *GOD* and they shall be *MY* people."**

8:11 **"And they shall not teach to the-one near him [associate, neighbor] and saying to each of his brother, "You know [become acquainted with] the *THE-MASTER* [Lord]" for all shall-be-acquainted [perceive, have knowledge] of *ME*, from the least to the greatest of them."**

8:12 **"For *I* shall be merciful and *I* will no longer recall to mind their unjustness and their sins and their lawlessness."** [Jer 31:31–34]

Section IV

8:13   By saying this [This means] *HE* has declared the former outdated [worn out by time and use, ancient, antiquated, old] by being outdated [obsolete] and failing [be obsolete, decaying, have no strength, deprived of force and authority] from age and is near destruction [disappearing].

HEBREWS 9

9:1   Truly the first (Covenant) also has the-ordinances [statutes, precepts concerning public worship] of divine service and an earthly holy place [sanctuary, temple].

9:2   For The-Booth [Tabernacle, Temple] is constructed such that in the front part [section, partition] has The-Lamp-Stand also The-Table displaying The-Showbread which is called The-Sanctuary.

9:3   And after the-second-curtain, (the) tabernacle is called the Holy-of-Holies,

9:4   having The-Golden Censor instrument and The-Ark-of-The-Covenant covered entirely in gold, with The-Golden Urn having The-Manna and The-Rod of Aaron, the-one germinating [sprouts, buds, bring forth leaves] and The-Tablets of The-Covenant.

9:5   And up-over her [it, The Ark] The-Cherubim of Glory cover with shade [shading] The-Propitiation [pardoning, covering, mercy]-Place [mercy-seat] about which now there is not a particular [special] thing to be saying [teaching].

9:6   Now indeed making things ready continually entering in The-front of The-Tabernacle executing [working, performing the sacrifices] the-divine-service are The-Priests.

9:7   For only once a year only The-Chief-Sacred-One [high priest] goes into the-second, never without blood which he offers for the sake of himself and for the-sins of the-people.

9:8   This signified the-spirit having not yet making a way known [manifesting, showing, to appear] into The-Holy-of-Holies, still having to stand in front of The-Booth [Tabernacle, Temple],

9:9   which is a parable [proverb, setting things side by side, comparing what is happening today] for the-present season [period] where both gifts and sacrifices being offered are not being able to perfect the conscience of The-One-offering-divine-services;

9:10   only over [in control of] foods and drinks with different washings and fleshly ordinances [statutes, laws] for the season [period] placed on (them) until restored-to-its-[their]-natural-and-normal-condition.

9:11 Yet *Anointed* came [was purposed] to be (the) *Chief-Sacred-One* [High Priest] of the good things to come, through the greater and more perfect Booth [Tabernacle, Temple], not hand-made, that is, not of-the-creation.

9:12 Not using the-blood of goats and calves but by (*His*) own blood entering once for all eonian into the Holy-places, finding [acquiring, obtaining, procuring] redemption [salvation, deliverance].

9:13 For if the-blood of bulls and male goats and ashes of The-Heifer sprinkling the-ones-having-been-contaminated hallows [makes-holy] purifying [cleansing] the-flesh,

9:14 how much to-an-infinite-degree the-blood of *The-Anointed* who through the-eonian-spirit, offering *Himself* un-flawed to THE-GOD, cleansing your conscience from dead acts [works, deeds] to be-offering-divine-service to THE-LIVNG-GOD.

9:15 For this reason *He-is-Mediator* [arbitrates, intervenes]. That by becoming dead loosened [took away, removed] transgressions [flaws, shortages, make available the corrective measures for] from the-first-Covenant [Will and Testament] so the-ones-having-been called may-be-obtaining [receiving] The-Enjoyment-of-The-Allotment of The-Eonian.

9:16 For where there is a covenant [a will and testament] it is necessary to bring death to the-covenant-victim [maker, appointer, testator [covenant-taker]],

9:17 for a covenant [last will and testament] is confirmed [executed] after dying since at-no-time it has enforcement when the-covenant-victim is living.

9:18 For this reason the first [covenant, testament] had not been dedicated [initiated, consecrated, renewed] without [was required to be] using blood.

9:19 For each-and-every direction of The-Law that was spoken by Moses to the-entire-people, (Moses, he) took the-blood of the-calves and he-goats and water and The-Scarlet-Wool and Hyssop and with them sprinkled both The-Scroll and the-entire people.

9:20 Saying [affirming, advising, directing], **"This is the blood of The-Covenant which THE-GOD directs [commands] towards [with regard to] you."** [Ex 24:8]

9:21 Also in the same manner sprinkling The Booth [Tabernacle] and all the-instruments of the-office [ministry]

9:22 for almost all is being cleansed with blood by The-Law and without pouring out blood is no pardoning.

9:23 Then it is indeed necessary by the-patterns [examples] in The-Heavens for these to be purified, but in The-Heaven-Temple is a more excellent sacrifice than these.

Section IV

9:24 For *The-Anointed* entered into (the) Holy-places of The-True-Type not made by hands, but into this same Heaven-Temple appearing [show one's self] to the face of *THE-GOD* now for the sake of us.

9:25 And not to be continually offering *Himself* even as the-high-priest entering into the-Holiest place each year with other's blood.

9:26 Since *His* continual suffering was necessary at [from] The-Foundation-[inception, beginning]-of-The-System [world] and now once for all unplacing [abolishing, annulling] sin through *His* appearance and sacrifice at The-Finish-[conclusion]-of-The-Eons.

9:27 And since it is reserved [awaiting] for men to die once then after this judgment,

9:28 so then *The-Anointed* was offered-up once for all carrying-up [bearing, burdened with] the-sins for the-many, waiting to be seen by the-ones by *His* salvation.

HEBREWS 10

10:1 For The-Law possesses a shadow of the good to come, not the-identical-image. The same for the-practices with a definite period of time, the same of sacrifices they are offering having a finality. Those never were able to bring the-ones to come being matured [perfected].

10:2 Why are they to ever cease being offered? Because the-ones-offering-divine-service have been cleansed [purged from being guilty] once and for all no longer having a consciousness [thoughtful-desire] for sins [will shun and avoid sins].

10:3 For in those {practices and sacrifices} is a memory [remembrance, recollection, a call to think back and reflect on] of sins each year

10:4 making-it-impossible for the-blood of bulls and he-goats to-be-lifting [eliminate] sins.

10:5 By entering into The-System [world] *He* says, **"Sacrifices and offerings YOU will not [you did not intend, are not fond of, take pleasure in, wished for], yet a body *You* adapted [completed, arranged] for me."**

10:6 **"Whole burnt offerings and all-about [all-around, all things and activities concerning about {not only sin but including the entire sacrificial systems}] sin YOU have no delight [pleasure in]."**

10:7 **"Then *I* said: "Look, *I-Am* arriving, as the volume of the scroll has written about [concerning] *Me* to do The-Will-of-*THE-GOD*!"** [Ps 40:6–8]

10:8	Saying further [Repeating again], **"That sacrifice and offering and whole-burnt-offerings and all-concerning sin *YOU* do not desire [wish for, take no pleasure with], neither do *YOU* seem well [delighted] with anything The-Law has been offering."**
10:9	Then *He* has declared, **"Look, *I-Am* arriving to do The-Will-of-*THE-GOD*."** For you *HE*-is-dispatching [abolishing, taking away] the-first that *HE* should be establishing the-second.
10:10	By will [God's wishes, choice, desire, pleasure] we having-been-hallowed [sanctified, made-holy] by the-offering of The-Body-of-*The-Savior*-[Jehovah is Salvation]-*Anointed* once for all.
10:11	For certain, everyday sacred-ones [priests] stand officiating [ministering] often the same offerings and sacrifices which can never be-taking-away sins.
10:12	Yet *He* for the sake of sins offered one sacrifice for ever sitting at the right by *THE-GOD*
10:13	now waiting to place under the footstool of *His* feet the-enemies.
10:14	For in one offering *He*-has-perfected [completed] eonian the-ones being hallowed [sanctified, made-holy].
10:15	And testifying [witnessing] to us is also The-Holy-spirit. For it has been declared before after [as] this,
10:16	**"This is The-Covenant which *I* shall covenant with them after those days is saying *MASTER*. *I* shall impart [give, grant, write] *MY* laws on their hearts, also inscribing in their comprehension [minds],"**
10:17	and, **"The sins of them and the lawlessnesses [iniquities, wickedness] of them *I* should no longer be reminded."** [Jer 31:33, 34]
10:18	For of these [Meaning this], where pardoned-and-forgotten (there is) no further offering for sin.
10:19	Then, Brothers, having boldness, make an entrance into the-Holiest-place by The-Blood-of-*Savior*
10:20	which he dedicated [initiated, consecrated] a way for us through this Curtain, that is *His* flesh, recently slain but living,
10:21	also a *Great-Sacred-One* [High Priest] over the house of *THE-GOD*.
10:22	May we come with a true [genuine, real] heart in assurance [certain or sure confidence] of-believing, having the-hearts being cleansed by sprinkling [purified] from a wicked conscience and the-body-bathed with clean [pure] water.

Section IV

10:23 May we retain [grasp firmly, keep secure] the-vow [confession] of The-Expectation [hope, eternal salvation, faith] without wavering, believing about *The-Promised-One*.

10:24 And may we be considering one another, to sharpen [incite] in acts of Godly-love and ideal acts.

10:25 Not forsaking the leading together of ourselves as the-custom of us but entreating and even greater in your observation [watching] for The-Day drawing near [approaching].

10:26 For if we voluntarily sin after getting [receiving, understand] the knowledge of The-Truth, no further offering for sins is left [left-behind, remains, can be done again, no second chance is available].

10:27 But certain fearful [terrible, formidable] judgment and of a fiery boiling [jealousy] is about, waiting to be-eating [consuming, cannibalizing] the Hostile-(Ones).

10:28 Now anyone disregarding [rejecting, refusing, thwarting] The-Law of Moses by two to three witnesses is put to death without pity [compassion, mercy, a heart for].

10:29 How much more worthy of a greater punishment do you suppose shall be for the-one trampling on [insulting, treat with rudeness, insulting neglect] *The-Son* of *THE-GOD* and treating [accounting, considering, thinking] the-blood of the-covenant contaminated that hallowed *Him* and in outraging [despising, insulting] the-spirit of *THE-GRACE*?

10:30 For we are acquainted with *THE-ONE* saying, **"Avenging is mine; *I* shall be repaying says *MASTER*,"** and also, **"(The) *MASTER* shall be judging *HIS* people."** [Deut 32:35–36]

10:31 To be falling into the hands of *THE-LIVNG-GOD*, fearful!

10:32 But call to remembrance the former days when being enlightened you endured the many [vast] hard trials, [combats, struggles] of sufferings [afflictions, evil].

10:33 So indeed, being made a gazing stock [publicly humiliated] by both reproaches [sufferings] and afflictions and by this have become companions with the-ones-behaving [walking, participating] also in this same manner.

10:34 You also sympathized with me in my bonds and with joy the-snatching [plundering, spoiling, robbing] of your possessions in anticipation knowing that in yourselves is in (the) Heavens a better property [possession] and is permanent [not departing].

10:35 Then do not be casting away your boldness which has a great reward,

10:36　for you have need of endurance that you should be obtaining The-Promised-Blessing doing The-Will-of-*THE-GOD*.

10:37　**"For in a very, very little while *The-One-Coming* shall be arriving and shall not be delaying"** [Isa 29:17]

10:38　and, **"The-just-one of shall-be-living of-believing [by belief, by faith] and if ever he-should-be-shrinking [withdraw]** *MY* **soul is not delighted with him."** [Hab 2:3]

10:39　But we are not shrinking back into destruction [utter-destruction] but by-believing [faith] procuring [preserving, securing] of (the) soul.

HEBREWS 11

11:1　Now believing is a confidence [conviction] of an accomplished feat not being observed [of that which is invisible, unseen, looked upon].

11:2　In this, the-seniors [elders, forefathers] were witnesses [testified to, were a witness to divine revelation or inspiration, showed an honorable testimony].

11:3　By-believing, we have perfect understanding to declare The-Eons [period of ages, time periods]-of-*GOD* from that which is not apparently-seen to that which is to coming to be seen.

11:4　By believing, Abel offered a better sacrifice than Cain to *THE-GOD* by which he was shown to-be-just [righteous] by *THE-GOD*. Because of his honored-gifts [presents] and by her {the accepted offerings} [it, them], he is still speaking in death.

11:5　By believing, Enoch was transplanted to avoid death and could not be found because before being transferred by *THE-GOD* he had been testified as [declared, witnessed, affirmed] to-have-well-pleased [been favored by] *THE-GOD*.

11:6　For without believing (its) powerless [impotent, unable to be done, impossible] to-please-well for the-one must believe coming to *THE-GOD* that *HE-IS* and becoming to the-ones seeking [crave, beg, scrutinize, investigate] *HIM* a *REWARDER*.

11:7　Noah by believing was warned [divinely-instructed] concerning things not-as-yet being observed. Being pious, constructs The-Ark saving his household by which he-condemned The-System [world] and by belief [faith] became righteous, an Enjoyer-of-The-Allotment.

11:8　By believing, Abraham being called, obeyed coming out into the place he was about to obtain as a possession and came out not knowing [being acquainted] where he was going.

Section IV

11:9 By believing he lived next to The-Land-of-Promise as a stranger [foreigner, an enemy], living in tents [tabernacles] with Isaac and Jacob, The-Joint-Participants of The-same-Promise.

11:10 For he waited [expected] for The-City, the-foundations whose artist [craftsman] and builder [author of the work, architect]—*THE-GOD*.

11:11 By believing, Sarah, she had strength [ability] to get [receive] injected semen beyond (her) season of prime, giving birth since she believed *THE-ONE-PROMISING* believable [faithful].

11:12 Though declared [considered] as dead [impotent, unable to bear a child] from one has been generated [born, birthed] just-as many as the multitude of constellations of the heaven and as the innumerable sand along the shoreline of the sea.

11:13 These all died in belief [faith] not obtaining The-Promises but from a distance from them knew and were persuaded and welcomed and vowed they are strangers and foreigners [expatriates of] on the earth.

11:14 For such the-ones openly said [declared] that they are seeking-diligently [clamoring for, craving, wishing] (the) *FATHER'S*-place [one's fatherland].

11:15 And if truly they remembered from where they came out of, they may [could] have had the opportunity to return.

11:16 But now, they are craving a better (place), this of heavenly origin where *THE-GOD* is not ashamed of them, to put the name of [be surnamed, be given the name, be named after, the title of] *God* on them, for them *HE-MAKES* ready a city.

11:17 By believing, Abraham being tested led [presented as an offering] Isaac, indeed the-only-begotten. After having led, [presented the offering] received The-Promises.

11:18 To who was spoken [declared], "That in Isaac your seed shall be called [invited, named, titled],"

11:19 {Abraham} calculated [reasoned and was thoroughly-convinced] that out of the-dead-ones *THE-GOD* is able to arouse [rise-up, resurrect] him and by parable [according-to the stories, the legends, the folklores] recover the-risk {receive Isaac from death}.

11:20 By believing, Isaac blessed Jacob and Esau concerning what will come to pass [is destined to be, about to be].

11:21 By believing, Jacob while dying blessed each of the sons of Joseph and worshiped [while leaning, propping himself up] on the top of his staff.

11:22   By believing, Joseph when dying called to remembrance concerning The-Exodus to The-Sons-of-Israel and commanded [ordered] concerning [what to do with] his bones.

11:23   By believing, Moses being born was hid three months by his parents because they saw the little boy was attractive-and-not-ordinary and was not afraid of the mandate of The-King.

11:24   By believing, Moses already with rank [power, importance] denied [abdicated, refused, rejected] being called The-Son-of-the-Daughter-of-Pharaoh

11:25   preferring rather to be sharing persecution with The-People-of-*THE-GOD* than for a season [temporarily] to have pleasure born from sins.

11:26   Deeming [accounting, believing, reasoning, regarding] The-Reproach [rebuking] of *The-Anointed* was of greater riches than the treasures in Egypt, steadfastly-gazing on that reward.

11:27   By believing, he left Egypt not being afraid of the-fury of The-King steadfastly paying-heed-to *THE-INVISIBLE-ONE*.

11:28   By believing, he carried out The-Passover and the-pouring of the-blood so that The-Exterminating-One of the firstborn would not injure them.

11:29   By believing, they crossed-over The-Red-Sea as if dry, which the-Egyptians while attempting to-reclaim [recapture] were-swallowed-up [drowned].

11:30   By belief, the-walls of Jericho fell after being surrounded seven days.

11:31   By believing, Rahab the-prostitute received the-spies with peace and was not destroyed [perished] with the-ones-being-stubborn [not believing].

11:32   And further-more, my lacking (time), I could speak relating the times concerning Gideon, Barak, also about Samson and Jephtha, David, also about Samuel and the-prophets.

11:33   Who through believing [faith] brought down kingdoms, worked righteousness, obtained [received] promises, barred the-mouths of lions,

11:34   extinguished fire's strength, escaped the sword's edge, from weakness [cowardice] became strong [valiant] in the line of battle routing foreigners.

11:35   Women received their dead-ones back to life and others were beaten up [tortured] not expecting [accepting, allowing access to] deliverance so they-may-be-obtaining [reach, getting, securing] of that best Resurrection.

11:36   Further other ones in trials of mockeries and scourging [whippings] and still more in bonds and imprisonment.

SECTION IV

11:37 They were stoned, they were sawn, they were tried for murder, they died from the sword, they wandered about in sheep and goatskins; being destitute, afflicted and treated evilly.

11:38 Of whom the-system [world] was not worthy; wandering in the wildernesses and mountain and cave and the holes in the earth.

11:39 And all of these were giving a witness [honorable testimony] by believing not having received The-Promise.

11:40 THE-GOD has something better to look forward to concerning us, that not apart from us [without us] they may be matured [perfected, complete].

HEBREWS 12

12:1 Surely then since we also have such a vast and encompassing cloud of witnesses for us, put off every encumbrance, [burden, weight] and long-standing sins that we may racing with endurance the-contest before us.

12:2 Turn your attention to *The-Origin* and *Leader* and *Perfecter* of The-Belief [faith], *Savior*. Who instead of the joyful-condition [appointed-state] at beforehand [he-possessed, was present with] *Him*, endured the-disgrace [dishonor] of the despised [contemptible and hated] Pale [crucifixion] and is seated to the right of The-Throne of THE-GOD.

12:3 Take this into account about *The-One* having endured such opposition by sinners to [against] *Him* that you may not be faltering and your souls fainting.

12:4 You have not as of yet resisted [battled] by [with, using] blood to fight against sin.

12:5 And you have been oblivious to the pleading which was discussed with you as a son: **"*MY* son, do not hate the disciplining [nurturing, instruction, chastening] of *MASTER*! Do not weaken [be faint hearted, despondent] being corrected by *HIM*."**

12:6 **"Whom the *MASTER* loves *HE* is disciplining and every son whom *HE* acknowledges *HE* scourges."** [Prov 3:11, 12]

12:7 If you endure the disciplining as sons, THE-GOD will carry you. For what father is there who does not discipline his son?

12:8 And if you go without disciplining, as all have become participants of, then you are bastards and not sons.

12:9 Further, indeed if our fleshly fathers we have are discipliners and we give them reverence, how much more then shall we be set under [yield to the admonition of] THE-FATHER of The-Spirits and we shall be living?

12:10   Indeed, for few are the-days for the-ones which seems to them as chastising, yet profitable for the-ones that are-to-be-participating in the-holiness of *HIM*.

12:11   For indeed all chastening in the-present is not seen to be as joy but painful [sorrowful, grievous] and yet for the-ones being vigorously exercised through her [it], peaceable fruit of righteousness is given back.

12:12   Therefore erect-up [stiffen, raise, elevate] the exhausted hands and the tottering [feeble, weakened] knees,

12:13   and make a straight path for your feet that no one lame be turned away [shunned, turned aside] but rather may be healed.

12:14   Be chasing [earnestly endeavoring to acquire] peace with all and the-holy, apart from which no one shall be seeing *THE-MASTER*.

12:15   Watching carefully that not any are left behind [fail to become a partner, come late or is tardy] from The-Grace-of-*THE-GOD*. Nor any root of bitterness to sprout up [be born, grow] where through this many are defiled [contaminated, stained].

12:16   Nor any unlawful sexual intercourse [fornication, male prostitution] or profanity [ungodliness] or as Esau, who for one meal [sustenance] gave away [rejected] his birthright.

12:17   For you are aware that afterwards he repented of his rejection [decision] seeking her [it] out with even great tears, yet no place was found for him in The-Blessing to enjoy The-Allotment.

12:18   For you have not come to a mountain [high ranking preeminent one] that can be stroked-touched [seeking tokens, be bought-off] and consumed by fire [motivated by enraged anger] and murkiness [being under-handed, say one thing but do another intentionally] and darkness [blindness, no regard for an action or damage caused] and a sudden storm [impulsive, not predictable]

12:19   and a blaring trumpet [clamorous, confusing] and authoritative [booming, frightening, ominous, scary] voice which the-ones hearing begged no more words be spoken any more.

12:20   For they could not carry out [stand, bear, endure] the assignment [demand, request, be open minded to, in agreement with]; "If at any time a wild beast may come into contact with The-Mountain it shall be stoned or shot down with an arrow."

12:21   And so fearful was the spectacle [appearance, event, demonstration] (even) Moses said, "I am terrified and quaking!"

Section IV

12:22   But you have come to Mount Zion [Sion] and to The-City-of-*(THE)-LIVING-GOD*, heavenly Jerusalem with tens of thousands [innumerable multitudes] of messengers [envoys, angels],

12:23   to a universal convocation [assembly] and brought forward first by The-Called-Out [ecclesia] with a registry [a pedigree, a lineage, a record, known] in heaven; and to *GOD-JUDGE-OF-ALL* and to Spirits as Just-Ones having been perfected,

12:24   and to *Savior, Mediator* of the-fresh [recently born, new] covenant, with blood appointed for sprinkling [purifying] more excellent than spoken of Abel.

12:25   You beware! Do not be refusing [rejecting, avoiding, shunning] *THE-ONE-REVEALING*. For if they will not flee [find safety, escape] refusing [rejecting] *The-One-Revealed* on earth, how much greater we {will not escape}, the-ones turning from [rejecting, deserting] *The-One* from Heavens?

12:26   Whose voice then tottered [violently-shakes, severely-earthquakes] the earth but now *HE*-has-promised saying, **"I will still once again quake not only The-Earth, but also The-Heaven**!" [Hag 2:6,7]

12:27   And that being shaken once again is to show [make clear, display openly, be obvious, leave no doubt] what being transferred [removed or replaced, change of things instituted or established] should be remaining and should not be shaken [are to be left in place, standing].

12:28   So that we may receive an unshakeable [permanent] Kingdom. May-we-have grace through which we-may-be-offering-well-pleasing-divine-service to *THE-GOD* with reverence [Godly-honor, respect] and piety [godly-fear, veneration].

12:29   For even *THE-GOD* also has a consuming-fire [burning passion] for us.

HEBREWS 13

13:1   Let the-brotherly-affection continue!

13:2   Do not forget hospitality, for in doing this we were oblivious we lodged some messengers [Angels].

13:3   Keep being mindful of the-bound-ones [prisoners] as being bound-together with them and the-ones being maltreated for you be [are] of the same Body.

13:4   Marriage is honorable for all and the-undefiled-bed. But male prostitution [fornicators, unlawful sexual intercourse] shall be judged by *THE-GOD*.

13:5 Do not love silver [money]; be satisfied with the present manner of life. *HE* has declared, **"*I* will not ever give up [let sink, send back] nor will I ever forsake [abandon, desert] you."** [Deut 31:6; Josh 1:5]

13:6 With us have courage to say, **"*THE MASTER* is my helper and what shall I be afraid of that a man can do to me?"** [Ps 27:1, 118:6]

13:7 Be remembering the-ones leading [before] you who speak [utter, talk, preach] *The-Word*-of-*THE-GOD* to you. Consider along with their behavior you-being-imitators of their believing [faith].

13:8 *Savior Anointed* [Christ], *The-Same-One* yesterday, today and also into the-eons.

13:9 Do not be carried off with various and strange teachings. For a purified [genuine] heart is established by grace [*GODLY*-gifting], not by food which has no benefit [profitability] for the-ones walking about.

13:10 We have an Altar which the-ones offering divine service at The-Tabernacle have no authority to be eating off of [from].

13:11 For the bodies [carcasses] of those animals, whose blood for sins is carried into The-Holy-of -Holies by The-Chief-Sacred-One [high priest] is burned-up outside The-Camp

13:12 where *Savior* suffered making-holy through his own blood the-people outside of The-Gate.

13:13 Now then, may we come forward to *Him*, (from) outside The-Camp, carrying *His* abasement [condemnation].

13:14 For we do not have here a permanent city, but we are diligently looking for [wish for, crave] The-One-Impending.

13:15 Through *Him* then may we be offering up continually sacrifices of praise to *THE-GOD*, this is fruit from the lips, confessing [declaring] *THE-NAME-OF-HIM*.

13:16 And also do not be forgetting fellowshipping [gathering together] and doing good to others for such sacrifices greatly-pleases *THE-GOD*.

13:17 Be convinced to yield to the-ones leading you. For they are watching over your souls and will give an account. That with joy may they be doing this and not ones groaning for this is disadvantageous for you.

13:18 Pray concerning about us that we have confidence with a pure conscience, that we are able to have in all honest behavior.

13:19 And to a greater degree I am begging to do this that I may return to you very quickly.

Section IV

13:20 Now *THE-GOD-OF-THE-PEACE*, *THE-ONE-LEADING* (navigating) out of the-dead-ones *The-Great-Shepherd*-of-The-Sheep through *The-Blood*-of-The-Eonian-Covenant, *The-Master*-of-us, *Savior*,

13:21 that *He* may equip you for every good act, in doing The-Will-of-*HIM*, working in you what is well-pleasing in *HIS* sight, through *Savior-Anointed* to who be glory [the-esteem] into The-Eons.

13:22 And I am calling on you, Brothers, to endure in *The-Word* and with encouragement for I have written to you in few words.

13:23 You know that Brother Timothy has been released, with whom, if ever he may come, shortly I will see you.

13:24 Greet all the-ones leading you and all the-Holy-Ones are greeting you, the-ones from Italy.

13:25 The-Grace to all of you.

Amen.

Section V

A WILL AND TESTAMENT, THE TRANSFER OF AUTHORITY

THE LETTERS OF I AND II TIMOTHY

I TIMOTHY COMMENTARY

THE FOLLOWING LETTERS OF Paul are first and foremost all personal in nature, directly written to Timothy and designed to provide personal instructions and warnings to the one revealed within the Ecclesia as the successor to Paul's position as The Commissioner for the Nations. Paul pours out all his godly-love, passion, and concern to Timothy, a father terribly anxious about his son's actions and success. It's just as if the originator of a successful business now needs to turn over all affairs to his son or successors.

I Timothy immediately reconfirms God and Christ, The-Belief, a reconfirmation that the Law of Moses does have its place but only for the truly righteous, The Secret, and to live according-to Godly-love for all.

If anyone doubts whether this letter has any legal authority, the first opening line by Paul says that his commission came directly from a "legal order of God." This also is not just an ordinary letter to a longtime friend. There is anxiousness and great concern in this letter. Therefore, all instructions which follow from Paul to Timothy will have the same binding authority as Paul speaking personally and directly to all or any. Paul reminds Timothy of the oath he took in front of many, and many of those were the prominent elders within the Ecclesia as witnesses. This swearing in ceremony for Timothy was attended by many because of its sensitivity and importance. As speculation, John or Paul may have even been part of this activity. Many people probably do not realize that all the remaining Apostles still communicated with each other despite distance and location. For instance, see Peter's discourse on understanding Paul and his writings (II Peter 3:16). Paul reminds him that he is obligated to keep his promise not only to them, but more importantly to God and Christ.

I Timothy provides the instructions for operating an effective Ecclesia and effective teaching of The-Belief. Also as the personal minister now, he instructs all the Ecclesia to first pray and give thanks for the sake of all men, next for those in authority, and then to lead a quiet and peaceable life.

Paul then offers advice for serving The Elders as a father, the elderly women as mothers, and others as a caring and ever-guarding elder brother for his younger brothers and sisters.

Section V

Paul instructs all to be done in modesty and then lays out the pattern for determining and selecting those wishing to serve The-Body-of-Christ, the position of women as leaders in the Ecclesia, and slaves wishing to serve.

Paul follows up with a direct prophecy of a great falling away and a disbelief in The-Secret.

Paul then turns his attention back to Timothy, specifically providing the plan to follow in order to insure his staying loyal and true and remaining in The-Belief.

The remaining topics deal with elders, widows, being gainfully employed, living with unbelievers, ordination practices, slavery with its slippery slope for both master and slave, and avoiding the deception that prosperity or those preaching this empty philosophy is a sign of God loving and blessing you.

In the end Paul just doesn't advise Timothy; he commands him to keep the instructions and orders handed to him. Paul is dead serious about Timothy's success and the great battle Paul knows is lying ahead for Timothy as the new lead of the Ecclesiae. Paul is preparing Timothy for the future and giving him direct marching orders as the principal attorney of The Body of Christ of the Nations and the Ecclesia in general. In effect, this is the will and testament of Paul himself to his predecessor, but for us today it is an effective and meaningful set of instruction and practices for those who are shepherding and guiding anyone.

I TIMOTHY AS A LETTER

PAUL, COMMISSIONER OF *SAVIOR Anointed* by the legal order of *GOD*, *SAVIOR* of us and of *Master Savior Anointed*, *The-Hope* of us. To Timotheus, a genuine offspring in belief; grace, mercy, peace from *GOD*, *FATHER* of us and *Savior-Anointed*, *The-Master* of us.

As I continued going to Macedonia, I instructed you to remain in Ephesus, that you-were-to-be-ordering certain-ones to-not-be-teaching-something different other than the edification in The-Belief of *THE-GOD*, nor pay-attention to-myths and endless genealogies or-be authors-of controversy.

For the complete-obedience of The-Law ends in Godly-love out of a clean heart and good conscience and an unhypocritical belief of-which some have deviated being-turned-aside by empty-teaching determined to-be Law-teachers with no understanding about what they-are-saying or any concern about what they-are-insisting.

For we-agree-and-confirm the laws are ideal if anyone can ever lawfully use it. Understanding this, the law was-not-provided for the righteous but for the lawless and disobedient, condemning ungodliness and sinners, maligners and profane, those committing patricide and matricide, murderers, male prostitutes, homosexuals, kidnappers, liars, false-swearers also with anything different to oppose sound teaching with which I was-entrusted, The-Well-Message-of-the-Glory-of-*THE-BLESSED-GOD*. And I have unbounding-thanks for *The-One-Strengthening* me, *Anointed Savior*, *The-Master* of us that believing in me placed me into this service who before was a blasphemer-and-slanderer and persecutor and filled-with-great-pride-and-greatly-insulting-others. But I-was-given-mercy for I did this being-ignorant and in unbelief.

But *THE-MASTER* in-exceeding-abundance-pours-out-on us The-Grace by The-Belief and Godly-love in *The-Anointed-Savior*. Believable is this saying and worthy of all acceptance that *Anointed Savior* came into The-System to save sinners of whom I am the first-in-rank-and-first-in-line. And it is because of this I-was-shown-mercy that to me first *Savior Anointed* might-be-displaying unlimited patience as a pattern for the-ones following believing in *Him* into life eonian.

Now to *THE-ETERNAL-KING*, *INCORRUPTIBLE*, *INVISIBLE*, the *ONLY-WISE-GOD* honor and glory into the Eons of the Eons.

Amen!

Section V

This instruction I am committing to you, son Timotheus, according-to the prophecies that were made concerning you that you are to wage a great warfare with them. Keep believing with a good conscience which some have discarded-and-abandoned concerning The-Belief. They-have-caused-a-shipwreck, just as Hymeneus and Alexander whom I-turned-over to The-Satan that-they-may-be-trained to not make-malicious-false-statements.

I encourage you therefore to first of all make confiding-requests, prayers, petitions, and giving-thanks for the sake of all men. For kings and all the-ones being in authority that we-may-lead mild and quiet lives in all godliness and dignity. For this is approved and agreeable in-view of *GOD, THE-SAVIOR* of us. Who intends to-save all men and to come to the Knowledge-of-Truth. For there is *ONE-GOD* and *One-Mediator-of-GOD* and men, *The-Man-Anointed-Savior, The-One-Giving* himself in exchange for a ransom for-the-sake of all, *The-Testimony* in the season appointed into which I was-appointed to proclaim and be-a commissioner. I declare this to be true by *Anointed*. I am not lying. A teacher in-Belief and Truth to the Nations. It-is-my-intentions that the-men be-praying in every place, lifting up holy hands without anger-due-to-punishment-received and hesitation.

Same also the-women, to dress well-decorated in regard-for-others and adorn themselves in self-control, not braided with gold or pearls or very-costly garments but that which fits women professing reverence-for-GOD through good actions. In quietness let a woman be-learning with all willing-subjection. And I am not permitting a woman to-be-teaching, nor to-be-domineering-and-have authority-over men and to not-be-meddling-in-the-affairs-of-others. For Adam was molded first, then Eve. For Adam was-not-seduced, but the woman being-seduced became the transgressor. Yet she-shall-be-rescued through child-bearing if ever they-should-continue-remaining in belief and Godly-love and holiness and self-control.

This is a true statement, if any covets-and-desires to supervise, he-is-desiring an honorable work. The-supervisor is obligated to-be-beyond-censure-or-criticism, the husband of one wife, sober, self-controlled, modest, hospitable, and able-to-skillfully-teach. Not a wine-drunkard, not quarrelsome, not greedy for gain, but patient, not a fighter or brawler, not driven for money, presiding properly over his own household, his-children well-behaved in all respects. For how can men care for the Ecclesia if anyone is not able to preside over his own household? Not a new-convert so-that he-should-not-be-falling into conceit and judgment by The-Adversary. More he must also have a good report from the-ones not in the Ecclesia that he-should-not-fall into criticism-and-accusations and trapped by The-Adversary.

The same for servants, honorable, not double-tongued, not addicted to excessive wine, not greedy-for-gain, firmly believing The-Secret-of-The-Belief with a clean conscience. And also, let-them-first-be-tested-and-proven blameless, then let-them-serve.

The same for their-wives, honorable, not gossipers, temperate with wine, faithful in all. Let the servers be husbands of one wife, presiding over their children and over their own households. For the-ones serving are getting-for-themselves a good position of dignity with great boldness in Belief in *The-Anointed-Savior*.

I wrote all of this hoping to come to you soon. Yet if I may-be-delayed-for-an-unusually-extended-time, you know how the house of-*GOD* is to conduct themselves which is The-Ecclesia-of-the-*LIVING-GOD*, *THE PILLAR* and *FOUNDATION* of *The-Truth*.

For there-is-no-possibility-for-deniably-arguing-about the holiness-and-purposeful-sureness of The-Secret! *God* was without-doubt-or-question in the flesh, was-declared-righteous in spirit, was-observed-and-watched by messengers, was exposed among the Nations, was-believed in by The-System, was-taken-up in majesty-and-the-most-exalted-state.

But the spirit is clearly-and-plainly affirming that in coming seasons some shall-be-withdrawing from The-Belief heeding to imposter spirits and teachings of demons. In hypocrisy, speaking lies, their own consciences cauterized. Forbidding marriage, to not have foods that *THE-GOD* created for receiving-and-use with thanksgiving for the-ones believing and know the truth. For every created-thing of *GOD* is good and nothing is to-be-rejected but eaten with thanksgiving. For it has-been-hallowed through *GOD*'s word and prayerful-conversations.

If you are supplying these things to the brothers, you-shall-be-a good servant of *Savior Anointed*. Forming-the-mind-and-educating in the instructions of The-Belief and the genuine-and-precious teaching which you-have-fully-followed. Yet you-refuse the unholy and you strive earnestly to become godly-with-piety-toward-God. For exercising the body has few benefits yet the-godliness is profitable for all, having the Promise-of-Life that is now and the Impending. These words are believable and worthy of all acceptance. For to this we-are-toiling also and we-are-being-reviled, that we rely on the *Living-God* who is the *Savior* of all men especially of-believing-ones. These things command and teach.

Let no man take-advantage of your youth; you become a model of the-believing-ones, in conversations-and-doctrine, in behavior, in Godly-love, in spirit, in belief, in purity.

Until I come, devote-thought-and-effort-to reading, to exhortation, to the-teaching. Do-not-not-be-careless with the gracious gift which was given to you when the elders placed their hands on you through a prophetic-message. Meditate on these things; devote yourself in these that your advancement-and-growth may be apparent to all. Take care to watch after yourself and be-persistent in the-teaching and doing them. For in this you-shall-be-saving yourself and the-ones hearing you.

Do not express disapproval with a senior but approach him like a father and those younger as brothers, the elderly women as mothers, and the younger-women as sisters with all propriety-and-purity.

Honor the widows that are really widows, and if any widow has children or grandchildren let them first teach at their own home to be pious and to return-in-like

Section V

what-is-due to the parents for this is good and acceptable in-the-sight of *GOD*. For the-one that is really a widow and is alone relies on *THE-GOD* and is continually in requests and prayers night and day. For the-one in-luxury-with-a-voluptuous-life is dead though living. And in this you be declaring that they may-be blameless.

And if anyone is not providing for their own, especially family-members, he-has rejected The-Belief and is worse than an unbeliever. No widow is-to-be-listed as a widow less than sixty years old, having been the wife of one husband, been-confirmed doing good actions or brought-up her children or lodging-strangers or washes the feet of the Holy-Ones or relieved the-ones afflicted or imitates every good deed. But refuse the younger widow for when they feel the impulses of sexual desires wishing to marry again have-placed-second-in-importance *The-Anointed* receiving judgment since they have done-away-with their first Belief. Further yet, they-are-learning to become idle-ones making-a-circuit between homes. Not only idle, but also gossipers and meddlers talking about-what is-not-right-and-proper. I desire then the younger widows remarry, to bear children, manage the household providing no incentive to The-One-Opposing to-insult-and-berate grace. For some have already returned after The-Satan. If a widow is with a believing man or woman, let them take care of her. Do not let her burden the Ecclesia so the-ones who are really widows should-be-attended to.

Ideally the presiding Elders should-be-counted-worthy of double honor, especially the-ones toiling in preaching and teaching. For the-writings say you shall not muzzle the threshing ox and the worker is worthy of the-wages of him.

Do not agree-to-allow an Elder's accusation without two or three witness. The-one's sinning, expose them in the-sight-of all so that the remaining may-have fear. I-am-commanding in-the-sight-of *THE-GOD* and *Master Savior Anointed* and the-chosen-messengers that you are to guard-and-not-violate these, without prejudice, doing nothing with a bias.

Do not place hands on anyone to quickly or participating in sin with others. Be keeping yourself pure. Do not drink water any longer but use a little wine because of your stomach and your frequent infirmities.

Some men's sins are openly-evident heading for judgment and others are to follow-imitating-them. Likewise, openly-evident also good work but those-not-doing-good wishing to be hid cannot hide.

Whoever may be under the yoke of slavery, let them deem all honor to their own owners that the name of *THE-GOD* and the doctrine may-not-be-blasphemed. And those having believing owners do-not-despise them knowing they are brothers. But rather let-them-slave knowing-that they-are believers and beloved, participants of The-Benefit. These things you teach and exhort. If anyone is teaching different and not agreeing-to-the true-and-incorruptible words of *The-Master* of us *Savior Anointed* or with the devout teaching, he is conceited, knows nothing other than about a-morbid-fondness-for creating-doubt and controversies out of which develops envy, strife, vile-verbal-abuse, wicked inferences-and-suspicions, constant-contentions. Men of corrupted minds deprived of *The-Truth*. Remove yourself from these holding-by-custom that to-be acquiring-wealth-and-being-wealthy is a sign-of-being favored by God.

But godliness with contentment is great gain. For we carried nothing into The-System; most certainly we not able to carry-out anything and we-shall-be-content with nourishment and clothing. But the-ones intending to-be-rich are-falling into many trials and traps and many foolish and harmful desires which swamp-and-drown men into complete-ruin and destruction. For the love-of-money is a root for all of the evils which some crave and were-led-astray from The-Belief and surround themselves in great sorrow-and-grief.

But you, oh man of *THE-GOD*, you flee from these things! You passionately-pursue godliness, belief, Godly-love, endurance, meekness. Fight the great battle of The-Belief, unrelentingly-hold on to the eonian life into which you are also called to and you confessed-declared-and-swore an approved-honorable promise in-the-sight-a multitude of witnesses.

I-am-commanding you before *THE-GOD, THE-ONE-MAKING-LIVE* The-All and *Anointed Savior, The-One-Testifying* to Pontius Pilate the true-factual-and-accurate public proclamation-claim-assertion-and-affirmation. You are-to-keep these directions free from vice, not-open-to-criticism until the appearance of *The-Master* of us *Savior Anointed* when at his own season shall-be-showing *The-Happy* and *Only-Potentate, The-King-of-Kings,* and *Lord-of-Lords The-Only-One* with immortality, dwelling in an-unapproachable light that no man has seen or can comprehend to whom is eonian honor-by-rank-state-and-reverence and dominion-power-and-might.

Instruct-and-warn the-ones who are currently wealthy to-not-be-proud or rely on uncertain riches but in *THE-GOD, THE-LIVING-ONE-SUPPLYING* us richly in all-things enjoyable. Those-doing-good-actions, be rich in good actions, ready-to-give, maintain communion and fellowship treasuring-up for-themselves an ideal foundation for The-Impending that they-may-insure-and-secure the eonian life.

Oh Timothy! You guard what-is-committed-to-your-trust, turn away from the ungodly useless discussions, and oppose false-so-called knowledge that some are-claiming. They-deviate from The-Belief.

The-Grace with you, Timothy.

Amen.

(I Timothy was written from Laodicea, which is the mother city of Phrygia Pacatiana)

I TIMOTHY STUDY NOTES

Note: Through my many translations, I have come to believe that the phrase or associated phrasing of "inheritance" [ex: Col 1:12] accurately translated as "the-allotment" in Scripture is not a good or proper translation (i.e., inheritance). Paul makes it clear that we are to be family members (I state: royal and godly) destined to be with HIM and HE with us and we in Christ and He in us. Inheritance has an implied connotation, an accepted concept that someone has died. THE-GOD is certainly not dead, and Christ has risen to life eonian (there are times of times of times) as well. I see this as a watering down of the intent and meaning of the Scriptures and have dropped using the word *inheritance* when speaking of THE-GOD's plan and purpose for us. We are to take rulership in an active kingdom with Christ at the head of the realm and we under Him, with THE-GOD over all of us.

Note The Greek word *agapen* translated as "love" in most translations is missing that this is Godly in nature and not of men or any other such creature. I have therefore carried the adjective to add clarity to the meaning of this word throughout this translation.

Note: In my research, nearly all translations have dropped "the" as a modifier, but the Greek word for "the" is in every text and not meant to be ignored or deleted. It is often specifically singular, and when attached to the noun, it is describing that noun as unique, one of a kind, a specific thing, the original, the one and only. It is for this reason that I carry "the" everywhere it appears in all translations. Whether of God, Jesus, Satan or any other entity, concept, or idea, the modifier "the" clears up a lot of generalized words, ideas, concepts, and entities.

Note: The root of the word *pnuemia*, translated as "spirit, wind, or breath," has no gender identity since this is a word that is neuter in gender. *Pnuemia* is an "it." The Greeks, as we of English language, often fix a gender to objects and things—for example: cars, boats, the moon, the sun. For the Greeks, *pnuemia* at times has a male gender affixed to it. *Pnuemia* in the Scriptures is never capitalized or designated as a standalone being, entity, principality, or sovereignty when used as the word "spirit." It is simply the power inherent in the

I TIMOTHY STUDY NOTES

being, whether of man, or God, or Christ, or any other entity. If anything is living, "it" possesses a spirit. The "Holy-spirit" is simply the power from and of The-God, giving and renewing life and performing The-God's will.

Note: Paul constantly claims and mentions "principles, powers, authorities, sovereignties not of our world." He quite clearly claims that these beings are the ones that certainly influence and control (predominately in a negative way) the systems of this world, people of the nations, and as individuals directly. You can find this concept also contained in The Old Testament through the implications of the first commandment. This claim and the concept of the warring factions in heaven makes a fascinating study.

Note: Time periods, eons, ages, millennia, eons, and eons—I stayed true to the Greek words associated with time and what we still use today in our common language. A study of time periods is fascinating but is also an area that can cause confusion. The-God always works on some kind of a timetable, but understanding which is which and when is when is a bit of a mystery. Some timetables are only known to The-God and made clear to man at God's will.

Note What is the difference between "expectation" and "hope?" Nearly all translations adopt the word "hope" for "expectation," but Paul uses almost exclusively the word "expectation." Here is why I constantly use "expectation." Having an expectation means you have no doubt at all. It is sure and certain with no ambiguity or doubt. Having a hope means you are not 100 percent convinced and convicted. I can tell you that Paul is undeniably convinced and convicted in what he delivers and talks about. Using "hope" sends a message that there is some possibility for "wiggle room," doubt, error, or excuses.

Even worse, much of the use of the word "expectation" in Paul's writings has the modifier "the" attached to "expectation," thus forming the proper translation and singular concept of "The-Expectation." This makes "The-Expectation" an event, not a philosophy or theological premise. Not recognizing "The-Expectation" as an event will lead the reader immediately down an incorrect understanding of what is being offered or discussed.

1:15 The phrase "The-System" is often substituted with the singular concept and word "world." But to substitute this in the translation would stop the reader from grasping the scope and breadth of "The-System." The-System is meant to include all intelligent creatures or creation; systems of operations throughout the universes, heavens, and earth; all creation itself and that which has been created. This verse causes great reflection on the majesty of God's plans, will, divine purpose, and actions.

2:9 This verse is a direct reference and summarization of "The-Secret" revealed to the Ecclesiae. See also verses 3:9, 3:16.

Section V

3:16   The Greek word *aggelois* translated as "messengers" here does not mean only angels but any of the heavenly agents. We know this because Satan was always looking for a way to dominate and rule over Christ, and he is more than a messenger.

3:16   The phrase "was believed by the System" is a testament, an incriminating charge, a decree by Paul stating that all of the creations of God, in the heavens, on the earth, and those below the earth know Christ is the Anointed Savior, Appointed King of Kings, Lords of Lords and preeminent in all matters, including knowledge, wisdom, and power.

4:2   "their own conscience's cauterized [branded] . . ." All translations agree that this is to be understood as the demons' souls are branded, as animals are branded with an identifying mark, with the marking of sins or carrying the continual consciousness of sin. Hence there is a searing or cauterizing in their minds and they have been removed the way medically something has been removed by cauterizing.

4:3   "believing and know the truth." This phrase also includes understanding how not to offend the weaker members of the Ecclesia concerning the burnt sacrifices offered to the temple idols. See all of Paul's progressive writings and instructions in his earlier letters.

4:6   "Yet you-refuse the profane [unhallowed, common]." The bracketed words are a direct Hebrew equivalent for the word "profane." With this understanding, the idea would be the Jewish attitude and approach toward anything to do with Gentile practices and interaction—that is, to clearly avoid a Gentile at all cost that could "taint" or "make them unclean."

4:10   "that we rely on the Living-God who is the Savior of all men especially of-believing-ones." Take note of the bolded words in this verse. I did not make the bolded words all capital letters, but I have identified both of these titles with Christ, not with THE-GOD. However, I want to focus on the title "Living-God." This is The Christ; a man now being called a God. This is equating Jesus with the same authority, power, and surname as THE-GOD. Christ made the claim by being God as all men are now stated to be in Psalm 82:6. This will be reiterated again in I Timothy 4:14 and throughout the letter. This is profound because we were created to follow Jesus and be in the image of GOD. We too upon our resurrection will also be called God. I shudder thinking about the responsibility and purpose we will have being a God. Meditating on this is overwhelming for me.

4:14   Was there a prophecy in the Old Testament concerning Timothy? Not directly, but commentaries recognize that in the New Testament Ecclesia prophets were provided to teach, receive proper interpretations of the Old Testament writing, provide predictions of future events, and encourage the struggling and blooming Ecclesia. There must have been some sort of revelations provided to the prophets in the Ecclesiae concerning Timothy. In his ordination Timothy must have not only received the Holy-sprit for his office in the ministry, but also the gifts associated with the role and needs of a prophet for the Ecclesia. The inference is that Timothy is to be the head of the Ecclesiae in the future, and a great responsibility lay ahead of him that needed to be carefully taken care of and nurtured.

5:2   The Greek word *hagneia*, translated as "chasteness" or "purity," is rooted to the Nazirite vow activities found within the Old Covenant.

5:10   "washing the feet." While it was common to wash the feet of anyone entering a house since sandals were in fashion as footwear, this is also a reference to the early practice of foot washing as introduced by Jesus at the last meal where he washed the feet of his disciples. The practice is a demonstration of one's willingness to serve others, whether they were insignificant or important. The fact that "The-Master" washed the feet of his disciples was a shock to the disciples. The cultural practice was that the lowest of the servants or family members always washed the eminent entering the house. Christ turned the cultural practice upside down to teach the disciples to have a new approach and perspective of serving everyone they met.

5:11   For a discussion concerning this verse, I offer the following and invite the reader to decide if the conclusion fits the needs and actions of the times when this letter was written to Timothy—and also its potential application for today: http://www.biblegateway.com/resources/commentaries/IVP-NT/1Tim/Young-Widow

613:   "*The-One-Testifying* to Pontius Pilate the ideal [true, factual, accurate, exact] profession [public proclamation, claim, assertion, affirmation]" (italics mine). Here Paul is retelling the tale of this historic meeting in one sentence. This is more than a face-to-face private meeting between men. It was done in front of Pilate's seat of authority at the Praetorian in Fort Antonia (today's present Dome of the Rock complex) located just north of the Temple which was connected via a colonnade. It was an easy walk and a short distance from the High Priest's quarters in the Temple and the Hall of the Sanhedrin at the Temple to the Praetorian. A mob of priests, Sanhedrin, and riotous temple worshippers followed the procession taking Christ to Pilate. This "court room trial" was held out in the open, in public, with Jesus standing on the "pediment" before the worldly power and seat of authority where all could witness the proceedings. Having already been condemned to death by the Jews for sedition and blasphemy, Christ was now presented to the "principality and power of the age": the Roman Empire. This was one of the most dramatic and climatic events in all of history. The importance of Paul's statement is this: Christ personally and publicly confirmed the fact of his Sonship, Divinity, and Kingship before the "entire system" (more than just the system of this world). And while declared "innocent" of sedition and blasphemy, everyone still agreed to allow the torturing and killing of Jesus as a common thief, a national heretic and threat to the world governments (I include the spiritual realm within this statement). I would be derelict if I did not mention that, in addition to Christ being hung in crucifixion fashion, the Roman's methodology, those Jews passing Christ on the way to or from the Temple would have stoned him just as they did Stephen since he was condemned to death by the High Priest and Sanhedrin. This meant that Jesus was excommunicated from the Jewish society. Stoning was the Jewish methodology for State-sponsored deaths. The Jews and the Gentiles participated jointly in the killing of The Messiah. For more on this, see Dr. Ernest L. Martin's book *The Secrets of Golgotha*.

6:19   The word translated as "foundation" means the principles and doctrines of Christianity as Paul instructed and taught.

I TIMOTHY IN VERSE

I TIMOTHY 1

1:1 Paul, Commissioner [apostle] of *Savior Anointed* by the injunction [legal order, command, mandate] of *GOD, SAVIOR* [Deliverer, Preserver] of us and of *Master Savior Anointed, The-Hope* of us.

1:2 To Timotheus, a genuine offspring [child] in belief [faith]; grace, mercy, peace from *GOD, FATHER* of us and *Savior Anointed, The-Master* of us.

1:3 As (I continued) going into Macedonia, I instructed you to remain in Ephesus, that you-were-to-be-ordering [commanding] certain-ones to-not-be-teaching-something different

1:4 nor pay-attention to-myths [fictional-stories] and never-ending [endless] genealogies, authors-of [causing, bringing] debates [matters of controversy] other than the edification in The-Belief [faith] of *THE-GOD*.

1:5 For the consummation of-the-charge [complete-obedience of The-Law ends] in Godly-love out of a clean heart and good conscience and unhypocritical [sincere] belief [faith]

1:6 of-which some deviated, being-turned-aside by empty-speaking [teaching]

1:7 wishing [desiring, determined] to-be Law-teachers with no understanding about what they-are-saying or any concern about (what) they-are-insisting [strongly-asserting, claiming].

1:8 For we-know [agree and confirm] the Laws are ideal if anyone can ever lawfully use it.

1:9 Understanding this, the law was-not-laid [given, provided] for the righteous but for the lawless and disobedient [the unruly, uncontrollable], condemning ungodliness and sinners, maligners and profane, patricide and matricide, murderers,

Section V

1:10 paramours [male prostitutes], sodomites [homosexuals], kidnappers, liars, perjurers [false swearers] also with anything different to oppose sound teaching [doctrine]

1:11 with which I was-entrusted, The-Well-Message-of-the-Glory-of-*THE-BLESSED-GOD* [The-Happy-God, The-Joyous-God].

1:12 And I have unbounding-thanks for *The-One-Strengthening* me, *Anointed Savior, The-Master* of us that believing in me placed (me) into this service

1:13 who before was a calumniator [make malicious false statements about, blasphemed, railed at, dishonored, slander] and persecutor and an-insolent-man [filled with great pride and given to great insulting by word or action to others]. But I-was-given-mercy for I did this being-ignorant and in unbelief.

1:14 But the-Grace-of-*THE-MASTER* overwhelms [in exceeding-abundance pours out on] us by [because of, through] The-Belief and Godly-love in *The-Anointed-Savior*.

1:15 Believable (is) this saying and worthy of all acceptance that *Anointed Savior* came into The-System to save sinners of whom I am the first in place [first in line, first in rank, supreme].

1:16 And it is because of this I-was-shown-mercy that to me first *Savior Anointed* might-be- displaying all [unlimited] patience as a pattern [example] for the-ones following believing in *Him* into life eonian.

1:17 Now to THE-ETERNAL-KING, INCORRUPTIBLE, INVISIBLE, the ONLY-WISE-GOD honor and glory into the Eons of the Eons.

Amen!

1:18 This message [instructions, charge] I am committing to you, son Timotheus [Honoring God], according-to the prophecies that were made concerning you, that you are to wage a great warfare with them.

1:19 Hold [Keep the] believing and a good conscience which [that] some have thrust-away [thrown away, discarded, abandoned] concerning The-Belief [faith]. They-nautical-wreck [have-caused-a-shipwreck]

1:20 just as Hymeneus [Nuptial, the god of marriage Ibhar] and Alexander [Defender of people, Defender of man], whom I-gave-up [turned-over] to The-Satan [Adversary] that-they-may-be-trained to not make-malicious-false-statements [blaspheme].

I TIMOTHY IN VERSE

I TIMOTHY 2

2:1 I encourage you therefore to first of all, make confident-requests, prayers, petitions, and giving-thanks for the sake of all men.

2:2 For kings and all the-ones being in superiority [authority, pre-eminence] that we-may-lead mild and quiet lives in all godliness and dignity.

2:3 For this is ideal [approved] and welcomed [agreeable] in-view of *God, The-Savior* of us.

2:4 Who intends [has in mind] to-save all men and to come to the Knowledge-of-Truth.

2:5 For (there is) ONE-GOD and *One-Mediator-of-GOD* and men, *The-Man-Anointed-Savior*,

2:6 *The-One-Giving* himself in exchange for a ransom for-the-sake of all, *The-Testimony* [Witness] in the season appointed

2:7 into which I was-appointed a herald [to proclaim, preacher] and be-a commissioner [apostle]. I declare this to be true by *Anointed*. I am not lying. A teacher in-Belief [faith] and truth to the Nations [Gentiles].

2:8 It-is-my-intentions [great desire] that the-men be-praying in every place, lifting up holy hands without indignation [anger due to punishment received] and doubt [hesitation].

2:9 Same also the-women, to dress well-arranged [decorated] in modesty [regard for others] and adorn themselves in self-control [modesty], not braided with gold or pearls or very-costly garments [apparel]

2:10 but that which fits women professing reverence-for-*GOD* through good actions.

2:11 In quietness let a woman be-learning with all obedience [willing-subjection].

2:12 And I am not permitting a woman to-be-teaching, nor to-be-controlling [domineering, have authority over] men and to be quiet [not meddling in the affairs of others, silence].

2:13 For Adam was molded first, then Eve.

2:14 For Adam was-not-seduced, but the woman being-seduced became the transgressor.

2:15 Yet she-shall-be-saved [rescued] through child-bearing if ever they-should-continue-remaining in Belief [faith] and Godly-love and holiness and self-control [virtue].

Section V

I TIMOTHY 3

3:1 This is a true statement, if any craves [covets, desires] to supervise [be a bishop] he-is-desiring an ideal [honorable] work [employment, business].

3:2 The-supervisor is bound [by-necessity, is obligated] to-be-beyond-reproach [blameless, not open to censure or criticism], the man [husband] of one woman [wife], sober, self-controlled, modest, hospitable, able-to-skillfully-teach.

3:3 Not a wine-drunkard, not quarrelsome, not greedy for gain, but patient, a pacifist [not a fighter or brawler], not-fond-of-silver [driven for money],

3:4 presiding properly over his own household, his-children well-behaved in all respects.

3:5 For how can men care for the Ecclesia if anyone is not able to preside over his own household?

3:6 Not a young-plant [new-convert, neophyte] so-that he-should-not-be-falling into conceit and judgment by The-Adversary.

3:7 More he must also have a good testimony [record, report] from the-ones outside [not in the Ecclesia] that he-should-not-fall into reproach [criticism, accusations] and trapped by The-Adversary.

3:8 The same for servants [deacons], honorable, not double-tongued, not addicted to excessive wine, not greedy-for-gain

3:9 keeping-in-mind [firmly believing] The-Secret-of-The-Belief [faith] with a clean conscience.

3:10 And also, let-them-first-be-tested [proven] blameless, then let-them-serve.

3:11 The same for their-wives, honorable, not slanderous [gossipers], temperate with wine, faithful in all.

3:12 Let the servers be husbands of one wife, presiding over their children and over their own households.

3:13 For the-ones serving [the deacons] are getting-for-themselves a good rank [place, position of dignity] with great boldness in Belief in *The-Anointed-Savior*.

3:14 I wrote all of this hoping to come to you soon.

3:15 Yet if I made-be-that-delayed [delayed for an unusually extended time] you know how the house of-*GOD* is to behave [conduct themselves] which is The-Ecclesia-of-the-*Living-God*, *The Pillar* [One Who Holds Up] and *Foundation* [Creates and Sustains] of *The-Truth*.

3:16 For without great controversy is [there is no possibility for deniably arguing about] the devoutness [holiness and purposeful-sureness] of The-Secret!

God was manifest [without-doubt-or-question] in the flesh, was-declared-righteous in spirit, was-viewed [observed-and-watched] by messengers, was proclaimed [exposed] among [to] the Nations [Gentiles], was-believed in by The-System, was-taken-up [raised, taken into heaven] in glory [majesty, splendor, the-most–exalted-state, most-glorious-condition].

I TIMOTHY 4

4:1 But the spirit expressly [clearly, plainly, definitely, specifically] is-affirming that in coming seasons [ages, eras] some shall-be-withdrawing from [leave, swayed from] The-Belief [faith] heeding to vagabond [imposter, corrupter, leading into error] spirits and teachings [precepts, doctrines] of demons.

4:2 In hypocrisy, speaking lies, their own consciences cauterized [branded].

4:3 Forbidding marriage, to not have foods that *The-God* created for taking [receiving and use] with thanksgiving for the-ones believing and know the truth.

4:4 For every created-thing of *GOD* is good and nothing is to-be-cast-away [thrown away, rejected] but eaten with thanksgiving.

4:5 For it has-been-hallowed through *GOD'S* word [instruction, revelation, teaching] and prayerful-conversations.

4:6 If you are supplying these things to the brothers, you-shall-be-a good servant of *Savior Anointed*. Nurturing [forming the mind, educating] in the instructions of The-Belief [faith] and the ideal [genuine, excellent in its nature, precious] teaching which you-have-fully-followed.

4:7 Yet you-refuse the profane [unholy, common] and you-be-exercising yourself [strive earnestly to become] toward devoutness [godliness, piety toward God].

4:8 For exercising the body has few benefits yet the-godliness is profitable for all, having the *Promise-of-Life* that is now and the Impending [things to come].

4:9 These words are believable and worthy of all welcome [acceptance].

4:10 For to this we-are-toiling also and we-are-being-reviled, that we rely on the *Living-God* who is the *Savior* of all men especially of-believing-ones.

4:11 These things command and teach.

4:12 Let no man take-advantage of your youth; you become a model [type, example] of The-Believing-Ones, in word [conversations, doctrine], in behavior, in Godly-love, in spirit, in belief [faith], in purity [sinless of life].

Section V

4:13   Until I come devote-thought-and-effort-to reading, to exhortation, to the-teaching [doctrine].

4:14   Do-not-not-be-careless with the gracious gift which was given to you when the elders placed their hands (on you) through a prophetic-message.

4:15   Meditate on these things; devote yourself in these that your progress [advancement, growth] may be apparent to all.

4:16   Take care to watch after yourself and be-persistent [preserve, continue in] in the-teaching [doctrine] and doing them. For in this you-shall-be-saving yourself and the-ones hearing you.

I TIMOTHY 5

5:1   Do not upbraid [chastise, express disapproval] with a senior [elder] but approach him like a father and those younger as brothers,

5:2   the elderly women as mothers, the younger-women as sisters with all chasteness [propriety, purity].

5:3   Honor the widows that are really widows,

5:4   and if any widow has children or grandchildren, let them first teach at their own home to be pious and to return-in-like what-is-due to the parents, for this is good and acceptable in-the-sight of *GOD*.

5:5   For the-one that is really a widow and is alone relies on *THE-GOD* and is continually in requests and prayers night and day.

5:6   For the-one squandering [in luxury, with a voluptuous life] is dead though living.

5:7   And in this you be declaring that they may-be blameless.

5:8   And if anyone is not providing for their own, especially family-members, he-has-disowned [refused, rejected] The-Belief [faith] and is worse than an unbeliever.

5:9   No widow is-to-be-listed as a widow less than sixty years old, having been the wife of one husband,

5:10   been-attested [confirmed] doing good actions [deeds] or brought-up her children or lodging-strangers or washes the feet of the Holy-Ones or relieved the-ones afflicted or imitates every good deed.

5:11   But refuse the younger widow for when they feel the impulses of sexual desires wishing to marry against [have alienated themselves from, have placed second in importance] *The-Anointed*

5:12	having [received] judgment since they have done-away-with their first belief.
5:13	Further yet, they-are-learning to become idle-ones making-a-circuit between homes. Not only idle, but also gossipers and meddlers talking about-what is-not-right-and-proper.
5:14	I desire then the younger widows remarry, to bear children, manage the household, providing no incentive to The-One-Opposing [an Adversary] to-revile [insult, berate] grace.
5:15	For some have already returned after The-Satan.
5:16	If a widow is with a believing man or woman, let them relieve [take care of] her. Do not let her burden the Ecclesia so the-ones who are really widows should-be-attended to.
5:17	Ideally the presiding elders should-be-counted-worthy of double honor, especially the-ones toiling in word [preaching] and teaching [doctrine].
5:18	For the-writings say you shall not muzzle the threshing ox and the worker is worthy of the-wages of him.
5:19	Do not agree-to-allow an elder's accusation without two or three witness.
5:20	The-ones sinning expose them in the-sight-of all so that the remaining may-have fear.
5:21	I-am-charging [commanding] before [in the sight of] *THE-GOD* and *Master Savior Anointed* and the-chosen-messengers that you are to guard [guard to not violate] these, without prejudice, doing nothing with a bias.
5:22	Do not place hands on anyone to quickly or participating in sin with others. Be keeping yourself pure.
5:23	Do not drink water any longer but use a little wine because of your stomach and your frequent infirmities.
5:24	Some men's sins are openly-evident heading for judgment and others are to follow-imitating-them.
5:25	Likewise openly-evident also good work but the-otherwise [those not doing good] having-it [wishing] to be hid but are unable [cannot hide].

I TIMOTHY 6

6:1	Whoever may be under the yoke of slavery, let them deem all honor to their own owners that the name of *THE-GOD* and the doctrine may-not-be-blasphemed.
6:2	And those having believing owners, do-not-despise them knowing they are brothers. But rather let-them-slave [be subject to, serve, obey] knowing-that

Section V

they-are believers and beloved, participants of The-Benefit. These things you teach and exhort.

6:3 If anyone is teaching different and not approaching [agreeing to the] sound [true and incorruptible] words of *The-Master* of us, *Savior Anointed* or with the devout [respect to, reverence to] teaching [doctrine],

6:4 he is conceited, being-versed-in [knows] nothing other than about diseased [a morbid fondness for] questionings [creating doubt] and controversies out of which comes [develops] envy, strife, vile-verbal-abuse, wicked surmising [guesswork, inference, assumptions, suspicions], constant-contentions.

6:5 Men of corrupted minds deprived of The-Truth. Remove yourself from those holding-by-custom supposing that to-be gaining [acquiring wealth, being wealthy] as godliness [a sign of devoutness, being favored by God].

6:6 But godliness with contentment is great gain.

6:7 For we carried nothing into The-System; most certainly we not able to carry-out anything,

6:8 and we-shall-be-content with sustenance [nourishment, food] and clothing.

6:9 But the-ones intending to-be-rich are-falling into many trials and traps and many foolish and harmful desires which submerge [swamp, drown] men into complete-ruin [total-extermination] and destruction.

6:10 For the love-of-money is a root for all of the evils which some crave and were-led-astray from The-Belief and on-all-sides to [surround] themselves in great pains [sorrow, grief].

6:11 But you, oh man of *THE-GOD*, you flee from these things! You chase [passionately-pursue] justice [righteousness], devoutness [godliness], belief [faith], Godly-love, endurance [perseverance], meekness.

6:12 Fight the great contest [battle, the trials] of The-Belief [faith], firmly-grasp [unrelentingly-hold on to] the eonian life into which you are also called to and you vowed [promised, confessed, declared, swore] an ideal [approved, precious, honorable] promise in-the-sight-of many [a multitude] of witnesses.

6:13 I-am-commanding you before *THE-GOD*, *THE-ONE-MAKING-LIVE* The-All and *Anointed Savior*, *The-One-Testifying* to Pontius Pilate the ideal [true, factual, accurate, exact] profession [public proclamation, claim, assertion, affirmation].

6:14 You are-to-keep these directions unspotted [free from vice], not-open-to-censure [with no criticism] until the appearance of *The-Master* of us *Savior Anointed*,

6:15	when at his own season shall-be-showing *The-Happy* [blessed] and *Only-Potentate, The-King-of-Kings* and *Lord-of-Lords*.
6:16	*The-Only-One* with immortality, dwelling in an-unapproachable light that no man has seen or can perceive [comprehend] to whom is eonian [age-lasting] honor [honor by rank and state, reverence] and force [dominion, power and might].
6:17	Charge [instruct and warn] the-ones who are currently rich [wealthy] to-not-be-haughty [proud] or rely on uncertain riches but in *THE-GOD, THE-LIVING-ONE-SUPPLYING* us richly in all-things enjoyable.
6:18	Those-doing-good-actions, be rich in good actions, liberal [ready to give], be sociable [maintain communion and fellowship]
6:19	treasuring-up for-themselves an ideal foundation for The-Impending that they-may-be-getting-hold [insure and secure] the eonian life.
6:20	Oh Timothy! You guard what-is-committed-to-your-trust, turn away from the profane [ungodly] useless [empty] discussions, and oppose false-so-called knowledge
6:21	that some are-claiming. They-deviate [swerve, err] from The-Belief [faith].

The-Grace with you, Timothy.
Amen.

(I Timothy was written from Laodicea, which is the mother city of Phrygia Pacatiana)

II TIMOTHY COMMENTARY

IN A TURN OF events, Paul realizes that his tenure as a Commissioner is coming to a very quick, very abrupt end. Since arrangements had been in the works for the transition of Timothy as the legal lead and authority for some time now, it clearly appears that Timothy is managing the daily affairs of the Ecclesiae. II Timothy is as much a reminder to continue shepherding the flock and holding to The-Belief as it is a call for last-minute arrangements. Essentially this letter has the sound of Paul calling on his personal attorney to come back to him to prepare his true last will and testament. "Bring back my personal effects as quickly as you can," we can almost hear Paul plead. "I need to put them in order!"

And this is exactly what Paul will do. He will readjust the letters to the Romans and Corinthians, adding the information of The-Secret for the Ecclesiae. He will decide what other letters are needed for posterity, meet with "The Commissioners" (which I understand to be Peter and John, since James was murdered some time previous), and turn over all his effects to them and to Timothy. It is also Paul's last opportunity to pass on to posterity the full understanding and knowledge he had, any last minute divine instructions, and clarify and answer any last-minute questions they may have had. Paul wanted to strengthen not only their belief for the coming heavy persecutions but also for the sake of the Ecclesia. And Peter had his own personal persecution occurring; stories of his "upside-down crucifixion" were of great consternation to all. They all needed to insure someone would keep all in order and to "pass it on," and that task eventually falls to John and the remaining elders.

So what makes this letter so unique? I contend that II Timothy is not only the last will and testament of Paul for the Ecclesia but also provides the clue to the assembly of the letters we will come to know commonly as the New Testament. This letter is historical as a high-level legal review for ministering to the Ecclesiae; it is also a record for the beginnings of the assembly of the entire New Testament canon. The aging corporate attorney is now finalizing the very final last-minute arrangements for completely stepping out of his role. It is Paul's final summation and effort.

But does Paul meet Nero's thumb-down decision? Paul had hinted it was Christ's will that he should go to Spain, and it is possible that may have occurred. The Letter of Acts ends quite abruptly, as if no one knew exactly what to record as the last acts or fate of "that good soldier who disappeared into the mists of time." Certainly, Mark or

Timothy or John would have had firsthand information if Paul was executed in Rome, and it would have been recorded in Acts to close out the letter. But nobody within this inner circle took the time to record Paul's last and final act, whether in Rome or elsewhere. And Mark was a recorder for the Ecclesiae.

Myths and legends exist that Paul did make it to Spain and eventually to Britain, only to be murdered there. If no members back in the Empire had any actual knowledge or proof of what happened to him, how could they end the book of Acts? Was his body brought back to Rome only to be interred there? It would allow for some of the stories of Paul's sarcophagus "being there" and for people to be able to "point to it" later in the ages. All of this is merely speculation, but one thing we do know for sure: This was a man that shook up the entire world along with the Twelve Apostles. He has left us a lasting legacy worth researching, discussing, and debating, and it's for you as a jurist to decide if you believe him or not. Paul, from start to finish, leaves all the necessary legal briefs, summations, understandings, debates, and arguments in order for you and I to come to "the full knowledge of The Secret of The-God and The Anointed Savior, The Messiah."

II TIMOTHY AS A LETTER

Paul, Commissioner of Savior *Anointed* by the will of *GOD* with the Promise-of-Life in *The-Anointed-Savior*. To Timothy, beloved child, grace, mercy, peace from *FATHER GOD* and *Anointed-Savior, The-Master* of us.

I have gratitude to *THE-GOD* to whom I-am-offering-divine-service as my-forefathers in clear conscience. I have unending concerns in remembrance of you in my supplications-and-prayers night and day, greatly desiring to see you, remembering you. That I may be filled with tears of joy when remembering having the pure-and-childlike belief in you which was first in the homes of your grandmother Lois and your mother Eunice. For I-have-been-convinced that this is also in you because I-am-reminding you to-be-rekindling the gracious-gift of *THE-GOD* which is in you through the placing on of the-hands of mine. For *THE-GOD* of us has not given us the spirit of timidity but of Godly-power and of Godly-love and of a sound-mind.

Then do not be-ashamed of the testimony-and-teaching of *The-Master* of us or yet me the prisoner of *Him*. But you endure the persecutions delivering the Well-Message using the Godly-power of *GOD, THE-ONE-SAVING* us and calling us to a holy calling not with our actions but according-to *HIS* own purpose and grace. Which-is-being-given to us in *Anointed Savior* before eonian times but now being-made-to-appear through the coming-appearance of *The-Savior* of us *Savior Anointed*. Indeed *The-One-Abolishing* The-Death; for causing-and-bringing into existence life and incorruption through the Well-Message.

Into this I was appointed to-be a heraldry and commissioner and teacher to the Nations. Because of this purpose and things, I-am-suffering, but not because I-am-ashamed, for I know whom I-have-believed and I-have-been-thoroughly-convinced that which-*He*-committed to me, *He-Is-Able*, that is, to guard it up-to The-Day.

You-copy the model, the true-and-incorruptible words which you heard from me in belief and Godly-love in *The-Anointed Savior*. Guard that-which-is-praiseworthy-and-the-godly which-is-committed-to-your trust through the Holy-spirit, the-one-making-its-home in us.

You-are-aware-of this that all were-turned-from me, the-ones in Asia of whom are Phygellus and Hermongenes. May *The-Master* be-granting mercy to the household of Onesiphorus for many times he-refreshed me and was-not-ashamed of my chains. Even when he came to Rome, he diligently sought me and found me. May *The-Master* be-granting to him to-be-finding mercy with *Master* in that, The-Day and how-many he served in Ephesus. You know this quite-well.

You then, my child, be-filled-with-strength in the grace in *The-Anointed Savior* and with that which you heard by me along-with the many witnesses. Commit these to believing men who shall-be competent also to teach to others.

You therefore endure the hardships of a good soldier of *Savior Anointed*. No man battling is-involved-in the business-and-affairs of the-course-of-life so that he should please the-one-enlisting him. And during the course of competing, no one is wreathed if he-is-not-competing lawfully. The farmer must be the first to take the fruits of his work.

Make sure you understand what-I-am-saying and *The-Master* give you all understanding in all things.

Remember *Savior Anointed*, *The-One-Having-Been-Raised* out of the dead, out of the seed of David according-to my well-message for which I-am-suffering-evil in bondage as if an evil-criminal. But *The-Word*-of-*THE-GOD* is not suppressed-and-locked-up. Because of this I-am-bearing-up-bravely-and-calmly because of The-Chosen-Ones that they also may-be-receiving the salvation in *Anointed Savior* with eonian glory.

These sayings are believable, for if we-died-together also we-shall-be-alive-together. If we-are-enduring, also we-shall-be-reigning-together. If we-are denying-and-leaving, also THE-ONE shall-be-disowning us. If we-are-being-unfaithful, THE-ONE is-remaining faithful; HE cannot prove-to-be-false-to-himself. Keep reminding yourself of these. Witness in-full-view of *The-Master*. Do not engage in worthless controversy meant to destroy-and-overthrow the-ones listening. Study to qualify yourself, to present to *THE-GOD* an unashamed worker, correctly-holding-to-a-straight-course.

And the unholy useless-discussions, you-don't-get-involved-with because they just-continue-increasing in ungodliness. And the teaching of those which come-from Hymeneus and Philetus shall-be-as a gangrene pasture who have deviated The-Truth saying the Resurrection has already occurred and have-subverted The-Belief of some.

And yet this, the solid foundation of *THE-GOD* is fixed-and-firmly-established having *The-Seal*. *The-Master* knows the-ones belonging to *Him* and let-them-completely-withdraw from injustice every one-of-the-ones calling the name of *Anointed*.

For in the-great-home are not only utensils of gold and silver but also wood, clay-ware, and indeed some-which have value and some-which have no value. When in time then if anyone should-thoroughly-clean himself from these, he-shall-be a utensil of value prepared for every good deed-and-act having-been-hallowed and useful for *The-Owner* having-been-prepared for every good deed.

Flee also youthful desires. Flee from these! But passionately-run-down justice, belief, Godly-love, and peace with the-ones-calling-on-their-behalf *The-Master* out of pure heart.

Section V

Again, you avoid stupid and uneducated-and-ignorant questioning! Be-aware they-are-creating fighting contentions-and-strife. For the slave of *Master* is-obligated to not create quarrels but be gentle to all, able to teach in patience-when-others-present-errors and mistreatment, in meekness, training the-ones-antagonizing to see whether *THE-GOD* may-give them repentance and an acknowledgment of truth and not-be-drinking with The-Adversary, having-been-captured-alive in his trap for his will.

Further know this, that in the last days, perilous periods shall-be-present. For the-men shall-be fond-of-themselves, fond-of-money, great-boasters, proud, making malicious false statements and slandering others, disobedient to parents, ungrateful, wicked, without-natural-affection, trucebreakers, adversaries, without self-control, fierce, haters of good, traitors, impulsive, highly-conceited, loving-self-gratification rather than loving-God having a form of godliness and at-the same time denying God's power. You absolutely-avoid these!

For from these are the-ones slipping into the houses and capturing the weak-minded-and-senseless women heaped-full of sins, being-led into-various-lusts, eager to learn but yet-not-at-any time being-able to come to understand truth. That is the method by-which Jannes and Jambres opposed-themselves-against Moses. They also opposed the truth, men of corrupted minds, unfit-for-use concerning The-Belief. But they shall-not-be-making-progress any more for their lack-of-understanding shall-be obvious to all as also those became.

However, you have-fully-followed my teaching, way of life with-a-purpose, in The-Belief, in patience, in Godly-love, in consistency-and-steadfastness, in persecutions, in sufferings just as what occurred to me in Antioch, in Iconium, in Lystra. Those persecutions I-endured and out of all of them *The-Master* rescued me. And all the-ones-willing to live in piety-and-godliness in *Anointed Savior* shall-be-being-persecuted.

But evil men and swindlers shall-be-increasing for the worse, deceiving and being-deceived. But you hold-true-and-stay-faithful in what you learned and were-entrusted with, remembering-and-not-forgetting by whom that you learned from and that from a baby you became acquainted with the holy-writings that are able to make you wise leading-to salvation through belief in *The Anointed Savior*.

All writings are inspired-by-*GOD* and beneficial for teaching, for convincing, for corrections, for training-and-education in the-justice that the man of *THE-GOD* may-be equipped, completely-furnished for every good deed.

I am commanding you in-the-sight of *THE-GOD* and *The-Master Savior Anointed*, *The-One* about to be-judging the living-ones and dead-ones with the reappearance of *Him* and The-Kingdom of *His*. Proclaim *The-Word*, stand-by-it! In-season out-of-season. Expose, rebuke, admonish-entreat-encourage with all patience and teaching. For there shall-be an era when the sound teachings shall-not-be-tolerated but after the desires of their own selves. They-will surround themselves with teachers to tickle the hearing and indeed will turn their ears away from *The-Truth*, again to be-turned-to The-Myths.

But you-be-wary-and-alert about all, endure-afflictions, do the work of a well-messenger, fulfill-in-entirety-every-part-of your service. For I already am-being-poured-out and the period of my death is imminent. I-have-raced the good running I have finished, I have kept The-Belief.

The-Rest is being reserved for me, the crown of justice which *The-Master, The-Just-Judge* shall-be-paying to me in that, The-Day. Not only to-me, but also to all the-ones having-loved the reappearance of *Him*. Strive quickly to come to me for Demas has abandoned me godly-loving the current eon and went to Thessalonica, Crescens to Galatia, Titus to Dalmatia. Only Luke is with me. Take Mark and bring him with you for he is very-useful for me in the service and Tichicus I dispatched to Ephesus.

Bring with you the traveling-chest which I left in Troas with Carpus and the letters, especially the parchments.

Alexander the Coppersmith displayed great evil to me; may *The-Master* repay him according-to his deeds. You also be be-guarding against him for he-has-withstood greatly the instructions-and-orders of us.

In the beginning no one came to my defense for all abandoned me. May it not be-accounted against them for *Master* stood-beside me and enabled me that through me the proclamation may-be-in-full-entirety-discharged and all the Nations should-be-told for I was rescued out of the mouth of a lion. And *The-Master* shall-be-rescuing me from every wicked deed and shall-be-saving-me to The-Kingdom-of-*His*, *The-Celestial-One* to whom is the-esteem into the Eons of the Eons.

Amen.

Greet Prisca and Aquila and the household of Onesiphorus. Erastus remains in Corinth; Trophimus I left in Miletus being-sick.

Prepare yourself to come before winter. Eubulus greets you and Pudens and Linus and Claudia and all the Brothers.

The-Master Savior Anointed be with the spirit of you.

The-Grace with you.

Amen.

II TIMOTHY STUDY NOTES

Note: Through my many translations, I have come to believe that the phrase or associated phrasing of "inheritance" [ex: Col 1:12] accurately translated as "the-allotment" in Scripture is not a good or proper translation (i.e., inheritance). Paul makes it clear that we are to be family members (I state: royal and godly) destined to be with HIM and HE with us and we in Christ and He in us. Inheritance has an implied connotation, an accepted concept that someone has died. THE-GOD is certainly not dead, and Christ has risen to life eonian (there are times of times of times) as well. I see this as a watering down of the intent and meaning of the Scriptures and have dropped using the word *inheritance* when speaking of THE-GOD's plan and purpose for us. We are to take rulership in an active kingdom with Christ at the head of the realm and we under Him, with THE-GOD over all of us.

Note   The Greek word *agapen* translated as "love" in most translations is missing that this is Godly in nature and not of men or any other such creature. I have therefore carried the adjective to add clarity to the meaning of this word throughout this translation.

Note: In my research, nearly all translations have dropped "the" as a modifier, but the Greek word for "the" is in every text and not meant to be ignored or deleted. It is often specifically singular, and when attached to the noun, it is describing that noun as unique, one of a kind, a specific thing, the original, the one and only. It is for this reason that I carry "the" everywhere it appears in all translations. Whether of God, Jesus, Satan or any other entity, concept, or idea, the modifier "the" clears up a lot of generalized words, ideas, concepts, and entities.

Note: The root of the word *pnuemia*, translated as "spirit, wind, or breath," has no gender identity since this is a word that is neuter in gender. *Pnuemia* is an "it." The Greeks, as we of English language, often fix a gender to objects and things— for example: cars, boats, the moon, the sun. For the Greeks, *pnuemia* at times has a male gender affixed to it. *Pnuemia* in the Scriptures is never capitalized or designated as a standalone being, entity, principality, or sovereignty when used as the word "spirit." It is simply the power inherent in the

II TIMOTHY STUDY NOTES

being, whether of man, or God, or Christ, or any other entity. If anything is living, "it" possesses a spirit. The "Holy-spirit" is simply the power from and of The-God, giving and renewing life and performing The-God's will.

Note: Paul constantly claims and mentions "principles, powers, authorities, sovereignties not of our world." He quite clearly claims that these beings are the ones that certainly influence and control (predominately in a negative way) the systems of this world, people of the nations, and as individuals directly. You can find this concept also contained in The Old Testament through the implications of the first commandment. This claim and the concept of the warring factions in heaven makes a fascinating study.

Note: Time periods, eons, ages, millennia, eons, and eons—I stayed true to the Greek words associated with time and what we still use today in our common language. A study of time periods is fascinating but is also an area that can cause confusion. The-God always works on some kind of a timetable, but understanding which is which and when is when is a bit of a mystery. Some timetables are only known to The-God and made clear to man at God's will.

Note What is the difference between "expectation" and "hope?" Nearly all translations adopt the word "hope" for "expectation," but Paul uses almost exclusively the word "expectation." Here is why I constantly use "expectation." Having an expectation means you have no doubt at all. It is sure and certain with no ambiguity or doubt. Having a hope means you are not 100 percent convinced and convicted. I can tell you that Paul is undeniably convinced and convicted in what he delivers and talks about. Using "hope" sends a message that there is some possibility for "wiggle room," doubt, error, or excuses.

Even worse, much of the use of the word "expectation" in Paul's writings has the modifier "the" attached to "expectation," thus forming the proper translation and singular concept of "The-Expectation." This makes "The-Expectation" an event, not a philosophy or theological premise. Not recognizing "The-Expectation" as an event will lead the reader immediately down an incorrect understanding of what is being offered or discussed.

1:9 Notice that Paul says your calling and acceptance by God is not done by your deeds, actions, or work. He provides all of this to you.

1:14 Your "trust" means as an overseer, protector, administrator or "trustee." Paul is reminding Timothy of his legal responsibilities.

1:12 "The-Day" is a direct reference to the-day of Christ's return.

2:4 Note that the word "practice" is still used today to describe a legal office or place of business.

Section V

2:9 "The-Word" here can display two meanings. First, the "scriptures" of The God cannot be suppressed, but I am more convinced of the second meaning to be Christ, and therefore I have capitalized and italicized the connected words. Jesus is also not bound or held by anything in heaven or earth other than The Father's will, purpose, and authority.

2:12 This verse alludes to one of the aspects revealed concerning "The-Secret."

2:20 "The great home" refers the New Jerusalem which comes from heaven.

3:6 Paul is never one to lightly walk through a flowerbed when it needs to be trampled and trounced on. He is brutal when he needs to be. The Greek word *gunaikaria*, translated commonly as "little-women," is such an occasion. Commentaries acknowledge that this is meant to be blunt and derogatory about how women were [and are being] led away. A better understanding of this phrase would be a weak-minded woman; a woman driven only by emotions and no rationale; a woman driven by the lust of her desires and senses; a woman, given into only herself and her selfish drives. I have provided a sense of all these meanings with the lexicon equivalents within the brackets following the phrase.

3:8 The Greek word *adokimoi* translated as "rejects" is from the striking of coinage that were rejected as flawed for a wide variety of reasons.

3:9 For a point of clarification, the verse "But they shall-not-be-making-progress any more. For their lack-of-understanding shall-be obvious to all as also those became" is better understood as: "Those deceiving everyone won't get much further. Their lack of understanding will be exposed to all, just as Jannes and Jambres."

4:2 The Greek sentence structure for "in [with] all patience and teaching [(the) instructions while He was teaching" requires some clarification. Commentaries state that the Greek is properly rendered "while he was teaching." The sentence is best translated then as follows: "with all patience and the instructions while He was teaching." The "He" is Jesus' instructions, and additionally some commentaries indicate that Paul is getting ready to reiterate those instructions in the next few sentences to Timothy. See *Strong's* G1322, definition 2, for a concise discussion.

4:4 "The-Myths"—what are they? To name a few: Christ is not a man in the flesh in Heaven today; Christ is not resurrected; Circumcision and The-Law are required; the Resurrection has already taken place; there is no spirit world or kingdom; worship of angels and playing with divinities; false and worthless genealogies; and the trinity.

4:6   The concept of "being-libationed" or "poured-out" is a direct reference to the drink offerings in the Temple and a reflection of Christ's life and blood being poured out. Specifically, Paul is well aware that his death sentence is not going to be commuted, according to many commentaries.

4:8   The-Rest Paul is referring to is his death.

4:13   The Greek word *phelonen* translates as an "outer covering, a cloak, bark." All three words describe a protective outer covering. To the English reader, using the words "cloak" or "coat" this would imply an outer weather garment, whereas in this verse Paul is protecting paper and letters. The more accurate translation is "carrying-case, attaché case, the protected-papers." A better explanation is provided in an article by Dr. Ernest L. Martin:[1]

> Vincent, in his *Word Studies in the New Testament, p. 326*, has this to say about the word *phelonen*.

> "Hesychius explains it as originally a case for keeping the mouthpieces of wind-instruments; thence, generally, a box. Phrynicus, a Greek sophist of the second half of the third century, defines it as `a receptacle for books, clothes, silver, or anything else.' Phelonen was a wrapper of parchments, and was translated figuratively in Latin by toga or paenula `a cloak,' sometimes of leather; also the wrapping which a shopkeeper put round fish or olives; also the parchment cover for papyrus rolls. Accordingly it is claimed that Timothy in 4:13 is bidden to bring, not a cloak, but a roll-case. So the Syriac Version."

While I am tempted to replace *phelonen* with "the protected papers" because I think this is also accurate and correct, I have used the term "traveling-case" because it has the closest relationship to the Greek. I hope the reader grasps what the contents inside the carrying-case were. However, this begs the question: How much of the New Testament that we use today was already developed and being used within the first forty years of the early Ecclesiae? If II Timothy is the last of Paul's epistles, that would only leave the letters of John and the Revelation of Jesus Christ to be added after AD 70. Essentially 90 percent of the New Testament was already in existence and being used no later than AD 65–68. The carrying-case contained these New Testament letters. This has to be the time when Chapters 15 and 16 of Romans were added to the original Romans letter by Paul so he could include "The-Secret" about all of God's creation, especially that the Nations (Gentiles) have the full divinity of God and Christ just as the called-ones and were to be allotted the heavens as part of their Godly reward. Note that of all the letters sent to the churches by Paul, only Galatians does not mention The-Secret.

---

1. Dr. Ernest L. Martin, PhD "Restoring the Bible; Chapter 24 Canonization of Paul's Epistles; The Cloak, The Scrolls, and The Parchment," © 1976 –2001 Associates for Scriptural Knowledge.

Section V

4:17   "Out of the mouth of a lion" is likely literal in meaning, but because Paul was under Caesar's arrest, this may have been as a subtext, a euphemism referring to Nero.

II TIMOTHY IN VERSE

II TIMOTHY 1

1:1 Paul, Commissioner of *Savior Anointed*, by the will of *GOD* with the Promise-of-Life in *The-Anointed-Savior*.

1:2 To Timothy, beloved child: grace, mercy, peace from *FATHER GOD*, and *Anointed Savior The-Master* of us.

1:3 I have gratitude to *THE-GOD* to whom I-am-offering-divine-service as my-forefathers [ancestors] in clear conscience. I have unending concerns in remembrance of you in my petitions [supplications and prayers] night and day,

1:4 greatly desiring to see you, remembering you. That I may be filled with tears of joy

1:5 when remembering having the unhypocritical [pure, childlike] belief [faith] in you which was first in the homes of your grandmother Lois [Superior] and your mother Eunice [Good Victory]. For I-have-been-convinced that this is also in you

1:6 because I-am-reminding you to-be-rekindling [keep firing back up] the gracious-gift of *THE-GOD* which is in you through the placing on of the-hands of mine.

1:7 For *THE-GOD* of us has not given us the spirit of timidity but of Godly-power and of Godly-love and of a sound-mind.

1:8 Then do not be-ashamed of the witness [testimony, teaching, doctrine] of *The-Master* of us or yet me the prisoner of *Him*. But you-suffer-with-the-evil [endure the persecutions delivering, suffer together (with me) in] of the Well-Message using the Godly-power of *GOD*,

1:9 *THE-ONE-SAVING* us and calling us to a holy calling not with our actions [works, deeds] but according-to (*HIS*) own purpose and grace. Which-is-being-given to us in *Anointed Savior* before eonian times

SECTION V

1:10 but now being-made-to-appear [displayed] through the coming-appearance of *The-Savior* of us *Savior Anointed*. Indeed *The-One-Abolishing* The-Death, for illuminating [causing, bringing into existence] life and incorruption through the Well-Message.

1:11 Into this I was appointed to-be a proclaimer [heraldry, preacher] and commissioner and teacher to the Nations [Gentiles].

1:12 Because of this cause [purpose] and things I-am-suffering, but not because I-am-ashamed for I know whom I-have-believed and I-have-been-thoroughly-convinced that which-*He*-committed to me *He-Is-Able*, that is to guard into The-Day.

1:13 You-copy the pattern [model, example], the sound [true and incorruptible] words which you heard from me in belief [faith] and Godly-love in *The-Anointed Savior*.

1:14 Guard the ideal [that which is praiseworthy, the godly] which-is-committed-to-your trust through (the) Holy-spirit, the-one-making-its-home in us.

1:15 You-are-aware-of this, that all were-turned-from me, the-ones in Asia of whom are Phygellus [Fugitive] and Hermongenes [Hermes' Heir].

1:16 May *The-Master* be-granting mercy to the household of Onesiphorus [Profit-Carrying-One] for many times he-refreshed me and was-not-ashamed of my chains [did not desert me because I was a prisoner].

1:17 Even when he came to Rome, he diligently sought me and found (me).

1:18 May *The-Master* be-granting to him to-be-finding mercy with *Master* in that, The-Day, and how-many he served in Ephesus. You know this quite-well.

II TIMOTHY 2

2:1 You then, my child, be-filled-with-strength in the grace in *The-Anointed Savior*

2:2 and with that which you heard by me along-with the many witnesses. Commit these to believing [faithful] men who shall-be competent [able to] also to teach to different-ones [others].

2:3 You therefore endure the suffering-evils [hardships] of a good soldier of *Savior Anointed*.

2:4 No man battling is-involved-in the practices [business, affairs] of livelihood [course of life, wealth, that which sustains life] so that he should please the-one-enlisting (him).

2:5 And if during the course of competing no one is wreathed if he-is-not-competing lawfully.

2:6 The farmer must be the first to take the fruits of his work.

2:7 Make sure you understand what-I-am-saying and *The-Master* give you all understanding in all (things).

2:8 Remember *Savior Anointed, The-One-Having-Been-Raised* out of the dead, out of the seed of David according-to my well-message

2:9 for which I-am-suffering-evil in bondage [captivity] as if a malefactor [evil-criminal]. But *The-Word-of-THE-GOD* is not captive [in chains, suppressed, locked-up].

2:10 Because of this I-am-enduring [remaining behind, fleeing, accept bravely and calmly] because of The-Chosen-Ones that they also may-be-receiving the salvation in *Anointed Savior* with eonian glory.

2:11 These sayings are believable [faithful] for if we-died-together also we-shall-be-alive-[living]-together.

2:12 If we-are-enduring, also we-shall-be-reigning-together. If we-are-disowning [denying and leaving, legally reject] also *THE-ONE* shall-be-disowning us.

2:13 If we-are-being-unfaithful, *THE-ONE* is-remaining faithful, *HE* cannot prove-to-be-false-to-himself [contradict, change one's character, deeds, purpose].

2:14 Keep reminding yourself of these. Witness in-full-view of *The-Master*. Do not engage in worthless controversy meant to upset [extinct the spirit, destroy, overthrow] the-ones listening.

2:15 Study to qualify yourself, to present to *THE-GOD* an unashamed worker, correctly-holding-to-a-straight-course [accurately dividing the word of the-truth].

2:16 And the unholy useless-discussions you-stand-away-from [don't get involved with] because they just-continue-increasing in irreverence [ungodliness].

2:17 And the teaching of those which come-from Hymeneus [Nuptial, (the god of marriage Ibhar)] and Philetus [Fond] shall-be-as a gangrene pasture

2:18 who have deviated The-Truth saying the Resurrection has already occurred and have-subverted The-Belief [faith] of some.

2:19 And yet this, the solid foundation of *THE-GOD* stands [is fixed, firmly-established] having *The-Seal. The-Master* knows the-ones belonging to *Him* and let-them-completely-withdraw from injustice every one-of-the-ones calling [as his Lord] the name of *Anointed*.

Section V

2:20 For in the great home are not only utensils of gold and silver but also wood, clay-ware [fired pottery, earthenware], and indeed some-which have value and some-which have no value.

2:21 When in time then if anyone should-purge [thoroughly-clean] himself from these, he-shall-be a utensil of value prepared for every good action [business, employment, deed, an act] having-been-hallowed and useful for *The-Owner* having-been-prepared for every good deed.

2:22 Flee also youthful desires [what is forbidden lusts]. Flee from these! But chase [passionately run-down] justice [righteousness], belief [faith], Godly-love, (and) peace with the-ones-appealing [calling on their behalf, mercy, and justice in front of a judge] *The-Master* out of clean [pure] heart.

2:23 Again, you avoid stupid [insipid, foolish] and undisciplined [uneducated, ignorant] questioning! Be-aware they-are-creating fighting [quarrels, contention, strife].

2:24 For the slave of *Master* is-obligated to not create quarrels but be gentle to all, able to teach in patience-of-wrongs [when others present errors] and mistreatment,

2:25 in meekness, training the-ones-antagonizing to see whether THE-GOD may-give them repentance and a realization [an acknowledgment] of truth

2:26 and be-sobering-up away from [not drinking with] The-Adversary, having-been-caught-[captured]-alive in his trap into [for] his will.

II TIMOTHY 3

3:1 Further know this, that in the last days, perilous seasons [periods] shall-be-present.

3:2 For the-men shall-be fond-of-themselves, fond-of-silver [money], ostentatious [great boasters], proud, making malicious false statements and slandering others, disobedient to parents, ungrateful, wicked,

3:3 without-natural-affection, trucebreakers, adversaries, without self-control, fierce [savage, untamed], haters of good,

3:4 traitors, impulsive [thoughtless, foolish], highly-conceited, loving-self-gratification rather than loving-God

3:5 having a form of godliness and also (at the) same (time) denying (God's) power. You absolutely-avoid these!

II TIMOTHY IN VERSE

3:6   For out of [from] these are the-ones slipping into the houses and capturing the little-women [weak-minded, senseless, ignorant] heaped-full of sins, being-led into-various-feelings [lusts],

3:7   eager to learn but yet-not-at-any time being-able to come to understand truth.

3:8   That is the method by-which Jannes [Gift from God] and Jambres [Poverty, Bitter, A Rebel] opposed [resisted, set themselves against] Moses. They also opposed the truth, men of corrupted minds, rejects [castaways, unfit for use] concerning The-Belief [faith].

3:9   But they shall-not-be-making-progress any more for their lack-of-understanding shall-be obvious to all as also those became.

3:10   However, you have-fully-followed my teaching [doctrine], way of life with-a-purpose, in The-Belief [faith], in patience, in Godly-love, in endurance [consistency, steadfastness],

3:11   in persecutions, in sufferings [evil, misfortune, calamity, afflictions] just as what occurred to me in Antioch, in Iconium, in Lystra. Those persecutions I-carried [endured] and out of all of them *The-Master* rescued me.

3:12   And all the-ones-willing to live devoutly [in piety, godly] in *Anointed Savior* shall-be-being-persecuted.

3:13   But wicked [evil] men and swindlers [deceivers] shall-be-waxing [increasing, making progress] for the worse, deceiving and being-deceived.

3:14   But you remain [hold true, stay faithful] in what you learned and were-entrusted with, being aware [remembering, not forgetting] by whom that you learned from

3:15   and that from a baby [new-born-child] you became acquainted with the holy-writings that are able to make you wise into [leading to] salvation through belief [faith] in *The-Anointed-Savior*.

3:16   All writings are *GOD*-spirited [filled with God's spirit, inspired by God] and beneficial for teaching, for convincing, for corrections, for disciplining [training and education] in the-justice [righteousness]

3:17   that the man of *THE-GOD* may-be equipped, fitted-out [completely-furnished] for every good deed.

SECTION V

II TIMOTHY 4

4:1 I am charging [commanding] you in-the-sight of *THE-GOD* and *The-Master Savior Anointed*, *The-One* about to be-judging the living-ones and dead-ones with the reappearance of *Him* and The-Kingdom of *His*.

4:2 Herald [proclaim, preach] *The-Word*, stand-by-it! In-season [when opportunity is given], out-of-season, expose, rebuke, exhort [admonish, entreat, encourage] in [with] all patience and teaching [(the) instructions while *He* was teaching].

4:3 For there shall-be a season [era] when the sound teachings shall-not-be-tolerated but after the desires of their own selves. They-shall-be-heaping-up [they will have a multitude of, they will surround themselves with] teachers to tickle the hearing [preach what they want to hear]

4:4 and indeed will turn their ears away from *The-Truth*, yet [again] to be-turned-to The-Myths.

4:5 But you-be-sober [wary, alert] about all, endure-afflictions, do the work of a well-messenger [evangelist], fully-discharge [fulfill in entirety every part of] your service [ministry].

4:6 For I already am-being-libationed [poured-out] and the season [period] of my loosening [release, departure, death] is imminent.

4:7 I-have-contended [fought, raced] the good running, [career] I have finished; I have kept The-Belief [faith].

4:8 The-Rest is being reserved for me, the wreath [crown] of justice [righteousness] which *The-Master*, *The-Just-Judge* shall-be-paying to me in that, The-Day. Not only to-me, but also to all the-ones having-loved the reappearance of *Him*.

4:9 Strive swiftly [quickly] to come to me

4:10 for Demas [Popular] has abandoned me godly-loving the current eon and went to Thessalonica, Crescens [Growing] to Galatia, Titus [Of the Giants] to Dalmatia.

4:11 Only Luke is with me. Take Mark and bring him with you, for he is very-useful for me in the service [ministry]

4:12 and Tichicus [Fortuitous] I dispatched to Ephesus.

4:13 Bring with you the traveling-chest which I left in Troas with Carpus [Fruit, Profit, My Bounty] and the scrollets [letters, small books, small scrolls], especially the parchments [vellums].

II TIMOTHY IN VERSE

4:14 Alexander the Coppersmith displayed great evil to me; may *The-Master* repay him according-to his deeds.

4:15 You also be-guarding against him, for he-has-withstood greatly the words [speaking, instructions, admonition, orders] of us.

4:16 In the beginning no one came to my defense, for all abandoned me. May it not be-accounted [charged] against them

4:17 for *Master* stood-beside me and enabled me that through me the proclamation may-be-full-in-entirety-discharged [completed] and all the Nations [Gentiles] should-be-hearing [told] for I was rescued out of the mouth of a lion.

4:18 And *The-Master* shall-be-rescuing me from every wicked deed [action, work] and shall-be-saving-me to The-Kingdom-of-*His*, *The-Celestial-(One)* to whom is the-esteem [glory] into the Eons of the Eons.

Amen.

4:19 Greet Prisca [Ancient] and Aquila [Eagle] and the household of Onesiphorus [Profit-Carrying].

4:20 Erastus [Loved] remains in Corinth, Trophimus [Well-educated, Well-brought-up] I left in Miletus being-sick.

4:21 Prepare yourself to come before winter. Eubulus [Prudent, Good-counselor] greets you and Pudens [Shame-faced] and Linus [Net] and Claudia [Lame] and all the Brothers.

4:22 *The-Master Savior Anointed* (be) with the spirit of you.

The-Grace with you.
Amen.

(To Timothy, the second letter, being selected [ordained] as the primary supervisor [overseer, elder, bishop] of the Called-Out of the Ephesians. Written from Rome when Paul stood a second time before to Caesar Nero.)

Section VII

POWER OF ATTORNEY ASSIGNMENT
(Titus)

The Letter of TITUS

TITUS COMMENTARY

THE LAST TWO LETTERS of Paul have been sent to individuals within "The-Out-Called" or "Called-Out." Titus is the first of these two direct letters to individuals, and each one—while the same in theme—are quite different in approach and purpose.

First in order is Titus. This letter to Titus actually gives him power of attorney and a proxy associated with the development of The-Body of Christ. In the name of Paul and by the authority given Paul in Christ, Titus is directed to create and reorder the management of personnel for the Ecclesiae in Crete. If anyone doubts that this is a power of attorney letter and a proxy, the Greek words translated as "injunction, unimpeachable, subordination, indictable, embezzle, statement," and "abstain" can be found as root words in several of Paul's instructions and directions to Titus. You and I have an insight into watching Paul order and maintain the affairs of Christ as the prime corporate attorney, and at the same time we are being given the footprint, the master plan, for the ordering and creating of an effective Ecclesia. Potentially we may have the chance to do the same. Titus was able to take this letter and read it directly to his audience not only as his letter of introduction but also direct authority. This letter would not have been placed in Titus' hand to be read only once and then retained within only his personal effects. Titus would have had a series of these power of attorney letters, leaving one behind at each Ecclesia. Such a letter would have been the same as Paul being there. We often think of the letters of Paul being individual in nature and hand-carried from place to place, but in reality, multiple copies would have gone out to be left behind for reference and instructions, whether of Romans or any of the other letters. The Letter of Titus is no different.

In addition to creating and fixing the management for serving, Paul restates several tenets Titus is to reconfirm and reiterate for what was and was not associated with The-Belief. One could argue that the tenets being readdressed here by Paul may have been specific to the Crete region, but the mention of circumcision indicates that this was still a problem that was not resolved in the minds and understanding of all. Therefore, the restatement of matters needing correction takes on a universal and age-sustaining provenance for us today.

It is necessary within this introduction to discuss the translation of the Greek word *theon*; I have taken *all* associated definitions and placed a negative stigma to these (italics mine for emphasis). This word occurs in Titus 1:16, and here Paul is discussing the false leaders claiming intimate knowledge and fellowship with that "of God," or being "God's representatives," or what "God is." My interpretation is that Paul is accusing those false leaders of lying about the claim that they have a direct relationship with The-God himself, with God's direct messengers, with the angels, or with The-God as a trinity. I realize the word "trinity" will send many into a complete shock and rage. Paul is claiming that all four applications are not teachings within The-Belief, and I leave it to the reader to investigate *Strong's* G2316 *theon* in context with Paul's statement and determine for yourself. My understanding is that Paul is calling the following lies and not a tenet of The Body of Christ: the worship and following of angels; anyone claiming to directly talk to God or God directly talking to them; or the concept of a trinity. I realize this is controversial, and if any of these three topics are to be observed or believed by those called, I welcome counterpoint and provable discussion with scriptural references.

Outside of this point of discussion, the remaining commentary stands on its own merits. We have a corporate letter going to a junior partner with the full rights and privileges to act in Paul's and Christ's behalf intended to be minimally "regional" in nature and intent, but universal in application in reality.

TITUS AS A LETTER

PAUL, A WILLING-BOUND-SLAVE OF *GOD*, a Commissioner of *Anointed-Jesus* with the Belief-of-the-Chosen-Ones-of-God with the Knowledge-of-Truth in reverence, in expectation of life eonian which *THE-TRUE-GOD* promised before the ages of time. Yet *HE-MAKES-APPEAR* in *HIS* own time and place, *The-Word*-of-*HIM* which I am committed by fidelity and trusted with to proclaim according-to the injunction-and-authority-and-mandate-and-command of *God*, *The-Savior* of us.

To Titus, a genuine offspring in common belief; grace, mercy, peace to you from *GOD-THE-FATHER* and *Master-Messiah-Anointed*, *The-Savior* of us. I left you in Crete for this purpose that you should be building and put in place what lacks in each city. To set in place seniors if anyone is unindictable and unimpeachable, a husband of one wife, having believing children not accused of decadence or insubordination. For a supervisor is bound and obligated to be unimpeachable as an administrator of God, not seeking or given in self-gratification, not indignant and irritating, not to excessive wine, not quarrelsome, not greedy for money. But hospitable, fond of goodness, sensible and sound-minded, just and upright, keeping-the-commands, free from wickedness, self-controlled, keeping and maintaining the faithful teaching according-to the *Word*. That he may be able to be factual and true in errorless teaching, to-be-convincing, exhorting and exposing The-Ones-Contradicting.

For indeed there are many insubordinate and disobedient ones uttering senseless things and imposters. Especially The-Ones concerning circumcision. Whose mouths must be stopped and silenced, who are subverting whole households. Teaching that which is not required-or-obligated concerning mosaic laws, circumcision, or what is required for salvation for their sordid and filthy dishonorable gain. And a certain-one of their own, their prophet, claims Cretans are forever falsifying, evil, wild beasts, lazy, and avoid work.

That testimony, this is true! Because of this you are to immediately expose and refute, call to account, and demand an explanation from them that they may be without error in grace and strengthened in The-Belief. Do not listen, obey, or consider Jewish myths and directions from men, the-ones leaving and abandoning The-Belief. All is indeed pure-and-ethical and not forbidden to-the-ones pure, yet to-the-ones having-been-defiled and unbelieving, nothing is clean and their mind and conscience has-been-defiled. They are swearing and claiming to-be-acquainted with deities,

Section VII

divinities, and yet they are disowning and denying *Him* being abominable and unpersuadable and not proving to have any good work.

Now you be speaking what is accurate-above-all-others-clear-plain-and-obvious, that being-sound teaching. That the aged men are to be sober, sane, be established and strong in The-Belief, in the-Godly-love with endurance. The aged-women similarly become sacred in behavior and demeanor, not adversaries, not in much wine. Give yourself in bonded service to teaching the-proper-behavior. That they may be instructing the young wives to be sensible, to Godly-love their husbands, to Godly-love their children, self-controlled, pure and chaste, watching the home, good, honorable, and upright, in willing voluntary submission to their own husbands that the saying of *THE-GOD* may not be-being-blasphemed. And you be directing and instructing the young men to be sober-minded.

About yourself, in all present yourself the model of properly acting, teaching with integrity and incorruptness, in reverence and respect and purity, in sincerity, sound speech not censured or condemnable; that the Contrary One may be-being-shamed having nothing wicked or bad to say about you.

Slaves, be obedient, align to your own owners, in all be well-pleasing and acceptable, not contradictory, not embezzling, but in belief displaying honor and uprightness in all that *The-Teaching-of-God-The-Savior* of us in all may be embellished with honor.

For the merciful kindness and good will of *THE-GOD* has appeared and clearly become known saving all men, training us to refuse and reject the ungodliness and The-Systems' worldly desires and lusts, that we should be living soberly, justly and righteously, and devoutly in the current eon anticipating The-happy-Expectation, even The-Appearance-of-the-Glory-of-*THE-GREAT-GOD* and our *Savior, Messiah-Anointed.* Who gives *Himself* for the sake of us, that *He-Redeems* us from all conditions-of-violating-the-law and *He-Cleans* a people for *Himself,* zealous with honorable-morally-good-noble-and-exceedingly-pleasing acts. Of this you be speaking and be addressing, instructing, and exposing, correcting, and explaining in all and with every mandate and authority. And let no-one be slighting, despise, or scorn you.

You keep reminding them they are to be yielding and are subject to the Powers, Sovereignties, and Authorities; ready to be doing all good acts. No-one is to be blaspheming or speaking evil, making malicious false statements, abstaining from fighting, be fair to all displaying to all men meekness. For we were once foolish and stubborn being deceived; slaving to the lusty-desires and various gratifications, in depravity, wickedness, and malice, injurious and for envy, passing on detestable hatred to one another.

But now *God-The-Savior* of us has appeared and shone kindness and love to mankind. Not by works of righteousness that we do, but according-to *HIS* mercy *HE-SAVES* us through the complete washing through the Holy-spirit. Becoming a new creation to a new birth, a pristine condition, a new life which *HE*-pours-out on us abundantly through *Messiah-Anointed*, *The-Savior* of us. That being justified by *HIS* grace, we may become Enjoyers-of-The-Allotment in The-Expectation of life eonian through the ages. True, accurate and believable are these words concerning this. I assert confidently and affirm and intend and purposefully desire that you understand to remain doing good acts; the-ones having believed in *THE-GOD*. These good acts are beneficial for men.

And avoid godless foolish questionings and genealogies, also strife and fighting about the Law. Stay away from these for it is without benefit and empty! After the first and second admonition, refuse to be with The-Man following false doctrine. Understand such a one is corrupted-perverted-inverted-and-turned-upside down and is sinning condemning himself.

Whenever I shall be sending Artemis or Tychicus for you, make haste to come to me to Nicopolis, for I have decided to winter there. Send immediately Zenas The-Lawyer and Apollos that nothing is short for their provisions. And let ours also be learning to produce good works for the necessary needs of the edification of the soul that they are not empty but yielding what they ought to produce. All the-ones with me are greeting you, the-ones that Godly-love us in the Belief.

The-Grace be with all of you.

Amen.

TITUS STUDY NOTES

Note: Through my many translations, I have come to believe that the phrase or associated phrasing of "inheritance" [ex: Col 1:12] accurately translated as "the-allotment" in Scripture is not a good or proper translation (i.e., inheritance). Paul makes it clear that we are to be family members (I state: royal and godly) destined to be with HIM and HE with us and we in Christ and He in us. Inheritance has an implied connotation, an accepted concept that someone has died. THE-GOD is certainly not dead, and Christ has risen to life eonian (there are times of times of times) as well. I see this as a watering down of the intent and meaning of the Scriptures and have dropped using the word *inheritance* when speaking of THE-GOD's plan and purpose for us. We are to take rulership in an active kingdom with Christ at the head of the realm and we under Him, with THE-GOD over all of us.

Note The Greek word *agapen* translated as "love" in most translations is missing that this is Godly in nature and not of men or any other such creature. I have therefore carried the adjective to add clarity to the meaning of this word throughout this translation.

Note: In my research, nearly all translations have dropped "the" as a modifier, but the Greek word for "the" is in every text and not meant to be ignored or deleted. It is often specifically singular, and when attached to the noun, it is describing that noun as unique, one of a kind, a specific thing, the original, the one and only. It is for this reason that I carry "the" everywhere it appears in all translations. Whether of God, Jesus, Satan or any other entity, concept, or idea, the modifier "the" clears up a lot of generalized words, ideas, concepts, and entities.

Note: The root of the word *pnuemia*, translated as "spirit, wind, or breath," has no gender identity since this is a word that is neuter in gender. *Pnuemia* is an "it." The Greeks, as we of English language, often fix a gender to objects and things— for example: cars, boats, the moon, the sun. For the Greeks, *pnuemia* at times has a male gender affixed to it. *Pnuemia* in the Scriptures is never capitalized or designated as a standalone being, entity, principality, or sovereignty when used as the word "spirit." It is simply the power inherent in the

being, whether of man, or God, or Christ, or any other entity. If anything is living, "it" possesses a spirit. The "Holy-spirit" is simply the power from and of The-God, giving and renewing life and performing The-God's will.

Note: Paul constantly claims and mentions "principles, powers, authorities, sovereignties not of our world." He quite clearly claims that these beings are the ones that certainly influence and control (predominately in a negative way) the systems of this world, people of the nations, and as individuals directly. You can find this concept also contained in The Old Testament through the implications of the first commandment. This claim and the concept of the warring factions in heaven makes a fascinating study.

Note: Time periods, eons, ages, millennia, eons, and eons—I stayed true to the Greek words associated with time and what we still use today in our common language. A study of time periods is fascinating but is also an area that can cause confusion. The-God always works on some kind of a timetable, but understanding which is which and when is when is a bit of a mystery. Some timetables are only known to The-God and made clear to man at God's will.

Note What is the difference between "expectation" and "hope?" Nearly all translations adopt the word "hope" for "expectation," but Paul uses almost exclusively the word "expectation." Here is why I constantly use "expectation." Having an expectation means you have no doubt at all. It is sure and certain with no ambiguity or doubt. Having a hope means you are not 100 percent convinced and convicted. I can tell you that Paul is undeniably convinced and convicted in what he delivers and talks about. Using "hope" sends a message that there is some possibility for "wiggle room," doubt, error, or excuses.

Even worse, much of the use of the word "expectation" in Paul's writings has the modifier "the" attached to "expectation," thus forming the proper translation and singular concept of "The-Expectation." This makes "The-Expectation" an event, not a philosophy or theological premise. Not recognizing "The-Expectation" as an event will lead the reader immediately down an incorrect understanding of what is being offered or discussed.

1:1 The phrase "willing-bound" has the implication of "as in the marriage of husband and wife."

1:16 The Greek word *theon* (Strong's G2316 or translated as "God") has also as a potential definition "The Trinity" (see definition "2"). If this is true, and supplementing "Trinity" for "God," Paul is clearly not acknowledging the Trinity Doctrine as correct, but rather as a false doctrine since he is quite clear about "THE-GOD" being a singular entity or being in every one of his letters including Titus. He is condemning this false teacher who claims to have the knowledge of "God."

Section VII

2:8 My translation of "Contrary One" is rather broad in who it is referencing. While this letter indicates there was an individual on Crete corrupting doctrine and insisting on circumcision, one could interpret the "Contrary One" as The-Adversary or Satan. If you see the letter of Titus written for and "talking" to you directly, then Satan becomes a much clearer choice.

2:11 "The merciful kindness" that appeared and was being spoken of is the Messiah Jesus.

2:11 "Saving all men" is a direct reference to "The-Secret."

2:13 "The-happy-Expectation" is an event much like in the United States where "Independence Day" or the "Fourth of July" or "Labor Day" are events. I have capitalized it as such, realizing this. Paul is talking about receiving your resurrection and spiritual body, Christ's return and setting up His Kingdom, and you receiving your Allotment reserved for you by God.

2:13 This portion of the verse, "even the-appearance of the glory of THE-GREAT-GOD and our Savior, Messiah-Anointed," is telling the reader that not only is Christ to come back to earth, but God Himself intends to do so also.

TITUS IN VERSE

TITUS 1

1:1 Paul, a slave [willing-bound-slave] of *GOD*, a Commissioner of *Anointed-Jesus* with the Belief [faith]-of-the-Chosen-Ones-of-*GOD*, with the Knowledge-of-Truth in devoutness [reverence]

1:2 in expectation of life eonian which *THE-TRUE-GOD* promised before times eonian [the ages of time].

1:3 Yet *HE-MAKES-APPEAR* in *HIS* own season [era, time and place], *The-Word* of *HIM* which I am entrusted [committed by fidelity, trusted with] to proclaim according-to the injunction [authority, mandate, command] of *God*, *The-Savior* of us.

1:4 To Titus, (a) genuine offspring [child] in common belief [faith]; grace, mercy, peace (to you) from *GOD-THE-FATHER* and *Master-Messiah-Anointed*, *The-Savior* of us.

1:5 I left you in Crete for this grace [this cause, on this account, purpose]. That you should be erecting [building, put in place, amending, repairing] what lacks in each city, to be constituting [set in place, appoint to office, place in charge] seniors [bishops, elders, presbyters].

1:6 If anyone is unindictable [unimpeachable], a husband of one wife, having believing children not accused of decadence [habitual extravagance wastefulness] or insubordination [unruly].

1:7 For a supervisor is bound to be unimpeachable, as an administrator of God, not seeking or given in self-gratification, not indignant [irritable], not to excessive wine, not quarrelsome, not greedy for money.

1:8 But a fond-lodger [hospitable], fond of goodness, sensible [sound-minded], just [upright, righteous, keeping the commands], free from wickedness [pious, moral], self-controlled,

Section VII

1:9 upholding [keeping, maintaining] the faithful teaching according-to the *Word*. That he may be able in sound [factual and true, errorless] teaching, to-be-entreating [convincing, exhort] and exposing The-Ones-Contradicting.

1:10 For indeed there are many insubordinates [disobedient] (ones) uttering senseless things and imposters. Especially The-Ones concerning about-cutting [Circumcision].

1:11 Whose mouths must be bridled [stopped, silenced, gagged], who are subverting whole households. Teaching that which is not binding [Mosaic Laws, circumcision, required or obligated concerning [required for salvation]] for their sordid [filthy, dishonorable] gain.

1:12 And a certain-one of their own, their prophet (claims, says): Cretans are ever falsifying, evil wild beasts, idle bellies [lazy, avoid work].

1:13 That testimony, this is true! Because of this you are to sharply [immediately] expose [refute, call to account, demand an explanation from] them that they may be sound [without error, in grace and strong] in The-Belief [faith].

1:14 Do not heed [listen, obey, consider] Jewish myths and directions from men, the ones turning from [leaving, abandoning] The-Belief.

1:15 All is indeed clean [pure, ethical, not forbidden] to-the-ones clean, yet to-the-ones having-been-defiled and unbelieving, nothing is clean and their mind and conscience has-been-defiled.

1:16 They are vowing [swearing, claiming, testifying] to-be-acquainted with God [deity, divinities], yet they-are disowning [denying] (HIM) being abominable and stubborn [unpersuadable] and untested [not proving to have, unfit as] every [all, any] good act [work].

TITUS 2

2:1 Now you be speaking what is the eminent [accurate above all others, conspicuous, clear, plain, obvious] being-sound teaching [doctrine].

2:2 That the seniors [aged men] are to be grave [sober], sane, being sound [established, strong] in The-Belief [faith], in the Godly-love, in endurance [steadfast].

2:3 The aged-women similarly become sacred in behavior and demeanor, not adversaries, not in much wine, enslaved [give yourself in bonded service [as a bondswoman]] to teaching the ideal [proper behavior],

2:4 that they may be instructing the young females [wives] to be sensible, to Godly-love their men [husband], to Godly-love their children;

TITUS IN VERSE

2:5   self-controlled, pure [chaste], watching the home, good [honorable, upright], in willing [voluntary] submission to their own men [husbands] that the saying of THE-GOD may not be-being-blasphemed.

2:6   And you be entreating [directing, instruct] the young men to be sober-minded.

2:7   About yourself, in all present yourself the model of properly acting, in teaching with integrity [incorruptness], gravely [reverence and respect, purity], in sincerity,

2:8   sound speech not censured or condemnable; that The-Contrary-One may be-being-shamed having nothing wicked [bad] to say about you.

2:9   Slaves, be obedient [arrange yourself, array, align] to your own owners, in all be well-pleasing [acceptable], not contradictory,

2:10   not embezzling, but in belief [faith] displaying honor [uprightness] in all; that the Teaching-[doctrine]-of-*The-Savior* of us, *God,* in all may be embellished with gain [honor].

2:11   For the grace [merciful kindness, good will] of *THE-GOD* has appeared [shown upon, clearly become known] saving all men,

2:12   training us to refuse [reject] the ungodliness and The-Systems' [worldly] desires [lusts], that we should be living sanely [soberly], justly [righteously], and devoutly in the current eon

2:13   anticipating The-happy-Expectation, even The-Appearance-of-the-Glory-of-*THE-GREAT-GOD* and our *Savior, Jesus-Anointed.*

2:14   *Who* gives *Himself* for the sake of us, that *He-Redeems* us from all lawlessness [conditions of violating the law] and *He-Cleans* a people for *Himself,* zealous with ideal [honorable, morally good, noble, exceedingly-pleasing] acts [works].

2:15   Of this you be speaking and be entreating [addressing, instructing] and exposing [correcting, explaining] in all [and with every] mandate [command, authority]. And let no-one be slighting [despise, condemn, scorn] you.

TITUS 3

3:1   You keep reminding them they are to be yielding and be subject to the Originals [powers, sovereignties] and Authorities, ready to be doing all good acts [works].

3:2   No-one is to (be)-blaspheming [speaking evil, make malicious false statements about], abstaining from fighting, be fair [and moderate] to all, displaying to all men meekness.

Section VII

3:3 For when we were foolish and stubborn, being deceived, slaving to the lusty-desires and various gratifications, in depravity [wickedness, malice, to injure], and for envy, passing on detestable hatred to one another.

3:4 But now *The-Savior* of us, *God*, has appeared and shone kindness and love to mankind.

3:5 Not by works of justice [righteousness] that we do, but according-to *His* mercy, *He-Saves* us through the bathing [complete washing] through the Holy-spirit. Becoming a new creation [new birth, to a pristine condition, new life]

3:6 which *HE*-pours-out on us abundantly through *Messiah-Anointed, The-Savior* of us.

3:7 That being justified by *HIS* grace, we may become Enjoyers-of-The-Allotment in The-Expectation of life eonian [through the ages].

3:8 True [accurate and believable] are these words concerning this. I assert confidently [affirming] and intend [purposefully desire] that you understand to maintain [remain doing] ideal [good] acts [works]; the-ones having believed in *THE-GOD*. These good acts are beneficial for men.

3:9 And avoid godless [foolish] questionings and genealogies, also strife and fighting about the Law. Stay away from these for it is without benefit and empty!

3:10 After the first and second admonition, refuse to be with The-Man following false doctrine [that is a heretic].

3:11 Understand such a one is corrupted [has been perverted, inverted] and is sinning, being self-condemned [condemning himself].

3:12 Whenever I shall be sending Artemis or Tychicus for you, give diligence [make haste] to come to me to Nicopolis [Conquer City], for I have decided to winter there.

3:13 Send immediately Zenas The-Lawyer and Apollos that nothing may be lacking [short on provisions, sustenance] for them {for their journey}.

3:14 And let ours also be learning to maintain [produce, preside over doing] good works for necessary needs [edification of the soul], that they are not unfruitful [empty, to be yielding what they ought to produce].

3:15 All the-ones with me are greeting you, the-ones that Godly-love us in (the) Belief [faith].

The-Grace (be) with all of you.
Amen.

Section IIX

A TORT
(Philemon)

The Letter of PHILEMON

PHILEMON COMMENTARY

PHILEMON RESTS AS THE last and fourteenth letter of Paul, and it is the shortest and the most personal also a tort. It is an interesting letter in that Paul to Philemon acknowledges that Paul has the authority as a power of attorney to insist and force Philemon in giving up his slave, but he chooses a completely different approach by returning Philemon's slave Onesimus to him. Forcing the issue with an iron glove just does not seem palatable to Paul, and in a letter of personal appeal, he sets the stage for Philemon to think about Onesimus' future, Philemon's future, and Paul's future needs and interests.

Within this letter Paul hints that Philemon has freedom, not only in what to do with Onesimus but also in Christ, and on a different level he is asking whether or not Onesimus should have this same freedom. This, then, is as such the beginning of a "trial balloon" case opposing slavery on many levels. You are getting a chance to see Paul question the eon standing practice of slavery. In another parallel line of thought, why continue the practice to be enslaved, which is part of a dying and fading operation of The-System of the Originals (see my comment about the "Originals" in my study notes)? Was slavery really ever intended or was this just another operation in place inside the "system" to prevent man from the true freedom intended at the inception of time? I would argue that today we are still enslaved, with many different operations all designed to keep us from freedom, which is reminiscent of the Roman letter. Hence Philemon comes full circle, reintroducing again from Romans the topic of freedom. We certainly have enslavement today, which I contend is to end upon the return of Christ.

Philemon is much more argumentative and challenging in purpose and intent then one would read just on the surface. I hope this sheds a different understanding on what Philemon is about and demonstrates that Paul, on a personal level takes on the role as the humbled "servant," willing to give up the most to serve Christ's purposes and yet challenges the thinking of that day and for our day as well.

Obvious to all in this letter is seeing Paul take a humble approach as a servant himself to Philemon's asking for special consideration on behalf of Onesimus, another servant. While this letter is also about repaying Philemon for Paul's use of this slave for the work in the Ecclesia and requesting his release to continue in that work, Paul proposes to the Nations a much bigger question: Is any slavery acceptable? For it is

Section IIX

certainly not what will exist in God's Kingdom. Paul asks Philemon, "What is your freedom worth? What is Onesimus' freedom worth? Are you in dominion of Onesimus in Christ?" Are any of us? Our true freedom is in Christ.

Closing out Paul's letters, we come back to the topic of freedom that I introduced in the Romans letter. Here we see a complete unity of all of Paul's letters from start to finish. All his letters relate to freedom in Christ, and all his letters are written as legal briefs, charges, debates, and summations for you.

Philemon, short and sweet, and most humbling in approach, offers a challenge from Paul, just as does Romans. Paul, in a last stand as an aging dominant male lion, roars into the ages and makes a final appeal for freedom. His argument is that this freedom in Christ is a free gift, given by God the Father, and we are not to be content with the things and systems in this life, not to take advantage of others, but rather to imitate Christ who slaved and sacrificed and served others and did not impose his will. This freedom comes from exercising godly-love, not by obeying commandments, rules, and regulations that only continue to enslave. This godly-love is also a gift from the Father.

I will make mention again in the Study Notes but it's worth mentioning it here in preface to reading the letter. I've talked about Paul's mastery of turning an idea, argument, practice in on itself showing the ineffectiveness of continuing the activity and to stop being enslaved to a dead or dying philosophy or event. That will be very obvious in this letter. For the name Onesimus is translated as "Profitable" in the common English language. I dropped using Onesimus' name in the letter for the use of Profitable so the reader can see Paul's brilliance in the crafted letter to Philemon. The "profitless-one" for Philemon is "profitable" for Paul and Christ.

Philemon sits as a fitting masterpiece to close out the career and tenure of Paul and his service for you and me and all those into the ages and eons to come.

God bless The-All.

PHILEMON AS A LETTER

PAUL, A CAPTIVE PRISONER of *Anointed-Savior*, and Timothy, The-Brother,
 to Philemon, the Godly-beloved and fellow-worker of us, and to Apphia and to Archippus, the fellow-warriors and associates of us, and to the Ecclesia in your house. Grace to you and peace from *GOD*, *FATHER* of us and *Master-Savior-Anointed*.

I am giving thanks to *THE-GOD* of mine, always making reminders about you in my prayer hearing of your Godly-love and The-Belief which you are having in the *Master-Savior* and to all the Holy-Ones. That the participation-and-sharing and proof of The-Belief operating in you may continue growing, be fuller, and have more of in-the-correct-and-precise, full-and-accurate knowledge of everything good which is in you for *Anointed-Savior*.

For we are having great joy and encouragement, comfort, and solace in the Godly-love for the Holy-Ones you have, having deep care and compassions for them, and they, having been helped to be refreshed and restored through you Brother. Because of this, in boldness, in direct and frank speech, unreserved and openly in *Anointed* I could have charged and ordered you out of convenience and out of duty since your conversion, but rather I come out of Godly-love.

I Paul am humbly requesting as such a one of an aged-man now, an elderly ambassador, also as a prisoner of *Savior-Anointed*, I am requesting with great consideration from you concerning the offspring of mine whom I converted during my imprisonment, Profitable (Onesimus) who once was profitless to you, yet now is profitable to you and me who I send back to you. As in my mercy and forgiveness for him, be taking him back to yourself whom I intended to retain for myself instead of replacing you, so he may be serving me in the willing-bondage of the Well-Message. Yet without your opinion about what to do, decree, and advice, and out of honor for you I will do nothing so this is not forced or imposed upon but from you of free will, without any reservations and forgiven in full.

For perhaps this reason he was separated for an hour, that you may then be having him back for eonian, the rest of the time. No longer as a slave, but a slave as *The-Beloved-Brother* from above, especially for me but much more for you in the flesh and for *Master*. If you consider me a companion, accept him as me, and if in anything he has injured you or owes you, be placing this to my account. I Paul, in my own handwriting, shall repay it, and I will never come back and say to you later that you

Section IIX

owe me anything at all. Yes, Brother, may I-profit and have joy from you in *Master* if out of my deep compassion and mercy for you I sooth-and-refresh and restore you through *Master*.

I write to you having confidence of your counsel, decision, and in observation of your counsel-and-decision that even over what I am asking you shall be doing more. And also, at the same time be preparing a lodging for me, for I am expecting that through your prayers I shall be graciously granted to be with you.

Epaphras is greeting you, my fellow-captive in *Anointed-Savior*, Marcus, Aristarchus, Demas, Lucas, my fellow-workers. The Grace of *The-Master* of us, *Savior-Anointed* be with your spirit.

Amen.

PHILEMON STUDY NOTES

Note: Through my many translations, I have come to believe that the phrase or associated phrasing of "inheritance" [ex: Col 1:12] accurately translated as "the-allotment" in Scripture is not a good or proper translation (i.e., inheritance). Paul makes it clear that we are to be family members (I state: royal and godly) destined to be with HIM and HE with us and we in Christ and He in us. Inheritance has an implied connotation, an accepted concept that someone has died. THE-GOD is certainly not dead, and Christ has risen to life eonian (there are times of times of times) as well. I see this as a watering down of the intent and meaning of the Scriptures and have dropped using the word *inheritance* when speaking of THE-GOD's plan and purpose for us. We are to take rulership in an active kingdom with Christ at the head of the realm and we under Him, with THE-GOD over all of us.

Note The Greek word *agapen* translated as "love" in most translations is missing that this is Godly in nature and not of men or any other such creature. I have therefore carried the adjective to add clarity to the meaning of this word throughout this translation.

Note: In my research, nearly all translations have dropped "the" as a modifier, but the Greek word for "the" is in every text and not meant to be ignored or deleted. It is often specifically singular, and when attached to the noun, it is describing that noun as unique, one of a kind, a specific thing, the original, the one and only. It is for this reason that I carry "the" everywhere it appears in all translations. Whether of God, Jesus, Satan or any other entity, concept, or idea, the modifier "the" clears up a lot of generalized words, ideas, concepts, and entities.

Note: The root of the word *pnuemia*, translated as "spirit, wind, or breath," has no gender identity since this is a word that is neuter in gender. *Pnuemia* is an "it." The Greeks, as we of English language, often fix a gender to objects and things— for example: cars, boats, the moon, the sun. For the Greeks, *pnuemia* at times has a male gender affixed to it. *Pnuemia* in the Scriptures is never capitalized or designated as a standalone being, entity, principality, or sovereignty when used as the word "spirit." It is simply the power inherent in the

Section IIX

being, whether of man, or God, or Christ, or any other entity. If anything is living, "it" possesses a spirit. The "Holy-spirit" is simply the power from and of The-God, giving and renewing life and performing The-God's will.

Note: Paul constantly claims and mentions "principles, powers, authorities, sovereignties not of our world." He quite clearly claims that these beings are the ones that certainly influence and control (predominately in a negative way) the systems of this world, people of the nations, and as individuals directly. You can find this concept also contained in The Old Testament through the implications of the first commandment. This claim and the concept of the warring factions in heaven makes a fascinating study.

Note: Time periods, eons, ages, millennia, eons, and eons—I stayed true to the Greek words associated with time and what we still use today in our common language. A study of time periods is fascinating but is also an area that can cause confusion. The-God always works on some kind of a timetable, but understanding which is which and when is when is a bit of a mystery. Some timetables are only known to The-God and made clear to man at God's will.

Note What is the difference between "expectation" and "hope?" Nearly all translations adopt the word "hope" for "expectation," but Paul uses almost exclusively the word "expectation." Here is why I constantly use "expectation." Having an expectation means you have no doubt at all. It is sure and certain with no ambiguity or doubt. Having a hope means you are not 100 percent convinced and convicted. I can tell you that Paul is undeniably convinced and convicted in what he delivers and talks about. Using "hope" sends a message that there is some possibility for "wiggle room," doubt, error, or excuses.

Even worse, much of the use of the word "expectation" in Paul's writings has the modifier "the" attached to "expectation," thus forming the proper translation and singular concept of "The-Expectation." This makes "The-Expectation" an event, not a philosophy or theological premise. Not recognizing "The-Expectation" as an event will lead the reader immediately down an incorrect understanding of what is being offered or discussed.

1:10–14 Paul is a master at turning that which is negative into a positive and vice versa. He takes Onesimus' name (Profitable) and weaves it in and out of these verses turning someone that was "unprofitable" into someone profitable for Philemon, Paul, and Christ. This section is ingeniously simple and direct, yet shows Paul's gift for masterfully crafting the request and point he needs to make using the very word or argument pro or con (also see verse 20).

1:19 The reminder at the end of this verse was not intended to "shame" Philemon into accepting Onesimus back, but instead is intended to encourage Philemon to continue to exercise and practice the gifts of godly-love, forgiveness, and mercy that he was already demonstrating, and moreover to the one who had slighted him. Are we not asked to do the same with those in our lives?

Note: While investigating, comparing, and researching this verse, two camps of thought became apparent depending on the resource. Camp one, the most common approach, is to imply that Philemon "owed" Paul since Paul was the one (either directly or indirectly) responsible for his conversion, and the opening salutation and immediately following verses certainly support this idea. I have, therefore, reflected this providing the following as an alternative for the word "yourself": [at all, *for your own life* [*salvation*]] (italics mine for this discussion).

But I agree with the second line of thinking, which is that the burden is totally Paul's without reservation, as if this were really his own honest debt to pay back, and no one else's. He "bought the goods"; he needed to pay for them. He had already stated his agenda early in the letter and is doing nothing more than walking the walk he constantly taught others to exercise: to demonstrate and live the pure and unadulterated Godly-love of Christ, humbling himself before Philemon and "taking on each other's burdens." In one defense of this, Paul stated that he was not going to force the "Profitable" one on him, but rather let him make his own decision, so Paul has no reason to come back later in the letter and subtly hint that Philemon "is obligated and owes" anyone to take back Onesimus. Paul says he was willing to keep him for his needs. I believe the first line of thinking does Paul and his teachings an injustice. I have translated this verse in keeping with pure and chaste motives. You decide for yourself, however, which fits the purpose and intent best.

1:20 Paul is truly trying to say "May we bless each other, which also blesses and honors Christ" in this request. Christ in return would bless them.

Note: I can't help but wonder if Paul somehow, sometime, taught Onesimus about the "Suffering Servant" Jesus Christ and how our Brother in Heaven served (and serves) us despite the way we may have honored and "treated" Him (hopefully only in the past). I then wonder if Paul did meet Philemon face-to-face and if he talked about what true leadership and administration over a household was supposed to be as Christ heads his body and Ecclesia. My suspicion is both required a realignment, as we all do.

PHILEMON IN VERSE

PHILEMON 1

1:1 Paul, a bound-one [captive, prisoner] of *Anointed-Savior*, and Timothy, The-Brother to Philemon [Fond-one], the Godly-beloved and fellow-worker of us,

1:2 and to Apphia [Fruitful] and to Archippus [Master of the Horse] the fellow-warrior [associate, soldier] of us, and to the Ecclesia in your house.

1:3 Grace to you and peace from *GOD*, *FATHER* of us and *Master-Savior-Anointed*.

1:4 I am giving thanks to *THE-GOD* of mine, always making reminders about you in my prayer

1:5 hearing of your Godly-love and The-Belief which you are having in the *Master-Savior* and to all the Holy-ones.

1:6 That the communion [participation, sharing, proof] of The-Belief operating in you may-be-becoming [continue growing, be fuller, have more] in the correct and precise [full and accurate] knowledge of everything good, which is in you for *Anointed-Savior*.

1:7 For we are having great joy and encouragement [comfort and solace] in the Godly-love for the Holy-Ones you have, having deep care and compassions for (them), and (they), having been helped to be restored [refreshed] through you Brother.

1:8 Because of this, in boldness [direct and frank speech, unreserved and openly] in *Anointed* I could have commanded, [charged, ordered] you out of convenience [out of duty [since your conversion]]

1:9 but rather (I come) out of Godly-love.

1:10 I Paul am entreating [humbly requesting] as such a one of an aged-man now, [an elderly ambassador], also as a prisoner of *Savior-Anointed*, I am entreating [praying, requesting/begging with great consideration from] you concerning the offspring [son, child] of mine whom I generated [converted, begat, birthed] in [during] my bonds [chains, imprisonment] Onesimus [Profitable, Useful]

1:11 who once was useless [profitless] to you, yet now is useful [profitable] to you and me

1:12 who I send back to you. As in my compassions [mercy and forgiveness] for him, be taking him (back) to yourself

1:13 whom I intended to retain for myself for the sake of [instead, to replace] you, so he may be serving me in the bonds [willing-bondage [as husband and wife]] of the Well-Message.

1:14 Yet without your opinion [about what to do, decree, advice] and out of good [honor] for you, I will do nothing so this is not out compulsion [forced, imposed upon] from you but voluntary [of free will, willingly without any reservations, forgiven in full].

1:15 For perhaps this reason he was separated for an hour, that you may then be having him back for eonian [the rest of the time].

1:16 No longer as a slave, but a slave as a beloved brother from above, especially for me, but much more for you in the flesh and for (the) *Master*.

1:17 If you are having [consider] me a companion [partner, comrade, associate], accept him as me.

1:18 And if in anything he has injured you or owes you, be placing this to my charge [account].

1:19 I Paul, in my own handwriting, shall repay [refund] it, and I will not even say [assert, acknowledge, have forgotten, come back] to you that you owe me for [from] yourself [anything at all, for your own life [salvation]].

1:20 Yes, Brother, may I-profit [have joy] from you in (the) *Master* if out of my deep compassion and mercy for you, I soothe [refresh and restore] you in [by way of, through] (the) *Master*.

1:21 I write to you having confidence of your counsel [decision and in observation of your Christianity] that even over what I am asking you shall be doing (more).

1:22 And also at the same time be preparing a lodging for me, for I am expecting that through your prayers I shall be graciously granted to be with you.

1:23 Epaphras [Lovely] is greeting you, my fellow-captive in *Anointed-Savior*;

1:24 Marcus [John (Jewish)—a defense], Aristarchus [the best ruler], Demas [governor of the people], Lucas [light-giving], my fellow-workers.

1:25 The Grace of The-Master of us, *Savior*-Anointed (be) with your spirit.

Amen.

Summary and Closing

Summary and Closing Comments

First, allow me to give credit where credit is due: to our Father God. When I started this project, it was an activity I never expected to take well over five years to complete. Each time I reread this private translation and compare it to the host of others, I continue to be challenged by what I was permitted to do and have come to understand. I claim no religion, and therefore I hope I've had a much more open mind when researching, analyzing, and reaching a supposition. I have been honest enough to tell the reader how I reached my decisions. I have done so that you may be convinced in your own mind about accepting or rejecting what has been offered. I am here to persuade no one, but I am willing to challenge everyone's thinking and actions. By the grace of God, I have grown and been allowed to dissolve many mis-teachings, errors, and outright lies by many claiming to represent Christ. But I see as Paul sees, and he has said that many are serving only their bellies and lusts. It is also so apparent today. But for my readers, what I hope is that you will appreciate my efforts and do your own research.

Additionally, I want you to recognize that Paul was not just another typical Jew of the day. He had credentials—credentials that went back to royal lineage—and he was a member of both the Sanhedrin and Pharisees. He had exclusive training at the feet of Gamaliel. What does this mean? He was at one time married and had at least one child. He sat in judgment in the highest court of the land and was a strikingly handsome man. For convenience, I have extracted selected passages and information from this excellent article found at https://www.aish.com/jl/m/pm/48936377.html:

> Qualifications for Membership
>
> Every member of the Sanhedrin had to be distinguished in Torah knowledge, wisdom, humility, fear of God, indifference to monetary gain, love of truth, love of fellow man, and good reputation. It is thus written, "You shall provide out of all the people, able men, who fear God, men of truth, disdaining unjust gain, and place them over [the people]" (Exodus 18:21). It is likewise written, "Take from each of your tribes, wise men, with understanding and full of knowledge, and I will make them your leaders" (Deut. 1:13).
>
> . . . be expert in all areas of the Torah. They also had to have enough knowledge of science and mathematics to be able to adapt Torah law to all possible problems.

Members of the Sanhedrin likewise had to have knowledge of other religions, as well as the teachings of idolatry and the occult arts, so as to be able to render judgment in cases involving these matters.

The Sanhedrin was required to hear all testimony directly, and not through an interpreter. It is therefore preferable that its members be familiar with all the languages spoken by Jews around the world.

In order that the Sanhedrin commands the utmost respect, its members must be of good appearance, and free of bodily defect. Therefore, a person who is blind, even in one eye, cannot be a member of the Sanhedrin (Now think about Paul's eye infirmary later while serving Christ).

Age and Lineage

Similarly, the members of the Sanhedrin must command respect as mature individuals. Therefore, it is preferable that each member be at least 40 years old, unless he is incomparable in wisdom and universally respected. Under no condition should a person under 18 be appointed to the Sanhedrin.

A person who is very old may not sit on the Sanhedrin, since he is apt to be too severe. The same is true of a man who is sterile, or even childless.

It is preferable that the members of the Sanhedrin be chosen from people of unbroken descent, as in the case of all positions of authority. It is required, however, that all members of the Sanhedrin be of Jewish parentage . . .

It is preferable that the Sanhedrin contain Kohen-priests and Levites as members.

The reader needs to be aware that Paul was all of these, and as I mentioned in the opening chapters, he was also a Pharisee, and this position and role had its own separate set of regulations my readers should explore on their own. Paul was not a pawn inside the Jewish system. He was the "Golden Boy." He was well known and highly respected, and when he was ordered to murder those opposing the Law of Moses, he had the full authority of Rome and the ruling party of the Jewish nation. He had a very clear conscience about this. He was eliminating sedition and preventing insurrection for Rome and preserving the Jewish state of affairs.

Second, he was a preeminent debater. This is clearly demonstrated in Acts 23 when he addressed both parties of the Sanhedrin and Pharisaic Councils and later the audience at Mars Hill in Greece. There is no doubt that Paul left both audiences in a quandary about how to refute the claims he presented. Under the influence of the generations of Jewish scholars and finally having been taught by Gamelial, Paul was able to present clearly and precisely the argument or dispute needing to be addressed. By using Scripture to defend or attack the issue, and with the clearest of logic, he again draws an irrefutable conclusion pro or con. One of the reasons I placed the writings into a letter format is that reading one verse at a time forces the reader to unconsciously accept each verse as a complete theme or concept. It also draws the reader

Summary and Closing Comments

away from the flow of the thought process and presentation, but not so when associated with the topic that is under scrutiny and embedded with the associated verses.

Paul remained a controversial person both inside and outside the Ecclesiae, and Peter notes that Paul's instructions and information was "difficult to understand." But make no mistake, Paul was and is in harmony with John, Peter, and all the other apostles.

Paul also sets the standard for behavior within the corporate body of Christ. This is, after all, a family business with Father God and Christ at the helm. As with any business, all have sets of values, all have an image, all have expectations of servicing the public, and all offer that something special. Paul presents the same for the Body of Christ in service to others by humbleness, meekness, godly-love, being responsible, and trying to not offend. He also recommends living a quiet and peaceable life, always ready to defend your belief and be prepared for the future.

Some other information that should be noted, studied, and discussed are:

- Paul's letters expand the knowledge of the quality and nature of Father God, His activities, what He expects, and His presence. Paul always places Him first in order of importance, recognition, praise, and worship.
- Paul expands the preeminence, role, activities, the quality and nature of Christ over all things.
- Notice that the "Holy-spirit" is completely ignored in all letters, everywhere. And it is identified as a source of power only, not an entity or being. To "blaspheme" the Holy-spirit is in fact blaspheming Father God, since this is his direct unlimited-inherent-power.
- The New Covenant is spiritual in nature and supersedes the Law of Moses.
- The letters are progressive in nature, from the basic to complete understanding for our day and time.
- Not all are called at the same time.
- Hebrews is an accusation against the beings in heaven defending the preeminence, titleship, ultimate authority and ownership of all things, and all of these and more belong only to the man Jesus. Hebrews is the bookend to Job. When Job exclaims, "Where is my Savior, who is the one to defend me?" Hebrews responds, conclusively proving it is only Jesus the Christ.
- You are called to serve.
- Paul's letters are dual in nature; they are meant to be as much about the spiritual as the physical.
- Paul's letters start off with the theme of freedom, and he ends with this topic.

Summary and Closing Comments

- Paul started off as the great attacker against the belief and then became the greatest defender of the belief.

- Paul writes in the superlative. His confidence is supreme, and he wants to impress his audience of the absolute sureness of the future and the coming kingdom of God and Christ.

- Paul writes in the active and active-future tenses. This grammatical feature is not taught by any theologians or scholars, and thus has been completely lost. Those who have not studied the language will not recognize or understand this. Paul's writings are full of superior, extreme, and fully developed adjectives and adverbs. In English we would use such words as infinite, to the power of (as in a mathematical concept), extreme, exponentially.

- Your being saved is a gift; you cannot earn it nor do anything to get it. It is strictly a gift given for and by God. This includes having the Holy-spirit, the character and nature of who and what you are.

- All are part of a divine lottery.

- Paul's writings are a description of the New Compact (Testament, Covenant); his writings provide the developmental history of this and show that it was intended from the time of Adam, the Apostles' times, the here and now, and for the future.

This list is not exhaustive. Within my study notes I've included a myriad of other themes and concepts worth exploring and developing. Also note that not all my lists and comments are all fully developed but rather are designed to allow the reader a jumping-off point for research and further exploration on your own.

In conclusion, I offer the following perspectives to pursue:

- Paul as an attorney
- Paul as a revealer
- Paul as a historian
- Paul a master of prose and poetry
- Paul as understanding the Government of God

Even more astonishing and needing to be recognized, understood, and reflected upon is the coming Government of God. The Father and Jesus The Christ form a bona fide legal entity, with legal activities and proceedings that will be active and used within that government. As it is here with worldly judicial systems, so it is in the spirit world.

May this all be found in HIS will and purpose, and may you be found with HIS glory, nature, quality, and divinity.

In Jesus' name,
Amen.

Honorarium and Acknowledgments

To THE-ONE-AND-ONLY-GOD AND FATHER of us be the glory and honor to offer this effort to you, and may it be HIS will and delight to call and grow you in and through our Master-Savior-Anointed, The-Messiah, and prepare you for His Coming-Kingdom/Government and your part in it.

This was Paul's wish for all mankind even to his last living breath, and who am I to not desire the same out of Godly-love to meet each one of you in The-Coming-Government?

I also desire to extend my sincerest love and affection to some people who have passed through my life bringing me to the place to have worked on this activity. To my father, Edwin, long since passed, who by the grace of God was lifted out of the gutters; a street urchin, he grew up without parents only to show me how a father devotes his time and entire being in love to be a family man. My affection and love for God, limited as it may be, comes directly from him. There has been no man greater in my life that I have known or will meet in this lifetime. I have tried and continue to try my best to imitate him daily.

My mother, Doris, who gave her whole life to her family. She knew very little of what the world had to offer, but rather always tried to live her life for God. Could there have been a better nurturer?

To my sons, Jarred and Brett, I have written this for you so that God may open your eyes as it may be in His will and purpose. Call upon Him to let you enter The-First. May GOD allow me to be the first to hold Jarred's hands and hug him at his resurrection as well as my father and mother.

To a beautiful woman, Bounthane Phothilath, whom had I not taken the time to meet, this project would have never occurred. In some respects, this is written for her, her family, and her country. May God reach out to you and bring you into his flock ahead of His intended schedule for you. *Huk Toun kau dawk-gu-làap kaao mii-kaa.*

To Stacia, a sister in Christ that God allowed me to meet. Stacia, I love you like a sister. May God continue to grow you in his grace, truth, and the full knowledge-of-Him.

To the ASKELM organization that encouraged me to dig deeper, and specifically to David Sielaff, Director of Associates for Scriptural Knowledge, who has devoted more time, resources, and caring to me than should have been offered. May God continue to bless you and yours.

God Bless All!

www.ingramcontent.com/pod-product-compliance
Lightning Source LLC
Chambersburg PA
CBHW081144290426
44108CB00018B/2437